# Handbook of Face Recognition

Stan Z. Li    Anil K. Jain

Editors

# Handbook of
# Face Recognition

With 210 Illustrations

 Springer

Stan Z. Li
Center for Biometrics Research and Testing &
    National Lab of Pattern Recognition
Institute of Automation
Chinese Academy of Sciences
Beijing 100080
China
szli@nlpr.ia.ac.cn

Anil K. Jain
Department of Computer Science
    & Engineering
Michigan State University
East Lansing, MI 48824-1226
USA
jain@cse.msu.edu

Library of Congress Cataloging-in-Publication Data
Handbook of face recognition / editors, Stan Z. Li & Anil K. Jain.
    p. cm.
    Includes bibliographical references and index.
    ISBN 0-387-40595-X (alk. paper)
    1. Human face recognition (Computer science    I. Li, S. Z., 1958–    II. Jain,
Anil K., 1948–
    TA1650.H36    2004
    006.4′2—dc22                                            2004052453

ISBN 0-387-40595-X         Printed on acid-free paper.

Printed in the United States of America.        (MP)

9 8 7 6 5 4 3 2 1        SPIN 10946602

springeronline.com

# Preface

Face recognition has a large number of applications, including security, person verification, Internet communication, and computer entertainment. Although research in automatic face recognition has been conducted since the 1960s, this problem is still largely unsolved. Recent years have seen significant progress in this area owing to advances in face modeling and analysis techniques. Systems have been developed for face detection and tracking, but reliable face recognition still offers a great challenge to computer vision and pattern recognition researchers.

There are several reasons for recent increased interest in face recognition, including rising public concern for security, the need for identity verification in the digital world, and the need for face analysis and modeling techniques in multimedia data management and computer entertainment. Recent advances in automated face analysis, pattern recognition, and machine learning have made it possible to develop automatic face recognition systems to address these applications.

This book was written based on two primary motivations. The first was the need for highly reliable, accurate face recognition algorithms and systems. The second was the recent research in image and object representation and matching that is of interest to face recognition researchers.

The book is intended for practitioners and students who plan to work in face recognition or who want to become familiar with the state-of-the-art in face recognition. It also provides references for scientists and engineers working in image processing, computer vision, biometrics and security, Internet communications, computer graphics, animation, and the computer game industry. The material fits the following categories: advanced tutorial, state-of-the-art survey, and guide to current technology.

The book consists of 16 chapters, covering all the subareas and major components necessary for designing operational face recognition systems. Each chapter focuses on a specific topic or system component, introduces background information, reviews up-to-date techniques, presents results, and points out challenges and future directions.

Chapter 1 introduces face recognition processing, including major components such as face detection, tracking, alignment, and feature extraction, and it points out the technical challenges of building a face recognition system. We emphasize the importance of subspace analysis and learning, not only providing an understanding of the challenges therein but also the most successful solutions available so far. In fact, most technical chapters represent subspace learning-based techniques for various steps in face recognition.

Chapter 2 reviews face detection techniques and describes effective statistical learning methods. In particular, AdaBoost-based learning methods are described because they often achieve practical and robust solutions. Techniques for dealing with nonfrontal face detection are discussed. Results are presented to compare boosting algorithms and other factors that affect face detection performance.

Chapters 3 and 4 discuss face modeling methods for face alignment. These chapters describe methods for localizing facial components (e.g., eyes, nose, mouth) and facial outlines and for aligning facial shape and texture with the input image. Input face images may be extracted from static images or video sequences, and parameters can be extracted from these input images to describe the shape and texture of a face. These results are based largely on advances in the use of active shape models and active appearance models.

Chapters 5 and 6 cover topics related to illumination and color. Chapter 5 describes recent advances in illumination modeling for faces. The illumination invariant facial feature representation is described; this representation improves the recognition performance under varying illumination and inspires further explorations of reliable face recognition solutions. Chapter 6 deals with facial skin color modeling, which is helpful when color is used for face detection and tracking.

Chapter 7 provides a tutorial on subspace modeling and learning-based dimension reduction methods, which are fundamental to many current face recognition techniques. Whereas the collection of all images constitutes high dimensional space, images of faces reside in a subspace of that space. Facial images of an individual are in a subspace of that subspace. It is of paramount importance to discover such subspaces so as to extract effective features and construct robust classifiers.

Chapter 8 addresses problems of face tracking and recognition from a video sequence of images. The purpose is to make use of temporal constraints present in the sequence to make tracking and recognition more reliable.

Chapters 9 and 10 present methods for pose and illumination normalization and extract effective facial features under such changes. Chapter 9 describes a model for extracting illumination invariants, which were previously presented in Chapter 5. Chapter 9 also presents a subregion method for dealing with variation in pose. Chapter 10 describes a recent innovation, called Morphable Models, for generative modeling and learning of face images under changes in illumination and pose in an analysis-by-synthesis framework. This approach results in algorithms that, in a sense, generalize the alignment algorithms described in Chapters 3 and 4 to the situation where the faces are subject to large changes in illumination and pose. In this work, the three-dimensional data of faces are used during the learning phase to train the model in addition to the normal intensity or texture images.

Chapters 11 and 12 provide methods for facial expression analysis and synthesis. The analysis part, Chapter 11, automatically analyzes and recognizes facial motions and facial feature changes from visual information. The synthesis part, Chapter 12, describes techniques on three-dimensional face modeling and animation, face lighting from a single image, and facial expression synthesis. These techniques can potentially be used for face recognition with varying poses, illuminations, and facial expressions. They can also be used for human computer interfaces.

Chapter 13 reviews 27 publicly available databases for face recognition, face detection, and facial expression analysis. These databases provide a common ground for development and evaluation of algorithms for faces under variations in identity, face pose, illumination, facial expression, age, occlusion, and facial hair.

Chapter 14 introduces concepts and methods for face verification and identification performance evaluation. The chapter focuses on measures and protocols used in FERET and FRVT (face recognition vendor tests). Analysis of these tests identifies advances offered by state-of-the-art technologies for face recognition, as well as the limitations of these technologies.

Chapter 15 offers psychological and neural perspectives suggesting how face recognition might go on in the human brain. Combined findings suggest an image-based representation that encodes faces relative to a global average and evaluates deviations from the average as an indication of the unique properties of individual faces.

Chapter 16 describes various face recognition applications, including face identification, security, multimedia management, and human-computer interaction. The chapter also reviews many face recognition systems and discusses related issues in applications and business.

## Acknowledgments

A number of people helped in making this book a reality. Vincent Hsu, Dirk Colbry, Xiaoguang Lu, Karthik Nandakumar, and Anoop Namboodiri of Michigan State University, and Shiguang Shan, Zhenan Sun, Chenghua Xu and Jiangwei Li of the Chinese Academy of Sciences helped proofread several of the chapters. We also thank Wayne Wheeler and Ann Kostant, editors at Springer, for their suggestions and for keeping us on schedule for the production of the book. This handbook project was done partly when Stan Li was with Microsoft Research Asia.

December 2004

*Stan Z. Li*
Beijing, China

*Anil K. Jain*
East Lansing, Michigan

# Contents

# Chapter 1. Introduction

Stan Z. Li[1] and Anil K. Jain[2]

[1] Center for Biometrics Research and Testing (CBRT) and National Laboratory of Pattern Recognition (NLPR), Chinese Academy of Sciences, Beijing 100080, China. szli@nlpr.ia.ac.cn *
[2] Michigan State University, East Lansing, MI 48824, USA. jain@cse.msu.edu

Face recognition is a task that humans perform routinely and effortlessly in their daily lives. Wide availability of powerful and low-cost desktop and embedded computing systems has created an enormous interest in automatic processing of digital images and videos in a number of applications, including biometric authentication, surveillance, human-computer interaction, and multimedia management. Research and development in automatic face recognition follows naturally.

Research in face recognition is motivated not only by the fundamental challenges this recognition problem poses but also by numerous practical applications where human identification is needed. Face recognition, as one of the primary biometric technologies, became more and more important owing to rapid advances in technologies such as digital cameras, the Internet and mobile devices, and increased demands on security. Face recognition has several advantages over other biometric technologies: It is natural, nonintrusive, and easy to use. Among the six biometric attributes considered by Hietmeyer [12], facial features scored the highest compatibility in a Machine Readable Travel Documents (MRTD) [18] system based on a number of evaluation factors, such as enrollment, renewal, machine requirements, and public perception, shown in Figure 1.1.

A face recognition system is expected to identify faces present in images and videos automatically. It can operate in either or both of two modes: (1) face verification (or authentication), and (2) face identification (or recognition). Face verification involves a one-to-one match that compares a query face image against a template face image whose identity is being claimed. Face identification involves one-to-many matches that compares a query face image against all the template images in the database to determine the identity of the query face. Another face recognition scenario involves a watch-list check, where a query face is matched to a list of suspects (one-to-few matches).

The performance of face recognition systems has improved significantly since the first automatic face recognition system was developed by Kanade [14]. Furthermore, face detection, facial feature extraction, and recognition can now be performed in "realtime" for images captured under *favorable* (i.e., constrained) situations.

---

* Part of this work was done when Stan Z. Li was with Microsoft Research Asia.

Although progress in face recognition has been encouraging, the task has also turned out to be a difficult endeavor, especially for unconstrained tasks where viewpoint, illumination, expression, occlusion, accessories, and so on vary considerably. In the following sections, we give a brief review on technical advances and analyze technical challenges.

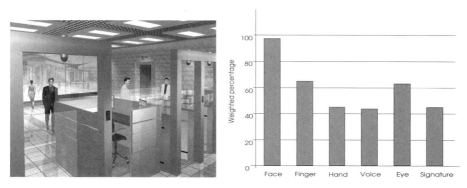

**Fig. 1.1.** A scenario of using biometric MRTD systems for passport control (left), and a comparison of various biometric features based on MRTD compatibility (right, from Hietmeyer [12] with permission).

# 1 Face Recognition Processing

Face recognition is a visual pattern recognition problem. There, a face as a three-dimensional object subject to varying illumination, pose, expression and so on is to be identified based on its two-dimensional image (three-dimensional images e.g., obtained from laser may also be used). A face recognition system generally consists of four modules as depicted in Figure 1.2: detection, alignment, feature extraction, and matching, where localization and normalization (face detection and alignment) are processing steps before face recognition (facial feature extraction and matching) is performed.

*Face detection* segments the face areas from the background. In the case of video, the detected faces may need to be tracked using a *face tracking* component. *Face alignment* is aimed at achieving more accurate localization and at normalizing faces thereby whereas face detection provides coarse estimates of the location and scale of each detected face. Facial components, such as eyes, nose, and mouth and facial outline, are located; based on the location points, the input face image is normalized with respect to geometrical properties, such as size and pose, using geometrical transforms or morphing. The face is usually further normalized with respect to photometrical properties such illumination and gray scale.

After a face is normalized geometrically and photometrically, *feature extraction* is performed to provide effective information that is useful for distinguishing between faces of different persons and stable with respect to the geometrical and photometrical variations. For *face matching*, the extracted feature vector of the input face is matched against those of enrolled faces in the database; it outputs the identity of the face when a match is found with sufficient confidence or indicates an unknown face otherwise.

Face recognition results depend highly on features that are extracted to represent the face pattern and classification methods used to distinguish between faces whereas face localization and normalization are the basis for extracting effective features. These problems may be analyzed from the viewpoint of face subspaces or manifolds, as follows.

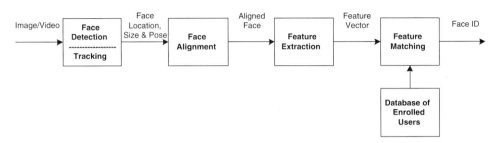

**Fig. 1.2.** Face recognition processing flow.

## 2 Analysis in Face Subspaces

Subspace analysis techniques for face recognition are based on the fact that a class of patterns of interest, such as the face, resides in a subspace of the input image space. For example, a small image of $64 \times 64$ has 4096 pixels can express a large number of pattern classes, such as trees, houses and faces. However, among the $256^{4096} > 10^{9864}$ possible "configurations," only a few correspond to faces. Therefore, the original image representation is highly redundant, and the dimensionality of this representation could be greatly reduced when only the face pattern are of interest.

With the eigenface or principal component analysis (PCA) [9] approach [28], a small number (e.g., 40 or lower) of eigenfaces [26] are derived from a set of training face images by using the Karhunen-Loeve transform or PCA. A face image is efficiently represented as a feature vector (i.e., a vector of weights) of low dimensionality. The features in such subspace provide more salient and richer information for recognition than the raw image. The use of subspace modeling techniques has significantly advanced face recognition technology.

The manifold or distribution of all faces accounts for variation in face appearance whereas the nonface manifold accounts for everything else. If we look into these manifolds in the image space, we find them highly nonlinear and nonconvex [4, 27]. Figure 1.3(a) illustrates face versus nonface manifolds and (b) illustrates the manifolds of two individuals in the entire face manifold. Face detection can be considered as a task of distinguishing between the face and nonface manifolds in the image (subwindow) space and face recognition between those of individuals in the face manifold.

Figure 1.4 further demonstrates the nonlinearity and nonconvexity of face manifolds in a PCA subspace spanned by the first three principal components, where the plots are drawn from

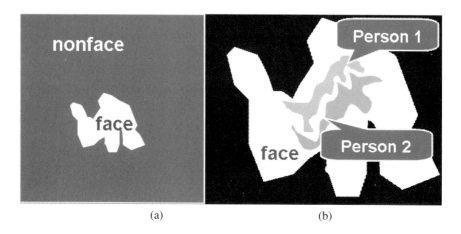

(a)                                    (b)

**Fig. 1.3.** (a) Face versus nonface manifolds. (b) Face manifolds of different individuals.

real face image data. Each plot depicts the manifolds of three individuals (in three colors). There are 64 original frontal face images for each individual. A certain type of transform is performed on an original face image with 11 gradually varying parameters, producing 11 transformed face images; each transformed image is cropped to contain only the face region; the 11 cropped face images form a sequence. A curve in this figure is the image of such a sequence in the PCA space, and so there are 64 curves for each individual. The three-dimensional (3D) PCA space is projected on three 2D spaces (planes). We can see the nonlinearity of the trajectories.

Two notes follow: First, while these examples are demonstrated in a PCA space, more complex (nonlinear and nonconvex) curves are expected in the original image space. Second, although these examples are subject the geometric transformations in the 2D plane and pointwise lighting (gamma) changes, more significant complexity is expected for geometric transformations in 3D (e.g.out-of-plane head rotations) transformations and lighting direction changes.

## 3 Technical Challenges

As shown in Figure 1.3, the classification problem associated with face detection is highly nonlinear and nonconvex, even more so for face matching. Face recognition evaluation reports (e.g., [8, 23]) and other independent studies indicate that the performance of many state-of-the-art face recognition methods deteriorates with changes in lighting, pose, and other factors [6, 29, 35]. The key technical challenges are summarized below.

**Large Variability in Facial Appearance**. Whereas shape and reflectance are intrinsic properties of a face object, the appearance (i.e., the texture look) of a face is also subject to several other factors, including the facial pose (or, equivalently, camera viewpoint), illumination, facial expression. Figure 1.5 shows an example of significant intrasubject variations caused by these

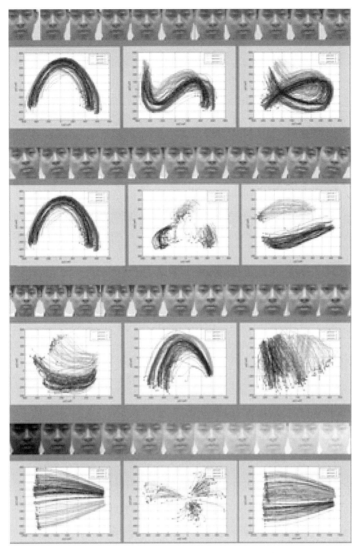

**Fig. 1.4.** Nonlinearity and nonconvexity of face manifolds under (from top to bottom) translation, rotation , scaling, and Gamma transformations.

factors. In addition to these, various imaging parameters, such as aperture, exposure time, lens aberrations, and sensor spectral response also increase intrasubject variations. Face-based person identification is further complicated by possible small intersubject variations (Figure 1.6). All these factors are confounded in the image data, so "the variations between the images of the same face due to illumination and viewing direction are almost always larger than the image variation due to change in face identity" [21]. This variability makes it difficult to extract the intrinsic information of the face objects from their respective images.

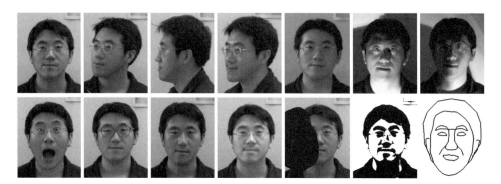

**Fig. 1.5.** Intrasubject variations in pose, illumination, expression, occlusion, accessories (e.g., glasses), color, and brightness. (Courtesy of Rein-Lien Hsu [13].)

(a)                                             (b)

**Fig. 1.6.** Similarity of frontal faces between (a) twins (downloaded from www.marykateandashley.com); and (b) a father and his son (downloaded from BBC news, news.bbc.co.uk).

**Highly Complex Nonlinear Manifolds**. As illustrated above, the entire face manifold is highly nonconvex, and so is the face manifold of any individual under various change. Linear methods such as PCA [26, 28], independent component analysis (ICA) [2], and linear discriminant analysis (LDA) [3]) project the data linearly from a high-dimensional space (e.g., the image space) to a low-dimensional subspace. As such, they are unable to preserve the nonconvex variations of face manifolds necessary to differentiate among individuals. In a linear subspace, Euclidean distance and more generally Mahalanobis distance, which are normally used for template matching, do not perform well for classifying between face and nonface manifolds and between manifolds of individuals (Figure 1.7(a)). This crucial fact limits the power of the linear methods to achieve highly accurate face detection and recognition.

**High Dimensionality and Small Sample Size**. Another challenge is the ability to generalize, illustrated by Figure 1.7(b). A canonical face image of $112 \times 92$ resides in a 10,304-dimensional feature space. Nevertheless, the number of examples per person (typically fewer than 10, even just one) available for learning the manifold is usually much smaller than the dimensionality of the image space; a system trained on so few examples may not generalize well to unseen instances of the face.

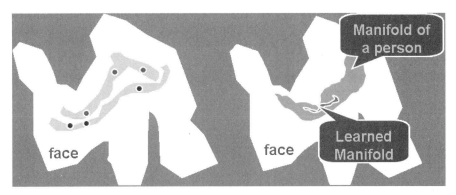

**Fig. 1.7.** Challenges in face recognition from subspace viewpoint. (a) Euclidean distance is unable to differentiate between individuals: In terms of Euclidean distance, an interpersonal distance can be smaller than an intrapersonal one. (b) The learned manifold or classifier is unable to characterize (i.e., generalize to) unseen images of the same individual face.

## 4 Technical Solutions

There are two strategies for dealing with the above difficulties: feature extraction and pattern classification based on the extracted features. One is to construct a "good" feature space in which the face manifolds become simpler i.e., less nonlinear and nonconvex than those in the other spaces. This includes two levels of processing: (1) normalize face images geometrically and photometrically, such as using morphing and histogram equalization; and (2) extract features in the normalized images which are stable with respect to such variations, such as based on Gabor wavelets.

The second strategy is to construct classification engines able to solve difficult nonlinear classification and regression problems in the feature space and to generalize better. Although good normalization and feature extraction reduce the nonlinearity and nonconvexity, they do not solve the problems completely and classification engines able to deal with such difficulties are still necessary to achieve high performance. A successful algorithm usually combines both strategies.

With the geometric feature-based approach used in the early days [5, 10, 14, 24], facial features such as eyes, nose, mouth, and chin are detected. Properties of and relations (e.g., areas, distances, angles) between the features are used as descriptors for face recognition. Advantages of this approach include economy and efficiency when achieving data reduction and insensitivity to variations in illumination and viewpoint. However, facial feature detection and measurement techniques developed to date are not reliable enough for the geometric feature-based recognition [7], and such geometric properties alone are inadequate for face recognition because rich information contained in the facial texture or appearance is discarded. These are reasons why early techniques are not effective.

The statistical learning approach learns from training data (appearance images or features extracted from appearance) to extract good features and construct classification engines. During the learning, both prior knowledge about face(s) and variations seen in the training data are taken into consideration. Many successful algorithms for face detection, alignment and matching nowadays are learning-based.

The appearance-based approach, such as PCA [28] and LDA [3] based methods, has significantly advanced face recognition techniques. Such an approach generally operates directly on an image-based representation (i.e., array of pixel intensities). It extracts features in a subspace derived from training images. Using PCA, a face subspace is constructed to represent "optimally" only the face object; using LDA, a discriminant subspace is constructed to distinguish "optimally" faces of different persons. Comparative reports (e.g., [3]) show that LDA-based methods generally yield better results than PCA-based ones.

Although these linear, holistic appearance-based methods avoid instability of the early geometric feature-based methods, they are not accurate enough to describe subtleties of original manifolds in the original image space. This is due to their limitations in handling nonlinearity in face recognition: there, protrusions of nonlinear manifolds may be smoothed and concavities may be filled in, causing unfavorable consequences

Such linear methods can be extended using nonlinear kernel techniques (kernel PCA [25] and kernel LDA [19]) to deal with nonlinearity in face recognition [11, 16, 20, 31]. There, a *nonlinear* projection (dimension reduction) from the image space to a feature space is performed; the manifolds in the resulting feature space become simple, yet with subtleties preserved. Although the kernel methods may achieve good performance on the training data, however, it may not be so for unseen data owing to their more flexibility than the linear methods and overfitting thereof.

Another approach to handle the nonlinearity is to construct a local appearance-based feature space, using appropriate image filters, so the distributions of faces are less affected by various changes. Local features analysis (LFA) [22], Gabor wavelet-based features (such as elastic graph bunch matching, EGBM) [15, 30, 17] and local binary pattern (LBP) [1] have been used for this purpose.

Some of these algorithms may be considered as combining geometric (or structural) feature detection and local appearance feature extraction, to increase stability of recognition performance under changes in viewpoint, illumination, and expression. A taxonomy of major face recognition algorithms in Figure 1.8 provides an overview of face recognition technology based on pose dependency, face representation, and features used for matching.

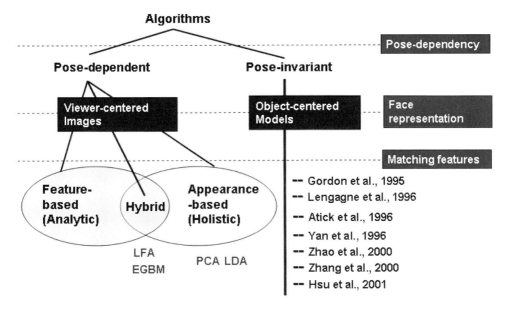

**Fig. 1.8.** Taxonomy of face recognition algorithms based on pose-dependency, face representation, and features used in matching (Courtesy of Rein-Lien Hsu [13]).

A large number of local features can be produced with varying parameters in the position, scale and orientation of the filters. For example, more than 100,000 local appearance features can be produced when an image of $100 \times 100$ is filtered with Gabor filters of five scales and eight orientation for all pixel positions, causing increased dimensionality. Some of these features are effective and important for the classification task whereas the others may not be so. AdaBoost methods have been used successfully to tackle the feature selection and nonlinear classification problems [32, 33, 34]. These works lead to a framework for learning both effective features and effective classifiers.

## 5 Current Technology Maturity

As introduced earlier, a face recognition system consists of several components, including face detection, tracking, alignment, feature extraction, and matching. Where are we along the road of making automatic face recognition systems? To answer this question, we have to assume some given constraints namely what the intended situation for the application is and how strong constraints are assumed, including pose, illumination, facial expression, age, occlusion, and facial hair. Although several chapters (14 and 16 in particular), provide more objective comments, we risk saying the following here: Real-time face detection and tracking in the normal indoor environment is relatively well solved, whereas more work is needed for handling outdoor scenes. When faces are detected and tracked, alignment can be done as well, assuming the image resolution is good enough for localizing the facial components, face recognition works well for cooperative frontal faces without exaggerated expressions and under illumination without much shadow. Face recognition in an unconstrained daily life environment without the user's cooperation, such as for recognizing someone in an airport, is currently a challenging task. Many years' effort is required to produce practical solutions to such problems.

## Acknowledgment

The authors thank Jörgen Ahlberg for his feedback on Chapters 1 and 2.

## References

1. T. Ahonen, A. Hadid, and M.Pietikainen. "Face recognition with local binary patterns. In *Proceedings of the European Conference on Computer Vision*, pages 469–481, Prague, Czech, 2004.
2. M. S. Bartlett, H. M. Lades, and T. J. Sejnowski. Independent component representations for face recognition. *Proceedings of the SPIE, Conference on Human Vision and Electronic Imaging III*, 3299:528–539, 1998.
3. P. N. Belhumeur, J. P. Hespanha, and D. J. Kriegman. Eigenfaces vs. Fisherfaces: Recognition using class specific linear projection. *IEEE Transactions on Pattern Analysis and Machine Intelligence*, 19(7):711–720, July 1997.
4. M. Bichsel and A. P. Pentland. Human face recognition and the face image set's topology. *CVGIP: Image Understanding*, 59:254–261, 1994.
5. R. Brunelli and T. Poggio. Face recognition: Features versus templates. *IEEE Transactions on Pattern Analysis and Machine Intelligence*, 15(10):1042–1052, 1993.
6. R. Chellappa, C. Wilson, and S. Sirohey. Human and machine recognition of faces: A survey. *Proceedings of IEEE*, 83:705–740, 1995.
7. I. J. Cox, J. Ghosn, and P. Yianilos. Feature-based face recognition using mixture-distance. In *Proceedings of IEEE Computer Society Conference on Computer Vision and Pattern Recognition*, pages 209–216, 1996.
8. Face Recognition Vendor Tests (FRVT). *http://www.frvt.org*.
9. K. Fukunaga. *Introduction to statistical pattern recognition*. Academic Press, Boston, 2 edition, 1990.
10. A. J. Goldstein, L. D. Harmon, and A. B. Lesk. Identification of human faces. *Proceedings of the IEEE*, 59(5):748–760, 1971.
11. G. D. Guo, S. Z. Li, and K. L. Chan. Face recognition by support vector machines. In *Proc. Fourth IEEE Int. Conf on Automatic Face and Gesture Recognition*, pages 196–201, Grenoble, 2000.
12. R. Hietmeyer. Biometric identification promises fast and secure processing of airline passengers. *The International Civil Aviation Organization Journal*, 55(9):10–11, 2000.
13. R.-L. Hsu. *Face Detection and Modeling for Recognition*. Ph.D. thesis, Michigan State University, 2002.
14. T. Kanade. *Picture Processing by Computer Complex and Recognition of Human Faces*. Ph.D. thesis, Kyoto University, 1973.
15. M. Lades, J. Vorbruggen, J. Buhmann, J. Lange, C. von der Malsburg, R. P. Wurtz, and W. Konen. Distortion invariant object recognition in the dynamic link architecture. *IEEE Transactions on Computers*, 42:300–311, 1993.
16. Y. Li, S. Gong, and H. Liddell. Recognising trajectories of facial identities using kernel discriminant analysis. In *Proc. British Machine Vision Conference*, pages 613–622, 2001.

17. C. Liu and H. Wechsler. Gabor feature based classification using the enhanced fisher linear discriminant model for face recognition. *IEEE Transactions on Image Processing*, 11(4):467–476, 2002.

18. Machine Readable Travel Documents (MRTD). http://www.icao.int/mrtd/overview/overview.cfm.

19. S. Mika, G. Ratsch, J. Weston, B. Scholkopf, and K.-R. Mller. Fisher discriminant analysis with kernels. *Neural Networks for Signal Processing IX*, pages 41–48, 1999.

20. B. Moghaddam. Principal manifolds and bayesian subspaces for visual recognition. In *International Conference on Computer Vision (ICCV'99)*, pages 1131–1136, 1999.

21. Y. Moses, Y. Adini, and S. Ullman. Face recognition: The problem of compensating for changes in illumination direction. In *Proceedings of the European Conference on Computer Vision*, volume A, pages 286–296, 1994.

22. P. Penev and J. Atick. Local feature analysis: A general statistical theory for object representation. *Neural Systems*, 7(3):477–500, 1996.

23. P. J. Phillips, H. Moon, S. A. Rizvi, and P. J. Rauss. The FERET evaluation methodology for face-recognition algorithms". *IEEE Transactions on Pattern Analysis and Machine Intelligence*, 22(10):1090–1104, 2000.

24. A. Samal and P. A.Iyengar. Automatic recognition and analysis of human faces and facial expressions: A survey. *Pattern Recognition*, 25:65–77, 1992.

25. B. Schölkopf, A. Smola, and K. R. Müller. Nonlinear component analysis as a kernel eigenvalue problem. *Neural Computation*, 10:1299–1319, 1999.

26. L. Sirovich and M. Kirby. Low-dimensional procedure for the characterization of human faces. *Journal of the Optical Society of America A*, 4(3):519–524, 1987.

27. M. Turk. A random walk through eigenspace. *IEICE Trans. Inf. & Syst.*, E84-D(12):1586–1695, 2001.

28. M. A. Turk and A. P. Pentland. Eigenfaces for recognition. *Journal of Cognitive Neuroscience*, 3(1):71–86, 1991.

29. D. Valentin, H. Abdi, A. J. O'Toole, and G. W. Cottrell. Connectionist models of face processing: A survey. *Pattern Recognition*, 27(9):1209–1230, 1994.

30. L. Wiskott, J. Fellous, N. Kruger, and C. v. d. malsburg. Face recognition by elastic bunch graph matching. *IEEE Transactions on Pattern Analysis and Machine Intelligence*, 19(7):775–779, 1997.

31. M.-H. Yang, N. Ahuja, and D. Kriegman. Face recognition using kernel eigenfaces. In *Proceedings of the IEEE International Conference on Image Processing*, volume 1, pages 37–40, 2000.

32. P. Yang, S. Shan, W. Gao, S. Z. Li, and D. Zhang. Face recognition using ada-boosted gabor features. In *Proceedings of International Conference on Automatic Face and Gesture Recognition*, Vancouver, 2004.

33. G. Zhang, X. Huang, S. Z. Li, and Y. Wang. Boosting local binary pattern (LBP)-based face recognition. In S. Z. Li, J. Lai, T. Tan, G. Feng, and Y. Wang, editors, *Advances in Biometric Personal Authentication*, volume 3338 of *Lecture Notes in Computer Science*, pages 180–187. Springer, 2004.

34. L. Zhang, S. Z. Li, Z. Qu, and X. Huang. Boosting local feature based classifiers for face recognition. In *Proceedings of First IEEE Workshop on Face Processing in Video*, Washington, D.C., 2004.

35. W. Zhao, R. Chellappa, P. Phillips, and A. Rosenfeld. Face recognition: A literature survey. *ACM Computing Surveys*, pages 399–458, 2000.

# Chapter 2. Face Detection

Stan Z. Li

Microsoft Research Asia, Beijing 100080, China. *

Face detection is the first step in automated face recognition. Its reliability has a major influence on the performance and usability of the entire face recognition system. Given a single image or a video, an ideal face detector should be able to identify and locate all the present faces regardless of their position, scale, orientation, age, and expression. Furthermore, the detection should be irrespective of extraneous illumination conditions and the image and video content.

Face detection can be performed based on several cues: skin color (for faces in color images and videos), motion (for faces in videos), facial/head shape, facial appearance, or a combination of these parameters. Most successful face detection algorithms are appearance-based without using other cues. The processing is done as follows: An input image is scanned at all possible locations and scales by a subwindow. Face detection is posed as classifying the pattern in the subwindow as either face or nonface. The face/nonface classifier is learned from face and nonface training examples using statistical learning methods.

This chapter focuses on appearance-based and learning-based methods. More attention is paid to AdaBoost learning-based methods because so far they are the most successful ones in terms of detection accuracy and speed. The reader is also referred to review articles, such as those of Hjelmas and Low [12] and Yang et al. [52], for other face detection methods.

## 1 Appearance-Based and Learning Based Approaches

With appearance-based methods, face detection is treated as a problem of classifying each scanned subwindow as one of two classes (i.e., face and nonface). Appearance-based methods avoid difficulties in modeling 3D structures of faces by considering possible face appearances under various conditions. A face/nonface classifier may be learned from a training set composed of face examples taken under possible conditions as would be seen in the running stage and nonface examples as well (see Figure 2.1 for a random sample of 10 face and 10 nonface subwindow images). Building such a classifier is possible because pixels on a face are highly correlated, whereas those in a nonface subwindow present much less regularity.

* Stan Z. Li is currently with Center for Biometrics Research and Testing (CBRT) and National Laboratory of Pattern Recognition (NLPR), Chinese Academy of Sciences, Beijing 100080, China. szli@nlpr.ia.ac.cn

However, large variations brought about by changes in facial appearance, lighting, and expression make the face manifold or face/nonface boundaries highly complex [4, 38, 43]. Changes in facial view (head pose) further complicate the situation. A nonlinear classifier is needed to deal with the complicated situation. The speed is also an important issue for realtime performance. Great research effort has been made for constructing complex yet fast classifiers and much progress has been achieved since 1990s.

**Fig. 2.1.** Face (top) and nonface (bottom) examples.

Turk and Pentland [44] describe a detection system based on principal component analysis (PCA) subspace or eigenface representation. Whereas only likelihood in the PCA subspace is considered in the basic PCA method, Moghaddam and Pentland [25] also consider the likelihood in the orthogonal complement subspace; using that system, the likelihood in the image space (the union of the two subspaces) is modeled as the product of the two likelihood estimates, which provide a more accurate likelihood estimate for the detection. Sung and Poggio [41] first partition the image space into several face and nonface clusters and then further decompose each cluster into the PCA and null subspaces. The Bayesian estimation is then applied to obtain useful statistical features. The system of Rowley et al. 's [32] uses retinally connected neural networks. Through a sliding window, the input image is examined after going through an extensive preprocessing stage. Osuna et al. [27] train a nonlinear support vector machine to classify face and nonface patterns, and Yang et al. [53] use the SNoW (Sparse Network of Winnows) learning architecture for face detection. In these systems, a bootstrap algorithm is used iteratively to collect meaningful nonface examples from images that do not contain any faces for retraining the detector.

Schneiderman and Kanade [35] use multiresolution information for different levels of wavelet transform. A nonlinear face and nonface classifier is constructed using statistics of products of histograms computed from face and nonface examples using AdaBoost learning [34]. The algorithm is computationally expensive. The system of five view detectors takes about 1 minute to detect faces for a $320 \times 240$ image over only four octaves of candidate size [35][1].

Viola and Jones [46, 47] built a fast, robust face detection system in which AdaBoost learning is used to construct nonlinear classifier (earlier work on the application of Adaboost for image classification and face detection can be found in [42] and [34]). AdaBoost is used to solve the following three fundamental problems: (1) learning effective features from a large feature set; (2) constructing weak classifiers, each of which is based on one of the selected features; and (3) boosting the weak classifiers to construct a strong classifier. Weak classifiers are

---

[1] During the revision of this article, Schneiderman and Kanade [36] reported an improvement in the speed of their system, using a coarse-to-fine search strategy together with various heuristics (re-using Wavelet Transform coefficients, color preprocessing, etc.). The improved speed is five seconds for an image of size $240 \times 256$ using a Pentium II at 450MHz.

based on simple scalar Haar wavelet-like features, which are steerable filters [28]. Viola and Jones make use of several techniques [5, 37] for effective computation of a large number of such features under varying scale and location, which is important for realtime performance. Moreover, the simple-to-complex cascade of classifiers makes the computation even more efficient, which follows the principles of pattern rejection [3, 6] and coarse-to-fine search [2, 8]. Their system is the first realtime frontal-view face detector, and it runs at about 14 frames per second on a $320 \times 240$ image [47].

Liu [23] presents a Bayesian Discriminating Features (BDF) method. The input image, its one-dimensional Harr wavelet representation, and its amplitude projections are concatenated into an expanded vector input of 768 dimensions. Assuming that these vectors follow a (single) multivariate normal distribution for face, linear dimension reduction is performed to obtain the PCA modes. The likelihood density is estimated using PCA and its residuals, making use of Bayesian techniques [25]. The nonface class is modeled similarly. A classification decision of face/nonface is made based on the two density estimates. The BDF classifier is reported to achieve results that compare favorably with state-of-the-art face detection algorithms, such as the Schneiderman-Kanade method. It is interesting to note that such good results are achieved with a single Gaussian for face and one for nonface, and the BDF is trained using relatively small data sets: 600 FERET face images and 9 natural (nonface) images; the trained classifier generalizes very well to test images. However, more details are needed to understand the underlying mechanism.

The ability to deal with nonfrontal faces is important for many real applications because approximately 75% of the faces in home photos are nonfrontal [17]. A reasonable treatment for the multiview face detection problem is the view-based method [29], in which several face models are built, each describing faces in a certain view range. This way, explicit 3D face modeling is avoided. Feraud et al. [7] adopt the view-based representation for face detection and use an array of five detectors, with each detector responsible for one facial view. Wiskott et al. [48] build elastic bunch graph templates for multiview face detection and recognition. Gong et al. [11] study the trajectories of faces (as they are rotated) in linear PCA feature spaces and use kernel support vector machines (SVMs) for multipose face detection and pose estimation [21, 26]. Huang et al. [14] use SVMs to estimate the facial pose. The algorithm of Schneiderman and Kanade [35] consists of an array of five face detectors in the view-based framework.

Li et al. [18, 19, 20] present a multiview face detection system, extending the work in other articles [35, 46, 47]. A new boosting algorithm, called FloatBoost, is proposed to incorporate Floating Search [30] into AdaBoost (RealBoost). The backtrack mechanism in the algorithm allows deletions of weak classifiers that are ineffective in terms of the error rate, leading to a strong classifier consisting of only a small number of weak classifiers. An extended Haar feature set is proposed for dealing with out-of-plane (left-right) rotation. A coarse-to-fine, simple-to-complex architecture, called a detector-pyramid, is designed for the fast detection of multiview faces. This work leads to the first realtime multiview face detection system. It runs at 200 ms per image ($320 \times 240$ pixels) on a Pentium-III CPU of 700 MHz.

Lienhart et al. [22] use an extended set of rotated Haar features for dealing with in-plane rotation and train a face detector using Gentle Adaboost [9] with small CART trees as base classifiers. The results show that this combination outperforms that of Discrete Adaboost with stumps.

In the following sections, we describe basic face-processing techniques and neural network-based and AdaBoost-based learning methods for face detection. Given that the AdaBoost learning with the Haar-like feature approach has achieved the best performance to date in terms of both accuracy and speed, our presentation focuses on the AdaBoost methods. Strategies are also described for efficient detection of multiview faces.

## 2 Preprocessing

### 2.1 Skin Color Filtering

Human skin has its own color distribution that differs from that of most of nonface objects. It can be used to filter the input image to obtain candidate regions of faces, and it may also be used to construct a stand-alone skin color-based face detector for special environments. A simple color-based face detection algorithm consists of two steps: (1) segmentation of likely face regions and (2) region merging.

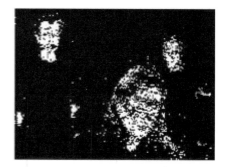

**Fig. 2.2.** Skin color filtering. Input image (left) and skin color-filtered map (right).

A skin color likelihood model, $p(color|face)$, can be derived from skin color samples. This may be done in the hue-saturation-value (HSV) color space or in the normalized red-green-blue (RGB) color space (see [24, 54] and Chapter 6 for comparative studies). A Gaussian mixture model for $p(color|face)$ can lead to better skin color modeling [49, 50]. Figure 2.2 shows skin color segmentation maps. A skin-colored pixel is found if the likelihood $p(H|face)$ is greater than a threshold (0.3), and S and V values are between some upper and lower bounds. A skin color map consists of a number of skin color regions that indicate potential candidate face regions. Refined face regions can be obtained by merging the candidate regions based on the color and spatial information. Heuristic postprocessing could be performed to remove false detection. For example, a human face contains eyes where the eyes correspond to darker regions inside the face region. A sophisticated color based face detection algorithm is presented in Hsu et al. [13].

Although a color-based face detection system may be computationally attractive, the color constraint alone is insufficient for achieving high accuracy face detection. This is due to large facial color variation as a result of different lighting, shadow, and ethic groups. Indeed, it is the appearance, albeit colored or gray level, rather than the color that is most essential for face detection. Skin color is often combined with the motion cue to improve the reliability for face detection and tracking on video [49, 50]. However, the most successful face detection systems do not rely on color or motion information, yet achieve good performance.

## 2.2 Image Normalization

Appearance-based methods operate on subwindows of a fixed size. Therefore, explicit or implicit resizing (e.g., to $20 \times 20$ pixels) is necessary. Normalization of pixel intensity helps correct variations in imaging parameters in cameras as well as changes in illumination conditions. The meaning of resizing is apparent; intensity normalization operations, including mean value normalization, histogram equalization, and illumination correction, are described below.

A simple intensity normalization operation is linear stretching. A histogram equalization helps reduce extreme illumination (Figure 2.3). In another simple illumination correction operation, the subwindow $I(x, y)$ is fitted to the best fitting plane $I'(x, y) = a \times x + b \times y + c$, where the values of the coefficients $a$, $b$ and $c$ may be estimated using the least-squares method; and then extreme illumination is reduced in the difference image $I''(x, y) = I(x, y) - I'(x, y)$ (Figure 2.4) [32, 41]. After normalization, the distribution of subwindow images becomes more compact and standardized, which helps reduce the complexity of the subsequent face/nonface classification. Note that these operations are "global" in the sense that all the pixels may be affected after such an operation. Intensity normalization may also be applied to local subregions, as is in the case for local Haar wavelet features [46] (See later in AdaBoost based methods).

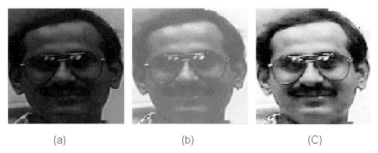

(a)                    (b)                    (C)

**Fig. 2.3.** Effect of linear stretching and and histogram equalization. (**a**) Original subwindow. (**b**) Linearly stretched. (**c**) Histogram equalized.

## 2.3 Gaussian Mixture Modeling

The distributions of face and nonface subwindows in a high dimensional space are complex. It is believed that a single Gaussian distribution cannot explain all variations. Sung and Poggio [41] propose to deal with this complexity by partitioning the face training data into several (six) face clusters, and nonface training data into several (six) nonface clusters, where the cluster

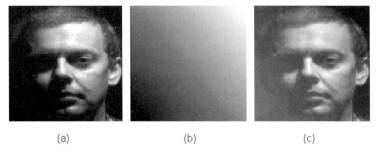

|     |     |     |
|:---:|:---:|:---:|
| (a) | (b) | (c) |

**Fig. 2.4.** Effect of illumination correction. (**a**) Original image subwindow $I$. (**b**) Best illumination plane $I'$. (**c**) Difference image $I''$.

numbers are chosen empirically. The clustering is performed by using a modified $k$-means algorithm based on the Mahalanobis distance [41] in the image space or some another space. Figure 2.5 shows the centroids of the resulting face and nonface clusters. Each cluster can be further modeled by its principal components using the PCA technique. Based on the multi-Gaussian and PCA modeling, a parametric classifier can be formulated based on the distances of the projection points within the subspaces and from the subspaces [41]. The clustering can also be done using factor analysis and self-organizing map (SOM) [51].

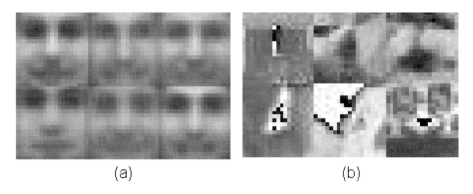

|     |     |
|:---:|:---:|
| (a) | (b) |

**Fig. 2.5.** Centroid images of six face clusters (a) and six nonface clusters (b).

It is believed that a few (e.g., six) Gaussian distributions are not enough to model the face distribution and even less sufficient to model the nonface distribution. However, it is reported in [23] that good results are achieved using a single Gaussian distribution for face and one for nonface, with a nonlinear kernel support vector machine classifier; and more interestingly, the BDF face/nonface classifier therein is trained using relatively small data sets: 600 FERET face images and 9 natural (nonface) images, and it generalizes very well to test images. The BDF work is worth more studies.

# 3 Neural Networks and Kernel Based Methods

Nonlinear classification for face detection may be performed using neural networks or kernel-based methods. With the neural methods [32, 41], a classifier may be trained directly using preprocessed and normalized face and nonface training subwindows. Rowley et al. [32] use the preprocessed 20×20 subwindow as an input to a neural network. The network has retinal connections to its input layer and two levels of mapping. The first level maps blocks of pixels to the hidden units. There are 4 blocks of 10×10 pixels, 16 blocks of 5×5 pixels, and 6 overlapping horizontal stripes of 20×5 pixels. Each block is input to a fully connected neural network and mapped to the hidden units. The 26 hidden units are then mapped to the final single-valued output unit and a final decision is made to classify the 20×20 subwindow into face or nonface. Several copies of the same networks can be trained and their outputs combined by arbitration (ANDing) [32].

The input to the system of Sung and Poggio [41] is derived from the six face and six nonface clusters. More specifically, it is a vector of $2 \times 6 = 12$ distances in the PCA subspaces and $2 \times 6 = 12$ distances from the PCA subspaces. The 24 dimensional feature vector provides a good representation for classifying face and nonface patterns. In both systems, the neural networks are trained by back-propagation algorithms.

Nonlinear classification for face detection can also be done using kernel SVMs [21, 26, 27], trained using face and nonface examples. Although such methods are able to learn nonlinear boundaries, a large number of support vectors may be needed to capture a highly nonlinear boundary. For this reason, fast realtime performance has so far been a difficulty with SVM classifiers thus trained. Although these SVM-based systems have been trained using the face and nonface subwindows directly, there is no reason why they cannot be trained using some salient features derived from the subwindows.

Yang et al. [53] use the SNoW learning architecture for face detection. SNoW is a sparse network of linear functions in which Winnow update rule is applied to the learning. The SNoW algorithm is designed for learning with a large set of candidate features. It uses classification error to perform multicative update of the weights connecting the target nodes.

# 4 AdaBoost-Based Methods

For AdaBoost learning, a complex nonlinear *strong classifier* $H_M(x)$ is constructed as a linear combination of $M$ simpler, easily constructible *weak classifiers* in the following form [9]

$$H_M(x) = \frac{\sum_{m=1}^{M} \alpha_m h_m(x)}{\sum_{m=1}^{M} \alpha_m} \tag{1}$$

where $x$ is a pattern to be classified, $h_m(x) \in \{-1, +1\}$ are the $M$ weak classifiers, $\alpha_m \geq 0$ are the combining coefficients in $\mathbb{R}$, and $\sum_{m=1}^{M} \alpha_m$ is the normalizing factor. In the discrete version, $h_m(x)$ takes a discrete value in $\{-1, +1\}$, whereas in the real version, the output of $h_m(x)$ is a number in $\mathbb{R}$. $H_M(x)$ is real-valued, but the prediction of class label for $x$ is obtained as $\hat{y}(x) = \text{sign}[H_M(x)]$ and the normalized confidence score is $|H_M(x)|$.

The AdaBoost learning procedure is aimed at learning a sequence of best weak classifiers $h_m(x)$ and the best combining weights $\alpha_m$. A set of $N$ labeled training examples

$\{(x_1, y_1), \dots, (x_N, y_N)\}$ is assumed available, where $y_i \in \{+1, -1\}$ is the class label for the example $x_i \in \mathbb{R}^n$. A distribution $[w_1, \dots, w_N]$ of the training examples, where $w_i$ is associated with a training example $(x_i, y_i)$, is computed and updated during the learning to represent the distribution of the training examples. After iteration $m$, harder-to-classify examples $(x_i, y_i)$ are given larger weights $w_i^{(m)}$, so that at iteration $m + 1$, more emphasis is placed on these examples. AdaBoost assumes that a procedure is available for learning a weak classifier $h_m(x)$ from the training examples, given the distribution $[w_i^{(m)}]$.

In Viola and Jones's face detection work [46, 47], a weak classifier $h_m(x) \in \{-1, +1\}$ is obtained by thresholding on a scalar feature $z_k(x) \in \mathbb{R}$ selected from an overcomplete set of Haar wavelet-like features [28, 42]. In the real versions of AdaBoost, such as RealBoost and LogitBoost, a real-valued weak classifier $h_m(x) \in \mathbb{R}$ can also be constructed from $z_k(x) \in \mathbb{R}$ [20, 22, 34]. The following discusses how to generate candidate weak classifiers.

## 4.1 Haar-like Features

Viola and Jones propose four basic types of scalar features for face detection [28, 47], as shown in Figure 2.6. Such a block feature is located in a subregion of a subwindow and varies in shape (aspect ratio), size, and location inside the subwindow. For a subwindow of size 20×20, there can be tens of thousands of such features for varying shapes, sizes and locations. Feature $k$, taking a scalar value $z_k(x) \in \mathbb{R}$, can be considered a transform from the $n$-dimensional space ($n = 400$ if a face example $x$ is of size 20×20) to the real line. These scalar numbers form an overcomplete feature set for the intrinsically low-dimensional face pattern. Recently, extended sets of such features have been proposed for dealing with out-of-plane head rotation [20] and for in-plane head rotation [22].

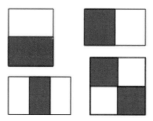

**Fig. 2.6.** Four types of rectangular Haar wavelet-like features. A feature is a scalar calculated by summing up the pixels in the white region and subtracting those in the dark region.

These Haar-like features are interesting for two reasons: (1) powerful face/nonface classifiers can be constructed based on these features (see later); and (2) they can be computed efficiently [37] using the summed-area table [5] or integral image [46] technique.

The integral image $II(x, y)$ at location $x, y$ contains the sum of the pixels above and to the left of $x, y$, defined as [46]

$$II(x, y) = \sum_{x' \leq x, \; y' \leq y} I(x, y) \tag{2}$$

The image can be computed in one pass over the original image using the the following pair of recurrences

$$S(x,y) = S(x, y-1) + I(x,y) \tag{3}$$
$$II(x,y) = II(x-1, y) + S(x,y) \tag{4}$$

where $S(x,y)$ is the cumulative row sum, $S(x,-1) = 0$ and $II(-1,y) = 0$. Using the integral image, any rectangular sum can be computed in four array references, as illustrated in Figure 2.7. The use of integral images leads to enormous savings in computation for features at varying locations and scales.

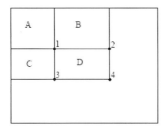

**Fig. 2.7.** The sum of the pixels within rectangle $D$ can be computed with four array references. The value of the integral image at location 1 is the sum of the pixels in rectangle $A$. The value at location 2 is $A + B$, at location 3 is $A + C$, and at location 4 is $A + B + C + D$. The sum within $D$ can be computed as (4+1) - (2+3). From Viola and Jones [46], © 2001 IEEE, with permission.

With the integral images, the intensity variation within a rectangle $D$ of any size and any location can be computed efficiently; for example $V_D = \sqrt{V * V}$ where $V = (4+1) - (2+3)$ is the sum within $D$, and a simple intensity normalization can be done by dividing all the pixel values in the subwindow by the variation.

### 4.2 Constructing Weak Classifiers

As mentioned ealrlier, the AdaBoost learning procedure is aimed at learning a sequence of best weak classifiers to combine $h_m(x)$ and the combining weights $\alpha_m$ in Eq.(1). It solves the following three fundamental problems: (1) learning effective features from a large feature set; (2) constructing weak classifiers, each of which is based on one of the selected features; and (3) boosting the weak classifiers to construct a strong classifier.

Adaboost assumes that a "weak learner" procedure is available. The task of the procedure is to select the most significant feature from a set of candidate features, given the current strong classifier learned thus far, and then construct the best weak classifier and combine it into the existing strong classifier. Here, the "significance" is with respect to some given criterion (see below).

In the case of discrete AdaBoost, the simplest type of weak classifiers is a "stump." A stump is a single-node decision tree. When the feature is real-valued, a stump may be constructed by thresholding the value of the selected feature at a certain threshold value; when the feature is discrete-valued, it may be obtained according to the discrete label of the feature. A more general decision tree (with more than one node) composed of several stumps leads to a more sophisticated weak classifier.

For discrete AdaBoost, a stump may be constructed in the following way. Assume that we have constructed $M - 1$ weak classifiers $\{h_m(x) | m = 1, \ldots, M - 1\}$ and we want to construct $h_M(x)$. The stump $h_M(x) \in \{-1, +1\}$ is determined by comparing the selected feature $z_{k^*}(x)$ with a threshold $\tau_M$ as follows

$$h_M(x) = +1 \quad \text{if } z_{k^*} > \tau_{k^*} \tag{5}$$
$$= -1 \quad \text{otherwise} \tag{6}$$

In this form, $h_M(x)$ is determined by two parameters: the type of the scalar feature $z_{k^*}$ and the threshold $\tau_{k^*}$. The two may be determined by some criterion, for example, (1) the minimum weighted classification error, or (2) the lowest false alarm rate given a certain detection rate.

Supposing we want to minimize the weighted classification error with real-valued features, then we can choose a threshold $\tau_k \in \mathbb{R}$ for each feature $z_k$ to minimize the corresponding weighted error made by the stump with this feature; we then choose the best feature $z_{k^*}$ among all $k$ that achieves the lowest weighted error.

Supposing that we want to achieve the lowest false alarm rate given a certain detection rate, we can set a threshold $\tau_k$ for each $z_k$ so a specified detection rate (with respect to $w^{M-1}$)) is achieved by $h_M(x)$ corresponding to a pair $(z_k, \tau_k)$. Given this, the false alarm rate (also with respect to $w^{M-1}$) due to this new $h_M(x)$ can be calculated. The best pair $(z_{k^*}, \tau_{k^*})$ and hence $h_M(x)$ is the one that minimizes the false alarm rate.

There is still another parameter that can be tuned to balance between the detection rate and the false alarm rate: The class label prediction $\hat{y}(x) = \text{sign}[H_M(x)]$ is obtained by thresholding the strong classifier $H_M(x)$ at the default threshold value 0. However, it can be done as $\hat{y}(x) = \text{sign}[H_M(x) - T_M]$ with another value $T_M$, which can be tuned for the balance.

The form of Eq.(6) is for Discrete AdaBoost. In the case of real versions of AdaBoost, such as RealBoost and LogitBoost, a weak classifier should be real-valued or output the class label with a probability value. For the real-value type, a weak classifier may be constructed as the log-likelihood ratio computed from the histograms of the feature value for the two classes. (See the literature for more details [18, 19, 20]). For the latter, it may be a decision stump or tree with probability values attached to the leaves [22].

### 4.3  Boosted Strong Classifier

AdaBoost learns a sequence of weak classifiers $h_m$ and boosts them into a strong one $H_M$ effectively by minimizing the upper bound on classification error achieved by $H_M$. The bound can be derived as the following exponential loss function [33]

$$J(H_M) = \sum_i e^{-y_i H_M(x_i)} = \sum_i e^{-y_i \sum_{m=1}^{M} \alpha_m h_m(x)} \tag{7}$$

where $i$ is the index for training examples. AdaBoost construct $h_m(x)$ $(m = 1, \ldots, M)$ by stagewise minimization of Eq.(7). Given the current $H_{M-1}(x) = \sum_{m=1}^{M-1} \alpha_m h_m(x)$, and the newly learned weak classifier $h_M$, the best combining coefficient $\alpha_M$ for the new strong classifier $H_M(x) = H_{M-1}(x) + \alpha_M h_M(x)$ minimizes the cost

$$\alpha_M = \arg\min_\alpha J(H_{M-1}(x) + \alpha_m h_M(x)) \tag{8}$$

The minimizer is

$$\alpha_M = \log\frac{1 - \epsilon_M}{\epsilon_M} \tag{9}$$

where $\epsilon_M$ is the weighted error rate

$$\epsilon_M = \sum_i w_i^{(M-1)} 1[\mathrm{sign}(H_M(x_i)) \neq y_i] \tag{10}$$

where $1[C]$ is 1 if $C$ is true but 0 otherwise.

Each example is reweighted after an iteration i.e., $w_i^{(M-1)}$ is updated according to the classification performance of $H_M$:

$$
\begin{aligned}
w^{(M)}(x, y) &= w^{(M-1)}(x, y) \exp\left(-y\alpha_M h_M(x)\right) \\
&= \exp\left(-y H_M(x)\right)
\end{aligned}
\tag{11}
$$

which is used for calculating the weighted error or another cost for training the weak classifier in the next round. This way, a more difficult example is associated with a larger weight so it is emphasized more in the next round of learning. The algorithm is summarized in Figure 2.8.

---

0. (Input)
    (1) Training examples $\mathcal{Z} = \{(x_1, y_1), \ldots, (x_N, y_N)\}$,
        where $N = a + b$; of which $a$ examples have $y_i = +1$
        and $b$ examples have $y_i = -1$.
    (2) The number $M$ of weak classifiers to be combined.
1. (Initialization)
    $w_i^{(0)} = \frac{1}{2a}$ for those examples with $y_i = +1$ or
    $w_i^{(0)} = \frac{1}{2b}$ for those examples with $y_i = -1$.
2. (Forward inclusion)
    For $m = 1, \ldots, M$:
    (1) Choose optimal $h_m$ to minimize the weighted error.
    (2) Choose $\alpha_m$ according to Eq. (9).
    (3) Update $w_i^{(m)} \leftarrow w_i^{(m)} \exp[-y_i \alpha_m h_m(x_i)]$ and
        normalize to $\sum_i w_i^{(m)} = 1$.
3. (Output)
    Classification function: $H_M(x)$ as in Eq.(1).
    Class label prediction: $\hat{y}(x) = \mathrm{sign}[H_M(x)]$.

---

**Fig. 2.8.** AdaBoost learning algorithm.

## 4.4 FloatBoost Learning

AdaBoost attempts to boost the accuracy of an ensemble of weak classifiers. The AdaBoost algorithm [9] solves many of the practical difficulties of earlier boosting algorithms. Each weak classifier is trained stage-wise to minimize the empirical error for a given distribution reweighted according to the classification errors of the previously trained classifiers. It is shown that AdaBoost is a sequential forward search procedure using the greedy selection strategy to minimize a certain margin on the training set [33].

A crucial heuristic assumption used in such a sequential forward search procedure is the monotonicity (i.e., that addition of a new weak classifier to the current set does not decrease the value of the performance criterion). The premise offered by the sequential procedure in AdaBoost breaks down when this assumption is violated (i.e., when the performance criterion function is nonmonotonic).

Floating Search [30] is a sequential feature selection procedure with backtracking, aimed to deal with nonmonotonic criterion functions for feature selection. A straight sequential selection method such as sequential forward search or sequential backward search adds or deletes one feature at a time. To make this work well, the monotonicity property has to be satisfied by the performance criterion function. Feature selection with a nonmonotonic criterion may be dealt with using a more sophisticated technique, called plus-$\ell$-minus-$r$, which adds or deletes $\ell$ features and then backtracks $r$ steps [16, 40].

The sequential forward floating search (SFFS) methods [30] allows the number of backtracking steps to be controlled instead of being fixed beforehand. Specifically, it adds or deletes a single ($\ell = 1$) feature and then backtracks $r$ steps, where $r$ depends on the current situation. It is this flexibility that overcomes the limitations due to the nonmonotonicity problem. Improvement on the quality of selected features is achieved at the cost of increased computation due to the extended search. The SFFS algorithm performs well in several applications [15, 30]. The idea of floating search is further developed by allowing more flexibility for the determination of $\ell$ [39].

Let $\mathcal{H}_M = \{h_1, \ldots, h_M\}$ be the current set of $M$ weak classifiers, $J(H_M)$ be the criterion that measures the overall cost (e.g., error rate) of the classification function $H_M$, and $J_m^{\min}$ be the minimum cost achieved so far with a linear combination of $m$ weak classifiers whose value is initially set to very large before the iteration starts.

The FloatBoost Learning procedure is shown in Figure 2.9. It is composed of several parts: the training input, initialization, forward inclusion, conditional exclusion, and output. In step 2 (forward inclusion), the currently most significant weak classifiers are added one at a time, which is the same as in AdaBoost. In step 3 (conditional exclusion), FloatBoost removes the least significant weak classifier from the set $\mathcal{H}_M$ of current weak classifiers, subject to the condition that the removal leads to a lower cost than $J_{M-1}^{\min}$. Supposing that the weak classifier removed was the $m'$-th in $\mathcal{H}_M$, then $h_{m'}, \ldots, h_{M-1}$ and the $\alpha_m$'s must be relearned. These steps are repeated until no more removals can be done.

For face detection, the acceptable cost $J^*$ is the maximum allowable risk, which can be defined as a weighted sum of the missing rate and the false alarm rate. The algorithm terminates when the cost is below $J^*$ or the maximum number $M$ of weak classifiers is reached.

FloatBoost usually needs a fewer number of weak classifiers than AdaBoost to achieve a given objective function value $J^*$. Based on this observation, one has two options: (1) Use

0. (Input)
    (1) Training examples $\mathcal{Z} = \{(\mathbf{x}_1, y_1), \ldots, (\mathbf{x}_N, y_N)\}$,
       where $N = a + b$; of which $a$ examples have
       $y_i = +1$ and $b$ examples have $y_i = -1$.
    (2) The maximum number $M_{\max}$ of weak classifiers.
    (3) The cost function $J(H_M)$, and the maximum acceptable cost $J^*$.
1. (Initialization)
    (1) $w_i^{(0)} = \frac{1}{2a}$ for those examples with $y_i = +1$ or
       $w_i^{(0)} = \frac{1}{2b}$ for those examples with $y_i = -1$.
    (2) $J_m^{\min} =$ max-value (for $m = 1, \ldots, M_{\max}$),
       $M = 0, \mathcal{H}_0 = \{\}$.
2. (Forward inclusion)
    (1) $M \leftarrow M + 1$.
    (2) Learn $h_M$ and $\alpha_M$.
    (3) Update $w_i^{(M)} \leftarrow w_i^{(M-1)} \exp[-y_i \alpha_M h_M(x_i)]$,
       normalize to $\sum_i w_i^{(M)} = 1$.
    (4) $\mathcal{H}_M = \mathcal{H}_{M-1} \cup \{h_M\}$;
       If $J_M^{\min} > J(H_M)$, then $J_M^{\min} = J(H_M)$.
3. (Conditional exclusion)
    (1) $h' = \arg \min_{h \in \mathcal{H}_M} J(H_M - h)$.
    (2) If $J(H_M - h') < J_{M-1}^{\min}$, then
       (a) $\mathcal{H}_{M-1} = \mathcal{H}_M - h'$.
          $J_{M-1}^{\min} = J(H_M - h'); M = M - 1$.
       (b) If $h' = h_{m'}$, then
          recalculate $w_i^{(j)}$ and $h_j$ for $j = m', \ldots, M$.
       (c) Go to 3.(1).
    (3) Else
       (a) If $M = M_{\max}$ or $J(\mathcal{H}_M) < J^*$, then go to 4.
       (b) Go to 2.(1).
4. (Output)
    Classification function: $H_M(x)$ as in Eq.(1).
    Class label prediction: $\hat{y}(x) = \text{sign}[H_M(x)]$.

**Fig. 2.9.** FloatBoost algorithm.

the FloatBoost-trained strong classifier with its fewer weak classifiers to achieve similar performance, as can be done by a AdaBoost-trained classifier with more weak classifiers; (2) continue FloatBoost learning to add more weak classifiers even if the performance on the training data does not increase. The reason for considering option (2) is that even if the performance does not improve on the training data, adding more weak classifiers may lead to improvements on test data [33]; however, the best way to determine how many weak classifiers to use for FloatBoost, as well as AdaBoost, is to use a validation set to generate a performance curve and then choose the best number.

### 4.5 Cascade of Strong Classifiers

A boosted strong classifier effectively eliminates a large portion of nonface subwindows while maintaining a high detection rate. Nonetheless, a single strong classifier may not meet the requirement of an extremely low false alarm rate (e.g., $10^{-6}$ or even lower). A solution is to arbitrate between several detectors (strong classifier) [32], for example, using the "AND" operation.

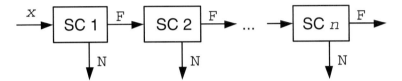

**Fig. 2.10.** A cascade of $n$ strong classifiers (SC). The input is a subwindow $x$. It is sent to the next SC for further classification only if it has passed all the previous SCs as the face (F) pattern; otherwise it exits as nonface (N). $x$ is finally considered to be a face when it passes all the $n$ SCs.

Viola and Jones [46, 47] further extend this idea by training a cascade consisting of a cascade of strong classifiers, as illustrated in Figure 2.10. A strong classifier is trained using bootstrapped nonface examples that pass through the previously trained cascade. Usually, 10 to 20 strong classifiers are cascaded. For face detection, subwindows that fail to pass a strong classifier are not further processed by the subsequent strong classifiers. This strategy can significantly speed up the detection and reduce false alarms, with a little sacrifice of the detection rate.

## 5 Dealing with Head Rotations

Multiview face detection should be able to detect nonfrontal faces. There are three types of head rotation: (1) out-of-plane (left-right) rotation; (2) in-plane rotation; and (3) up-and-down nodding rotation. Adopting a coarse-to-fine view-partition strategy, the detector-pyramid architecture consists of several levels from the coarse top level to the fine bottom level.

Rowley et al. [31] propose to use two neural network classifiers for detection of frontal faces subject to in-plane rotation. The first is the router network, trained to estimate the orientation of an assumed face in the subwindow, though the window may contain a nonface pattern. The inputs to the network are the intensity values in a preprocessed $20\times20$ subwindow. The angle of rotation is represented by an array of 36 output units, in which each unit represents an anglar range. With the orientation estimate, the subwindow is derotated to make the potential face upright. The second neural network is a normal frontal, upright face detector.

Li et al. [18, 20] constructed a detector-pyramid to detect the presence of upright faces, subject to out-of-plane rotation in the range $\Theta = [-90°, +90°]$ and in-plane rotation in $\Phi = [-45°, +45°]$. The in-plane rotation in $\Phi = [-45, +45]$ may be handled as follows: (1) Divide $\Phi$ into three subranges: $\Phi_1 = [-45, -15]$, $\Phi_2 = [-15, +15]$, and $\Phi_3 = [+15, +45]$. (2) Apply the detector-pyramid on the original image and two images derived from the original one; the two images are derived by rotating the original one in the image plane by $\pm 30$ (Figure 2.11). This effectively covers in-plane-rotation in $[-45, +45]$. The up-and-down nodding rotation is dealt with by the tolerance of the face detectors to this.

**Fig. 2.11.** Middle: An image containing frontal faces subject to in-plane rotation. Left and right: In-plane rotated by $\pm 30°$.

The design of the detector-pyramid adopts the coarse-to-fine and simple-to-complex strategy [2, 8]. The architecture is illustrated in Figure 2.12. This architecture design is for the detection of faces subject to out-of-plane rotation in $\Theta = [-90°, +90°]$ and in-plane rotation in $\Phi_2 = [-15°, +15°]$. The full in-plane rotation in $\Phi = [-45°, +45°]$ is dealt with by applying the detector-pyramid on the images rotated $\pm 30°$, as mentioned earlier.

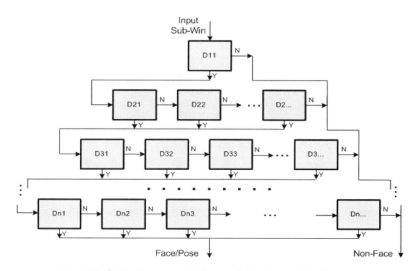

**Fig. 2.12.** Detector-pyramid for multiview face detection.

**<u>Coarse-to-fine</u>** The partitions of the out-of-plane rotation for the three-level detector-pyramid is illustrated in Figure 2.13. As the the level goes from coarse to fine, the full range $\Theta$ of out-of-plane rotation is partitioned into increasingly narrower ranges. Although there are no overlaps between the partitioned view subranges at each level, a face detector trained for one view may detect faces of its neighboring views. Therefore, faces detected by the seven channels at the bottom level of the detector-pyramid must be merged to obtain the final result. This is illustrated in Figure 2.14.

| -90 | -80 | -70 | -60 | -50 | -40 | -30 | -20 | -10 | 0 | 10 | 20 | 30 | 40 | 50 | 60 | 70 | 80 | 90 |
|-----|-----|-----|-----|-----|-----|-----|-----|-----|---|----|----|----|----|----|----|----|----|----|

**Fig. 2.13.** Out-of-plane view partition. Out-of-plane head rotation (row 1), the facial view labels (row 2), and the coarse-to-fine view partitions at the three levels of the detector-pyramid (rows 3 to 5).

**Simple-to-complex** A large number of subwindows result from the scan of the input image. For example, there can be tens to hundreds of thousands of them for an image of size $320 \times 240$, the actual number depending on how the image is scanned (e.g., regarding the scale increment factor). For the purpose of efficiency, it is crucial to discard as many nonface subwindows as possible at the earliest possible stage so as few as possible subwindows are processed further at later stages. Therefore, the detectors in the early stages are designed to be simple so that they can reject nonface subwindows quickly with little computation, whereas those at the later stage are more complex and require more computation.

**Fig. 2.14.** Merging from different channels. From left to right: Outputs of fontal, left, and right view channels and the final result after the merge.

# 6 Postprocessing

A single face in an image may be detected several times at close locations or on multiple scales. False alarms may also occur but usually with less consistency than multiple face detections. The number of multiple detections in a neighborhood of a location can be used as an effective indication for the existence of a face at that location. This assumption leads to a heuristic for resolving the ambiguity caused by multiple detections and eliminating many false detections.

A detection is confirmed if the number of multiple detections is greater than a given value; and given the confirmation, multiple detections are merged into a consistent one. This is practiced in most face detection systems [32, 41]. Figure 2.15 gives an illustration. The image on the left shows a typical output of initial detection, where the face is detected four times with four false alarms on the cloth. On the right is the final result after merging. After the postprocessing, multiple detections are merged into a single face and the false alarms are eliminated. Figures 2.16 and 2.17 show some typical frontal and multiview face detection examples; the multiview face images are from the Carnegie Mellon University (CMU) face database [45].

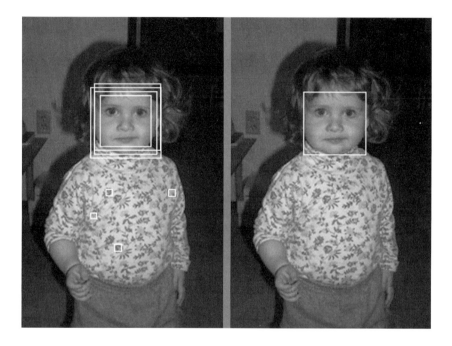

**Fig. 2.15.** Merging multiple detections.

## 7 Performance Evaluation

The result of face detection from an image is affected by the two basic components: the face/nonface classifier and the postprocessing (merger). To understand how the system works, it is recommended that the two components be evaluateed separately [1], with two types of test data. The first consists of face icons of a fixed size (as are used for training). This process aims to evaluate the performance of the face/nonface classifier (preprocessing included), without being affected by merging. The second type of test data consists of normal images. In this case, the face detection results are affected by both trained classifier and merging; the overall system performance is evaluated.

**Fig. 2.16.** Results of frontal face detection.

## 7.1 Performance Measures

The face detection performance is primarily measured by two rates: the correct detection rate (which is 1 minus the miss detection rate) and the false alarm rate. The performance can be observed by plotting on the receiver operating characteristic ROC curves. Figure 2.18 shows a typical ROC curve for face detection. An ideal face detection system should have a detection rate of 100%, with a false alarm rate of 0, though none of the current systems can achieve this generally. In practical systems, increasing the detection rate is usually accompanied by an increase in the false alarm rate. In the case where a confidence function is used to distinguish between the face and nonface subwindows, with the high output value indicating the detection of face and low value nonface, a trade-off between the two rates can be made by adjusting the decisional threshold. In the case of the AdaBoost learning method, the threshold for Eq.(1) is learned from the training face icons and bootstrapped nonface icons, so a specified rate (usually the false alarm rate) is under control for the training set. Remember that performance numbers of a system are always with respect to the data sets used (the reader is referred to Chapter 13 for face detection databases); two algorithms or systems cannot be compared directly unless the same data sets are used.

**Fig. 2.17.** Results of multiview face detection.

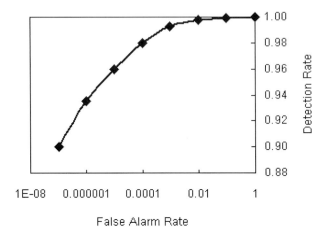

**Fig. 2.18.** Typical ROC curve for face detection.

## 7.2 Comparison of Boosting-Based Algorithms

As AdaBoost-based methods (with local Haar wavelet features) have so far provided the best face detection solutions in terms of the statistical rates and the speed, the following provides a comparative evaluation on different boosting algorithms (DAB: discrete Adaboost; RAB: real Adaboost; and GAB: gentle Adaboost), different training sets preparations, and different weak classifiers [22]. The results provide empirical references for face detection engineers.

### Boosting Algorithms

Three 20-stage cascade classifiers were trained with DAB, RAB, and GAB using the Haar-like feature set of Viola and Jones [46, 47] and stumps as the weak classifiers. It is reported that GAB outperformed the other two boosting algorithms [22]; for instance, at an absolute false alarm rate of 10 on the CMU test set, RAB detected only 75.4% and DAB only 79.5% of all frontal faces, and GAB achieved 82.7% at a rescale factor of 1.1. Also, a smaller rescaling factor of 1.1 for scanning images was beneficial for a high detection rate. For example, at 10 false alarms on the CMU test set, GAB improved from a detection rate of 68.8% to that of 82.7% when the rescaling factor was decreased from 1.2 to 1.1.

### Weak Classifiers: Tree versus Stumps

Stumps are the simplest tree type of weak classifiers (WCs) that can be used in discrete AdaBoost. A stump, as in Eq.(6), is a single-node tree that does not allow learning dependence between features. In general, $n$ split nodes are needed to model dependence between $n-1$ variables. Table 2.1 compares the CART tree weak classifiers of varying number of nodes in terms of the effectiveness of rejecting nonface subwindows. It is observed that RAB is most effective.

**Table 2.1.** Average number of features evaluated per nonface subwindow of size 20×20 (Reproduced from Lienhart et al. [22]).

| AdaBoost Type | Number of Splits | | | |
|---|---|---|---|---|
| | 1 | 2 | 3 | 4 |
| DAB | 45.09 | 44.43 | 31.86 | 44.86 |
| GAB | 30.99 | 36.03 | 28.58 | 35.40 |
| RAB | 26.28 | 33.16 | 26.73 | 35.71 |

**Basic versus Extended Haar-like Features**

Two face detection systems were trained: one with the basic Haar-like feature set of Viola and Jones [46, 47], and one with the extended haar-like feature set in which rotated versions of the basic Haar features are added. On average the false alarm rate was about 10% lower for the extended haar-like feature set at comparable hit rates. At the same time the computational complexity was comparable. This suggests that whereas the larger Haar-like feature set makes it more complex in both time and memory in the boosting learning phase, gain is obtained in the detection phase.

**Subwindow Size**

Different subwindow sizes, ranging from $16 \times 16$ up to $32 \times 32$, have been used on face detection. The experiments [22] show that a subwindow size of $20{\times}20$ achieves the highest detection rate at an absolute number of false alarms between 5 and 100 on the CMU test set of frontal faces. A subwindow size of $24 \times 24$ worked better for false alarms fewer than five.

# 8 Conclusions

Face detection is the first step in automated face recognition and has applications in biometrics and multimedia management. Owing to the complexity of the face and nonface manifolds, highly accurate face detection with a high detection rate and low false alarm rate has been challenging. Now this difficult problem has almost been solved to meet the minimum requirements of most practical applications, bebcause of the advances in face recognition research and machine learning.

AdaBoost learning-based face detection methods [18, 20, 22, 46, 47] have been the most effective of all those developed so far. In terms of detection and false alarm rates, they are comparable to the neural network method of Rowley et al. [32], but are several times faster.

Regarding the AdaBoost approach, the following conclusions can be drawn in terms of feature sets, boosting algorithms, weak classifiers, subwindow sizes, and training set sizes according to reported studies [18, 20, 22, 46, 47]:

- An over-complete set of Haar-like features are effective for face detection. The use of the integral image method makes computation of these features efficient and achieves scale invariance. Extended Haar-like features help detect nonfrontal faces.

- AdaBoost learning can select best subset from a large feature set and construct a powerful nonlinear classifier.
- The cascade structure significantly improves the detection speed and effectively reduces false alarms, with a little sacrifice of the detection rate.
- FloatBoost effectively improves boosting learning result. It results in a classifier that needs fewer weaker classifiers than the one obtained using AdaBoost to achieve a similar error rate, or achieve a lower error rate with the same number of weak classifiers. This run time improvement is obatined at the cost of longer training time (about times times longer).
- Less aggressive versions of Adaboost, such as GentleBoost and LogitBoost, may be preferable to discrete and real Adaboost in dealing with training data containing outliers [10].
- Representationally, more complex weak classifiers such as small CART trees can model second-order and/or third-order dependencies, and may be beneficial for the nonlinear task of face detection.
- The optimal input subwindow size for frontal face detection appears to be $20 \times 20$.

Although face detection technology is now sufficiently mature to meet the minimum requirements of many practical applications, much work is still needed before automatic face detection can achieve performance comparable to the human performance. The Haar+AdaBoost approach is effective and efficient. However, the current approach has almost reached its power limit. Within such a framework, possible improvements may be possible by designing additional sets of features that are complementary to the existing ones and adopting more advanced learning techniques, which could lead to more complex classifiers while avoiding the overfitting problem.

## Acknowledgment

The author thanks Rainer Lienhart for useful discussions on the evaluation of AdaBoost-based methods.

## References

1. M. Alvira and R. Rifkin. An empirical comparison of SNoW and svms for face detection". Technical Report AI Momo 2001-004 & CBCL Memo 193, MIT, 2001.
2. Y. Amit, D. Geman, and K. Wilder. Joint induction of shape features and tree classifiers. *IEEE Transactions on Pattern Analysis and Machine Intelligence*, 19:1300–1305, 1997.
3. S. Baker and S. Nayar. Pattern rejection. In *Proceedings of IEEE Computer Society Conference on Computer Vision and Pattern Recognition*, pages 544–549,1996.
4. M. Bichsel and A. P. Pentland. Human face recognition and the face image set's topology. *CVGIP: Image Understanding*, 59:254–261, 1994.
5. F. Crow. Summed-area tables for texture mapping. In *SIGGRAPH*, volume 18(3), pages 207–212, 1984.
6. M. Elad, Y. Hel-Or, and R. Keshet. Pattern detection using a maximal rejection classifier. *Pattern Recognition Letters*, 23:1459–1471, 2002.
7. J. Feraud, O. Bernier, and M. Collobert. A fast and accurate face detector for indexation of face images. In *Proc. Fourth IEEE Int. Conf on Automatic Face and Gesture Recognition*, Grenoble 2000.

8. F. Fleuret and D. Geman. Coarse-to-fine face detection. *International Journal of Computer Vision*, 20:1157–1163, 2001.

9. Y. Freund and R. Schapire. A decision-theoretic generalization of on-line learning and an application to boosting. *Journal of Computer and System Sciences*, 55(1):119–139, August 1997.

10. J. Friedman, T. Hastie, and R. Tibshirani. Additive logistic regression: a statistical view of boosting. Technical report, Department of Statistics, Sequoia Hall, Stanford Univerity, July 1998.

11. S. Gong, S. McKenna, and J. Collins. An investigation into face pose distribution. In *Proc. IEEE International Conference on Face and Gesture Recognition*, Vermont, 1996.

12. E. Hjelmas and B. K. Low. Face detection: A survey. *Computer Vision and Image Understanding*, 3(3):236–274, September 2001.

13. R.-L. Hsu, M. Abdel-Mottaleb, and A. K. Jain. Face detection in color images. *IEEE Transactions on Pattern Analysis and Machine Intelligence*, 24(5):696–706, 2002.

14. J. Huang, X. Shao, and H. Wechsler. Face pose discrimination using support vector machines (SVM). In *Proceedings of International Conference Pattern Recognition*, Brisbane, Queensland, Australia, 1998.

15. A. Jain and D. Zongker. Feature selection: evaluation, application, and samll sample performance. *IEEE Transactions on Pattern Analysis and Machine Intelligence*, 19(2):153–158, 1997.

16. J. Kittler. Feature set search algorithm. In C. H. Chen, editor, *Pattern Recognition in Practice*, pages 41–60. NorthHolland, Sijthoff and Noordhoof, 1980.

17. A. Kuchinsky, C. Pering, M. L. Creech, D. Freeze, B. Serra, and J. Gwizdka. FotoFile: A consumer multimedia organization and retrieval system. In *Proceedings of ACM SIG CHI'99 Conference*, Pittsburg, May 1999.

18. S. Z. Li and Z. Zhang. FloatBoost learning and statistical face detection. *IEEE Transactions on Pattern Analysis and Machine Intelligence*, 26(9):1112–1123, 2004.

19. S. Z. Li, Z. Q. Zhang, H.-Y. Shum, and H. Zhang. FloatBoost learning for classification. In *Proceedings of Neural Information Processing Systems*, Vancouver, 2002.

20. S. Z. Li, L. Zhu, Z. Q. Zhang, A. Blake, H. Zhang, and H. Shum. Statistical learning of multi-view face detection. In *Proceedings of the European Conference on Computer Vision*, volume 4, pages 67–81, Copenhagen, Denmark, May 28 - June 2 2002.

21. Y. M. Li, S. G. Gong, and H. Liddell. Support vector regression and classification based multi-view face detection and recognition. In *IEEE Int. Conf. Oo Face & Gesture Recognition*, pages 300–305, Grenoble, 2000.

22. R. Lienhart, A. Kuranov, and V. Pisarevsky. Empirical analysis of detection cascades of boosted classifiers for rapid object detection. MRL Technical Report, Intel Labs, December 2002.

23. C. Liu. A Bayesian discriminating features method for face detection. *IEEE Transactions on Pattern Analysis and Machine Intelligence*, 25(6):725–740, 2003.

24. B. Martinkauppi. *Face colour under varying illumination - analysis and applications*. Ph.D. thesis, Department of Electrical and Information Engineering, University of Oulu, Finland, 2002.

25. B. Moghaddam and A. Pentland. Probabilistic visual learning for object representation. *IEEE Transactions on Pattern Analysis and Machine Intelligence*, 7:696–710, 1997.

26. J. Ng and S. Gong. Performing multi-view face detection and pose estimation using a composite support vector machine across the view sphere. In *Proc. IEEE International Workshop on Recognition, Analysis, and Tracking of Faces and Gestures in Real-Time Systems*, pages 14–21, Corfu, 1999.

27. E. Osuna, R. Freund, and F. Girosi. Training support vector machines: An application to face detection. In *CVPR*, pages 130–136, 1997.

28. C. P. Papageorgiou, M. Oren, and T. Poggio. A general framework for object detection. In *Proceedings of IEEE International Conference on Computer Vision*, pages 555–562, Bombay, 1998.

29. A. P. Pentland, B. Moghaddam, and T. Starner. View-based and modular eigenspaces for face recognition. In *Proceedings of IEEE Computer Society Conference on Computer Vision and Pattern Recognition*, pages 84–91, 1994.

30. P. Pudil, J. Novovicova, and J. Kittler. Floating search methods in feature selection. *Pattern Recognition Letters*, 15(11):1119–1125, 1994.

31. H. Rowley, S. Baluja, and T. Kanade. Rotation invariant neural network-based face detection. In *Proceedings of IEEE Computer Society Conference on Computer Vision and Pattern Recognition*, 1998.

32. H. A. Rowley, S. Baluja, and T. Kanade. Neural network-based face detection. *IEEE Transactions on Pattern Analysis and Machine Intelligence*, 20(1):23–28, 1998.

33. R. Schapire, Y. Freund, P. Bartlett, and W. S. Lee. Boosting the margin: A new explanation for the effectiveness of voting methods. *Annals of Statistics*, 26(5):1651–1686, 1998.

34. H. Schneiderman. *A Statistical Approach to 3D Object Detection Applied to Faces and Cars (CMU-RI-TR-00-06)*. PhD thesis, RI, 2000.

35. H. Schneiderman and T. Kanade. A statistical method for 3D object detection applied to faces and cars. In *Proceedings of IEEE Computer Society Conference on Computer Vision and Pattern Recognition*, 2000.

36. H. Schneiderman and T. Kanade. Object detection using the statistics of parts. *International Journal of Computer Vision*, 56(3):151–177, Feb 2004.

37. P. Y. Simard, L. Bottou, P. Haffner, and Y. L. Cun. Boxlets: a fast convolution algorithm for signal processing and neural networks. In M. Kearns, S. Solla, and D. Cohn, editors, *Advances in Neural Information Processing Systems*, volume 11, pages 571–577. MIT Press, 1998.

38. P. Y. Simard, Y. A. L. Cun, J. S. Denker, and B. Victorri. Transformation invariance in pattern recognition - tangent distance and tangent propagation. In G. B. Orr and K.-R. Muller, editors, *Neural Networks: Tricks of the Trade*. Springer, New York, 1998.

39. P. Somol, P. Pudil, J. Novoviova, and P. Paclik. Adaptive floating search methods in feature selection. *Pattern Recognition Letters*, 20:1157–1163, 1999.

40. S. D. Stearns. On selecting features for pattern classifiers. In *Proceedings of International Conference Pattern Recognition*, pages 71–75, 1976.

41. K.-K. Sung and T. Poggio. Example-based learning for view-based human face detection. *IEEE Transactions on Pattern Analysis and Machine Intelligence*, 20(1):39–51, 1998.

42. K. Tieu and P. Viola. Boosting image retrieval. In *Proceedings of IEEE Computer Society Conference on Computer Vision and Pattern Recognition*, volume 1, pages 228–235, 2000.

43. M. Turk. A random walk through eigenspace. *IEICE Trans. Inf. & Syst.*, E84-D(12):1586–1695, 2001.

44. M. A. Turk and A. P. Pentland. Eigenfaces for recognition. *Journal of Cognitive Neuroscience*, 3(1):71–86, 1991.

45. Various. Face Detection Databases, www.ri.cmu.edu/projects/project_419.html.

46. P. Viola and M. Jones. Rapid object detection using a boosted cascade of simple features. In *Proceedings of IEEE Computer Society Conference on Computer Vision and Pattern Recognition*, Kauai, Hawaii, 12-14 2001.

47. P. Viola and M. Jones. Robust real time object detection. In *IEEE ICCV Workshop on Statistical and Computational Theories of Vision*, Vancouver, 2001.

48. L. Wiskott, J. Fellous, N. Kruger, and C. v. d. malsburg. Face recognition by elastic bunch graph matching. *IEEE Transactions on Pattern Analysis and Machine Intelligence*, 19(7):775–779, 1997.

49. J. Yang, W. Lu, and A. Waibel. Skin-color modeling and adaptation. In *Proceedings of the First Asian Conference on Computer Vision*, pages 687–694, 1998.

50. M.-H. Yang and N. Ahuja. Gaussian mixture model for human skin color and its application in image and video databases. In *Proc. of the SPIE Conf. on Storage and Retrieval for Image and Video Databases*, volume 3656, pages 458–466, San Jose, 1999.

51. M.-H. Yang, N. Ahuja, and D. Kriegman. Face detection using mixtures of linear subspaces. In *Proceedings of the 4-th IEEE International Conference on Automatic Face and Gesture Recognition*, pages 70–76, Grenoble, 2000.

52. M.-H. Yang, D. Kriegman, and N. Ahuja. Detecting faces in images: a survey. *IEEE Transactions on Pattern Analysis and Machine Intelligence*, 24(1):34–58, 2002.

53. M.-H. Yang, D. Roth, and N. Ahuja. A SNoW-based face detector. In *Proceedings of Neural Information Processing Systems*, pages 855–861, 2000.

54. B. D. Zarit, B. J. Super, and F. K. H. Quek. Comparison of five color models in skin pixel classification. In *IEEE ICCV Workshop on Recognition, Analysis and Tracking of Faces and Gestures in Real-time Systems*, pages 58–63, Corfu, Greece, September 1999.

# Chapter 3. Modeling Facial Shape and Appearance

Tim Cootes, Chris Taylor, Haizhuang Kang, Vladimir Petrović

Imaging Science and Biomedical Engineering, University of Manchester, UK

To interpret images of faces, it is important to have a model of how the face can appear. Faces can vary widely, but the changes can be broken down into two parts: changes in shape and changes in the texture (patterns of pixel values) across the face. Both shape and texture can vary because of differences between individuals and due to changes in expression, viewpoint, and lighting conditions. In this chapter we will describe a powerful method of generating compact models of shape and texture variation and describe how such models can be used to interpret images of faces.

## 1 Statistical Models of Appearance

We wish to build models of facial appearance and its variation. We adopt a statistical approach, learning the ways in which the shape and texture of the face vary across a range of images. We rely on obtaining a suitably large, representative training set of facial images, each of which is annotated with a set of feature points defining correspondences across the set. The positions of the feature points are used to define the shape of the face and are analyzed to learn the ways in which the shape can vary. The patterns of intensities are then analyzed to learn the ways in which the texture can vary. The result is a model capable of synthesizing any of the training images and generalizing from them, but it is specific enough that only face-like images are generated.

### 1.1 Statistical Shape Models

To build a statistical model, we require a set of training images. The set should be chosen so it covers the types of variation we wish the model to represent. For instance, if we are interested only in faces with neutral expressions, we should include only neutral expressions in the model. If, however, we wish to be able to synthesize and recognize a range of expressions, the training set should include images of people smiling, frowning, winking, and so on. The faces in the training set should be of a resolution at least as high as those in the images we wish to synthesize or interpret.

Each face must then be annotated with a set of points defining the key facial features. These points are used to define the correspondences across the training set and represent the shape of the face in the image. Thus the same number of points should be placed on each image and with the same set of labels. For instance, the first point might be the center of the left eye, the second the center of the right eye, and so on. Figure 3.1 shows a set of 68 points used to annotate frontal faces. The more points used, the more subtle are the variations in shape that can be represented. Typically, one would place points around the main facial features (eyes, nose, mouth, eyebrows) together with points around the outline to define the boundary of the face.

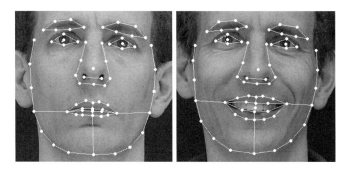

**Fig. 3.1.** Example of 68 points defining facial features.

Shape is usually defined as the quality of a configuration of points that is invariant under some transformation. In two or three dimensions we usually consider either the similarity transformation (translation, rotation, scaling) or the affine transformation.

Let $S_\mathbf{t}(\mathbf{x})$ apply a transformation defined by parameters in vector $\mathbf{t}$. In two-dimensional similarity transformations have four parameters, affine transformations are defined by six parameters. The configurations of points defined by $\mathbf{x}$ and $S_\mathbf{t}(\mathbf{x})$ are considered to have the same *shape*. Shape differences are those changes that cannot be explained by application of such a global transformation. Advances in the statistics of shape allow formal statistical techniques to be applied to sets of shapes, making possible analysis of shape differences and changes [15].

Our aim is to derive models that allow us to both analyze new shapes and synthesize shapes similar to those in a training set.

If we use $n$ points, $\{(x_i, y_i)\}$, to describe the face shape, we can represent the shape as the $2n$ element vector, $\mathbf{x}$, where

$$\mathbf{x} = (x_1, \dots, x_n, y_1, \dots, y_n)^T \tag{1}$$

Given $s$ training examples, we generate $s$ such vectors $\mathbf{x}_j$. Before we can perform statistical analysis on these vectors it is important that the shapes represented are in the same coordinate frame. We wish to remove variation that could be attributable to the allowed global transformation, $S(\mathbf{x})$.

**Aligning Sets of Shapes**

There is considerable literature on methods of aligning shapes into a common coordinate frame, the most popular approach being Procrustes analysis [17]. This transforms each shape in a set, $\mathbf{x}_i$, so the sum of squared distances of the shape to the mean ($D = \sum |S(\mathbf{x}_i) - \bar{\mathbf{x}}|^2$) is minimized. It is poorly defined unless constraints are placed on the alignment of the mean (for instance, ensuring that it is centered on the origin and has unit scale and some fixed but arbitrary orientation).

To align a single shape $\mathbf{x}$ to the mean, $\bar{\mathbf{x}}$, choose the parameters, $\mathbf{t}$, which minimize $|S_{\mathbf{t}}(\mathbf{x}) - \bar{\mathbf{x}}|^2$.

Although analytic solutions exist to the alignment of a *set* of shapes, a simple iterative approach is as follows.

1. Translate each example so its center of gravity is at the origin.
2. Choose one example as an initial estimate of the mean shape and scale so $|\bar{\mathbf{x}}| = 1$.
3. Record the first estimate as $\bar{\mathbf{x}}_0$ to define the default reference frame.
4. Align all the shapes with the current estimate of the mean shape.
5. Reestimate the mean from aligned shapes.
6. Apply constraints on the current estimate of the mean by aligning it with $\bar{\mathbf{x}}_0$ and scaling so $|\bar{\mathbf{x}}| = 1$.
7. If not converged, return to step 4.

Convergence is declared if the estimate of the mean does not change significantly after an iteration. On convergence, all the examples are aligned in a common coordinate frame and can be analyzed for shape change.

**Statistical Models of Variation**

Suppose now we have $s$ sets of $n$ points $\mathbf{x}_i$ in $d$ dimensions (usually two or three) that are aligned into a common coordinate frame. These vectors form a distribution in $nd$ dimensional space. If we can model this distribution, we can generate new examples similar to those in the original training set, and we can examine new shapes to determine if they are plausible examples.

In particular we seek a parameterized model of the form $\mathbf{x} = M(\mathbf{b})$, where $\mathbf{b}$ is a vector of parameters of the model. Such a model can be used to generate new vectors, $\mathbf{x}$. If we can model the distribution of parameters, $p_b(\mathbf{b})$, we can limit them so the generated $\mathbf{x}$'s are similar to those in the training set. Similarly it should be possible to estimate $p_x(\mathbf{x})$ using the model.

To simplify the problem, we first wish to reduce the dimensionality of the data from $nd$ to something more manageable. An effective approach is to apply principal component analysis (PCA) to the data. The data form a cloud of points in the $nd$-D space. PCA computes the main axes of this cloud, allowing one to approximate any of the original points using a model with fewer than $nd$ parameters. The approach is as follows.

1. Compute the mean of the data.

$$\bar{\mathbf{x}} = \frac{1}{s} \sum_{i=1}^{s} \mathbf{x}_i \tag{2}$$

2. Compute the covariance of the data.

$$\mathbf{S} = \frac{1}{s-1} \sum_{i=1}^{s} (\mathbf{x}_i - \bar{\mathbf{x}})(\mathbf{x}_i - \bar{\mathbf{x}})^T \tag{3}$$

3. Compute the eigenvectors, $\phi_i$ and corresponding eigenvalues $\lambda_i$ of $\mathbf{S}$ (sorted so $\lambda_i \geq \lambda_{i+1}$). Efficient methods of computing the eigenvectors and values exist for the case in which there are fewer samples than dimensions in the vectors [11].

We can approximate any example from the training set, $\mathbf{x}$ using

$$\mathbf{x} \approx \bar{\mathbf{x}} + \mathbf{P}_s \mathbf{b}_s \tag{4}$$

where $\mathbf{P}_s = (\phi_1 | \phi_2 | \dots | \phi_t)$ contains the $t$ eigenvectors corresponding to the largest eigenvalues, and $\mathbf{b}_s$ is a $t$ dimensional vector given by

$$\mathbf{b}_s = \mathbf{P}_s^T (\mathbf{x} - \bar{\mathbf{x}}) \tag{5}$$

$\mathbf{P}^T \mathbf{P} = \mathbf{I}$ because the eigenvectors are orthonormal.

The vector $\mathbf{b}_s$ defines a set of parameters of a deformable model. By varying the elements of $\mathbf{b}_s$ we can vary the shape, $\mathbf{x}$, using Eq. (4). The variance of the $i^{th}$ parameter, $b_i$, across the training set is given by $\lambda_i$. By applying suitable limits (for instance $\pm 3\sqrt{\lambda_i}$ to the parameter $b_i$) we ensure that the shape generated is similar to those in the original training set.

If the original data, $\{\mathbf{x}_i\}$, is distributed as a multivariate Gaussian, the parameters $\mathbf{b}$ are distributed as an axis-aligned Gaussian, $p(\mathbf{b}) - N(\mathbf{0}, \Lambda)$ where $\Lambda = diag(\lambda_1, \dots, \lambda_t)$. Our experiments on 2D images suggest that the Gaussian assumption is a good approximation to the face shape distribution, so long as the training set contains only modest viewpoint variation. Large viewpoint variation tends to introduce nonlinear changes into the shape [10].

A shape in the image frame, $\mathbf{X}$, can be generated by applying a suitable transformation to the points, $\mathbf{x}$: $\mathbf{X} = S_{\mathbf{t}}(\mathbf{x})$. Typically $S_{\mathbf{t}}$ is a similarity transformation described by a scaling, $s$, an in-plane rotation, $\theta$, and a translation $(t_x, t_y)$. For linearity we represent the scaling and rotation as $(s_x, s_y)$, where $s_x = (s \cos \theta - 1)$, $s_y = s \sin \theta$. The pose parameter vector $\mathbf{t} = (s_x, s_y, t_x, t_y)^T$ is then zero for the identity transformation, and $S_{\mathbf{t}}(\mathbf{x})$ is linear in the parameters.

**Choice of Number of Modes**

The number of modes to retain, $t$, can be chosen in several ways. A simple approach is to choose $t$ to explain a given proportion (e.g., 98%) of the variance exhibited in the training set.

Let $\lambda_i$ be the eigenvalues of the covariance matrix of the training data. Each eigenvalue gives the variance of the data about the mean in the direction of the corresponding eigenvector. The total variance in the training data is the sum of all the eigenvalues, $V_T = \sum \lambda_i$.

We can then choose the $t$ largest eigenvalues such that

$$\sum_{i=1}^{t} \lambda_i \geq f_v V_T \qquad (6)$$

where $f_v$ defines the proportion of the total variation one wishes to explain.

If the noise on the measurements of the (aligned) point positions has a variance of $\sigma_n^2$, we could choose the largest $t$ such that $\lambda_t > \sigma_n^2$, assuming that the eigenvalues are sorted into descending order.

An alternative approach is to choose enough modes that the model can approximate any training example to within a given accuracy. For instance, we may wish that the best approximation to an example has every point within one pixel of the corresponding example points.

To achieve this we build models with increasing numbers of modes, testing the ability of each to represent the training set. We choose the first model that passes our desired criteria.

Additional confidence can be obtained by performing this test in a miss-one-out manner. We choose the smallest $t$ for the full model such that models built with $t$ modes from all but any one example can approximate the missing example sufficiently well.

**Face Shape Variation**

Figure 3.2 shows the first two most significant modes of face shape variation of a model built from examples of a single individual with different viewpoints and expressions. The model has learned that the 2D shape change caused by 3D head rotation causes the largest shape change.

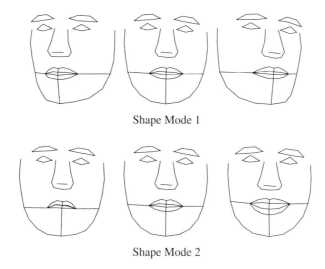

Shape Mode 1

Shape Mode 2

**Fig. 3.2.** Two modes of a face shape model (parameters varied by $\pm 2\sigma$ from the mean).

**Fitting the Model to New Points**

Suppose now we wish to find the best pose and shape parameters to match a model instance $\mathbf{x}$ to a new set of image points, $\mathbf{Y}$. minimizing the sum of square distances between corresponding model and image points is equivalent to minimizing the expression

$$E_{pts} = |\mathbf{Y} - S_{\mathbf{t}}(\bar{\mathbf{x}} + \mathbf{\Phi}_s \mathbf{b}_s)|^2 \tag{7}$$

More generally, we can allow different weights for different points by minimizing

$$E_{pts} = [\mathbf{Y} - S_{\mathbf{t}}(\bar{\mathbf{x}} + \mathbf{\Phi}_s \mathbf{b}_s)]^T \mathbf{W}_{pts}[\mathbf{Y} - S_{\mathbf{t}}(\bar{\mathbf{x}} + \mathbf{\Phi}_s \mathbf{b}_s)] \tag{8}$$

If the allowed global transformation $S_{\mathbf{t}}(.)$ is more complex than a simple translation, this is a nonlinear equation with no analytic solution. However a good approximation can be found rapidly using a two-stage iterative approach.

1. Solve for the pose parameters $\mathbf{t}$ assuming a fixed shape $\mathbf{b}_s$.
2. Solve for the shape parameters, $\mathbf{b}_s$, assuming a fixed pose.
3. Repeat until convergence.

Each of the steps reduces to the solution of a linear equation for common choices of transformation (e.g., similarity or affine) [19].

If the weights are chosen to relate to the uncertainty in the estimates of positions of target points $\mathbf{Y}$, $E_{pts}$ can be considered as a log likelihood. Priors on the shape parameters can then be included by minimizing

$$E'_{pts} = E_{pts} + \log p(\mathbf{b}_s) \tag{9}$$

If we assume a Gaussian distribution of shapes,

$$\log p(\mathbf{b}_s) \propto \sum_{i=1}^{t} b_i^2 / \lambda_i \tag{10}$$

## 1.2 Statistical Models of Texture

To build a statistical model of the texture (intensity or color over an image patch) we warp each example image so its feature points match a reference shape (typically the mean shape). The warping can be achieved using any continuous deformation, such as piece-wise affine using a triangulation of the region or an interpolating spline. Warping to a reference shape removes spurious texture variation due to shape differences that would occur if we simply performed eigenvector decomposition on the un-normalized face patches (as in the eigen-face approach [24, 31]). The intensity information is sampled from the *shape-normalized* image over the region covered by the mean shape to form a texture vector, $\mathbf{g}_{im}$. For example, Figure 3.3 shows a labeled face image and the face patch warped into the mean shape. Although the main shape changes due to smiling have been removed, there is considerable texture difference from a purely neutral face.

In practice, the texture sample $\mathbf{g}_{im}$ is obtained as follows. Assume that the points defining the shape of the object in the target image are given by $\mathbf{X}$.

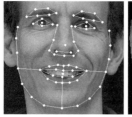 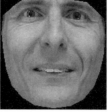

Original image        Warped to mean shape

**Fig. 3.3.** Example of face warped to mean shape.

- Precompute the pixel positions of the sample in the model reference frame, $(x_{s,i}, y_{s,i})$ (typically all the pixels in the region of interest).
- Construct a warping function, $W_{\mathbf{X}}(x, y)$, that maps the points of the mean shape onto the target points, $\mathbf{X}$.
- For each element $i$ in $\mathbf{g}_{im}$, sample the target image at $W_{\mathbf{X}}(x_{s,i}, y_{s,i})$ using interpolation if appropriate.

The texture sample has a fixed number of pixels, independent of the size of the object in the target image.

The texture sample is then normalized to remove global lighting effects. A simple approach is to apply a linear transformation

$$\mathbf{g} = (\mathbf{g}_{im} - \beta \mathbf{1})/\alpha \tag{11}$$

The values of $\alpha$ and $\beta$ can be chosen so the sum of the elements is zero and the variance of the elements is unity,

$$\beta = (\mathbf{g}_{im}.\mathbf{1})/n$$
$$\alpha = |\mathbf{g}_{im}|^2/n - \beta^2 \tag{12}$$

where $n$ is the number of elements in the vectors. For color images, each plane can be normalized separately.

By applying PCA to the normalized data, we obtain a linear model

$$\mathbf{g} = \bar{\mathbf{g}} + \mathbf{P}_g \mathbf{b}_g \tag{13}$$

where $\bar{\mathbf{g}}$ is the mean normalized gray-level vector, $\mathbf{P}_g$ is a set of orthogonal *modes of variation*, and $\mathbf{b}_g$ is a set of gray-level parameters.

The texture in the image frame can be generated from the texture parameters, $\mathbf{b}_g$, and the normalization parameters $\alpha, \beta$. The texture in the image frame is then given by

$$\mathbf{g}_{im} = \alpha(\bar{\mathbf{g}} + \mathbf{P}_g \mathbf{b}_g) + \beta \mathbf{1} \tag{14}$$

We generalize this to a texture transformation $T_{\mathbf{u}}(\mathbf{g})$ with parameters $\mathbf{u}$. So in the case above $\mathbf{u}' = (\alpha - 1, \beta)$ and

$$\mathbf{g}_{im} = T_{\mathbf{u}}(\mathbf{g}) = (1 + u_1)(\mathbf{g}) + u_2 \mathbf{1} \tag{15}$$

This form is chosen so $\mathbf{u} = \mathbf{0}$ gives the identity that allows the update scheme used in the active appearance model (below) to have a simpler description.

By varying the elements of the texture parameter vector $\mathbf{b}_g$ within limits learned from the training set, we can generate a variety of plausible shape-normalized face textures. For instance, Figure 3.4 shows the first four modes of a texture model built from 400 images of 100 individuals (including neutral, smiling, frowning, and surprised expressions of each). The model represents about 20,000 pixels.

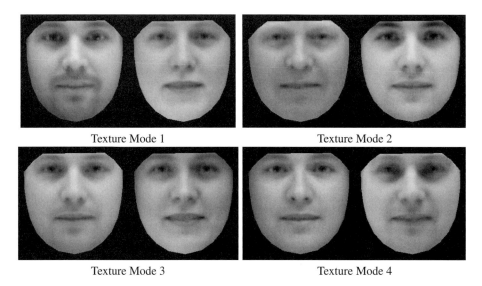

Texture Mode 1                    Texture Mode 2

Texture Mode 3                    Texture Mode 4

**Fig. 3.4.** Four modes of a face texture model (parameters varied by $\pm 2\sigma$ from the mean).

### 1.3 Combined Models of Appearance

The shape and texture of any example can thus be summarized by the parameter vectors $\mathbf{b}_s$ and $\mathbf{b}_g$. Because there may be correlations between the shape and texture variations, we apply a further PCA to the data as follows. For each example we generate the concatenated vector

$$\mathbf{b} = \begin{pmatrix} \mathbf{W}_s \mathbf{b}_s \\ \mathbf{b}_g \end{pmatrix} = \begin{pmatrix} \mathbf{W}_s \mathbf{P}_s^T (\mathbf{x} - \bar{\mathbf{x}}) \\ \mathbf{P}_g^T (\mathbf{g} - \bar{\mathbf{g}}) \end{pmatrix} \tag{16}$$

where $\mathbf{W}_s$ is a diagonal matrix of weights for each shape parameter, allowing for the difference in units between the shape and gray models (see below). We apply a PCA to these vectors, giving a further model

$$\mathbf{b} = \mathbf{P}_c \mathbf{c} \tag{17}$$

where $\mathbf{P}_c$ are the eigenvectors, and $\mathbf{c}$ is a vector of *appearance* parameters controlling both the shape and gray levels of the model. By the nature of its construction, $\mathbf{c}$ has a zero mean across the training set.

Note that the linear nature of the model allows us to express the shape and gray-levels directly as functions of $\mathbf{c}$

$$\mathbf{x} = \bar{\mathbf{x}} + \mathbf{P}_s \mathbf{W}_s^{-1} \mathbf{P}_{cs} \mathbf{c} \quad, \quad \mathbf{g} = \bar{\mathbf{g}} + \mathbf{P}_g \mathbf{P}_{cg} \mathbf{c} \qquad (18)$$

where

$$\mathbf{P}_c = \begin{pmatrix} \mathbf{P}_{cs} \\ \mathbf{P}_{cg} \end{pmatrix} \qquad (19)$$

This can be summarized as

$$\begin{aligned} \mathbf{x} &= \bar{\mathbf{x}} + \mathbf{Q}_s \mathbf{c} \\ \mathbf{g} &= \bar{\mathbf{g}} + \mathbf{Q}_g \mathbf{c} \end{aligned} \qquad (20)$$

where

$$\begin{aligned} \mathbf{Q}_s &= \mathbf{P}_s \mathbf{W}_s^{-1} \mathbf{P}_{cs} \\ \mathbf{Q}_g &= \mathbf{P}_g \mathbf{P}_{cg} \end{aligned} \qquad (21)$$

An example image can be synthesized for a given $\mathbf{c}$ by generating the shape-free gray-level image from the vector $\mathbf{g}$ and warping it using the control points described by $\mathbf{x}$.

## Choice of Shape Parameter Weights

The elements of $\mathbf{b}_s$ have units of distance, and those of $\mathbf{b}_g$ have units of intensity so they cannot be compared directly. Because $\mathbf{P}_g$ has orthogonal columns, varying $\mathbf{b}_g$ by one unit moves $\mathbf{g}$ by one unit. To make $\mathbf{b}_s$ and $\mathbf{b}_g$ commensurate, we must estimate the effect of varying $\mathbf{b}_s$ on the sample $\mathbf{g}$. To do this one can systematically displace each element of $\mathbf{b}_s$ from its optimum value on each training example and sample the image given the displaced shape. The RMS change in $\mathbf{g}$ per unit change in shape parameter $b_s$ gives the weight $w_s$ to be applied to that parameter in equation (16).

A simpler alternative is to set $\mathbf{W}_s = r\mathbf{I}$ where $r^2$ is the ratio of the total intensity variation to the total shape variation (in the normalized frames). In practice the synthesis and search algorithms are relatively insensitive to the choice of $\mathbf{W}_s$.

## Example: Facial Appearance Model

Figure 3.5 shows the first four modes of a combined-appearance model built from the same 400 face images as described above. The modes combine the variation due to lighting, viewpoint, identity, and expression.

## Separating Sources of Variability

Because we know the identity of the person in each training image, we can compute within-identity and between-identity covariance matrices for the parameters associated with each image. The eigenvectors, $\mathbf{P}_w$, of the within-identity covariance matrix give us a (linear) way of manipulating the face of an individual. Varying the elements of the vector $\mathbf{c}_w$ varies the appearance parameters $\mathbf{c}$,

$$\mathbf{c} = \mathbf{P}_w \mathbf{c}_w \qquad (22)$$

and thus the appearance of the face, in ways that an individual's face can change. Figure 3.6 shows the first two such modes for the data described above. These are predominantly expression changes.

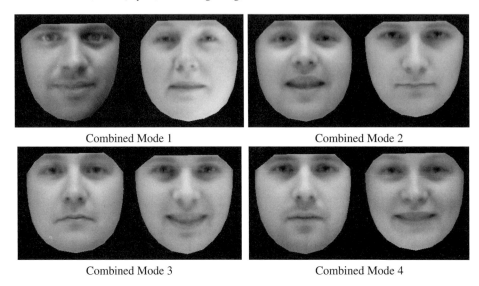

Combined Mode 1          Combined Mode 2

Combined Mode 3          Combined Mode 4

**Fig. 3.5.** Four modes of combined shape and texture model (parameters varied by $\pm 2\sigma$ from the mean).

Similarly those of the between-identity matrix, $\mathbf{P}_b$, allow us to examine the differences between individuals with fewer confounding effects from individual face variation. Figure 3.7 shows the first two such modes for the data described above. These modes should cause minimal apparent expression change but describe the differences in face shape and texture between people.

In this case the between-class covariance matrix is formed from the mean for each class (identity), which may not be a good representative of the individual and may itself be corrupted by some nonreference expression or head pose. For instance, the first identity mode in Figure 3.7 includes a small amount of expression change, so is not a pure identity variation. Costen et al. [12] describe an iterative approach to separating different sources of variability to obtain better linear models of facial variation.

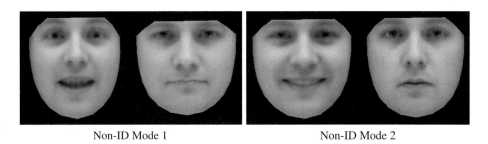

Non-ID Mode 1          Non-ID Mode 2

**Fig. 3.6.** Two modes of individual face variation (nonidentity modes).

ID Mode 1                                      ID Mode 2

**Fig. 3.7.** Two modes of variation between individuals (identity modes).

In the following sections we describe two approaches for matching the models to new images. The first matches only the shape model to the data; the second matches the full appearance model.

## 2 Active Shape Models

Given a rough starting approximation, the parameters of an instance of a model can be modified to better fit the model to a new image. By choosing a set of shape parameters, $\mathbf{b}_s$, for the model we define the shape of the object in an object-centred coordinate frame. We can create an instance $\mathbf{X}$ of the model in the image frame by defining the position, orientation, and scale parameters, $\mathbf{t}$.

An iterative approach to improving the fit of the instance, $\mathbf{X} = S_\mathbf{t}(\mathbf{x})$, to an image proceeds as follows.

1. Examine a region of the image around each point $\mathbf{X}_i$ to find the best nearby match for the point $\mathbf{X}_i'$.
2. Update the parameters $(\mathbf{t}, \mathbf{b}_s)$ to best fit to the new found points $\mathbf{X}'$.
3. Repeat until convergence.

In practice we look along profiles normal to the model boundary through each model point (Figure 3.8). If we expect the model boundary to correspond to an edge, we can simply locate the strongest edge (including orientation if known) along the profile. Its position gives the new suggested location for the model point.

However, model points are not always placed on the strongest edge in the locality – they may represent a weaker secondary edge or some other image structure. The best approach is to learn from the training set what to look for in the target image. One approach is to sample along the profile normal to the boundary in the training set and build a statistical model of the gray-level structure.

### 2.1 Modeling Local Structure

Suppose for a given point we sample along a profile $k$ pixels either side of the model point in the $i^{th}$ training image. We have $2k + 1$ samples, which can be put in a vector $\mathbf{g}_i$. To reduce the

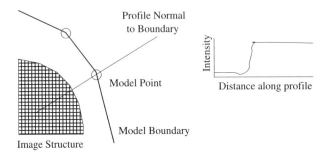

**Fig. 3.8.** At each model point, sample along a profile normal to the boundary.

effects of global intensity changes, we sample the derivative along the profile, rather than the absolute gray-level values. We then normalize the sample by dividing through by the sum of absolute element values.

$$\mathbf{g}_i \rightarrow \frac{1}{\sum_j |g_{ij}|} \mathbf{g}_i \tag{23}$$

We repeat this for each training image to obtain a set of normalized samples $\{\mathbf{g}_i\}$ for the given model point. We assume that they are distributed as multivariate Gaussian and estimate their mean $\bar{\mathbf{g}}$ and covariance $\mathbf{S}_g$. This gives a statistical model for the gray-level profile about the point. This is repeated for every model point, giving one gray-level model for each point.

The quality of fit of a new sample, $\mathbf{g}_s$, to the model is given by

$$f(\mathbf{g}_s) = (\mathbf{g}_s - \bar{\mathbf{g}})^T \mathbf{S}_g^{-1} (\mathbf{g}_s - \bar{\mathbf{g}}) \tag{24}$$

This is the Mahalanobis distance of the sample from the model mean and is linearly related to the log of the probability that $\mathbf{g}_s$ is drawn from the distribution. minimizing $f(\mathbf{g}_s)$ is equivalent to maximizing the probability that $\mathbf{g}_s$ comes from the distribution.

During the search we sample a profile $m$ pixels either side of the current point ($m > k$). We then test the quality of fit of the corresponding gray-level model at each of the $2(m - k) + 1$ possible positions along the sample (Fig. 3.9) and choose the one that gives the best match [lowest value of $f(\mathbf{g}_s)$].

This is repeated for each model point, giving a suggested new position for each point. We then compute the pose and shape parameters that best match the model to the new points, effectively imposing shape constraints on the allowed point positions (see "Fitting the Model to New Points", above).

Details of how weightings can be included in this model parameter updating are described by Hill et al. [19]. This allows different points to be weighted according to one's belief in their reliability. Van Ginneken et al. [32] show that an effective way to search for improved point positions is to use nonlinear two class classifiers. One classifier is trained for each point, aiming to distinguish between the image information around the target point from that around nearby incorrect points.

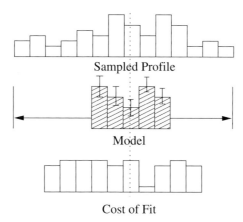

Fig. 3.9. Search along sampled profile to find best fit of gray-level model.

## 2.2 Multiresolution Active Shape Models

To improve the efficiency and robustness of the algorithm, it is implemented in a multiresolution framework. This involves first searching for the object in a coarse image and then refining the location in a series of finer resolution images. This leads to a faster algorithm and one that is less likely to get stuck on the wrong image structure. Local models for each point are trained on each level of a Gaussian image pyramid.

## 2.3 Examples of Search

Figure 3.10 demonstrates using an Active Shape Model to locate the features of a face. The model instance is placed near the center of the image and a coarse to fine search performed. The search starts on the third level of a Gaussian pyramid (1/8 the resolution in $x$ and $y$ compared to the original image). Large movements are made during the first few iterations, getting the position and scale roughly correct. As the search progresses to finer resolutions, more subtle adjustments are made. The final convergence (after a total of 18 iterations) gives a good match to the target image. In this case, at most, 10 iterations were allowed at each resolution, and the algorithm converges in much less than a second (on a modern personal computer).

Figure 3.11 demonstrates the ASM failing. The main facial features have been found, but the local models searching for the edges of the face have failed to locate their correct positions, perhaps because they are too far away. The ASM is a local method and prone to local minima.

The ASM only uses relatively sparse local information around the points of interest. In addition it treats the information at each point as independent, which is often not the case. In the following we describe a method for using all of the image information in the region of a face to match an appearance model to the data.

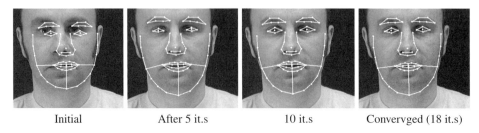

Initial          After 5 it.s          10 it.s          Convervged (18 it.s)

**Fig. 3.10.** Search using an active shape model of a face.

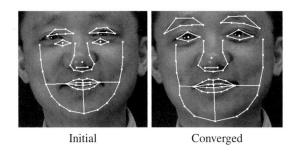

Initial                    Converged

**Fig. 3.11.** Example of ASM search failure. The search profiles are not long enough to locate the edges of face.

## 3 Active Appearance Models

We can use the combined models of appearance described above for image interpretation using the *interpretation through synthesis* paradigm. Given a new image of a face, we wish to locate the facial features and extract information we can use for face verification, recognition, and so on. If a facial appearance model is trained on a sufficiently general set of data it is able to synthesise faces similar to that in the target image. If we can find the model parameters that generate a face similar to the target, those parameters imply the position of the facial features and can be used directly for face interpretation.

In the following sections we describe an algorithm (known as the active appearance model, or AAM algorithm), which employs a useful approximation to achieve rapid and accurate matching of an appearance model to a new image. We first describe the original formulation of the algorithm and then give an overview of a variety of closely related alternative approaches.

### 3.1 Quality of Match

If we choose a particular set of model parameters $\mathbf{c}$, a set of pose parameters $\mathbf{t}$, and a set of texture normalization parameters $\mathbf{u}$, we can synthesize a new face image, $I(\mathbf{c}, \mathbf{t}, \mathbf{u})$. We concatenate the parameters into a single vector, $\mathbf{p} = (\mathbf{c}^T | \mathbf{t}^T | \mathbf{u}^T)^T$. If our aim is to generate a face matching that in a target image, we must define some measure to determine the quality of fit. The simplest approach is to compute the sum of squares difference of the target image and synthesized image.

The steps are as follows.

1. Use Eq. (20) to compute the shape $\mathbf{x}$ and model texture $\mathbf{g}_m$ in the model reference frame.
2. Compute the shape in the image frame by applying $\mathbf{X} = S_\mathbf{t}(\mathbf{x})$
3. Sample the target image in the region defined by $\mathbf{X}$ to obtain $\mathbf{g}_{im}$ (see Section 1.2).
4. Project the texture into the model frame using $\mathbf{g}_s = T_\mathbf{u}^{-1}(\mathbf{g}_{im})$
5. Compute the residual $\mathbf{r}(\mathbf{p}) = \mathbf{g}_s - \mathbf{g}_m$

A simple measure of the quality of the fit is then

$$E_{sos}(\mathbf{p}) = |\mathbf{r}(\mathbf{p})|^2 = \mathbf{r}(\mathbf{p})^T \mathbf{r}(\mathbf{p}) \tag{25}$$

Note that by making assumptions about the distributions of residuals we can estimate $p(\mathbf{r}|\mathbf{p})$ and place the matching in a Bayesian framework (for more details, see Cootes and Taylor [9]). However, for simplicity in the following we only consider minimizing the simple sum of squares error function.

Given an initial estimate of the parameters $\mathbf{p}$, we wish to modify them by some $\delta\mathbf{p}$ so as to minimize $|\mathbf{r}(\mathbf{p} + \delta\mathbf{p})|^2$.

A first-order Taylor expansion of $\mathbf{r}(\mathbf{p})$ gives

$$\mathbf{r}(\mathbf{p} + \delta\mathbf{p}) = \mathbf{r}(\mathbf{p}) + \frac{\partial\mathbf{r}}{\partial\mathbf{p}}\delta\mathbf{p} \tag{26}$$

where the $ij^{th}$ element of matrix $\frac{\partial\mathbf{r}}{\partial\mathbf{p}}$ is $\frac{dr_i}{dp_j}$.

By equating Eq. (26) to zero, we obtain the RMS solution.

$$\delta\mathbf{p} = -\mathbf{R}\mathbf{r}(\mathbf{p}) \; where \; \mathbf{R} = (\frac{\partial\mathbf{r}}{\partial\mathbf{p}}^T \frac{\partial\mathbf{r}}{\partial\mathbf{p}})^{-1}\frac{\partial\mathbf{r}}{\partial\mathbf{p}}^T \tag{27}$$

In a standard optimization scheme it would be necessary to recalculate $\frac{\partial\mathbf{r}}{\partial\mathbf{p}}$ at every step, an expensive operation. However, we assume that because it is being computed in a normalized reference frame, it can be considered approximately fixed. We can thus estimate it once from our training set. We estimate $\frac{\partial\mathbf{r}}{\partial\mathbf{p}}$ by numerical differentiation, systematically displacing each parameter from the known optimal value on typical images and computing an average over the training set. Residuals at displacements of differing magnitudes are measured (typically up to 0.5 standard deviations of each parameter) and combined with a Gaussian kernel to smooth them.

We then precompute $\mathbf{R}$ and use it in all subsequent searches with the model.

Images used in the calculation of $\frac{\partial\mathbf{r}}{\partial\mathbf{p}}$ can be either examples from the training set or synthetic images generated using the appearance model itself. When synthetic images are used, one can use a suitable (e.g., random) background or can detect the areas of the model that overlap the background and remove those samples from the model-building process. The latter makes the final relationship more independent of the background.

## 3.2 Iterative Model Refinement

Using Eq. (27) we can suggest a correction in the model parameters based on a measured residual $\mathbf{r}$. This allows us to construct an iterative algorithm for solving our optimization problem.

Given a current estimate of the model parameters $\mathbf{c}$, the pose $\mathbf{t}$, the texture transformation $\mathbf{u}$, and the image sample at the current estimate, $\mathbf{g}_{im}$, the steps of the iterative procedure are as follows.

1. Project the texture sample into the texture model frame using $\mathbf{g}_s = T_{\mathbf{u}}^{-1}(\mathbf{g}_{im})$.
2. Evaluate the error vector, $\mathbf{r} = \mathbf{g}_s - \mathbf{g}_m$, and the current error, $E = |\mathbf{r}|^2$.
3. Compute the predicted displacements, $\delta\mathbf{p} = -\mathbf{R}\mathbf{r}(\mathbf{p})$.
4. Update the model parameters $\mathbf{p} \to \mathbf{p} + k\delta\mathbf{p}$, where initially $k = 1$.
5. Calculate the new points, $\mathbf{X}'$ and model frame texture $\mathbf{g}'_m$.
6. Sample the image at the new points to obtain $\mathbf{g}'_{im}$.
7. Calculate a new error vector, $\mathbf{r}' = T_{\mathbf{u}'}^{-1}(\mathbf{g}'_{im}) - \mathbf{g}'_m$.
8. If $|\mathbf{r}'|^2 < E$, accept the new estimate, otherwise try at $k = 0.5$, $k = 0.25$, and so on.

This procedure is repeated until no improvement is made in the error, $|\mathbf{r}|^2$, and convergence is declared.

**Incrementing Model Parameters**

When we modify the parameter vector $\mathbf{p} = (\mathbf{c}^T|\mathbf{t}^T|\mathbf{u}^T)^T$ by a small increment $\delta\mathbf{p} = (\delta\mathbf{c}^T|\delta\mathbf{t}^T|\delta\mathbf{u}^T)^T$, the simplest approach is to use addition, $\mathbf{p}_1 = \mathbf{p} + \delta\mathbf{p}$. However, the parameters controlling the pose $\mathbf{t}$ and texture transformation $\mathbf{u}$ should really be updated by computing the composition of the resulting transformations. Thus we should choose new pose parameters $\mathbf{t}_1$ such that $S_{\mathbf{t}_1}(\mathbf{x}) = S_{\mathbf{t}}[S_{\delta\mathbf{t}}(\mathbf{x})]$ and new texture transformation parameters $\mathbf{u}_1$ such that $T_{\mathbf{u}_1}(\mathbf{g}) = T_{\mathbf{u}}[T_{\delta\mathbf{u}}(\mathbf{g})]$. This is because the update step estimates corrections in the model frame, which must then be projected into the image frame using the current pose and texture transformations. This updating should be used during training when estimating the update matrices and during the search algorithm above.

**Multiresolution Search**

Both models and update matrices can be estimated at a range of image resolutions (training on a Gaussian image pyramid). We can then use a multiresolution search algorithm in which we start at a coarse resolution and iterate to convergence at each level before projecting the current solution to the next level of the model. This is more efficient and can converge to the correct solution from further away than search at a single resolution.

The complexity of the algorithm is $O(n_{pixels}n_{modes})$ at a given level. Essentially each iteration involves sampling $n_{pixels}$ points from the image and then multiplying by a $n_{modes}$ x $n_{pixel}$ matrix.

**3.3 Examples of AAM Search**

Figures 3.12 and 3.13 show the stages from an AAM search, matching a gray-scale model to images of people not included in the training set. We have found that, in general, gray-scale models are able to generalize to unseen images more effectively than color models.

Figure 3.14 demonstrates how the AAM can fail if initialized too far from the true position. It is only a local optimization and can fall into local minima. In this case the model has matched the eye and eyebrow to the wrong side of the face, and attempted to mimic the dark background by shading one side of the reconstructed face.

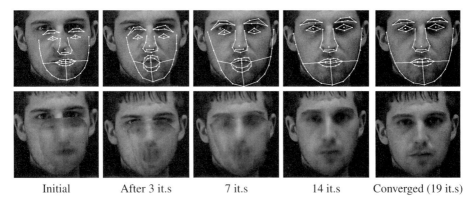

Fig. 3.12. Search using active appearance model (AAM) of a face, showing evolution of the shape and the reconstructed image. Initial iterations are performed using a low resolution model. Resolution increases as search progresses. Person not in training set.

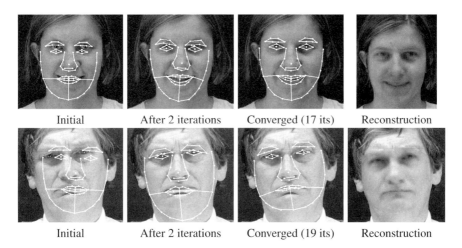

Fig. 3.13. Matching appearance models to new people using the AAM.

## 3.4 Alternative Strategies

A variety of related approaches to matching models of shape and texture have been suggested. Here we summarize some of the key contributions.

**Shape AAM**

Rather than have residuals driving the appearance model parameters **c**, they could be used to drive the pose **t** and shape model parameters $\mathbf{b}_s$ alone. The texture model parameters could then be directly estimated by fitting to the current texture. This is closely related to the 'active blob'

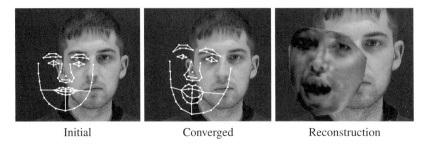

| Initial | Converged | Reconstruction |

**Fig. 3.14.** Example of AAM search failure. The initialization was too far from true position.

of Sclaroff and Isidoro [29], which uses an elastic deformation model rather than a statistical model of shape.

In a training phase one learns the relationships

$$
\begin{aligned}
d\mathbf{t} &= \mathbf{R}_t \mathbf{r} \\
d\mathbf{b}_s &= \mathbf{R}_s \mathbf{r}
\end{aligned}
\tag{28}
$$

During the search the update step is modified as follows.

1. Normalize the current texture sample to obtain $\mathbf{g}_s$.
2. Fit the texture model to the sample using $\mathbf{b}_g = \mathbf{P}_g^T(\mathbf{g}_s - \bar{\mathbf{g}})$.
3. Compute the residual as $\mathbf{r} = \mathbf{g}_s - \mathbf{g}_m$.
4. Predict the pose and shape parameter updates using Eq. (28).
5. Apply and test the updates as for the basic algorithm.

The linear nature of the relationships allows one to predict the shape and pose updates from the normalized texture sample, avoiding fitting the texture model [6]. This can improve the efficiency of the process. However, one must fit the texture model if the total error is to be computed (e.g., to test for improvements). If required, a combined model of shape and texture can be used to apply constraints to the relative shape and texture parameter vectors.

**Compositional Approach**

Baker and Matthews [2, 3] point out that the essentially additive method of updating the parameters in the basic framework can be problematic, and propose an alternative *inverse compositional* updating scheme. They consider the case in which separate (independent) shape and texture models are used (essentially the shape AAM above). The shape model Eq. (4) can be thought of as a parameterized transformation of the mean shape.

$$
\mathbf{x} = T_{\mathbf{b}_s}(\bar{\mathbf{x}})
\tag{29}
$$

Using an additive update of the form $\mathbf{b}_s \rightarrow \mathbf{b}_s + \delta$, leads to a new transformation

$$
\mathbf{x}_{new} = T_{\mathbf{b}_s + \delta}(\bar{\mathbf{x}})
\tag{30}
$$

However, it is more natural to think of the update itself as a transformation.

$$\mathbf{x}_{new} = T_{\mathbf{b}_s}(T_\delta(\bar{\mathbf{x}})) \tag{31}$$

In this case we must compute the new parameters, $\mathbf{b}'_s$ such that

$$T_{\mathbf{b}'_s}(\bar{\mathbf{x}}) = T_{\mathbf{b}_s}(T_\delta(\bar{\mathbf{x}})) \tag{32}$$

One way to achieve this is to approximate the transformation using thin-plate splines [5] as follows

1. Compute the thin plate spline, $T_{tps}(.)$, which maps the points $\bar{\mathbf{x}}$ to $\mathbf{x}$.
2. Compute the modified mean points, $\mathbf{x}_\delta = \bar{\mathbf{x}} + \mathbf{P}_s\delta$.
3. Apply the transformation, $\mathbf{x}' = T_{tps}(\mathbf{x}_\delta)$.
4. Find the shape parameters that best match, $\mathbf{b}'_s = \mathbf{P}_s^T(\mathbf{x}' - \bar{\mathbf{x}})$.

The sampling and updating is otherwise identical to that for the shape AAM described above. An excellent extended description of this approach, demonstrating that the compositional method leads to more accurate results than additive methods, is given by Baker and Matthews [2, 3].

### Direct AAMs

Hou et al. [20] suggest that in some cases it is possible to predict the shape directly from the texture, when the two are sufficiently correlated. Combining Eqs. (17), (19), and (16) we obtain

$$\begin{aligned}\mathbf{b}_s &= \mathbf{W}_w^{-1}\mathbf{P}_{cs}\mathbf{c} \\ \mathbf{b}_g &= \mathbf{P}_{cg}\mathbf{c}\end{aligned} \tag{33}$$

Equating $\mathbf{c}$ gives

$$\mathbf{b}_s = \mathbf{S}\mathbf{b}_g = \mathbf{W}_w^{-1}\mathbf{P}_{cs}\mathbf{P}_{cg}^{-1}\mathbf{b}_g \tag{34}$$

where $\mathbf{P}_{cg}^{-1}$ is the pseudo-inverse of $\mathbf{P}_{cg}$. Thus we can predict the shape parameters from the texture accurately if the rank of $\mathbf{P}_{cg}$ is larger than the number of shape parameters. Hou et al. demonstrated that this was the case for a face model.

One iteration of the matching procedure is then as follows.

1. Fit the texture model to the normalized sample using $\mathbf{b}_g = \mathbf{P}_g^T(\mathbf{g}_s - \bar{\mathbf{g}})$.
2. Compute the residual as $\mathbf{r} = \mathbf{g}_s - \mathbf{g}_m$.
3. Predict the pose using $d\mathbf{t} = \mathbf{R}_t\mathbf{r}$.
4. Predict the shape using $\mathbf{b}_s = \mathbf{S}\mathbf{b}_g$.
5. Apply and test the updates as for the basic algorithm.

### 3.5  Choice of Texture Representation

The examples above all assumed that the raw image intensities (or RGB values) are modeled, and that matching involves reconstructing the intensities. However, intensities can be highly sensitive to lighting conditions and camera parameters. More robust results can be obtained by modeling some filtered version of the original image.

Edge-based representations tend to be less sensitive to lighting conditions than raw intensity measures. Thus an obvious alternative to modeling the intensity values directly is to record the local image gradient in each direction at each pixel. Although this yields more information at each pixel and at first glance might seem to favor edge regions over flatter regions, it is only a linear transformation of the original intensity data. Where model building involves applying a linear PCA to the samples, the resulting model is almost identical to one built from raw intensities, apart from some effects around the border, where computing the gradients includes some background information into the model.

However, nonlinear normalization of the gradient at each pixel in the region to be modeled has been found to be a useful representation. If the local gradients at a pixel are $g_x$, $g_y$, we compute normalized features $(g'_x, g'_y) = (g_x, g_y)/(g + g_0)$, where $g$ is the magnitude of the gradient, and $g_0$ is the mean gradient magnitude over a region. Building texture models of this normalized value has been shown to give more robust matching than matching intensity models [30].

Stegmann and Larsen [26] demonstrated that combining multiple feature bands (e.g., intensity, hue, and edge information) improved face feature location accuracy. Scott et al. [21] have shown that including features derived from "cornerness" measures can further improve performace.

## 3.6  Estimating the Update Matrix

All the methods above rely on estimating a matrix, $\mathbf{R}$, that predicts the parameter updates from the current texture error, $\delta\mathbf{p} = \mathbf{R}\mathbf{r}$. The original work on AAMs [16] used a regression-based approach to compute this. Later it was suggested that a better method was to compute the gradient matrix $\frac{\partial \mathbf{r}}{\partial \mathbf{p}}$ [7], which was claimed to be more stable, had a clearer mathematical interpretation and allowed extra constraints to be easily incorporated [9].

The regression-based approach assumes that we have repeatedly displaced the model parameters and computed the resulting residual. If the parameter displacements are stored in the columns of $\mathbf{C}$ and the corresponding residuals in the columns of $\mathbf{V}$, we require a matrix $\mathbf{R}$ such that $\mathbf{C} = \mathbf{R}\mathbf{V}$. This can then be used in the update method.

A simple approach to obtaining $\mathbf{R}$ is to compute

$$\mathbf{R} = \mathbf{C}\mathbf{V}^+ \tag{35}$$

where $\mathbf{V}^+$ is the pseudo-inverse of $\mathbf{V}$.

However, this tends to overfit to the training data unless there are more displacements than pixels modeled (a rare occurrence). Various techniques have been proposed to correct for this, a simple one being to apply PCA to reduce the dimensionality of the residuals before performing the regression. It has been demonstrated (e.g., Hou et al. [20]) that this leads to better performance, presumably because the result is smoother and less likely to be overtrained.

However, an alternative approach is to attempt to compute the gradient matrix, $\frac{\partial \mathbf{r}}{\partial \mathbf{p}}$, such that $\mathbf{r} = \frac{\partial \mathbf{r}}{\partial \mathbf{p}}\delta\mathbf{p}$. This can be estimated directly by displacing each parameter in turn [7]. An alternative novel approach is to estimate it from randomly displaced data as follows. Using the same data as described above (multiple random displacements), we can determine the gradient matrix using

$$\frac{\partial \mathbf{r}}{\partial \mathbf{p}} = \mathbf{V}\mathbf{C}^+ \tag{36}$$

Because of their relative sizes, it is usually much quicker to compute the pseudoinverse $\mathbf{C}^+$ than $\mathbf{V}^+$. In this case we can compute the update matrix simply as $\mathbf{R} = \frac{\partial \mathbf{r}}{\partial \mathbf{p}}^+$ [9]. This approach avoids the danger of over-fitting exhibited by the simple regression approach. For tests comparing the different approaches [8] the last method (estimating the gradient using regression) gave the best localization performance, but the direct numerical estimate of the gradient led to the lowest mean residual texture errors during the search.

## 4 Related Work

Benson and Perrett [4] were among the first to generate synthetic faces by warping textures. Statistical models of the texture and shape were constructed by Craw and Cameron [13], who began investigating their use for face recognition [14].

Jones and Poggio [23] described an alternative model of appearance (independent shape and texture variation) they term a "morphable model." An optical flow based algorithm is used here to match the model onto new images and can be used in a "boot-strapping" mode in which the model is matched to new examples which can then be added to the training set [34].

Yan et al. [35] suggested an iterative matching scheme in which a shape prediction from an ASM-like search is combined with one from a texture model (as with the direct AAM approach). This is claimed to provide more accurate results than either an ASM or an AAM.

Romdhani et al. have proposed a nonlinear extension to the ASM [28]. Stegmann et al. have done extensive work with Active Appearance Models, and have made their software available [25]. Ahlberg [22] demonstrated using an AAM-like algorithm to track faces using a 3D textured head model (see Chapter 4). Vetter [33] built 3D models of the head combining 3D shape models with surface texture models (for full details, see Chapter 10). Batur and Hayes demonstrated that modifying the update matrix $\mathbf{R}$, depending on the current estimates of the model parameters, can lead to more accurate and reliable matching [1].

## 5 Face Verification Using Combined Appearance Models

Given a face image, we can estimate the model parameters, $\mathbf{c}$, that best match the model to it (those that synthesize a face as similar as possible to the target face). If the model is sufficiently complex, the parameters should summarize almost all the important information required to describe the face and can thus be used for face interpretation.

In particular, it is possible to use the parameters for face verification or recognition. By comparing the vectors representing two images, $\mathbf{c}_1$ and $\mathbf{c}_2$, we can measure how similar they are. Experiments suggest that an effective measure of difference is the normalized dot product.

$$d = 1 - \frac{\mathbf{c}_1}{|\mathbf{c}_1|} \cdot \frac{\mathbf{c}_2}{|\mathbf{c}_2|} \tag{37}$$

This is zero for a perfect match. This method outperforms other simple metrics such as the euclidean distance or the un-normalized dot product [18].

As mentioned above, the model parameters encode a range of variations, due to differences between people and those due to changes in an individual face. The changes of one individual's face can be larger than those between two people and can confound simple verification algorithms. An effective method for dealing with these changes is to explicitly model the changes of an individual (see Section 1.3). The eigenvectors, $\mathbf{P}_w$, of the within-individual covariance matrix describe the most significant facial changes (Figure 3.6).

Given a set of face parameters, $\mathbf{c}$, we can estimate the within-individual variation as $\mathbf{c}_w = \mathbf{P}_w^T \mathbf{c}$ and remove it to give a set of parameters that represent the face in a standard pose, expression, and lighting.

$$\mathbf{c}_n = \mathbf{c} - \mathbf{P}_w \mathbf{c}_w = \mathbf{c} - \mathbf{P}_w \mathbf{P}_w^T \mathbf{c} \qquad (38)$$

If we then compare these corrected vectors from different images, we obtain much better discrimination between individuals. This approach has been found to perform better than using linear discriminant analysis to select a suitable subspace for face verification [18].

Experiments applying this technique to the XM2VTS data set [27] suggest that this approach can achieve equal error rates of 0.8% when using hand annotations of the data set. This result was obtained using a face model trained on a completely separate data set of 1800 images. The within-individual variation models were estimated from 600 images in the XM2VTS registration set and tested on the 960 images from the XM2VTS test set. The result is sensitive to the number of modes used in the model of within-identity variation, and the choice points used to align the shape model (using only points from the eyes, nose, and mouth during shape alignment gives better performance than using all the points, perhaps because they tend to be more stable).

It should be noted that the above results were performed with hand annotation of 68 points on each image and thus give some measure of the upper limit of the technique. When search is used, the performance degrades significantly. This is because the search algorithm introduces extra errors (and sometimes completely fails to converge).

The inclusion of shape variation allows additional flexibility, which makes the models more specific and more compact than rigid approaches such as "eigen-face" approaches [24, 31]. However, the resulting models require that more parameters be estimated during the search, potentially leading to more frequent search failures. In cases in which the faces tend to be well constrained, such as frontal images with neutral expressions (e.g., the XM2VTS database), the inclusion of shape variation can roughly halve the equal error rate (we obtained a rate of about 2% when repeating the experiment reported above with a rigid shape model). However, it is possible that the increased uncertainty when matching a flexible model due the the larger number of parameters may lead to worse results overall for a full system. This is less likely to be the case for faces exhibiting larger pose or expression changes, for which rigid models are inappropriate.

# 6 Discussion and Conclusions

We have described statistical models of the shape and texture of faces capable of synthesizing convincing face images. They are capable of representing a wide range of variations exhibited by faces and can be used to distingush the sources of variation (such as those due to differences between individuals from those due to changes of expression, head pose, or lighting).

Algorithms such as the ASM and AAM and their variants can be used to match the models rapidly to images of interest. The parameters of the models and the facial features found can then be used for further analysis.

Both the matching algorithms presented above and their variations are local optimization techniques and tend to fall into local minima. Thus initialization is important. The accuracy required of the initial model placement tends to be highly data-dependent. When independent estimates of feature point positions are available, they can be incorporated into the matching schemes and tend to lead to more reliable matching [9].

It should be noted, however, that the approach relies on establishing correspondences across a training set, and between models and new images. As a result, it can deal effectively only with certain types of change. In particular, variation that cannot be corresponded because it tends to vary from person to person (e.g., wrinkles on the forehead or the appearance of moles) will tend to get blurred out by the averaging process inherent in the modeling. This suggests that the method can be improved by adding further layers of information to the model to represent individual differences that are poorly represented by the pooling used in the current models.

Open questions regarding the models include

- How does one obtain accurate correspondences across the training set?
- What is the optimal choice of model size and number of model modes?
- Which representation of image structure should be modeled?
- What is the best method for matching the model to the image?

To conclude, statistical models of shape and appearance are powerful tools for face interpretation and have been shown to be effective in many applications.

**Acknowledgments**

The authors thank their numerous colleagues who have contributed to the research summarised in this chapter, including C. Beeston, F. Bettinger, D. Cooper, D. Cristinacce, G. Edwards, A. Hill, J. Graham, and P. Kittipanya-ngam. Thanks also to Martin Roberts for reviewing the manuscript.

# References

1. A.U.Batur and M.H.Hayes. A novel convergence scheme for active appearance models. In *Proc. Computer Vision and Pattern Recognition*, volume 1, pages 359–366, 2003.
2. S. Baker and I. Matthews. Equivalence and efficiency of image alignment algorithms. In *Proc. Computer Vision and Pattern Recognition*, volume 1, pages 1090–1097, 2001.
3. S. Baker and I. Matthews. Lucas-kanade 20 years on: A unifying framework part 1: The quantity approximated, the warp update rule, and the gradient descent approximation. *International Journal of Computer Vision*, 2004.
4. P. Benson and D. Perrett. Synthesizing continuous-tone caricatures. *Image and Vision Computing*, 9:123–129, 1991.
5. F. Bookstein. Principal warps: Thin-plate splines and the decomposition of deformations. *IEEE Transactions on Pattern Analysis and Machine Intelligence*, 11(6):567–585, 1989.

6. T. Cootes, G. Edwards, and C. Taylor. A comparative evaluation of active appearance model algorithms. In P. Lewis and M. Nixon, editors, *Proc. British Machine Vision Conference*, volume 2, pages 680–689. BMVA Press, UK, Sept. 1998.

7. T. Cootes, G. Edwards, and C. Taylor. Active appearance models. *IEEE Transactions on Pattern Analysis and Machine Intelligence*, 23(6):681–685, 2001.

8. T. Cootes and P.Kittipanya-ngam. Comparing variations on the active appearance model algorithm. In P.L.Rosin and D. Marshall, editors, *Proc. British Machine Vision Conference*, volume 2, pages 837–846, 2002.

9. T. Cootes and C. Taylor. Constrained active appearance models. In *Proc. International Conference on Computer Vision*, volume 1, pages 748–754. IEEE Computer Society Press, 2001.

10. T. F. Cootes, G.V.Wheeler, K.N.Walker, and C. J. Taylor. View-based active appearance models. *Image and Vision Computing*, 20:657–664, 2002.

11. T. F. Cootes, C. J. Taylor, D. Cooper, and J. Graham. Active shape models - their training and application. *Computer Vision and Image Understanding*, 61(1):38–59, Jan. 1995.

12. N. Costen, T. Cootes, and C. Taylor. Compensating for ensemble-specificity effects when building facial models. *Image and Vision Computing*, 20:673–682, 2002.

13. I. Craw and P. Cameron. Parameterising images for recognition and reconstruction. In *Proc. British Machine Vision Conference*, pages 367–370. Springer, London, 1991.

14. I. Craw and P. Cameron. Face recognition by computer. In D. Hogg and R. Boyle, editors, *Proc. British Machine Vision Conference*, pages 489–507. Springer, London, 1992.

15. I. Dryden and K. V. Mardia. *The Statistical Analysis of Shape*. Wiley, London, 1998.

16. G. Edwards, C. Taylor, and T. Cootes. Interpreting face images using active appearance models. In *Proc. Conf. on Automatic Face and Gesture Recognition*, pages 300–305, 1998.

17. C. Goodall. Procrustes methods in the statistical analysis of shape. *Journal of the Royal Statistical Society B*, 53(2):285–339, 1991.

18. T. C. H. Kang and C. Taylor. A comparison of face verification algorithms using appearance models. In P.L.Rosin and D. Marshall, editors, *Proc. British Machine Vision Conference*, volume 2, pages 477–486. BMVA Press, UK, 2002.

19. A. Hill, T. F. Cootes, and C. J. Taylor. Active shape models and the shape approximation problem. In *Proc. British Machine Vision Conference*, pages 157–166. BMVA Press, UK, Sept. 1995.

20. X. Hou, S. Li, H. Zhang, and Q. Cheng. Direct appearance models. In *Proc. Computer Vision and Pattern Recognition*, volume 1, pages 828–833, 2001.

21. I.M.Scott, T.F.Cootes, and C.J.Taylor. Improving appearance model matching using local image structure. In *Proc. Information Processing in Medical Imaging*, pages 258–269. Springer-Verlag, New York, 2003.

22. J.Ahlberg. Using the active appearance algorithm for face and facial feature tracking. In *Proc. Workshop on Recognition, Analysis and Tracking of Faces and Gestures in Realtime Systems*, 2001.

23. M. J. Jones and T. Poggio. Multidimensional morphable models : A framework for representing and matching object classes. *International Journal of Computer Vision*, 2(29):107–131, 1998.

24. M. Kirby and L. Sirovich. Application of the Karhumen-Loeve procedure for the characterization of human faces. *IEEE Transactions on Pattern Analysis and Machine Intelligence*, 12(1):103–108, 1990.

25. M.B.Stegmann, B.K.Ersbøll, and R.Larsen. FAME - a flexible appearance modelling environment. *IEEE Trans. on Medical Imaging*, 22(10), 2003.

26. M.B.Stegmann and R.Larsen. Multi-band modelling of appearance. *Image and Vision Computing*, 21(1):66–67, 2003.

27. K. Messer, J. Matas, J. Kittler, J. Luettin, and G. Maitre. XM2VTSdb: The extended m2vts database. In *Proc. 2nd Conf. on Audio and Video-based Biometric Personal Verification*. Springer-Verlag, New York, 1999.

28. S. Romdhani, S. Gong, and A. Psarrou. A multi-view non-linear active shape model using kernel PCA. In T. Pridmore and D. Elliman, editors, *Proc. British Machine Vision Conference*, volume 2, pages 483–492, 1999.

29. S. Sclaroff and J. Isidoro. Active blobs. In *International Journal of Computer Vision*, pages 1146–53, 1998.

30. T.F.Cootes and C.J.Taylor. On representing edge structure for model matching. In *Proc. Computer Vision and Pattern Recognition*, volume 1, pages 1114–1119, 2001.

31. M. Turk and A. Pentland. Eigenfaces for recognition. *Journal of Cognitive Neuroscience*, 3(1):71–86, 1991.

32. B. van Ginneken, A. Frangi, J. Stall, and B. ter Haar Romeny. Active shape model segmentation with optimal features. *IEEE-TMI*, 21:924–933, 2002.

33. T. Vetter. Learning novel views to a single face image. In *Proc. Conf. on Automatic Face and Gesture Recognition*, pages 22–27, 1996.

34. T. Vetter, M. Jones, and T. Poggio. A bootstrapping algorithm for learning linear models of object classes. In *Proc. Computer Vision and Pattern Recognition*, pages 40–46, 1997.

35. S. Yan, C. Liu, S. Li, H. Zhang, H.-Y. Shum, and Q.Cheng. Face alignment using texture-constrained active shape models. *Image and Vision Computing*, 21(1):69–75, 2003.

# Chapter 4. Parametric Face Modeling and Tracking

Jörgen Ahlberg[1] and Fadi Dornaika[2]

[1] Dept. of IR Systems, Div. of Sensor Technology, Swedish Defence Research Agency (FOI),
P. O. Box 1165, SE-581 11 Linköping, Sweden. `jorahl@foi.se`
[2] Computer Vision Center, Universitat Autònoma de Barcelona, ES-081 93 Bellaterra, Spain.
`dornaika@cvc.uab.es`

## 1 Introduction

In the previous chapter, models for describing the (two-dimensional) appearance of faces were discussed. In this chapter, we continue to discuss models of facial images, this time, however, with the focus on three-dimensional models and how they are used for face tracking.

Whether we want to analyze a facial image (face detection, tracking, recognition) or synthesize one (computer graphics, face animation), we need a model for the appearance and/or structure of the human face. Depending on the application, the model can be simple (e.g., just an oval shape) or complex (e.g., thousands of polygons in layers simulating bone and layers of skin and muscles). We usually wish to control appearance, structure, and motion of the model with a small number of parameters, chosen so as to best represent the variability likely to occur in the application.

When analyzing facial images, we try to identify our model with the face in the image, find the model parameters that makes the model describe the image as well as possible, and regard the found model parameters as parameters of the face in the image. For example, if our face model is just an oval shape within a certain size range, we look for such a shape in the image, measure its position and size, and assume that the measured values are measurements of the position and size of the face.

When analyzing a *sequence* of images (or *frames*), showing a moving face, the model might describe not only the static appearance of the face but also its dynamic behavior (i.e., the motion).

To be able to execute any further analysis of a facial image (e.g., recognition), the position of the face in the image is helpful, as is the pose (i.e., the 3D position and orientation) of the face. The process of estimating position and pose parameters, and maybe others as well, from each frame in a sequence is called *tracking*. In contrast to face detection, we can utilize the knowledge of position, pose, and so on, of the face in the previous image in the sequence. Tracking of faces has received significant attention for quite some time but is still not a completely solved problem.

This chapter explains the basics of parametric face models used for face tracking as well as fundamental strategies and methodologies for tracking. Three tracking algorithms are described in some detail.

The chapter is organized as follows: In the next section, we provide a short review of the contemporary research in face tracking. Then, in Section 3, parametric face modeling is described. Various strategies for tracking are discussed in Section 4, and three trackers are described in Sections 5–7. A summary is given in Section 8.

## 2 Previous Work

A plethora of face trackers are available in the literature, but only a few of them can be mentioned here. They differ in how they model the face, how they track changes from one frame to the next, if and how changes in illumination and structure are handled, if they are susceptible to drift, and if realtime performance is possible. The presentation here is limited to monocular systems (in contrast to stereo-vision) and 3D tracking.

Li et al. [25] estimated face motion in a simple 3D model by a combination of prediction and a model-based least-squares solution to the optical flow constraint equation. A render-feedback loop was used to combat drift. Eisert and Girod [14] determined a set of facial animation parameters based on the MPEG-4 facial animation standard (see Section 3.3) from two successive video frames using a hierarchical optical flow based method. Tao et al. [40] derived the 3D head pose from 2D-to-3D feature correspondences. The tracking of nonrigid facial features such as the eyebrows and the mouth was achieved via a probabilistic network approach. Pighin et al. [31] derived the face position (rigid motion) and facial expression (nonrigid motion) using a continuous optimization technique. The face model was based on a set of 3D face models.

LaCascia et al. [24] used a cylindrical face model with a parameterized texture being a linear combination of texture warping templates and orthogonal illumination templates. The 3D head pose was derived by registering the texture map captured from the new frame with the model texture. Stable tracking was achieved via regularized, weighted least-squares minimization of the registration error.

Malciu and Prêteux [27] used an ellipsoidal (alternatively an ad hoc Fourier synthesized) textured wireframe model and minimized the registration error and/or used the optical flow to estimate the 3D pose. DeCarlo and Metaxas [9] used a sophisticated face model parameterized in a set of deformations. Rigid and nonrigid motion was tracked by integrating optical flow constraints and edge-based forces, thereby preventing drift. Wiles et al. [43] tracked a set of hyperpatches (i.e., represensations of surface patches invariant to motion and changing lighting).

Gokturk et al. [18] developed a two-stage approach for 3D tracking of pose and deformations. The first stage learns the possible deformations of 3D faces by tracking stereo data. The second stage simultaneously tracks the pose and deformation of the face in the monocular image sequence using an optical flow formulation associated with the tracked features. A simple face model using 19 feature points was utilized.

Ström [37] used an extended Kalman filter and structure from motion to follow the 3D rigid motion of the head. The face model is a simple 3D wireframe model onto which the texture from the first frame is mapped. The texture is extended when new parts of the head are seen. A reinitialization step in case of tracker failure was developed as well.

Ahlberg and Forchheimer [4] represented the face using a deformable wireframe model with a statistical texture. The active appearance models described in Chapter 3 were used to minimize the registration error. Because the model allows deformation, rigid and nonrigid motions are tracked. Dornaika and Ahlberg [12] extend the tracker with a step based on random sampling and consensus to improve the rigid 3D pose estimate.

We return (Section 4) to different kinds of tracking, after briefly discussing various ways to model the face.

# 3 Parametric Face Modeling

There are many ways to parameterize and model the appearance and behavior of the human face. The choice depends on, among other things, the application, the available resources, and the display device. In Chapter 3, statistical models for analyzing and synthesizing facial images were described, providing an excellent way to model the 2D appearance of a face. Here, other modeling techniques for different purposes are mentioned as well.

What all models have in common is that a compact representation (few parameters) describing a wide variety of facial images is desirable. The parameter sets can vary considerably depending on the variability being modeled. The many kinds of variability being modeled/parameterized include the following.

- *Three-dimensional motion and pose*—the dynamic, 3D position and rotation of the head. Tracking involves estimating these parameters for each frame in the video sequence.
- *Facial action*—facial feature motion such as lip and eyebrow motion.
- *Shape and feature configuration*—the shape of the head, face and the facial features (e.g., mouth, eyes). This could be estimated or assumed to be known by the tracker.
- *Illumination*—the variability in appearance due to different lighting conditions. See Chapter 5.
- *Texture and color*—the image pattern describing the skin. See Chapter 6.
- *Expression*—muscular synthesis of emotions making the face look happy or sad, for example. See Chapter 11.

For a head tracker, the purpose is typically to extract the 3D motion parameters and be invariant to all other parameters. Whereas, for example, a user interface being sensitive to the mood of the user would need a model extracting the expression parameters, a recognition system should typically be invariant to all but the shape and texture parameters.

## 3.1 Eigenfaces

Statistical texture models in the form of *eigenfaces* [23, 34, 41] have been popular for facial image analysis. The basic idea is that a training set of facial images are collected and registered, each image is reshaped into a vector, and a principal component analysis (PCA)(see Chapter 3) is performed on the training set. The principal components are called eigenfaces. A facial image (in vector form), $\mathbf{x}$, can then be approximated by a linear combination, $\hat{\mathbf{x}}$, of these eigenfaces (i.e.,

$$\mathbf{x} \approx \hat{\mathbf{x}} = \bar{\mathbf{x}} + \mathbf{\Phi}_x \xi \qquad (1)$$

where $\bar{\mathbf{x}}$ is the average of the training set, $\mathbf{\Phi}_x = (\phi_1|\phi_2|\dots|\phi_t)$ contain the eigenfaces, and $\xi$ is a vector of weights or eigenface parameters). The parameters minimizing $||\mathbf{x} - \hat{\mathbf{x}}||^2$ are given by

$$\xi = \mathbf{\Phi}_x^T (\mathbf{x} - \bar{\mathbf{x}}) \qquad (2)$$

Commonly, some kind of image normalization is performed prior to eigenface computation (see, for example, Chapter 2, Section 2.2, and Chapter 3, Section 1.2).

The space spanned by the eigenfaces is called the *face space*. Unfortunately, the manifold of facial images has a highly nonlinear structure, as described in Chapter 1, and is thus not well modeled by a linear subspace. Linear and nonlinear techniques are available in the literature and often used for face recognition (a thorough treatment follows in Chapter 7). For face tracking, it has been more popular to linearize the face manifold by warping the facial images to a standard pose and/or shape, thereby creating *shape-free* [8], *geometrically normalized* [36], or *shape-normalized* (see Chapter 3) images and eigenfaces (texture templates, texture modes) that can be warped to any face shape or texture-mapped onto a wireframe face model.

## 3.2  Facial Action Coding System

During the 1960s and 1970s, a system for parameterizing minimal facial actions was developed by psychologists trying to analyze facial expressions. The system was called the *Facial Action Coding System* (FACS) [15] and describes each facial expression as a combination of around 50 *action units* (AUs). Each AU represents the activation of one facial muscle.

The FACS has been a popular tool not only for psychology studies but also for computerized facial modeling (an example is given in Section 3.5). There are also other models available in the literature. (See, for example, Park and Waters [30] who describe modeling skin and muscles in detail, which falls outside the scope of this chapter).

## 3.3  MPEG-4 Facial Animation

MPEG-4, since 1999 an international standard for coding and representation of audiovisual objects, contains definitions of face model parameters [29]. There are two sets of parameters: *facial definition parameters* (FDPs), which describe the static appearance of the head, and *facial animation parameters* (FAPs), which describe the dynamics.

The FAPs describe the motion of certain feature points, such as lip corners. Points on the face model not directly affected by the FAPs are then interpolated according to the face model's own motion model, which is not defined by MPEG-4 (complete face models can also be specified and transmitted). Typically, the FAP coefficients are used as morph target weights, provided the face model has a morph target for each FAP. The FDPs describe the static shape of the face by the 3D coordinates of each feature point (MPEG-4 defines 84 feature points) and the texture as an image with the corresponding texture coordinates.

## 3.4  Computer Graphics Models

When synthesizing faces using computer graphics (for user interfaces [20], web applications [28], or special effects in movies), the most common model is a *wireframe model* or a *polygonal mesh*. The face is then described as a set of vertices connected with lines forming polygons (usually triangles). The polygons are shaded or texture-mapped, and illumination is added. The texture could be parameterized or fixed—in the latter case facial appearance is changed by moving the vertices only. To achieve life-like animation of the face, a large number (thousands) of vertices and polygons are commonly used. Each vertex can move in three dimensions, so the model requires a large number of degrees of freedom. To reduce this number, some kind of parameterization is needed.

A commonly adopted solution is to create a set of *morph targets* and blend between them. A morph target is a predefined set of vertex positions, where each morph target represents, for example, a facial expression or a viseme. Thus, the model shape is defined by the morph targets $\mathbf{A}$ and controlled by the parameter vector $\alpha$

$$\begin{aligned} \mathbf{g} &= \mathbf{A}\alpha \\ \sum \alpha_i &= 1 \end{aligned} \qquad (3)$$

The $3N$-dimensional vector $\mathbf{g}$ contains the 3D coordinates of the $N$ vertices; the columns of the $3N \times M$-matrix $\mathbf{A}$ contains the $M$ morph targets; and $\alpha$ contains the $M$ morph target coefficients. To limit the required computational complexity, most $\alpha_i$ values are usually zero.

To render the model on the screen, we need to find a correspondence from the model coordinates to image pixels. The projection model (see Section 3.6), which is not defined by the face model, defines a function $P(\cdot)$ that projects the vertices on the image plane

$$(u, v) = P(x, y, z) \qquad (4)$$

The image coordinate system is typically defined over the range $[-1, 1] \times [-1, 1]$ or $[0, w - 1] \times [0, h - 1]$, where $(w, h)$ is the image dimensions in pixels.

To texturize the model, each vertex is associated with a (prestored) texture coordinate $(s, t)$ defined on the unit square. Using some interpolating scheme (e.g., piecewise affine transformations), we can find a correspondence from any point $(x, y, z)$ on the model surface to a point $(s, t)$ in the texture image and a point $(u, v)$ in the rendered image. Texture mapping is executed by copying (interpolated) pixel values from the texture $I_t(s, t)$ to the rendered image of the model $I_m(u, v)$. We call the coordinate transform $T_{\mathbf{u}}(\cdot)$, and thus

$$I_m(u, v) = T_{\mathbf{u}}[I_t(s, t)] \qquad (5)$$

More on computerized facial animation can be found in Chapters 10 and 12 and in refs. 29 and 30. Texture mapping is treated in [19].

## 3.5 Candide: A Simple Wireframe Face Model

Candide is a simple face model that has been a popular research tool for many years. It was originally created by Rydfalk [33] and later extended by Welsh [42] to cover the entire head (Candide-2) and by Ahlberg [2, 3] to correspond better to MPEG-4 facial animation (Candide-3). The simplicity of the model makes it a good pedagogic example.

Candide is a wireframe model with 113 vertices connected by lines forming 184 triangular surfaces. The geometry (shape, structure) is determined by the 3D coordinates of the vertices in a model-centered coordinate system $(x, y, z)$. To modify the geometry, Candide-1 and Candide-2 implement a set of action units from FACS. Each action unit is implemented as a list of vertex displacements, an *action unit vector*, describing the change in face geometry when the action unit is fully activated. The geometry is thus parameterized as

$$\mathbf{g}(\alpha) = \bar{\mathbf{g}} + \mathbf{\Phi}_a\alpha, \qquad 0 \leq \alpha_i \leq 1 \tag{6}$$

where the resulting vector $\mathbf{g}$ contains the $(x, y, z)$ coordinates of the vertices of the model, $\bar{\mathbf{g}}$ is the standard shape of the model, and the columns of $\mathbf{\Phi}_a$ are the action unit vectors. The $\alpha_i$ values are the action unit activation levels.

Candide-3 is parameterized slightly differently generalizing the action unit vectors to animation modes that implements action units or FAPs and adding shape modes. The parameterization is

$$\mathbf{g}(\alpha, \sigma) = \bar{\mathbf{g}} + \mathbf{\Phi}_a\alpha + \mathbf{\Phi}_s\sigma \tag{7}$$

The difference between $\alpha$ and $\sigma$ is that the shape parameters control the static deformations cause individuals to differ from each other. The animation parameters control the dynamic deformations due to facial expression changes.

This kind of linear model is, in different variations, a common way to model facial geometry. For example, in the previous chapter, a PCA was performed to find a matrix that described 2D shape and animation modes combined, and Gokturk et al. [18] estimated 3D animation modes using a stereo-vision system.

To change the pose, the model coordinates are rotated, scaled and translated so

$$\mathbf{g}(\alpha, \sigma, \pi) = s\,\mathbf{R}\,\mathbf{g}(\alpha, \sigma) + \mathbf{t} \tag{8}$$

where $\pi$ contains the six pose/global motion parameters plus a scaling factor.

## 3.6 Projection Models

The function $(u, v) = P(x, y, z)$, above, is a general projection model representing the camera. There are various projection models from which to chose, each with a set of parameters that may be known (calibrated camera) or unknown (uncalibrated camera). In most applications, the camera is assumed to be at least partly calibrated. We stress that only simple cases are treated here, neglecting such camera parameters as skewness and rotation. For more details, consult a computer vision textbook [35]. Two projection models are used in this chapter.

- The most common camera model is the *perspective projection*, which can be expressed as

$$\begin{cases} (u', v', w') = \mathbf{P}(x, y, z, 1)^T \\ (u, v) = (u'/w', v'/w') \end{cases} \tag{9}$$

where

$$\mathbf{P} = \begin{pmatrix} a_u & 0 & 0 & c_x \\ 0 & a_v & 0 & c_y \\ 0 & 0 & 1/f & c_z \end{pmatrix}, \tag{10}$$

$(c_x, c_y, c_z)$ is the focus of expansion (FOE), and $f$ is the focal length of the camera; $(a_u, a_v)$ determines the pixel size. Commonly, a simple expression for $\mathbf{P}$ is obtained where $(c_x, c_y, c_z) = \mathbf{0}$ and $a_u = a_v = 1$ are used. In this case, Eq. (9) is simply

$$(u, v) = (f\frac{x}{z}, f\frac{y}{z}). \tag{11}$$

- The *weak perspective projection* is a zero-order approximation to the perspective projection. It is suitably used for an object where the internal depth variation is small compared to the distance $z_{ref}$ from the camera to the object.

$$\begin{pmatrix} u \\ v \end{pmatrix} = \begin{pmatrix} a_u/z_{ref} & 0 & 0 & c_x \\ 0 & a_v/z_{ref} & 0 & c_y \end{pmatrix} \begin{pmatrix} x \\ y \\ z \\ 1 \end{pmatrix}. \tag{12}$$

## 4 Tracking Strategies

A face tracking system estimates the rigid or nonrigid motion of a face through a sequence of image frames. In the following, we discuss the two-frame situation, where we have an estimate of the model parameters $\hat{\mathbf{p}}_{k-1}$ in the old frame, and the system should estimate the parameters $\hat{\mathbf{p}}_k$ in the new frame (i.e., how to transform the model from the old frame to the new frame).

As mentioned in the Introduction, we discuss only monocular realtime trackers here. That is, we do not look into any stereo-vision systems, and we only consider trackers that can process several frames per second without dedicated hardware.

### 4.1  Motion Versus Model-Based Trackers

Tracking systems can be said to be either *motion-based* or *model-based*, sometimes referred to as *feed-forward* or *feed-back* motion estimation. A *motion-based* tracker estimates the displacements of pixels (or blocks of pixels) from one frame to another. The displacements might be estimated using optical flow methods (giving a dense optical flow field), block-based motion estimation methods (giving a sparse field but using less computational power), or motion estimation in a few image patches only (giving a few motion vectors only but at very low computational cost).

The estimated motion field is used to compute the motion of the object model using, for example, a least-squares method or extended Kalman filtering. The motion estimation in such a method is consequently dependent on the pixels in two frames; the object model is used only for transforming the 2D motion vectors to 3D object model motion. The problem with such methods is the *drifting* or the *long sequence motion problem*. A tracker of this kind accumulates motion errors and eventually loses track of the face. Examples of such trackers can be found in the literature [6, 7, 32].

A *model-based* tracker, on the other hand, uses a model of the object's appearance and tries to change the object model's pose (and possibly shape) parameters to fit the new frame. The motion estimation is thus dependent on the object model and the new frame—the old frame is not regarded except for constraining the search space. Such a tracker does not suffer from drifting; instead, problems arise when the model is not strong or flexible enough to cope with the situation in the new frame. Trackers of this kind can be found in certain articles [4, 24, 25, 37]. Other trackers [9, 11, 18, 27] are motion-based but add various model-based constraints to improve performance and combat drift.

## 4.2 Model-Based Trackers: First-Frame Models or Statistical Models

In general, the word *model* refers to any prior knowledge about the 3D structure, the 3D motion/dynamics, and the 2D facial appearance. One of the main issues when designing a model-based tracker is the appearance model. An obvious approach is to capture a reference image of the object at the beginning of the sequence. The image could then be geometrically transformed according to the estimated motion parameters, so one can compensate for changes in scale and rotation (and possibly nonrigid motion). Because the image is captured, the appearance model is deterministic, object-specific, and (potentially) accurate. Thus, trackers of this kind can be precise, and systems working in real time have been demonstrated [18, 37, 43].

A drawback with such a first-frame model is the lack of flexibility—it is difficult to generalize from one sample only (cf. Fig. 8 in Chapter 1). This can cause problems with changing appearance due to variations in illumination, facial expression, and other factors. Another drawback is that the initialization is critical; if the captured image was for some reason not representative for the sequence (due to partial occlusion, facial expression, or illumination) or simply not the correct image (i.e., if the object model was not correctly placed/shaped in the first frame) the tracker does not work well. Such problems can usually be solved by manual interaction but may be hard to automate.

Note that the model could be renewed continuously, so the model always is based on the previous frame. In this way the problems with flexibility are reduced, but the tracker is then motion-based and might drift. A solution, as adopted by Gokturk at al. [18], is to estimate the parameters with respect to the previous frame *and* the first frame of the sequence.

Another property is that the tracker does not know what it is tracking. This could be an advantage—the tracker can track different kinds of objects—or a disadvantage. A relevant example is when the goal is to extract some higher level information from a human face, such as facial expression or lip motion. In that case we need a tracker that identifies and tracks specific facial features (e.g., lip contours or feature points).

A different approach is a *statistical model-based tracker*. Here, the appearance model relies on previously captured images combined with knowledge of which parts or positions of the images correspond to the various facial features. When the model is transformed to fit the new frame, we thus obtain information about the estimated positions of those specific facial features.

The appearance model may be person specific or general. A specific model could, for example, be trained on a database containing images of one person only, resulting in an accurate model for this person. It could cope, to some degree, with the illumination and expression changes present in the database. A more general appearance model could be trained on a database containing many faces in different illuminations and with different facial expressions. Such a model would have a better chance to enable successful tracking of a previously unseen face in a new environment, whereas a specific appearance model presumably would result in better performance on the person and environment for which it was trained. Trackers using statistical models of appearance can be found in the literature [4, 24].

## 4.3 Appearance-Based Versus Feature-Based Tracking

An *appearance-based* or *featureless* tracker matches a model of the entire facial appearance with the input image, trying to exploit all available information in the model as well as the image. Generally, we can express this as follows:

Assume a parametric face model and an input image $I$ of a face from which we want to estimate a set of parameters. The parameters to be extracted should form a subset of the parameter set controlling the model. Given a vector $\mathbf{p}$ with $N$ parameters, the face model can generate an image $I_m(\mathbf{p})$. The principle of analysis-by-synthesis then states that the best estimates of the facial parameters are the ones minimizing the distance between the generated image and the input image

$$\mathbf{p}^* = \arg\min_{\mathbf{p}} \delta[I, I_m(\mathbf{p})] \tag{13}$$

for some distance measure $\delta(\cdot)$.

The problem of finding the optimal parameters is a high-dimensional ($N$ dimensions) search problem and thus of high computional complexity. By using clever search heuristics (e.g., the active appearance models described in the previous chapter), we can reduce the search time. Some trackers described by other investigators [4, 24, 25, 27] are appearance-based.

A *feature-based* tracker , on the other hand, choses a few facial features that are, supposedly, easily and robustly tracked. Features such as color, specific points or patches, and edges can be used. Typically, a tracker based on feature points tries, in the rigid motion case, to estimate the 2D position of a set of points and from these points compute the 3D pose of the face. Feature-based trackers are described by others [9, 12, 21, 37, 43].

In the following sections we describe three trackers found in the literature. They represent the classes mentioned above.

# 5  Feature-Based Tracking Using Extended Kalman Filtering and Structure from Motion

The tracker described in this section tracks a set of feature points in an image sequence and uses the 2D measurements to calulate the 3D structure and motion of the head. The tracker is based on the structure from motion (SfM) algorithm by Azerbayejani and Pentland [5]. The face tracker was then developed by Jebara and Pentland [21] and further by Ström et al. [39] and Ström [36, 37].

The tracker estimates the 3D pose and structure of a rigid object as well as the camera's focal length. With the terminology above, it is a first-frame model-based and feature-based tracker. We stress that the presentation here is somewhat simplified.

## 5.1  Face Model Parameterization

The tracker designed by Jebara and Pentland [21] estimated a model as a set of points with no surface. Ström et al. [39] extended the system to include a wireframe face model. A set of feature points are placed on the surface of the model, not necessarily coinciding with the model vertices. The face model gives the system several advantages, such as being able to predict the surface angle relative to the camera as well as self-occlusion. Thus, the tracker can predict when some measurements should not be trusted. The face model used by Ström was a modified version of Candide.

## Pose Parameterization

The pose in the $k^{th}$ frame is parameterized with three rotation angles $(r_x, r_y, r_z)$, three translation parameters $(t_x, t_y, t_z)$, and the inverse focal length $\phi = 1/f$ of the camera. In practice, the $z$-translation should be parameterized by $\zeta = t_z \phi$ instead of $t_z$ for stability reasons.

Azerbayejani and Pentland [5] chose to use a perspective projection model where the origin of the 3D coordinate system is placed in the center of the image plane instead of at the focal point, that is, the FOE is set to $(0, 0, 1)$ (see Section 3.6). This projection model has several advantages; for example, there is only one unknown parameter per feature point (as becomes apparent below).

Thus, the 2D (projected) screen coordinates are computed as

$$\begin{pmatrix} u \\ v \end{pmatrix} = \frac{1}{1 + z\phi} \begin{pmatrix} x \\ y \end{pmatrix} \tag{14}$$

## Structure Parameterization

The structure of the face is represented by the image coordinates $(u_0, v_0)$ and the depth values $z_0$ of the feature points in the first frame. If the depths $z_0$ are known, the 3D coordinates of the feature points can be computed for the first frame as

$$\begin{pmatrix} x_0 \\ y_0 \end{pmatrix} = (1 + z_0 \phi) \begin{pmatrix} u_0 \\ v_0 \end{pmatrix} \tag{15}$$

and for all following frames as

$$\begin{pmatrix} x \\ y \\ z \end{pmatrix} = \mathbf{R} \begin{pmatrix} x_0 \\ y_0 \\ z_0 \end{pmatrix} + \begin{pmatrix} t_x \\ t_y \\ t_z \end{pmatrix} \tag{16}$$

where $\mathbf{R}$ is the rotation matrix created from a quaternion. For clarity of presentation, the frame indices on all the parameters are omitted.

All put together, the model parameter vector is

$$\mathbf{p} = (t_x, t_y, t_z, r_x, r_y, r_z, \phi, z_1, \dots, z_N)^T \tag{17}$$

where $N$ is the number of feature points and $r_x, r_y, r_z$ are used to update the quaternion. Combining Eqs. (15), (16), and (14), we get a function from the parameter vector to screen coordinates

$$(u_1, v_1, \dots, u_N, v_N)^T = h_k(\mathbf{p}) \tag{18}$$

Note that the parameter vector has $N + 7$ degrees of freedom, and that we get $2N$ values if we measure the image coordinates for each feature point. Thus, the problem of estimating the parameter vector from image coordinates is overconstrained when $N > 7$.

## 5.2 Extended Kalman Filters and Structure from Motion

A Kalman filter is used to estimate the dynamic changes of a state vector of which only a function can be observed. When the function is nonlinear, we must use an extended Kalman filter (EKF). The literature on Kalman filtering is plentiful [17, 22, 35, 36], so we only summarize the approach here.

In our case, the state vector is the model parameter vector $\mathbf{p}$ and we observe, for each frame, the screen coordinates $\mathbf{u}_k = h_k(\mathbf{p}_k)$. Because we cannot measure the screen coordinates exactly, measurement noise $\mathbf{v}_k$ is added as well. We can summarize the dynamics of the system as

$$\begin{cases} \mathbf{p}_{k+1} = f_k(\mathbf{p}_k) + \mathbf{w}_k, & \mathbf{w}_k \sim N(\mathbf{0}, \mathbf{W}_k) \\ \hat{\mathbf{u}}_k = h_k(\mathbf{p}_k) + \mathbf{v}_k, & \mathbf{v}_k \sim N(\mathbf{0}, \mathbf{V}_k) \end{cases} \tag{19}$$

where $f_k(\cdot)$ is the dynamics function, $h_k(\cdot)$ is the measurement function, and $\mathbf{w}$ and $\mathbf{v}$ are zero-mean Gaussian random variables with known covariances $\mathbf{W}_k$ and $\mathbf{V}_k$.

The job for the Kalman filter is to estimate the state vector $\mathbf{p}_k$ given the measurement vector $\hat{\mathbf{u}}_k$ and the previous estimate $\hat{\mathbf{p}}_{k-1}$. Choosing the trivial dynamics function $f_k(\mathbf{p}_k) = \mathbf{p}_k$ the state estimate is updated using

$$\hat{\mathbf{p}}_k = \hat{\mathbf{p}}_{k-1} + \mathbf{K}_k[\hat{\mathbf{u}}_k - h_k(\hat{\mathbf{p}}_{k-1})] \tag{20}$$

where $\mathbf{K}_k$ is the Kalman gain matrix. It is updated every time step depending on $f_k(\cdot)$, $h_k(\cdot)$, $\mathbf{W}_k$, and $\mathbf{V}_k$. The covariances are given by initial assumptions or estimated during the tracking.

## 5.3 Tracking Process

The tracker must be initialized, for example by letting the user place his head in a certain position and with the face toward the camera or by using a face detection algorithm as described in Chapter 2. The model texture is captured from the image and stored as a reference, and feature points are automatically extracted. To select feature points that could be reliably tracked, points where the determinant of the Hessian

$$det(H) = \begin{vmatrix} I_{xx}(x,y) & I_{xy}(x,y) \\ I_{xy}(x,y) & I_{yy}(x,y) \end{vmatrix} \tag{21}$$

is large are used. The determinant is weighted with the cosine of the angle between the model surface normal and the camera direction. The number of feature points to select is limited only by the available computational power and the realtime requirements. At least seven points are needed for the tracker to work, and more are preferable. Ström [36] used 24 feature points and was able to achieve realtime performance.

The initial feature point depth values $(z_1, \ldots, z_N)$ are given by the face model. Then, for each frame, the model is rendered using the current model parameters. Around each feature point, a small ($7 \times 7$ pixels) patch is extracted from the rendered image. The patches are matched with the new frame using a zero-mean normalized cross correlation. The best match, with sub-pixel precision, for each feature point is collected in the measurement vector $\hat{\mathbf{u}}_k$ and fed into the Kalman filter update equation Eq. (20).

Using the face model and the values from the normalized template matching, the measurement noise covariance matrix can be estimated making the Kalman filter rely on some measurements more than others. Note that this also tells the Kalman filter in which directions in the image the measurements are reliable. For example, a feature point on an edge (e.g., the mouth outline) can reliably be placed in the direction perpendicular to the edge but less reliably along the edge. The system is illustrated in Figure 4.1.

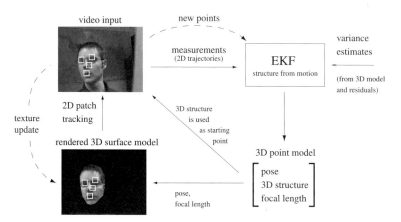

**Fig. 4.1.** Patches from the rendered image (lower left) are matched with the incoming video. The two-dimensional feature point trajectories are fed through the structure from motion (SfM) extended Kalman filter, which estimates the pose information needed to render the next model view. For clarity, only 4 of 24 patches are shown. Illustration courtesy of J. Ström.

## 5.4 Additional Features

The tracker described by Ström [36, 37] also uses several heuristics to improve reliability. For example, as the head rotates close to 90° many of the original feature points are lost. Therefore, new feature points are chosen, and texture from the side of the head is added to the texture model.

In the case of tracker failure, the system uses the information acquired from the original initialization to reinitialize. Tracking failure is detected by monitoring the feature point matches.

The system is evaluated in terms of accuracy, convergence speed, and robustness to occlusion. An experiment on synthetic data has shown a good following of the (known) model parameters.

## 6 Active Appearance-Based Real-Time Tracker

In this section we describe a statistical model-based and appearance-based tracker estimating the 3D pose and deformations of the face. It is based on the active appearance models (AAMs) described in Chapter 3. The tracker was first presented by Ahlberg [1], and improved versions for realtime performance were presented by Ahlberg and Forchheimer [4] and by Dornaika and Ahlberg [13].

To use the AAM search algorithm, we must first decide on a geometry for the face model, its parameterization of shape and texture, and how we use the model for warping images. Here, we use the face model Candide-3 described in Section 3.5.

## 6.1 Face Model Parameterization

### Geometry Parameterization

The geometry (structure) $\mathbf{g}(\sigma, \alpha)$ of the Candide model is parameterized according to Eq. (7). There are several techniques to estimate the shape parameters $\sigma$ (e.g., an AAM search or a feature-based algorithm). When adapting a model to a video sequence, the shape parameters should be changed only in the first frame(s)—the head shape does not vary during a conversation—whereas the pose and animation parameters naturally change at each frame. Thus, during the tracking process we can assume that $\sigma$ is fixed (and known), and let the shape depend on $\alpha$ only.

$$\begin{cases} \bar{\mathbf{g}}_\sigma = \bar{\mathbf{g}} + \mathbf{\Phi}_s \sigma \\ \mathbf{g}_\sigma(\alpha) = \bar{\mathbf{g}}_\sigma + \mathbf{\Phi}_a \alpha \end{cases} \tag{22}$$

### Pose Parameterization

To perform global motion (i.e., pose change), we need six parameters plus a scaling factor according to Eq. (8). Adopting the weak perspective projection, the model coordinates $\mathbf{g}_i = (x_i, y_i, z_i)^T$ of the $i^{th}$ vertex is projected according to

$$\mathbf{u}_i = \mathbf{P} \begin{pmatrix} s\mathbf{R}\mathbf{g}_i + \mathbf{t} \\ 1 \end{pmatrix} \tag{23}$$

where $\mathbf{P}$ is given by Eq. (12).

Using the model's $z$-translation as the reference plane (i.e., $z_{ref} = t_z$), this can be written as

$$\mathbf{u}_i = \mathbf{M} \begin{pmatrix} \mathbf{g}_i \\ 1 \end{pmatrix} \tag{24}$$

where

$$\mathbf{M} = \begin{pmatrix} \frac{a_u}{t_z} s\mathbf{r}_1 & \frac{a_u}{t_z} t_x + c_x \\ \frac{a_v}{t_z} s\mathbf{r}_2 & \frac{a_v}{t_z} t_y + c_y \end{pmatrix} \tag{25}$$

where $\mathbf{r}_1$ and $\mathbf{r}_2$ are the two first rows of the rotation matrix $\mathbf{R}$. Assuming square pixels ($a_u = a_v$) and using $\zeta = \frac{a_u}{t_z} s$ as a scale factor incorporating face model size as well as pixel size and $z$-translation we get

$$\mathbf{M} = \begin{pmatrix} \zeta \mathbf{r}_1 & \lambda t_x + c_x \\ \zeta \mathbf{r}_2 & \lambda t_y + c_y \end{pmatrix} \tag{26}$$

where $\lambda = \frac{a_u}{t_z}$. Using the 2D translation vector $\mathbf{t}' = \lambda(t_x, t_y)^T + \mathbf{c}$ and the three Euler angles for the rotation matrix $\mathbf{R}$, our pose parameter vector is

$$\pi = (r_x, r_y, r_z, \zeta, t'_x, t'_y)^T \tag{27}$$

We can thus easily retrieve the pose parameters from the projection matrix, and vice versa, as is needed later.

**Texture Parameterization**

We use a statistical model of the texture and control the texture with a small set of texture parameters $\xi$. The model texture vector $\hat{\mathbf{x}}$ is generated according to Eq. (1) (see Section 3.1). The synthesized texture vector $\hat{\mathbf{x}}$ has for each element a corresponding $(s, t)$ coordinate and is equivalent to the texture image $I_t(s, t)$: the relation is just lexicographic ordering, $\hat{\mathbf{x}} = L[I_t(s, t)]$. $I_t(s, t)$ is mapped on the wireframe model to create the generated image $I_m(u, v)$ according to Eq. (5).

The entire appearance of the model can now be controlled using the parameters $(\xi, \pi, \alpha, \sigma)$. However, as we assume that the shape $\sigma$ is fixed during the tracking session, and the texture $\xi$ depends on the other parameters, the parameter vector we optimize below is

$$\mathbf{p} = (\pi^T, \alpha^T)^T \tag{28}$$

## 6.2 Tracking Process

The tracker should find the optimal adaptation of the model to each frame in a sequence as described in Section 4.3. That is, we wish to find the parameter vector $\mathbf{p}_k^*$ that minimizes the distance between image $I_m$ generated by the model and each frame $I_k$. Here, an iterative solution is presented, and as an initial value of $\mathbf{p}$ we use $\hat{\mathbf{p}}_{k-1}$ (i.e., the estimated parameter vector from the previous frame).

Instead of directly comparing the generated image $I_m(u, v)$ to the input image $I_k(u, v)$, we back-project the input image to the model's parametric surface coordinate system $(s, t)$ using the inverse of the texture mapping transform $T_\mathbf{u}$.

$$I_{\mathbf{u}(\mathbf{p})}(s, t) = T_{\mathbf{u}(\mathbf{p})}^{-1}[I_k(u, v)] \tag{29}$$

$$\mathbf{x}(\mathbf{p}) = L[I_{\mathbf{u}(\mathbf{p})}(s, t)] \tag{30}$$

We then compare the normalized input image vector $\mathbf{x}(\mathbf{p})$ to the generated model texture vector $\hat{\mathbf{x}}(\mathbf{p})$. $\hat{\mathbf{x}}(\mathbf{p})$ is generated in the face space as closely as possible to $\mathbf{x}(\mathbf{p})$ (see Eq. (1)), and we compute a residual image $\mathbf{r}(\mathbf{p}) = \mathbf{x}(\mathbf{p}) - \hat{\mathbf{x}}(\mathbf{p})$. The process from input image to residual, is illustrated in Figure 4.2.

As the distance measure according to Eq. (13), we use the squared norm of the residual image

$$\delta[I_k, I_m(\mathbf{p})] = ||\mathbf{r}(\mathbf{p})||^2 \tag{31}$$

From the residual image we also compute the update vector

$$\Delta\mathbf{p} = -\mathbf{U}\mathbf{r}(\mathbf{p}) \tag{32}$$

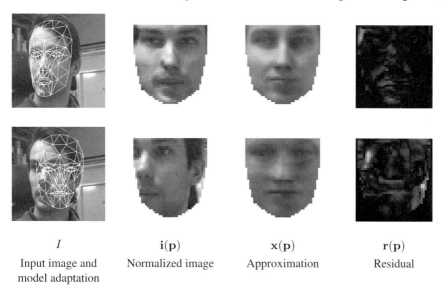

|           $I$          |        $\mathbf{i}(\mathbf{p})$        |     $\mathbf{x}(\mathbf{p})$    |     $\mathbf{r}(\mathbf{p})$    |
| Input image and model adaptation | Normalized image | Approximation | Residual |

**Fig. 4.2.** Analysis-synthesis process. A good and a bad model adaptation. The normalized image and its approximation should be more similar the better the model adaptation is.

where $\mathbf{U} = (\frac{\delta \mathbf{r}}{\delta \mathbf{p}})^{\dagger}$ is the precomputed active appearance update matrix (i.e., the pseudo-inverse of the estimated gradient matrix $\frac{\delta \mathbf{r}}{\delta \mathbf{p}}$). It is created by numeric differentiation, systematically displacing each parameter and computing an average over the training set, as explained in Chapter 3.

We then compute the estimated new parameter vector as

$$\hat{\mathbf{p}}_k = \mathbf{p} + \varDelta \mathbf{p} \tag{33}$$

In most cases, the model fitting is improved if the entire process is iterated a few times.

### 6.3 Tracking Results

Two video sequences of a previously unseen person were recorded using the same camera as when capturing the training set. In the first sequence, the illumination was the same as for the training set, in the second it differed somewhat. The Candide-3 model was manually adapted to the first frame of the sequence by changing the pose parameters and the static shape parameters (recall that the shape parameter vector $\sigma$ is assumed to be known). The model parameter vector $\mathbf{p}$ was then iteratively optimized for each frame. The results are shown in Figure 4.3. As can be seen, the pose estimates are good most of the time, and the mouth and eyebrow parameters behave well. However, note the tracker failure in the first sequence. Between frames 17 and 18 there is a head movement too fast for the tracker (actually, the image capturing device lost a few frames) and the face has moved out of the AAM's convergence area. Note also that the tracker recovers by itself around 30 frames later.

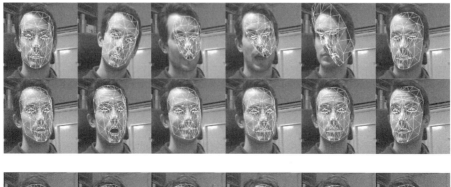

**Fig. 4.3.** Tracking results on two test sequences. Every tenth frame is shown.

This initial test shows that the system is able to track a previously unseen person in a subjectively accurate way. Some important issues remain to be addressed, though.

- Speed. Can the system run in real time? This is addressed in Section 6.4.
- Robustness. Can the system cope with varying illumination, facial expressions, and large head motion? Apparently, track is sometimes lost. One way to increase robustness is to combine the tracker with a feature-based step, as described in Section 6.5. To improve robustness to varying illumination conditions, an illumination basis could be added to the texture parameterization [24].
- Accuracy. How accurate is the tracking? Ahlberg and Forchheimer [4] describe a system that tracks a synthetic sequence where the true parameters are known.

### 6.4 Real-Time Tracking

The speed of the algorithm is of course critical for realtime applications, but an important observation is that the algorithm works better if the frame rate is high. When processing frames captured at a low frame rate, the algorithm suffers from being greedy and sometimes getting stuck in a local optimum. Typically, this results in the model not being able to follow fast moves, such as when the mouth is closed too fast or when the head is moved away quickly. If the frame rate is high, the motion between each frame is smaller, and thus the initial $\mathbf{p}_k(=\hat{\mathbf{p}}_{k-1})$ is closer to $\mathbf{p}_k^*$. A few (maybe five) frames per second seems to be sufficient for handling normal head motion.

A second observation is that when the motion between the frames is small, fewer iterations are usually needed, and the algorithm thus requires less time per frame.

When running the algorithm on live video (i.e., with input directly from a camera), the computation time is critical. Assuming that the video input device can provide new frames as fast as the tracking system can process them, a reduced computation time would increase the frame rate. As observed above, this would improve the performance of the tracking and decrease the average number of iterations needed per frame, which would increase the possible frame rate even more.

In conclusion, it is important to optimize the algorithm as much as possible. Studying the algorithm, we find that there are three potentially time-consuming parts within each iteration.

- *Shape normalization.* Using dedicated graphics hardware for texture mapping (i.e., letting the graphics card perform the image warping), or performing certain parts of the computation offline, we can do the shape normalization in less than a millisecond on a consumer desktop computer [3].
- *Analysis-synthesis.* The projection of the shape-normalized input image onto the texture modes and generation of the model texture has a complexity that grows linearly with the number of texture modes used. Fortunately, this step can be avoided almost completely. Instead of computing $\hat{\mathbf{x}}(\mathbf{p})$ we use the texture generated by the estimated parameters in the old frame, $\hat{\mathbf{x}}(\hat{\mathbf{p}}_{k-1})$. Thus, the analysis-synthesis step needs to be done only once per frame instead of once per iteration, speeding up the tracker significantly as well as removing the dependence of the number of texture modes used. As shown by Dornaika and Ahlberg [13], this can be done without any deterioration of the tracker's accuracy—on the contrary, the tracking can be improved as more texture modes can be used at almost no additional computational cost.
- *Residual image and update vector computation.* The complexity grows linearly with the number of parameters to extract. However, it can be performed very quickly (less than a millisecond) by exploiting the vector instructions available in many modern central processing units (CPUs) (e.g., Intel's SSE2 or Motorola's Altivec).

In total, we can thus perform an iteration in less than 2 msec. Because typically fewer than 10 iterations are needed per frame, the algorithm is able to run in real time.

## 6.5 Feature/Motion-Based Extensions

To combine the strengths of appearance/model-based trackers and feature/motion-based trackers, a motion estimation algorithm could be added to the tracker described above. The idea is to use a simple, fast motion estimator to obtain a quick and rough estimate of the global motion of the face which is refined by the AAM search. The face model would then be moved according to this estimate, and the iterative model adaptation process starts at this new position. Thus, the tracker would be able to do a "jump" to a position closer to the correct position, and the risk of getting stuck in a local (suboptimal) optimum is reduced.

There are a number of fast motion estimators available in the literature on video coding (e.g., [26]) using various difference measures, search algorithms, block shapes, and so forth. Ahlberg and Forchheimer [4] used a simple estimator where a single image block cut from the old frame is sought in the new frame. As pointed out by Ström [38], the region between the eyes is suitable for tracking, being quite robust to changes in scale and rotation.

Running the tracker on the test sequence that included a tracking failure shows good improvement when the motion estimation is used; the part with fast head motion is now correctly tracked (Figure 4.4). To introduce more tracking failures, the tracker was given every third frame only in order to simulate very fast head motion. This led to tracking failure a few times during the sequence, but using motion estimation the whole sequence is correctly tracked.

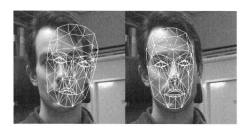

**Fig. 4.4.** Model adaptation after too-fast head movement with and without motion estimation.

Dornaika and Ahlberg [10] chose six features to be able to estimate the full 3D motion. The six corresponding vertices of the model are first projected onto the old frame $I_{k-1}$. The obtained image points are then matched with the new frame, and the six computed 2D correspondences give the set of six 3D-to-2D correspondences, from which a rough estimation of the projection matrix $\mathbf{M}$ is computed. Eventually, the retrieved pose parameters $\hat{\pi}_k$ as well as the animation parameters $\hat{\alpha}_{k-1}$ are handed over to the active appearance model search for further refinement.

## 7 Feature/Appearance-Based Tracker

In this section, we describe the feature/appearance-based tracker introduced by Dornaika and Ahlberg [12, 11]. As above, we assume two frames from a sequence, $I_{k-1}$ and $I_k$, and estimated model parameters $\hat{\mathbf{p}}_{k-1}$ from the old frame. As in Section 6, we use a weak perspective projection with a $2 \times 4$ projection matrix $\mathbf{M}$(see Eq. (26)), that can be recovered from the model parameters (and vice versa). The head pose is estimated using a RANdom SAmpling Consensus (RANSAC) technique [16] combined with a texture consistency measure to avoid drifting. Once the 3D head pose $\pi$ is estimated, the facial animation parameters $\alpha$ can be estimated using the scheme described in Section 6. The whole adaptation process is summarized in Figure 4.5. The face model and its parameterization is similar to that in the previous section.

### 7.1 Feature-Based Head Pose Estimation

Given two consecutive images, *previmg* and *curimg*, of a face undergoing rigid and nonrigid motion, one can still find a set of facial features that are affected only by the rigid motion. Features undergoing local deformation (facial animation) can be considered as outliers. Thus, by identifying the inlier features (whose motion is fully described by the rigid motion), the

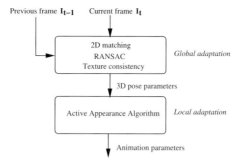

Fig. 4.5. Summary of the feature/appearance-based tracker.

projection matrix can be recovered thanks to the 3D deformable wireframe model. Because facial deformation tends to exist in some localized areas, the globally consistent inlier features can be considered to be from the dominant head motion.

Computing the projection matrix requires a set of correspondences between the 3D face model and the new frame $I_k$. Because a direct match between 3D features and 2D images is extremely difficult, we use the previous adaptation $\hat{\mathbf{p}}_{k-1}$ and project the 3D vertices of the model onto the old frame $I_{k-1}$.

$$\mathbf{u}_{i(k-1)} = \begin{pmatrix} u_{i(k-1)} \\ v_{i(k-1)} \end{pmatrix} = \mathbf{M}_{k-1} \begin{pmatrix} \mathbf{g}_{i(k-1)} \\ 1 \end{pmatrix} \tag{34}$$

is the projection of the $i^{th}$ vertex in the $(k-1)^{th}$ frame.

Dornaika and Ahlberg kept 101 vertices belonging to the central part of the face model. The patches of *previmg* centered on the obtained projections $\mathbf{u}_{i(k-1)}$ are then matched with the new frame using the zero-mean normalized cross correlation with subpixel accuracy within a certain search region. The computed matches $\mathbf{u}_{i(k-1)} \leftrightarrow \mathbf{u}_{i(k)}$ give the set of 3D-to-2D correspondences $\mathbf{g}_{i(k-1)} \leftrightarrow \mathbf{u}_{i(k)}$, which are handed over to the RANSAC method, integrating the statistical facial texture model, which estimates the projection matrix. The hybrid technique is described below.

The 2D matching process is made reliable and fast by adopting a multistage scheme. First, three features are matched in the frames *previmg* and *curimg* (the two inner eye corners and the philtrum top) from which a 2D affine transform is computed between *previmg* and *curimg*. Second, the 2D features $\mathbf{u}_{i(k-1)}$ are then matched in *curimg* using a small search window centered on their 2D affine transform.

## 7.2  Tracking Process

Retrieving the projection matrix $\mathbf{M}$ (the matrix $\mathbf{M}$ encapsulates the 3D head pose) from the obtained set of putative 3D-to-2D correspondences is carried out in two steps. The *exploration step* explores the set of 3D-to-2D correspondences using the conventional RANSAC paradigm. The output of this step is a set of solutions (matrices $\mathbf{M}$) together with their consensus measure. The *search step* selects the solution according to a consensus measure and the texture consistency with the appearance model (i.e., the distance between the geometrically normalized image and its closest image in the face space). The goals of these two steps are to (1) remove possible mismatches and locally deformed features from the computation of the projection matrix, and (2) prevent the tracker from drifting. Note that relying on the consensus measure alone may lead to a drifting tracker—it would then be a pure motion-based tracker.

Finally, as a third step, the active appearance algorithm is used as described in the previous section. Here, it is used to optimize the animation (local motion) parameters $\alpha$ only.

The algorithm can be summarized as follows. Let $n_c$ be the total number of the putative 3D-to-2D correspondences. For the sake of simplicity the subscript $(k)$ has been omitted.

- *Exploration step: random sampling and consensus*

  1. Randomly sample four 3D-to-2D feature correspondences $\mathbf{g} \leftrightarrow \mathbf{u}$ (noncoplanar configuration). The image points of this sample are chosen such that the mutual distance is large enough.
  2. Compute the projection matrix $\mathbf{M}$ using this sample.
  3. For all feature correspondences, compute the distance between the image features $\mathbf{u}$ and the projection $\hat{\mathbf{u}} = \mathbf{M} \begin{pmatrix} \mathbf{g} \\ 1 \end{pmatrix}$.
  4. Count the number of features for which the distance $|\mathbf{u} - \hat{\mathbf{u}}|$ is below some threshold. This number is denoted by $n_I$. Empirical tests have shown that a threshold value between 1.0 and 2.0 pixels works well.

- *Search step: consensus measure and texture consistency*

  1. Sort the projection matrices according to their $n_I$ in descending order.
  2. For the best solutions (e.g., 10 solutions), refit the matrix $\mathbf{M}$ using its inliers.
  3. For each such solution, compute the residual error between the remapped texture and its approximation as in Eqs. (29) to (31).
  4. Select the $\mathbf{M}$ with the smallest residual error.
  5. Retrieve the pose parameters $\pi$ from $\mathbf{M}$ as described in Section 6.1.

The number of random samples is capped at the number of feature correspondences $n_c$. Also, $n_c$ is variable, as matches are filtered out by thresholding their normalized cross-correlation. Typically, $n_c$ is between 70 and 101 features, assuming a total of 101 features. Note that the random sampling step described above is cheap because, for each random sample, we solve for eight unknowns using eight linear equations.

Once the 3D pose of the face is recovered by the hybrid technique, the animation parameters are recovered using the paradigm of the AAM search. The process is illustrated in Figure 4.6.

## 7.3 Results

Compared to the previous tracker, the pose estimation is improved, especially for out-of-plane rotations, as illustrated in Figure 4.7. With an improved pose estimation the estimation of animation parameters is improved as well. Both trackers were evaluated by Dornaika and Ahlberg [11].

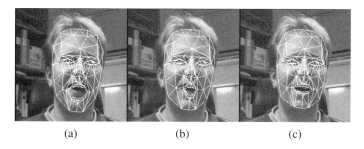

(a)                    (b)                    (c)

**Fig. 4.6.** Adaptation process applied to an input image at different stages. *a.* Global adaptation. *b.* Local adaptation (first iteration). *c.* Local adaptation (convergence).

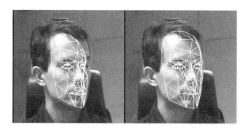

**Fig. 4.7.** Comparison of two tracking methods: Simultaneous estimation of the pose and animation parameters as described in Section 6 (left); feature/appearance-based method (right).

# 8 Conclusions

We have described some strategies for tracking and distinguished between model- and motion-based tracking as well as between appearance- and feature-based tracking. Whereas motion-based trackers may suffer from drifting, model-based trackers do not have that problem. Appearance- and feature-based trackers follow different basic principles and have different characteristics.

Three trackers have been described: one using extended Kalman filtering (EKF) and structure from motion (SfM), one using AAM, and one using AAM and RANSAC. The EKF/SfM tracker is a good example of a feature-based tracker: It tracks a few feature points and infers the motion of the feature points to the model. The AAM tracker is clearly appearance-based, and the RANSAC/AAM tracker seeks to combine the strengths of both strategies.

The three trackers are all model-based and thus do not suffer from drifting. The RANSAC tracker is basically a motion-based tracker, with an additional model-based step that prevents drift. The main advantage of this tracker is that accurate tracking can be obtained even when the 3D wireframe model is slightly inaccurate.

The three trackers differ in how they model the face. The EKF/SfM tracker use a deterministic texture model captured from the first frame, and the two others use a statistical texture model based on previously captured face images. In principle, however, they could all use the same deterministic or statistical texture models.

# References

1. J. Ahlberg. An active model for facial feature tracking. In *European Workshop on Image Analysis for Multimedia Interactive Services*, pages 63–67, Tampere, Finland, 2001.
2. J. Ahlberg. Candide-3: An updated parameterized face. Technical Report LiTH-ISY-R-2326, Linköping University, Sweden, 2001.
3. J. Ahlberg. *Model-based Coding—Extraction, Coding and Evaluation of Face Model Parameters*. Ph.D. thesis, Linköping University, Sweden, 2002.
4. J. Ahlberg and R. Forchheimer. Face tracking for model-based coding and face animation. *International Journal on Imaging Systems and Technology*, 13(1):8–22, 2003.
5. A. Azerbayejani and A. Pentland. Recursive estimation of motion, structure, and focal length. *IEEE Transactions on Pattern Analysis and Machine Intelligence*, 17(6):562–575, 1995.
6. S. Basu, I. Essa, and A. Pentland. Motion regularization for model-based head-tracking. In *International Conference on Computer Vision and Pattern Recognition*, pages 611–616, Vienna, 1996.
7. M.J. Black and Y. Yacoob. Recognizing facial expressions in image sequences using local parameterized models of image motion. *International Journal on Computer Vision*, 25(1):23–48, 1997.
8. I. Craw and P. Cameron. Parameterising images for recognition and reconstruction. In *British Machinve Vision Conference*, pages 367–370. Springer, London, 1991.
9. D. DeCarlo and D. Metaxas. Optical flow constraints on deformable models with applications to face tracking. *International Journal on Computer Vision*, 38(72):99–127, 2000.
10. F. Dornaika and J. Ahlberg. Active appearance model search with motion compensation for 3d face tracking. In *European Workshop on Image Analysis for Multimedia Interactive Services*, pages 359–364, London, 2003.
11. F. Dornaika and J. Ahlberg. Face and facial feature tracking using deformable models. *International Journal of Image and Graphics*, 4(3):499–532, 2004.
12. F. Dornaika and J. Ahlberg. Face model adaptation using robust matching and the active appearance algorithm. In *IEEE International Workshop on Applications of Computer Vision*, pages 3–7, Orlando, 2002.
13. F. Dornaika and J. Ahlberg. Fast and reliable active appearance model search for 3D face tracking. *IEEE Transactions on Systems, Man, and Cybernetics–Part B: Cybernetics*, 34(4):1838–1853, 2004.
14. P. Eisert and B. Girod. Model-based estimataion of facial expression parameters from image sequences. In *International Conference on Image Processing*, pages 418–421, Santa Barbara, CA, 1997.
15. P. Ekman and W. V. Friesen. *Facial Action Coding System*. Consulting Psychologists Press, Palo Alto, 1977.
16. M.A. Fischler and R.C. Bolles. Random sample consensus: A paradigm for model fitting with applications to image analysis and automated cartography. *Communcations of the ACM*, 24(6):381–395, 1981.
17. A. Gelb. *Applied Optimal Estimation*. MIT Press, Cambridge, MA, 1974.
18. S.B. Gokturk, J.Y. Bouguet, and R. Grzeszczuk. A data-driven model for monocular face tracking. In *International Conference on Computer Vision*, pages 701–708, Vancouver, 2001.
19. P. Heckbert. Survey of texture mapping. *IEEE Computer Graphics and Applications*, 1986.
20. InterFace. European union 5th framework IST project, 2000–2002.
21. T. Jebara and A. Pentland. Parameterized structure from motion for 3d adaptive feedback tracking of faces. In *International Conference on Computer Vision and Pattern Recognition*, pages 144–150, San Juan, 1997.
22. R.E. Kalman. A new approach to linear filtering and prediction problems. *Trans. ASME Journal Basic Engineering*, 82D:25–45, 1960.
23. M. Kirby and L. Sirovich. Application of the Karhunen-Loeve procedure for the characterization of human faces. *IEEE Transactions on Pattern Analysis and Machine Intelligence*, 12(1):103–108, 1990.

24. M. La Cascia, S. Sclaroff, and V. Athitsos. Fast, reliable head tracking under varying illumination: An approach based on registration of texture-mapped 3D models. *IEEE Transactions on Pattern Analysis and Machine Intelligence*, 22(4):322–336, 2000.

25. H. Li, P. Roivanen, and R. Forchheimer. 3-D motion estimation in model-based facial image coding. *IEEE Transactions on Pattern Analysis and Machine Intelligence*, 15(6):545–555, 1993.

26. A. Lundmark. *Hierarchical Structures and Extended Motion Information for Video Coding*. Ph.D. thesis, Linköping University, Sweden, 2001.

27. M. Malciu and F. Prêteux. A robust model-based approach for 3d head tracking in video sequences. In *International Conference on Automatic Face and Gesture Recognition*, pages 169–174, Grenoble, France, 2000.

28. I.S. Pandzic. Life on the web. *Software Focus Journal*, 2(2):52–59, 2001.

29. I.S. Pandzic and R. Forchheimer, editors. *MPEG-4 Facial Animation: The Standard, Implementations, and Applications*. Wiley, Chichester, 2002.

30. F.I. Parke and K. Waters. *Computer Facial Animation*. AK Peters, Wellesley, MA, 1996.

31. F. Pighin, S. Szeliski, and S. Salesin. Resynthesizing facial animation through 3D model-based tracking. In *International Conference on Computer Vision*, pages 143–150, Kerkyra, Greece, 1999.

32. P. Roivanen. *Motion estimation in model-based coding of human faces*. Licentiate thesis, Linköping University, Sweden, 1990.

33. M. Rydfalk. Candide, a parameterized face. Technical Report LiTH-ISY-I-866, Linköping University, Sweden, 1987.

34. L. Sirovich and M. Kirby. Low-dimensional procedure for the characterization of human faces. *Journal of the Optical Society of America*, 4(3):519–524, 1987.

35. M. Sonka, V. Hlavac, and R. Boyle. *Image processing, analysis, and machine vision*. PWS Publishing, Brooks/Cole, Pacific Grove, CA, 1998.

36. J. Ström. *Model-Based Head Tracking and Coding*. Ph.D. thesis, Linköping University, Sweden, 2002.

37. J. Ström. Model-based real-time head tracking. *EURASIP Journal on Applied Signal Processing*, 2002(10):1039–1052, 2002.

38. J. Ström. Reinitialization of a model-based face tracker. In *International Conference Augmented Virtual Environments and 3-D Imaging*, pages 128–131, Mykonos, Greece, 2001.

39. J. Ström, T. Jebara, S. Basu, and A. Pentland. Real time tracking and modeling of faces: an EKF-based analysis by synthesis approach. In *IEEE ICCV Workshop on Modelling People*, Kerkyra, Greece, 1999.

40. H. Tao, R. Lopez, and T. Huang. Tracking of face features using probabilistic network. In *International Conference on Automatic Face and Gesture Recognition*, Nara, Japan, 1998.

41. M. Turk and A. Pentland. Eigenfaces for recognition. *International Journal on Cognitive Neuroscience*, 3(1):71–86, 1991.

42. B. Welsh. *Model-Based Coding of Images*. Ph.D. thesis, British Telecom Research Lab, 1991.

43. C. S. Wiles, A. Maki, and N. Matsuda. Hyperpatches for 3D model acquisition. *IEEE Transactions on Pattern Analysis and Machine Intelligence*, 23(12):1391–1403, 2001.

# Chapter 5. Illumination Modeling for Face Recognition

Ronen Basri[1] and David Jacobs[2]

[1] The Weizmann Institute of Science, Rehovot 76100, Israel. ronen.basri@weizmann.ac.il
[2] University of Maryland, College Park, MD 20742, USA. djacobs@umiacs.umd.edu

## 1 Introduction

Changes in lighting can produce large variability in the appearance of faces, as illustrated in Figure 5.1. Characterizing this variability is fundamental to understanding how to account for the effects of lighting on face recognition. In this chapter*, we will discuss solutions to a problem: Given (1) a three-dimensional description of a face, its pose, and its reflectance properties, and (2) a 2D query image, how can we efficiently determine whether lighting conditions exist that can cause this model to produce the query image? We describe methods that solve this problem by producing simple, linear representations of the set of all images a face can produce under all lighting conditions. These results can be directly used in face recognition systems that capture 3D models of all individuals to be recognized. They also have the potential to be used in recognition systems that compare strictly 2D images but that do so using generic knowledge of 3D face shapes.

**Fig. 5.1.** Same face under different lighting conditions.

One way to measure the difficulties presented by lighting, or any variability, is the number of degrees of freedom needed to describe it. For example, the pose of a face relative to the camera has six degrees of freedom - three rotations, and three translations. Facial expression has a few tens of degrees of freedom if one considers the number of muscles that may contract to change expression. To describe the light that strikes a face, we must describe the intensity of

---

* Portions of this chapter are reprinted, with permission, from Basri and Jacobs [5], © 2004 IEEE.

light hitting each point on the face from each direction. That is, light is a function of position and direction, meaning that light has an infinite number of degrees of freedom. In this chapter, however, we will show that effective systems can account for the effects of lighting using fewer than 10 degrees of freedom. This can have considerable impact on the speed and accuracy of recognition systems.

Support for low-dimensional models is both empirical and theoretical. Principal component analysis (PCA) on images of a face obtained under various lighting conditions shows that this image set is well approximated by a low-dimensional, linear subspace of the space of all images (e.g., [18]). Experimentation shows that algorithms that take advantage of this observation can achieve high performance (e.g., [16, 21]). In addition, we describe theoretical results that, with some simplifying assumptions, prove the validity of low-dimensional, linear approximations to the set of images produced by a face. For these results we assume that light sources are distant from the face, but we do allow arbitrary combinations of point sources (e.g., the sun) and diffuse sources (e.g., the sky). We also consider only diffuse components of reflectance, modeled as Lambertian reflectance, and we ignore the effects of cast shadows, such as those produced by the nose. We do, however, model the effects of attached shadows, as when one side of a head faces away from a light. Theoretical predictions from these models provide a good fit to empirical observations and produce useful recognition systems. This suggests that the approximations made capture the most significant effects of lighting on facial appearance. Theoretical models are valuable not only because they provide insight into the role of lighting in face recognition but also because they lead to analytically derived, low-dimensional, linear representations of the effects of lighting on facial appearance, which in turn can lead to more efficient algorithms.

An alternate stream of work attempts to compensate for lighting effects without the use of 3D face models. This work matches directly 2D images using representations of images that are found to be insensitive to lighting variations. These include image gradients [11], Gabor jets [26], the direction of image gradients [12, 23], and projections to subspaces derived from linear discriminants [8]. These methods are certainly of interest, especially for applications in which 3D face models are not available. However, methods based on 3D models may be more powerful, as they have the potential to compensate completely for lighting changes, whereas 2D methods cannot achieve such invariance [1, 12, 32]. Another approach of interest, discussed in Chapter 10 in this volume, is to use general 3D knowledge of faces to improve methods of image comparison.

## 2 Background on Reflectance and Lighting

Throughout this chapter, we consider only distant light sources. By a *distant* light source we mean that it is valid to make the approximation that a light shines on each point in the scene from the same angle and with the same intensity (this also rules out, for example, slide projectors).

We consider two lighting conditions. A *point* source is described by a single direction, represented by the unit vector $u_l$, and intensity, $l$. These factors can be combined into a vector with three components, $\bar{l} = lu_l$. Lighting may also come from multiple sources, including diffuse sources such as the sky. In that case we can describe the intensity of the light as a function of its direction, $\ell(u_l)$, which does not depend on the position in the scene. Light, then, can be thought of as a nonnegative function on the surface of a sphere. This allows us to represent scenes in which light comes from multiple sources, such as a room with a few lamps, and also to represent light that comes from extended sources, such as light from the sky, or light reflected off a wall.

Most of the analysis in this chapter accounts for *attached shadows*, which occur when a point in the scene faces away from a light source. That is, if a scene point has a surface normal $v_r$, and light comes from the direction $u_l$, when $u_l \cdot v_r < 0$ none of the light strikes the surface. We also discuss methods of handling *cast shadows*, which occur when one part of a face blocks the light from reaching another part of the face. Cast shadows have been treated by methods based on rendering a model to simulate shadows [17], whereas attached shadows can be accounted for with analytically derived linear subspaces.

Building truly accurate models of the way the face reflects light is a complex task. This is in part because skin is not homogeneous; light striking the face may be reflected by oils or water on the skin, by melanin in the epidermis, or by hemoglobin in the dermis, below the epidermis (see, for example, [2, 3, 30], which discuss these effects and build models of skin reflectance) (see also the Chapter 6). Based on empirical measurements of skin, Marschner et al. [29] state: "The BRDF itself is quite unusual; at small incidence angles it is almost Lambertian, but at higher angles strong forward scattering emerges." Furthermore, light entering the skin at one point may scatter below the surface of the skin, and exit from another point. This phenomenon, known as subsurface scattering, cannot be modeled by a bidirectional reflectance function (BRDF), which assumes that light leaves a surface from the point that it strikes it. Jensen et al.[24] presented one model of subsurface scattering.

For purposes of realistic computer graphics, this complexity must be confronted in some way. For example, Borshukov and Lewis [10] reported that in *The Matrix Reloaded*, they began by modeling face reflectance using a Lambertian diffuse component and a modified Phong model to account for a Fresnel-like effect. "As production progressed it became increasingly clear that realistic skin rendering couldn't be achieved without subsurface scattering simulations."

However, simpler models may be adequate for face recognition. They also lead to much simpler, more efficient algorithms. This suggests that even if one wishes to model face reflectance more accurately, simple models may provide useful, approximate algorithms that can initialize more complex ones. In this chapter we discuss analytically derived representation of the images produced by a convex, Lambertian object illuminated by distant light sources. We restrict ourselves to convex objects so we can ignore the effect of shadows cast by one part of the object on another part of it. We assume that the surface of the object reflects light according to Lambert's law [27], which states that materials absorb light and reflect it uniformly in all directions. The only parameter of this model is the *albedo* at each point on the object, which describes the fraction of the light reflected at that point.

Specifically, according to Lambert's law, if a light ray of intensity $l$ coming from the direction $u_l$ reaches a surface point with albedo $\rho$ and normal direction $v_r$, the intensity $i$ reflected by the point due to this light is given by

$$i = l(u_l)\rho \max(u_l \cdot v_r, 0) \tag{1}$$

If we fix the lighting and ignore $\rho$ for now, the reflected light is a function of the surface normal alone. We write this function as $r(\theta_r, \phi_r)$, or $r(v_r)$. If light reaches a point from a multitude of directions, the light reflected by the point would be the integral over the contribution for each direction. If we denote $k(u \cdot v) = \max(u \cdot v, 0)$, we can write:

$$r(v_r) = \int_{S^2} k(u_l \cdot v_r)\ell(u_l)du_l \tag{2}$$

where $\int_{S^2}$ denotes integration over the surface of the sphere.

## 3 Using PCA to Generate Linear Lighting Models

We can consider a face image as a point in a high-dimensional space by treating each pixel as a dimension. Then one can use PCA to determine how well one can approximate a set of face images using a low-dimensional, linear subspace. PCA was first applied to images of faces by Sirovitch and Kirby [40], and used for face recognition by Turk and Pentland [41]. Hallinan [18] used PCA to study the set of images that a single face in a fixed pose produces when illuminated by a floodlight placed in various positions. He found that a five- or six-dimensional subspace accurately models this set of images. Epstein et al. [13] and Yuille et al. [43] described experiments on a wide range of objects that indicate that images of Lambertian objects can be approximated by a linear subspace of between three and seven dimensions. Specifically, the set of images of a basketball were approximated to 94.4% by a 3D space and to 99.1% by a 7D space, whereas the images of a face were approximated to 90.2% by a 3D space and to 95.3% by a 7D space. This work suggests that lighting variation has a low-dimensional effect on face images, although it does not make clear the exact reasons for it.

Because of this low-dimensionality, linear representations based on PCA can be used to compensate for lighting variation. Georghiades et al.[17] used a 3D model of a face to render images with attached or with cast shadows. PCA is used to compress these images to a low-dimensional subspace, in which they are compared to new images (also using nonnegative lighting constraints we discuss in Section 5). One issue raised by this approach is that the linear subspace produced depends on the face's pose. Computing this on-line, when pose is determined, it is potentially expensive. Georghiades et al.[16] attacked this problem by sampling pose space and generating a linear subspace for each pose. Ishiyama and Sakamoto [21] instead generated a linear subspace in a model-based coordinate system, so this subspace can be transformed in 3D as the pose varies.

## 4 Linear Lighting Models: Without Shadows

The empirical study of the space occupied by the images of various real objects was to some degree motivated by a previous result that showed that Lambertian objects, in the absence of *all* shadows, produce a set of images that form a three-dimensional linear subspace [31, 37]. To visualize this, consider a Lambertian object illuminated by a point source described by the vector $\bar{l}$. Let $p_i$ denote a point on the object, let $n_i$ be a unit vector describing the surface normal at $p_i$, let $\rho_i$ denote the albedo at $p_i$, then define $\bar{n}_i = \rho_i n_i$. In the absence of attached shadows, Lambertian reflectance is described by $\bar{l}^T \bar{n}_i$. If we combine all of an object's surface normals into a single matrix $N$, so the $i$'th column of $N$ is $\bar{n}_i$, the entire image is described by

$I = \bar{l}^T N$. This implies that any image is a linear combination of the three rows of $N$. These are three vectors consisting of the $x$, $y$, and $z$ components of the object's surface normals, scaled by albedo. Consequently, all images of an object lie in a three-dimensional space spanned by these three vectors. Note that if we have multiple light sources, $\bar{l}_1...\bar{l}_d$, we have

$$I = \sum_i (\bar{l}_i N) = (\sum_i \bar{l}_i) N$$

so this image, too, lies in this three-dimensional subspace. Belhumeur et al. [8] reported face recognition experiments using this 3D linear subspace. They found that this approach partially compensates for lighting variation, but not as well as methods that account for shadows.

Hayakawa [19] used factorization to build 3D models using this linear representation. Koenderink and van Doorn [25] augmented this space to account for an additional, perfect diffuse component. When in addition to a point source there is also an ambient light, $\ell(u_l)$, which is constant as a function of direction, and we ignore cast shadows, it has the effect of adding the albedo at each point, scaled by a constant to the image. This leads to a set of images that occupy a four-dimensional linear subspace.

## 5 Attached Shadows: Nonlinear Models

Belhumeur and Kriegman [7] conducted an analytic study of the images an object produces when shadows are present. First, they pointed out that for arbitrary illumination, scene geometry, and reflectance properties, the set of images produced by an object forms a convex cone in image space. It is a cone because the intensity of lighting can be scaled by any positive value, creating an image scaled by the same positive value. It is convex because two lighting conditions that create two images can always be added together to produce a new lighting condition that creates an image that is the sum of the original two images. They call this set of images the *illumination cone*.

Then they showed that for a convex, Lambertian object in which there are attached shadows but no cast shadows the dimensionality of the illumination cone is $O(n^2)$, where $n$ is the number of distinct surface normals visible on the object. For an object such as a sphere, in which every pixel is produced by a different surface normal, the illumination cone has volume in image space. This proves that the images of even a simple object do not lie in a low-dimensional linear subspace. They noted, however, that simulations indicate that the illumination cone is "thin"; that is, it lies near a low-dimensional image space, which is consistent with the experiments described in Section 3. They further showed how to construct the cone using the representation of Shashua [37]. Given three images obtained with lighting that produces no attached or cast shadows, they constructed a 3D linear representation, clipped all negative intensities at zero, and took convex combinations of the resulting images.

Georghiades and colleagues [17, 16] presented several algorithms that use the illumination cone for face recognition. The cone can be represented by sampling its extremal rays; this corresponds to rendering the face under a large number of point light sources. An image may be compared to a known face by measuring its distance to the illumination cone, which they showed can be computed using nonnegative least-squares algorithms. This is a convex optimization guaranteed to find a global minimum, but it is slow when applied to a high-dimensional image space. Therefore, they suggested running the algorithm after projecting the query image and the extremal rays to a lower-dimensional subspace using PCA.

Also of interest is the approach of Blicher and Roy [9], which buckets nearby surface normals and renders a model based on the average intensity of image pixels that have been matched to normals within a bucket. This method assumes that similar normals produce similar intensities (after the intensity is divided by the albedo), so it is suitable for handling attached shadows. It is also extremely fast.

# 6 Linear Lighting Models: Spherical Harmonic Representations

The empirical evidence showing that for many common objects the illumination cone is "thin" even in the presence of attached shadows has remained unexplained until recently, when Basri and Jacobs [4, 5], and in parallel Ramamoorthi and Hanrahan [35], analyzed the illumination cone in terms of spherical harmonics. This analysis showed that, when we account for attached shadows, the images of a convex Lambertian object can be approximated to high accuracy using nine (or even fewer) basis images. In addition, this analysis provides explicit expressions for the basis images. These expressions can be used to construct efficient recognition algorithms that handle faces under arbitrary lighting. At the same time these expressions can be used to construct new shape reconstruction algorithms that work under unknown combinations of point and extended light sources. We next review this analysis. Our discussion is based primarily on the work of Basri and Jacobs [5].

## 6.1 Spherical Harmonics and the Funk-Hecke Theorem

The key to producing linear lighting models that account for attached shadows lies in noting that Eq. (2), which describes how lighting is transformed to reflectance, is analogous to a convolution on the surface of a sphere. For every surface normal, $v_r$ reflectance is determined by integrating the light coming from all directions weighted by the kernel $k(u_l \cdot v_r) = \max(u_l \cdot v_r, 0)$. For every $v_r$ this kernel is just a rotated version of the same function, which contains the positive portion of a cosine function. We denote the (unrotated) function $k(u_l)$ (defined by fixing $v_r$ at the north pole) and refer to it as the *half-cosine* function. Note that on the sphere convolution is well defined only when the kernel is rotationally symmetrical about the north pole, which indeed is the case for this kernel.

Just as the Fourier basis is convenient for examining the results of convolutions in the plane, similar tools exist for understanding the results of the analog of convolutions on the sphere. We now introduce these tools, and use them to show that when producing reflectance, $k$ acts as a low-pass filter.

The *surface spherical harmonics* are a set of functions that form an orthonormal basis for the set of all functions on the surface of the sphere. We denote these functions by $Y_{nm}$, with $n = 0, 1, 2, \ldots$ and $-n \leq m \leq n$

$$Y_{nm}(\theta, \phi) = \sqrt{\frac{(2n+1)}{4\pi} \frac{(n-|m|)!}{(n+|m|)!}} P_{n|m|}(\cos \theta) e^{im\phi} \tag{3}$$

where $P_{nm}$ represents the *associated Legendre functions*, defined as

$$P_{nm}(z) = \frac{(1-z^2)^{m/2}}{2^n n!} \frac{d^{n+m}}{dz^{n+m}} (z^2-1)^n \tag{4}$$

We say that $Y_{nm}$ is an $n$'th *order* harmonic.

It is sometimes convenient to parameterize $Y_{nm}$ as a function of space coordinates $(x, y, z)$ rather than angles. The spherical harmonics, written $Y_{nm}(x, y, z)$, then become polynomials of degree $n$ in $(x, y, z)$. The first nine harmonics then become

$$
\begin{aligned}
Y_{00} &= \frac{1}{\sqrt{4\pi}} & Y_{10} &= \sqrt{\frac{3}{4\pi}}\, z \\
Y_{11}^e &= \sqrt{\frac{3}{4\pi}}\, x & Y_{11}^o &= \sqrt{\frac{3}{4\pi}}\, y \\
Y_{20} &= \tfrac{1}{2}\sqrt{\frac{5}{4\pi}}(3z^2-1) & Y_{21}^e &= 3\sqrt{\frac{5}{12\pi}}\, xz \\
Y_{21}^o &= 3\sqrt{\frac{5}{12\pi}}\, yz & Y_{22}^e &= \tfrac{3}{2}\sqrt{\frac{5}{12\pi}}(x^2-y^2) \\
Y_{22}^o &= 3\sqrt{\frac{5}{12\pi}}\, xy,
\end{aligned}
\tag{5}
$$

where the superscripts $e$ and $o$ denote the even and odd components of the harmonics, respectively (so $Y_{nm} = Y_{n|m|}^e \pm iY_{n|m|}^o$, according to the sign of $m$; in fact the even and odd versions of the harmonics are more convenient to use in practice because the reflectance function is real).

Because the spherical harmonics form an orthonormal basis, any piecewise continuous function, $f$, on the surface of the sphere can be written as a linear combination of an infinite series of harmonics. Specifically, for any $f$,

$$f(u) = \sum_{n=0}^{\infty} \sum_{m=-n}^{n} f_{nm} Y_{nm}(u) \tag{6}$$

where $f_{nm}$ is a scalar value, computed as

$$f_{nm} = \int_{S^2} f(u) Y_{nm}^*(u)\, du \tag{7}$$

and $Y_{nm}^*(u)$ denotes the complex conjugate of $Y_{nm}(u)$.

Rotating a function $f$ results in a phase shift. Define for every $n$ the $n$'th order amplitude of $f$ as

$$A_n \stackrel{\text{def}}{=} \sqrt{\frac{1}{2n+1} \sum_{m=-n}^{n} f_{nm}^2} \tag{8}$$

Then rotating $f$ does not change the amplitude of a particular order. It may shuffle values of the coefficients, $f_{nm}$, for a particular order, but it does not shift energy between harmonics of different orders.

Both the lighting function, $\ell$, and the Lambertian kernel, $k$, can be written as sums of spherical harmonics. Denote by

$$\ell = \sum_{n=0}^{\infty} \sum_{m=-n}^{n} l_{nm} Y_{nm} \tag{9}$$

the harmonic expansion of $\ell$, and by

$$k(u) = \sum_{n=0}^{\infty} k_n Y_{n0} \tag{10}$$

Note that, because $k(u)$ is circularly symmetrical about the north pole, only the zonal harmonics participate in this expansion, and

$$\int_{S^2} k(u) Y_{nm}^*(u) du = 0, \quad m \neq 0 \tag{11}$$

Spherical harmonics are useful for understanding the effect of convolution by $k$ because of the Funk-Hecke theorem, which is analogous to the convolution theorem. Loosely speaking, the theorem states that we can expand $\ell$ and $k$ in terms of spherical harmonics, and then convolving them is equivalent to multiplication of the coefficients of this expansion (see Basri and Jacobs [5] for details).

Following the Funk-Hecke theorem, the harmonic expansion of the reflectance function, $r$, can be written as:

$$r = k * \ell = \sum_{n=0}^{\infty} \sum_{m=-n}^{n} \left( \sqrt{\frac{4\pi}{2n+1}} k_n l_{nm} \right) Y_{nm} \tag{12}$$

## 6.2  Properties of the Convolution Kernel

The Funk-Hecke theorem implies that when producing the reflectance function, $r$, the amplitude of the light, $\ell$, at every order $n$ is scaled by a factor that depends only on the convolution kernel, $k$. We can use this to infer analytically what frequencies dominate $r$. To achieve this we treat $\ell$ as a signal and $k$ as a filter and ask how the amplitudes of $\ell$ change as it passes through the filter.

The harmonic expansion of the Lambertian kernel (Eq. 10) can be derived [5] yielding

$$k_n = \begin{cases} \frac{\sqrt{\pi}}{2} & n = 0 \\ \sqrt{\frac{\pi}{3}} & n = 1 \\ (-1)^{\frac{n}{2}+1} \frac{\sqrt{(2n+1)\pi}}{2^n (n-1)(n+2)} \binom{n}{\frac{n}{2}} & n \geq 2, \text{ even} \\ 0 & n \geq 2, \text{ odd} \end{cases} \tag{13}$$

The first few coefficients, for example, are

$$\begin{array}{ll} k_0 = \frac{\sqrt{\pi}}{2} \approx 0.8862 & k_1 = \sqrt{\frac{\pi}{3}} \approx 1.0233 \\ k_2 = \frac{\sqrt{5\pi}}{8} \approx 0.4954 & k_4 = -\frac{\sqrt{\pi}}{16} \approx -0.1108 \\ k_6 = \frac{\sqrt{13\pi}}{128} \approx 0.0499 & k_8 = \frac{\sqrt{17\pi}}{256} \approx -0.0285 \end{array} \tag{14}$$

($k_3 = k_5 = k_7 = 0$), $|k_n|$ approaches zero as $O(n^{-2})$. A graphic representation of the coefficients may be seen in Figure 5.2.

The energy captured by every harmonic term is measured commonly by the square of its respective coefficient divided by the total squared energy of the transformed function. The total squared energy in the half cosine function is given by

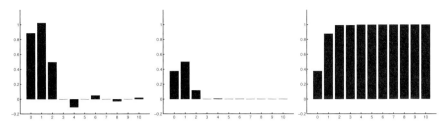

**Fig. 5.2.** From left to right: the first 11 coefficients of the Lambertian kernel; the relative energy captured by each of the coefficients; and the cumulative energy.

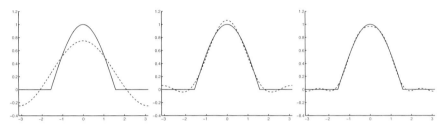

**Fig. 5.3.** A slice of the Lambertian kernel (solid line) and its approximations (dashed line) of first (left), second (middle), and fourth (right) order.

$$\int_0^{2\pi} \int_0^{\pi} k^2(\theta) \sin\theta d\theta d\phi = 2\pi \int_0^{\frac{\pi}{2}} \cos^2\theta \sin\theta d\theta = \frac{2\pi}{3} \qquad (15)$$

(Here we simplify our computation by integrating over $\theta$ and $\phi$ rather than $u$. The $\sin\theta$ factor is needed to account for the varying length of the latitude over the sphere.) Figure 5.2 shows the relative energy captured by each of the first several coefficients. It can be seen that the kernel is dominated by the first three coefficients. Thus, a second-order approximation already accounts for $(\frac{\pi}{4} + \frac{\pi}{3} + \frac{5\pi}{64})/\frac{2\pi}{3} \approx 99.22\%$ of the energy. With this approximation the half cosine function can be written as:

$$k(\theta) \approx \frac{3}{32} + \frac{1}{2}\cos\theta + \frac{15}{32}\cos^2\theta \qquad (16)$$

The quality of the approximation improves somewhat with the addition of the fourth-order term (99.81%) and deteriorates to 87.5% when a first order approximation is used. Figure 5.3 shows a one-dimensional slice of the Lambertian kernel and its various approximations.

### 6.3 Approximating the Reflectance Function

Because the Lambertian kernel, $k$, acts as a low-pass filter, the high frequency components of the lighting have little effect on the reflectance function. This implies that we can approximate the reflectance function that occurs under any lighting conditions using only low-order spherical harmonics. In this section, we show that this leads to an approximation that is always quite accurate.

We achieve a low-dimensional approximation to the reflectance function by truncating the sum in Eq. (12). That is, we have:

$$r = k * \ell \approx \sum_{n=0}^{N} \sum_{m=-n}^{n} \left( \sqrt{\frac{4\pi}{2n+1}} \, k_n l_{nm} \right) Y_{nm} \tag{17}$$

for some choice of order $N$. This means considering only the effects of the low order components of the lighting on the reflectance function. Intuitively, we know that because $k_n$ is small for large $n$, this approximation should be good. However, the accuracy of the approximation also depends on $l_{nm}$, the harmonic expansion of the lighting.

To evaluate the quality of the approximation, consider first, as an example, lighting, $\ell = \delta$, generated by a unit directional (distant point) source at the $z$ direction ($\theta = \phi = 0$). In this case the lighting is simply a delta function whose peak is at the north pole ($\theta = \phi = 0$). It can be readily shown that

$$r(v) = k * \delta = k(v) \tag{18}$$

If the sphere is illuminated by a single directional source in a direction other than the $z$ direction, the reflectance obtained would be identical to the kernel but shifted in phase. Shifting the phase of a function distributes its energy between the harmonics of the same order $n$ (varying $m$), but the overall energy in each $n$ is maintained. The quality of the approximation therefore remains the same, but now for an $N$'th order approximation we need to use all the harmonics with $n \leq N$ for all $m$. Recall that there are $2n+1$ harmonics in every order $n$. Consequently, a first-order approximation requires four harmonics. A second-order approximation adds five more harmonics, yielding a 9D space. The third-order harmonics are eliminated by the kernel, so they do not need to be included. Finally, a fourth order approximation adds nine more harmonics, yielding an 18D space.

We have seen that the energy captured by the first few coefficients $k_i$ ($1 \leq i \leq N$) directly indicates the accuracy of the approximation of the reflectance function when the light consists of a single point source. Other light configurations may lead to different accuracy. Better approximations are obtained when the light includes enhanced diffuse components of low frequency. Worse approximations are anticipated if the light includes mainly high frequency patterns.

However, even if the light includes mostly high frequency, patterns the accuracy of the approximation is still high. This is a consequence of the nonnegativity of light. A lower bound on the accuracy of the approximation for *any* light function is given by

$$\frac{k_0^2}{\frac{2\pi}{3} - \sum_{n=1}^{N} k_n^2} \tag{19}$$

(Proof appears in Basri and Jacobs [5].)

It can be shown that using a second order approximation (involving nine harmonics) the accuracy of the approximation for any light function exceeds 97.96%. With a fourth order approximation (involving 18 harmonics) the accuracy exceeds 99.48%. Note that the bound computed in Eq. (19) is not tight, as the case that all the higher order terms are saturated yields a function with negative values. Consequently, the worst case accuracy may even be higher than the bound.

## 6.4 Generating Harmonic Reflectances

Constructing a basis to the space that approximates the reflectance functions is straightforward: We can simply use the low order harmonics as a basis (see Eq. 17). However, in many cases we want a basis vector for the $nm$ component of the reflectances to indicate the reflectance produced by a corresponding basis vector describing the lighting, $Y_{nm}$. This makes it easy for us to relate reflectances and lighting, which is important when we want to enforce the constraint that the reflectances arise from nonnegative lighting (see Section 7.1). We call these reflectances *harmonic reflectances* and denote them by $r_{nm}$. Using the Funk-Hecke theorem, $r_{nm}$ is given by

$$r_{nm} = k * Y_{nm} = \left( \sqrt{\frac{4\pi}{2n+1}} k_n \right) Y_{nm} \tag{20}$$

Then, following Eq. (17),

$$r = k * \ell \approx \sum_{n=0}^{N} \sum_{m=-n}^{n} l_{nm} r_{nm} \tag{21}$$

The first few harmonic reflectances are given by

$$\begin{array}{lll} r_{00} = \pi Y_{00} & r_{1m} = \frac{2\pi}{3} Y_{1m} & r_{2m} = \frac{\pi}{4} Y_{2m} \\ r_{4m} = \frac{\pi}{24} Y_{4m} & r_{6m} = \frac{\pi}{64} Y_{6m} & r_{8m} = \frac{\pi}{128} Y_{8m} \end{array} \tag{22}$$

for $-n \leq m \leq n$ (and $r_{3m} = r_{5m} = r_{7m} = 0$).

## 6.5 From Reflectances to Images

Up to this point we have analyzed the reflectance functions obtained by illuminating a unit albedo sphere by arbitrary light. Our objective is to use this analysis to represent efficiently the set of images of objects seen under varying illumination. An image of an object under certain illumination conditions can be constructed from the respective reflectance function in a simple way: Each point of the object inherits its intensity from the point on the sphere whose normal is the same. This intensity is further scaled by its albedo.

We can write this explicitly as follows. Let $p_i$ denote the $i$'th object point. Let $n_i$ denote the surface normal at $p_i$, and let $\rho_i$ denote the albedo of $p_i$. Let the illumination be expanded with the coefficients $l_{nm}$ (Eq. 9). Then the image, $I_i$ of $p_i$ is

$$I_i = \rho_i r(n_i) \tag{23}$$

where

$$r(n_i) = \sum_{n=0}^{\infty} \sum_{m=-n}^{n} l_{nm} r_{nm}(n_i) \tag{24}$$

Then any image is a linear combination of *harmonic images*, $b_{nm}$, of the form

$$b_{nm}(p_i) = \rho_i r_{nm}(n_i) \tag{25}$$

with

**Fig. 5.4.** First nine harmonic images for a model of a face. The top row contains the zero'th harmonic (left) and the three first order harmonic images (right). The second row shows the images derived from the second harmonics. Negative values are shown in black, positive values in white.

$$I_i = \sum_{n=0}^{\infty} \sum_{m=-n}^{n} l_{nm} b_{nm}(p_i) \tag{26}$$

Figure 5.4 shows the first nine harmonic images derived from a 3D model of a face.

We now discuss how the accuracy of our low dimensional linear approximation to a model's images can be affected by the mapping from the reflectance function to images. The accuracy of our low dimensional linear approximation can vary according to the shape and albedos of the object. Each shape is characterized by a different distribution of surface normals, and this distribution may significantly differ from the distribution of normals on the sphere. Viewing direction also affects this distribution, as all normals facing away from the viewer are not visible in the image. Albedo further affects the accuracy of our low dimensional approximation, as it may scale each pixel by a different amount. In the worst case, this can make our approximation arbitrarily poor. For many objects it is possible to illuminate the object by lighting configurations that produce images for which low order harmonic representations provide a poor approximation.

However, generally, things are not so bad. In general, occlusion renders an arbitrary half of the normals on the unit sphere invisible. Albedo variations and curvature emphasize some normals and deemphasize others. In general, though, the normals whose reflectances are poorly approximated are not emphasized more than any other reflectances, and we can expect our approximation of reflectances on the entire unit sphere to be about as good over those pixels that produce the intensities visible in the image.

The following argument shows that the lower bound on the accuracy of a harmonic approximation to the reflectance function also provides a lower bound on the average accuracy of the harmonic approximation for *any* convex object. (This result was derived by Frolova et al. [14].) We assume that lighting is equally likely from all directions. Given an object, we can construct a matrix $M$ whose columns contain the images obtained by illuminating the object by a single point source, for all possible source directions. (Of course there are infinitely many such directions, but we can sample them to any desired accuracy.) The average accuracy of a low rank representation of the images of the object then is determined by

$$\min_{M^*} \frac{\|M^* - M\|^2}{\|M\|^2} \tag{27}$$

where $M^*$ is low rank. Now consider the rows of $M$. Each row represents the reflectance of a single surface point under all point sources. Such reflectances are identical to the reflectances of a sphere with uniform albedo under a single point source. (To see this, simply let the surface normal and the lighting directions change roles.) We know that under a point source the reflectance function can be approximated by a combination of the first nine harmonics to 99.22%. Because by this argument every row of $M$ can be approximated to the same accuracy, there exists a rank nine matrix $M^*$ that approximates $M$ to 99.22%. This argument can be applied to convex objects of any shape. Thus, on average, nine harmonic images approximate the images of an object by at least 99.22%, and likewise four harmonic images approximate the images of an objet by at least 87.5%. Note that this approximation can even be improved somewhat by selecting optimal coefficients to better fit the images of the object. Indeed, simulations indicate that optimal selection of the coefficients often increases the accuracy of the second order approximation up to 99.5% and that of the first order approximation to about 95%.

Ramamoorthi [34] further derived expressions to calculate the accuracies obtained with spherical harmonics for orders less than nine. His analysis, in fact, demonstrates that generically the spherical harmonics of the same order are not equally significant. The reason is that the basis images of an object are not generally orthogonal, and in some cases are quite similar. For example, if the $z$ components of the surface normals of an object do not vary much, some of the harmonic images are quite similar, such as $b_{00} = \rho$ versus $b_{10} = \rho z$. Ramamoorthi's calculations show a good fit (with a slight overshoot) to the empirical results. With his derivations the accuracy obtained for a 3D representation of a human face is 92% (in contrast to 90.2% in empirical studies) and for 7D 99% (in contrast to 95.3%). The somewhat lower accuracies obtained in empirical studies may be attributed to the presence of specularities, cast shadows, and noisy measurements.

Finally, it is interesting to compare the basis images determined by our spherical harmonic representation with the basis images derived for the case of no shadows. As mentioned in Section 4, Shashua [37] and Moses [31] pointed out that in the absence of attached shadows every possible image of an object is a linear combination of the $x$, $y$, and $z$ components of the surface normals scaled by the albedo. They therefore proposed using these three components to produce a 3D linear subspace to represent a model's images. Interestingly, these three vectors are identical, up to a scale factor, to the basis images produced by the first-order harmonics in our method.

We can therefore interpret Shashua's method as also making an analytic approximation to a model's images using low-order harmonics. However, our previous analysis tells us that the images of the first harmonic account for only 50% of the energy passed by the half-cosine kernel. Furthermore, in the worst case it is possible for the lighting to contain *no* component in the first harmonic. Most notably, Shashua's method does not make use of the zero'th harmonic (commonly referred to as the DC component). These are the images produced by a perfectly diffuse light source. Nonnegative lighting must always have a significant DC component. We noted in Section 4 that Koenderink and van Doorn [25] suggested augmenting Shashua's method with this diffuse component. This results in a linear method that uses the four most significant harmonic basis images, although Koenderink and van Doorn proposed it as apparently a heuristic suggestion, without analysis or reference to a harmonic representation of lighting.

# 7 Applications

We have developed an analytic description of the linear subspace that lies near the set of images an object can produce. We now show how to use this description in various tasks, including object recognition and shape reconstruction. We begin by describing methods for recognizing faces under different illuminations and poses. Later we briefly describe reconstruction algorithms for stationary ("photometric stereo") and moving objects.

## 7.1 Recognition

In a typical recognition problem, the 3D shape and reflectance properties (including surface normals and albedos) of faces may be available. The task then is, given an image of a face seen under unknown pose and illumination, to recognize the individual. Our spherical harmonic representation enables us to perform this task while accounting for complicated, unknown lighting that includes combinations of point and extended sources. Below we assume that the pose of the object is already known but that its identity and lighting conditions are not. For example, we may wish to identify a face that is known to be facing the camera; or we may assume that either a human or an automatic system has identified features, such as the eyes and the tip of the nose, that allow us to determine the pose for each face in the database, but that the database is too large to allow a human to select the best match.

Recognition proceeds by comparing a new query image to each model in turn. To compare to a model, we compute the distance between the query image and the nearest image the model can produce. We present two classes of algorithms that vary in their representation of a model's images. The linear subspace can be used directly for recognition, or we can restrict ourselves to a subset of the linear subspace that corresponds to physically realizable lighting conditions.

We stress the advantages we gain by having an *analytic* description of the subspace available, in contrast to previous methods in which PCA could be used to derive a subspace from a sample of an object's images. One advantage of an analytic description is that we know it provides an accurate representation of an object's possible images, not subject to the vagaries of a particular sample of images. A second advantage is efficiency; we can produce a description of this subspace much more rapidly than PCA would allow. The importance of this advantage depends on the type of recognition problem we tackle. In particular, we are interested in recognition problems in which the position of an object is not known in advance but can be computed at run-time using feature correspondences. In this case, the linear subspace must also be computed at run-time, and the cost of doing this is important.

### Linear Methods

The most straightforward way to use our prior results for recognition is to compare a novel image to the linear subspace of images that correspond to a model, as derived by our harmonic representation. To do this, we produce the harmonic basis images of each model, as described in Section 6.5. Given an image $I$ we seek the distance from $I$ to the space spanned by the basis images. Let $B$ denote the basis images. Then we seek a vector $a$ that minimizes $\|Ba - I\|$. $B$ is $p \times r$, $p$ is the number of points in the image, and $r$ is the number of basis images used. As discussed above, nine is a natural value to use for $r$, but $r = 4$ provides greater efficiency and

$r = 18$ offers even better potential accuracy. Every column of $B$ contains one harmonic image $b_{nm}$. These images form a basis for the linear subspace, though not an orthonormal one. Hence we apply a QR decomposition to $B$ to obtain such a basis. We compute $Q$, a $p \times r$ matrix with orthonormal columns, and $R$, an $r \times r$ matrix so that $QR = B$ and $Q^T Q$ is an $r \times r$ identity matrix. Then $Q$ is an orthonormal basis for $B$, and $Q^T QI$ is the projection of $I$ into the space spanned by $B$. We can then compute the distance from the image, $I$, and the space spanned by $B$ as $\|QQ^T I - I\|$. The cost of the $QR$ decomposition is $O(pr^2)$, assuming $p >> r$.

The use of an analytically derived basis can have a substantial effect on the speed of the recognition process. In previous work, Georghiades et al. [16] performed recognition by rendering the images of an object under many possible lightings and finding an 11D subspace that approximates these images. With our method this expensive rendering step is unnecessary. When $s$ sampled images are used (typically $s >> r$), with $s << p$ PCA requires $O(ps^2)$. Also, in MATLAB, PCA of a thin, rectangular matrix seems to take exactly twice as long as its QR decomposition. Therefore, in practice, PCA on the matrix constructed by Georghiades et al. would take about 150 times as long as using our method to build a 9D linear approximation to a model's images. (This is for $s = 100$ and $r = 9$. One might expect $p$ to be about 10,000, but this does not affect the relative costs of the methods.) This may not be significant if pose is known ahead of time and this computation takes place off line. When pose is computed at run time, however, the advantages of our method can become significant.

## Enforcing Nonnegative Light

When we take arbitrary linear combinations of the harmonic basis images, we may obtain images that are not physically realizable. This is because the corresponding linear combination of the harmonics representing lighting may contain negative values. That is, rendering these images may require negative "light," which of course is physically impossible. In this section we show how to use the basis images while enforcing the constraint of nonnegative light.

When we use a 9D approximation to an object's images, we can efficiently enforce the nonnegative lighting constraint in a manner similar to that proposed by Belhumeur and Kriegman[7], after projecting everything into the appropriate 9D linear subspace. Specifically, we approximate any arbitrary lighting function as a nonnegative combination of a fixed set of directional light sources. We solve for the best such approximation by fitting to the query image a non-negative combination of images each produced by a single, directional source.

We can do this efficiently using the 9D subspace that represents an object's images. We project into this subspace a large number of images of the object, in which each image is produced by a single directional light source. Such a light source is represented as a delta function; we can derive the representation of the resulting image in the harmonic basis simply by taking the harmonic transform of the delta function that represents the lighting. Then we can also project a query image into this 9D subspace and find the nonnegative linear combination of directionally lit images that best approximate the query image. Finding the nonnegative combination of vectors that best fit a new vector is a standard, convex optimization problem. We can solve it efficiently because we have projected all the images into a space that is only 9D.

Note that this method is similar to that presented in Georghiades et al. [17]. The primary difference is that we work in a low dimensional space constructed for each model using its harmonic basis images. Georghiades et al. performed a similar computation after projecting all images into a 100-dimensional space constructed using PCA on images rendered from models in a 10-model database. Also, we do not need to explicitly render images using a point source and project them into a low-dimensional space. In our representation, the projection of these images is given in closed form by the spherical harmonics.

A further simplification can be obtained if the set of images of an object is approximated only up to first order. Four harmonics are required in this case. One is the DC component, representing the appearance of the object under uniform ambient light, and three are the basis images also used by Shashua. In this case, we can reduce the resulting optimization problem to one of finding the roots of a sixth degree polynomial, which is extremely efficient. Further details of both methods can be found elsewhere [5].

## Specularity

Other work has built on this spherical harmonic representation to account for non-Lambertian reflectance [33]. The method first computes Lambertian reflectance, which constrains the possible location of a dominant compact source of light. Then it extracts highlight candidates as pixels that are brighter than we can predict from Lambertian reflectance. Next, we determine which of these candidates is consistent with a known 3D object. A general model of specular reflectance is used that implies that the surface normals of specular points obtained by thresholding intensity form a disk on the Gaussian sphere. Therefore, the method proceeds by selecting candidate specularities consistent with such a disk. It maps each candidate specularity to the point on the sphere having the same surface normal. Next, a plane is found that separates the specular pixels from the other pixels with a minimal number of misclassifications. The presence of specular reflections that are consistent with the object's known 3D structure then serves as a cue that the model and image match.

This method has succeeded in recognizing shiny objects, such as pottery. However, informal face recognition experiments with this method, using the data set described in the next section, have not shown significant improvements. Our sense is that most of our recognition errors are due to misalignments in pose, and that when a good alignment is found between a 3D model and image a Lambertian model is sufficient to produce good performance on a data set of 42 individuals.

In other work, Georghiades [15] augmented the recognition approach of Georghiades et al. [16] to include specular reflectance. After initialization using a Lambertian model, the position of a single light source and parameters of the Torrance-Sparrow model of specular reflectance are optimized to fit a 3D model of an individual. Face recognition experiments with a data set of 10 individuals show that this produces a reduction in overall errors from 2.96% to 2.47%. It seems probable that experiments with data sets containing large numbers of individuals are needed to truly gauge the value of methods that account for specular reflectance.

## Experiments

We have experimented with these recognition methods using a database of faces collected at NEC in Japan. The database contains models of 42 faces, each including the 3D shape of the face (acquired using a structured light system) and estimates of the albedos in the red, green,

**Fig. 5.5.** Test images used in the experiments.

and blue color channels. As query images, we use 42 images each of 10 individuals taken across seven poses and six lighting conditions (shown in Figure 5.5). In our experiment, each of the query images is compared to each of the 42 models, and then the best matching model is selected.

In all methods, we first obtain a 3D alignment between the model and the image using the algorithm of Blicher and Roy [9]. In brief, a dozen or fewer features on the faces were identified by hand, and then a 3D rigid transformation was found to align the 3D features with the corresponding 2D image features.

In all methods, we only pay attention to image pixels that have been matched to some point in the 3D model of the face. We also ignore image pixels that are of maximum intensity, as they may be saturated and provide misleading values. Finally, we subsample both the model and the image, replacing each $m \times m$ square with its average values. Preliminary experiments indicate that we can subsample quite a bit without significantly reducing accuracy. In the experiments below, we ran all algorithms subsampling with $16 \times 16$ squares, while the original images were $640 \times 480$.

Our methods produce coefficients that tell us how to combine the harmonic images linearly to produce the rendered image. These coefficients were computed on the sampled image but then applied to harmonic images of the full, unsampled image. This process was repeated separately for each color channel. Then a model was compared to the image by taking the root mean squared error derived from the distance between the rendered face model and all corresponding pixels in the image.

Figure 5.6 shows Receiver operating characteristic (ROC) curves for three recognition methods: the 9D linear method and the methods that enforce positive lighting in 9D and 4D. The curves show the fraction of query images for which the correct model is classified among the top $k$, as $k$ varies from 1 to 40. The 4D positive lighting method performs significantly less well

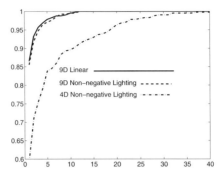

**Fig. 5.6.** Receiver operating characteristic (ROC) curves for our recognition methods. The vertical axis shows the percentage of times the correct model was found among the $k$ best matching models; the horizontal axis shows $k$.

than the others, getting the correct answer about 60% of the time. However, it is much faster and seems to be quite effective under simpler pose and lighting conditions. The 9D linear method and 9D positive lighting method each pick the correct model first 86% of the time. With this data set, the difference between these two algorithms is quite small compared to other sources of error. Such errors may include limitations in our model for handling cast shadows and specularities, but they also include errors in the model building and pose determination processes. In fact, on examining our results, we found that one pose (for one person) was grossly wrong because a human operator selected feature points in the wrong order. We eliminated from our results the six images (under six lighting conditions) that used this pose.

## 7.2 Modeling

The recognition methods described in the previous section require detailed 3D models of faces, as well as their albedos. Such models can be acquired in various ways. For example, in the experiments described above we used a laser scanner to recover the 3D shape of a face, and we estimated the albedos from an image taken under ambient lighting (which was approximated by averaging several images of a face). As an alternative, it is possible to recover the shape of a face from images illuminated by structured light or by using stereo reconstruction, although stereo algorithms may give somewhat inaccurate reconstructions for nontextured surfaces. Finally, other studies have developed reconstruction methods that use the harmonic formulation to recover both the shape and the albedo of an object simultaneously. In the remainder of this section we briefly describe two such methods. We first describe how to recover the shape of an object when the input images are obtained with a stationary object illuminated by variable lighting, a problem commonly referred to as "photometric stereo." Later, we discuss an approach for shape recovery of a moving object.

### Photometric Stereo

In photometric stereo, we are given a collection of images of a stationary object under varying illumination. Our objective is to recover the 3D shape of the object and its reflectance properties, which for a Lambertian object include the albedo at every surface point. Previous approaches to photometric stereo under unknown lighting generally assume that in every image the object is illuminated by a dominant point source (e.g., [19, 25, 43]). However, by using spherical harmonic representations it is possible to reconstruct the shape and albedo of an object under unknown lighting configurations that include arbitrary collections of point and extended sources. In this section we summarize this work, which is described in more detail elsewhere [6].

We begin by stacking the input images into a matrix $M$ of size $f \times p$, in which every input image of $p$ pixels occupies a single row, and $f$ denotes the number of images in our collection. The low dimensional harmonic approximation then implies that there exist two matrices, $L$ and $S$, of sizes $f \times r$ and $r \times p$ respectively, that satisfy

$$M \approx LS \qquad (28)$$

where $L$ represents the lighting coefficients, $S$ is the harmonic basis, and $r$ is the dimension used in the approximation (usually 4 or 9). If indeed we can recover $L$ and $S$, obtaining the surface normals and albedos of the shape is straightforward using Eqs. (22) and (25).

We can attempt to recover $L$ and $S$ using singular value decomposition (SVD). This produces a factorization of $M$ into two matrices $\tilde{L}$ and $\tilde{S}$, which are related to the correct lighting and shape matrices by an unknown, arbitrary $r \times r$ ambiguity matrix $A$. We can try to reduce this ambiguity. Consider the case that we use a first-order harmonic approximation ($r = 4$). Omitting unnecessary scale factors, the zero-order harmonic contains the albedo at every point, and the three first-order harmonics contain the surface normal scaled by the albedo. For a given point we can write these four components in a vector: $p = (\rho, \rho n_x, \rho n_y, \rho n_z)^T$. Then $p$ should satisfy $p^T J p = 0$, where $J = diag\{-1, 1, 1, 1\}$. Enforcing this constraint reduces the ambiguity matrix from 16 degrees of freedom to just 7. Further resolution of the ambiguity matrix requires additional constraints, which can be obtained by specifying a few surface normals or by enforcing integrability.

A similar technique can be applied in the case of a second order harmonic approximation ($r = 9$). In this case there are many more constraints on the nine basis vectors, and they can be satisfied by applying an iterative procedure. Using the nine harmonics, the surface normals can be recovered up to a rotation, and further constraints are required to resolve the remaining ambiguity.

An application of these photometric stereo methods is demonstrated in Figure 5.7. A collection of 32 images of a statue of a face illuminated by two point sources in each image were used to reconstruct the 3D shape of the statue. (The images were simulated by averaging pairs of images obtained with single light sources taken by researchers at Yale.) Saturated pixels were removed from the images and filled in using Wiberg's algorithm [42]; see also [22, 38]. We resolved the remaining ambiguity by matching some points in the scene with hand-chosen surface normals.

Photometric stereo is one way to produce a 3D model for face recognition. An alternative approach is to determine a discrete set of lighting directions that produce a set of images that span the 9D set of harmonic images of an object. In this way, the harmonic basis can be constructed directly from images, without building a 3D model. This problem was addressed by Lee et al. [28] and by Sato et al. [36]. Other approaches use harmonic representations to cluster the images of a face under varying illumination [20] or determine the harmonic images of a

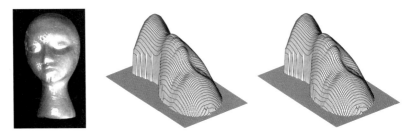

**Fig. 5.7.** Left: two face images averaged together to produce an image with two point sources. Saturated pixels shown in white. Center: the surface produced by the 4D method. Right: the surface from the 9D method. From Basri and Jacobs [6], © 2004 IEEE, with permission.

face from just one image using a statistical model derived from a set of 3D models of other faces [44].

## Objects in Motion

Photometric stereo methods require a still object while the lighting varies. For faces this requires a cooperative subject and controlled lighting. An alternative approach is to use video of a moving face. Such an approach, presented by Simakov et al. [39], is briefly described below.

We assume that the motion of a face is known, for example by tracking a few feature points such as the eyes and the tips of the mouth. Thus we know the epipolar constraints between the images and (in case the cameras are calibrated) also the mapping from 3D to each of the images. To obtain a dense shape reconstruction we need to find correspondences between points in all images. Unlike stereo, in which we can expect corresponding points to maintain approximately the same intensity, in the case of a moving object we expect points to change their intensity as they turn away from or toward light sources.

We therefore adopt the following strategy. For every point in 3D we associate a "correspondence measure," which indicates if its projections in all the images could come from the same surface point. To this end we collect all the projections and compute the residual of the following set of equations.

$$I_j = \rho l^T R_j Y(n) \tag{29}$$

In this equation, $1 \leq j \leq f$, $f$ is the number of images, $I_j$ denotes the intensity of the projection of the 3D point in the $j$'th image, $\rho$ is the unknown albedo, $l$ denotes the unknown lighting coefficients, $R_j$ denotes the rotation of the object in the $j$'th image, and $Y(n)$ denotes the spherical harmonics evaluated for the unknown surface normal. Thus to compute the residual we need to find $l$ and $n$ that minimize the difference between the two sides of this equation. (Note that for a single 3D point $\rho$ and $l$ can be combined to produce a single vector.)

Once we have computed the correspondence measure for each 3D point we can incorporate the measure in any stereo algorithm to extract the surface that minimizes the measure, possibly subject to some smoothness constraints.

The algorithm of Simakov et al. [39] described above assumes that the motion between the images is known. Zhang et al. [45] proposed an iterative algorithm that simultaneously recovers the motion assuming infinitesimal motion between images and modeling reflectance using a first order harmonic approximation.

## 8 Conclusions

Lighting can be arbitrarily complex, but in many cases its effect is not. When objects are Lambertian, we show that a simple, 9D linear subspace can capture the set of images they produce. This explains prior empirical results. It also gives us a new and effective way to understand the effects of Lambertian reflectance as that of a low-pass filter on lighting.

Moreover, we show that this 9D space can be directly computed from a model, as low-degree polynomial functions of its scaled surface normals. This description allows us to produce efficient recognition algorithms in which we know we are using an accurate approximation of the model's images. In addition, we can use the harmonic formulation to develop reconstructions algorithms to recover the 3D shape and albedos of an object. We evaluate the effectiveness of our recognition algorithms using a database of models and images of real faces.

## Acknowledgments

Major portions of this research were conducted while Ronen Basri and David Jacobs were at the NEC Research Institute, Princeton, NJ. At the Weizmann Institute Ronen Basri is supported in part by European Community grants IST-2000-26001 VIBES and IST-2002-506766 Aim Shape and by the Israel Science Foundation grant 266/02. The vision group at the Weizmann Institute is supported in part by the Moross Foundation.

## References

1. Y. Adini, Y. Moses, S. Ullman. Face Recognition: The Problem of Compensating for Changes in Illumination Direction. *IEEE Trans. on Pattern Analysis and Machine Intelligence* 19(7):721–732, 1997.
2. E. Angelopoulou. Understanding the color of human skin. *Proc. SPIE Conf. on Human Vision and Electronic Imaging VI* SPIE 4299:243–251, 2001.
3. E. Angelopoulou, R. Molana, and K. Daniilidis. Multispectral skin color modeling. *IEEE Conf. on Computer Vision and Patt. Rec.*, 635–642, 2001.
4. R. Basri, D.W. Jacobs. Lambertian reflectances and linear subspaces. *IEEE Int. Conf. on Computer Vision*, II:383–390, 2001.
5. R. Basri, D.W. Jacobs. Lambertian reflectances and linear subspaces. *IEEE Trans. on Pattern Analysis and Machine Intelligence*, 25(2):218–233, 2003.
6. R. Basri and D.W. Jacobs. Photometric stereo with general, unknown lighting. *IEEE Conf. on Computer Vision and Pattern Recognition*, II:374–381, 2001.
7. P. Belhumeur and D. Kriegman. What is the set of images of an object under all possible lighting conditions? *International Journal of Computer Vision*, 28(3):245–260, 1998.
8. P. Belhumeur, J. Hespanha, and D. Kriegman. Eigenfaces vs. fisherfaces: recognition using class specific linear projection. IEEE Trans. on Pattern Analysis and Machine Intelligence 19(7):711–720, 1997.

9. A.P. Blicher and S. Roy. Fast lighting/rendering solution for matching a 2D image to a database of 3D models: "LightSphere." *IEICE Trans. on Information and Systems*, E84-D(12):1722–1727, 2001.

10. G. Borshukov and J.P. Lewis. Realistic human face rendering for "The Matrix Reloaded," *SIGGRAPH-2003 Sketches and Applications Program*, 2003.

11. R. Brunellim and T. Poggio. Face recognition: Features versus templates. *IEEE Trans. on Pattern Analysis and Machine Intelligence*, **15**(10):1042–1062, 1993.

12. H. Chen, P. Belhumeur, and D. Jacobs. In search of illumination invariants. *IEEE Proc. Computer Vision and Pattern Recognition*, I:254–261, 2000.

13. R. Epstein, P. Hallinan, and A. Yuille. $5 \pm 2$ eigenimages suffice: an empirical investigation of low-dimensional lighting models. *IEEE Workshop on Physics-Based Vision*, 108–116, 1995.

14. D. Frolova, D. Simakov, and R. Basri, "Accuracy of spherical harmonic approximations for images of Lambertian objects under far and near lighting," *European Conf. on Computer Vision*, 574–587, 2004.

15. A. Georghiades. Incorporating the Torrance and Sparrow model of reflectance in uncalibrated photometric stereo. *Int. Conf. on Computer Vision*, II:816–823, 2003.

16. A. Georghiades, P. Belhumeur, and D. Kriegman. From few to many: generative models for recognition under variable pose and illumination. *IEEE Trans. on Pattern Analysis and Machine Intelligence*, 23(6):643-660, 2001.

17. A. Georghiades, D. Kriegman, and P. Belhumeur. Illumination cones for recognition under variable lighting: faces. *IEEE Conf. on Computer Vision and Pattern Recognition*, 52–59, 1998.

18. P. Hallinan. A low-dimensional representation of human faces for arbitrary lighting conditions. *IEEE Conf. on Computer Vision and Pattern Recognition*, 995–999, 1994.

19. H. Hayakawa. Photometric stereo under a light source with arbitrary motion. *Journal of the Optical Society of America*, 11(11):3079–3089, 1994.

20. J. Ho, M. Yang, J. Lim, K. Lee, and D. Kriegman. Clustering appearances of objects under varying illumination conditions. *IEEE Conf. on Computer Vision and Pattern Recognition*, I:11–18, 2003.

21. R. Ishiyama and S. Sakamoto. Geodesic illumination basis: compensating for illumination variations in any pose for face recognition. *IEEE Int. Conf. on Pattern Recognition*, 4:297–301, 2002.

22. D, Jacobs. Linear fitting with missing data for structure-from-motion. *Computer Vision and Image Understanding*, 82(1):57–81, 2001.

23. D. Jacobs, P. Belhumeur, and R. Basri. Comparing images under variable illumination. *IEEE Proc. Computer Vision and Pattern Recognition*, 610–617, 1998.

24. H.W. Jensen, S.R. Marschner, M. Levoy, and P. Hanrahan. "A practical model for subsurface light transport". In *Proc. SIGGRAPH*, 511–518, 2001.

25. J. Koenderink and A. Van Doorn. The generic bilinear calibration-estimation problem. *International Journal of Computer Vision*, 23(3):217–234, 1997.

26. M. Lades, J. Vorbruggen, J. Buhmann, J. Lange, C. von der Malsburg, R. Wurtz, and W. Konen. Distortion invariant object recognition in the dynamic link architecture. *IEEE Trans. on Computers*, 42(3):300–311, 1993.

27. J. Lambert. Photometria sive de mensura et gradibus luminus, colorum et umbrae. Eberhard Klett, 1760.

28. K.C. Lee, J. Ho, and D. Kriegman. Nine points of light: acquiring subspaces for face recognition under variable lighting. *IEEE Conf. on Computer Vision and Pattern Recognition*, 519–526, 2001.

29. S. Marschner, S. Westin, E. Lafortune, K. Torrance, and D. Greenberg. Image-based BRDF measurement including human skin. *10th Eurographics Workshop on Rendering*, 131–144, 1999.

30. I.V. Meglinski and S.J. Matcher. Quantitative assessment of skin layers absorption and skin reflectance spectra simulation in the visible and near-infrared spectral regions. Physiol. Meas. 23:741–753, 2002.

31. Y. Moses. *Face recognition: generalization to novel images*. Ph.D. Thesis, Weizmann Institute of Science, 1993.

32. Y. Moses and S. Ullman. Limitations of Non Model-Based Recognition Schemes. *European Conference on Computer Vision*, 820–828, 1992.

33. M. Osadchy, D. Jacobs, and R. Ramamoorthi. Using specularities for recognition. *International Conference on Computer Vision*, II:1512–1519, 2003.

34. R. Ramamoorthi. Analytic PCA construction for theoretical analysis of lighting variability in a single image of a Lambertian object. *IEEE Trans. on Pattern Analysis and Machine Intelligence*, 24(10),:1322–1333, 2002.

35. R. Ramamoorthi and P. Hanrahan. On the relationship between radiance and irradiance: determining the illumination from images of convex Lambertian object. *Journal of the Optical Society of America*, 18(10): 2448–2459, 2001.

36. I. Sato, T. Okabe, Y. Sato, and K. Ikeuchi. Appearance sampling for obtaining a set of basis images for variable illumination. *IEEE Int. Conf. on Computer Vision*, II:800–807, 2003.

37. A. Shashua. On photometric issues in 3d visual recognition from a single 2D image. *International Journal of Computer Vision*, 21(1-2):99–122, 1997.

38. H.Y. Shum, K. Ikeuchi, and R. Reddy. Principal component analysis with missing data and its application to polyhedral object modeling. *IEEE Trans. on Pattern Analysis and Machine Intelligence*, 17(9):854–867, 1995.

39. D. Simakov, D. Frolova, and R. Basri. Dense shape reconstruction of a moving object under arbitrary, unknown lighting. *IEEE Int. Conf. on Computer Vision*, 1202–1209, 2003.

40. L. Sirovitch and M. Kirby. Low-dimensional procedure for the characterization of human faces. *Journal of the Optical Society of America*, 2:586–591, 1987.

41. M. Turk and A. Pentland. Eigenfaces for recognition. *Journal of Cognitive Neuroscience*, 3(1):71–96, 1991.

42. T. Wiberg. Computation of principal components when data are missing. *Proc. Second Symp. Computational Statistics*, 229–236, 1976.

43. A. Yuille, D. Snow, R. Epstein, and P. Belhumeur. Determining generative models of objects under varying illumination: shape and albedo from multiple images using SVD and integrability. *International Journal of Computer Vision*, 35(3):203–222, 1999.

44. L. Zhang and D. Samaras. Face recognition under variable lighting using harmonic image exemplars. *IEEE Conf. on Computer Vision and Pattern Recognition*, I:19–25, 2003.

45. L. Zhang, B. Curless, A. Hertzmann, and S.M. Seitz. Shape and motion under varying illumination: unifying structure from motion, photometric stereo, and multi-view stereo. *IEEE Int. Conf. on Computer Vision*, 618–625, 2003.

# Chapter 6. Facial Skin Color Modeling

J. Birgitta Martinkauppi, Matti Pietikäinen

University of Oulu, Department of Electrical and Information Engineering, PO Box 4500, Oulu
FIN-90014, Finland, jbm@cs.joensuu.fi, mkp@ee.oulu.fi

Color information has been commonly used to assist face detection. Its popularity can be attributed to several factors such as computational efficiency and discrimination power. However, because of its sensitivity to illumination variations, changes in illumination (especially in chromaticity) can be detrimental to some models.

Use of color in facial skin detection may not be enough: It cannot necessarily distinguish faces from other objects (e.g., hands, wood) with a similar appearance. Other cues are therefore needed to verify that the selected area is indeed a face. Color is, however, still useful as a preprocessing step because it may significantly reduce the number of candidates by eliminating obviously false targets.

In this chapter, we try to answer the following questions: What factors should be taken into account when selecting a skin color model? How can we find a suitable model?

The chapter is organized in the following way: Section 1 provides an introduction to the problem. In Section 2, the behavior of skin color in different color spaces is considered. Section 3 presents a review of skin color models, and Section 4 describes the skin locus approach and compares it to other methods. Finally, discussion is presented in Section 5.

## 1 Introduction

Color is a low level feature that can be a powerful, highly discriminative and computationally fast cue. It is easy to understand and robust toward some geometric changes. A typical geometric change, such as rotation, scaling, or translation, hardly affects the color information observed under a uniform illumination field. It is also well known that we humans tend to spot easily any color changes in the skin tones [15, 22]. Furthermore, skin color is in some situations distinctive from the surroundings. It is therefore not surprising that color has been an intriguing and popular cue for face detection.

The main obstacle for universal color use in machine vision applications is that the cameras are not able to distinguish changes of surface colors from color shifts caused by varying illumination spectra. The effect of changing illumination can be observed in Figure 1 in which 16 face images are obtained under four prevailing and white balancing illuminations [23]. In this figure, a row contains images obtained with one calibration under four light sources (columns). As this example demonstrates, the change in color depends on the relationship between the calibration and prevailing lighting conditions. If the prevailing illumination has an elevated color temperature, the color appearance of the objects is shifted toward blue because a high color temperature of a light source is related to an increase in the blue component of its spectra. In the case of a lower color temperature, the colors appear more reddish because the illumination now has a redder component.

The illumination can affect the color appearance also via white calibration. A surface imaged under different white balancing light sources does not necessarily have the same color appearance in the images: Successful white balancing guarantees only the same appearance of true grays for a camera with linear response. For example, deviation of skin tones can be observed from the images in the diagonal axis of Figure 6.1. In Figure 6.2, the skin chromaticities from a person's canonical face images are shown and confirm the observation.

All this indicates one major factor to be considered when employing a skin color model: the illumination. If knowledge is available about possible prevailing and calibration lighting, it can be used for choosing or tuning the color model further. For example, a general skin color model used under stable, uniform lighting might also select obviously false candidates that are not possible due to illumination conditions. This is a natural consequence for a general model, which tolerates skin appearance with nonskin tones. On the other hand, a pure skin tone model fails when the colors of the objects shift owing to the illumination (especially chromaticity) variation in time or in the spatial domain. Again, the selected model is the limiting factor: If skin pixels can have only skin tones according to the model, a shift in colors may cause skin colors to fall into nonskin tones. Although many theories have been suggested for color correction and constancy, none has been proved to produce generally successful results for machine vision. On the contrary: Funt et al. found a failure of state-of-the-art color constancy algorithms for color indexing applications [13].

Other factors causing varying skin color appearances in images are, for example, differences in spectral sensitivities of cameras, interreflections, and the parameters and settings of the camera(s). However, one can generally state that these other factors usually cause smaller changes in appearance than the illumination. Objects imaged under different balancing conditions also vary less than those obtained under drastically varying prevailing illumination.

## 2  Skin Colors in Different Color Spaces

Numerous color spaces have been developed and suggested for various applications and purposes. They are usually obtained via a transform from RGB space or other "basic" color space. Unlike the basic color spaces, many of the derived ones split the color information into intensity and chromaticity components. However, the separation is not necessarily complete: The chromaticity part may depend on the intensity of the RGB values. There is an easy way to evaluate linear or linearized camera data for establishing if the components are independent: In the transform to the color space, one can make the substitution $R \rightarrow cR$, $G \rightarrow cG$, and $B \rightarrow cB$ in which $c$ describes a uniform change in the intensity levels. If the factor $c$ does not cancel out for chromaticity descriptors, the separation is incomplete. Obviously, using only the chromaticity part in this case does not offer robustness against intensity variations. If one does not find a

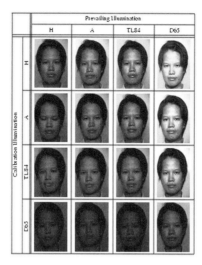

**Fig. 6.1.** A 16 image series has been obtained with four white balancing conditions (rows) and four prevailing illumination options (columns) [23]. The lights used were H, Horizon Planckian 2300 K; A, CIE A 2856 K; TL84, a fluorescent source modeling F11; and D65, daylight 6500 K. As can be observed, the color of the object depends on the white balancing condition and the relation between white balancing and prevailing illumination. (See insert for color reproduction of this figure)

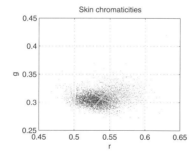

**Fig. 6.2.** Skin chromaticities from the calibrated (canonical) cases of Figure 6.1 are plotted in normalized r and g coordinates. Different colors for chromaticities in the figure refer to the light source used for white balancing of the camera. (See insert for color reproduction of this figure)

suitable color space from the mass of already formed ones, it is also possible to design a new one to fulfill the requirements. An example of this is tint/saturation/lightness (TSL), a color space designed especially for skin detection by Terrillon et al. for their camera [42].

The use of only chromaticity descriptors is suggested in many studies as a way of providing robustness against changing intensity. It allows us to detect an object appearing with varying intensity levels caused, for example, by shadowing or changing distance from the lighting. Of course, this is strictly valid only for a linear camera and for color spaces with intensity-independent chromaticity coordinates. Naturally, the discrimination is no longer possible between colors separated only by their intensity values. For skin detection, omitting the intensity component is especially attractive, as many research studies (e.g., [14, 17, 50]) have shown that skin tones differ mainly in their intensity values. Similarity of skin tones is not surprising, as the spectral reflectances of different skin tone groups are alike, as shown in Figure 6.3 [25] (see also [47]). As can be observed, the skin reflectances are smooth and similar. The main differ-

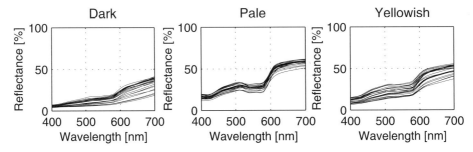

**Fig. 6.3.** Appearance of skin complexions can be roughly divided into three groups: dark, pale, and yellowish. As the spectra examples of each group demonstrates, the reflectances of these groups are similar and mainly separated by their level.

ence is in the level not the shape. The similarity of skin reflectances has also been demonstrated [18, 29] wherein skin spectra were reconstructed with high quality using only three basis vectors. The natural reason for the closeness of skin reflectances is that the skin color appearance for all ethnic groups is formed from three colorants: melanin, carotene and hemoglobin [11].

Several studies have been made to evaluate color spaces for skin detection [3, 5, 25, 36]. (Equations for many color spaces can be found elsewhere [27, 47].) Some of these consider only images with limited variations (e.g., many Internet images) [3, 5], whereas others took into account more drastic illumination changes [25, 36]. In the first case, the studies did not particularly consider the color shifts from skin tones, or at least they did not address these shifts clearly. They were more targeted to applications in which the illumination changes are minor and skin appears approximately in skin tone chromaticities. Skin tones in this chapter refer to skin color values that represent skin with an acceptable quality for humans. Commonly, the white balancing and prevailing illumination conditions are not mentioned, although this might be difficult for some images such as those downloaded from Internet.

Brand and Mason [3] compared the following three methods with the images of the Compaq skin and nonskin database: ratios between RGB channels; a one-dimensional indicator from IQ components of YIQ space, as suggested by Wang and Brandstein [45]; and an RGB probability map. They concluded that the RGB probability map gives the lowest false error rates when the true positive rate (the rate of correctly detected skin pixels) is fixed at 95% for the training set. RGB space has also been compared to YUV and HSV color models in [44] for principal component analysis (PCA) based face recognition. In that research, RGB and luminance Y produced equal recognition rates, but better performance was obtained with the SV components and YUV space. Furthermore, Jones and Rehg demonstrated in their large-scale experiment that in RGB space the histogram provides slightly better results than the mixture of Gaussians [20].

For color histogram-based skin classification, five color spaces (CIE Lab, Fleck HS, HSV, normalized RGB, YCrCb) were compared by Zarit et al. [52]. Their approaches were based on a look-up table and Bayesian decision theory. According to their study, the look-up table method applied in the HS-spaces performed best, whereas the performance in the CIE Lab and YCbCr spaces was poorer. For Bayesian decision-based classification, the choice of color space did not matter, but the maximum likelihood method produced a better result than the maximum a posteriori method.

Terrillon et al. compared the performance of a single Gaussian function and Gaussian mixtures for modeling skin chromaticity distributions in nine color spaces (TSL, NCC rgb, CIE xy, CIE SH, HSV, YIQ, YES, CIE Luv, CIE Lab) [42]. They made an interesting observation: the saturation S in HSV space took almost all values for a limited hue H range because it is sensitive to skin colors from different ethnic groups. Furthermore, the normalized spaces CIE SH and HS-space were found to have the highest discrimination rate between skin and non-skin classes. The single Gaussian model provided the best results in illumination normalized color spaces, whereas the use of Gaussian mixture models improved results with nonnormalized color spaces. However, the use of a Gaussian mixture in a normalized color space produced results comparable to those of a single Gaussian model. The Gaussian mixtures were better in unnormalized spaces because in these spaces the shape of skin color distributions were more complex. The conclusion was that illumination normalization produced skin distributions that were simpler to model, confined, and more efficient for skin color segmentation. Later [41], they showed that NCC rgb and CIE xy were most efficient for skin segmentation because the skin chromaticities occupied a smaller area in them. These two spaces were recognized as the most portable color spaces between two cameras and the most effective for face detection; and of the two, NCC rgb had the higher correct face detection rate and correct nonface rejection rate.

Contrary evaluations for single Gaussian and Gaussian mixtures models have been reported [5, 49]. Caetano et al. compared both models in normalized rg coordinates using skin pixels extracted from face, arms, and leg areas of different ethnic groups. According to the study, the Gaussian mixtures with two to eight components have similar behavior. When a higher rate of false positives is allowed, the amount of true positives is higher for the mixtures than the single Gaussian. Yang and Ahuja [49] concluded that same based on the shape of the skin color distribution. Gaussian mixtures have been also compared with self-organizing maps (SOMs) in four color spaces: HSV, Cartesian HS, TSL, and normalized rg [4]. The Gaussian mixtures provided better results only in normalized rg space, but overall the SOM produced a more consistent detection rate.

The previous comparative studies indicate that the normalized rgb space should be suitable for many applications using skin tones. However, any general recommendation about the best model is difficult to give because of the contradicting results, which may be due to different material (for example, cameras may have different properties and settings such as gamma) or the different modeling parameters used. At least for the Internet images, the models provided by Jones and Rehg [20] should be highly valid.

A more complex situation for skin detection is the case in which the illumination chromaticity varies. This leads naturally to more overlap between skin and nonskin classes due to the enlarged area of possible color appearances for different objects. So far, only two studies have been conducted, and neither of them evaluated the effect of drastic intensity changes in real or simulated images, or at least it was not mentioned.

Shin et al. compared eight color spaces (normalized rgb, CIE XYZ, CIE Lab, HSI, Spherical coordinate transform, YCbCr, YIQ, YUV) with three criteria: separability between skin and nonskin classes; compactness of skin colors; and robustness against illumination variations [36]. They evaluated the behavior of a space using its two color descriptors and all three descriptors. The RGB space performance was used as a baseline. The evaluation was done with Purdue's AR data set and the Physics-based Face Database from the University of Oulu [23]-[25]. The nonskin class was approximated using the University of Washington's Content-based Image Retrieval data set [2]. For all classes, the color space components were used in the range of 0 to 255 with quantization to 256 levels. This may not be such a good choice because at least for the three component case there are more than 16 million combinations, whereas the nonskin data set has "only" 59 million pixels. The conclusion was that the preferable space is RGB and that the illumination component increases separability. This is of course true if one can assume that the object has a limited intensity range under the illumination conditions used or one would have enough data to assess reliably all possible intensity cases.

The other study compared chromaticity coordinates of several color spaces which were I1I2I3 (Ohta's features), YES, YIQ, YUV, YCbCr (Rec 601-5 and Rec 709), normalized rgb, modified version of normalized rgb, ln-chromaticity, P1P2, l1l2l3, ratios between channels (G/R, B/R, and B/G), modified ab, HSV, HSL, TSL, and Yuv [25]. Only the chromaticity coordinates were compared because the speed for 2D skin detection is preferable in many face detection applications and because of the limited range of intensity changes. Of course, this makes the results for color spaces with incomplete RGB intensity separation from chromaticities only indicative.

For the evaluation, the facial pixels were obtained from the Physics-based Face Database [23] and from the Face Video database [25]. These databases contain images taken under 16 white balancing/prevailing illumination combinations obtained using four common light sources (Horizon 2300K, incandescent A, fluorescent TL84, daylight 6500K). The images were obtained with four cameras (one 3CCD and three 1CCDs). After the conversion from RGB to another color space, the data were quantized with 1% accuracy of the full range because there was not enough material to support lower accuracy; quantization is also commonly used to speed up the detection step. The results were evaluated using the following criteria: the overlap between two ethnic groups (Asian and Caucasian), the overlaps between cameras, and the continuity of regions.

When comparing the results from different cameras, it became obvious that the gain (brightness) control helps prevent smearing of the skin chromaticity region (Figure 6.4). This smearing was caused by color bleaching; in other words, the color value of a channel is unreliably low.

It was also noted that the commonly made mistake of displaying an HS-space in Cartesian coordinates causes the skin chromaticities to split into two separate regions. The color spaces except TSL and HS spaces in Cartesian coordinates were found to form a uniform skin chromaticity cluster. Most of the clusters could be modeled with quadratic functions or straight lines. The overlap of clusters between all four cameras was low, but better results were obtained when comparing cameras with and without brightness control only against each other. Also the relative areas occupied by skin colors were calculated, but this is not a good measure for all spaces. Although it allows evaluation without making a nonskin class, for sparse, large-range,

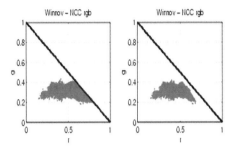

**Fig. 6.4.** The image on the left displays the normalized rg chromaticities of skin for a Winnov camera. Because the camera has no gain control, under a drastic illumination change the blue channel had values near zero or zero, causing an enlarged skin chromaticity region. The image on the right demonstrates the skin region constructed from only those skin color values for which the intensity level of every channel is more than 25. As this example shows, skin detection with some cameras may also be affected by the properties of the camera.

and nonuniformly distributed color spaces such as ratios, it gives too optimistic results. For normalized rgb the relative area was 14%, which was among the top results. The overlaps between skin colors from different ethnic groups were relatively good in all color spaces.

# 3 Skin Color Models

There are many ways to categorize the color detection algorithms. Here we used as a criterion the information needed from other images: An approach may be targeted at single images or an image series. In Section 4, we describe an approach based on a skin locus that can be adapted to both cases.

## 3.1 Single Images

Approaches for single images classify pixels based on either probabilities assigned to the colors of different object class(es) or spatial limitation of object's colors in a color space. It is also possible to combine one of these methods with some kind of preprocessing of the image, such as color constancy.

The basic assumption behind statistical procedures is that certain color tones belong to an object's pixels more often than others. The probabilities for color tones are usually calculated off-line from a "representative" training data set; however, for example, an on-line reconstruction of skin color histograms has been suggested using a manually selected initial skin patch [33]. To classify pixels a threshold value is needed, and it is also often obtained from the training data set. Unfortunately, universally valid thresholds are difficult to set or determine beforehand; usually they need to be modified to specific images or image sets.

The spatial limitation approach has an opposite starting point: It is not possible to determine reliably whether certain color tones of an object have higher probability than others in all cases. Instead, the goal is to find a color space region in which the object color pixels typically fall.

The color tones inside this region can be considered to have equal probability to belong to the skin class, whereas for the other tones, the probability is set to zero.

## Statistics-Based Classification

Many statistical techniques have been employed for skin detection: parametric, such as a Gaussian or Gaussian mixtures (e.g., [1, 42, 48]); semiparametric, such as the Self-Organizing Map (e.g., [31]) and neural networks [37]; and nonparametric, such as a histogram (e.g., [34, 20]). (Note that although the number of bins must be selected and it has been demonstrated to influence the outcome of the application, histograms are still generally called nonparametric.)

Gaussians and histograms are easy to implement. Their decision boundaries and operation can be studied and understood quite straightforwardly, so they are popular. For a histogram-based approach, the probabilities for object colors can be obtained using the following equation

$$P(C) = \frac{count[C]}{T_{count}} \tag{1}$$

where $C$ is the representation of color data used, $count[C]$ expresses the count in the histogram bin obtained from the object or objects, and $T_{count}$ is the total number of pixels belonging to the object or objects.

A Gaussian mixture model is defined as

$$P(C; \mu, \Sigma) = \sum_{k=1}^{n} \alpha_k \frac{1}{\sqrt{(2 * \pi)^d |\Sigma_k|}} exp^{-0.5(C-\mu_k)^T (\Sigma_k)^{-1}(C-\mu_k)} \tag{2}$$

where $n$ is the number of Gaussians used, $\alpha$ is the weight for the $k$th Gaussian, $\Sigma$ is the covariance matrix, $\mu$ is a mean vector, and $d$ is the dimension of the data ($C$). For single, unimodal Gaussian function, the n and $\alpha$ are set to 1. The parameters can be estimated for the unimodal Gaussian by using maximum likelihood, whereas for the multimodal Gaussian mixture they are determined using a more complex maximum likelihood approach, an expectation-maximization (EM) algorithm [10, 20, 48].

Both Gaussian- and histogram-based approaches can either work only on skin color or take into account the other objects. In the former case, the training data are used to form the distribution parameters; additionally the data have been used in some cases to determine the thresholding parameters. Typically, a pixel is classified as skin if its skin class probability exceeds the given threshold. A reliable distribution for the nonskin class may be difficult to obtain, but at least it has been done for Internet images [20]. Once the skin and nonskin classes are defined with the essential parameters, a thresholding method must be selected. For example, a Bayesian classifier may be employed even with suitably defined costs for false positives and negatives. An alternative is to penalize the skin colors that occur too often in the background. For instance, a ratio model can be computed by dividing the skin model probabilities by those from the nonskin class. Once again, a threshold value must be selected for the approach.

The SOM [21] has also been used to discriminate skin from other, nonskin objects. One of the strengths of SOM usage is in the interpretation and visualization of high dimensional data by projecting it to a low dimensional space. The user may select the classification boundaries. One important issue is the choice of input features which seems to depend on the application. SOM has been applied to both videos [31] and single images [4].

The previous methods were selected only as representative examples of statistical approaches to skin detection. There are many other types, such as the fuzzy-based skin color model [46] and maximum entropy model [19]. The common procedure for statistical approaches appears to consist of two steps: Selection of the training images and applying your favorite statistical methods to them. Typical for all these approaches is that they have been developed with images having no drastic prevailing illumination changes.

### Selection-Based on a Region in a Color Space

A region in the color space is determined from an image set considered to represent varying skin appearances. After the region is determined, it can be used directly to separate skin pixels from nonskin pixels. The region can be implemented in many ways: as a look-up table or as threshold values [6]. The shape of the region varies from simple [7] to complex [16]. It is not even necessary to determine a region: The possibilities for skin candidates can be limited by selecting a range from one of the chrominance components [9]. Once again, the procedure seems to contain two steps: Selecting the training images and finding the skin area. A problem related to these approaches occurs when determining the boundary of the skin region. Some values at the boundary can be caused by noise, and one might remove them, for example, on the basis of statistics. On the other hand, if a high true-positive rate is preferable, one might want to increase the area.

### Color Correction for a Region-Based Approach

Hsu [16] suggested combining a color correction step with skin detection processing. The color correction part should remove color shifts due to reflections and illumination variation so skin colors have skin tone appearances.

The lighting compensation technique used is called reference white [16]. As the name indicates, it is based on an assumption that there is always at least one white object in the image. The "white" pixels are recognized using their nonlinear gamma-corrected luminance values. The top 5% of these values are assumed to be from the white object(s); and if this 5% of values gets support for more than 100 pixels, the color correction stage is used. If there is not enough support, this stage is eliminated. The color shifts are corrected by applying coefficients to RGB channels. The coefficients are obtained from scaling the reference white pixels to 255. Note that there is no mention about how to handle clipped pixels or if they should be excluded.

The skin detection itself is done by an elliptical model in a modified $C_bC_r$ space which is obtained from a nonlinear transform applied to $YC_bC_r$ space. The weakest part of the method is the color correction, which can fail [13, 28] because of invalid assumptions and loss of data caused, for example, by clipping.

### 3.2 Image Sequences

A typical approach for image sequences is to track an object based on temporally slowly varying or fixed features. One feature is color, which can be used as a fixed model [8] or an adaptive model [32, 51]. A fixed model handles images in a sequence simply as single, separate images. It can be implemented as any method presented in the previous section.

An adaptive model is based on the assumption that the features extracted from sequential images resemble each other enough. For color-based skin detection, the update of the color model can be done by utilizing restriction(s) in temporal domain and spatial domain. For example, illumination can have temporal changes, or it may be spatially nonuniform but the skin color distributions between two frames overlap each other at least partially in the color space. The length of the time interval should be set so the movement of the face in a nonuniform illumination field or temporal illumination variation does not cause too large changes in skin color appearances. Otherwise, the images should be handled as separate images.

Up to now, two adaptive approaches applicable only on image sequences have been shown to track successfully. They both use spatial constraints in the image domain to select pixels for a skin color model update. With the approach of Raja et al. [32], these pixels were selected inside the face localization, whereas Yoo and Oh [51] utilize all pixels inside an elliptical face localization, as shown in Figure 6.5. The previous method provides some robustness against the localization error, because even in the case of reasonable minor localization error the inner area consists of facial pixels. However, problems may occur, for example, under a nonuniform illumination field when the pixels used during adaptation do not represent well the color change [25]. Yoo and Oh's method avoids this problem by using all pixels, but it is more sensitive to the localization quality. Both methods may start to track nonskin-colored objects because they do not set any limitations on the allowed colors [25].

**Fig. 6.5.** The image on the left demonstrates the method suggested by Raja et al. [32]. The skin color model is updated by the area (inner box) calculated from the face localization (outer box). The elliptical constraint used to select pixels for adaptation by Yoo and Oh [51] is shown in the image on the right.

## 4 Skin Color Modeling with a Skin Locus

The skin locus approach has its background in physical phenomena related to image formation. It is based on experiments on how the skin color appearance is affected by different illuminations. Therefore, the illumination conditions in which this modeling method is applicable are set clearly and unambiguously. The name "skin locus" came from Störring et al. [39], who showed that the track of skin chromaticities follows the curve of Planckian radiator's chromaticities in normalized rgb space in case of using one white balancing. The color data for these results were acquired so the clipping was avoided by manually adjusting the lens opening and shutter speed.

The main goal of a skin locus is to provide robustness against changing intensity and tolerance toward varying illumination chromaticity. This knowledge itself does not assume any probability for certain colors to belong to skin; it only defines the area for possible chromaticities and in this way tolerates inherently nonuniform illumination fields. However, it can be used for selecting pixels in probability-based face tracking as shown in [38]. Furthermore, skin locus has been shown to operate better under lighting variations than other state-of-the-art methods [16, 20, 32], which fail in some cases [26, 28].

## 4.1  Creating a Skin Locus

The skin locus for a camera can be calculated based on spectral information or obtained directly from an image set. To calculate the locus, one needs spectral knowledge of the camera, illumination conditions and skin. Whereas the spectral information of the two last factors can be easily obtained [25, 30], the camera characteristics are often unavailable. It is then necessary to take face images in the illumination range with the allowed camera settings.

In any case, the illumination range must be based on the given application. Typically, it is enough to take the illuminants with minimum and maximum color temperatures and a couple from the middle range. Then one has to know the number of possible white balancings and the lighting conditions under which they are done.

### Spectral-Based Approach

The skin reflectances can be obtained via simulation [30] or from measurements [25]. The same is true for spectral power distribution of illuminations (e.g., [47]). The spectral responses of the cameras can be difficult to acquire from the manufacturer, but techniques have been developed to estimate them using the Macbeth chart [12].

The spectral data can be substituted in to the basic color equation

$$O_i = K \frac{\sum_{\lambda=400}^{700} S_i(\lambda) \times I_{prevailing}(\lambda) \times \sigma(\lambda)}{\sum_{\lambda=400}^{700} S_i(\lambda) \times I_{calibration}(\lambda)} \tag{3}$$

where $O$ is the output; $i$ is the red, green, or blue channel; $K$ is a scaling coefficient used to determine the range of the output data; $\lambda$ is the wavelength range, which is typically from 400 to 700 nm; $S$ is the spectral sensitivity of a channel; $I$ is the spectral power distribution of the illumination; and $\sigma$ describes the spectral reflectance of an object. The numerator expresses the response of the camera for the surface observed under the current lighting. The denominator describes the scaling of the channel determined under the white balancing conditions. Sometimes $K$ and the denominator are presented as one constant factor for the prevailing conditions. When the prevailing illumination is not the same as in the calibration, a color shift is likely to occur. One should also note that the normalization methods for the illumination spectra may lead to different output values. The spectra may be normalized just by dividing all values by the value at 560 nm and multiplying by the constant 100. Alternatively, all values may be divided using the scaling obtained using a norm such as the Euclidean norm.

Equation (3) can be used to compute the response of a camera for a white target and skin. The results can be used further to simulate highlights, matte skin parts, and their combination. The simulations of combinations can be done in RGB or in normalized rg space. In the latter case, the combinations are directly on the line connecting the illumination chromaticity and respective skin chromaticity under the present conditions (e.g., [39]). This is based on the dichromatic reflection model [35]: The color observed from dielectric nonhomogeneous material, the group in which skin generally belongs, consists of light reflected at the surface and light filtered by the colorants. Furthermore, for materials such as skin, it can be assumed that the spectrum of surface-reflected light is equal to the spectrum of the lighting (neutral interface reflection [43]) as was done Störring ct al. [39]. When the camera parameters and settings are used in the simulations the results obtained correspond very well with the measurements according to Störring et al. [39].

Another approach for calculating the skin locus is to employ basis functions of skin color signal (Figure 6.6) [25]. Skin color signals are the spectra reflected from the skin. At least in theory, they are device-independent. The basis functions were calculated from these signals to get the skin locus of different cameras easily. By combining weights of different illumination cases, it is straightforward to simulate mixed conditions, as shown in Figure 6.7. Therefore, the number of light sources used to calculate the basis function can be smaller than the actual number of them used to compute the locus itself. Naturally, the camera settings and parameters should be addressed separately for the locus calculation.

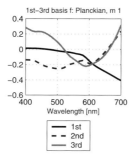

**Fig. 6.6.** The three first basis functions are computed using skin reflectances and Planckian illuminants. The color temperature range of the Planckians was from 2300 K to 6500 K by 100 K steps. Note that because both illuminant and reflectance data are smooth, the basis functions show the same characteristic.

**Image-Based Approach**

When the illumination range in which the application operates is determined and the possible white balancing conditions are known, the next step is to acquire the images. The number of white balancing conditions is determined by those commonly used in the applications. For some cameras, there might be just one, fixed balancing, whereas for others more calibrations need to be tolerated. The illumination range is obtained from the minimum and maximum color temperature range of possible lighting of the location(s). Note that the fluorescent light sources with strong green components should be taken into account when creating the locus because their light cast may shift skin chromaticities to outside the locus. The fluorescent lights with

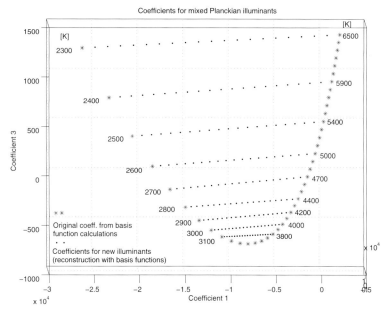

**Fig. 6.7.** The first three coefficients of basis functions (see Figure 6.6) form a quadratic slope. The coefficient for the original illuminants are marked with asterisks. The black points indicate the coefficients needed to reconstruct a new skin color signal, which is obtained using a combination of two illuminants with different degrees, such as Planckians of 2300 K and 6500 K. These new coefficients fall into a straight line between the "old" coefficients of the single illuminants' color signals. This indicates that the old coefficients can be used to simulate cases when there is more than one light source. Note that the axis of the second coefficient is almost perpendicular because the viewing angle was set to maximize the visibility of the slope.

strong blue and red components are not as worrying because usually color shifts caused by these two components are smaller than the shifts caused by changing color temperature.

It is sometimes difficult and cumbersome to obtain the image set but using at least one facial image on each condition gives quite a reliable locus. Figure 6.8 demonstrates the procedure: (1) Image acquisition under the chosen illumination conditions; (2) extraction of the skin areas; and (3) transformation of the skin RGB to the chromaticity space and modeling it with a suitable function. The use of chromaticity coordinates reduces the number of images needed because the intensity component can be ignored because of the linear camera approximation (or the global intensity variation in input RGB does not affect the chromaticity components). It is quite clear that the size of the locus depends on the selected illumination range and the number of calibrations. The obtained locus is dependent on the camera used, as shown in Figure 6.9. Some of the boundary chromaticities may be due to noise, so in some cases one might prefer a tighter locus. On the other hand, a wider locus may be preferred in applications in which the high correct detection rate is far more important than the low false detection rate. To achieve a tighter locus one must decide how to exclude chromaticities, which may be difficult because the skin chromaticity distribution obtained from the image series may be invalid for the distribution at other images: Chromaticities rarely appearing in one image set may be common in another set.

Once again, however, if there is enough material, one can use a statistical approach to exclude seldomly appearing values.

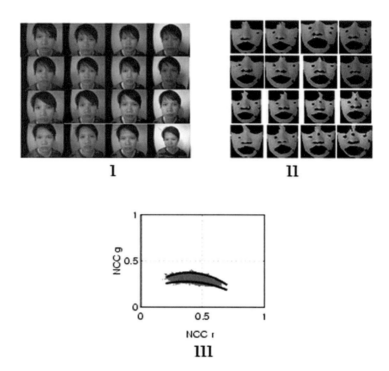

**Fig. 6.8.** The procedure to obtain a skin locus consists of three steps. **I.** Collecting the image material for different camera calibrations and prevailing conditions. Here four calibration conditions and four prevailing illuminations (Horizon 2300 K, CIE A 2856 K, fluorescent TL84, daylight 6500 K). Each row represents images obtained under one calibration condition while varying the prevailing lighting. Note that some cameras have limited capability of white balancing, as shown in the first and second rows. **II.** Selecting the skin areas for further processing. The selection can be manual or automatic. **III.** Converting the selected skin RGBs into a chromaticity space and modeling them using a polynomial, for example.

## 4.2 Applying a Skin Locus: Examples

The face detection application may be dealing with single images, videos, or both. These approaches need different considerations, which are addressed in the next two sections.

### Still Images

The skin locus is applied for still images as a filter, which simply describes possible skin chromaticities for a camera under given conditions. Because no additional constraint for color is

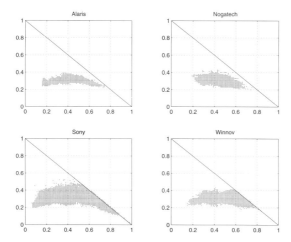

**Fig. 6.9.** The camera and its properties determine the skin locus, as indicated by the loci of four cameras. However, some regions are common to all, most notable the region of skin tones.

available, one must use the whole range. Further processing is needed to determine if the skin-colored area(s) is a face(s). This implementation of the skin locus is suitable not only for the single-image approach but also for approaches that handle both single images and videos. The images in the next two examples were taken from videos in which frames were handled as separate images. Figure 6.10 shows a successful example of the filtering applied for detecting several persons. Comparative results with other methods are shown in Figure 6.11 [28]. The

**Fig. 6.10.** A skin locus can be applied to images with one or more persons. The detection results are good for pure skin regions. (See insert for color reproduction of this figure)

skin locus produced good results under drastic illumination changes, whereas the other methods seemed to work well only under mild illumination variations.

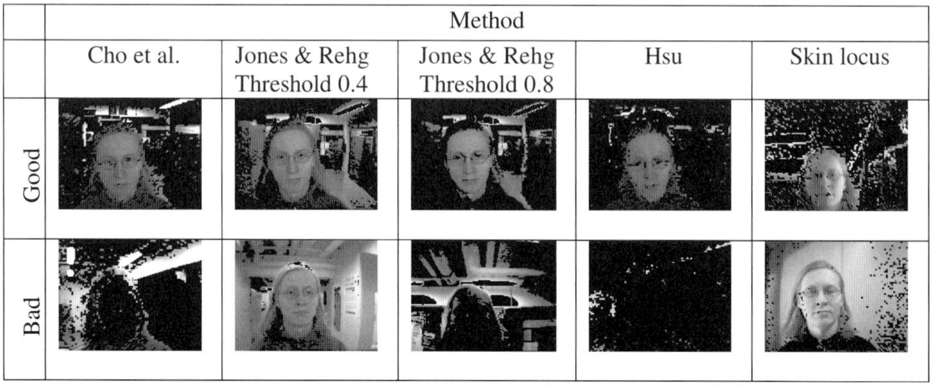

| | Method | | | | |
|---|---|---|---|---|---|
| | Cho et al. | Jones & Rehg Threshold 0.4 | Jones & Rehg Threshold 0.8 | Hsu | Skin locus |
| Good | | | | | |
| Bad | | | | | |

**Fig. 6.11.** Four state-of-the-art methods are compared using images with drastic illumination change. The upper row of images displays an example of good skin detection; the lower one shows a problematic case. Cho et al. [7] used an initial, fixed skin detection range as a pre-processing step for adaptive skin detection. As the second column shows, it is capable of working well under limited conditions. The Gaussian approach of Jones and Rehg [20] has been implemented with the parameters given in for skin and nonskin classes. The thresholds are selected based on a set of images, but for videos subjected to drastic change they are difficult to determine [28]. If the threshold is too low (see third column), the obviously nonskin-colored pixels can be selected. A higher threshold results in better discrimination at the cost of tolerance toward illumination variation, as shown in the fourth column. The fifth column shows the results of Hsu's method, the color correction part of which could not correct too drastic color changes. All three methods produce reasonably good results when there is no great illumination variation. Only a skin locus is able to work under real, large lighting variation, as shown in the sixth column. Colors that are defined as possible skin candidates should be distinguished using cues other than color. (See insert for color reproduction of this figure)

**Videos**

Videos are subject to varying illumination fields in time and spatial domains but generally between succeeding frames the variation range is somewhat limited. Therefore, knowledge about the skin color distribution of the previous frame may be used for the current frame. For example, the skin locus has been implemented as a filter in histogram back-projection [40] modified for adaptive tracking of one person [38]. Of course, it would be possible to extend the method for tracking multiple persons as well.

In experiments, the skin locus-based tracking was initialized by manually selecting the face from the first frame [25]; alternatively, an automatic method for selecting the facial region could be implemented to verify the facial areas with several cues. The accuracy of the selection needs not be high because the skin locus is used to filter out obvious nonskin-colored pixels. For statistical representation of the obtained skin color distribution, the skin color ratio histogram is used in rg space. This ratio histogram is obtained by dividing the skin color histogram by the histogram of the whole image. After the histogram is calculated, the next frame is converted to normalized rg and subjected to histogram back-projection. The histogram back-projection [40] is used with the ratio histogram scaled in the range 0 to 1 to form a new gray-level image: The pixel value in the gray-level image corresponds to the probability of the pixel rg values. The gray-level image was thresholded, and the binary image obtained was then subjected to morphologic operations to enhance the face blobs. The largest blob found was assumed to be the face and was localized with a bounding box. The localization was filtered with a skin locus and utilized for adapting the skin ratio histogram to the prevailing conditions. The adaptation was done using a moving average. The current and previous ratio histogram were weighted equally in this application. The moving average was selected because it provides a smooth transition between frames and may reduce the effect of values changed by noise. The obtained ratio histogram was applied to the next frame (but not in the calculation of the next moving average). Figure 6.12 shows how this implementation succeeded in tracking the person despite the drastic color changes (compare the results to those in Figure 6.13). Of course, an automatic initialization could have been employed by using additional features, which would most likely also improve the tracking accuracy. The tracking quality can be compared using, for example, the following measure of the overlap $A$.

$$A = \frac{|A_{gt} \bigcap A_c|}{\sqrt{|A_{gt}| \times |A_c|}} \tag{4}$$

The $|A_{gt}|$ refers to the area of the ground truth bounding box selected by human preference, while the $|A_c|$ is the area of the computed bounding box. The numerator is the area of the overlap between these two localization. The denominator is a scaling factor related to areas of ground truth and calculated bounding boxes. This measure has been calculated for the results of the indoor video (Figures 6.12 and 6.13) and is shown in Figure 6.14. An alternative option for the denominator would be the total area surrounded by these two boxes ($|A_c| + |A_{gt}| - |A_{gt} \bigcap A_c|$). However, neither of these methods necessarily correspond well to the localization goodness evaluation done by a human.

The skin locus can be combined also to other tracking methods such as the mean shift [25, 26]. With this implementation, no morphologic operations were employed, and the range of skin chromaticities inside the skin locus was also tracked. Figure 6.15 displays a couple of frames from the tracking using the skin locus. For comparison, Figure 6.16 shows the tracking results of the same video utilizing the constraint of Raja et al. As can be noted, the skin locus provides good performance, whereas the other implemented methods fail [25, 26].

## 5 Discussion

Up to the present time, several methods have been suggested for skin color detection and have been used successfully at least with their own test material. Their performance in general depends on many factors including illumination conditions which are often not mentioned or are vaguely described. Therefore, one may have to try several methods. Useful factors for selecting a suitable approach are illumination variations, the number of white balancings, properties such

**Fig. 6.12.** The image on the left shows tracking results for an indoor movie and the one on the right for an outdoor movie. The skin locus approach was able to track despite widely varying illumination. (See insert for color reproduction of this figure)

**Fig. 6.13.** The image on the left shows tracking with a fixed skin color model obtained from the first frame. This model is valid so long as the illumination variation is small. The right image displays adaptive tracking using the elliptical constraint suggested by Yoo and Oh. As can be observed from these images, this constraint is sensitive to the localization quality and may start to track other objects. (See insert for color reproduction of this figure)

as the sensitivities of the camera(s) used, the choice of suitable color spaces, the applicability of probabilities for skin tones, and the format of image data (video versus single images).

The range in which the illumination over the face (skin) may change is a major factor. It determines the generality needed for the approach: A too general model selects many clearly nonskin-class pixels under restricted conditions, whereas a too specific model cannot tolerate the color shifts. Obviously, different white balancings of the camera may also affect the color appearance. Even a successful white balancing of the camera for different illumination does not guarantee that the skin "tones" will be the same between the images obtained under different conditions. The same is true for the color output between different cameras and camera settings. However, the lighting variations usually cause the biggest color shifts, and the only approach that has been shown to tolerate drastic but real changes is the skin locus. In general, the available knowledge on illumination-related issues can be utilized for fine-tuning the skin color model.

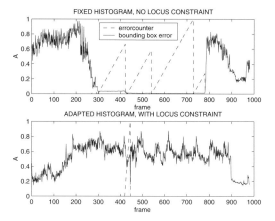

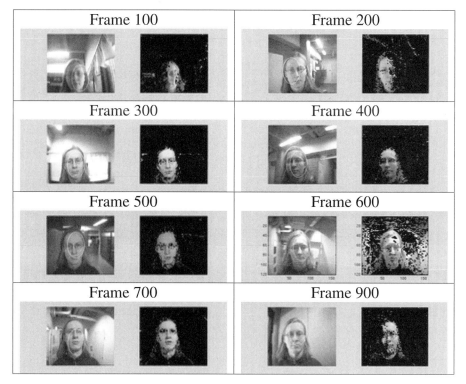

**Fig. 6.14.** As the overlap measure indicates, the fixed skin color model is valid only for the illumination conditions in which it is obtained. The skin locus is designed for varying illumination and therefore is superior in the indoor video.

**Fig. 6.15.** The skin locus combined with the mean shift produced good results despite changing conditions. The images on the left side show the localization over the original frame, and those on the right show the segmented frame. (See insert for color reproduction of this figure)

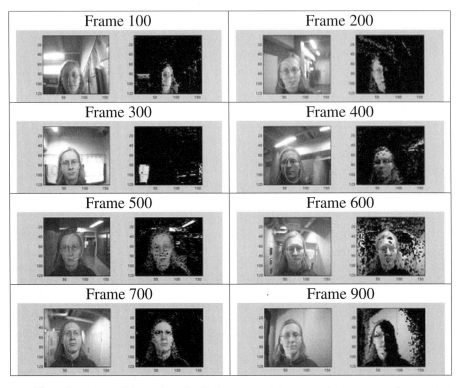

**Fig. 6.16.** The adaptive tracking using the Raja constraint succeeded in some frames but also was subjected to tracking failure as shown in the images. On the left side is shown the original frame with the localization, and the adaptation box inside the localization. The right side images show the segmented frame. (See insert for color reproduction of this figure.)

The evaluation results for different color spaces and skin color modeling are partially contradictory, but this may be due to different data set and test parameters. However, the results obtained so far indicate that the color space of the normalized color coordinates is suitable when the illumination intensity is allowed to vary in an unlimited manner. It is difficult to give a general recommendation for color modeling. The advantage of the region-based approaches is their insensitivity to the skin color distribution of the current image. On the other hand, the statistical methods can exclude the values that have lower than the selected threshold probability. The choice of statistical approach seems to be related to the application.

If skin pixels need be to detected in videos, one can usually utilize the causal relation between frames. Because the previous frame often has a close resemblance to the next frame, this can be used for tuning the skin color model for detection. Few approaches have used this relation to adapt the skin color model to the illumination change, but methods other than the skin locus have been demonstrated to fail under drastic but real lighting variations.

## Acknowledgments

The financial support of the Academy of Finland is gratefully acknowledged. We thank also the following individuals (in alphabetical order): Abdenour Hadid, Sami Huovinen, Mika Laaksonen, and Maricor Soriano.

# References

1. L.M Bergasa, M. Mazo, A. Gardel, M.A. Sotelo, and L. Boquete. Unsupervised and adaptive Gaussian skin-color model. *Image and Vision Computing*, 18(12):987-1003, 2000.
2. A. Berman and L.G. Shapiro. A flexible image database system for content-based retrieval. *Computer Vision and Image Understanding*, 72(1-2):175-195, 1999.
3. J. Brand and J.S. Mason. A comparative assessment of three approaches to pixel-level human skin-detection. In *Proceedings of International Conference on Pattern Recognition*, Barcelona, 1:5056-5059, 2000.
4. D. Brown, I. Craw, and J. Lewthwaite. A SOM based approach to skin detection with application in real time systems. In *Proceedings of the British Machine Vision Conference 2001*, University of Manchester, UK, pages 491-500, 2001.
5. T.S. Caetano, S.D. Olabarriaga, and D.A.C. Barone. Do mixture models in chromaticity space improve skin detection?. *Pattern Recognition*, 36(12):3019-3021, 2003.
6. D. Chai and K.N. Ngan. Locating facial region of a head-and-shoulders color image. In *Proceedings of 3rd International Conference on Automatic Face and Gesture Recognition*, Nara, Japan, pages 124-129, 1998.
7. K.M. Cho, J.H. Jang, and K.S. Hong. Adaptive skin-color filter. *Pattern Recognition*, 34(5):1067-1073, 2001.
8. D. Comaniciu and V. Ramesh. Robust detection and tracking of human faces with an active camera. In *Proceedings of 3rd IEEE International Workshop on Visual Surveillance*, Dublin, pages 11-18, 2000.
9. Y. Dai and Y. Nakano. Face-texture model-based on SGLD and its application in face detection in a color scene. *Pattern Recognition*, 29(6):1007-1017, 1996.
10. A.P. Dempster, N.M. Laird, and D.B. Rubin. Maximum likelihood from incomplete data via the EM algorithm. *Journal of the Royal Statistical Society: Series B. Methodological*, 39:1-38, 1977.
11. E.A. Edwards and S.Q. Duntley. The pigments and color of living human skin. *The American Journal of Anatomy*, 65(1):1-33, 1939.
12. G.D. Finlayson, S. Hordley, and P.M. Hubel. Recovering device sensitivities using quadratic programming. In *Proceedings of IS&T/SID 6th Color Imaging Conference: Color Science, Systems and Applications*, Scottsdale, Arizona, pages 90-95, 1998.
13. B. Funt, K. Barnard, and L. Martin. Is machine colour constancy good enough?. In *Proceedings of 5th European Conference on Computer Vision*, University of Freiburg, Germany, pages 445-459, 1998.
14. H.P. Graf, T. Chen, E. Petajan, and E. Cosatto. Locating faces and facial parts. In *Proceedings of 1st International Workshop Automatic Face and Gesture Recognition*, Zurich, pages 41-46, 1995.
15. L.A. Harwood. A chrominance demodulator IC with dynamic flesh correction. *IEEE Transaction on Consumer Electronics*, CE-22:111-117, 1976.
16. R.L. Hsu. *Face Detection and Modeling for Recognition*. Ph.D. thesis, Michigan State University, 2002.
17. M. Hunke and A. Waibel. Face locating and tracking for human-computer interaction. In *Proceedings of 1994 Conference Record of the Twenty-Eighth Asilomar Conference on Signals, Systems and Computers*, Pacific Grove, CA, 2:1277-1281, 1994.

18. F.H. Imai, N. Tsumura, H. Haneishi, and Y. Miyake. Principal component analysis of skin color and its application to colorimetric reproduction on CRT display and hardcopy. *Journal of Imaging Science and Technology*, 40(5):422-430, 1996.

19. B. Jedynak, H. Zheng, M. Daoudi, and D. Barret. Maximum entropy models for skin detection. Technical Report publication IRMA, 57(XIII), Universite des Sciences et Technologies de Lille, France, 2002.

20. M.J. Jones and J.M. Rehg. Statistical color models with application to skin detection. *International Journal of Computer Vision*, 46(1):81-96, 2002.

21. T. Kohonen. *Self-Organizing Maps*. Springer, New York, 1995.

22. E.J. Lee and Y.H. Ha. Automatic flesh tone reappearance for color enhancement in TV. *IEEE Transactions on Consumer Electronics*, 43(4):1153-1159, 1997.

23. E. Marszalec, B. Martinkauppi, M. Soriano, and M. Pietikäinen. A physics-based face database for color research. *Journal of Electronic Imaging*, 9(1):32-38, 2000.

24. A.M. Martinez and R. Benavente. The AR Face Database. CVC Technical Report 24. AVL, Purdue University, 1998.

25. B. Martinkauppi. *Face Colour under Varying Illumination - Analysis and Applications*. Ph.D. thesis, University of Oulu, 2002. Available at: http://herkules.oulu.fi/isbn9514267885/.

26. B. Martinkauppi, P. Sangi, M. Soriano, M. Pietikäinen, S. Huovinen, and M. Laaksonen. Illumination invariant face tracking with mean shift and skin locus. In *Proceedings of IEEE International Workshop on Cues in Communication*, Kauai, Hawaii, pages 44-49, 2001.

27. B. Martinkauppi, M. Soriano, and M. Laaksonen. Behaviour of skin color under varying illumination seen by different cameras in different color spaces. In *Proceedings of SPIE, Vol. 4301: Machine Vision in Industrial Inspection IX*, San Jose, CA, pages 102-113, 2001.

28. B. Martinkauppi, M. Soriano, and M. Pietikäinen. Detection of skin color under changing illumination: a comparative study. In *Proceedings of 12th International Conference on Image Analysis and Processing*, Mantova, Italy, pages 652-657, 2003.

29. H. Nakai, Y. Manabe, and S. Inokuchi. Simulation and analysis of spectral distribution of human skin. In *Proceedings of 14th International Conference on Pattern Recognition*, Brisbane, 2:1065-1067, 1998.

30. T. Ohtsuki and G. Healey. Using color and geometric models for extracting facial features. *Journal of Imaging Science and Technology*, 42(6):554-561, 1998.

31. T. Piirainen, O. Silvén, and V. Tuulos. Layered self-organizing maps based video content classification. In *Proceedings of Workshop on Real-time Image Sequence Analysis*, Oulu, Finland, pages 89-98, 2000.

32. Y. Raja, S.J. McKenna, and G. Gong. Tracking and segmenting people in varying lighting conditions using colour. In *Proceedings of IEEE 3rd International Conference on Automatic Face and Gesture Recognition*, Nara, Japan, pages 228-233, 1998.

33. D. Saxe and R. Foulds. Toward robust skin identification in video images. In *Proceedings of 2nd International Conference on Automatic Face and Gesture Recognition*, Killington, VT, pages 379-384, 1996.

34. B. Schiele and A. Waibel. Gaze tracking based on face-color. In *Proceedings of International Workshop on Automatic Face- and Gesture-Recognition*, Zurich, pages 344-348, 1995.

35. S.A. Shafer. Using color to separate reflection components. *Color Research and Application*, 10(4):210-218, 1985.

36. M.C. Shin, K.I. Chang, and L.V. Tsap. Does colorspace transformation make any difference on skin detection?. In *Proceedings of 6th IEEE Workshop on Applications of Computer Vision*, University of North Carolina, Charlotte, pages 275-279, 2002.

37. L.M. Son, D. Chai, and A. Bouzerdoum. A universal and robust human skin color model using neural networks. In *Proceedings of International Joint Conference on Neural Networks*, Washington, DC, 4:2844-2849, 2001.

38. M. Soriano, B. Martinkauppi, S. Huovinen, and M. Laaksonen. Adaptive skin color modeling using the skin locus for selecting training pixels. *Pattern Recognition*, 36(3):681-690, 2003.

39. M. Störring, H.J. Andersen, and E. Granum. Physics-based modelling of human skin colour under mixed illuminants. *Journal of Robotics and Autonomous Systems*, 35(3-4):131-142, 2001.

40. M. Swain and D. Ballard. Color indexing. *International Journal of Computer Vision*, 7(1):11-32, 1991.

41. J.C. Terrillon, Y. Niwa, and K. Yamamoto. On the selection of an efficient chrominance space for skin color-based image segmentation with an application to face detection. In *Proceedings of International Conference on Quality Control by Artificial Vision*, Bourgougne, France, 2:409-414, 2001.

42. J.C. Terrillon, M.N. Shirazi, H. Fukamachi, and S. Akamatsu. Comparative performance of different skin chrominance models and chrominance spaces for the automatic detection of human faces in color images. In *Proceedings of 4th IEEE International Conference on Automatic Face and Gesture Recognition*, Grenoble, France, pages 54-61, 2000.

43. S. Tominaga. Dichromatic reflection models for a variety of materials. *Color Research and Application*, 19(4):277-285, 1994.

44. L. Torres, J.Y. Reutter, and L. Lorente. The importance of the color information in face recognition. In *Proceedings of IEEE International Conference on Image Processing*, Kobe, Japan, pages 25-29, 1999.

45. C. Wang and M. Brandstein. Multi-source face tracking with audio and visual data. In *Proceedings of IEEE 3rd Workshop on Multimedia Signal Processing*, Copenhagen, pages 169-174, 1999.

46. H. Wu, Q. Chen, and M. Yachida. Face detection from color images using a fuzzy pattern matching method. *IEEE Transactions on Pattern Analysis and Machine Intelligence*, 21(6):557-563, 1999.

47. G. Wyszecki and W.S. Stiles. *Color Science Concepts and Methods, Quantitative Data and Formulae, Second Edition*. Wiley, New York, 2000.

48. M.H. Yang and N. Ahuja. Detecting human faces in color images. In *Proceedings of International Conference on Image Processing*, Chicago, 1:127-130, 1998.

49. M.H. Yang and N. Ahuja. *Face Detection and Gesture Recognition for Human-Computer Interaction*. Kluwer Academic, New York, 2001.

50. J. Yang and A. Waibel. A real-time face tracker. In *Proceedings of 3rd IEEE Workshop on Applications of Computer Vision*, Sarasota, Florida, pages 142-147, 1996.

51. T.W. Yoo and I.S. Oh. A fast algorithm for tracking human faces based on chromaticity histograms. *Pattern Recognition Letters*, 20(10):967-978, 1999.

52. B.D. Zarit, B.J. Super, and F.K.H. Quek. Comparison of five color models in skin pixel classification. In *Proceedings of International Workshop on Recognition, Analysis, and Tracking of Faces and Gestures in Real-Time Systems*, Corfu, Greece, pages 58-63, 1999.

# Color Plates for Chapters 6 and 15

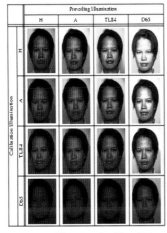

Chapter 6 : Fig. 6.1

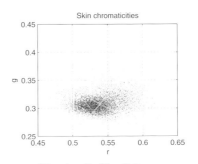

Chapter 6 : Fig. 6.2

Chapter 6 : Fig. 6.10

| | Method | | | | |
|---|---|---|---|---|---|
| | Cho et al. | Jones & Rehg Threshold 0.4 | Jones & Rehg Threshold 0.8 | Hsu | Skin locus |
| Good | | | | | |
| Bad | | | | | |

Chapter 6 : Fig. 6.11

Chapter 6 : Fig. 6.12

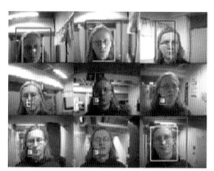

Chapter 6 : Fig. 6.13

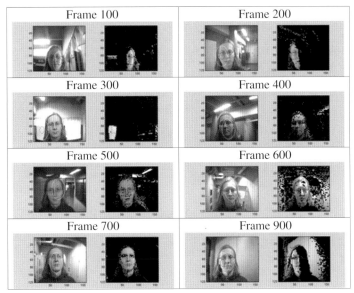

Chapter 6 : Fig. 6.15

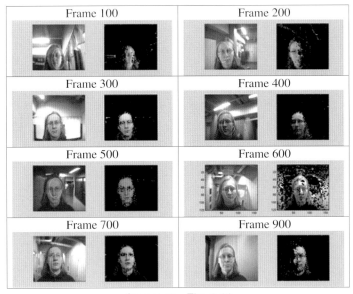

Chapter 6 : Fig. 6.16

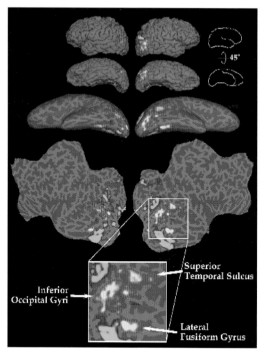

Chapter 15 : Fig. 15.9

# Chapter 7. Face Recognition in Subspaces

Gregory Shakhnarovich[1] and Baback Moghaddam[2]

[1] Computer Science and Artificial Intelligence Laboratory, MIT, Cambridge MA 02139, USA.
gregory@ai.mit.edu

[2] Mitsubishi Electric Research Labs, Cambridge MA 02139, USA. baback@merl.com

Images of faces, represented as high-dimensional pixel arrays, often belong to a manifold of intrinsically low dimension. Face recognition, and computer vision research in general, has witnessed a growing interest in techniques that capitalize on this observation and apply algebraic and statistical tools for extraction and analysis of the underlying manifold. In this chapter we describe in roughly chronologic order techniques that identify, parameterize, and analyze linear and nonlinear subspaces, from the original Eigenfaces technique to the recently introduced Bayesian method for probabilistic similarity analysis. We also discuss comparative experimental evaluation of some of these techniques as well as practical issues related to the application of subspace methods for varying pose, illumination, and expression.

## 1 Face Space and Its Dimensionality

Computer analysis of face images deals with a visual signal (light reflected off the surface of a face) that is registered by a digital sensor as an array of pixel values. The pixels may encode color or only intensity. In this chapter we assume the latter case (i.e., gray-level imagery). After proper normalization and resizing to a fixed $m$-by-$n$ size, the pixel array can be represented as a point (i.e., vector) in an $mn$-dimensional *image space* by simply writing its pixel values in a fixed (typically raster) order. A critical issue in the analysis of such multidimensional data is the *dimensionality*, the number of coordinates necessary to specify a data point. Below we discuss the factors affecting this number in the case of face images.

### 1.1 Image Space Versus Face Space

To specify an arbitrary image in the image space, one needs to specify every pixel value. Thus the "nominal" dimensionality of the space, dictated by the pixel representation, is $mn$, a high number even for images of modest size. Recognition methods that operate on this representation suffer from a number of potential disadvantages, most of them rooted in the so-called curse of dimensionality.

- Handling high-dimensional examples, especially in the context of similarity- and matching-based recognition, is computationally expensive.

- For parametric methods, the number of parameters one needs to estimate typically grows exponentially with the dimensionality. Often this number is much higher than the number of images available for training, making the estimation task in the image space ill-posed.
- Similarly, for nonparametric methods, the sample complexity–the number of examples needed to represent the underlying distribution of the data efficiently–is prohibitively high.

However, much of the surface of a face is smooth and has regular texture. Therefore, per-pixel sampling is in fact unnecessarily dense: The value of a pixel is typically highly correlated with the values of the surrounding pixels. Moreover, the appearance of faces is highly constrained; for example, any frontal view of a face is roughly symmetrical, has eyes on the sides, nose in the middle, and so on. A vast proportion of the points in the image space does not represent physically possible faces. Thus, the natural constraints dictate that the face images are in fact confined to a subspace referred to as the *face space*.

### 1.2 Principal Manifold and Basis Functions

It is common to model the face space as a (possibly disconnected) *principal manifold* embedded in the high-dimensional image space. Its *intrinsic* dimensionality is determined by the number of degrees of freedom within the face space; the goal of subspace analysis is to determine this number and to extract the *principal modes* of the manifold. The principal modes are computed as functions of the pixel values and referred to as *basis functions* of the principal manifold.

To make these concepts concrete, consider a straight line in $\mathbb{R}^3$, passing through the origin and parallel to the vector $\mathbf{a} = [a_1, a_2, a_3]^T$. Any point on the line can be described by three coordinates; nevertheless, the subspace that consists of all points on the line has a single degree of freedom, with the principal mode corresponding to translation along the direction of $\mathbf{a}$. Consequently, representing the points in this subspace requires a single basis function: $\phi(x_1, x_2, x_3) = \sum_{j=1}^{3} a_j x_j$. The analogy here is between the line and the face space and between $\mathbb{R}^3$ and the image space.

Note that, in theory, according to the described model any face image should fall in the face space. In practice, owing to sensor noise, the signal usually has a nonzero component outside the face space. This introduces uncertainty into the model and requires algebraic and statistical techniques capable of extracting the basis functions of the principal manifold in the presence of noise. In Section 1.3 we briefly describe principal component analysis, which plays an important role in many of such techniques. For a more detailed discussion, see Gerbrands [12] and Joliffe [17].

### 1.3 Principal Component Analysis

Principal component analysis (PCA) [17] is a dimensionality reduction technique based on extracting the desired number of *principal components* of the multidimensional data. The first principal component is the linear combination of the original dimensions that has the maximum variance; the $n$-th principal component is the linear combination with the highest variance, subject to being orthogonal to the $n - 1$ first principal components.

The idea of PCA is illustrated in Figure 7.1a; the axis labeled $\phi_1$ corresponds to the direction of maximum variance and is chosen as the first principal component. In a two-dimensional case, the second principal component is then determined uniquely by the orthogonality constraints; in a higher-dimensional space the selection process would continue, guided by the variances of the projections.

PCA is closely related to the Karhunen-Loève Transform (KLT) [21], which was derived in the signal processing context as the orthogonal transform with the basis $\mathbf{\Phi} = [\phi_1, \ldots, \phi_N]^T$ that for any $k \leq N$ minimizes the average $L_2$ *reconstruction error* for data points $\mathbf{x}$

$$\epsilon(\mathbf{x}) = \left\| \mathbf{x} - \sum_{i=1}^{k} \left( \phi_i^T \mathbf{x} \right) \phi_i \right\| \tag{1}$$

One can show [12] that, under the assumption that the data are zero-mean, the formulations of PCA and KLT are identical. Without loss of generality, we hereafter assume that the data are indeed zero-mean; that is, the mean face $\bar{\mathbf{x}}$ is always subtracted from the data.

The basis vectors in KLT can be calculated in the following way. Let $\mathbf{X}$ be the $N \times M$ data matrix whose columns $\mathbf{x}_1, \ldots, \mathbf{x}_M$ are *observations* of a signal embedded in $\mathbb{R}^N$; in the context of face recognition, $M$ is the number of available face images, and $N = mn$ is the number of pixels in an image. The KLT basis $\mathbf{\Phi}$ is obtained by solving the eigenvalue problem $\mathbf{\Lambda} = \mathbf{\Phi}^T \mathbf{\Sigma} \mathbf{\Phi}$, where $\mathbf{\Sigma}$ is the covariance matrix of the data

$$\mathbf{\Sigma} = \frac{1}{M} \sum_{i=1}^{M} \mathbf{x}_i \mathbf{x}_i^T \tag{2}$$

$\mathbf{\Phi} = [\phi_1, \ldots, \phi_m]^T$ is the eigenvector matrix of $\mathbf{\Sigma}$, and $\mathbf{\Lambda}$ is the diagonal matrix with eigenvalues $\lambda_1 \geq \ldots \geq \lambda_N$ of $\mathbf{\Sigma}$ on its main diagonal, so $\phi_j$ is the eigenvector corresponding to the $j$-th largest eigenvalue. Then it can be shown that the eigenvalue $\lambda_i$ is the variance of the data projected on $\phi_i$.

Thus, to perform PCA and extract $k$ principal components of the data, one must project the data onto $\mathbf{\Phi}_k$, the first $k$ columns of the KLT basis $\mathbf{\Phi}$, which correspond to the $k$ highest eigenvalues of $\mathbf{\Sigma}$. This can be seen as a linear projection $\mathbb{R}^N \to \mathbb{R}^k$, which retains the maximum energy (i.e., variance) of the signal. Another important property of PCA is that it *decorrelates* the data: the covariance matrix of $\mathbf{\Phi}_k^T \mathbf{X}$ is always diagonal.

The main properties of PCA are summarized by the following

$$\mathbf{x} \approx \mathbf{\Phi}_k \mathbf{y} , \ \mathbf{\Phi}_k^T \mathbf{\Phi}_k = \mathbf{I} , \ E\{y_i y_j\}_{i \neq j} = 0 \tag{3}$$

namely, approximate reconstruction, orthonormality of the basis $\mathbf{\Phi}_k$, and decorrelated principal components $y_i = \phi_i^T \mathbf{x}$, respectively. These properties are illustrated in Figure 7.1, where PCA is successful in finding the principal manifold, and in Figure 7.8a (see later), where it is less successful, owing to clear nonlinearity of the principal manifold.

PCA may be implemented via singular value decomposition (SVD). The SVD of an $M \times N$ matrix $\mathbf{X}$ ($M \geq N$) is given by

$$\mathbf{X} = \mathbf{U} \, \mathbf{D} \, \mathbf{V}^T \tag{4}$$

where the $M \times N$ matrix $\mathbf{U}$ and the $N \times N$ matrix $\mathbf{V}$ have orthonormal columns, and the $N \times N$ matrix $\mathbf{D}$ has the singular values[3] of $\mathbf{X}$ on its main diagonal and zero elsewhere.

---

[3] A singular value of a matrix $\mathbf{X}$ is the square root of an eigenvalue of $\mathbf{X}\mathbf{X}^T$.

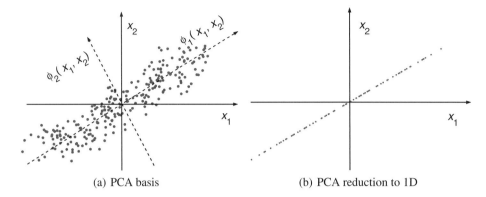

(a) PCA basis                                    (b) PCA reduction to 1D

**Fig. 7.1.** The concept of PCA/KLT. $a$. Solid lines, the original basis; dashed lines, the KLT basis. The dots are selected at regularly spaced locations on a straight line rotated at $30^\circ$ and then perturbed by isotropic 2D Gaussian noise. $b$. The projection (1D reconstruction) of the data using only the first principal component.

It can be shown that $\mathbf{U} = \mathbf{\Phi}$, so SVD allows efficient and robust computation of PCA without the need to estimate the data covariance matrix $\mathbf{\Sigma}$ (Eq. 2). When the number of examples $M$ is much smaller than the dimension $N$, this is a crucial advantage.

### 1.4 Eigenspectrum and Dimensionality

An important largely unsolved problem in dimensionality reduction is the choice of $k$, the intrinsic dimensionality of the principal manifold. No analytical derivation of this number for a complex natural visual signal is available to date. To simplify this problem, it is common to assume that in the noisy embedding of the signal of interest (in our case, a point sampled from the face space) in a high-dimensional space, the *signal-to-noise ratio* is high. Statistically, that means that the variance of the data along the principal modes of the manifold is high compared to the variance within the complementary space.

This assumption relates to the *eigenspectrum*, the set of eigenvalues of the data covariance matrix $\mathbf{\Sigma}$. Recall that the $i$-th eigenvalue is equal to the variance along the $i$-th principal component; thus, a reasonable algorithm for detecting $k$ is to search for the location along the decreasing eigenspectrum where the value of $\lambda_i$ drops significantly. A typical eigenspectrum for a face recognition problem, and the natural choice of $k$ for such a spectrum, is shown in Figure 7.3b (see later).

In practice, the choice of $k$ is also guided by computational constraints, related to the cost of matching within the extracted principal manifold and the number of available face images. See Penev and Sirovich [29] as well as Sections 2.2 and 2.4 for more discussion on this issue.

## 2 Linear Subspaces

Perhaps the simplest case of principal manifold analysis arises under the assumption that the principal manifold is linear. After the origin has been translated to the *mean face* (the average

**Fig. 7.2.** Eigenfaces: the average face on the left, followed by seven top eigenfaces. From Turk and Pentland [36], with permission.

image in the database) by subtracting it from every image, the face space is a linear subspace of the image space. In this section we describe methods that operate under this assumption and its generalization, a multilinear manifold.

## 2.1 Eigenfaces and Related Techniques

In their ground-breaking work in 1990 Kirby and Sirovich [19] proposed the use of PCA for face analysis and representation. Their paper was followed by the "eigenfaces" technique by Turk and Pentland [35], the first application of PCA to face recognition. Because the basis vectors constructed by PCA had the same dimension as the input face images, they were named "eigenfaces." Figure 7.2 shows an example of the mean face and a few of the top eigenfaces. Each face image was projected (after subtracting the mean face) into the principal subspace; the coefficients of the PCA expansion were averaged for each subject, resulting in a single $k$-dimensional representation of that subject. When a test image was projected into the subspace, Euclidean distances between its coefficient vector and those representing each subject were computed. Depending on the distance to the subject for which this distance would be minimized, and the PCA reconstruction error (Eq. 1), the image was classified as belonging to one of the familiar subjects, as a new face, or as a nonface. The latter demonstrates the dual use of subspace techniques for *detection*: When the appearance of an object class (e.g. faces) is modeled by a subspace, the distance from this subspace can serve to classify an object as a member or a nonmember of the class.

## 2.2 Probabilistic Eigenspaces

The role of PCA in the original Eigenfaces was largely confined to dimensionality reduction. The similarity between images $\mathbf{I}_1$ and $\mathbf{I}_2$ was measured in terms of the Euclidean norm of the difference $\mathbf{\Delta} = \mathbf{I}_1 - \mathbf{I}_2$ projected to the subspace, essentially ignoring the variation modes within the subspace and outside it. This was improved in the extension of eigenfaces proposed by Moghaddam and Pentland [26, 27], which uses a *probabilistic* similarity measure based on a parametric estimate of the probability density $p(\mathbf{\Delta}|\Omega)$.

A major difficulty with such estimation is that normally there are not nearly enough data to estimate the parameters of the density in a high dimensional space. Moghaddam and Pentland overcame this problem by using PCA to divide the vector space $\mathbb{R}^N$ into two subspaces, as shown in Figure 7.3: the principal subspace $F$, obtained by $\mathbf{\Phi}_k$ (the first $k$ columns of $\mathbf{\Phi}$) and its orthogonal complement $\bar{F}$ spanned by the remaining columns of $\mathbf{\Phi}$. The operating assumption here is that the data have intrinsic dimensionality $k$ (at most) and thus reside in $F$, with the exception of additive white Gaussian noise within $\bar{F}$. Every image can be decomposed into

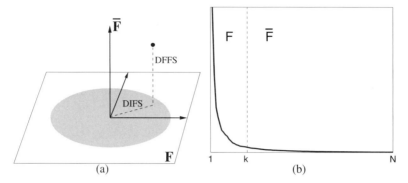

**Fig. 7.3.** *a*. Decomposition of $\mathbb{R}^N$ into the principal subspace $F$ and its orthogonal complement $\bar{F}$ for a Gaussian density. *b*. Typical eigenvalue spectrum and its division into the two orthogonal subspaces.

two orthogonal components by projection into these two spaces. Figure 7.3a shows the decomposition of $\Delta$ into distance *within* face space (DIFS) and the distance *from* face space (DFFS). Moreover, the probability density can be decomposed into two orthogonal components.

$$P(\Delta|\Omega) = P_F(\Delta|\Omega) \cdot P_{\bar{F}}(\Delta|\Omega) \tag{5}$$

In the simplest case, $P(\Delta|\Omega)$ is a Gaussian density. As derived by Moghaddam and Pentland [26], the complete likelihood estimate in this case can be written as the product of two independent marginal Gaussian densities

$$\hat{P}(\Delta|\Omega) = \left[ \frac{\exp\left(-\frac{1}{2}\sum_{i=1}^{k}\frac{y_i^2}{\lambda_i}\right)}{(2\pi)^{k/2}\prod_{i=1}^{k}\lambda_i^{1/2}} \right] \cdot \left[ \frac{\exp\left(-\frac{\epsilon^2(\Delta)}{2\rho}\right)}{(2\pi\rho)^{(N-k)/2}} \right] \tag{6}$$

$$= P_F(\Delta|\Omega)\,\hat{P}_{\bar{F}}(\Delta|\Omega;\rho)$$

where $P_F(\Delta|\Omega)$ is the true marginal density in $F$; $\hat{P}_{\bar{F}}(\Delta|\Omega;\rho)$ is the estimated marginal density in $\bar{F}$; $y_i = \phi_i^T\Delta$ are the principal components of $\Delta$; and $\epsilon(\Delta)$ is the PCA reconstruction error (Eq. 1). The information-theoretical optimal value for the noise density parameter $\rho$ is derived by minimizing the Kullback-Leibler (KL) divergence [8] and can be shown to be simply the average of the $N - k$ smallest eigenvalues

$$\rho = \frac{1}{N-k}\sum_{i=k+1}^{N}\lambda_i \tag{7}$$

This is a special case of the recent, more general factor analysis model called probabilistic PCA (PPCA) proposed by Tipping and Bishop [34]. In their formulation, the above expression for

$\rho$ is the maximum-likelihood solution of a latent variable model in contrast to the minimal-divergence solution derived by Moghaddam and Pentland [26].

In practice, most of the eigenvalues in $\bar{F}$ cannot be computed owing to insufficient data, but they can be estimated, for example, by fitting a nonlinear function to the available portion of the eigenvalue spectrum and estimating the average of the eigenvalues beyond the principal subspace. Fractal power law spectra of the form $f^{-n}$ are thought to be typical of "natural" phenomenon and are often a good fit to the decaying nature of the eigenspectrum, as illustrated by Figure 7.3b.

In this probabilistic framework, the recognition of a test image $\mathbf{x}$ is carried out in terms of computing for every database example $\mathbf{x}_i$ the difference $\mathbf{\Delta} = \mathbf{x} - \mathbf{x}_i$ and its decomposition into the $F$ and $\bar{F}$ components and then ranking the examples according to the value in Eq. (6).

## 2.3 Linear Discriminants: Fisherfaces

When substantial changes in illumination and expression are present, much of the variation in the data is due to these changes. The PCA techniques essentially select a subspace that retains most of that variation, and consequently the similarity in the face space is not necessarily determined by the identity.

Belhumeur et al. [2] propose to solve this problem with "Fisherfaces", an application of Fisher's linear discriminant (FLD). FLD selects the linear subspace $\mathbf{\Phi}$, which maximizes the ratio

$$\frac{\left|\mathbf{\Phi}^T \mathbf{S_b} \mathbf{\Phi}\right|}{\left|\mathbf{\Phi}^T \mathbf{S_w} \mathbf{\Phi}\right|} \tag{8}$$

where

$$\mathbf{S_b} = \sum_{i=1}^{m} N_i (\bar{\mathbf{x}}_i - \bar{\mathbf{x}})(\bar{\mathbf{x}}_i - \bar{\mathbf{x}})^T$$

is the *between-class* scatter matrix, and

$$\mathbf{S_w} = \sum_{i=1}^{m} \sum_{\mathbf{x} \in \mathbf{X}_i} (\mathbf{x} - \bar{\mathbf{x}}_i)(\mathbf{x} - \bar{\mathbf{x}}_i)^T$$

is the *within-class* scatter matrix; $m$ is the number of subjects (classes) in the database. Intuitively, FLD finds the projection of the data in which the classes are most linearly separable. It can be shown that the dimension of $\mathbf{\Phi}$ is at most $m - 1$.[4]

Because in practice $\mathbf{S_w}$ is usually singular, the Fisherfaces algorithm first reduces the dimensionality of the data with PCA so Eq.(8) can be computed and then applies FLD to further reduce the dimensionality to $m - 1$. The recognition is then accomplished by a NN classifier in this final subspace. The experiments reported by Belhumeur et al. [2] were performed on data sets containing frontal face images of 5 people with drastic lighting variations and another set with faces of 16 people with varying expressions and again drastic illumination changes. In all the reported experiments Fisherfaces achieve a lower error rate than eigenfaces.

---

[4] For comparison, note that the objective of PCA can be seen as maximizing the total scatter across all the images in the database.

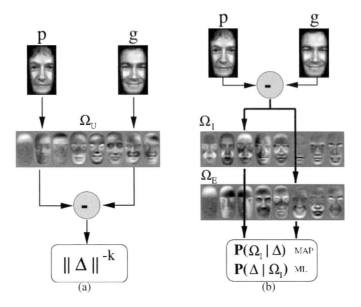

**Fig. 7.4.** Signal flow diagrams for computing the similarity g between two images. *a*. Original eigenfaces. *b*. Bayesian similarity. The difference image is projected through both sets of (intra/extra) eigenfaces to obtain the two likelihoods.

### 2.4 Bayesian Methods

Consider now a feature space of $\boldsymbol{\Delta}$ vectors, the differences between two images ($\boldsymbol{\Delta} = \mathbf{I}_j - \mathbf{I}_k$). One can define two classes of facial image variations: *intrapersonal* variations $\Omega_I$ (corresponding, for example, to different facial expressions and illuminations of the *same* individual) and *extrapersonal* variations $\Omega_E$ (corresponding to variations between *different* individuals). The similarity measure $S(\boldsymbol{\Delta})$ can then be expressed in terms of the intrapersonal *a posteriori* probability of $\boldsymbol{\Delta}$ belonging to $\Omega_I$ given by the Bayes rule.

$$S(\boldsymbol{\Delta}) \;=\; P(\Omega_I|\boldsymbol{\Delta}) \;=\; \frac{P(\boldsymbol{\Delta}|\Omega_I)P(\Omega_I)}{P(\boldsymbol{\Delta}|\Omega_I)P(\Omega_I) + P(\boldsymbol{\Delta}|\Omega_E)P(\Omega_E)} \tag{9}$$

Note that this particular Bayesian formulation, proposed by Moghaddam et al [25], casts the standard face recognition task (essentially an $m$-ary classification problem for $m$ individuals) into a *binary* pattern classification problem with $\Omega_I$ and $\Omega_E$.

The densities of both classes are modeled as high-dimensional Gaussians, using an efficient PCA-based method described in Section 2.2.

$$P(\boldsymbol{\Delta}|\Omega_E) = \frac{e^{-\frac{1}{2}\boldsymbol{\Delta}^T \Sigma_E^{-1} \boldsymbol{\Delta}}}{(2\pi)^{D/2}|\Sigma_E|^{1/2}}$$

$$P(\boldsymbol{\Delta}|\Omega_I) = \frac{e^{-\frac{1}{2}\boldsymbol{\Delta}^T \Sigma_I^{-1} \boldsymbol{\Delta}}}{(2\pi)^{D/2}|\Sigma_I|^{1/2}} \tag{10}$$

These densities are zero-mean, because for each $\mathbf{\Delta} = \mathbf{I}_j - \mathbf{I}_i$ there exists a $\mathbf{I}_i - \mathbf{I}_j$.

By PCA, the Gaussians are known to occupy only a subspace of image space (face space); thus, only the top few eigenvectors of the Gaussian densities are relevant for modeling. These densities are used to evaluate the similarity in Eq. (9). Computing the similarity involves first subtracting a candidate image $\mathbf{I}$ from a database example $\mathbf{I}_j$. The resulting $\mathbf{\Delta}$ image is then projected onto the eigenvectors of the extrapersonal Gaussian and also the eigenvectors of the intrapersonal Gaussian. The exponentials are computed, normalized, and then combined as in Eq. (9). This operation is iterated over all examples in the database, and the example that achieves the maximum score is considered the match. For large databases, such evaluations are expensive and it is desirable to simplify them by off-line transformations.

To compute the likelihoods $P(\mathbf{\Delta}|\Omega_I)$ and $P(\mathbf{\Delta}|\Omega_E)$, the database images $\mathbf{I}_j$ are pre-processed with *whitening* transformations [11]. Each image is converted and stored as a set of two whitened subspace coefficients: $\mathbf{y}_{\Phi_I}$ for intrapersonal space and $\mathbf{y}_{\Phi_E}$ for extrapersonal space

$$\mathbf{y}_{\Phi_I}^j = \mathbf{\Lambda}_I^{-\frac{1}{2}} \mathbf{V}_I \mathbf{I}_j \ , \qquad \mathbf{y}_{\Phi_E}^j = \mathbf{\Lambda}_E^{-\frac{1}{2}} \mathbf{V}_E \mathbf{I}_j \tag{11}$$

where $\mathbf{\Lambda}_X$ and $\mathbf{V}_X$ are matrices of the largest eigenvalues and eigenvectors, respectively, of $\mathbf{\Sigma}_X$ ($X$ being a substituting symbol for $I$ or $E$).

After this preprocessing, evaluating the Gaussians can be reduced to simple Euclidean distances as in Eq. (12). Denominators are of course precomputed. These likelihoods are evaluated and used to compute the *maximum a posteriori* (MAP) similarity $S(\mathbf{\Delta})$ in Eq. (9). Euclidean distances are computed between the $k_I$-dimensional $\mathbf{y}_{\Phi_I}$ vectors as well as the $k_E$-dimensional $\mathbf{y}_{\Phi_E}$ vectors. Thus, roughly $2 \times (k_E + k_I)$ arithmetic operations are required for each similarity computation, avoiding repeated image differencing and projections

$$P(\mathbf{\Delta}|\Omega_I) = P(\mathbf{I} - \mathbf{I}_j|\Omega_I) = \frac{e^{-\|\mathbf{y}_{\Phi_I} - \mathbf{y}_{\Phi_I}^j\|^2/2}}{(2\pi)^{k_I/2}|\mathbf{\Sigma}_I|^{1/2}}$$

$$P(\mathbf{\Delta}|\Omega_E) = P(\mathbf{I} - \mathbf{I}_j|\Omega_E) = \frac{e^{-\|\mathbf{y}_{\Phi_E} - \mathbf{y}_{\Phi_E}^j\|^2/2}}{(2\pi)^{k_E/2}|\mathbf{\Sigma}_E|^{1/2}} \tag{12}$$

The *maximum likelihood* (ML) similarity matching is even simpler, as only the intrapersonal class is evaluated, leading to the following modified form for the similarity measure.

$$S'(\mathbf{\Delta}) = P(\mathbf{\Delta}|\Omega_I) = \frac{e^{-\|\mathbf{y}_{\Phi_I} - \mathbf{y}_{\Phi_I}^j\|^2/2}}{(2\pi)^{k_I/2}|\mathbf{\Sigma}_I|^{1/2}} \tag{13}$$

The approach described above requires two projections of the difference vector $\mathbf{\Delta}$, from which likelihoods can be estimated for the Bayesian similarity measure. The computation flow is illustrated in Figure 7.4b. The projection steps are linear while the posterior computation is nonlinear. Because of the double PCA projections required, this approach has been called a "dual eigenspace" technique. Note the projection of the difference vector $\mathbf{\Delta}$ onto the "dual eigenfaces" ($\Omega_I$ and $\Omega_E$) for computation of the posterior in Eq. (9).

It is instructive to compare and contrast LDA (Fisherfaces) and the dual subspace technique by noting the similar roles of the between-class/within-class and extrapersonal/intrapersonal

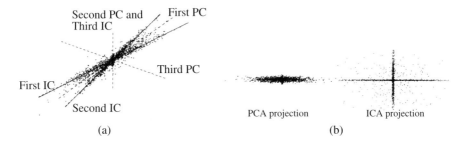

**Fig. 7.5.** ICA vs. PCA decomposition of a 3D data set. *a*. the bases of PCA (orthogonal) and ICA (non-orthogonal). *b*. Left: the projection of the data onto the top two principal components (PCA). Right: the projection onto the top two independent components (ICA). (From Bartlett et al. [1], with permission.)

subspaces. One such analysis was presented by Wang and Tang [39] where PCA, LDA, and Bayesian methods were "unified" under a three-parameter subspace method. Ultimately, the optimal probabilistic justification of LDA is for the case of two Gaussian distributions of equal covariance (although LDA tends to perform rather well even when this condition is not strictly true). In contrast, the dual formulation is entirely general and probabilistic by definition, and it makes no appeals to geometry, Gaussianity, or symmetry of the underlying data or, in fact, the two "meta classes" (intra-, and extrapersonal). These two probability distributions can take on any form (e.g., arbitrary mixture models), not just single Gaussians, although the latter case does make for easy visualization by diagonalizing the dual covariances as two sets of "eigenfaces".

### 2.5 Independent Component Analysis and Source Separation

While PCA minimizes the sample covariance (second-order dependence) of the data, independent component analysis (ICA) [6, 18] minimizes higher-order dependencies as well, and the components found by ICA are designed to be non-Gaussian. Like PCA, ICA yields a linear projection $\mathbb{R}^N \to \mathbb{R}^M$ but with different properties

$$\mathbf{x} \approx \mathbf{A}\mathbf{y} \,, \ \mathbf{A}^T\mathbf{A} \neq \mathbf{I} \,, \ P(\mathbf{y}) \approx \prod p(y_i) \tag{14}$$

that is, approximate reconstruction, *nonorthogonality* of the basis $\mathbf{A}$, and the near-factorization of the joint distribution $P(\mathbf{y})$ into marginal distributions of the (non-Gaussian) ICs.

An example of ICA basis is shown in Figure 7.5, where it is computed from a set of 3D points. The 2D subspace recovered by ICA appears to reflect the distribution of the data much better than the subspace obtained with PCA. Another example of an ICA basis is shown in Figure 7.8b where we see two unordered nonorthogonal IC vectors, one of which is roughly aligned with the first principal component vector in Figure 7.8a (see later), (i.e., the direction of maximum variance). Note that the actual non-Gaussianity and statistical independence achieved in this toy example are minimal at best, and so is the success of ICA in recovering the principal modes of the data.

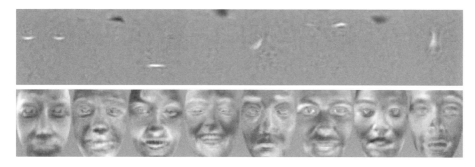

**Fig. 7.6.** Basis images obtained with ICA: Architecture I (*top*) and II (*bottom*). (From Draper et al. [10], with permission.)

ICA is intimately related to the *blind source separation* problem: decomposition of the input signal (image) $\mathbf{x}$ into a linear combination (mixture) of independent source signals. Formally, the assumption is that $\mathbf{x}^T = \mathbf{A}\mathbf{s}^T$, with $\mathbf{A}$ the unknown mixing matrix. ICA algorithms [5] try to find $\mathbf{A}$ or the *separating matrix* $\mathbf{W}$ such that $\mathbf{u}^T = \mathbf{W}\mathbf{x}^T = \mathbf{W}\mathbf{A}\mathbf{s}^T$. When the data consist of $M$ observations with $N$ variables, the input to ICA is arranged in an $N \times M$ matrix $\mathbf{X}$.

Bartlett et al. [1, 10] investigated the use of ICA framework for face recognition in two fundamentally different architectures:

**Architecture I** Rows of $\mathbf{S}$ are *independent basis images*, which combined by $\mathbf{A}$ yield the input images $\mathbf{X}$. Learning $\mathbf{W}$ allows us to estimate the basis images in the rows of $\mathbf{U}$. In practice, for reasons of computational tractability, PCA is first performed on the input data $\mathbf{X}$ to find the top $K$ eigenfaces; these are arranged in the columns of a matrix $\mathbf{E}$.[6] Then ICA is performed on $\mathbf{E}^T$; that is, the images are variables, and the pixel values are observations. Let $\mathbf{C}$ be the PCA coefficient matrix, that is, $\mathbf{X} = \mathbf{C}\mathbf{E}^T$. Then the $k$ independent ICA basis images (Fig. 7.6, top) are estimated by the rows of $\mathbf{U} = \mathbf{W}\mathbf{E}^T$, and the coefficients for the data are computed from $\mathbf{X} = \mathbf{E}\mathbf{W}^{-1}\mathbf{U}$.

**Architecture II** This architecture assumes that the sources in $\mathbf{S}$ are independent coefficients, and the columns of the mixing matrix $\mathbf{A}$ are the basis images; that is, the variables in the source separation problem are the pixels. Similar to Architecture I, ICA is preceded by PCA; however, in this case the input to ICA is the coefficient matrix $\mathbf{C}$. The resulting ICA basis consists of the columns of $\mathbf{E}\mathbf{A}$ (Fig. 7.6, bottom), and the coefficients are found in the rows of $\mathbf{U} = \mathbf{W}\mathbf{C}^T$. These coefficients give the *factorial representation* of the data.

Generally, the bases obtained with Architecture I reflect more local properties of the faces, whereas the bases in Architecture II have global properties and much more resemble faces (Fig. 7.6).

---

[5] A number of algorithms exist; most notable are Jade [5], InfoMax, and FastICA [16].

[6] These eigenfaces are linear combination of the original images, which under the assumptions of ICA should not affect the resulting decomposition.

## 2.6 Multilinear SVD: "Tensorfaces"

The linear analysis methods discussed above have been shown to be suitable when pose, illumination, or expression are fixed across the face database. When any of these parameters is allowed to vary, the linear subspace representation does not capture this variation well (see Section 5.1). In Section 3 we discuss recognition with nonlinear subspaces. An alternative, *multilinear* approach, called "tensorfaces," has been proposed by Vasilescu and Terzopoulos in [37, 38].

Tensor is a multidimensional generalization of a matrix: a *n-order tensor* $\mathcal{A}$ is an object with $n$ indices, with elements denoted by $a_{i_1,\ldots,i_n} \in \mathbb{R}$. Note that there are $n$ ways to *flatten* this tensor (i.e., to rearrange the elements in a matrix): The $i$-th row of $\mathcal{A}_{(s)}$ is obtained by concatenating all the elements of $\mathcal{A}$ of the form $a_{i_1,\ldots,i_{s-1},i,i_{s+1},\ldots,i_n}$.

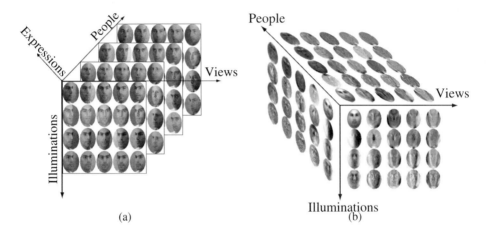

(a)    (b)

**Fig. 7.7.** Tensorfaces. *a*. Data tensor; the four dimensions visualized are identity, illumination, pose, and the pixel vector. The fifth dimension corresponds to expression (only the subtensor for neutral expression is shown). *b*. Tensorfaces decomposition. (From Vasilescu and Terzopoulos [37], with permission.)

A generalization of matrix multiplication for tensors is the *l-mode* product $\mathcal{A} \times_l \mathbf{M}$ of a tensor $\mathcal{A}$ and an $m \times k$ matrix $\mathbf{M}$, where $k$ is the $l$-th dimension of $\mathcal{A}$.

$$(\mathcal{A} \times_l \mathbf{M})_{i_1,\ldots i_{l-1},j,i_{l+1},\ldots i_n} = \sum_{i=1}^{k} a_{i_1,\ldots i_{l-1},i,i_{l+1},\ldots i_n} m_{ji} \tag{15}$$

Under this definition, Vasilescu and Terzopoulos [38] proposed an algorithm they called *n-mode SVD*, which decomposes an $n$-dimensional tensor $\mathcal{A}$ into

$$\mathcal{A} = \mathcal{Z} \times_1 \mathbf{U}_1 \times_2 \mathbf{U}_2 \cdots \times_n \mathbf{U}_n \tag{16}$$

The role of the *core tensor* $\mathcal{Z}$ in this decomposition is similar to the role of the singular value matrix $\mathbf{\Sigma}$ in SVD (Eq. 4): It governs the interactions between the *mode matrices* $\mathbf{U}_1, \ldots, \mathbf{U}_n$, which contain the orthonormal bases for the spaces spanned by the corresponding dimensions of the data tensor. The mode matrices can be obtained by flattening the tensor across the corresponding dimension and performing PCA on the columns of the resulting matrix; then the core tensor is computed as

$$\mathcal{Z} \; = \; \mathcal{A} \times_1 \mathbf{U}_1^T \times_2 \mathbf{U}_2^T \cdots \times_N \mathbf{U}_n^T$$

The notion of tensor can be applied to a face image ensemble in the following way [38]: Consider a set of $N$-pixel images of $N_p$ people's faces, each photographed in $N_v$ viewpoints, with $N_i$ illuminations and $N_e$ expressions. The entire set may be arranged in an $N_p \times N_v \times N_i \times N_e \times N$ tensor of order 5. Figure 7.7a illustrates this concept: Only four dimensions are shown; to visualize the fifth one (expression), imagine that the four-dimensional tensors for different expressions are "stacked."

In this context, the face image tensor can be decomposed into

$$\mathcal{A} \; = \; \mathcal{Z} \times_1 \mathbf{U}_p \times_2 \mathbf{U}_v \times_3 \mathbf{U}_i \times_4 \mathbf{U}_e \times_5 \mathbf{U}_{\text{pixels}} \tag{17}$$

Each mode matrix represents a parameter of the object appearance. For example, the columns of the $N_e \times N_e$ matrix $\mathbf{U}_e$ span the space of expression parameters. The columns of $\mathbf{U}_{\text{pixels}}$ span the image space; these are exactly the eigenfaces that would be obtained by direct PCA on the entire data set.

Each person in the database can be represented by a single $N_p$ vector, which contains coefficients with respect to the bases comprising the tensor

$$\mathcal{B} \; = \; \mathcal{Z} \times_2 \mathbf{U}_v \times_3 \mathbf{U}_i \times_4 \mathbf{U}_e \times_5 \mathbf{U}_{\text{pixels}}$$

For a given viewpoint $v$, illumination $i$, and expression $e$, an $N_p \times N$ matrix $\mathbf{B}_{v,i,e}$ can be obtained by indexing into $\mathcal{B}$ for $v, i, e$ and flattening the resulting $N_p \times 1 \times 1 \times 1 \times N$ subtensor along the identity (people) mode. Now a training image $\mathbf{x}_{p,v,e,i}$ of a person $j$ under the given conditions can be written as

$$\mathbf{x}_{p,v,e,i} \; = \; \mathbf{B}_{v,i,e}^T \, \mathbf{c}_p \tag{18}$$

where $\mathbf{c}_j$ is the $j$-th row vector of $\mathbf{U}_p$.

Given an input image $\mathbf{x}$, a candidate coefficient vector $\mathbf{c}_{v,i,e}$ is computed for all combinations of viewpoint, expression, and illumination, solving Eq. (18). The recognition is carried out by finding the value of $j$ that yields the minimum Euclidean distance between $\mathbf{c}$ and the vectors $\mathbf{c}_j$ across all illuminations, expressions and viewpoints.[7]

Vasilescu and Terzopoulos [38] reported experiments involving the data tensor consisting of images of $N_p = 28$ subjects photographed in $N_i = 3$ illumination conditions from $N_v = 5$ viewpoints, with $N_e = 3$ different expressions; the images were resized and cropped so they contain $N = 7493$ pixels. The performance of tensorfaces is reported to be significantly better than that of standard eigenfaces described in Section 2.1.

## 3 Nonlinear Subspaces

In this section we describe a number of techniques that do not assume that the principal manifold is linear.

---

[7] This also provides an estimate of the parameters (e.g., illumination) for the input image.

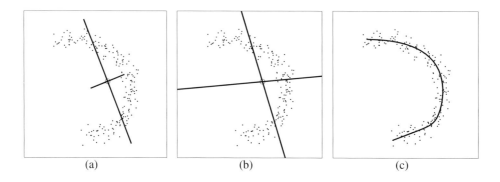

(a)                              (b)                              (c)

**Fig. 7.8.** *a*. PCA basis (linear, ordered, and orthogonal) *b*. ICA basis (linear, unordered, and nonorthogonal), *c*. Principal curve (parameterized nonlinear manifold). The circle shows the data mean.

### 3.1 Principal Curves and Nonlinear PCA

The defining property of nonlinear principal manifolds is that the *inverse image* of the manifold in the original space $\mathbb{R}^N$ is a nonlinear (curved) lower-dimensional surface that "passes through the middle of the data" while minimizing the sum total distance between the data points and their projections on that surface. Often referred to as *principal curves* [14], this formulation is essentially a nonlinear regression on the data. An example of a principal curve is shown in Figure 7.8c.

   One of the simplest methods for computing nonlinear principal manifolds is the nonlinear PCA (NLPCA) autoencoder multilayer neural network [9, 20] shown in Figure 7.9. The "bottleneck" layer forms a lower-dimensional manifold representation by means of a nonlinear *projection* function $f(\mathbf{x})$, implemented as a weighted sum-of-sigmoids. The resulting principal components $\mathbf{y}$ have an inverse mapping with a similar nonlinear *reconstruction* function $g(\mathbf{y})$, which reproduces the input data as accurately as possible. The NLPCA computed by such a multilayer sigmoidal neural network is equivalent (with certain exceptions[8]) to a *principal surface* under the more general definition [13, 14]. To summarize, the main properties of NLPCA are

$$\mathbf{y} = f(\mathbf{x}) \ , \ \mathbf{x} \approx g(\mathbf{y}) \ , \ P(\mathbf{y}) = ? \tag{19}$$

corresponding to nonlinear projection, approximate reconstruction, and typically no prior knowledge regarding the joint distribution of the components, respectively (however, see Zemel and Hinton [43] for an example of devising suitable priors in such cases). The principal curve in Figure 7.8c was generated with a 2-4-1-4-2 layer neural network of the type shown in Figure 7.9. Note how the principal curve yields a compact, relatively accurate representation of the data, in contrast to the linear models (PCA and ICA).

---

[8] The class of functions attainable by this neural network restricts the projection function $f()$ to be smooth and differentiable, and hence suboptimal in some cases [22].

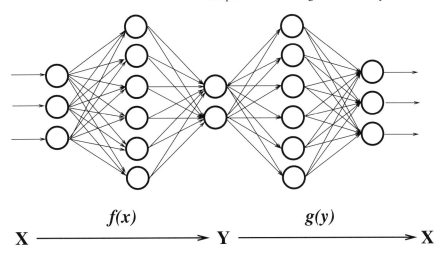

$f(x)$ $g(y)$

**X** ──────────────► **Y** ──────────────► **X**

**Fig. 7.9.** Autoassociative ("bottleneck") neural network for computing principal manifolds $\mathbf{y} \in \mathbb{R}^k$ in the input space $\mathbf{x} \in \mathbb{R}^N$.

### 3.2 Kernel-PCA and Kernel-Fisher Methods

Recently nonlinear principal component analysis has been revived with the "kernel eigenvalue" method of Schölkopf et al. [32]. The basic methodology of KPCA is to apply a nonlinear mapping to the input $\Psi(\mathbf{x}) : \mathbb{R}^N \to \mathbb{R}^L$ and then solve for a linear PCA in the resulting feature space $\mathbb{R}^L$, where $L$ is larger than $N$ and possibly infinite. Because of this increase in dimensionality, the mapping $\Psi(\mathbf{x})$ is made implicit (and economical) by the use of kernel functions satisfying Mercer's theorem [7]

$$k(\mathbf{x_i}, \mathbf{x_j}) = [\Psi(\mathbf{x_i}) \cdot \Psi(\mathbf{x_j})] \tag{20}$$

where kernel evaluations $k(\mathbf{x_i}, \mathbf{x_j})$ in the input space correspond to dot-products in the higher dimensional feature space. Because computing covariance is based on dot-products, performing a PCA in the feature space can be formulated with kernels in the input space without the explicit (and possibly prohibitively expensive) direct computation of $\Psi(\mathbf{x})$. Specifically, assuming that the projection of the data in feature space is zero-mean ("centered"), the covariance is given by

$$\Sigma_K = \ < \Psi(\mathbf{x_i}), \Psi(\mathbf{x_i})^T > \tag{21}$$

with the resulting eigenvector equation $\lambda \mathbf{V} = \Sigma_K \mathbf{V}$. Since the eigenvectors (columns of $\mathbf{V}$) must lie in the span of the training data $\Psi(\mathbf{x_i})$, it must be true that for each training point

$$\lambda(\Psi(\mathbf{x_i}) \cdot \mathbf{V}) = (\Psi(\mathbf{x_i}) \cdot \Sigma_K \mathbf{V}) \ \text{ for } i = 1, \dots T \tag{22}$$

and that there must exist coefficients $\{w_i\}$ such that

$$\mathbf{V} = \sum_{i=1}^{T} w_i \Psi(\mathbf{x_i}) \tag{23}$$

Using the definition of $\Sigma_K$, substituting the above equation into Eq. 22 and defining the resulting $T$-by-$T$ matrix $\mathbf{K}$ by $\mathbf{K}_{ij} = [\Psi(\mathbf{x_i}) \cdot \Psi(\mathbf{x_j})]$ leads to the equivalent eigenvalue problem formulated in terms of kernels in the input space

$$T\lambda\mathbf{w} \;=\; \mathbf{Kw} \qquad (24)$$

where $\mathbf{w} = (w_1, ..., w_T)^T$ is the vector of expansion coefficients of a given eigenvector $\mathbf{V}$ as defined in Eq. (23). The kernel matrix $\mathbf{K}_{ij} = k(\mathbf{x_i}, \mathbf{x_j})$ is then diagonalized with a standard PCA[9]. Orthonormality of the eigenvectors, $(\mathbf{V}^n \cdot \mathbf{V}^n) = 1$, leads to the equivalent normalization of their respective expansion coefficients, $\lambda_n(\mathbf{w}^n \cdot \mathbf{w}^n) = 1$.

Subsequently, the KPCA principal components of any input vector can be efficiently computed with simple kernel evaluations against the dataset. The $n$-th principal component $y_n$ of $\mathbf{x}$ is given by

$$y_n \;=\; (\mathbf{V}_n \cdot \Psi(\mathbf{x})) \;=\; \sum_{i=1}^{T} w_i^n \, k(\mathbf{x}, \mathbf{x_i}) \qquad (25)$$

where $\mathbf{V}_n$ is the $n$-th eigenvector of the feature space defined by $\Psi$. As with PCA, the eigenvectors $\mathbf{V}_n$ can be ranked by decreasing order of their eigenvalues $\lambda_n$ and a $d$-dimensional manifold projection of $\mathbf{x}$ is $\mathbf{y} = (y_1, ..., y_d)^T$, with individual components defined by Eq. (25).

A significant advantage of KPCA over neural network and principal curves is that KPCA does not require nonlinear optimization, is not subject to overfitting, and does not require prior knowledge of network architecture or the number of dimensions. Furthermore, unlike traditional PCA, one can use more eigenvector projections than the input dimensionality of the data (because KPCA is based on the matrix $\mathbf{K}$, the number of eigenvectors or features available is $T$). On the other hand, the selection of the optimal kernel (and its associated parameters) remains an "engineering problem." Typical kernels include Gaussians $\exp(-\|\mathbf{x_i} - \mathbf{x_j}\|)^2/\sigma^2)$, polynomials $(\mathbf{x_i} \cdot \mathbf{x_j})^d$ and sigmoids $\tanh(a(\mathbf{x_i} \cdot \mathbf{x_j}) + b)$, all of which satisfy Mercer's theorem [7].

Similar to the derivation of KPCA, one may extend the Fisherfaces method (see Section 2.3) by applying the FLD in the feature space. Yang [42] derived the kernel Fisherfaces algorithm, which maximizes the between-scatter to within-scatter ratio in the feature space through the use of the kernel matrix $\mathbf{K}$. In experiments on two data sets that contained images from 40 and 11 subjects, respectively, with varying pose, scale, and illumination, this algorithm showed performance clearly superior to that of ICA, PCA, and KPCA and somewhat better than that of the standard Fisherfaces.

## 4 Empirical Comparison of Subspace Methods

Moghaddam [23] reported on an extensive evaluation of many of the subspace methods described above on a large subset of the FERET data set [31] (see also Chapter 13). The experimental data consisted of a training "gallery" of 706 individual FERET faces and 1123 "probe"

---

[9] However, computing $\Sigma_K$ in Eq. (21) requires "centering" the data by computing the mean of $\Psi(\mathbf{x_i})$. Because there is no explicit computation of $\Psi(\mathbf{x_i})$, the equivalent must be carried out when computing the kernel matrix $\mathbf{K}$. For details on "centering" $\mathbf{K}$, see Schölkopf et al [32].

images containing one or more views of every person in the gallery. All these images were aligned and normalized as described by Moghaddam and Pentland [27]. The multiple probe images reflected various expressions, lighting, glasses on/off, and so on. The study compared the Bayesian approach described in Section 2.4 to a number of other techniques and tested the limits of the recognition algorithms with respect to image resolution or equivalently the amount of visible facial detail. Because the Bayesian algorithm was independently evaluated in DARPA's 1996 FERET face recognition competition [31] with medium resolution images ($84 \times 44$ pixels)—achieving an accuracy of $\approx 95\%$ on $O(10^3)$ individuals—it was decided to lower the resolution (the number of pixels) by a factor 16. Therefore, the aligned faces in the data set were downsampled to $21 \times 12$ pixels, yielding input vectors in a $\mathbb{R}^{N=252}$ space. Several examples are shown in Figure 7.10a,b.

The reported results were obtained with a fivefold Cross-Validation (CV) analysis. The total data set of 1829 faces (706 unique individuals and their collective 1123 probes) was randomly partitioned into five subsets with unique (nonoverlapping) individuals and their associated probes. Each subset contained both gallery and probe images of $\approx 140$ unique individuals. For each of the five subsets, the recognition task was correctly matching the multiple probes to the $\approx 140$ gallery faces using the other four subsets as training data. Note that with $N = 252$ and using 80% of the entire dataset for training, there are nearly three times as many training samples than the data dimensionality; thus, parameter estimations (for PCA, ICA, KPCA, and the Bayesian method) were properly overconstrained.

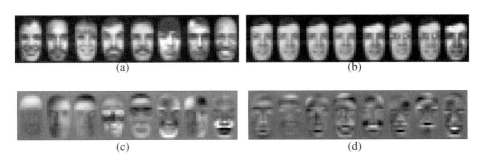

**Fig. 7.10.** Experiments on FERET data. $a$. Several faces from the gallery. $b$. Multiple probes for one individual, with different facial expressions, eyeglasses, variable ambient lighting, and image contrast. $c$. Eigenfaces. $d$. ICA basis images.

The resulting five experimental trials were pooled to compute the mean and standard deviation of the recognition rates for each method. The fact that the training and testing sets had no overlap in terms of individual identities led to an evaluation of the algorithms' *generalization* performance—the ability to recognize new individuals who were not part of the manifold computation or density modeling with the training set.

The baseline recognition experiments used a default manifold dimensionality of $k = 20$. This choice of $k$ was made for two reasons: It led to a reasonable PCA reconstruction error of MSE = 0.0012 (or 0.12% per pixel with a normalized intensity range of [0,1]) and a baseline PCA recognition rate of $\approx 80\%$ (on a different 50/50 partition of the dataset), thereby leaving a sizable margin for improvement. Note that because the recognition experiments were essentially a 140-way classification task, chance performance was approximately 0.7%.

### 4.1 PCA-Based Recognition

The baseline algorithm for these face recognition experiments was standard PCA (eigenface) matching. The first eight principal eigenvectors computed from a single partition are shown in Figure 7.10c. Projection of the test set probes onto the 20-dimensional linear manifold (computed with PCA on the training set only) followed by nearest-neighbor matching to the $\approx 140$ gallery images using a Euclidean metric yielded a mean recognition rate of 77.31%, with the highest rate achieved being 79.62% (Table 7.1). The full image-vector nearest-neighbor (template matching) (i.e., on $\mathbf{x} \in \mathbb{R}^{252}$) yielded a recognition rate of 86.46% (see dashed line in Figure 7.11). Clearly, performance is degraded by the $252 \rightarrow 20$ dimensionality reduction, as expected.

### 4.2 ICA-Based Recognition

For ICA-based recognition (Architecture II, see Section 2.5) two algorithms based on fourth-order cumulants were tried: the "JADE" algorithm of Cardoso [5] and the fixed-point algorithm of Hyvärinen and Oja [15]. In both algorithms a PCA whitening step ("sphering") preceded the core ICA decomposition. The corresponding *nonorthogonal* JADE-derived ICA basis is shown in Figure 7.10d. Similar basis faces were obtained with the method of Hyvärinen and Oja. These basis faces are the columns of the matrix $\mathbf{A}$ in Eq. (14), and their linear combination (specified by the ICs) reconstructs the training data. The ICA manifold projection of the test set was obtained using $\mathbf{y} = \mathbf{A}^{-1}\mathbf{x}$. Nearest-neighbor matching with ICA using the Euclidean $L_2$ norm resulted in a mean recognition rate of 77.30% with the highest rate being 82.90% (Table 7.1). We found little difference between the two ICA algorithms and noted that ICA resulted in the largest performance variation in the five trials (7.66% SD). Based on the mean recognition rates it is unclear whether ICA provides a systematic advantage over PCA or whether "more non-Gaussian" and/or "more independent" components result in a better manifold for *recognition* purposes with this dataset.

Note that the experimental results of Bartlett et al. [1] with FERET faces did favor ICA over PCA. This seeming disagreement can be reconciled if one considers the differences in the experimental setup and in the choice of the similarity measure. First, the advantage of ICA was seen primarily with more difficult time-separated images. In addition, compared to the results of Bartlett et al. [1] the faces in this experiment were cropped much tighter, leaving no information regarding hair and face shape, and they were much lower in resolution, factors that when combined make the recognition task much more difficult.

The second factor is the choice of the distance function used to measure similarity in the subspace. This matter was further investigated by Draper et al. [10]. They found that the best results for ICA are obtained using the cosine distance, whereas for eigenfaces the $L_1$ metric appears to be optimal; with $L_2$ metric, which was also used in the experiments of Moghaddam [23], the performance of ICA (Architecture II) was similar to that of eigenfaces.

**Table 7.1.** Recognition accuracies with $k = 20$ subspace projections using fivefold cross validation. Results are in percents

| Partition | PCA | ICA | KPCA | Bayes |
|-----------|-----|-----|------|-------|
| 1 | 78.00 | 82.90 | 83.26 | 95.46 |
| 2 | 79.62 | 77.29 | 92.37 | 97.87 |
| 3 | 78.59 | 79.19 | 88.52 | 94.49 |
| 4 | 76.39 | 82.84 | 85.96 | 92.90 |
| 5 | 73.96 | 64.29 | 86.57 | 93.45 |
| Mean | 77.31 | 77.30 | 87.34 | 94.83 |
| SD | 2.21 | 7.66 | 3.39 | 1.96 |

**Table 7.2.** Comparison of the subspace techniques across multiple attributes ($k = 20$).

|  | PCA | ICA | KPCA | Bayes |
|--|-----|-----|------|-------|
| Accuracy | 77% | 77% | 87% | 95% |
| Computation | $10^8$ | $10^9$ | $10^9$ | $10^8$ |
| Uniqueness | Yes | No | Yes | Yes |
| Projections | Linear | Linear | Nonlinear | Linear |

### 4.3 KPCA-Based Recognition

For KPCA, the parameters of Gaussian, polynomial, and sigmoidal kernels were first fine-tuned for best performance with a different 50/50 partition validation set, and Gaussian kernels were found to be the best for this data set. For each trial, the kernel matrix was computed from the corresponding training data. Both the test set gallery and probes were projected onto the kernel eigenvector basis (Eq. 25) to obtain the nonlinear principal components which were then used in nearest-neighbor matching of test set probes against the test set gallery images. The mean recognition rate was found to be 87.34%, with the highest rate being 92.37% (Table 7.1). The standard deviation of the KPCA trials was slightly higher (3.39) than that of PCA (2.21), but Figure 7.11 indicates that KPCA does in fact do better than both PCA and ICA, hence justifying the use of nonlinear feature extraction.

### 4.4 MAP-Based Recognition

For Bayesian similarity matching, appropriate training $\mathbf{\Delta}$s for the two classes $\Omega_I$ (Fig. 7.10b) and $\Omega_E$ (Fig. 7.10a) were used for the dual PCA-based density estimates $P(\mathbf{\Delta}|\Omega_I)$ and $P(\mathbf{\Delta}|\Omega_E)$, which were both modeled as single Gaussians with subspace dimensions of $k_I$ and $k_E$, respectively. The total subspace dimensionality $k$ was divided evenly between the two densities by setting $k_I = k_E = k/2$ for modeling.[10]

---

[10] In practice, $k_I > k_E$ often works just as well. In fact as $k_E \to 0$, one obtains a maximum-likelihood similarity $S = P(\mathbf{\Delta}|\Omega_I)$ with $k_I = k$, which for this data set is only a few percent less accurate than MAP [24].

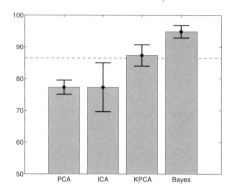

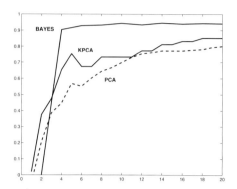

**Fig. 7.11.** Recognition performance of PCA, ICA, and KPCA manifolds versus Bayesian (MAP) similarity matching with a $k = 20$ dimensional subspace. Dashed line indicates the performance of nearest-neighbor matching with the full-dimensional image vectors.

**Fig. 7.12.** Recognition accuracy $R(k)$ of PCA, KPCA, and Bayesian similarity with increasing dimensionality $k$ of the principal subspace. ICA results, not shown, are similar to those of PCA.

With $k = 20$, Gaussian subspace dimensions of $k_I = 10$ and $k_E = 10$ were used for $P(\Delta|\Omega_I)$ and $P(\Delta|\Omega_E)$, respectively. Note that $k_I + k_E = 20$, thus matching the total number of projections used with the three principal manifold techniques. Using the maximum *a posteriori* (MAP) similarity in Eq. (9), the Bayesian matching technique yielded a mean recognition rate of 94.83%, with the highest rate achieved being 97.87% (Table 7.1). The standard deviation of the five partitions for this algorithm was also the lowest (1.96) (Fig 7.11).

### 4.5 Compactness of Manifolds

The performance of various methods with different size manifolds can be compared by plotting their recognition rates $R(k)$ as a function of the first $k$ principal components. For the manifold matching techniques, this simply means using a subspace dimension of $k$ (the first $k$ components of PCA/ICA/KPCA), whereas for the Bayesian matching technique this means that the subspace Gaussian dimensions should satisfy $k_I + k_E = k$. Thus all methods used the same number of subspace projections. This test was the premise for one of the key points investigated by Moghaddam [23]: Given the *same* number of subspace projections, which of these techniques is better at data modeling and subsequent recognition? The presumption is that the one achieving the highest recognition rate with the smallest dimension is preferred.

For this particular dimensionality test, the total data set of 1829 images was partitioned (split) in half: a training set of 353 gallery images (randomly selected) along with their corresponding 594 probes and a testing set containing the remaining 353 gallery images and their corresponding 529 probes. The training and test sets had no overlap in terms of individuals' identities. As in the previous experiments, the test set probes were matched to the test set gallery images based on the projections (or densities) computed with the training set. The results of this experiment are shown in Figure 7.12, which plots the recognition rates as a function of the dimensionality of the subspace $k$. This is a more revealing comparison of the relative performance of the methods, as *compactness* of the manifolds—defined by the lowest acceptable value of $k$—is an important consideration in regard to both generalization error (overfitting) and computational requirements.

### 4.6 Discussion

The relative performance of the principal manifold techniques and Bayesian matching is summarized in Table 7.1 and Figure 7.11. The advantage of probabilistic matching over metric matching on both linear and nonlinear manifolds is quite evident ($\approx$18% increase over PCA and $\approx$8% over KPCA). Note that the dimensionality test results in Figure 7.12 indicate that KPCA outperforms PCA by a $\approx$10% margin, and even more so with only few principal components (a similar effect was reported by Schölkopf et al. [32] where KPCA outperforms PCA in low-dimensional manifolds). However, Bayesian matching achieves $\approx$ 90% with only four projections—two for each $P(\Delta|\Omega)$—and dominates both PCA and KPCA throughout the entire range of subspace dimensions in Figure 7.12.

A comparison of the subspace techniques with respect to multiple criteria is shown in Table 7.2. Note that PCA, KPCA, and the dual subspace density estimation are uniquely defined for a given training set (making experimental comparisons repeatable), whereas ICA is not unique owing to the variety of techniques used to compute the basis and the iterative (stochastic) optimizations involved. Considering the relative computation (of training), KPCA required $\approx 7 \times 10^9$ floating-point operations compared to PCA's $\approx 2 \times 10^8$ operations. On the average, ICA computation was one order of magnitude larger than that of PCA. Because the Bayesian similarity method's learning stage involves two separate PCAs, its computation is merely twice that of PCA (the same order of magnitude).

Considering its significant performance advantage (at low subspace dimensionality) and its relative simplicity, the dual-eigenface Bayesian matching method is a highly effective subspace modeling technique for face recognition. In independent FERET tests conducted by the U.S. Army Laboratory [31], the Bayesian similarity technique outperformed PCA and other subspace techniques, such as Fisher's linear discriminant (by a margin of at least 10%). Experimental results described above show that a similar recognition accuracy can be achieved using mere "thumbnails" with 16 times fewer pixels than in the images used in the FERET test. These results demonstrate the Bayesian matching technique's robustness with respect to image resolution, revealing the surprisingly small amount of facial detail required for high accuracy performance with this learning technique.

## 5 Methodology and Usage

In this section we discuss issues that require special care from the practitioner, in particular, the approaches designed to handle database with varying imaging conditions. We also present a number of extensions and modifications of the subspace methods.

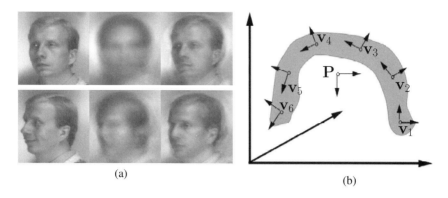

(a)                                                    (b)

**Fig. 7.13.** Parametric versus view-based eigenspace methods. *a.* Reconstructions of the input image (left) with parametric (middle) and view-based (right) eigenspaces. Top: training image; bottom: novel (test) image. *b.* Difference in the way the two approaches span the manifold.

## 5.1 Multiple View-based Approach for Pose

The problem of face recognition under general viewing conditions (change in pose) can also be approached using an eigenspace formulation. There are essentially two ways to approach this problem using an eigenspace framework. Given $M$ individuals under $C$ different views, one can do recognition and pose estimation in a universal eigenspace computed from the combination of $MC$ images. In this way, a single parametric eigenspace encodes identity as well as pose. Such an approach, for example, has been used by Murase and Nayar [28] for general 3D object recognition.

Alternatively, given $M$ individuals under $C$ different views, we can build a view-based set of $C$ distinct eigenspaces, each capturing the variation of the $M$ individuals in a common view. The view-based eigenspace is essentially an extension of the eigenface technique to multiple sets of eigenvectors, one for each combination of scale and orientation. One can view this architecture as a set of parallel observers, each trying to explain the image data with their set of eigenvectors. In this view-based, multiple-observer approach, the first step is to determine the location and orientation of the target object by selecting the eigenspace that best describes the input image. This can be accomplished by calculating the likelihood estimate using each viewspace's eigenvectors and then selecting the maximum.

The key difference between the view-based and parametric representations can be understood by considering the geometry of face space, illustrated in Figure 7.13b. In the high-dimensional vector space of an input image, multiple-orientation training images are represented by a set of $C$ distinct regions, each defined by the scatter of $M$ individuals. Multiple views of a face form nonconvex (yet connected) regions in image space [3]. Therefore, the resulting ensemble is a highly complex and nonseparable manifold.

The parametric eigenspace attempts to describe this ensemble with a projection onto a single low-dimensional linear subspace (corresponding to the first $k$ eigenvectors of the $MC$ training images). In contrast, the view-based approach corresponds to $C$ independent subspaces, each describing a particular region of the face space (corresponding to a particular view of a face).

**Fig. 7.14.** Multiview face image data used in the experiments described in Section 5.1. (From Moghaddam and Pentland [27], with permission.)

The principal manifold $\mathbf{v}_c$ of each region $c$ is extracted separately. The relevant analogy here is that of modeling a complex distribution by a single cluster model or by the union of several component clusters. Naturally, the latter (view-based) representation can yield a more accurate representation of the underlying geometry.

This difference in representation becomes evident when considering the quality of reconstructed images using the two methods. Figure 7.13 compares reconstructions obtained with the two methods when trained on images of faces at multiple orientations. In the top row of Figure 7.13a, we see first an image in the training set, followed by reconstructions of this image using first the parametric eigenspace and then the view-based eigenspace. Note that in the parametric reconstruction, neither the pose nor the identity of the individual is adequately captured. The view-based reconstruction, on the other hand, provides a much better characterization of the object. Similarly, in the bottom row of Figure 7.13a, we see a novel view ($+68^o$) with respect to the training set ($-90^o$ to $+45^o$). Here, both reconstructions correspond to the nearest view in the training set ($+45^o$), but the view-based reconstruction is seen to be more representative of the individual's identity. Although the quality of the reconstruction is not a direct indicator of the recognition power, from an information-theoretical point-of-view, the multiple eigenspace representation is a more accurate representation of the signal content.

The view-based approach was evaluated [27] on data similar to that shown in Figure 7.14 which consisted of 189 images: nine views of 21 people. The viewpoints were evenly spaced from $-90^o$ to $+90^o$ along the horizontal plane. In the first series of experiments, the interpolation performance was tested by training on a subset of the available views ($\pm90^o$, $\pm45^o$, $0^o$) and testing on the intermediate views ($\pm68^o$, $\pm23^o$). A 90% average recognition rate was obtained. A second series of experiments tested the extrapolation performance by training on a range of views (e.g., $-90^o$ to $+45^o$) and testing on novel views outside the training range (e.g., $+68^o$ and $+90^o$). For testing views separated by $\pm23^o$ from the training range, the average recognition rate was 83%. For $\pm45^o$ testing views, the average recognition rate was 50%.

## 5.2 Modular Recognition

The eigenface recognition method is easily extended to facial features [30], as shown in Figure 7.15a. This leads to an improvement in recognition performance by incorporating an addi-

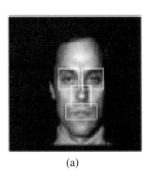

(a)

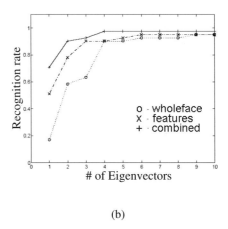

(b)

**Fig. 7.15.** Modular eigenspaces. *a*. Rectangular patches whose appearance is modeled with eigenfeatures. *b*. Performance of eigenfaces, eigenfeatures, and the layered combination of both as a function of subspace dimension. (From Pentland et al. [30], with permission.)

tional layer of description in terms of facial features. This can be viewed as either a modular or layered representation of a face, where a coarse (low-resolution) description of the whole head is augmented by additional (higher resolution) details in terms of salient facial features. Pentland et al. [30] called the latter component *eigenfeatures*. The utility of this layered representation (eigenface plus eigenfeatures) was tested on a small subset of a large face database: a representative sample of 45 individuals with two views per person, corresponding to different facial expressions (neutral vs. smiling). This set of images was partitioned into a training set (neutral) and a testing set (smiling). Because the difference between these particular facial expressions is primarily articulated in the mouth, this feature was discarded for recognition purposes.

Figure 7.15b shows the recognition rates as a function of the number of eigenvectors for eigenface-only, eigenfeature only, and the combined representation. What is surprising is that (for this small dataset at least) the eigenfeatures alone were sufficient to achieve an (asymptotic) recognition rate of 95% (equal to that of the eigenfaces).

More surprising, perhaps, is the observation that in the lower dimensions of eigenspace eigenfeatures outperformed the eigenface recognition. Finally, by using the combined representation, one gains a slight improvement in the asymptotic recognition rate (98%). A similar effect was reported by Brunelli and Poggio [4], where the cumulative normalized correlation scores of templates for the face, eyes, nose, and mouth showed improved performance over the face-only templates.

A potential advantage of the eigenfeature layer is the ability to overcome the shortcomings of the standard eigenface method. A pure eigenface recognition system can be fooled by gross variations in the input image (e.g., hats, beards). However, the feature-based representation may still find the correct match by focusing on the characteristic nonoccluded features (e.g., the eyes and nose).

## 5.3 Recognition with Sets

An interesting recognition paradigm involves the scenario in which the input consists not of a single image but of a *set* of images of an unknown person. The set may consist of a contiguous *sequence* of frames from a video or a noncontiguous, perhaps unordered, set of photographs extracted from a video or obtained from individual snapshots. The former case is discussed in Chapter 8 (recognition from video). In the latter case, which we consider here, no temporal information is available. A possible approach, and in fact the one often taken until recently, has been to apply standard recognition methods to every image in the input set and then combine the results, typically by means of voting.

However, a large set of images contains more information than every individual image in it: It provides clues not only on the possible appearance on one's face but also on the typical patterns of variation. Technically, just as a set of images known to contain an individual's face allows one to represent that individual by an estimated intrinsic subspace, so the unlabeled input set leads to a subspace estimate that represents the unknown subject. The recognition task can then be formulated in terms of matching the subspaces.

One of the first approaches to this task has been the mutual subspace method (MSM) [41], which extracts the principal linear subspace of fixed dimension (via PCA) and measures the distance between subspaces by means of *principal angles* (the minimal angle between any two vectors in the subspaces). MSM has the desirable feature that it builds a compact model of the distribution of observations. However, it ignores important statistical characteristics of the data, as the eigenvalues corresponding to the principal components, as well as the means of the samples, are disregarded in the comparison. Thus its decisions may be statistically suboptimal.

A probabilistic approach to measuring subspace similarity has been proposed [33]. The underlying statistical model assumes that images of the $j$-th person's face have probability density $p_j$; the density of the unknown subject's face is denoted by $p_0$. The task of the recognition system is then to find the class label $j^*$, satisfying

$$j^* = \operatorname*{argmax}_{j} \Pr(p_0 = p_j) \qquad (26)$$

Therefore, given a set of images distributed by $p_0$, solving Eq. (26) amounts to choosing optimally between $M$ hypotheses of the form in statistics is sometimes referred to as the two-sample hypothesis: that two sets of examples come from the same distribution. A principled way to solve this task is to choose the hypothesis $j$ for which the *Kullback-Leibler divergence* between $p_0$ and $p_j$ is minimized.

In reality, the distributions $p_j$ are unknown and must be estimated from data, as well as $p_0$. Shakhnarovich et al. [33] modeled these distributions as Gaussians (one per subject), which are estimated according to the method described in Section 2.2. The KL divergence is then computed in closed form. In the experiments reported by these authors [33], this method significantly outperformed the MSM.

Modeling the distributions by a single Gaussian is somewhat limiting; Wolf and Shashua [40] extended this approach and proposed a nonparametric discriminative method: *kernel principal angles*. They devised a positive definite kernel that operates on pairs of data matrices by projecting the data (columns) into a feature space of arbitrary dimension, in which principal angles can be calculated by computing inner products between the examples (i.e., application of the kernel). Note that this approach corresponds to nonlinear subspace analysis in the original space;

for instance, one can use polynomial kernels of arbitrary degree. In experiments that included a face recognition task on a set of nine subjects, this method significantly outperformed both MSM and the Gaussian-based KL-divergence model of Shakhnarovich et al. [33].

# 6 Conclusion

Subspace methods have been shown to be highly successful in face recognition, as they have in many other vision tasks. The exposition in this chapter roughly follows the chronologic order in which these methods have evolved. Two most notable directions in this evolution can be discerned: (1) the transition from linear to general, possibly nonlinear, and disconnected manifolds; and (2) the introduction of probabilistic and specifically Bayesian methods for dealing with the uncertainty and with similarity. All of these methods share the same core assumption: that ostensibly complex visual phenomena such as images of human faces, represented in a high-dimensional measurement space, are often intrinsically low-dimensional. Exploiting this low dimensionality allows a face recognition system to simplify computations and to focus the attention on the features of the data relevant for the identity of a person.

# Acknowledgments

We thank M.S. Bartlett and M.A.O. Vasilescu for kind permission to use figures from their published work and for their comments. We also acknowledge all who contributed to the research described in this chapter.

# References

1. M. Bartlett, H. Lades, and T. Sejnowski. Independent component representations for face recognition. In *Proceedings of the SPIE: Conference on Human Vision and Electronic Imaging III*, volume 3299, pages 528–539, 1998.
2. V. Belhumeur, J. Hespanha, and D. Kriegman. Eigenfaces vs. Fisherfaces: Recognition using class specific linear projection. *IEEE Transactions on Pattern Analysis and Machine Intelligence*, 19(7):711–720, July 1997.
3. M. Bichsel and A. Pentland. Human face recognition and the face image set's topology. *CVGIP: Image Understanding*, 59(2):254–261, 1994.
4. R. Brunelli and T. Poggio. Face recognition: Features vs. templates. *IEEE Transactions on Pattern Analysis and Machine Intelligence*, 15(10):1042–1052, 1993.
5. J.-F. Cardoso. High-order contrasts for independent component analysis. *Neural Computation*, 11(1):157–192, 1999.
6. P. Comon. Independent component analysis - a new concept? *Signal Processing*, 36:287–314, 1994.
7. R. Courant and D. Hilbert. *Methods of Mathematical Physics*, volume 1. Interscience, New-York, 1953.
8. M. Cover and J. Thomas. *Elements of Information Theory*. Wiley & Sons, New York, 1994.
9. D. DeMers and G. Cottrell. Nonlinear dimensionality reduction. In *Advances in Neural Information Processing Systems*, pages 580–587, San Francisco, 1993. Morgan Kaufmann.

10. B. A. Draper, K. Baek, M. S. Bartlett, and J. R. Beveridge. Recognizing faces with PCA and ICA. *Computer Vision and Image Understanding*, 91(1–2):115–137, July/Aug. 2003.

11. K. Fukunaga. *Introduction to Statistical Pattern Recognition*. Academic, San Diego, 2nd edition, 1990.

12. J. J. Gerbrands. On the relationships between SVD, KLT and PCA. *Pattern Recognition*, 14:375–381, 1981.

13. T. Hastie. *Principal Curves and Surfaces*. PhD thesis, Stanford University, 1984.

14. T. Hastie and W. Stuetzle. Principal curves. *Journal of the American Statistical Association*, 84(406):502–516, 1989.

15. A. Hyvärinen and E. Oja. A family of fixed-point algorithms for independent component analysis. Technical Report A40, Helsinki University of Technology, 1996.

16. A. Hyvärinen and E. Oja. Independent component analysis: algorithms and applications. *Neural Networks*, 13(4-5):411–430, 2000.

17. I. T. Jolliffe. *Principal Component Analysis*. Springer, New York, 1986.

18. C. Jutten and J. Herault. Blind separation of sources, part I: An adaptive algorithm based on neuromimetic architecture. *Signal Processing*, 24:1–10, 1991.

19. M. Kirby and L. Sirovich. Application of the Karhunen-Loéve procedure for the characterization of human faces. *IEEE Transactions on Pattern Analysis and Machine Intelligence*, 12(1):103–108, Jan. 1990.

20. M. A. Kramer. Nonlinear principal components analysis using autoassociative neural networks. *AIChE Journal*, 32(2):233–243, 1991.

21. M. M. Loève. *Probability Theory*. Van Nostrand, Princeton, 1955.

22. E. C. Malthouse. Some theoretical results on nonlinear principal component analysis. Technical report, Northwestern University, 1998.

23. B. Moghaddam. Principal manifolds and bayesian subspaces for visual recognition. *IEEE Transactions on Pattern Analysis and Machine Intelligence*, 24(6):780–788, June 2002.

24. B. Moghaddam, T. Jebara, and A. Pentland. Efficient MAP/ML similarity matching for face recognition. In *Proceedings of International Conference on Pattern Recognition*, pages 876–881, Brisbane, Australia, Aug. 1998.

25. B. Moghaddam, T. Jebara, and A. Pentland. Bayesian face recognition. *Pattern Recognition*, 33(11):1771–1782, Nov. 2000.

26. B. Moghaddam and A. Pentland. Probabilistic visual learning for object detection. In *Proceedings of IEEE International Conference on Computer Vision*, pages 786–793, Cambridge, MA, June 1995.

27. B. Moghaddam and A. Pentland. Probabilistic visual learning for object representation. *IEEE Transactions on Pattern Analysis and Machine Intelligence*, 19(7):696–710, July 1997.

28. H. Murase and S. K. Nayar. Visual learning and recognition of 3D objects from appearance. *International Journal of Computer Vision*, 14(1):5–24, Jan. 1995.

29. P. Penev and L.Sirovich. The global dimensionality of face space. In *Proc. of IEEE Internation Conf. on Face and Gesture Recognition*, pages 264–270, Grenoble, France, 2000.

30. A. Pentland, B. Moghaddam, and T. Starner. View-based and modular eigenspaces for face recognition. In *Proceedings of IEEE Computer Vision and Pattern Recognition*, pages 84–91, Seattle, WA, June 1994. IEEE Computer Society Press.

31. P. J. Phillips, H. Moon, P. Rauss, and S. Rizvi. The FERET evaluation methodology for face-recognition algorithms. In *Proceedings of IEEE Computer Vision and Pattern Recognition*, pages 137–143, June 1997.

32. B. Schölkopf, A. Smola, and K.-R. Muller. Nonlinear component analysis as a kernel eigenvalue problem. *Neural Computation*, 10(5):1299–1319, 1998.

33. G. Shakhnarovich, J. W. Fisher, and T. Darrell. Face recognition from long-term observations. In *Proceedings of European Conference on Computer Vision*, pages 851–865, Copenhagen, Denmark, May 2002.

34. M. Tipping and C. Bishop. Probabilistic principal component analysis. Technical Report NCRG/97/010, Aston University, Sept. 1997.
35. M. Turk and A. Pentland. Eigenfaces for recognition. *Journal of Cognitive Neuroscience*, 3(1):71–86, 1991.
36. M. Turk and A. Pentland. Face recognition using eigenfaces. In *Proceedings of IEEE Computer Vision and Pattern Recognition*, pages 586–590, Maui, Hawaii, Dec. 1991.
37. M. Vasilescu and D. Terzopoulos. Multilinear Subspace Analysis of Image Ensembles. In *Proceedings of IEEE Computer Vision and Pattern Recognition*, pages 93–99, Madison, WI, June 2003.
38. M. A. O. Vasilescu and D. Terzopoulos. Multilinear analysis of image ensembles: TensorFaces. In *Proceedings of European Conference on Computer Vision*, pages 447–460, Copenhagen, Denmark, May 2002.
39. X. Wang and X. Tang. Unified subspace analysis for face recognition. In *Proceedings of IEEE International Conference on Computer Vision*, pages 318–323, Nice, France, Oct. 2003.
40. L. Wolf and A. Shashua. Learning over Sets using Kernel Principal Angles. *Journal of Machine Learning Research*, 4:913–931, Oct. 2003.
41. O. Yamaguchi, K. Fukui, and K.-i. Maeda. Face recognition using temporal image sequence. In *Proc. of IEEE Internation Conf. on Face and Gesture Recognition*, pages 318–323, Nara, Japan, Apr. 1998.
42. M.-H. Yang. Kernel eigenfaces vs. kernel fisherfaces: Face recognition using kernel methods. In *Proc. of IEEE Internation Conf. on Face and Gesture Recognition*, pages 215–220, Washington, DC, May 2002.
43. R. S. Zemel and G. E. Hinton. Developing population codes by minimizing description length. In J. D. Cowan, G. Tesauro, and J. Alspector, editors, *Advances in Neural Information Processing Systems*, volume 6, pages 11–18, San Francisco, 1994. Morgan Kaufmann.

# Chapter 8. Face Tracking and Recognition from Video

Rama Chellappa and Shaohua Kevin Zhou

Center for Automation Research   Siemens Corporate Research
University of Maryland            755 College Road East
College Park, MD 20742, USA      Princeton, NJ 08540, USA
rama@cfar.umd.edu                kzhou@scr.siemens.com

Most face recognition algorithms take still images as probe inputs. This chapter presents a video-based face recognition approach that takes video sequences as inputs. Because the detected face might be moving in the video sequence, we inevitably have to deal with uncertainty in tracking as well as in recognition. Rather than resolving these two uncertainties separately, our strategy is to perform simultaneous tracking and recognition of human faces from a video sequence.

In general, a video sequence is a collection of still images; so still-image-based recognition algorithms can always be applied. An important property of a video sequence is its temporal continuity. Although this property has been exploited for tracking, it has not been used for recognition. In this chapter, we systematically investigate how temporal continuity can be incorporated for video-based recognition.

Our probabilistic approach solves still-to-video recognition, where the gallery consists of still images and the probes are video sequences. A time series state space model is proposed to fuse temporal information in a probe video, which simultaneously characterizes the kinematics and identity using a motion vector and an identity variable, respectively. The joint posterior distribution of the motion vector and the identity variable is estimated at each time instant and then propagated to the next time instant. Marginalization over the motion vector yields a robust estimate of the posterior distribution of the identity variable. A computationally efficient sequential importance sampling (SIS) algorithm is used to estimate the posterior distribution. Empirical results demonstrate that, owing to the propagation of the identity variable over time, degeneracy in posterior probability of the identity variable is achieved.

The organization of the chapter is as follows: Section 1 sets the framework for face recognition in video. Section 2 covers in detail all the components of the simultaneous tracking and recognition approach. Section 3 presents some techniques for enhancing tracking and recognition accuracy via modeling interframe appearance and appearance changes between video frames and gallery images. Section 4 addresses future research issues and discussion.

# 1 Review

Probabilistic video analysis has recently gained significant attention in the computer vision community since the seminal work of Isard and Blake [16]. In their effort to solve the problem of visual tracking, they introduced a time series state space model parameterized by a tracking motion vector (e.g., affine transformation parameters), denoted by $\theta_t$. The CONDENSATION algorithm was developed to provide a numerical approximation to the posterior distribution of the motion vector at time $t$ given the observations up to $t$ [i.e., $p(\theta_t|z_{0:t})$ where $z_{0:t} = (z_0, z_1, \ldots, z_t)$ and $z_t$ is the observation at time $t$] and to propagate it over time according to the kinematics. The CONDENSATION algorithm, also known as the particle filter, was originally proposed [14] in the signal processing literature and has been used to solve many other vision tasks [5, 28], including human face recognition [22]. In this chapter, we systematically investigate the application of the particle filter for face recognition in a video sequence.

Face recognition has been an active research area for a long time. Refer to Chellappa *et al.* [8] and Zhao *et al.* [34] for surveys and Phillips *et al.* [27] for reports on experiments. Experiments reported in [27] evaluated still-to-still scenarios, where the gallery and the probe set consist of both still facial images. Some well-known still-to-still face recognition approaches include principal component analysis [33], linear discriminant analysis [3, 13], and elastic graph matching [20]. Typically, recognition is performed based on an abstract representation of the face image after suitable geometric and photometric transformations and corrections.

Following Phillips *et al.* [27], we define a still-to-video scenario as follows. The gallery consists of still facial templates, and the probe set consists of video sequences containing the facial region. Denote the gallery as $\mathcal{I} = \{I_1, I_2, \ldots, I_N\}$, indexed by the identity variable $n$, which lies in a finite sample space $\mathcal{N} = \{1, 2, \ldots, N\}$. Though significant research has been conducted on still-to-still recognition, research efforts on still-to-video recognition are relatively fewer owing to the following challenges [34] in typical surveillance applications: poor video quality, significant illumination and pose variations, and low image resolution. Most existing video-based recognition systems [9, 34] attempt the following: The face is first detected and then tracked over time. Only when a frame satisfying certain criteria (size, pose) is acquired is recognition performed using still-to-still recognition technique. For this, the face part is cropped from the frame and transformed or registered using appropriate transformations. This tracking-then-recognition approach attempts to resolve uncertainties in tracking and recognition sequentially and separately and requires a criterion for selecting good frames and estimation of parameters for registration. Also, still-to-still recognition does not effectively exploit temporal information.

To overcome these difficulties, we propose a tracking-and-recognition approach that attempts to resolve uncertainties in tracking and recognition simultaneously in a unified probabilistic framework. To fuse temporal information, the time series state space model is adopted to characterize the evolving kinematics and identity in the probe video. Three basic components of the model are the following.

- A motion equation governing the kinematic behavior of the tracking motion vector
- An identity equation governing the temporal evolution of the identity variable
- An observation equation establishing a link between the motion vector and the identity variable

Using the SIS [12, 19, 23] technique, the joint posterior distribution of the motion vector and the identity variable [i.e., $p(n_t, \theta_t | z_{0:t})$] is estimated at each time instant and then propagated to the next time instant governed by motion and identity equations. The marginal distribution of the identity variable [i.e., $p(n_t | z_{0:t})$] is estimated to provide the recognition result. An SIS algorithm is presented to approximate the distribution $p(n_t | z_{0:t})$ in the still-to-video scenario. It achieves computational efficiency over its CONDENSATION counterpart by considering the discrete nature of the identity variable.

It is worth emphasizing that (1) our model can take advantage of any still-to-still recognition algorithm [3, 13, 20, 33] by embedding distance measures used therein in our likelihood measurement; and (2) it allows a variety of image representations and transformations. Section 3 presents an enhancement technique that incorporates more sophisticated appearance-based models. The appearance models are used for tracking (modeling interframe appearance changes) and recognition (modeling appearance changes between video frames and gallery images), respectively. Table 8.1 summarizes the proposed approach and others in terms of using temporal information.

| Process | Function | Use of temporal information |
|---|---|---|
| Visual tracking | Modeling the interframe differences | In tracking |
| Visual recognition | Modeling the difference between probe and gallery images | Not related |
| Tracking then recognition | Combining tracking and recognition sequentially | Only in tracking |
| Tracking and recognition | Unifying tracking and recognition | In both tracking and recognition |

**Table 8.1.** Summary of the proposed approach and other methods.

## 2 Simultaneous Tracking and Recognition from Video

In this section, we first present the details on the propagation model for recognition and discuss its impact on the posterior distribution of identity variable. We then proceed to solve the model using the SIS algorithms.

### 2.1 Time Series State Space Model for Recognition

The recognition model consists of the following components.

- *Motion equation*
  In its most general form, the motion model can be written as

$$\theta_t = g(\theta_{t-1}, u_t); \quad t \geq 1 \tag{1}$$

where $u_t$ is noise in the motion model, whose distribution determines the motion state transition probability $p(\theta_t | \theta_{t-1})$. The function $g(.,.)$ characterizes the evolving motion, and it could be a function learned offline or given a priori. One of the simplest choices is an additive function (i.e., $\theta_t = \theta_{t-1} + u_t$), which leads to a first-order Markov chain.

The choice of $\theta_t$ is dependent on the application. Affine motion parameters are often used when there is no significant pose variation available in the video sequence. However, if a three-dimensional (3D) face model is used, 3D motion parameters should be used accordingly.

- *Identity equation*
  Assuming that the identity does not change as time proceeds, we have

$$n_t = n_{t-1}; \ t \geq 1 \tag{2}$$

In practice, one may assume a small transition probability between identity variables to increase the robustness.

- *Observation equation*
  By assuming that the transformed observation is a noise-corrupted version of some still template in the gallery, the observation equation can be written as

$$\mathcal{T}_{\theta_t}\{z_t\} = I_{n_t} + v_t; \ t \geq 1 \tag{3}$$

where $v_t$ is observation noise at time $t$, whose distribution determines the observation likelihood $p(z_t|n_t, \theta_t)$, and $\mathcal{T}_{\theta_t}\{z_t\}$ is a transformed version of the observation $z_t$. This transformation could be geometric, photometric, or both. However, when confronting sophisticated scenarios, this model is far from sufficient. One should use a more realistic likelihood function as shown in Section 3.

- *Statistical independence*
  We assume statistical independence between all noise variables $u_t$ and $v_t$.
- *Prior distribution*
  The prior distribution $p(n_0|z_0)$ is assumed to be uniform.

$$p(n_0|z_0) = \frac{1}{N}; \ n_0 = 1, 2, \ldots, N \tag{4}$$

In our experiments, $p(\theta_0|z_0)$ is assumed to be Gaussian: its mean comes from an initial detector or manual input and its covariance matrix is manually specified.

Using an overall state vector $x_t = (n_t, \theta_t)$, Eqs. (1) and (2) can be combined into one state equation (in a normal sense) that is completely described by the overall state transition probability

$$p(x_t|x_{t-1}) = p(n_t|n_{t-1})p(\theta_t|\theta_{t-1}) \tag{5}$$

Given this model, our goal is to compute the posterior probability $p(n_t|z_{0:t})$. It is in fact a probability mass function (PMF), as $n_t$ only takes values from $\mathcal{N} = \{1, 2, ..., N\}$, as well as a marginal probability of $p(n_t, \theta_t|z_{0:t})$, which is a mixed distribution. Therefore, the problem is reduced to computing the posterior probability.

**Posterior Probability of Identity Variable**

The evolution of the posterior probability $p(n_t|z_{0:t})$ as time proceeds is interesting to study, as the identity variable does not change by assumption [i.e., $p(n_t|n_{t-1}) = \delta(n_t - n_{t-1})$, where $\delta(.)$ is a discrete impulse function at zero; that is, $\delta(x) = 1$ if $x = 0$; otherwise $\delta(x) = 0$].

Using time recursion, Markov properties, and statistical independence embedded in the model, we can easily derive

$$p(n_{0:t}, \theta_{0:t}|z_{0:t}) = p(n_{0:t-1}, \theta_{0:t-1}|z_{0:t-1}) \frac{p(z_t|n_t, \theta_t)p(n_t|n_{t-1})p(\theta_t|\theta_{t-1})}{p(z_t|z_{0:t-1})}$$

$$= p(n_0, \theta_0|z_0) \prod_{i=1}^{t} \frac{p(z_i|n_i, \theta_i)p(n_i|n_{i-1})p(\theta_i|\theta_{i-1})}{p(z_i|z_{0:i-1})}$$

$$= p(n_0|z_0)p(\theta_0|z_0) \prod_{i=1}^{t} \frac{p(z_i|n_i, \theta_i)\delta(n_i - n_{i-1})p(\theta_i|\theta_{i-1})}{p(z_i|z_{0:i-1})} \qquad (6)$$

Therefore, by marginalizing over $\theta_{0:t}$ and $n_{0:t-1}$, we obtain the marginal posterior distribution for the identity $j$.

$$p(n_t = j|z_{0:t}) = p(n_0 = j|z_0) \int_{\theta_0} \cdots \int_{\theta_t} p(\theta_0|z_0) \prod_{i=1}^{t} \frac{p(z_i|j, \theta_i)p(\theta_i|\theta_{i-1})}{p(z_i|z_{0:i-1})} d\theta_t \ldots d\theta_0 \qquad (7)$$

Thus, $p(n_t = j|z_{0:t})$ is determined by the prior distribution $p(n_0 = j|z_0)$ and the product of the likelihood functions $\prod_{i=1}^{t} p(z_i|j, \theta_i)$. If a uniform prior is assumed, then $\prod_{i=1}^{t} p(z_i|j, \theta_i)$ is the only determining factor.

If we further assume that, for the correct identity $l \in \mathcal{N}$, there exists a constant $\eta > 1$ such that

$$p(z_t|n_t = l, \theta_t) \geq \eta p(z_t|n_t = j, \theta_t); \quad t \geq 1, j \in \mathcal{N}, j \neq l \qquad (8)$$

we have been able to show [37] that the posterior probability for the correct identity $l$, $p(n_t = l|z_{0:t})$, is lower-bounded by an increasing curve that converges to 1.

To measure the evolving uncertainty remaining in the identity variable as observations accumulate, we use the notion of entropy [10]. In the context of this problem, conditional entropy $H(n_t|z_{0:t})$ is used. However, the knowledge of $p(z_{0:t})$ is needed to compute $H(n_t|z_{0:t})$. We assume that it degenerates to an impulse at the actual observations $\tilde{z}_{0:t}$ because we observe only this particular sequence, that is, $p(z_{0:t}) = \delta(z_{0:t} - \tilde{z}_{0:t})$. Now

$$H(n_t|z_{0:t}) = - \sum_{n_t \in \mathcal{N}} p(n_t|\tilde{z}_{0:t}) \log_2 p(n_t|\tilde{z}_{0:t}) \qquad (9)$$

We expect that $H(n_t|z_{0:t})$ decreases as time proceeds, as we start from an equiprobable distribution to a degenerate one.

## 2.2 Sequential Importance Sampling Algorithm

Consider a general time series state space model fully determined by (1) the overall state transition probability $p(x_t|x_{t-1})$; (2) the observation likelihood $p(z_t|x_t)$; and (3) prior probability

$p(x_0)$ and statistical independence among all noise variables. We wish to compute the posterior probability $p(x_t|z_{0:t})$.

If the model is linear with Gaussian noise, it is analytically solvable by a Kalman filter, which essentially propagates the mean and variance of a Gaussian distribution over time. For nonlinear and non-Gaussian cases, an extended Kalman filter and its variants have been used to arrive at an approximate analytic solution [2]. Recently, the SIS technique, a special case of the Monte Carlo method [12, 19, 23] has been used to provide a numerical solution and propagate an arbitrary distribution over time.

**Importance Sampling**

The essence of the Monte Carlo method is to represent an arbitrary probability distribution $\pi(x)$ closely by a set of discrete samples. It is ideal to draw i.i.d. samples $\{x^{(m)}\}_{m=1}^M$ from $\pi(x)$. However it is often difficult to implement, especially for nontrivial distributions. Instead, a set of samples $\{x^{(m)}\}_{m=1}^M$ is drawn from an importance function $g(x)$ from which it is easy to sample; then a weight

$$w^{(m)} = \pi(x^{(m)})/g(x^{(m)}) \tag{10}$$

is assigned to each sample. This technique is called importance sampling. It can be shown [23] that the importance sample set $\mathcal{S} = \{(x^{(m)}, w^{(m)})\}_{m=1}^M$ is properly weighted to the target distribution $\pi(x)$. To accommodate a video, importance sampling is used in a sequential fashion, which leads to SIS. SIS propagates $\mathcal{S}_{t-1}$ according to the sequential importance function, say $g(x_t|x_{t-1})$, and calculates the weight using

$$w_t = w_{t-1} p(z_t|x_t) p(x_t|x_{t-1})/g(x_t|x_{t-1}) \tag{11}$$

In the CONDENSATION algorithm, $g(x_t|x_{t-1})$ is taken to be $p(x_t|x_{t-1})$ and Eq. (11) becomes

$$w_t = w_{t-1} p(z_t|x_t) \tag{12}$$

In fact, Eq. (12) is implemented by first resampling the sample set $\mathcal{S}_{t-1}$ according to $w_{t-1}$ and then updating the weight $w_t$ using $p(z_t|x_t)$. For a complete description of the SIS method, refer to Doucet *et al.* [12] and Liu and Chen [23].

The following two propositions are useful for guiding the development of the SIS algorithm.

**Proposition 1.** *When $\pi(x)$ is a PMF defined on a finite sample space, the proper sample set should exactly include all samples in the sample space.*

**Proposition 2.** *If a set of weighted random samples $\{(x^{(m)}, y^{(m)}, w^{(m)})\}_{m=1}^M$ is proper with respect to $\pi(x, y)$, a new set of weighted random samples $\{(y'^{(k)}, w'^{(k)})\}_{k=1}^K$, which is proper with respect to $\pi(y)$ or the marginal of $\pi(x, y)$ can be constructed as follows.*
*1. Remove the repetitive samples from $\{y^{(m)}\}_{m=1}^M$ to obtain $\{y'^{(k)}\}_{k=1}^K$, where all $y'^{(k)}$ values are distinct.*
*2. Sum the weight $w^{(m)}$ belonging to the same sample $y'^{(k)}$ to obtain the weight $w'^{(k)}$.*

$$w'^{(k)} = \sum_{m=1}^M w^{(m)} \ \delta(y^{(m)} - y'^{(k)}) \tag{13}$$

**Algorithms and Computational Efficiency**

In the context of this framework, the posterior probability $p(n_t, \theta_t | z_{0:t})$ is represented by a set of indexed and weighted samples

$$\mathcal{S}_t = \{(n_t^{(m)}, \theta_t^{(m)}, w_t^{(m)})\}_{m=1}^M \tag{14}$$

with $n_t$ as the above index. By Proposition 2, we can sum the weights of the samples belonging to the same index $n_t$ to obtain a proper sample set $\{n_t, \beta_{n_t}\}_{n_t=1}^N$ with respect to the posterior PMF $p(n_t | z_{0:t})$.

Straightforward implementation of the CONDENSATION algorithm for simultaneous tracking and recognition is not efficient in terms of its computational load. Because $\mathcal{N} = \{1, 2, \ldots, N\}$ is a countable sample space, we need $N$ samples for the identity variable $n_t$ according to Proposition 1. Assume that, for each identity variable $n_t$, $J$ samples are needed to represent $\theta_t$. Hence, we need $M = J * N$ samples in total. Further assume that one resampling step takes $T_r$ seconds (s), one predicting step $T_p$ s, computing one transformed image $T_t$ s, evaluating likelihood once $T_l$ s, one updating step $T_u$ s. Obviously, the bulk of computation is $J * N * (T_r + T_p + T_t + T_l)$ s to deal with one video frame as the computational time for the normalizing step and the marginalizing step is negligible. It is well known that computing the transformed image is much more expensive than other operations, that is, $T_t >> \max(T_r, T_p, T_l)$. Therefore, as the number of templates $N$ grows, the computational load increases dramatically.

There are various approaches in the literature for reducing the computational complexity of the CONDENSATION algorithm. In the study [32], random particles were guided by deterministic search. The assumed density filtering approach [6], different from CONDENSATION, is even more efficient. Those approaches are general and do not explicitly exploit the special structure of the distribution in this setting: a mixed distribution of continuous and discrete variables. To this end, we propose the following algorithm.

As the sample space $\mathcal{N}$ is countable, an exhaustive search of sample space $\mathcal{N}$ is possible. Mathematically, we release the random sampling in the identity variable $n_t$ by constructing samples as follows. For each $\theta_t^{(j)}$

$$(1, \theta_t^{(j)}, w_{t,1}^{(j)}), (2, \theta_t^{(j)}, w_{t,2}^{(j)}), \ldots, (N, \theta_t^{(j)}, w_{t,N}^{(j)})$$

We in fact use the following notation for the sample set

$$\mathcal{S}_t = \{(\theta_t^{(j)}, w_t^{(j)}, w_{t,1}^{(j)}, w_{t,2}^{(j)}, \ldots, w_{t,N}^{(j)})\}_{j=1}^J \tag{15}$$

with $w_t^{(j)} = \sum_{n=1}^N w_{t,n}^{(j)}$. The proposed algorithm is summarized in Figure 8.1.

Thus, instead of propagating random samples on both the motion vector and identity variable, we can keep the samples on the identity variable fixed and let those on the motion vector be random. Although we propagate only the marginal distribution for motion tracking, we still propagate the joint distribution for recognition purposes.

The bulk of computation of the proposed algorithm is $J * (T_r + T_p + T_t) + J * N * T_l$ s, a tremendous improvement over the traditional CONDENSATION algorithm when dealing with a large database, as the dominant computational time $J * T_t$ does not depend on $N$.

**Initialize** *a sample set* $\mathcal{S}_0 = \{(\theta_0^{(j)}, N, 1, ..., 1)\}_{j=1}^J$ *according to prior distribution* $p(\theta_0|z_0)$.
**For** $t = 1, 2, \ldots$
  **For** $j = 1, 2, \ldots, J$
    **Resample** $\mathcal{S}_{t-1} = \{(\theta_{t-1}^{(j)}, w_{t-1}^{(j)})\}_{j=1}^J$ *to obtain a new sample* $(\theta_{t-1}^{'(j)}, 1, w_{t-1,1}^{'(j)}, \ldots, w_{t-1,N}^{'(j)})$, *where* $w_{t-1,n}^{'(j)} = w_{t-1,n}^{(j)}/w_{t-1}^{(j)}$ *for* $n = 1, 2, \ldots, N$.
    **Predict** *the sample by drawing* $(\theta_t^{(j)})$ *from* $p(\theta_t|\theta_{t-1}^{'(j)})$.
    **Compute** *the transformed image* $\mathcal{T}_{\theta_t^{(j)}}\{z_t\}$.
    **For** $n = 1, \ldots, N$
      **Update** *the weight using* $\alpha_{t,n}^{(j)} = w_{t-1,n}^{'(j)} * p(z_t|n, \theta_t^{(j)})$.
    **End**
  **End**
  **Normalize** *each weight using* $w_{t,n}^{(j)} = \alpha_{t,n}^{(j)}/\sum_{n=1}^N \sum_{j=1}^J \alpha_{t,n}^{(j)}$ *and* $w_t^{(j)} = \sum_{n=1}^N w_{t,n}^{(j)}$.
  **Marginalize** *over* $\theta_t$ *to obtain weight* $\beta_{n_t}$ *for* $n_t$.
**End**

**Fig. 8.1.** Computationally efficient SIS algorithm.

## 2.3 Experimental Results

In this section we describe the still-to-video scenarios used in our experiments and model choices, followed by a discussion of results. Two databases are used in the still-to-video experiments.

Database-0 was collected outside a building. We mounted a video camera on a tripod and requested subjects to walk straight toward the camera to simulate typical scenarios for visual surveillance. Database-0 includes one face gallery and one probe set. The images in the gallery are listed in Figure 8.2. The probe contains 12 videos, one for each individual. Figure 8.2 gives some frames in a probe video.

In Database-1, we have video sequences with subjects walking in a slant path toward the camera. There are 30 subjects, each having one face template. The face gallery is shown in Figure 8.3. The probe contains 30 video sequences, one for each subject. Figure 8.3 shows some frames extracted from one probe video. As far as imaging conditions are concerned, the gallery is quite different from the probe, especially in terms of lighting. This is similar to the "FC" test protocol of the FERET test [27]. These images/videos were collected as part of the HumanID project by the National Institute of Standards and Technology and University of South Florida researchers. Table 8.2 summarizes the features of the two databases.

| Parameter | Database-0 | Database-1 |
|---|---|---|
| No. of subjects | 12 | 30 |
| Gallery | Frontal face | Frontal face |
| Motion in probe | Walking straight toward the camera | Walking straight toward the camera |
| Illumination variation | No | Large |
| Pose variation | No | Slight |

**Table 8.2.** Summary of the two databases.

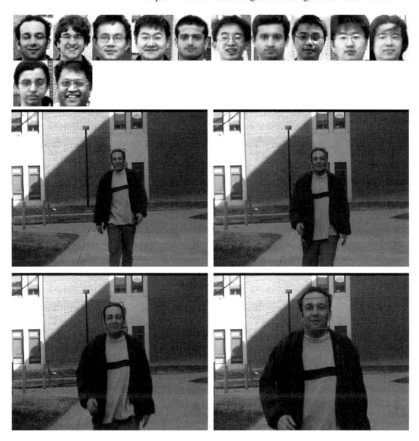

**Fig. 8.2.** Database-0. First row: the face gallery with image size of 30 x 26. Second and third rows: four frames in one probe video with image size of 320 x 240; the actual face size ranged approximately from 30 x 30 in the first frame to 50 x 50 in the last frame. Note that the sequence is taken under a well controlled condition so there are no significant illumination or pose variations between the gallery and the probe.

## Results for Database-0

We now consider affine transformation. Specifically, the motion is characterized by $\theta = (a_1, a_2, a_3, a_4, t_x, t_y)$, where $\{a_1, a_2, a_3, a_4\}$ are deformation parameters and $\{t_x, t_y\}$ are 2D translation parameters. It is a reasonable approximation because there is no significant out-of-plane motion as the subjects walk toward the camera. Regarding the photometric transformation, only the zero-mean-unit-variance operation is performed to compensate partially for contrast variations. The complete transformation $\mathcal{T}_\theta\{z\}$ is processed as follows. Affine transform $z$ using $\{a_1, a_2, a_3, a_4\}$, crop out the interested region at position $\{t_x, t_y\}$ with the same size as the still template in the gallery, and perform the zero-mean-unit-variance operation.

**Fig. 8.3.** Database-1. First row: the face gallery with image size of 30 x 26. Second and third rows: four frames in one probe video with image size of 720 x 480; the actual face size ranged from approximately 20 x 20 in the first frame to 60 x 60 in the last frame. Note the significant illumination variations between the probe and the gallery.

A time-invariant first-order Markov Gaussian model with constant velocity is used for modeling motion transition. Given that the subject is walking toward the camera, the scale increases with time. However, under perspective projection, this increase is no longer linear, causing the constant-velocity model to be not optimal. However, experimental results show that so long as the samples of $\theta$ can cover the motion, this model is sufficient.

The likelihood measurement is simply set as a "truncated" Laplacian

$$p_1(z_t|n_t, \theta_t) = \mathsf{L}(\|\mathcal{T}_{\theta_t}\{z_t\} - I_{n_t}\|; \sigma_1, \tau_1) \tag{16}$$

where $\|.\|$ is sum of absolute distance, $\sigma_1$ and $\lambda_1$ are manually specified, and

$$L(x; \sigma, \tau) = \begin{cases} \sigma^{-1} \exp(-x/\sigma) & \text{if } x \le \tau\sigma \\ \sigma^{-1} \exp(-\tau) & \text{otherwise} \end{cases} \tag{17}$$

Gaussian distribution is widely used as a noise model, accounting for sensor noise and digitization noise among others. However, given the observation equation: $v_t = \mathcal{T}_{\theta_t}\{z_t\} - I_{n_t}$, the dominant part of $v_t$ becomes the high-frequency residual if $\theta_t$ is not proper; and it is well known that the high-frequency residual of natural images is more Laplacian-like. The "truncated" Laplacian is used to give a "surviving" chance for samples to accommodate abrupt motion changes.

Figure 8.4 presents the plot of the posterior probability $p(n_t|z_{0:t})$, the conditional entropy $H(n_t|z_{0:t})$, and the minimum mean square error (MMSE) estimate of the scale parameter $sc = \sqrt{(a_1^2 + a_2^2 + a_3^2 + a_4^2)/2}$, all against $t$. The tracked face in Figure 8.2 is superimposed on the image using a bounding box.

Suppose the correct identity for Figure 8.2 is $l$. From Figure 8.4, we can easily observe that the posterior probability $p(n_t = l|z_{0:t})$ increases as time proceeds and eventually approaches 1, and all others $p(n_t = j|z_{0:t})$ for $j \ne l$ go to 0. Figure 8.4 also plots the decrease in conditional entropy $H(n_t|z_{0:t})$ and the increase in scale parameter, which matches with the scenario of a subject walking toward a camera.

Table 8.3 summarizes the average recognition performance and computational time of the CONDENSATION and the proposed algorithm when applied to Database-0. Both algorithms achieved 100% recognition rate with top match. However, the proposed algorithm is more than 10 times faster than the CONDENSATION algorithm. This experiment was implemented in C++ on a PC with P-III 1G CPU and 512M RAM with the number of motion samples $J$ chosen to be 200, the number of templates in the gallery $N$ to be 12.

| Algorithm | CONDENSATION | Proposed |
|---|---|---|
| Recognition rate within top one match | 100% | 100% |
| Time per frame | 7 seconds | 0.5 seconds |

**Table 8.3.** Recognition performance of algorithms when applied to Database-0.

**Results on Database-1**

*Case 1: Tracking and Recognition Using Laplacian Density*

We first investigate the performance using the same setting as described in Section 2.3. Table 8.4 shows that the recognition rate is poor: only 13% are correctly identified using the top match. The main reason is that the "truncated" Laplacian density is not able to capture the appearance difference between the probe and the gallery, indicating a need for more effective appearance modeling. Nevertheless, the tracking accuracy [1] is reasonable, with 83% successfully tracked

---

[1] We manually inspect the tracking results by imposing the MMSE motion estimate on the final frame as shown in Figures 8.2 and 8.3 and determine if tracking is successful or not for this sequence. This is done for all sequences, and the tracking accuracy is defined as the ratio of the number of sequences successfully tracked to the total number of all sequences.

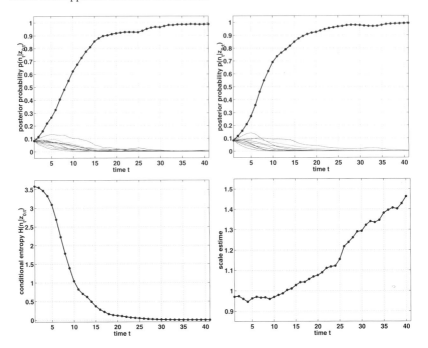

**Fig. 8.4.** Posterior probability $p(n_t|z_{0:t})$ against time $t$, obtained by the CONDENSATION algorithm (top left) and the proposed algorithm (top right). Conditional entropy $H(n_t|z_{0:t})$ (bottom left) and MMSE estimate of scale parameter $sc$ (bottom right) against time $t$. The conditional entropy and the MMSE estimate are obtained using the proposed algorithm.

because we are using multiple face templates in the gallery to track the specific face in the probe video. After all, faces in both the gallery and the probe belong to the same class of human face, and it seems that the appearance change is within the class range.

*Case 2: Pure Tracking Using Laplacian Density*

In Case 2, we measure the appearance change within the probe video as well as the noise in the background. To this end, we introduce a dummy template $T_0$, a cut version in the first frame of the video. Define the observation likelihood for tracking as

$$q(z_t|\theta_t) = \mathsf{L}(\|\mathcal{T}_{\theta_t}\{z_t\} - T_0\|; \sigma_2, \tau_2) \tag{18}$$

where $\sigma_2$ and $\tau_2$ are set manually. The other setting, such as motion parameter and model, is the same as in Case 1. We still can run the CONDENSATION algorithm to perform pure tracking. Table 8.4 shows that 87% are successfully tracked by this simple tracking model, which implies that the appearance within the video remains similar.

*Case 3: Tracking and Recognition Using Probabilistic Subspace Density*

As mentioned in Case 1, we need a new appearance model to improve the recognition accuracy. Of the many approaches suggested in the literature, we decided to use the approach

| Case | Case 1 | Case 2 | Case 3 | Case 4 | Case 5 |
|---|---|---|---|---|---|
| Tracking accuracy | 83% | 87% | 93% | 100% | NA |
| Recognition within top 1 match | 13% | NA | 83% | 93% | 57% |
| Recognition within top 3 matches | 43% | NA | 97% | 100% | 83% |

**Table 8.4.** Performances of algorithms when applied to Database-1.

suggested by Moghaddam *et al.* [26] because of its computational efficiency and high recognition accuracy. However, here we model only the intrapersonal variations. Modeling both intra/extrapersonal variations is considered in Section 3.2.

We need at least two facial images for one identity to construct the intrapersonal space (IPS). Apart from the available gallery, we crop out the second image from the video ensuring no overlap with the frames actually used in probe videos. Figure 8.5 (top row) shows a list of such images. Compare with Figure 8.3 to see how the illumination varies between the gallery and the probe.

We then fit a probabilistic subspace density [25] on top of the IPS. It proceeds as follows: A regular PCA is performed for the IPS. Suppose the eigensystem for the IPS is $\{(\lambda_i, e_i)\}_{i=1}^d$, where $d$ is the number of pixels and $\lambda_1 \geq ... \geq \lambda_d$. Only top $r$ principal components corresponding to top $r$ eigenvalues are then kept while the residual components are considered isotropic. We refer the reader to Moghaddam and Pentland [25] for full details. Figure 8.5 (middle row) shows the eigenvectors for the IPS. The density is written as follows

$$\mathbf{Q}(x) = \{\frac{exp(-\frac{1}{2}\sum_{i=1}^{r}\frac{y_i^2}{\lambda_i})}{(2\pi)^{r/2}\prod_{i=1}^{r}\lambda_i^{1/2}}\}\{\frac{exp(-\frac{\epsilon^2}{2\rho})}{(2\pi\rho)^{(d-r)/2}}\} \tag{19}$$

where the principal components $y_i$, the reconstruction error $\epsilon^2$, and the isotropic noise variance $\rho$ are defined as

$$y_i = e_i^{\mathsf{T}}x, \quad \epsilon^2 = \|x\|^2 - \sum_{i=1}^{r}y_i^2, \quad \rho = (d-r)^{-1}\sum_{i=r+1}^{d}\lambda_i \tag{20}$$

It is easy to write the likelihood as follows:

$$p_2(z_t|n_t, \theta_t) = \mathbf{Q}_{IPS}(\mathcal{T}_{\theta_t}\{z_t\} - I_{n_t}) \tag{21}$$

Table 8.4 lists the performance using this new likelihood measurement. It turns out that the performance is significantly better than in Case 1, with 93% tracked successfully and 83% correctly recognized within the top match. If we consider the top three matches, 97% are correctly identified.

*Case 4: Tracking and Recognition using Combined Density*

In Case 2, we studied appearance changes within a video sequence. In Case 3, we studied the appearance change between the gallery and the probe. In Case 4, we attempt to take advantage of both cases by introducing a combined likelihood defined as follows.

$$p_3(z_t|n_t, \theta_t) = p_2(z_t|n_t, \theta_t)q(z_t|\theta_t) \tag{22}$$

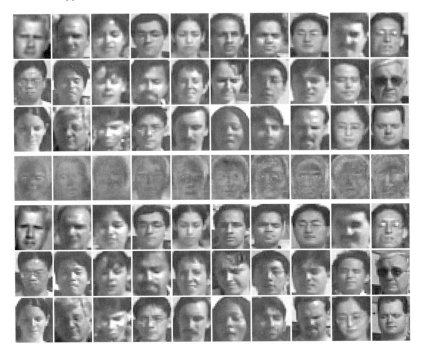

**Fig. 8.5.** Database-1. Top row: second facial images for training probabilistic density. Middle row: top 10 eigenvectors for the IPS. Bottom row: the facial images cropped out from the largest frontal view.

Again, all other settings are the same as in Case 1. We now obtain the best performance so far: no tracking error, 93% are correctly recognized as the first match, and no error in recognition when the top three matches are considered.

*Case 5: Still-to-Still Face Recognition*

We also performed an experiment for still-to-still face recognition. We selected the probe video frames with the best frontal face view (i.e., biggest frontal view) and cropped out the facial region by normalizing with respect to the eye coordinates manually specified. This collection of images is shown in Figure 8.5 (bottom row), and it is fed as probes into a still-to-still face recognition system with the learned probabilistic subspace as in Case 3. It turns out that the recognition result is 57% correct for the top match and 83% for the top three matches. Clearly, Case 4 is the best of all.

## 3 Enhancing Tracking and Recognition Accuracy

The general formulation of our recognition model leaves room for enhancing tracking and recognition accuracy. In other words, one can employ model choices tuned for specific scenarios. However, here we present [36] rather general appearance-based models. This technique includes enhanced approaches to modeling interframe appearance changes for accurate tracking and modeling appearance changes between probe video frames and gallery images for accurate recognition.

## 3.1 Modeling Interframe Appearance Changes

To model interframe appearance changes, a certain appearance model $A_t$ is needed. In the work of Hager and Belhumeur [15] and in Section 2, a fixed template, $A_t = T_0$, is matched with observations to minimize a cost function in the form of the sum of the squared distance (SSD). This is equivalent to assuming that the noise $V_t$ is a normal random vector with zero mean and a diagonal (isotropic) covariance matrix. At the other extreme, one could use a rapidly changing model, for example, taking $A_t$ as the "best" patch of interest in the previous frame. However, a fixed template cannot handle appearance changes in the video, and a rapidly changing model is susceptible to drift. Thus, it is necessary to have a model that is a compromise between these two cases, which leads to an online appearance model [17].

Interframe appearance changes are also related to the motion transition model. For a visual tracking problem, it is ideal to have an exact motion model governing the kinematics of the object. In practice, however, approximate models are used. There are two types of approximation commonly found in the literature. One is to learn a motion model directly from a training video [16]. However, such a model may overfit the training data and may not necessarily succeed when presented with testing videos containing objects arbitrarily moving at different times and places. Also, one cannot always rely on the availability of training data in the first place. The second is a fixed constant-velocity model with fixed noise variance fitted for simplicity as in Section 2. Let $r_0$ be a fixed constant measuring the extent of noise. If $r_0$ is small, it is difficult to model rapid movements; if $r_0$ is large, it is computationally inefficient because many more particles are needed to accommodate large noise variance. All these factors make the use of such a model ineffective. In our work, we overcome this by introducing an adaptive-velocity model.

### Adaptive Appearance Model

The adaptive appearance model assumes that the observations are explained by different causes, thereby indicating the use of a mixture density of components. Jepson *et al.* [17] used three components: the $W$ component characterizing two-frame variations, the $S$ component depicting the stable structure within all past observations (though it is slowly-varying), and the $L$ component accounting for outliers such as occluded pixels. In our implementation, we have incorporated only the $S$ and $W$ components.

As an option, to further stabilize our tracker one could use an $F$ component, which is a fixed template that one is expecting to observe most often. For example, in face tracking this could be just the facial image as seen from a frontal view. In the sequel, we derive the equations as if there is an $F$ component. However, the effect of this component can be ignored by setting its initial mixing probability to zero.

We now describe our mixture appearance model. The appearance model at time $t$, $A_t = \{W_t, S_t, F_t\}$, is a time-varying one that models the appearances present in all observations up to time $t - 1$. It obeys a mixture of Gaussians, with $W_t, S_t, F_t$ as mixture centers $\{\mu_{i,t}; \ i =$

$w, s, f$} and their corresponding variances {$\sigma^2_{i,t}$; $i = w, s, f$} and mixing probabilities {$m_{i,t}$; $i = w, s, f$}. Note that {$m_{i,t}, \mu_{i,t}, \sigma^2_{i,t}$; $i = w, s, f$} are "images" consisting of $d$ pixels that are assumed to be independent of each other.

In summary, the observation likelihood is written as

$$p(Y_t|\theta_t) = p(Z_t|\theta_t) = \prod_{j=1}^{d} \{ \sum_{i=w,s,f} m_{i,t}(j) \text{N}[Z_t(j); \mu_{i,t}(j), \sigma^2_{i,t}(j)] \} \tag{23}$$

where $\text{N}(x; \mu, \sigma^2)$ is a normal density

$$\text{N}(x; \mu, \sigma^2) = (2\pi\sigma^2)^{-1/2} \exp\{-\rho(\frac{x-\mu}{\sigma})\}, \quad \rho(x) = \frac{1}{2}x^2 \tag{24}$$

*Model Update*

To keep our chapter self-contained, we show how to update the current appearance model $A_t$ to $A_{t+1}$ after $\hat{Z}_t$ becomes available; that is, we want to compute the new mixing probabilities, mixture centers, and variances for time $t + 1$, {$m_{i,t+1}, \mu_{i,t+1}, \sigma^2_{i,t+1}$; $i = w, s, f$}.

It is assumed that the past observations are exponentially "forgotten" with respect to their contributions to the current appearance model. Denote the exponential envelope by $\mathcal{E}_t(k) = \alpha \exp[-\tau^{-1}(t-k)]$ for $k \leq t$, where $\tau = n_h/\log 2$, $n_h$ is the half-life of the envelope in frames, and $\alpha = 1 - \exp(-\tau^{-1})$ to guarantee that the area under the envelope is 1. We sketch the updating equations as below and refer the interested readers to Jepson *et al.* [17] for more technical details and justifications.

The EM algorithm [11] is invoked. Because we assume that the pixels are independent of each other, we can deal with each pixel separately. The following computation is valid for $j = 1, 2, \ldots, d$, where $d$ is the number of pixels in the appearance model.

Firstly, the posterior responsibility probability is computed as

$$o_{i,t}(j) \propto m_{i,t}(j)\text{N}(\hat{Z}_t(j); \mu_{i,t}(j), \sigma^2_{i,t}(j)); \quad i = w, s, f, \quad and \quad \sum_{i=w,s,f} o_{i,t}(j) = 1 \tag{25}$$

Then the mixing probabilities are updated as

$$m_{i,t+1}(j) = \alpha \, o_{i,t}(j) + (1-\alpha) \, m_{i,t}(j); \quad i = w, s, f \tag{26}$$

and the first- and second-order moment images {$M_{p,t+1}$; $p = 1, 2$} are evaluated as

$$M_{p,t+1}(j) = \alpha \, \hat{Z}^p_t(j) o_{s,t}(j) + (1-\alpha) \, M_{p,t}(j); \quad p = 1, 2 \tag{27}$$

Finally, the mixture centers and the variances are updated as

$$S_{t+1}(j) = \mu_{s,t+1}(j) = \frac{M_{1,t+1}(j)}{m_{s,t+1}(j)}, \quad \sigma^2_{s,t+1}(j) = \frac{M_{2,t+1}(j)}{m_{s,t+1}(j)} - \mu^2_{s,t+1}(j) \tag{28}$$

$$W_{t+1}(j) = \mu_{w,t+1}(j) = \hat{Z}_t(j), \quad \sigma^2_{w,t+1}(j) = \sigma^2_{w,1}(j) \tag{29}$$

$$F_{t+1}(j) = \mu_{f,t+1}(j) = F_1(j), \quad \sigma^2_{f,t+1}(j) = \sigma^2_{f,1}(j) \tag{30}$$

*Model Initialization*

To initialize $A_1$, we set $W_1 = S_1 = F_1 = T_0$ (with $T_0$ supplied by a detection algorithm or manually), $\{m_{i,1}, \sigma_{i,1}^2; \ i = w, s, f\}$, and $M_{1,1} = m_{s,1} T_0$ and $M_{2,1} = m_{s,1} \sigma_{s,1}^2 + T_0^2$.

## Adaptive Velocity State Model

The state transition model we use has a term for modeling adaptive velocity. The adaptive velocity in the state parameter is calculated using a first-order linear prediction based on the appearance difference between two successive frames. The previous particle configuration is incorporated in our prediction scheme.

   Construction of the particle configuration involves the costly computation of image warping (in our experiments, it usually takes about half of the computation load). In a conventional particle filter, the particle configuration is used only to update the weight; that is, computing the weight for each particle by comparing the warped image with the online appearance model using the observation equation. Our approach, in addition, uses the particle configuration in the state transition equation. In some sense, we "maximally" utilize the information contained in the particles (without wasting the costly computation of image warping) because we use it in both state and observation models.

*Adaptive Velocity*

With the availability of the sample set $\Theta_{t-1} = \{\theta_{t-1}^{(j)}\}_{j=1}^J$ and the image patches of interest $\mathcal{Y}_{t-1} = \{y_{t-1}^{(j)}\}_{j=1}^J$ with $y_{t-1}^{(j)} = \mathcal{T}_{\theta_t^{(j)}}\{z_t\}$, for a new observation $z_t$, we can predict the shift in the motion vector (or adaptive velocity) $\nu_t = \theta_t - \hat{\theta}_{t-1}$ using a first-order linear approximation [4, 15, 18], which essentially comes from the constant brightness constraint; there exists a $\theta_t$ such that

$$\mathcal{T}_{\theta_t}\{z_t\} \simeq \hat{y}_{t-1} \tag{31}$$

Approximating $\mathcal{T}_{\theta_t}\{z_t\}$ via a first-order Taylor series expansion around $\hat{\theta}_{t-1}$ yields

$$\mathcal{T}_{\theta_t}\{z_t\} \simeq \mathcal{T}_{\hat{\theta}_{t-1}}\{z_t\} + C_t(\theta_t - \hat{\theta}_{t-1}) = \mathcal{T}_{\hat{\theta}_{t-1}}\{z_t\} + C_t \nu_t \tag{32}$$

where $C_t$ is the Jacobian matrix.

   Combining Eqs. (31) and (32) gives

$$\hat{y}_{t-1} \simeq \mathcal{T}_{\hat{\theta}_{t-1}}\{z_t\} + C_t \nu_t \tag{33}$$

that is

$$\nu_t \simeq -B_t(\mathcal{T}_{\hat{\theta}_{t-1}}\{z_t\} - \hat{y}_{t-1}) \tag{34}$$

where $B_t$ is the pseudo-inverse of the $C_t$ matrix, which can be efficiently estimated from the available data $\Theta_{t-1}$ and $\mathcal{Y}_{t-1}$.

   Specifically, to estimate $B_t$ we stack into matrices the differences in motion vectors and image patches using $\hat{\theta}_{t-1}$ and $\hat{y}_{t-1}$ as pivotal points.

$$\begin{cases} \Theta_{t-1}^{\delta} = [\theta_{t-1}^{(1)} - \hat{\theta}_{t-1}, \ \ldots, \ \theta_{t-1}^{(J)} - \hat{\theta}_{t-1}] \\ \mathcal{Y}_{t-1}^{\delta} = [y_{t-1}^{(1)} - \hat{y}_{t-1}, \ \ldots, \ y_{t-1}^{(J)} - \hat{y}_{t-1}] \end{cases} \tag{35}$$

The least-squares solution for $B_t$ is

$$B_t = (\Theta_{t-1}^{\delta} \mathcal{Y}_{t-1}^{\delta \ \mathrm{T}})(\mathcal{Y}_{t-1}^{\delta} \mathcal{Y}_{t-1}^{\delta \ \mathrm{T}})^{-1} \tag{36}$$

However, it turns out that the matrix $\mathcal{Y}_{t-1}^{\delta} \mathcal{Y}_{t-1}^{\delta \ \mathrm{T}}$ is often rank-deficient owing to the high dimensionality of the data (unless the number of the particles exceeds the data dimension). To overcome this, we use the singular value decomposition.

$$\mathcal{Y}_{t-1}^{\delta} = USV^{\mathrm{T}} \tag{37}$$

It can be easily shown that

$$B_t = \Theta_{t-1}^{\delta} V S^{-1} U^{\mathrm{T}} \tag{38}$$

To gain some computational efficiency, we can further approximate

$$B_t = \Theta_{t-1}^{\delta} V_q S_q^{-1} U_q^{\mathrm{T}} \tag{39}$$

by retaining the top $q$ components. Note that if only a fixed template is used [18] the $B$ matrix is fixed and precomputable. In our case, the appearance is changing so we have to compute the $B_t$ matrix in each time step.

We also calculate the prediction error $\epsilon_t$ between $\tilde{y}_t = \mathcal{T}_{\hat{\theta}_{t-1}+\nu_t}\{z_t\}$ and the updated appearance model $A_t$. The error $\epsilon_t$ is defined as

$$\epsilon_t = \phi(\tilde{y}_t, A_t) = \sum_{i=w,s,f} \frac{2}{d} \sum_{j=1}^{d} m_{i,t}(j) \rho(\frac{\tilde{y}_t(j) - \mu_{i,t}(j)}{\sigma_{i,t}(j)}) \tag{40}$$

To summarize, we use the following state model

$$\theta_t = \hat{\theta}_{t-1} + \nu_t + u_t \tag{41}$$

where $\nu_t$ is the predicted shift in the motion vector. The choice of $u_t$ is discussed below.

*Adaptive Noise*

The value of $\epsilon_t$ determines the quality of prediction. Therefore, if $\epsilon_t$ is small, which implies a good prediction, we only need noise with small variance to absorb the residual motion; if $\epsilon_t$ is large, which implies a poor prediction, we then need noise with large variance to cover potentially large jumps in the motion state.

To this end, we use $u_t$ of the form $u_t = r_t * u_0$, where $r_t$ is a function of $\epsilon_t$, and $u_0$ is a "standardized" random vector. In practice, we take $u_0$ as a Gaussian random vector with zero mean and a given covariance matrix. Because $\epsilon_t$ is "variance"-type measure, we use

$$r_t = \max(\min(r_0 \sqrt{\epsilon_t}, r_{max}), r_{min}) \tag{42}$$

where $r_{min}$ is the lower bound to maintain a reasonable sample coverage, and $r_{max}$ is the upper bound to constrain the computational load.

## 3.2 Modeling Appearance Changes between Frames and Gallery Images

We adopt the maximum a posteriori (MAP) rule developed in [26] for the recognition score $p_n(z_t|n_t, \theta_t)$. Two subspaces are constructed to model appearance variations. The intrapersonal space (IPS) is meant to cover all the variations in appearances belonging to the same person, whereas the extrapersonal space (EPS) is used to cover all the variations in appearances belonging to different people. More than one facial image per person is needed to construct the IPS. Apart from the available gallery, we crop out four images from the video ensuring no overlap with frames used in probe videos. The probabilistic subspace density (Eq. 19) estimation method is applied separately to the IPS and the EPS, yielding two different eigensystems. Assuming equal priors on the IPS and the EPS, the recognition score $p_n(z_t|n_t, \theta_t)$ is finally computed as

$$p_n(z_t|n_t, \theta_t) = \frac{\mathbf{Q}_{IPS}(\mathcal{T}_{\theta_t}\{z_t\} - I_{n_t})}{\mathbf{Q}_{IPS}(\mathcal{T}_{\theta_t}\{z_t\} - I_{n_t}) + \mathbf{Q}_{EPS}(\mathcal{T}_{\theta_t}\{z_t\} - I_{n_t})} \tag{43}$$

## 3.3 Complete Observation Likelihood

As in Section 2.3, we can construct a combined likelihood by taking the product of $p_a(z_n|\theta_t)$ and $p_n(z_t|n_t, \theta_t)$. To fully exploit the fact that all gallery images are in frontal view, we also compute how likely the patch $y_t$ is in frontal view and denote this score by $p_f(z_t|\theta_t)$. We simply measure this by fitting a PS density on top of the gallery images [25], assuming that they are i.i.d. samples from the frontal face space (FFS). It is easy to write $p_f(z_t|\theta_t)$ as follows.

$$p_f(z_t|\theta_t) = \mathbf{Q}_{FFS}(\mathcal{T}_{\theta_t}\{z_t\}) \tag{44}$$

If the patch is in frontal view, we accept a recognition score. Otherwise, we simply set the recognition score as equiprobable among all identities (i.e., $1/N$). The complete likelihood $p(z_t|n_t, \theta_t)$ is now defined as

$$p(z_t|n_t, \theta_t) \propto p_a \left\{ p_f\, p_n + (1 - p_f)\, N^{-1} \right\} \tag{45}$$

We also adjust the particle number $J_t$ based on the following two considerations. (1) If the noise variance $r_t$ is large, we need more particles; conversely, fewer particles are needed for noise with small variance $r_t$. Based on the principle of asymptotic relative efficiency [7], we should adjust the particle number $J_t$ in a similar fashion (i.e., $J_t = J_0 r_t/r_0$). (2) As shown in Section 2.1, the uncertainty in the identity variable $n_t$ is characterized by an entropy measure $H_t$ for $p(n_t|z_{0:t})$, and $H_t$ is a nonincreasing function (under one weak assumption). Accordingly, we increase the number of particles by a fixed amount $J_{fix}$ if $H_t$ increases; otherwise we deduct $J_{fix}$ from $J_t$. Combining these two, we have

$$J_t = J_0 \frac{r_t}{r_0} + J_{fix} * (-1)^{i[H_{t-1} < H_{t-2}]} \tag{46}$$

where $i[.]$ is an indication function.

## 3.4 Experimental Results

We have applied our algorithm to tracking and recognizing human faces captured by a hand-held video camera in office environments. There are 29 subjects in the database. Figure 8.6 shows all the images in the galley set and the top 10 eigenvectors for the FFS, IPS, and EPS, respectively. Figure 8.7 presents some frames (with tracking results) in the video sequence for Subject-2 featuring quite large pose variations, moderate illumination variations, and quick scale changes (back and forth toward the end of the sequence).

**Fig. 8.6.** Rows 1∼3: the gallery set with 29 subjects in frontal view. Rows 4∼6: the top 10 eigenvectors for the FFS, IPS, and EPS, respectively.

Tracking is successful for all the video sequences, and a 100% recognition rate is achieved, whereas the approach in Section 2 fails to track in several video sequences owing to its inability to handle significant appearance changes caused by pose and illumination variations. The posterior probabilities $p(n_t|z_{0:t})$ with $n_t = 1, 2, ...N$ obtained for the Subject-2 sequence are plotted in Figure 8.8a. It is very fast, taking about less than 10 frames, to reach above the 0.9 level for the posterior probability corresponding to Subject-2, whereas all other posterior probabilities corresponding to other identities approach zero. This is mainly attributed to the discriminative power of the MAP recognition score induced by the IPS and EPS modeling. The approach in Section 2 usually takes about 30 frames to reach the 0.9 level because only intrapersonal modeling is adopted. Figure 8.8(b) captures the scale change in the Subject-2 sequence.

## 4 Issues and Discussions

We have presented a probabilistic model for recognizing human faces present in a video sequence and derived several important features embedded in this framework: (1) the temporal fusion of tracking and recognition; (2) the evolution of the posterior probability of the identity

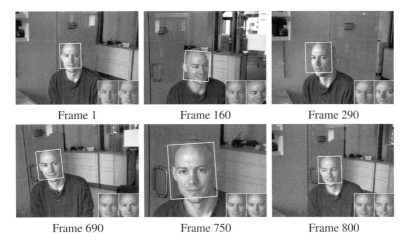

Frame 1     Frame 160     Frame 290

Frame 690     Frame 750     Frame 800

**Fig. 8.7.** Example images in the Subject-2 probe video sequence and the tracking results.

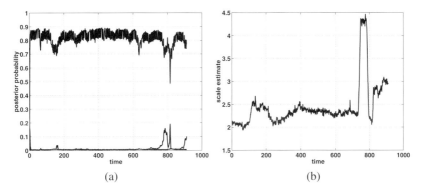

(a)     (b)

**Fig. 8.8.** Results on the Subject-2 sequence. a. Posterior probabilities against time $t$ for all identities $p(n_t|z_{0:t})$, $n_t = 1, 2, ..., N$. The line close to 1 is for the true identity. b. Scale estimate against time $t$.

variable; (3) the computational efficiency of the SIS algorithm for solving this model; and (4) the generality of this model by incorporating more sophisticated appearance models.

Our current approach is appearance-based (to be more accurate, image-intensity-based). One limitation of the appearance-based learning approach is its difficulty dealing with novel appearances not present in the training stage. Such novel appearances are easily produced by illumination, pose and facial expression variations, especially when a video sequence is used. To overcome the above limitations, the following issues are worthy of further investigations.

1. Feature-based approach. It is ideal to have features derived from the image intensities invariant to the above variations. A good example is the elastic graph matching (EGM) algorithm [20]. Filter responses from Gabor wavelets are computed to form a sparse graph representation and recognition is based on graph-matching results. This representation is

known to be more resistant to illumination and pose variations. It is also robust to variations in facial expression.

2. We have used only one template for each person in the gallery. Obviously, we can use multiple templates per person. The still templates in the gallery can be further generalized to video sequences to realize video-to-video recognition. In the article of Zhou *et al.* [37], exemplars and their prior probabilities can be learned from the gallery videos to serve as still templates in the still-to-video scenario. A person $n$ may have a collection of $K_n$ exemplars, such as $\mathcal{C}^n = \{c_1^n, \ldots, c_k^n, \ldots, c_{K_n}^n\}$ indexed by $k$. The likelihood is modified as a mixture density with exemplars as mixture centers. The joint distribution $p(n_t, k_t, \theta_t | z_{0:t})$ is computed using the SIS algorithm and is marginalized to yield $p(n_t | z_{0:t})$. In the experiments reported by Zhou *et al.* [37], the subjects walked on a treadmill with their faces moving naturally, giving rise to significant variations across poses. However, the proposed method successfully copes with these pose variations (using exemplars) as evidenced by the experimental results. Other learning methods can be applied to the gallery videos. For example, a mixture of Gaussians can be used to replace the exemplar-learning procedure. Hidden Markov models can also be used if the person is involved in a particular activity. Liu and Chen [24] showed that hidden Markov models can be used to learn the dynamics among successive appearances. Matching video sequences is equivalent to comparing two Markov models. In the work of Lee *et al.* [21], pose variations were handled by learning the view-discretized appearance manifolds from the training ensemble. Transition probabilities from one view to another view are used to regularize the search space. However, the cropped images are used for testing [21, 24]. Recently, a linear dynamical system model [31], a special type of dynamic model, was used to model the video sequence and the system model coefficients were used in face recognition [1].

3. The use of 3D face model. There are some recent efforts on handling pose and illumination variation that invoke the 3D face model, either explicitly or implicitly. Romdhani *et al.* [29] showed that the 3D face model can be used explicitly to recover the unknown pose. Zhou and Chellappa [35] used 3D model implicitly to recover the unknown illumination. However, the above two methods are still-image-based. Incorporation of these methods into our video-based recognition framework is appealing. If explicit 3D models are needed, how to capture such a model becomes an issue. All 3D models were recorded separately by Romdhani *et al.* [29]. The obtained 3D models are highly accurate but they need a manual operator. The alternative is to use a structure from motion algorithm [30].

## Acknowledgments

Partially supported by DARPA/ONR grant N00014-00-1-0908. The work was done when Zhou was at Maryland. We thank Dr. Baback Moghaddam at Mitsubishi Electric Research Labs.

## References

1. G. Aggarwal, A. Roy-Chowdhury, and R. Chellappa. A system identification approach for video-based face recognition. *Internation Conference on Pattern Recognition*, Cambridge, UK, 2004.

2. B. Anderson and J. Moore. *Optimal Filtering*. Prentice Hall, Englewood Cliffs, NJ, 1979.

3. P.N. Belhumeur, J.P. Hespanha, and D.J. Kriegman. Eigenfaces vs. Fisherfaces: Recognition using class specific linear projection. *IEEE Transactions on Pattern Analysis and Machine Intelligence*, 19:711–720, 1997.

4. J. Bergen, P. Anadan, K. Hanna, and R. Hingorani. Hierarchical model-based motion estimation. European Conference on Computer Vision, pages 237–252, 1992.

5. M.J. Black and A.D. Jepson. A probabilistic framework for matching temporal trajectories. *European Conference on Computer Vision*, pages 909–924, 1998.

6. X. Boyen and D. Koller. Tractable inference for complex stochastic processes. *Uncertainty in AI (UAI)*, pages 33-42, 1998.

7. G. Casella and R. L. Berger. *Statistical Inference*. Duxbury, Belmont, CA, 2002.

8. R. Chellappa, C.L. Wilson, and S. Sirohey. Human and machine recognition of faces: A survey. *Proceedings of IEEE*, 83:705–740, 1995.

9. T. Choudhury, B. Clarkson, T. Jebara, and A. Pentland. Multimodal person recognition using unconstrained audio and video. *International Conference on Audio- and Video-Based Person Authentication*, pages 176–181, 1999.

10. T.M. Cover and J.A. Thomas. *Elements of Information Theory*. Wiley, New York, 1991.

11. A.P. Dempster, N.M. Laird, and D.B. Rubin. Maximum likelihood from incomplete data via the em algorithm. *Journal of Royal Statistical Society B*, 39:1-38, 1977.

12. A. Doucet, S.J. Godsill, and C. Andrieu. On sequential Monte Carlo sampling methods for Bayesian filtering. *Statistics and Computing*, 10:197–208, 2000.

13. K. Etemad and R. Chellappa. Discriminant analysis for recognition of human face images. *Journal of Optical Society of America A* , pages 1724–1733, 1997.

14. N.J. Gordon, D.J. Salmond, and A.F.M. Smith. Novel approach to nonlinear/non-Gaussian Bayesian state estimation. *IEE Proceedings on Radar and Signal Processing*, 140:107–113, 1993.

15. G.D. Hager and P.N. Belhumeur. Efficient region tracking with parametric models of geometry and illumination. *IEEE Transactions on Pattern Analysis and Machine Intelligence*, 20:1025–1039, 1998.

16. M. Isard and A. Blake. Contour tracking by stochastic propagation of conditional density. *European Conference on Computer Vision*, pages 343–356, 1996.

17. A.D. Jepson, D.J. Fleet, and T.F. El-Maraghi. Robust online appearance model for visual tracking. *IEEE Computer Society Conference on Computer Vision and Pattern Recognition*, 1:415–422, 2001.

18. F. Jurie and M. Dhome. A simple and efficient template matching algorithm. *IEEE Internatonal Conference on Computer Vision*, 2:544–549, 2001.

19. G. Kitagawa. Monte Carlo filter and smoother for non-Gaussian nonlinear state space models. *Journal of Computational and Graphical Statistics*, 5:1–25, 1996.

20. M. Lades, J.C. Vorbruggen, J. Buhmann, J. Lange, C. van der Malsburg, R.P. Wurtz, and W. Konen. Distortion invariant object recognition in the dynamic link architecture. *IEEE Transactions on Computers*, 42:300–311, 1993.

21. K. Lee, J. Ho, M. Yang, and D. Kriegman. Video-based face recognition using probabilistic appearance manifolds. *IEEE Conference on Computer Vision and Pattern Recognition*, 2003.

22. B. Li and R. Chellappa. A generic approach to simultaneous tracking and verification in video. *IEEE Transactions on Image Processing*, 11:530–544, 2002.

23. J.S. Liu and R. Chen. Sequential Monte Carlo for dynamic systems. *Journal of the American Statistical Association*, 93:1032–1044, 1998.

24. X. Liu and T. Chen. Video-based face recognition using adaptive hidden Markov models. *IEEE Conference on Computer Vision and Pattern Recognition*, 2003.

25. B. Moghaddam and A. Pentland. Probabilistic visual learning for object representation. *IEEE Transactions on Pattern Analysis and Machine Intelligence*, 19:696–710, 1997.

26. B. Moghaddam, T. Jebara, and A. Pentland. Bayesian modeling of facial similarity. *Advances in Neural Information Processing Systems*, 11:910–916, 1999.

27. P.J. Phillips, H. Moon, S. Rivzi, and P. Rauss. The FERET evaluation methodology for face-recognition algorithms. *IEEE Transactions on Pattern Analysis and Machine Intelligence*, 22:1090–1104, 2000.

28. G. Qian and R. Chellappa. Structure from motion using sequential Monte Carlo methods. *IEEE Internation Conference on Computer Vision*, pages 614–621, 2001.

29. S. Romdhani, V. Blanz, and T. Vetter. Face identification by fitting a 3D morphable model using linear shape and texture errror functions. *European Conference on Computer Vision*, 2002.

30. A. Roy-Chowdhury and R. Chellappa. Face reconstruction from video using uncertainty analysis and a generic model. *Computer Vision and Image Understanding*, 91:188-213, 2003.

31. S. Soatto, G. Doretto, and Y.N. Wu. Dynamic textures. *IEEE Internation Conference on Computer Vision*, 2001.

32. J. Sullivan and J. Rittscher. Guiding random particle by deterministic search. *IEEE International Conference on Computer Vision*, pages 323 –330, 2001.

33. M. Turk and A. Pentland. Eigenfaces for recognition. *Journal of Cognitive Neuroscience*, 3:71–86, 1991.

34. W.Y. Zhao, R. Chellappa, A. Rosenfeld, and P.J. Phillips. Face recognition: A literature survey. *ACM Computing Surveys*, 35:399–458, 2003.

35. S. Zhou, R. Chellappa, D. Jacobs. Characterization of human faces under illumination variations using rank, integrability, and symmetry constraints. *European Conference on Computer Vision*, Prague, Czech, 2004.

36. S. Zhou, R. Chellappa, and B. Moghaddam. Visual tracking and recognition using appearance-adaptive models in particle filters. *IEEE Transactions on Image Processing*, November, 2004.

37. S. Zhou, V. Krueger, and R. Chellappa. Probabilistic recognition of human faces from video. *Computer Vision and Image Understanding*, 91:214-245, 2003.

# Chapter 9. Face Recognition Across Pose and Illumination

Ralph Gross, Simon Baker, Iain Matthews, and Takeo Kanade

Robotics Institute, Carnegie Mellon University, Pittsburgh, PA 15213, USA.
{rgross, simonb, iainm, tk}@cs.cmu.edu

The last decade has seen automatic face recognition evolve from small-scale research systems to a wide range of commercial products. Driven by the FERET face database and evaluation protocol, the currently best commercial systems achieve verification accuracies comparable to those of fingerprint recognizers. In these experiments, only frontal face images taken under controlled lighting conditions were used. As the use of face recognition systems expands toward less restricted environments, the development of algorithms for view and illumination invariant face recognition becomes important. However, the performance of current algorithms degrades significantly when tested across pose and illumination, as documented in a number of evaluations. In this chapter we review previously proposed algorithms for pose and illumination invariant face recognition. We then describe in detail two successful appearance-based algorithms for face recognition across pose, eigen light-fields, and Bayesian face subregions. We furthermore show how both of these algorithms can be extended toward face recognition across pose and illumination.

## 1 Introduction

The most recent evaluation of commercial face recognition systems shows the level of performance for face verification of the best systems to be on par with fingerprint recognizers for frontal, uniformly illuminated faces [38]. Recognizing faces reliably across changes in pose and illumination has proved to be a much more difficult problem [9, 24, 38]. Although most research has so far focused on frontal face recognition, there is a sizable body of work on pose invariant face recognition and illumination invariant face recognition. However, face recognition across pose *and* illumination has received little attention.

### 1.1 Multiview Face Recognition and Face Recognition Across Pose

Approaches addressing pose variation can be classified into two categories depending on the type of gallery images they use. Multiview face recognition is a direct extension of frontal face recognition in which the algorithms require gallery images of every subject at every pose. In face recognition across pose we are concerned with the problem of building algorithms to recognize a face from a novel viewpoint (i.e., a viewpoint from which it has not previously been seen). In both categories we furthermore distinguish between model-based and appearance-based algorithms. Model-based algorithms use an explicit two-dimensional (2D) [12] or 3D [11, 15] model of the face, whereas appearance-based methods directly use image pixels or features derived from image pixels [36].

One of the earliest appearance-based multiview algorithms was described by Beymer [6]. After a pose estimation step, the algorithm geometrically aligns the probe images to candidate poses of the gallery subjects using the automatically determined locations of three feature points. This alignment is then refined using optical flow. Recognition is performed by computing normalized correlation scores. Good recognition results are reported on a database of 62 subjects imaged in a number of poses ranging from -30° to +30° (yaw) and from -20° to +20° (pitch). However, the probe and gallery poses are similar. Pentland et al. [37] extended the popular eigenface approach of Turk and Pentland [47] is extended to handle multiple views. The authors compare the performance of a parametric eigenspace (computed using all views from all subjects) with view-based eigenspaces (separate eigenspaces for each view). In experiments on a database of 21 people recorded in nine evenly spaced views from minus 90° to +90°, view-based eigenspaces outperformed the parametric eigenspace by a small margin.

A number of 2D model-based algorithms have been proposed for face tracking through large pose changes. In one study [13] separate active appearance models were trained for profile, half-profile, and frontal views, with models for opposing views created by simple reflection. Using a heuristic for switching between models, the system was able to track faces through wide angle changes. It has been shown that linear models are able to deal with considerable pose variation so long as all the modeled features remained visible [32]. A different way of dealing with larger pose variations is then to introduce nonlinearities into the model. Romdhani et al. extended active shape models [41] and active appearance models [42] using a kernel PCA to model shape and texture nonlinearities across views. In both cases models were successfully fit to face images across a full 180° rotation. However, no face recognition experiments were performed.

In many face recognition scenarios the pose of the probe and gallery images are different. For example, the gallery image might be a frontal "mug shot," and the probe image might be a three-quarter view captured from a camera in the corner of a room. The number of gallery and probe images can also vary. For example, the gallery might consist of a pair of images for each subject, a frontal mug shot and full profile view (like the images typically captured by police departments). The probe might be a similar pair of images, a single three-quarter view, or even a collection of views from random poses. In these scenarios multiview face recognition algorithms cannot be used. Early work on face recognition across pose was based on the idea of linear object classes [48]. The underlying assumption is that the 3D shape of an object (and 2D projections of 3D objects) can be represented by a linear combination of prototypical objects. It follows that a rotated view of the object is a linear combination of the rotated views of the prototype objects. Using this idea the authors were able to synthesize rotated views of face images from a single-example view. This algorithm has been used to create virtual views from a single input image for use in a multiview face recognition system [7]. Lando and Edelman used a comparable example-based technique to generalize to new poses from a single view [31].

A completely different approach to face recognition across pose is based on the work of Murase and Nayar [36]. They showed that different views of a rigid object projected into an eigenspace fall on a 2D manifold. Using a model of the manifold they could recognize objects from arbitrary views. In a similar manner Graham and Allison observed that a densely sampled image sequence of a rotating head forms a characteristic *eigensignature* when projected into an eigenspace [19]. They use radial basis function networks to generate eigensignatures based on a single view input. Recognition is then performed by distance computation between the projection of a probe image into eigenspace and the eigensignatures created from gallery views. Good generalization is observed from half-profile training views. However, recognition rates for tests across wide pose variations (e.g., frontal gallery and profile probe) are weak.

One of the early model-based approaches for face recognition is based on elastic bunch graph matching [49]. Facial landmarks are encoded with sets of complex Gabor wavelet coefficients called jets. A face is then represented with a graph where the various jets form the nodes. Based on a small number of hand-labeled examples, graphs for new images are generated automatically. The similarity between a probe graph and the gallery graphs is determined as average over the similarities between pairs of corresponding jets. Correspondences between nodes in different poses is established manually. Good recognition results are reported on frontal faces in the FERET evaluation [39]. Recognition accuracies decrease drastically, though, for matching half profile images with either frontal or full profile views. For the same framework a method for transforming jets across pose has been introduced [35]. In limited experiments the authors show improved recognition rates over the original representation.

## 1.2 Illumination Invariant Face Recognition

In addition to face pose, illumination is the next most significant factor affecting the appearance of faces. Ambient lighting changes greatly within and between days and among indoor and outdoor environments. Due to the 3D structure of the face, a direct lighting source can cast strong shadows that accentuate or diminish certain facial features. It has been shown experimentally [2] and theoretically for systems based on principal component analysis (PCA) [50] that differences in appearance induced by illumination are larger than differences between individuals. Because dealing with illumination variation is a central topic in computer vision, numerous approaches for illumination invariant face recognition have been proposed.

Early work in illumination invariant face recognition focused on image representations that are mostly insensitive to changes in illumination. In one study [2] various image representations and distance measures were evaluated on a tightly controlled face database that varied the face pose, illumination, and expression. The image representations include edge maps, 2D Gabor-like filters, first and second derivatives of the gray-level image, and the logarithmic transformations of the intensity image along with these representations. However, none of the image representations was found to be sufficient by itself to overcome variations due to illumination changes. In more recent work it was shown that the ratio of two images from the same object is simpler than the ratio of images from different objects [27]. In limited experiments this method outperformed both correlation and PCA but did not perform as well as the illumination cone method described below. A related line of work attempted to extract the object's surface reflectance as an illumination invariant description of the object [25, 30]. We discuss the most recent algorithm in this area in more detail in Section 4.2. Sashua and Riklin-Raviv [44] proposed a different illumination invariant image representation, the quotient image. Computed from a small set of example images, the quotient image can be used to re-render an object of the same class under a different illumination condition. In limited recognition experiments the method outperforms PCA.

A different approach to the problem is based on the observation that the images of a Lambertian surface, taken from a fixed viewpoint but under varying illumination, lie in a 3D linear subspace of the image space [43]. A number of appearance-based methods exploit this fact to model the variability of faces under changing illumination. Belhumeur et al.[4] extended the eigenface algorithm of Turk and Pentland [47] to fisherfaces by employing a classifier based on Fisher's linear discriminant analysis. In experiments on a face database with strong variations in illumination fisherfaces outperform eigenfaces by a wide margin. Further work in the area by Belhumeur and Kriegman showed that the set of images of an object in fixed pose but under varying illumination forms a convex cone in the space of images [5]. The illumination cones of human faces can be approximated well by low-dimensional linear subspaces [16]. An algorithm based on this method outperforms both eigenfaces and fisherfaces. More recently Basri and Jacobs showed that the illumination cone of a convex Lambertian surface can be approximated by a nine-dimensional linear subspace [3]. In limited experiments good recognition rates across illumination conditions are reported.

Common to all these appearance-based methods is the need for training images of database subjects under a number of different illumination conditions. An algorithm proposed by Sim and Kanade overcomes this restriction [45]. They used a statistical shape-from-shading model to recover the face shape from a single image and synthesize the face under a new illumination. Using this method they generated images of the gallery subjects under many different illumination conditions to serve as gallery images in a recognizer based on PCA. High recognition rates are reported on the illumination subset of the CMU PIE database [46].

### 1.3 Algorithms for Face Recognition across Pose and Illumination

A number of appearance and model-based algorithms have been proposed to address the problems of face recognition across pose and illumination simultaneously. In one study [17] a variant of photometric stereo was used to recover the shape and albedo of a face based on seven images of the subject seen in a fixed pose. In combination with the illumination cone representation introduced in [5] the authors can synthesize faces in novel pose and illumination conditions. In tests on 4050 images from the Yale Face Database B, the method performed almost without error. In another study [10] a morphable model of 3D faces was introduced. The model was created using a database of Cyberware laser scans of 200 subjects. Following an analysis-by-synthesis paradigm, the algorithm automatically recovers face pose and illumination from a single image. For initialization, the algorithm requires the manual localization of seven facial feature points. After fitting the model to a new image, the extracted model parameters describing the face shape and texture are used for recognition. The authors reported excellent recognition rates on both the FERET [39] and CMU PIE [46] databases. Once fit, the model could also be used to synthesize an image of the subject under new conditions. This method was used in the most recent face recognition vendor test to create frontal view images from rotated views [38]. For 9 of 10 face recognition systems tested, accuracies on the synthesized frontal views were significantly higher than on the original images.

## 2 Eigen Light-Fields

We propose an appearance-based algorithm for face recognition across pose. Our algorithm can use any number of gallery images captured at arbitrary poses and any number of probe images also captured with arbitrary poses. A minimum of one gallery and one probe image are needed, but if more images are available the performance of our algorithm generally improves.

Our algorithm operates by estimating (a representation of) the light-field [34] of the subject's head. First, generic training data are used to compute an eigenspace of head light-fields, similar to the construction of eigenfaces [47]. Light-fields are simply used rather than images. Given a collection of gallery or probe images, the projection into the eigenspace is performed by setting up a least-squares problem and solving for the projection coefficients similar to approaches used to deal with occlusions in the eigenspace approach [8, 33]. This simple linear algorithm can be applied to any number of images captured from any poses. Finally, matching is performed by comparing the probe and gallery eigen light-fields.

### 2.1 Light-Fields Theory

#### Object Light-Fields

The *plenoptic function* [1] or *light-field* [34] is a function that specifies the radiance of light in free space. It is a 5D function of position (3D) and orientation (2D). In addition, it is also sometimes modeled as a function of time, wavelength, and polarization, depending on the application in mind. In 2D, the light-field of a 2D object is actually 2D rather than the 3D that might be expected. See Figure 9.1 for an illustration.

#### Eigen Light-Fields

Suppose we are given a collection of light-fields $L_i(\theta, \phi)$ of objects $O_i$ (here faces of different subjects) where $i = 1, \ldots, N$. See Figure 9.1 for the definition of this notation. If we perform an eigendecomposition of these vectors using PCA, we obtain $d \leq N$ eigen light-fields $E_i(\theta, \phi)$ where $i = 1, \ldots, d$. Then, assuming that the eigenspace of light-fields is a good representation of the set of light-fields under consideration, we can approximate any light-field $L(\theta, \phi)$ as

$$L(\theta, \phi) \approx \sum_{i=1}^{d} \lambda_i E_i(\theta, \phi) \tag{1}$$

where $\lambda_i = \langle L(\theta, \phi), E_i(\theta, \phi) \rangle$ is the inner (or dot) product between $L(\theta, \phi)$ and $E_i(\theta, \phi)$. This decomposition is analogous to that used for face and object recognition [36, 47]. The mean light-field could also be estimated and subtracted from all of the light-fields.

Capturing the complete light-field of an object is a difficult task, primarily because it requires a huge number of images [18, 34]. In most object recognition scenarios it is unreasonable to expect more than a few images of the object (often just one). However, any image of the object corresponds to a curve (for 3D objects, a surface) in the light-field. One way to look at this curve is as a highly occluded light-field; only a small part of the light-field is visible. Can the eigen coefficients $\lambda_i$ be estimated from this highly occluded view? Although this may seem

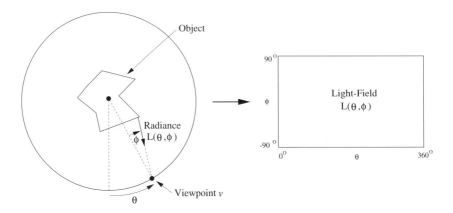

**Fig. 9.1.** The object is conceptually placed within a circle. The angle to the viewpoint $v$ around the circle is measured by the angle $\theta$, and the direction the viewing ray makes with the radius of the circle is denoted $\phi$. For each pair of angles $\theta$ and $\phi$, the radiance of light reaching the viewpoint from the object is then denoted by $L(\theta, \phi)$, the *light-field*. Although the light-field of a 3D object is actually 4D, we continue to use the 2D notation of this figure in this chapter for ease of explanation.

hopeless, consider that light-fields are highly redundant, especially for objects with simple reflectance properties such as Lambertian. An algorithm has been presented [33] to solve for the unknown $\lambda_i$ for eigen *images*. A similar algorithm was implicitly used by Black and Jepson [8]. Rather than using the inner product $\lambda_i = \langle L(\theta, \phi), E_i(\theta, \phi) \rangle$, Leonardis and Bischof [33] solved for $\lambda_i$ as the least-squares solution of

$$L(\theta, \phi) - \sum_{i=1}^{d} \lambda_i E_i(\theta, \phi) = 0 \tag{2}$$

where there is one such equation for each pair of $\theta$ and $\phi$ that are unoccluded in $L(\theta, \phi)$. Assuming that $L(\theta, \phi)$ lies *completely within the eigenspace* and that enough pixels are unoccluded, the solution of Eq. (2) is exactly the same as that obtained using the inner product [21]. Because there are $d$ unknowns ($\lambda_1 \ldots \lambda_d$) in Eq. (2), at least $d$ unoccluded light-field pixels are needed to overconstrain the problem, but more may be required owing to linear dependencies between the equations. In practice, two to three times as many equations as unknowns are typically required to get a reasonable solution [33]. Given an image $I(m, n)$, the following is then an algorithm for estimating the eigen light-field coefficients $\lambda_i$.

1. For each pixel $(m, n)$ in $I(m, n)$, compute the corresponding light-field angles $\theta_{m,n}$ and $\phi_{m,n}$. (This step assumes that the camera intrinsics are known, as well as the relative orientation of the camera to the object.)
2. Find the least-squares solution (for $\lambda_1 \ldots \lambda_d$) to the set of equations

$$I(m, n) - \sum_{i=1}^{d} \lambda_i E_i(\theta_{m,n}, \phi_{m,n}) = 0 \tag{3}$$

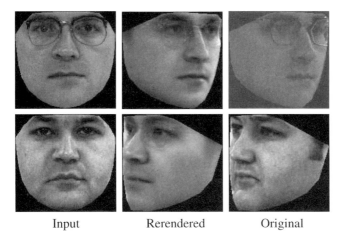

|        |           |          |
|--------|-----------|----------|
| Input  | Rerendered | Original |

**Fig. 9.2.** Our eigen light-field estimation algorithm for re-rendering a face across pose. The algorithm is given the left-most (frontal) image as input from which it estimates the eigen light-field and then creates the rotated view shown in the middle. For comparison, the original rotated view is shown in the right-most column. In the figure we show one of the better results (top) and one of the worst (bottom.) Although in both cases the output looks like a face, the identity is altered in the second case.

where $m$ and $n$ range over their allowed values. (In general, the eigen light-fields $E_i$ need to be interpolated to estimate $E_i(\theta_{m,n}, \phi_{m,n})$. Also, all of the equations for which the pixel $I(m, n)$ does not image the object should be excluded from the computation.)

Although we have described this algorithm for a single image $I(m, n)$, any number of images can obviously be used (so long as the camera intrinsics and relative orientation to the object are known for each image). The extra pixels from the other images are simply added in as additional constraints on the unknown coefficients $\lambda_i$ in Eq. (3). The algorithm can be used to estimate a light-field from a collection of images. Once the light-field has been estimated, it can then be used to render new images of the same object under different poses. (See Vetter and Poggio [48] for a related algorithm.) We have shown [21] that the algorithm correctly re-renders a given object assuming a Lambertian reflectance model. The extent to which these assumptions are valid are illustrated in Figure 9.2, where we present the results of using our algorithm to re-render faces across pose. In each case the algorithm received the left-most (frontal) image as input and created the rotated view in the middle. For comparison, the original rotated view is included as the right-most image. The re-rendered image for the first subject is similar to the original. Although the image created for the second subject still shows a face in the correct pose, the identity of the subject is not as accurately recreated. We conclude that overall our algorithm works fairly well but that more training data are needed so the eigen light-field of faces can more accurately represent any given face light-field.

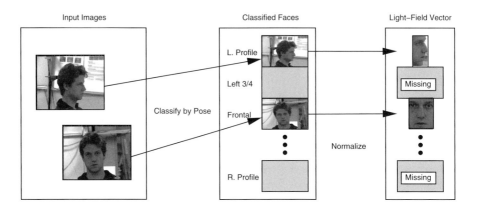

**Fig. 9.3.** Vectorization by normalization. Vectorization is the process of converting a set of images of a face into a light-field vector. Vectorization is performed by first classifying each input image into one of a finite number of poses. For each pose, normalization is then applied to convert the image into a subvector of the light-field vector. If poses are missing, the corresponding part of the light-field vector is missing.

## 2.2 Application to Face Recognition Across Pose

The eigen light-field estimation algorithm described above is somewhat abstract. To be able to use it for face recognition across pose we need to do the following things.

*Vectorization:* The input to a face recognition algorithm consists of a collection of images (possibly just one) captured from a variety of poses. The eigen light-field estimation Algorithm operates on light-field vectors (light-fields represented as vectors). Vectorization consists of converting the input images into a light-field vector (with missing elements, as appropriate.)

*Classification:* Given the eigen coefficients $a_1 \ldots a_d$ for a collection of gallery faces and for a probe face, we need to classify which gallery face is the most likely match.

*Selecting training and testing sets:* To evaluate our algorithm we have to divide the database used into (disjoint) subsets for training and testing.

We now describe each of these tasks in turn.

### Vectorization by Normalization

Vectorization is the process of converting a collection of images of a face into a light-field vector. Before we can do this we first have to decide how to discretize the light-field into pixels. Perhaps the most natural way to do this is to uniformly sample the light-field angles ($\theta$ and $\phi$ in the 2D case of Figure 9.1). This is not the only way to discretize the light-field. Any sampling, uniform or nonuniform, could be used. All that is needed is a way to specify what is the allowed set of light-field pixels. For each such pixel, there is a corresponding index in the light-field vector; that is, if the light-field is sampled at $K$ pixels, the light-field vectors are $K$ dimensional vectors.

We specify the set of light-field pixels in the following manner. We assume that there are only a finite set of poses $1, 2, \ldots, P$ in which the face can occur. Each face image is first classified into the nearest pose. (Although this assumption is clearly an approximation, its validity is demonstrated by the empirical results in Section 2.3. In both the FERET [39] and PIE [46] databases, there is considerable variation in the pose of the faces. Although the subjects are asked to place their face in a fixed pose, they rarely do this perfectly. Both databases therefore contain considerable variation away from the finite set of poses. Our algorithm performs well on both databases, so the approximation of classifying faces into a finite set of poses is validated.)

Each pose $i = 1, \ldots, P$ is then allocated a fixed number of pixels $K_i$. The total number of pixels in a light-field vector is therefore $K = \sum_{i=1}^{P} K_i$. If we have images from poses 3 and 7, for example, we know $K_3 + K_7$ of the $K$ pixels in the light-field vector. The remaining $K - K_3 - K_7$ are unknown, missing data. This vectorization process is illustrated in Figure 9.3.

We still need to specify how to sample the $K_i$ pixels of a face in pose $i$. This process is analogous to that needed in appearance-based object recognition and is usually performed by "normalization." In eigenfaces [47], the standard approach is to find the positions of several canonical points, typically the eyes and the nose, and to warp the input image onto a coordinate frame where these points are in fixed locations. The resulting image is then masked. To generalize eigenface normalization to eigen light-fields, we just need to define such a normalization for each pose.

We report results using two different normalizations. The first is a simple one based on the location of the eyes and the nose. Just as in eigenfaces, we assume that the eye and nose locations are known, warp the face into a coordinate frame in which these canonical points are in a fixed location, and finally crop the image with a (pose-dependent) mask to yield the $K_i$ pixels. For this simple three-point normalization, the resulting masked images vary in size between 7200 and 12,600 pixels, depending on the pose.

The second normalization is more complex and is motivated by the success of active appearance models (AAMs) [12]. This normalization is based on the location of a large number (39–54 depending on the pose) of points on the face. These canonical points are triangulated and the image warped with a piecewise affine warp onto a coordinate frame in which the canonical points are in fixed locations. The resulting masked images for this multipoint normalization vary in size between 20,800 and 36,000 pixels. Although currently the multipoint normalization is performed using hand-marked points, it could be performed by fitting an AAM [12] and then using the implied canonical point locations.

## Classification Using Nearest Neighbor

The eigen light-field estimation algorithm outputs a vector of eigen coefficients $(a_1, \ldots, a_d)$. Given a set of gallery faces, we obtain a corresponding set of vectors $(a_1^{\mathrm{id}}, \ldots, a_d^{\mathrm{id}})$, where id is an index over the set of gallery faces. Similarly, given a probe face, we obtain a vector $(a_1, \ldots, a_d)$ of eigen coefficients for that face. To complete the face recognition algorithm we need an algorithm that classifies $(a_1, \ldots, a_d)$ with the index id, which is the most likely match. Many classification algorithms could be used for this task. For simplicity, we use the nearest-neighbor algorithm, that classifies the vector $(a_1, \ldots, a_d)$ with the index.

$$\arg\min_{\text{id}} \text{dist}\left((a_1, \ldots, a_d), (a_1^{\text{id}}, \ldots, a_d^{\text{id}})\right) \;=\; \arg\min_{\text{id}} \sum_{i=1}^{d} \left(a_i - a_i^{\text{id}}\right)^2 \qquad (4)$$

All of the results reported in this chapter use the Euclidean distance in Eq. (4). Alternative distance functions, such as the Mahalanobis distance, could be used instead if so desired.

**Selecting the Gallery, Probe, and Generic Training Data**

In each of our experiments we divided the database into three disjoint subsets:

*Generic training data:* Many face recognition algorithms such as eigenfaces, and including our algorithm, require "generic training data" to build a generic face model. In eigenfaces, for example, generic training data are needed to compute the eigenspace. Similarly, in our algorithm, generic data are needed to construct the eigen light-field.

*Gallery:* The gallery is the set of reference images of the people to be recognized (i.e., the images given to the algorithm as examples of each person who might need to be recognized).

*Probe:* The probe set contains the "test" images (i.e., the images to be presented to the system to be classified with the identity of the person in the image).

The division into these three subsets is performed as follows. First we randomly select half of the subjects as the generic training data. The images of the remaining subjects are used for the gallery and probe. There is therefore never any overlap between the generic training data and the gallery and probe.

After the generic training data have been removed, the remainder of the databases are divided into probe and gallery sets based on the pose of the images. For example, we might set the gallery to be the frontal images and the probe set to be the left profiles. In this case, we evaluate how well our algorithm is able to recognize people from their profiles given that the algorithm has seen them only from the front. In the experiments described below we choose the gallery and probe poses in various ways. The gallery and probe are always disjoint unless otherwise noted.

## 2.3 Experimental Results

**Databases**

We used two databases in our face recognition across pose experiments, the CMU Pose, Illumination, and Expression (PIE) database [46] and the FERET database [39]. Each of these databases contains substantial pose variation. In the pose subset of the CMU PIE database (Fig. 9.4), the 68 subjects are imaged simultaneously under 13 poses totaling 884 images. In the FERET database, the subjects are imaged nonsimultaneously in nine poses. We used 200 subjects from the FERET pose subset, giving 1800 images in total. If not stated otherwise, we used half of the available subjects for training of the generic eigenspace (34 subjects for PIE, 100 subjects for FERET) and the remaining subjects for testing. In all experiments (if not stated otherwise) we retain a number of eigenvectors sufficient to explain 95% of the variance in the input data.

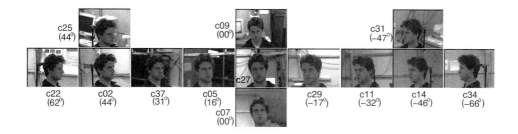

**Fig. 9.4.** Pose variation in the PIE database. The pose varies from full left profile (c34) to full frontal (c27) and to full right profile (c22). Approximate pose angles are shown below the camera numbers.

## Comparison with Other Algorithms

We compared our algorithm with eigenfaces [47] and FaceIt, the commercial face recognition system from Identix (formerly Visionics).[1]

We first performed a comparison using the PIE database. After randomly selecting the generic training data, we selected the gallery pose as one of the 13 PIE poses and the probe pose as any other of the remaining 12 PIE poses. For each disjoint pair of gallery and probe poses, we computed the average recognition rate over all subjects in the probe and gallery sets. The details of the results are shown in Figure 9.5 and are summarized in Table 9.1.

In Figure 9.5 we plotted color-coded $13 \times 13$ "confusion matrices" of the results. The row denotes the pose of the gallery, the column the pose of the probe, and the displayed intensity the average recognition rate. A lighter color denotes a higher recognition rate. (On the diagonals the gallery and probe images are the same so all three algorithms obtain a 100% recognition rate.)

Eigen light-fields performed far better than the other algorithms, as witnessed by the lighter color of Figure 9.5a,b compared to Figures 9.5c,d. Note how eigen light-fields was far better able to generalize across wide variations in pose, and in particular to and from near-profile views.

Table 9.1 includes the average recognition rate computed over all disjoint gallery-probe poses. As can be seen, eigen light-fields outperformed both the standard eigenfaces algorithm and the commercial FaceIt system.

We next performed a similar comparison using the FERET database [39]. Just as with the PIE database, we selected the gallery pose as one of the nine FERET poses and the probe pose as any other of the remaining eight FERET poses. For each disjoint pair of gallery and probe poses, we computed the average recognition rate over all subjects in the probe and gallery sets, and then averaged the results. The results are similar to those for the PIE database and are summarized in Table 9.2. Again, eigen light-fields performed significantly better than either FaceIt or eigenfaces.

Overall, the performance improvement of eigen light-fields over the other two algorithms is more significant on the PIE database than on the FERET database. This is because the PIE

---

[1] Version 2.5.0.17 of the FaceIt recognition engine was used in the experiments.

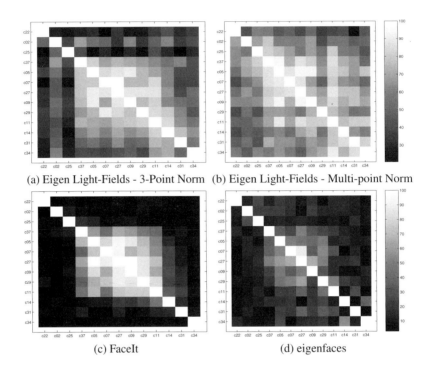

(a) Eigen Light-Fields - 3-Point Norm   (b) Eigen Light-Fields - Multi-point Norm

(c) FaceIt                                (d) eigenfaces

**Fig. 9.5.** Comparison with FaceIt and eigenfaces for face recognition across pose on the CMU PIE [46] database. For each pair of gallery and probe poses, we plotted the color-coded average recognition rate. The row denotes the pose of the gallery and the column the pose of the probe. The fact that the images in a and b are lighter in color than those in c and d implies that our algorithm performs better.

database contains more variation in pose than the FERET database. For more evaluation results see Gross et al. [23].

**Table 9.1.** Comparison of eigen light-fields with FaceIt and eigenfaces for face recognition across pose on the CMU PIE database. The table contains the average recognition rate computed across all disjoint pairs of gallery and probe poses; it summarizes the average performance in Figure 9.5.

| Algorithm | Average recognition accuracy (%) |
|---|---|
| Eigenfaces | 16.6 |
| FaceIt | 24.3 |
| Eigen light-fields | |
|     Three-point norm | 52.5 |
|     Multipoint norm | 66.3 |

**Table 9.2.** Comparison of eigen light-fields with FaceIt and eigenfaces for face recognition across pose on the FERET database. The table contains the average recognition rate computed across all disjoint pairs of gallery and probe poses. Again, eigen light-fields outperforms both eigenfaces and FaceIt.

| Algorithm | Average recognition accuracy (%) |
|---|---|
| Eigenfaces | 39.4 |
| FaceIt | 59.3 |
| Eigen light-fields three-point normalization | 75.0 |

# 3 Bayesian Face Subregions

Owing to the complicated 3D nature of the face, differences exist in how the appearance of various face regions change for different face poses. If, for example, a head rotates from a frontal to a right profile position, the appearance of the mostly featureless cheek region only changes little (if we ignore the influence of illumination), while other regions such as the left eye disappear, and the nose looks vastly different. Our algorithm models the appearance changes of the different face regions in a probabilistic framework [28]. Using probability distributions for similarity values of face subregions; we compute the likelihood of probe and gallery images coming from the same subject. For training and testing of our algorithm we use the CMU PIE database [46].

## 3.1 Face Subregions and Feature Representation

Using the hand-marked locations of both eyes and the midpoint of the mouth, we warp the input face images into a common coordinate frame in which the landmark points are in a fixed location and crop the face region to a standard $128 \times 128$ pixel size. Each image $I$ in the database is labeled with the identity $i$ and pose $\phi$ of the face in the image: $I = (i, \phi), i \in \{1, \ldots, 68\}, \phi \in \{1, \ldots, 13\}$. As shown in Figure 9.6, a $7 \times 3$ lattice is placed on the normalized faces, and $9 \times 15$ pixel subregions are extracted around every lattice point. The intensity values in each of the 21 subregions are normalized to have zero mean and unit variance.

As the similarity measure between subregions we use SSD (sum of squared difference) values $s_j$ between corresponding regions $j$ for all image pairs. Because we compute the SSD after image normalization, it effectively contains the same information as normalized correlation.

## 3.2 Modeling Local Appearance Change Across Pose

For probe image $I_{i,p} = (i, \phi_p)$ with unknown identity $i$ we compute the probability that $I_{i,p}$ is coming from the same subject $k$ as gallery image $I_{k,g}$ for each face subregion $j, j \in \{1, \ldots, 21\}$. Using Bayes' rule we write:

$$P(i = k | s_j, \phi_p, \phi_g) = \frac{P(s_j | i = k, \phi_p, \phi_g) P(i = k)}{P(s_j | i = k, \phi_p, \phi_g) P(i = k) + P(s_j | i \neq k, \phi_p, \phi_g) P(i \neq k)} \quad (5)$$

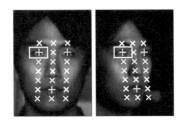

**Fig. 9.6.** Face subregions for two poses of the CMU PIE database. Each face in the database is warped into a normalized coordinate frame using the hand-labeled locations of both eyes and the midpoint of the mouth. A $7 \times 3$ lattice is placed on the normalized face, and $9 \times 15$ pixel subregions are extracted around every lattice point, resulting in a total of 21 subregions.

We assume the conditional probabilities $P(s_j | i = k, \phi_p, \phi_g)$ and $P(s_j | i \neq k, \phi_p, \phi_g)$ to be Gaussian distributed and learn the parameters from data. Figure 9.7 shows histograms of similarity values for the right eye region. The examples in Figure 9.7 show that the discriminative power of the right eye region diminishes as the probe pose changes from almost frontal (Figure 9.7a) to right profile (Figure 9.7c).

It is reasonable to assume that the pose of each gallery image is known. However, because the pose $\phi_p$ of the probe images is in general not known, we marginalize over it. We can then compute the conditional densities for similarity value $s_j$ as

$$ P(s_j | i = k, \phi_g) = \sum_p P(\phi_p) P(s_j | i = k, \phi_p, \phi_g) $$

and

$$ P(s_j | i \neq k, \phi_g) = \sum_p P(\phi_p) P(s_j | i \neq k, \phi_p, \phi_g) $$

If no other knowledge about the probe pose is given, the pose prior $P(\phi_p)$ is assumed to be uniformly distributed. Similar to the posterior probability defined in Eq. (5) we compute the probability of the unknown probe image coming from the same subject (given similarity value $s_j$ and gallery pose $\phi_g$) as

$$ P(i = k | s_j, \phi_g) = \frac{P(s_j | i = k, \phi_g) P(i = k)}{P(s_j | i = k, \phi_g) P(i = k) + P(s_j | i \neq k, \phi_g) P(i \neq k)} \qquad (6) $$

To decide on the most likely identity of an unknown probe image $I_{i,p} = (i, \phi_p)$ we compute match probabilities between $I_{i,p}$ and all gallery images for all face subregions using Eq. (5) or (6). We currently do not model dependencies between subregions, so we simply combine the different probabilities using the sum rule [29] and choose the identity of the gallery image with the highest score as the recognition result.

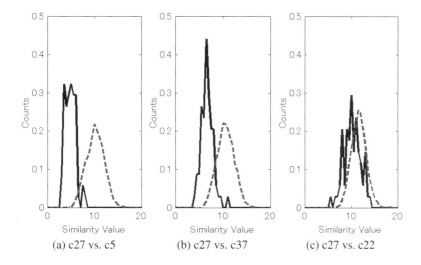

(a) c27 vs. c5          (b) c27 vs. c37          (c) c27 vs. c22

**Fig. 9.7.** Histograms of similarity values $s_j$ for the right eye region across multiple poses. The distribution of similarity values for identical gallery and probe subjects are shown with solid curves, the distributions for different gallery and probe subjects are shown with broken curves.

### 3.3  Experimental Results

We used half of the 68 subjects in the CMU PIE database for training of the models described in Section 3.2. The remaining 34 subjects are used for testing. The images of all 68 subjects are used in the gallery. We compare our algorithm to eigenfaces [47] and the commercial FaceIt system.

#### Experiment 1: Unknown Probe Pose

For the first experiment we assume the pose of the probe images to be unknown. We therefore must use Eq. (6) to compute the posterior probability that probe and gallery images come from the same subject. We assume $P(\phi_p)$ to be uniformly distributed, that is, $P(\phi_p) = \frac{1}{13}$. Figure 9.8 compares the recognition accuracies of our algorithm with eigenfaces and FaceIt for frontal gallery images. Our system clearly outperforms both eigenfaces and FaceIt. Our algorithm shows good performance up until $45°$ head rotation between probe and gallery image (poses 02 and 31). The performance of eigenfaces and FaceIt already drops at $15°$ and $30°$ rotation, respectively.

#### Experiment 2: Known Probe Pose

In the case of known probe pose we can use Eq. (5) to compute the probability that probe and gallery images come from the same subject. Figure 9.9 compares the recognition accuracies of our algorithm for frontal gallery images for known and unknown probe poses. Only small differences in performances are visible.

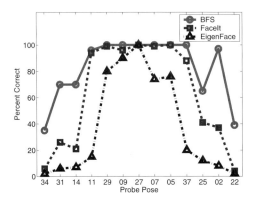

**Fig. 9.8.** Recognition accuracies for our algorithm (labeled BFS), eigenfaces, and FaceIt for frontal gallery images and unknown probe poses. Our algorithm clearly outperforms both eigenfaces and FaceIt.

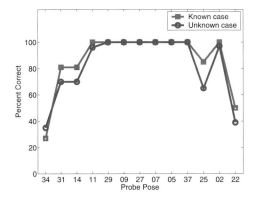

**Fig. 9.9.** Comparison of recognition accuracies of our algorithm for frontal gallery images for known and unknown probe poses. Only small differences are visible.

Figure 9.10 shows recognition accuracies for all three algorithms for all possible combinations of gallery and probe poses. The area around the diagonal in which good performance is achieved is much wider for our algorithm than for either eigenfaces or FaceIt. We therefore conclude that our algorithm generalizes much better across pose than either eigenfaces or FaceIt.

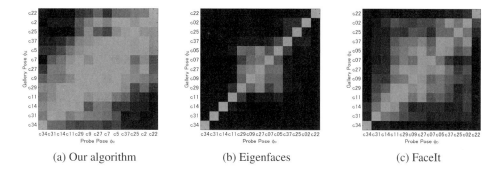

(a) Our algorithm          (b) Eigenfaces          (c) FaceIt

**Fig. 9.10.** Recognition accuracies for our algorithm, eigenfaces, and FaceIt for all possible combinations of gallery and probe poses. Here lighter pixel values correspond to higher recognition accuracies. The area around the diagonal in which good performance is achieved is much wider for our algorithm than for either eigenfaces or FaceIt.

## 4 Face Recognition Across Pose and Illumination

Because appearance-based methods use image intensities directly, they are inherently sensitive to variations in illumination. Drastic changes in illumination such as between indoor and outdoor scenes therefore cause significant problems for appearance-based face recognition algorithms [24, 38]. In this section we describe two ways to handle illumination variations in facial imagery. The first algorithm extracts illumination invariant subspaces by extending the previously introduced eigen light-fields to Fisher light-fields [22], mirroring the step from eigenfaces [47] to fisherfaces [4]. The second approach combines Bayesian face subregions with an image preprocessing algorithm that removes illumination variation prior to recognition [20]. In both cases we demonstrate results for face recognition across pose *and* illumination.

### 4.1 Fisher Light-Fields

Suppose we are given a set of light-fields $L_{i,j}(\theta, \phi)$, $i = 1, \ldots, N$, $j = 1, \ldots, M$ where each of $N$ objects $O_i$ is imaged under $M$ different illumination conditions. We could proceed as described in Section 2.1 and perform PCA on the whole set of $N \times M$ light-fields. An alternative approach is Fisher's linear discriminant (FLD) [14], also known as linear discriminant analysis (LDA) [51], which uses the available class information to compute a projection better suited for discrimination tasks. Analogous to the algorithm described in Section 2.1, we now find the least-squares solution to the set of equations

$$L(\theta, \phi) - \sum_{i=1}^{m} \lambda_i W_i(\theta, \phi) = 0 \tag{7}$$

where $W_i, i = 1, \ldots, m$ are the generalized eigenvectors computed by LDA.

**Table 9.3.** Performance of eigen light-fields and Fisher light-fields with FaceIt on three face recognition across pose and illumination scenarios. In all three cases, eigen light-fields and Fisher light-fields outperformed FaceIt by a large margin.

| Conditions | Eigen light-fields | Fisher light-fields | FaceIt |
|---|---|---|---|
| Same pose, different illumination | - | 81.1% | 41.6% |
| Different pose, same illumination | 72.9% | - | 25.8% |
| Different pose, different illumination | - | 36.0% | 18.1% |

**Experimental Results**

For our face recognition across pose and illumination experiments we used the pose and illumination subset of the CMU PIE database [46]. In this subset, 68 subjects are imaged under 13 poses and 21 illumination conditions. Many of the illumination directions introduce fairly subtle variations in appearance, so we selected 12 of the 21 illumination conditions that span the set widely. In total we used $68 \times 13 \times 12 = 10,608$ images in the experiments.

We randomly selected 34 subjects of the PIE database for the generic training data and then removed the data from the experiments (see Section 2.2). There were then a variety of ways to select the gallery and probe images from the remaining data.

Same pose, different illumination: The gallery and probe poses are the same. The gallery and probe illuminations are different. This scenario is like traditional face recognition across illumination but is performed separately for each pose.

Different pose, same illumination: The gallery and probe poses are different. The gallery and probe illuminations are the same. This scenario is like traditional face recognition across pose but is performed separately for each possible illumination.

Different pose, different illumination: Both the pose and illumination of the probe and gallery are different. This is the most difficult and most general scenario.

We compared our algorithms with FaceIt under these three scenarios. In all cases we generated every possible test scenario and then averaged the results. For "same pose, different illumination," for example, we consider every possible pose. We generated every pair of disjoint probe and gallery illumination conditions. We then computed the average recognition rate for each such case. We averaged over every pose and every pair of distinct illumination conditions. The results are included in Table 9.3. For "same-pose, different illumination," the task is essentially face recognition across illumination separately for each pose. In this case, it makes little sense to try eigen light-fields because we know how poorly eigenfaces performs with illumination variation. Fisher light-fields becomes fisherfaces for each pose, which empirically we found outperforms FaceIt. Example illumination "confusion matrices" are included for two poses in Figure 9.11.

For "different pose, same illumination," the task reduces to face recognition across pose but for a variety of illumination conditions. In this case there is no intraclass variation, so it makes little sense to apply Fisher light-fields. This experiment is the same as Experiment 1 in Section 2.3 but the results are averaged over every possible illumination condition. As we found for Experiment 1, eigen light-fields outperforms FaceIt by a large amount.

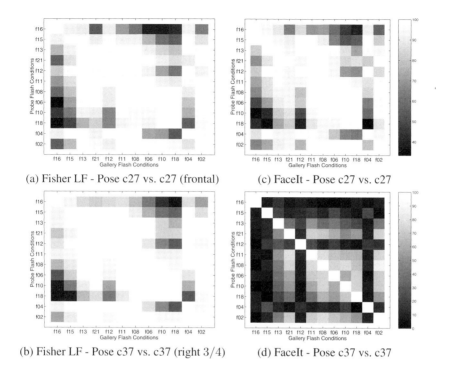

(a) Fisher LF - Pose c27 vs. c27 (frontal)    (c) FaceIt - Pose c27 vs. c27

(b) Fisher LF - Pose c37 vs. c37 (right 3/4)    (d) FaceIt - Pose c37 vs. c37

**Fig. 9.11.** Example "confusion matrices" for the "same-pose, different illumination" task. For a given pose, and a pair of distinct probe and gallery illumination conditions, we color-code the average recognition rate. The superior performance of Fisher light-fields is witnessed by the lighter color of (a–b) over (c–d).

Finally, in the "different pose, different illumination" task both algorithms perform fairly poorly. However, the task is difficult. If the pose and illumination are both extreme, almost none of the face is visible. Because this case might occur in either the probe or the gallery, the chance that such a difficult case occurs is large. Although more work is needed on this task, note that Fisher light-fields still outperforms FaceIt by a large amount.

### 4.2  Illumination Invariant Bayesian Face Subregions

In general, an image $I(x, y)$ is regarded as product $I(x, y) = R(x, y)L(x, y)$, where $R(x, y)$ is the reflectance and $L(x, y)$ is the illuminance at each point $(x, y)$ [26]. Computing the reflectance and the illuminance fields from real images is, in general, an ill-posed problem. Our approach uses two widely accepted assumptions about human vision to solve the problem: (1) human vision is *mostly* sensitive to scene reflectance and *mostly* insensitive to the illumination conditions; and (2) human vision responds to local changes in contrast rather than to global brightness levels. Our algorithm computes an estimate of $L(x, y)$ such that when it divides $I(x, y)$ it produces $R(x, y)$ in which the local contrast is appropriately enhanced. We find a

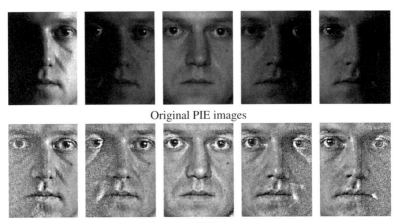

Original PIE images

Processed PIE images

**Fig. 9.12.** Result of removing illumination variations with our algorithm for a set of images from the PIE database.

solution for $L(x, y)$ by minimizing

$$J(L) = \iint_{\Omega} \rho(x, y)(L - I)^2 dxdy + \lambda \iint_{\Omega} (L_x^2 + L_y^2)dxdy \qquad (8)$$

Here $\Omega$ refers to the image. The parameter $\lambda$ controls the relative importance of the two terms. The space varying permeability weight $\rho(x, y)$ controls the anisotropic nature of the smoothing constraint. See Gross and Brajovic [20] for details. Figure 9.12 shows examples from the CMU PIE database before and after processing with our algorithm. We used this algorithm to normalize the images of the combined pose and illumination subset of the PIE database. Figure 9.13 compares the recognition accuracies of the Bayesian face subregions algorithm for original and normalized images using gallery images with frontal pose and illumination. The algorithm achieved better performance on normalized images across all probe poses. Overall the average recognition accuracy improved from 37.3% to 44%.

## 5 Conclusions

One of the most successful and well studied approaches to object recognition is the *appearance-based* approach. The defining characteristic of appearance-based algorithms is that they directly use the pixel intensity values in an image of the object as the features on which to base the recognition decision. In this chapter we described an appearance-based method for face recognition across pose based on an algorithm to estimate the eigen light-field from a collection of images. Unlike previous appearance-based methods, our algorithm can use any number of gallery images captured from arbitrary poses and any number of probe images also captured from arbitrary poses. The gallery and probe poses do not need to overlap. We showed that our

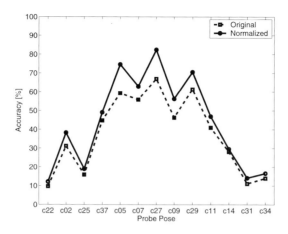

**Fig. 9.13.** Recognition accuracies of the Bayesian face subregions algorithm on original and normalized images using gallery images with frontal pose and illumination. For each probe pose the accuracy is determined by averaging the results for all 21 illumination conditions. The algorithm achieves better performance on normalized images across all probe poses. The probe pose is assumed to be known.

algorithm can reliably recognize faces across pose and also take advantage of the additional information contained in widely separated views to improve recognition performance if more than one gallery or probe image is available.

In eigen light-fields all face pixels are treated equally. However, differences exist in how the appearance of various face regions change across face poses. We described a second algorithm, Bayesian face subregions, which derives a model for these differences and successfully employs it for face recognition across pose. Finally, we demonstrated how to extend both algorithms toward face recognition across both pose and illumination. Note, however, that for this task recognition accuracies are significantly lower, suggesting that there still is room for improvement. For example, the model-based approach of Romdhani et al.[40] achieved better results across pose on the PIE database than the appearance-based algorithms described here.

## Acknowledgments

The research described here was supported by U.S. Office of Naval Research contract N00014-00-1-0915 and in part by U.S. Department of Defense contract N41756-03-C4024. Portions of the research in this paper used the FERET database of facial images collected under the FERET program.

# References

1. E. Adelson and J. Bergen. The plenoptic function and elements of early vision. In Landy and Movshon, editors, *Computational Models of Visual Processing*. MIT Press, Cambridge, MA, 1991.

2. Y. Adini, Y. Moses, and S. Ullman. Face recognition: The problem of compensating for changes in illumination direction. *IEEE Transactions on Pattern Analysis and Machine Intelligence*, 19(7):721–732, 1997.

3. R. Basri and D. Jacobs. Lambertian reflectance and linear subspaces. *IEEE Transactions on Pattern Analysis and Machine Intelligence*, 25(2):218–233, 2003.

4. P. Belhumeur, J. Hespanha, and D. Kriegman. Eigenfaces vs. fisherfaces: recognition using class specific linear projection. *IEEE Transactions on Pattern Analysis and Machine Intelligence*, 19(7):711–720, 1997.

5. P. Belhumeur and D. Kriegman. What is the set of images of an object under all possible lighting conditions. *Int. J. of Computer Vision*, 28(3):245–260, 1998.

6. D. Beymer. Face recognition under varying pose. Technical Report 1461, MIT AI Laboratory, Cambridge, MA, 1993.

7. D. Beymer and T. Poggio. Face recognition from one example view. A.I. Memo No. 1536, MIT AI Laboratory, Cambridge, MA, 1995.

8. M. Black and A. Jepson. Eigen-tracking: robust matching and tracking of articulated objects using a view-based representation. *International Journal of Computer Vision*, 36(2):101–130, 1998.

9. D. Blackburn, M. Bone, and P. Phillips. Facial recognition vendor test 2000: evaluation report, 2000.

10. V. Blanz and T. Vetter. Face recognition based on fitting a 3D morphable model. *IEEE Transactions on Pattern Analysis and Machine Intelligence*, 25(9):1063–1074, 2003.

11. V. Blanz, S. Romdhani, and T. Vetter. Face identification across different poses and illumination with a 3D morphable model. In *Proceedings of the Fifth International Conference on Face and Gesture Recognition*, pages 202–207, 2002.

12. T. Cootes, G. Edwards, and C. Taylor. Active appearance models. *IEEE Transactions on Pattern Analysis and Machine Intelligence*, 23(6):681–685, 2001.

13. T. Cootes, G. Wheeler, K. Walker, and C. Taylor. View-based active appearance models. *Image and Vision Computing*, 20:657–664, 2002.

14. K. Fukunaga. *Introduction to Statistical Pattern Recognition*. Academic Press, San Diego, CA, 1990.

15. A. Georghiades, P. Belhumeur, and D. Kriegman. From few to many: Generative models for recognition under variable pose and illumination. In *Proceedings of the Fourth International Conference on Face and Gesture Recognition*, pages 277–284, 2000.

16. A. Georghiades, D. Kriegman, and P. Belhumeur. Illumination cones for recognition under variable lighting: faces. In *Proceedings of the IEEE Conference on Computer Vision and Pattern Recognition*, 1998.

17. A. Georghiades, D. Kriegman, and P. Belhumeur. From few to many: generative models for recognition under variable pose and illumination. *IEEE Transactions on Pattern Analysis and Machine Intelligence*, 23(6):643–660, 2001.

18. S. Gortler, R. Grzeszczuk, R. Szeliski, and M. Cohen. The lumigraph. In *Computer Graphics Proceedings, Annual Conference Series (SIGGRAPH)*, pages 43–54, 1996.

19. D. Graham and N. Allison. Face recognition from unfamiliar views: subspace methods and pose dependency. In *3rd International Conference on Automatic Face and Gesture Recognition*, pages 348–353, 1998.

20. R. Gross and V. Brajovic. An image pre-processing algorithm for illumination invariant face recognition. In *4th International Conference on Audio- and Video Based Biometric Person Authentication (AVBPA)*, pages 10–18, June 2003.

21. R. Gross, I. Matthews, and S. Baker. Eigen light-fields and face recognition across pose. In *Proceedings of the Fifth International Conference on Face and Gesture Recognition*, pages 1–7, 2002.

22. R. Gross, I. Matthews, and S. Baker. Fisher light-fields for face recognition across pose and illumination. In *Proceedings of the German Symposium on Pattern Recognition (DAGM)*, pages 481–489, 2002.

23. R. Gross, I. Matthews, and S. Baker. Appearance-based face recognition and light-fields. *IEEE Transactions on Pattern Analysis and Machine Intelligence*, 26(4):449–465, 2004.

24. R. Gross, J. Shi, and J. Cohn. Quo vadis face recognition? In *Third Workshop on Empirical Evaluation Methods in Computer Vision*, 2001.

25. B. Horn. Determining lightness from an image. *Computer Graphics and Image Processing*, 3(1):277–299, 1974.

26. B. Horn. *Robot Vision*. MIT Press, Cambridge, MA, 1986.

27. D. Jacobs, P. Belhumeur, and R. Basri. Comparing images under variable illumination. In *IEEE Conference on Computer Vision and Pattern Recognition*, pages 610–617, 1998.

28. T. Kanade and A. Yamada. Multi-subregion based probabilistic approach toward pose-invariant face recognition. In *IEEE International Symposium on Computational Intelligence in Robotics and Automation (CIRA2003)*, pages 954–959, 2003.

29. J. Kittler, M. Hatef, R. Duin, and J. Matas. On combining classifiers. *IEEE Trans. on Pattern Analysis and Machine Intelligence*, 20(3):226–239, 1998.

30. E. Land and J. McCann. Lightness and retinex theory. *Journal of the Optical Society of America*, 61(1):1–11, 1971.

31. M. Lando and S. Edelman. Generalization from a single view in face recognition. In *International Workshop on Automatic Face-and Gesture-Recognition*, 1995.

32. A. Lanitis, C. Taylor, and T. Cootes. Automatic interpretation and coding of face images using flexible models. *IEEE Transactions on Pattern Analysis and Machine Intelligence*, 19(7):743–756, 1997.

33. A. Leonardis and H. Bischof. Robust recognition using eigenimages. *Computer Vision and Image Understanding*, 78(1):99–118, 2000.

34. M. Levoy and M. Hanrahan. Light field rendering. In *Computer Graphics Proceedings, Annual Conference Series (SIGGRAPH)*, pages 31–41, 1996.

35. T. Maurer and C. von der Malsburg. Single-view based recognition of faces rotated in depth. In *International Workshop on Automatic Face and Gesture Recogition*, pages 248–253, 1995.

36. H. Murase and S. Nayar. Visual learning and recognition of 3-D objects from appearance. *International Journal of Computer Vision*, 14:5–24, 1995.

37. A. Pentland, B. Moghaddam, and T. Starner. View-based and modular eigenspaces for face recognition. In *Proceedings of the IEEE Conference on Computer Vision and Pattern Recognition*, pages 84–91, 1994.

38. P. J. Phillips, P. Grother, J. Ross, D. Blackburn, E. Tabassi, and M. Bone. Face recognition vendor test 2002: evaluation report, March 2003.

39. P. J. Phillips, H. Moon, S. Rizvi, and P. Rauss. The FERET evaluation methodology for face-recognition algorithms. *IEEE Transactions on Pattern Analysis and Machine Intelligence*, 22(10):1090–1104, 2000.

40. S. Romdhani, V. Blanz, and T. Vetter. Face identification by matching a 3D morphable model using linear shape and texture error functions. In *Proceedings of the European Conference on Computer Vision*, pages 3–19, 2002.

41. S. Romdhani, S. Gong, and A. Psarrou. Multi-view nonlinear active shape model using kernel PCA. In *10th British Machine Vision Conference*, volume 2, pages 483–492, 1999.

42. S. Romdhani, A. Psarrou, and S. Gong. On utilising template and feature-based correspondence in multi-view appearance models. In *6th European Conference on Computer Vision*, volume 1, pages 799–813, 2000.

43. A. Shashua. *Geometry and Photometry in 3D visual recognition*. PhD thesis, MIT, 1994.

44. A. Shashua and T. Riklin-Raviv. The Quotient image: class-based re-rendering and recognition with varying illumination conditions. *IEEE Transactions on Pattern Analysis and Machine Intelligence*, 23(2):129–139, 2001.

45. T. Sim and T. Kanade. Combining models and exemplars for face recognition: an illuminating example. In *Workshop on Models versus Exemplars in Computer Vision*, 2001.

46. T. Sim, S. Baker, and M. Bsat. The CMU pose, illumination, and expression database. *IEEE Transactions on Pattern Analysis and Machine Intelligence*, 25(12):1615–1618, 2003.

47. M. Turk and A. Pentland. Face recognition using eigenfaces. In *Proceedings of the IEEE Conference on Computer Vision and Pattern Recognition*, 1991.

48. T. Vetter and T. Poggio. Linear object classes and image synthesis from a single example image. *IEEE Transactions on Pattern Analysis and Machine Intelligence*, 19(7):733–741, 1997.

49. L. Wiskott, J. Fellous, N. Kruger, and C. von der Malsburg. Face recognition by elastic bunch graph matching. *IEEE Transactions on Pattern Analysis and Machine Intelligence*, 19(7):775–779, 1997.

50. W. Zhao and R. Chellappa. Robust face recognition using symmetric shape-from-shading. Technical report, Center for Automation Research, University of Maryland, 1999.

51. W. Zhao, A. Krishnaswamy, R. Chellappa, D. Swets, and J. Weng. Discriminant analysis of principal components for face recognition. In H. Wechsler, P. J. Phillips, V. Bruce, and T. Huang, editors, *Face Recognition: From Theory to Applications*. Springer, New York, 1998.

# Chapter 10. Morphable Models of Faces

Sami Romdhani[1], Volker Blanz[2], Curzio Basso[1], and Thomas Vetter[1]

[1] University of Basel, Computer Science Department, Bernoullistrasse 16, CH-4056 Basel, Switzerland.
`{sami.romdhani, curzio.basso, thomas.vetter}@unibas.ch`
[2] Max-Planck-Institut für Informatik, Stuhlsatzenhausweg 85, 66123 Saarbrücken, Germany.
`blanz@mpi-sb.mpg.de`

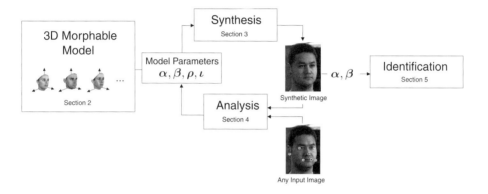

## 1 Morphable Model for Face Analysis

Our approach is based on an *analysis by synthesis* framework. The idea of this framework is to synthesize an image of a face that resembles the face in an input image. This framework requires a generative model able to accurately synthesize face images. The parameters of the image generated by the model are then used for high-level tasks such as identification.

To be applicable on any input face image, a good model must be able to generate any face images. Face images vary widely with respect to the imaging conditions (illumination and angle from which the face is viewed, called pose) and with respect to the identity and the expression of the face. A generative model must not only allow for these variations but must also clearly separate the source of variations to make, say, identification tasks invariant to the other sources of variation.

We explain in this section that a thrre-dimensional (3D) representation enables the accurate modeling of any illumination and pose as well as the separation of these variations from the rest (identity and expression). The generative model must be able to synthesize images from any individual. In a morphable model, the identity variation is modeled by making linear combinations of faces of a small set of persons. In this section, we show why linear combinations yield a realistic face only if the set of example faces is in correspondence. A good generative model should be restrictive in the sense that unlikely faces should be rarely instantiated. To achieve this the probability density function of human faces must be learned and used as a prior probability to synthesize faces.

Based on these principles, we detail the construction of a 3D morphable face model in Section 2. The main step of the model construction is computation of the correspondences of a set of example 3D laser scan of faces with a reference 3D face laser scan. We also introduce the *regularized* morphable model, which improves the correspondences. The synthesis of a face image from the model is presented in Section 3.

The generative model is half of the work. The other half is the analyzing algorithm (the *fitting algorithm*). The fitting algorithm finds the parameters of the model that synthesize an image as close as possible to the input image. We detail two fitting algorithms in Section 4. The main difference between these two algorithms is their trade-off between accuracy and computational load. Based on these two fitting algorithms, identification results are presented in Section 5 for face images varying in illumination and pose.

## 1.1  Three-dimensional Representation

Each individual face can generate a variety of images. This huge diversity of face images makes their analysis difficult. In addition to the general differences between individual faces, the appearance variations in images of a single faces can be separated into the following four sources.

- Pose changes can result in dramatic changes in images. Due to occlusions different parts of the object become visible or invisible. Additionally, the parts seen in two views change their spatial configuration relative to each other.
- Illumination changes influence the appearance of a face even if the pose of the face is fixed. Positions and distribution of light sources around a face have the effect of changing the brightness distribution in the images, the locations of attached shadows, and specular reflections. Additionally, cast shadows can generate prominent contours in facial images.
- Facial expressions, an important tool in human communication, are another source of variations in images. Only a few facial landmarks that are directly coupled with the bony structure of the skull, such as the interoccular distance or the general position of the ears, are constant in a face. Most other features can change their spatial configuration or position via articulation of the jaw or muscle action (e.g, a moving eyebrows, lips or cheeks).
- In the long term, a face changes because of aging, changing a hairstyle, or use of makeup or accessories.

The isolation and explicit description of all these sources of variations must be the ultimate goal of a face analysis system. For example, it is desirable that the parameters that code the identity of a person are not perturbed by a modification of pose. In an analysis by synthesis framework this implies that a face model must account for each of these variations independently by explicit parameters.

The main challenge for the design of such systems is to find or choose a description of these parameters that allows the appropriate modeling of images on the one hand and gives a precise description of an image on the other.

Some of the sources of variations, such as illumination and pose, obey the physical laws of nature. These laws reflect constraints derived from the three-dimensional geometry of faces and the interaction of their surfaces with light. They are optimally imposed by a 3D representation, which was therefore chosen for the morphable model.

On the other hand, there are additional regularities between faces that are not formulated as physical laws but can be obtained by exploiting the general statistics of faces. These methods are also denoted as learning from examples. It is expected that learning schemes that conform or incorporate the physical constraints are more successful in tasks such as generalizing from a single image of a face to novel views or to different illumination conditions.

As a result, the 3D morphable model uses physical laws to model pose and illumination as well as statistical methods to model identity and expression. As we see in the next two sections, these statistical methods require the faces to be put into correspondence.

## 1.2  Correspondence-Based Representation

For ease of visualization, we motivate the correspondence based representation on a 2D image example, and the same argument can be made on 3D faces. As seen in other chapters of this book, the crucial assumption of most of the model-based face analysis techniques is that any facial image can be generated by linear combinations of a few faces. However, linear operations such as a simple addition of raw images, pixel by pixel, is not very meaningful, as shown in Figure 10.1. Already the average of two images of a face does not result in the image of a face. Instead, the average appears blurry with double contours. Hence, facial images in their pixel representation do not form a vector space. For correct image modeling and synthesis, it is not sufficient to consider only image intensities, it is also necessary to consider the spatial locations of object features. That is, the correspondence between images has to be established. Only a separate addition of the shape and texture information satisfies the vector space requirements. Hence, shape alone forms a vector space, and texture alone forms another vector space. The face vector space is the combination of these two vector spaces.

So, correspondence separates texture information from two-dimensional shape information in an image. Correspondence is the basic requirement for the modeling of facial images in a vector space. The utilization of correspondence for image modeling was proposed by several authors [5, 11, 15, 18, 32]; for a review see Beymer and Poggio [4]. The common feature of these methods is that they all derive their facial model, used for the analysis and synthesis of facial images, from separate texture and shape vector spaces. It should be noted that some of these approaches do not extract the correspondence of *physical* points: Lanitis *et al.* [18], for instance, put into correspondence the 2D occluding contour, which varies from pose to pose. In contrast, our approach puts in correspondence 3D points that are equivalent across object instances.

The *appearance-based representation* is another one opposed to the correspondence-based representation. This representation is used by methods known as eigenface techniques [28, 30], and their generalized version is introduced as appearance-based models [22]. These techniques have been demonstrated to be successful when applied to images of a set of very different objects or, as in the case of faces, when viewpoint or lighting conditions are kept close to constant. Contrasting with our approach, these appearance-based models do not rely on shape features but, rather, only on pixel features. Also, they are learned by exploring the statistics of example data represented in the pixel space of the images. However, none of these techniques uses correspondences that exploit an object-centered representation.

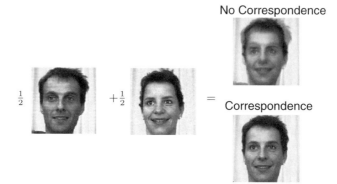

**Fig. 10.1.** Computing the average of two face images using different image representations. No correspondence information is used (Top right) and using correspondence (Bottom right).

In contrast to the techniques based on point correspondence between images or objects, these appearance-based models use linear combinations of images directly. This lack of correspondence information between the images is the crucial disadvantage of these methods. It disables the methods from any generalization abilities that go beyond a direct comparison of a novel image to stored images. Because of the truncated representation in a principal component space (see Section 1.3) and the missing correspondences, these techniques have limited image synthesis capabilities. Already the mixture of two instances of the same object results in an extremely blurry image ( Fig. 10.1). Although we show the advantages of a correspondence-based representation on a 2D image example, the validity of the argument extends to 3D faces.

### 1.3 Face Statistics

In the previous section, we explained that correspondences enable the generation of faces by simple linear combination of several faces. However, the coefficients of the linear combination do not have a uniform distribution. This distribution is learned from example faces using the currently widely accepted assumption that the face space is Gaussian. Under this assumption, PCA is used to learn a probability model of faces that is used as prior probability at the analysis step (see Section 4.1). More details about the face statistics of our model are given in Sections 2.3 and 2.4.

## 2  3D Morphable Model Construction

The construction of a 3D morphable model requires a set of example 3D faces (e.g., laser scans). The results presented in this chapter were obtained with a morphable model constructed with 200 laser scans acquired by a *Cyberware* 3030PS laser scanner. The constructions is performed in three steps: First, the laser scans are preprocessed. This semiautomatic step aims to remove the scanning artifacts and to select the part of the head that is to be modeled (from one ear to the other and from the neck to the forehead). In the second step, the correspondences are computed between one scan chosen as the reference scan, and each of the other scans. Then a principal components analysis is performed to estimate the statistics of the 3D shape and color of the faces.

In Section 2.4, a novel procedure to construct a *regularized* morphable model is introduced that yields better correspondences. It is shown in Section 5.1 that the regularized morphable model improves the identification performance. The original morphable model computes correspondences between a pair of laser scans. However, the regularized morphable model uses a prior probability derived from other face scans to constraint the correspondences. This can be seen as simultaneously putting a laser scan in correspondence with a *set* of laser scans.

## 2.1  Preprocessing Laser Scans

Preprocessing laser scans is a semiautomatic step that aims to remove the scanning artifacts and select the part of the head that is to be modeled. It is performed in three consecutive stages.

1. Holes are filled, and spikes (i.e., scan artifacts) are removed using an interactive tool.
2. The faces are aligned in 3D using the 3D-3D absolute orientation method [16].
3. The parts of the head that we do not wish to model (e.g., the back of the head behind the ears, the hair area, and the region underneath the throat) are trimmed.

## 2.2  Dense Correspondences Computed by Optical Flow

To compute dense point-to-point correspondences between two 3D laser scans of faces automatically, we use optical flow. The scans are recorded by a laser scanner, measuring the radius (i.e., depth), $r$, along with the color $R, G, B$ of faces. Optical flow is computed on a cylindrical representation, $\mathbf{I}(h, \phi)$, of the colored 3D scans:

$$\mathbf{I}(h, \phi) = [r(h, \phi), R(h, \phi), G(h, \phi), B(h, \phi)] \tag{1}$$

Correspondences are given by a dense vector field $\mathbf{v}(h, \phi) = [\Delta h(h, \phi), \Delta\phi(h, \phi)]$, such that each point of the first scan, $\mathbf{I}_1(h, \phi)$, corresponds to the point $\mathbf{I}_2(h + \Delta h, \phi + \Delta\phi)$ on the second scan. A modified optical flow algorithm [6] is used to estimate this vector field.

### Optical flow on gray-level images

Many optical flow algorithms (e.g. [3], [17], [19]) are based on the assumption that objects in an image sequence $I(x, y, t)$ conserve their brightness as they move across the images at a velocity $(v_x, v_y)^{\mathrm{T}}$.

$$\frac{dI}{dt} = v_x \frac{\partial I}{\partial x} + v_y \frac{\partial I}{\partial y} + \frac{\partial I}{\partial t} = 0 \tag{2}$$

For a pair of images, $I_1$ and $I_2$, taken at two discrete moments, the temporal derivatives, $v_x$, $v_y$ and $\frac{\partial I}{\partial t}$, in Eq. (2), are approximated by finite differences $\Delta x$, $\Delta y$, and $\Delta I = I_2 - I_1$. If the images are not from a temporal sequence but show two different objects, corresponding points can no longer be assumed to have equal brightnesses. Still, optical flow algorithms may be applied successfully.

A unique solution for both components of $\mathbf{v} = (v_x, v_y)^T$ from Eq. (2) can be obtained if $\mathbf{v}$ is assumed to be constant on each neighborhood $R(x_0, y_0)$, and the following expression [3, 19] is minimized at each point $(x_0, y_0)$.

$$E(x_0, y_0) = \sum_{x,y \in R(x_0,y_0)} \left[ v_x \frac{\partial I(x,y)}{\partial x} + v_y \frac{\partial I(x,y)}{\partial y} + \Delta I(x,y) \right]^2 \qquad (3)$$

We used a $5 \times 5$ pixel neighborhood $R(x_0, y_0)$. In each point $(x_0, y_0)$, $\mathbf{v}(x_0, y_0)$ can be found by solving a $2 \times 2$ linear system (see Blanz and Vetter [7] for details). To deal with large displacements $\mathbf{v}$, the algorithm of Bergen and Hingorani [3] employs a coarse-to-fine strategy using a Gaussian pyramid of down-sampled images: With the gradient-based method described above, the algorithm computes the flow field on the lowest level of resolution and refines it on each subsequent level.

**Generalization to 3D colored surfaces**

For processing 3D laser scans $\mathbf{I}(h, \phi)$, Eq. (3) is replaced by

$$E = \sum_{h,\phi \in R} \left\| v_h \frac{\partial \mathbf{I}(h, \phi)}{\partial h} + v_\phi \frac{\partial \mathbf{I}(h, \phi)}{\partial \phi} + \Delta \mathbf{I} \right\|^2 \qquad (4)$$

with a norm $\|\mathbf{I}\|^2 = w_r r^2 + w_R R^2 + w_G G^2 + w_B B^2 \qquad (5)$

Weights $w_r$, $w_R$, $w_G$, and $w_B$ compensate for variations in the radius data and the red, green, and blue texture components; and they control the overall weighting of shape versus texture information. The weights are chosen heuristically. The minimum of Eq. (4) is again given by a $2 \times 2$ linear system (see [7]).

Correspondences between scans of different individuals, who may differ in overall brightness and size, are improved by using Laplacian pyramids (band-pass filtering) rather than Gaussian pyramids (low-pass filtering). Additional quantities, such as Gaussian curvature, mean curvature, or the surface normal, may be incorporated in $\mathbf{I}(h, \phi)$ to improve the results. To obtain reliable results even in regions of the face with no salient structures, a specifically designed smoothing and interpolation algorithm [7] is added to the matching procedure on each level of resolution.

### 2.3  Face Space Based on Principal Components Analysis

We mentioned that the correspondences enable the formulation of a face space. The face space is constructed by putting a set of $M$ example 3D laser scans into correspondence with a reference laser scan. This introduces a consistent labeling of all $N_v$ 3D vertices across all the scans. The shape and texture surfaces are parameterized in the $(u, v)$ reference frame, where one pixel corresponds to one 3D vertex (Fig. 10.2). The 3D position in Cartesian coordinates of the $N_v$ vertices of a face scan are arranged in a shape matrix, $\mathbf{S}$; and their color in a texture matrix, $\mathbf{T}$.

$$\mathbf{S} = \begin{pmatrix} x_1 & x_2 & \cdots & x_{N_v} \\ y_1 & y_2 & \cdots & y_{N_v} \\ z_1 & z_2 & \cdots & z_{N_v} \end{pmatrix}, \qquad \mathbf{T} = \begin{pmatrix} r_1 & r_2 & \cdots & r_{N_v} \\ g_1 & g_2 & \cdots & g_{N_v} \\ b_1 & b_2 & \cdots & b_{N_v} \end{pmatrix} \qquad (6)$$

Having constructed a linear face space, we can make linear combinations of the shapes, $\mathbf{S}_i$, and the textures, $\mathbf{T}_i$ of $M$ example individuals to produce faces of new individuals.

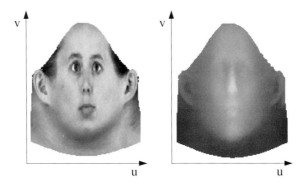

**Fig. 10.2.** Texture and shape in the reference space $(u, v)$.

$$\mathbf{S} = \sum_{i=1}^{M} \alpha_i \cdot \mathbf{S}_i, \qquad \mathbf{T} = \sum_{i=1}^{M} \beta_i \cdot \mathbf{T}_i \tag{7}$$

Equation (7) assumes a uniform distribution of the shapes and the textures. We know that this distribution yields a model that is not restrictive enough: If some $\alpha_i$ or $\beta_i$ are $\gg 1$, the face produced is unlikely. Therefore, we assume that the shape and the texture spaces have a Gaussian probability distribution function. Principal component analysis (PCA) is a statistical tool that transforms the space such that the covariance matrix is diagonal (i.e., it decorrelates the data). PCA is applied separately to the shape and texture spaces, thereby ignoring the correlation between shape and texture, in contrast to other techniques (see Section 1.3 of Chapter 3). We describe the application of PCA to shapes; its application to textures is straightforward. After subtracting their average, $\overline{\mathbf{S}}$, the exemplars are arranged in a data matrix $\mathbf{A}$ and the eigenvectors of its covariance matrix $\mathbf{C}$ are computed using the singular value decomposition [25] of $\mathbf{A}$.

$$\overline{\mathbf{S}} = \tfrac{1}{M} \sum_{i=1}^{M} \mathbf{S}_i, \quad \mathbf{a}_i = \mathrm{vec}(\mathbf{S}_i - \overline{\mathbf{S}}), \quad \mathbf{A} = (\mathbf{a}_1, \mathbf{a}_2, \ldots, \mathbf{a}_M) = \mathbf{U}\mathbf{\Lambda}\mathbf{V}^{\mathsf{T}}$$

$$\mathbf{C} = \tfrac{1}{M}\mathbf{A}\mathbf{A}^{\mathsf{T}} = \tfrac{1}{M}\mathbf{U}\mathbf{\Lambda}^2\mathbf{U}^{\mathsf{T}} \tag{8}$$

The component $\mathrm{vec}(\mathbf{S})$ vectorizes $\mathbf{S}$ by stacking its columns. The $M$ columns of the orthogonal matrix $\mathbf{U}$ are the eigenvectors of the covariance matrix $\mathbf{C}$, and $\sigma_i^2 = \frac{\lambda_i^2}{M}$ are its eigenvalues, where the $\lambda_i$ are the elements of the diagonal matrix $\mathbf{\Lambda}$, arranged in decreasing order. Let us denote $\mathbf{U}_{\cdot,i}$, the column $i$ of $\mathbf{U}$, and the principal component $i$, reshaped into a $3 \times N_v$ matrix, by $\mathbf{S}^i = \mathbf{U}_{\cdot,i}^{(3)}$. The notation $\mathbf{a}_{m \times 1}^{(n)}$ [21] folds the $m \times 1$ vector $\mathbf{a}$ into an $n \times (m/n)$ matrix.

Now, instead of describing a novel shape and texture as a linear combination of examples, as in Eq. 7, we express them as a linear combination of $N_S$ shape and $N_T$ texture principal components.

$$\mathbf{S} = \overline{\mathbf{S}} + \sum_{i=1}^{N_S} \alpha_i \cdot \mathbf{S}^i, \qquad \mathbf{T} = \overline{\mathbf{T}} + \sum_{i=1}^{N_T} \beta_i \cdot \mathbf{T}^i \tag{9}$$

The advantage of this formulation is that the probabilities of a shape and a texture are readily available.

$$p(\mathbf{S}) \sim e^{-\frac{1}{2}\sum_i \frac{\alpha_i^2}{\sigma_{S,i}^2}}, \qquad p(\mathbf{T}) \sim e^{-\frac{1}{2}\sum_i \frac{\beta_i^2}{\sigma_{T,i}^2}} \tag{10}$$

## 2.4 Regularized Morphable Model

The correspondence estimation computed by optical flow, detailed in Section 2.2, may, for some laser scans, be wrong in some regions. These bad correspondences are visualized on shape caricatures (i.e., faces for which the shape is obtained by multiplying the flow field by a coefficient higher than 1), as seen on the top row of Figure 10.3. These problems arise because the scans' boundaries are artificially set and sometimes some of these boundaries do not correspond with the boundaries set on other scans. This leads to errors in correspondence estimated by optical flow. In this section, we present a scheme aiming to improve the correspondence by regularizing it using statistics derived from scans that do not present correspondence errors. This is achieved by modifying the model construction in two ways: First, probabilistic PCA [29] is used instead of PCA, which regularizes the model by allowing the exemplars to be noisy. Second, a bootstrapping technique is used whereby the model is iteratively estimated.

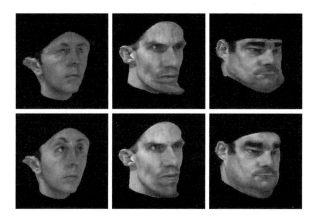

**Fig. 10.3.** Correspondence artifacts are visualized by making shape caricatures (i.e., extending the shape deviations from the average). Top row: Three caricatures yielded by the original morphable model are shown. Bottom row: Caricatures of the same scans obtained by the regularized morphable model are presented. Clearly, the bottom row is less perturbed by correspondence artifacts.

## Probabilistic PCA

Instead of assuming a linear model for the shape, as in previous section, we assume a linear Gaussian model

$$\operatorname{vec} \mathbf{S} = \operatorname{vec} \overline{\mathbf{S}} + \mathbf{C}_S \cdot \boldsymbol{\alpha} + \boldsymbol{\epsilon} \tag{11}$$

where $\mathbf{C}_S$, whose columns are the regularized shape principal components, has dimensions $3N_v \times N_S$, and the shape coefficients $\boldsymbol{\alpha}$ and the noise $\boldsymbol{\epsilon}$ have a Gaussian distribution with zero mean and covariance $\mathbf{I}$ and $\sigma^2 \mathbf{I}$, respectively.

Tipping and Bishop [29] use the EM algorithm [12] to iteratively estimate $\mathbf{C}_S$ and the projection of the example vectors to the model, $\mathbf{K} = [\boldsymbol{\alpha}_1 \boldsymbol{\alpha}_2 \dots \boldsymbol{\alpha}_M]$. The algorithm starts with $\mathbf{C}_S = \mathbf{A}$; and then at each iteration it computes a new estimate of the shape coefficients $\mathbf{K}$ (expectation step, or *e-step*) and of the regularized principal components $\mathbf{C}_S$ (maximization step, or *m-step*). The coefficients of the example shapes, the unobserved variables, are estimated at the *e-step*.

$$\mathbf{K} = \mathbf{B}^{-1}\mathbf{C}_S^{\mathrm{T}}\mathbf{A} \quad \text{with} \quad \mathbf{B} = \mathbf{C}_S^{\mathrm{T}}\mathbf{C}_S + \sigma^2\mathbf{I} \tag{12}$$

This is the maximum a posteriori estimator of $\mathbf{K}$; that is, the expected value of $\mathbf{K}$ given the posterior distribution $p(\boldsymbol{\alpha}|\mathbf{C}_S)$. At the *m-step*, the model is estimated by computing the $\mathbf{C}_S$, which maximizes the likelihood of the data, given the current estimate of $\mathbf{K}$ and $\mathbf{B}$.

$$\mathbf{C}_S = \mathbf{A} \cdot \mathbf{K}^{\mathrm{T}} \cdot \left(\sigma^2 \cdot M \cdot \mathbf{B}^{-1} + \mathbf{K} \cdot \mathbf{K}^{\mathrm{T}}\right)^{-1} \tag{13}$$

These two steps are iterated in sequence until the algorithm is judged to have converged. In the original algorithm the value of $\sigma^2$ is also estimated at the m-step as

$$\sigma^2 = \frac{1}{3N_v \cdot M} \operatorname{tr}\left(\mathbf{A}\mathbf{A}^{\mathrm{T}} - \mathbf{C}_s\mathbf{K}\mathbf{A}^{\mathrm{T}}\right) \tag{14}$$

but in our case, with $M \ll 3N_v$, this would yield an estimated value of zero. Therefore, we prefer to estimate $\sigma^2$ by replacing $\mathbf{A}$ and $\mathbf{K}$ in Eq. (14) with a data matrix of test vectors (vectors not used in estimating $\mathbf{C}_s$) and its corresponding coefficients matrix obtained via Eq. (12). If a test set is not available, we can still get an estimate of $\sigma^2$ by cross validation.

### Bootstrapping

The bootstrapping aims to constrain the correspondences using face statistics. The idea, which was first reported by Vetter et al. [33] and applied to the 3D morphable model by Blanz and Vetter [6] is to put some of the 3D scans in correspondence with optical flow as explained in Section 2.2. Then a morphable model is constructed using only the subset of the laser scans for which the correspondences are deemed to be correct by a human expert. The rest of the laser scans (those for which the correspondences are not good enough) are fitted to the model in a similar method as the one explained in Section 4. The method is different though, as here the morphable model is fitted to a 3D laser scan and not to a 2D image. The fitting produces, for each laser scan, a face in correspondence with the reference face and that more resembles the original scan than the reference does. This face is called the approximation (Fig. 10.4). Then the correspondences between the approximations and its original face are computed by optical flow. These correspondences are more likely to be good than the one computed between the reference face and the original. This procedure is applied iteratively. At each iteration the faces for which correspondences are judged adequate are added to the morphable model. The process stops when all the correspondences are judge satisfactory.

### 2.5 Segmented Morphable Model

As mentioned, our morphable model is derived from statistics computed on 200 example faces. As a result, the dimensions of the shape and texture spaces, $N_S$ and $N_T$, are limited to 199. This

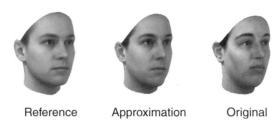

Reference          Approximation          Original

**Fig. 10.4.** Images of rendering of 3D lasers scans. The first is the reference with which correspondences are to be estimated. The second is the fitting of the original with a morphable model constructed with a subset of the scan for which correspondences were correct. The last one is the original scan.

might not be enough to account for the rich variations of individualities present in humankind. Naturally, one way to augment the dimension of the face space would be to use 3D scans of more persons but they are not available. Hence we resort to another scheme: We segment the face into four regions (nose, eyes, mouth and the rest) and use a separate set of shape and texture coefficients to code them [6]. This method multiplies by four the expressiveness of the morphable model. The fitting results in Section 4 and the identification results in Section 5 are based on a segmented morphable model with $N_S = N_T = 100$ for all segments. In the rest of the chapter, we denote the shape and texture parameters by $\alpha$ and $\beta$ when they can be used interchangeably for the global and the segmented parts of the model. When we want to distinguish them, we use, for the shape parameters, $\alpha^g$ for the global model (full face) and $\alpha^{s_1}$ to $\alpha^{s_4}$ for the segmented parts (the same notation is used for the texture parameters).

## 3  Morphable Model to Synthesize Images

One part of the analysis by synthesis loop is the synthesis (i.e., the generation of accurate face images viewed from any pose and illuminated by any condition). This process is explained in this section.

### 3.1  Shape Projection

To render the image of a face, the 3D shape must be projected to the 2D image frame. This is performed in two steps. First, a 3D rotation and translation (i.e., a rigid transformation) maps the object-centered coordinates, $\mathbf{S}$, to a position relative to the camera.

$$\mathbf{W} = \mathbf{R}_\gamma \mathbf{R}_\theta \mathbf{R}_\phi \mathbf{S} + \mathbf{t_w} \mathbf{1}_{1 \times N_v} \tag{15}$$

The angles $\phi$ and $\theta$ control in-depth rotations around the vertical and horizontal axis, and $\gamma$ defines a rotation around the camera axis; $\mathbf{t_w}$ is a 3D translation. A projection then maps a vertex $k$ to the image plane in $(x_j, y_j)$. We typically use two projections: the perspective and the weak perspective projection.

$$\text{Perspective}: \begin{cases} x_j = t_x + f\dfrac{\mathbf{W}_{1,j}}{\mathbf{W}_{3,j}} \\ y_j = t_y + f\dfrac{\mathbf{W}_{2,j}}{\mathbf{W}_{3,j}} \end{cases} \qquad \text{Weak perspective}: \begin{cases} x_j = t_x + f\mathbf{W}_{1,j} \\ y_j = t_y + f\mathbf{W}_{2,j} \end{cases} \quad (16)$$

where $f$ is the focal length of the camera, which is located in the origin; and $(t_x, t_y)$ defines the image-plane position of the optical axis.

For ease of explanation, the shape transformation parameters are denoted by the vector $\boldsymbol{\rho} = [f\ \phi\ \theta\ \gamma\ t_x\ t_y\ \mathbf{t}_\mathbf{w}^\mathsf{T}]^\mathsf{T}$, and $\boldsymbol{\alpha}$ is the vector whose elements are the $\alpha_i$. In the remainder of the chapter, the projection of the vertex $i$ to the image frame $(x, y)$ is denoted by the vector valued function $\mathbf{p}(u_i, v_i; \boldsymbol{\alpha}, \boldsymbol{\rho})$. This function is clearly continuous in $\boldsymbol{\alpha}, \boldsymbol{\rho}$. To provide continuity in the $(u, v)$ space as well, we use a triangle list and interpolate between neighboring vertices, as is common in computer graphics. Note that only $N_{vv}$ vertices, a subset of the $N_v$ vertices, are visible after the 2D projection (the remaining vertices are hidden by self-occlusion). We call this subset the domain of the shape projection $\mathbf{p}(u_i, v_i; \boldsymbol{\alpha}, \boldsymbol{\rho})$ and denote it by $\Omega(\boldsymbol{\alpha}, \boldsymbol{\rho}) \in (u, v)$.

In conclusion, the shape modeling and its projection provides mapping from the parameter space $\boldsymbol{\alpha}, \boldsymbol{\rho}$ to the image frame $(x, y)$ via the reference frame $(u, v)$. However to synthesize an image, we need the inverse of this mapping, detailed in the next section.

### 3.2  Inverse Shape Projection

The shape projection aforementioned maps a $(u, v)$ point from the reference space to the image frame. To synthesize an image, we need the inverse mapping: An image is generated by looping on the pixels $(x, y)$. To know which color must be drawn on that pixel, we must know where this pixel is mapped into the reference frame. This is the aim of the inverse shape mapping explained in this section.

The inverse shape projection, $\mathbf{p}^{-1}(x, y; \boldsymbol{\alpha}, \boldsymbol{\rho})$, maps an image point $(x, y)$ to the reference frame $(u, v)$. Let us denote the composition of a shape projection and its inverse by the symbol $\circ$; hence, $\mathbf{p}(u, v; \boldsymbol{\alpha}, \boldsymbol{\rho}) \circ \mathbf{p}^{-1}(x, y; \boldsymbol{\alpha}, \boldsymbol{\rho})$ is equal to $\mathbf{p}(\mathbf{p}^{-1}(x, y; \boldsymbol{\alpha}, \boldsymbol{\rho}); \boldsymbol{\alpha}, \boldsymbol{\rho})$, but we prefer the former notation for clarity. The inverse shape projection is defined by the following equation, which specifies that under the same set of parameters the shape projection composed with its inverse is equal to the identity.

$$\begin{aligned} \mathbf{p}(u, v; \boldsymbol{\alpha}, \boldsymbol{\rho}) \circ \mathbf{p}^{-1}(x, y; \boldsymbol{\alpha}, \boldsymbol{\rho}) &= (x, y) \\ \mathbf{p}^{-1}(x, y; \boldsymbol{\alpha}, \boldsymbol{\rho}) \circ \mathbf{p}(u, v; \boldsymbol{\alpha}, \boldsymbol{\rho}) &= (u, v) \end{aligned} \qquad (17)$$

Because of the discretization of the shape, it is not easy to express $\mathbf{p}^{-1}$ analytically as a function of $\mathbf{p}$, but it can be computed using the triangle list: The domain of the plane $(x, y)$ for which there exists an inverse under the parameters $\boldsymbol{\alpha}$ and $\boldsymbol{\rho}$, denoted by $\Psi(\boldsymbol{\alpha}, \boldsymbol{\rho})$, is the range of $\mathbf{p}(u, v; \boldsymbol{\alpha}, \boldsymbol{\rho})$. Such a point of $(x, y)$ lies in a single visible triangle under the projection $\mathbf{p}(u, v; \boldsymbol{\alpha}, \boldsymbol{\rho})$. Therefore, the point in $(u, v)$ under the inverse projection has the same relative position in this triangle in the $(u, v)$ space. This process is depicted in Figure 10.5.

### 3.3  Illumination and Color Transformation

*Ambient and Directed Light*

We simulate the illumination of a face using an ambient light and a directed light. The effects of the illumination are obtained using the standard Phong model, which approximately describes

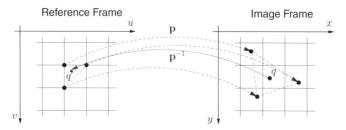

**Fig. 10.5.** Inverse shape function $\mathbf{p}^{-1}(x, y; \boldsymbol{\alpha}, \boldsymbol{\rho})$ maps the point $q$ defined in the $(x, y)$ coordinate system, onto the point $q'$ in $(u, v)$. This is done by recovering the triangle that would contain the pixel $q$ under the mapping $\mathbf{p}(u, v; \boldsymbol{\alpha}, \boldsymbol{\rho})$. Then the relative position of $q$ in that triangle is the same as the relative position of $q'$ in the same triangle in the $(u, v)$ space.

the diffuse and specular reflection on a surface [14]; see [7] for further details. The parameters of this model are the intensity of the ambient light ($L_{r,amb}$, $L_{g,amb}$, $L_{b,amb}$), the intensity of the directed light ($L_{r,dir}$, $L_{g,dir}$, $L_{b,dir}$), its direction ($\theta_l$ and $\phi_l$), the specular reflectance of human skin ($k_s$), and the angular distribution of the specular reflections of human skin ($\nu$).

*Color Transformation*

Input images may vary a lot with respect to the overall tone of color. To be able to handle a variety of color images as well as gray level images and even paintings, we apply gains $g_r$, $g_g$, $g_b$, offsets $o_r$, $o_g$, $o_b$, and a color contrast $c$ to each channel [6]. This is a linear transformation that multiplies the RGB color of a vertex (after it has been illuminated) by the matrix $\mathbf{M}$ and adds the vector $\mathbf{o} = [o_r,\ o_g,\ o_b]^{\mathrm{T}}$, where

$$\mathbf{M}(c, g_r, g_g, g_b) = \begin{pmatrix} g_r & 0 & 0 \\ 0 & g_g & 0 \\ 0 & 0 & g_b \end{pmatrix} \cdot \left[ \mathbf{I} + (1 - c) \begin{pmatrix} 0.3 & 0.59 & 0.11 \\ 0.3 & 0.59 & 0.11 \\ 0.3 & 0.59 & 0.11 \end{pmatrix} \right] \tag{18}$$

For brevity, the illumination and color transformation parameters are regrouped in the vector $\boldsymbol{\iota}$. Hence the illuminated texture depends on the coefficients of the linear combination regrouped in $\boldsymbol{\beta}$, on the light parameters $\boldsymbol{\iota}$, and on $\boldsymbol{\alpha}$ and $\boldsymbol{\rho}$ used to compute the normals and the viewing direction of the vertices required for the Phong illumination model. Similarly to the shape, we denote the color of a vertex $i$ by the vector valued function $\mathbf{t}(u_i, v_i; \boldsymbol{\beta}, \boldsymbol{\iota}, \boldsymbol{\alpha}, \boldsymbol{\rho})$, which is extended to the continuous function $\mathbf{t}(u, v; \boldsymbol{\beta}, \boldsymbol{\iota}, \boldsymbol{\alpha}, \boldsymbol{\rho})$ by using the triangle list and interpolating.

### 3.4 Image Synthesis

Synthesizing the image of a face is performed by mapping a texture from the reference to the image frame using an inverse shape projection

$$\mathbf{I}(x_j, y_j; \boldsymbol{\alpha}, \boldsymbol{\beta}, \boldsymbol{\rho}, \boldsymbol{\iota}) = \mathbf{t}(u, v; \boldsymbol{\beta}, \boldsymbol{\iota}, \boldsymbol{\alpha}, \boldsymbol{\rho}) \circ \mathbf{p}^{-1}(x_j, y_j; \boldsymbol{\alpha}, \boldsymbol{\rho}) \tag{19}$$

where $j$ runs over the pixels that belong to $\Psi(\boldsymbol{\alpha}, \boldsymbol{\rho})$ (i.e., the pixels for which a shape inverse exist, as defined in Section 3.2).

# 4   Image Analysis with a 3D Morphable Model

In the analysis by synthesis framework, an algorithm seeks the parameters of the model that render a face as close to the input image as possible. These parameters explain the image and can be used for high-level tasks such as identification. This algorithm is called a *fitting algorithm*. It is characterized by the following four features.

- **Efficient**: The computational load allowed for the fitting algorithm is clearly dependent on the applications. Security applications, for instance, require fast algorithms (i.e., near real time).
- **Robust** (against non-Gaussian noise): The assumption of normality of the difference between the image synthesized by the model and the input image is generally violated owing to the presence of accessories or artifacts (glasses, hair, specular highlight).
- **Accurate**: As we have already pointed out, accuracy is crucial for the application that is to use the fitting results (and generally the level of accuracy required depends thereon).
- **Automatic**: The fitting should require as little human intervention as possible, optimally with no initialization.

An algorithm capable of any of the four aforementioned features is difficult to set up. An algorithm capable of *all* four features is the holy grail of model-based computer vision. In this chapter we present two fitting algorithms. The first one, called *stochastic newton optimization* (SNO) is accurate but computationally expensive: a fitting takes 4.5 minutes on a 2 GHz Pentium IV. SNO is detailed elsewhere [7]. The second fitting algorithm is a 3D extension of the *inverse compositional image alignment* (ICIA) algorithm introduced by Baker and Matthews [1]. It is more efficient than SNO, and a fitting requires 30 seconds on the same machine. Our ICIA algorithm was introduced by Romdhani and Vetter [26].

As initialization, the algorithms require the correspondences between some of the model vertices (typically eight) and the input image. These correspondences are set manually. They are required to obtain a good initial condition for the iterative algorithm. The 2D positions in the image of these $N_l$ points are set in the matrix $\mathbf{L}_{2 \times N_l}$. They are in correspondence with the vertex indices set in the vector $\mathbf{v}_{N_l \times 1}$. The positions of these landmarks for three views are shown in Figure 10.6.

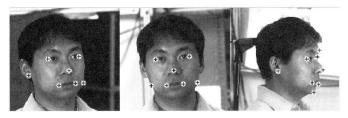

**Fig. 10.6. Initialization**: Seven landmarks for front and side views and eight for the profile view are manually labeled for each input image.

Both algorithms use optimization techniques to minimize a cost function. The main difference between them is that SNO is an *additive* algorithm whereby the update is added to the current parameters, whereas ICIA is an *inverse compositional* algorithm (see Section 4.3). The advantage of ICIA is that it uses derivatives computed in one point of the parameter space. Hence the derivatives must not be recomputed at each iteration as is the case with SNO. This is the reason of the efficiency of ICIA.

## 4.1   Maximum A Posteriori Estimation of the Parameters

Both algorithms aim to find the model parameters $\alpha, \rho, \beta, \iota$ that explain an input image. To increase the robustness of the algorithms, these parameters are estimated by a *maximum a posteriori* (MAP) estimator, which maximizes $p(\alpha, \rho, \beta, \iota \mid \mathbf{I}_{\text{input}}, \mathbf{L})$ [6]. Applying the Bayes rule and neglecting the dependence between parameters yield:

$$p(\alpha, \beta, \rho, \iota \mid \mathbf{I}_{\text{input}}, \mathbf{L}) \sim p(\mathbf{I}_{\text{input}} \mid \alpha, \beta, \rho, \iota) \cdot p(\mathbf{L} \mid \alpha, \rho) \cdot p(\alpha) \cdot p(\beta) \cdot p(\rho) \cdot p(\iota) \quad (20)$$

The expression of the priors $p(\alpha)$ and $p(\beta)$, is given by Eq. (10). For each shape projection and illumination parameter, we assume a Gaussian probability distribution with the means $\bar{\rho}_i$ and $\bar{\iota}_i$ and with variances $\sigma^2_{\rho,i}$ and $\sigma^2_{\iota,i}$. These values are set manually.

Assuming that the $x$ and $y$ coordinates of the landmark points are independent and that they have the same Gaussian distribution with variance $\sigma^2_L$, it gives:

$$E_L = -2 \log p(\mathbf{L} \mid \alpha, \rho) = \frac{1}{\sigma^2_L} \sum_{j}^{N_l} \left\| \mathbf{L}_{\cdot, j} - \begin{pmatrix} x_{\mathbf{v}_j} \\ y_{\mathbf{v}_j} \end{pmatrix} \right\|^2 \quad (21)$$

The difference between our two algorithms lies in the formulation of the likelihood $p(\mathbf{I}_{\text{input}} \mid \alpha, \rho, \beta, \iota)$, which results in different maximization schemes.

## 4.2   Stochastic Newton Optimization

The likelihood of the input image given the model parameters is expressed in the image frame. Assuming that all the pixels are independent and that they have the same Gaussian distribution with variance $\sigma^2_I$, gives:

$$E_I = -2 \log p(\mathbf{I}_{\text{input}} \mid \alpha, \beta, \rho, \iota) = \frac{1}{\sigma^2_I} \sum_{x,y} \left\| \mathbf{I}_{\text{input}}(x, y) - \mathbf{I}(x, y; \alpha, \beta, \rho, \iota) \right\|^2 \quad (22)$$

The sum is carried out over the pixels that are projected from the vertices in $\Omega(\alpha, \rho)$. At one pixel location, the norm is computed over the three color channels. The overall energy to be minimized is then:

$$E = \frac{1}{\sigma^2_I} E_I + \frac{1}{\sigma^2_L} E_L + \sum_i \frac{\alpha^2_i}{\sigma^2_{S,i}} + \sum_i \frac{\beta^2_i}{\sigma^2_{T,i}} + \sum_i \frac{(\rho_i - \bar{\rho}_i)^2}{\sigma^2_{\rho,i}} + \sum_i \frac{(\iota_i - \bar{\iota}_i)^2}{\sigma^2_{\iota,i}} \quad (23)$$

This log-likelihood is iteratively minimized by performing a Taylor expansion up to the second order (i.e., approximating the log-likelihood by a quadratic function) and computing the update that minimizes the quadratic approximation. The update is added to the current parameter to obtain the new parameters.

We use a stochastic minimization to decrease the odds of getting trapped in a local minima and to decrease the computational time: Instead of computing $E_I$ and its derivatives on all pixels of $\Psi(\alpha, \rho)$, it is computed only on a subset of 40 pixels thereof. These pixels are randomly chosen at each iteration. The first derivatives are computed analytically using the chain rule. The Hessian is approximated by a diagonal matrix computed by numeric differentiation every 1000 iterations. This algorithm was further detailed by Blanz and Vetter [7].

The SNO algorithm is extremely accurate (see the experiments in Section 5). However, its main drawback is its poor efficiency due to the fact that the derivatives are computed at each iteration. In the next section we present a fitting algorithm that uses constant derivatives. It is hence faster.

### Fitting Results

Several fitting results and reconstructions are shown in Figure 10.7. They were obtained with the SNO algorithm on some of the PIE images (see Section 1.5 of Chapter 13). These images are illuminated with ambient light and one directed light source. The algorithm was initialized with seven or eight landmark points (depending on the pose of the input image) (Figure 10.6). In the third column, the separation between the albedo of the face and the illumination is not optimal: part of the specular reflections were attributed to the texture by the algorithm. This may be due to shortcomings of the Phong illumination model for reflections at grazing angles or to a prior probability inappropriate for this illumination condition. (The prior probabilities of the illumination and rigid parameters, $\sigma_{\rho,i}^2$ and $\sigma_{\iota,i}^2$, are kept constant for fitting the 4488 PIE images.)

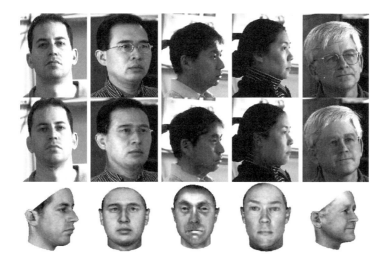

**Fig. 10.7.** Stochastic Newton optimization fitting results: Three-dimensional reconstruction from CMU-PIE images using the SNO fitting algorithm. Top: originals. Middle: reconstructions rendered into original. Bottom: novel views. The pictures shown here are difficult to fit due to harsh illumination, profile views, or eyeglasses. Illumination in the third image is not fully recovered, so part of the reflections are attributed to texture.

### 4.3 Inverse Compositional Image Alignment

We present here a second fitting algorithm whose major feature compared to the previous SNO algorithm is its improved efficiency. The efficiency comes from the fact that throughout the algorithm the derivatives needed are always computed at the same point in the parameter space. Hence the derivatives do not change across iterations and can be precomputed. We introduced this algorithm elsewhere [26]. The original inverse compositional image alignment (ICIA) algorithm was introduced [1] as an efficient algorithm for fitting 2D correspondence-based models. The authors derived a first-order approximation to fit flexible appearance models (i.e., sparse correspondence-based 2D models). In this section, we extend this algorithm to 3D morphable models.

#### ICIA Log-Likelihood

In contrast to the SNO algorithm, the log-likelihood of the input image is computed in the reference frame $(u, v)$. Another difference is that the parameters' update is inverted and composed with the current estimate instead of simply added to the current estimate.

We derived this algorithm for the case where the face is illuminated by ambient light only (i.e., without directed light). Then the texture depends on $\beta$ and on $\iota$. To formulate the log-likelihood, we introduce the inverse texture mapping, using the color transformation matrices $\mathbf{M}$ and $\mathbf{o}$ defined in Eq. (18).

$$\mathbf{t}^{-1}(\mathbf{t}(u_i, v_i); \boldsymbol{\beta}, \boldsymbol{\iota}) = \mathbf{t}(u_i, v_i) - \mathbf{M}^{-1} \cdot \sum_{k=1}^{N_t} \beta_k \cdot \mathbf{T}_{\cdot,i}^k - \mathbf{o} \cdot \mathbf{1}_{1 \times N_v} \tag{24}$$

This definition is chosen for the texture inverse because then a texture composed with its inverse under the same set of parameters is equal to the mean texture: $\mathbf{t}^{-1}(\mathbf{t}(u_i, v_i; \boldsymbol{\beta}, \boldsymbol{\iota}); \boldsymbol{\beta}, \boldsymbol{\iota}) = \mathbf{T}_{\cdot,i}^0$. Denoting by $\boldsymbol{\gamma} = [\boldsymbol{\alpha}^\mathsf{T} \boldsymbol{\rho}^\mathsf{T}]^\mathsf{T}$ the shape and projection parameters, the log-likelihood is expressed as:

$$E_I = \frac{1}{2\sigma_I^2} \cdot \sum_{u_i, v_i \in \Omega(\boldsymbol{\gamma}^d)} \left[ \mathbf{t}(u, v; \Delta\boldsymbol{\beta}, \Delta\boldsymbol{\iota}) \circ \mathbf{p}^{-1}(x, y; \boldsymbol{\gamma}^d) \circ \mathbf{p}(u_i, v_i; \boldsymbol{\gamma}^d + \Delta\boldsymbol{\gamma}) \right.$$
$$\left. - \mathbf{t}^{-1}(\mathbf{I}_{\text{input}}(x, y) \circ \mathbf{p}(u_i, v_i; \boldsymbol{\gamma}^c); \boldsymbol{\beta}^c, \boldsymbol{\iota}^c) \right]^2 \tag{25}$$

where the parameters superscripted by $^d$ refer to the parameters at which the derivatives are computed, and the parameters superscripted by $^c$ refer to the current parameters. The log-likelihood is to be minimized with respect to the model parameters update $\Delta\boldsymbol{\gamma}$, $\Delta\boldsymbol{\beta}$, and $\Delta\boldsymbol{\iota}$. The current estimate of the model parameters are $\boldsymbol{\gamma}^c$, $\boldsymbol{\beta}^c$, and $\boldsymbol{\iota}^c$. A simple example of this log-likelihood computation is given in Figure 10.8. The top row shows the mean texture in the reference space that is to be put in correspondence with an input image (displayed on its right). The input image is mapped to the reference frame using the current shape parameters (middle row): For a point $(u_i, v_i)$ in $\Omega(\boldsymbol{\gamma}^d)$, the image is sampled at the pixel $\mathbf{p}(u_i, v_i; \boldsymbol{\gamma}^c)$. Then, the update, which minimizes $E_I$, is a transformation of the reference space given by $\mathbf{p}^{-1}(x, y; \boldsymbol{\gamma}^d) \circ \mathbf{p}(u_i, v_i; \boldsymbol{\gamma}^d + \Delta\boldsymbol{\gamma})$ (bottom row).

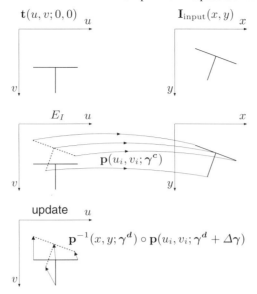

**Fig. 10.8.** Example of the computation of the log-likelihood for a reference texture and an input image given at the first row. On the second row, the image is sampled at the position given by the current shape projection estimate. On the third row, the parameters $\Delta\gamma$ that minimize $E_I$ are computed. This update is a transformation of the reference frame.

There are two novelties with respect to the original ICIA [1] formulation. The first is the presence of the inverse shape projection $\mathbf{p}^{-1}(x, y; \gamma^d)$ between the shape update and the texture update. This inverse shape projection must be present because it is not possible to compose a shape (projecting to the image frame) with a texture (whose domain is the reference frame). The second novelty is the update of the texture and illumination parameters as well, $\Delta\beta$ and $\Delta\iota$.

Let us now compute the derivative of the ICIA log-likelihood (Eq. 25) with respect to the shape and projection parameter update $\Delta\gamma$ at the point $\Delta\gamma = 0, \Delta\beta = 0, \Delta\iota = 0$. In the remaining, we omit the dependent variables, assuming that it is clear that the dependents of $\mathbf{p}$ and $\mathbf{t}$ are $(u, v)$ and the dependents of $\mathbf{p}^{-1}$ and $I$ are $(x, y)$.

$$\frac{\partial E_I}{\partial \Delta\gamma_k} = \sum_i \frac{\partial(t(0,0) \circ \mathbf{p}^{-1}(\gamma^d) \circ \mathbf{p}_i(\gamma^d + \Delta\gamma))}{\partial \Delta\gamma_k}\bigg|_{\Delta\gamma=0}^{\mathrm{T}}$$
$$\cdot \, [t(0,0) \circ \mathbf{p}^{-1}(\gamma^d) \circ \mathbf{p}_i(\gamma^d) - \mathbf{t}^{-1}(I \circ \mathbf{p}_i(\gamma^c); \beta^c, \iota^c)] \quad (26)$$

Note that, using Eq. (19) and the chain rule:

$$\mathbf{t}(0,0) \circ \mathbf{p}^{-1}(\gamma^d) = \mathbf{I^d}(x, y; \alpha^d, 0, \rho^d, 0) \quad (27)$$

$$\frac{\partial(t(0,0) \circ \mathbf{p}^{-1}(\gamma^d) \circ \mathbf{p}_i(\gamma))}{\partial \gamma_k} = \nabla\mathbf{I^d} \cdot \frac{\partial \mathbf{p}_i(\gamma)}{\partial \gamma_k} \quad (28)$$

We refer to the second factor of the right member of Eq. (26) in squared brackets as the *texture error* at the vertex $i$, $\mathbf{e}_i$. The texture error, $\mathbf{e}$, is a column vector of length $3N_{vv}$. It is a difference of two terms: The first is the mean texture (the projection and inverse projection cancel each other using Eq. 17). The second term is the image to be fitted mapped to the reference frame $(u, v)$ using the current shape and projection parameters and inverse-texture mapped with the current texture and illumination parameters. At the optimum (and if the face image can be fully explained by the model), this term is equal to the mean texture, and hence the texture error is null. The first factor of Eq. (26) is the element of the shape Jacobian, $\mathbf{J^s}$, at the row $i$ and column $k$. The dimensions of the shape Jacobian matrix are $3N_{vv} \times N_s$. As the parameters' update is composed with the current estimate, the Taylor expansion of Eq. (25) is always performed in $\Delta\gamma = 0, \Delta\boldsymbol{\beta} = 0, \Delta\boldsymbol{\iota} = 0$. Hence, the Jacobian depends only on $\gamma^d$, which is constant across iterations. This is the key feature of the ICIA algorithm: the Jacobian and the Gauss approximation of the Hessian can be precomputed, in contrast to those of the SNO algorithm, which depend on the current parameters. As a result, what is to be computed at each iteration is a matrix-vector product and a shape projection composition (explained in the next section).

The derivatives with respect to the texture parameters update $\Delta\boldsymbol{\beta}$ and illumination parameters $\Delta\boldsymbol{\iota}$ take a form similar to those of the shape parameters. The combined Jacobian of the shape and texture model is then $\mathbf{J} = [\mathbf{J^s J^t}]$. The Gauss approximation of the Hessian is $\mathbf{H} = \mathbf{J^T J}$, leading to the Gauss-Newton update.

$$\begin{pmatrix} \Delta\gamma \\ \Delta\boldsymbol{\beta} \\ \Delta\boldsymbol{\iota} \end{pmatrix} = -\mathbf{H}^{-1} \cdot \mathbf{J}^\mathrm{T} \cdot \mathbf{e} \tag{29}$$

### Parameters at Which the Derivatives Are Computed

The derivatives of Eq. (28) are computed using an image of the mean texture $\mathbf{I^d}$. This image is rendered in a particular image frame set by $\phi^d$ and $\theta^d$. The gradient of this image is multiplied by the derivative of the 3D shape model projected in the same image frame. As the shape model is 3D, in various image frames, the vertices move in different directions with $\boldsymbol{\alpha}$. This means that the Jacobian depends on the image frame in which it is computed. For the second-order Taylor expansion (performed to obtain Eq. 29) to be valid, this image frame must be close to the image frame of the optimum; that is, $\phi^d$ and $\theta^d$ must be close to the optimum $\phi$ and $\theta$. We conducted synthetic experiments to understand the impact of poor $\phi^d$ and $\theta^d$ on the fitting result. Figure 10.9 shows a plot of the error in correspondence obtained after fitting synthetic face images with various $\phi^d$ values different from the optimal $\phi$. The synthetic face image is generated with one morphable model and fitted with another morphable model. As the optimum face image is synthetic, we know exactly its pose and the 2D position of its vertices. The Figure 10.9 shows that if a set of derivatives is precomputed at $20°$ intervals, the error in correspondence is less than a pixel. As a result, a set of Jacobians is computed for a series of different $\phi^d, \theta^d$ values. During the iterative fitting, the derivatives used are the ones closest to the current estimation of $\phi, \theta$. Note that, at first, this approach might seem close to the view-based approach [10, 22, 23]. The difference, however, is fundamental. With this approach, the extraneous (rotation) parameters are clearly separated from the intrinsic (identity, i.e., $\boldsymbol{\alpha}, \boldsymbol{\beta}$) parameters. They are, however, convolved with one another in the view-based approach.

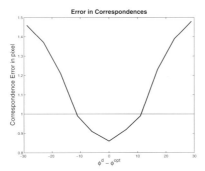

**Fig. 10.9.** Error in correspondence using derivatives computed at azimuths different from the optimum.

## Shape Projection Composition

In the ICIA algorithm the shape projection update is *composed* with the current shape projection estimate. This composition, detailed in this section, is performed in two steps. The first step computes the correspondences after composition between the model vertices and the image pixels; that is, it yields a mapping from $(u_i, v_i)$ to $(x, y)$, denoted by $\mathbf{p}^*(u_i, v_i)$. The second step maps this set of vertices-pixels correspondence to the shape model, yielding the model parameters after composition, $\boldsymbol{\alpha}^*$ and $\boldsymbol{\rho}^*$.

*Correspondences After Composition*

The update obtained after an iteration is a transformation of the reference frame $(u, v)$: $\mathbf{p}^{-1}(x, y; \boldsymbol{\gamma^d}) \circ \mathbf{p}(u_i, v_i; \boldsymbol{\gamma^d} + \Delta\boldsymbol{\gamma})$ (see Eq. 25). It is this transformation that must be composed with the current shape projection to obtain the new correspondences. The result of the shape projection composition is a shape projection, $\mathbf{p}^*(u_i, v_i)$, mapping the points of the reference frame $(u_i, v_i)$ to the image frame, $(x_i^*, y_i^*)$, equal to:

$$\mathbf{p}^*(u_i, v_i) = \mathbf{p}(u, v; \boldsymbol{\gamma^c}) \circ \mathbf{p}^{-1}(x, y; \boldsymbol{\gamma^d}) \circ \mathbf{p}(u_i, v_i; \boldsymbol{\gamma^d} + \Delta\boldsymbol{\gamma}) \tag{30}$$

Taking the example of Figure 10.8, the composition of its update with the current parameter is shown in Figure 10.10. Under the first shape projection, the rightmost on the above equation, the vertex $i$ is mapped to the image frame, say the point $(x_i^+, y_i^+)$, under the parameters $\boldsymbol{\gamma^d} + \Delta\boldsymbol{\gamma}$ using Eqs. (9), (15), and (16). Then, under the inverse shape projection, this point $(x_i^+, y_i^+)$ is mapped to the reference frame, say the point $(u_i^+, v_i^+)$, using the procedure described in Section 3.2. Finally, $(u_i^+, v_i^+)$ is mapped to $(x_i^*, y_i^*)$ using the shape projection with the parameter $\boldsymbol{\gamma^c}$.

*Correspondences Mapping to the Shape Model*

The first step of the composition yields a set of correspondences between the model vertices $(u_i, v_i)$ and the points in the image frame $(x_i^*, y_i^*)$. To recover the model parameters, $\boldsymbol{\alpha}$ and $\boldsymbol{\rho}$, explaining these correspondences, Eqs. (9), (15), and (16) must be inverted. In the case of

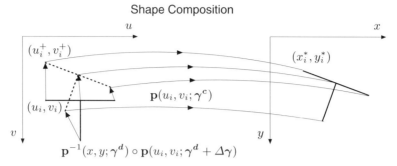

**Fig. 10.10.** Composition of the shape projection update with the current shape projection.

perspective projection, the equation governing the projection is nonlinear and hence the parameters are recovered by minimizing a nonlinear function. Alternatively, if a weak-perspective projection is used, the equation is bilinear. A closed form solution to this problem is presented elsewhere [27]. This algorithm is a novel *selective* approach that addresses this problem more accurately than the former method based on singular value decomposition factorization [2]. The rotation matrix and the focal length are recovered using Eq. (15) of [27] and the 2D translation using Eq. (16) of [27]; then the shape parameters $\alpha$ are recovered by inverting the linear system of equations using the estimated rotation matrix and focal length.

It should be noted that neither with the weak perspective nor with the perspective projections, can these equations be fully inverted, as there would remain a small residual called the *correspondences mapping error*. This is due to the fact that the shape model is not closed under composition.

*Deferred Correspondence Mapping*

It is to be noted that the correspondences are not required to be projected to the shape model, thereby extracting the shape projection parameters explaining a shape composition at each iteration. As seen in the middle row of Figure 10.8, the inputs of an iteration are the current correspondences (needed to sample the image at the correct location), not the current shape parameters $\gamma^c$. Then, at the end of the fitting, the correspondences are mapped to retrieve the final shape parameters. This scheme, called deferred correspondence mapping, has two advantages. First, there is no correspondence mapping error introduced at each iteration. Second, the algorithm is more efficient, as Eqs. (9), (15), and (16) are not inverted at each iteration.

The ICIA algorithm applied to 3D morphable models was detailed by Romdhani et al. [26], who also presented a robust version, using a Talwar function instead of the sum of square, thereby alleviating the Gaussian assumption of the image formation and allowing the fitting to be independent of attributes that are not modeled, such as eyeglasses.

**Comparison with the Active Appearance Model Fitting**

The active appearance model (AAM) search algorithm is presented in Section 3 of Chapter 3. The AAM is a 2D correspondence-based model. Its fitting algorithm has a feature similar to that of the ICIA algorithm presented here. Similar to Eq. (29), it uses a constant, linear relation between the texture error and the model update. However, in contrast to the ICIA algorithm, the update is not composed with the current parameters but added to them. Matthews and Baker [20] showed why this additive update is inappropriate and therefore has limited applicability.

**Fitting Results**

Some fitting results and reconstructions obtained with the ICIA algorithm are presented on Figure 10.11. The input images are part of the PIE face database (ambient light at 13 poses). Similar to the SNO algorithm, the initialization is provided by landmark points.

View 31      View 09      View 27      View 07      View 05      View 37      View 22

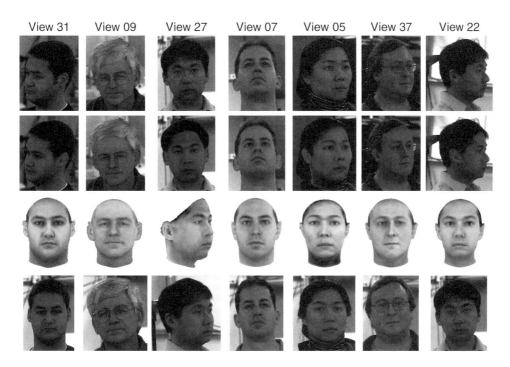

**Fig. 10.11.** Inverse compositional image alignment fitting results. Three-dimensional reconstruction from CMU-PIE images using the ICIA fitting algorithm. Top row. Originals. Second row. Reconstructions rendered into originals. Third row. Novel views. Bottom row. Images at approximately the same pose as in the third row provided for comparison.

# 5 Identification and Verification

We evaluated the 3D morphable model and the fitting algorithms on two applications: identification and verification. In the identification task, an image of an unknown person is provided to our system. The unknown face image is then compared to a database of known people, called the gallery set. The ensemble of unknown images is called the probe set. In the identification task, it is assumed that the individual in the unknown image is in the gallery. In a verification task, the individual in the unknown image claims an identity. The system must then accept or reject the claimed identity. Verification performance is characterized by two statistics: The verification rate is the rate at which legitimate users are granted access. The false alarm rate is the rate at which impostors are granted access. See section 1 of Chapter 14 for more detailed explanations of these two tasks.

We evaluated our approach on three data sets. **Set 1**: a portion of the FERET data set containing images with various poses. In the FERET nomenclature these images correspond to the series ba through bk. We omitted the images bj as the subjects present an expression that is not accounted for by our 3D morphable model. This data set includes 194 individuals across nine poses at constant lighting condition except for the series bk, which used a frontal view at another illumination condition than the rest of the images. **Set 2**: a portion of the CMU–PIE data set including images of 68 individuals at a neutral expression viewed from 13 different angles at ambient light. **Set 3**: another portion of the CMU–PIE data set containing images of the same 68 individuals at three poses (frontal, side, and profile) and illuminated by 21 different directions and by ambient light only. Among the 68 individuals in Set 2 and 3, a total of 28 wear glasses, which are not modeled and could decrease the accuracy of the fitting. None of the individuals present in these three sets was used to construct the 3D morphable model. These sets cover a large ethnic variety, not present in the set of 3D scans used to build the model. Refer to Chapter 13 for a formal description of the FERET and PIE set of images.

Identification and verification are performed by fitting an input face image to the 3D morphable model, thereby extracting its identity parameters, $\alpha$ and $\beta$. Then recognition tasks are achieved by comparing the identity parameters of the input image with those of the gallery images. We defined the identity parameters of a face image, denoted by the vector $\mathbf{c}$, by stacking the shape and texture parameters of the global and segmented models (see Section 2.5) and rescaling them by their standard deviations.

$$\mathbf{c} = \left[ \frac{\alpha_1^g}{\sigma_{S,1}}, \ldots, \frac{\alpha_{99}^g}{\sigma_{S,99}}, \frac{\beta_1^g}{\sigma_{T,1}}, \ldots, \frac{\beta_{99}^g}{\sigma_{T,99}}, \frac{\alpha_1^{s_1}}{\sigma_{S,1}}, \ldots, \frac{\alpha_{99}^{s_1}}{\sigma_{S,99}}, \ldots, \ldots, \frac{\beta_{99}^{s_4}}{\sigma_{T,99}} \right]^{\mathrm{T}} \quad (31)$$

We defined two distance measures to compare two identity parameters $\mathbf{c}_1$ and $\mathbf{c}_2$. The first measure, $d_A$, is based on the angle between the two vectors (it can also be seen as a normalized correlation), and is insensitive to the norm of both vectors. This is favorable for recognition tasks, as increasing the norm of $\mathbf{c}$ produces a caricature (see Section 2.4) which does not modify the perceived identity. The second distance [7], $d_W$, is based on discriminant analysis [13] and favors directions where identity variations occur. Denoting by $\mathbf{C}_W$ the pooled within-class covariance matrix, these two distances are defined by:

$$d_A = \frac{\mathbf{c}_1^{\mathrm{T}} \cdot \mathbf{c}_2}{\sqrt{(\mathbf{c}_1^{\mathrm{T}} \cdot \mathbf{c}_1)(\mathbf{c}_2^{\mathrm{T}} \cdot \mathbf{c}_2)}} \quad \text{and} \quad d_W = \frac{\mathbf{c}_1^{\mathrm{T}} \cdot \mathbf{C}_W \cdot \mathbf{c}_2}{\sqrt{(\mathbf{c}_1^{\mathrm{T}} \cdot \mathbf{C}_W \cdot \mathbf{c}_1)(\mathbf{c}_2^{\mathrm{T}} \cdot \mathbf{C}_W \cdot \mathbf{c}_2)}} \quad (32)$$

Results on Sets 1 and 3 use the distance $d_W$ with, for Set 1, a within-class covariance matrix learned on Set 3, and vice versa.

## 5.1  Pose Variation

In this section, we present identification and verification results for images of faces that vary in pose. Table 10.1 lists percentages of correct rank 1 identification obtained with the SNO fitting algorithm on Set 1 (FERET). The 10 poses were used to constitute gallery sets. The results are detailed for each probe pose. The results for the front view gallery (here in bold) were first reported in [7]. The first plot of Figure 10.12 shows the ROC for a verification task for the front view gallery and the nine other poses in the probe set. The verification rate for a false alarm rate of 1% is 87.9%.

**Table 10.1.** SNO identification performances on Set 1 (FERET).

| Parameter | Performance (%) by probe view | | | | | | | | | | Mean |
|---|---|---|---|---|---|---|---|---|---|---|---|
|  | $bi$ | $bh$ | $bg$ | $bf$ | $ba$ | $be$ | $bd$ | $bc$ | $bb$ | $bk$ | |
| $\phi$ | $-37.9°$ | $-26.5°$ | $-16.3°$ | $-7.1°$ | $1.1°$ | $11.2°$ | $18.9°$ | $27.4°$ | $38.9°$ | $0.1°$ | |
| Gallery view | | | | | | | | | | | |
| $bi$ | - | 98.5 | 94.8 | 87.6 | 85.6 | 87.1 | 87.1 | 84.0 | 77.3 | 76.8 | 86.5 |
| $bh$ | 99.5 | - | 97.4 | 95.9 | 91.8 | 95.9 | 94.8 | 92.3 | 83.0 | 86.1 | 93.0 |
| $bg$ | 97.9 | 99.0 | - | 99.0 | 95.4 | 96.9 | 96.9 | 91.2 | 81.4 | 89.2 | 94.1 |
| $bf$ | 95.9 | 99.5 | 99.5 | - | 97.9 | 96.9 | 99.0 | 94.8 | 88.1 | 95.4 | 96.3 |
| **$ba$** | **90.7** | **95.4** | **96.4** | **97.4** | **-** | **99.5** | **96.9** | **95.4** | **94.8** | **96.9** | **95.9** |
| $be$ | 91.2 | 95.9 | 96.4 | 97.4 | 100.0 | - | 99.5 | 99.0 | 96.4 | 94.3 | 96.7 |
| $bd$ | 88.7 | 97.9 | 96.9 | 99.0 | 97.9 | 99.5 | - | 99.5 | 98.5 | 92.3 | 96.7 |
| $bc$ | 87.1 | 90.7 | 91.2 | 94.3 | 96.4 | 99.0 | 99.5 | - | 99.0 | 87.6 | 93.9 |
| $bb$ | 78.9 | 80.4 | 77.8 | 80.9 | 87.6 | 94.3 | 94.8 | 99.0 | - | 74.7 | 85.4 |
| $bk$ | 83.0 | 88.1 | 92.3 | 95.4 | 96.9 | 94.3 | 93.8 | 88.7 | 79.4 | - | 90.2 |

The overall mean of the table is 92.9%. $\phi$ is the average estimated azimuth pose angle of the face. Ground truth for $\phi$ is not available. Condition $bk$ has different illumination than the others. The row in bold is the front view gallery (condition $ba$).

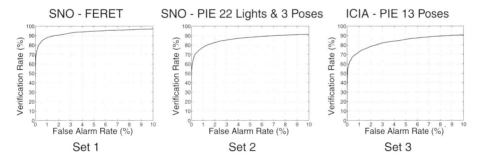

**Fig. 10.12.** Receiver operator characteristic for a verification task obtained with the SNO and ICIA algorithms on different sets of images. These plots should not be used as a comparison between SNO and ICIA as they reflect results obtained on different images.

The ICIA algorithm was evaluated on Set 2, images from 68 individuals at ambient illumination seen from 13 poses. These images are part of the CMU–PIE face database. The rank 1 identification percentages are presented in Table 5.1 for each pose taken as gallery and probe sets. These results were obtained using the distance $d_A$. The third plot of Figure 10.12 is the ROC for a verification task obtained using the pose 11 as gallery set and all other poses as probe set. The verification rate for 1% false alarm rate is 72.9%. These results were obtained using a regularized morphable model (see Section 2.4). They are on average 6% better than the one obtained using the original morphable model. Note that the results presented here should not be used as a comparison between the two fitting algorithms as they were applied on different sets of images.

**Table 10.2.** ICIA identification performances on the Set 2 (PIE data set across 13 poses, illuminated by ambient light).

| | Performance (%) by probe view | | | | | | | | | | | | | |
|---|---|---|---|---|---|---|---|---|---|---|---|---|---|---|
| | 34 | 31 | 14 | 11 | 29 | 9 | 27 | 7 | 5 | 37 | 25 | 2 | 22 | Mean |
| Azimuth | -66 | -47 | -46 | -32 | -17 | 0 | 0 | 0 | 16 | 31 | 44 | 44 | 62 | |
| Altitude | 3 | 13 | 2 | 2 | 2 | 15 | 2 | 2 | 2 | 2 | 2 | 13 | 3 | |
| Gallery view | | | | | | | | | | | | | | |
| 34 | - | 100 | 100 | 100 | 94 | 74 | 75 | 72 | 71 | 69 | 66 | 71 | 75 | 81 |
| 31 | 99 | - | 100 | 100 | 100 | 99 | 96 | 85 | 91 | 91 | 88 | 87 | 78 | 93 |
| 14 | 99 | 100 | - | 100 | 100 | 97 | 97 | 94 | 93 | 90 | 88 | 91 | 76 | 94 |
| 11 | 96 | 100 | 100 | - | 100 | 100 | 100 | 99 | 96 | 90 | 85 | 84 | 72 | 93 |
| 29 | 88 | 97 | 100 | 100 | - | 100 | 100 | 100 | 99 | 96 | 88 | 84 | 71 | 94 |
| 9 | 79 | 97 | 94 | 97 | 100 | - | 100 | 100 | 100 | 94 | 84 | 93 | 68 | 92 |
| 27 | 76 | 93 | 99 | 99 | 100 | 100 | - | 99 | 100 | 96 | 85 | 85 | 79 | 93 |
| 7 | 71 | 91 | 96 | 99 | 100 | 100 | 100 | - | 100 | 97 | 85 | 88 | 74 | 92 |
| 5 | 88 | 99 | 97 | 99 | 100 | 99 | 100 | 100 | - | 100 | 100 | 99 | 90 | 97 |
| 37 | 81 | 91 | 96 | 97 | 94 | 99 | 97 | 96 | 100 | - | 100 | 100 | 99 | 96 |
| 25 | 81 | 96 | 97 | 93 | 96 | 96 | 87 | 87 | 97 | 100 | - | 100 | 100 | 94 |
| 2 | 76 | 82 | 93 | 90 | 84 | 90 | 85 | 87 | 94 | 100 | 100 | - | 100 | 90 |
| 22 | 85 | 84 | 87 | 87 | 76 | 81 | 85 | 76 | 90 | 99 | 100 | 100 | - | 88 |

The overall mean of the table is 91.9%.

## 5.2 Pose and Illumination Variations

In this section we investigate the performance of our method in the presence of combined pose and illumination variations. The SNO algorithm was applied to the images of Set 3, CMU–PIE images of 68 individuals varying with respect to three poses, 21 directed light and ambient light conditions. Table 5.2 presents the rank 1 identification performance averaged over all lighting conditions for front, side, and profile view galleries. Illumination 13 was selected for the galleries. The second plot of Figure 10.12 shows the ROC for a verification using as gallery a side view illuminated by light 13 and using all other images of the set as probes. The verification rate for a 1% false alarm rate was 77.5%. These results were first reported by Blanz and Vetter [7].

**Table 10.3.** Mean percentage of correct identification obtained after a SNO fitting on Set 3, averaged over all lighting conditions for front, side, and profile view galleries.

| Gallery view | Performance (%) by probe view | | | Mean |
|:---:|:---:|:---:|:---:|:---:|
| | Front | Side | Profile | |
| Front | 99.8% (97.1–100) | 97.8% (82.4–100) | 79.5% (39.7–94.1) | 92.3 % |
| Side | 99.5% (94.1–100) | 99.9% (98.5–100) | 85.7% (42.6–98.5) | 95.0 % |
| Profile | 83.0% (72.1–94.1) | 86.2% (61.8–95.6) | 98.3% (83.8–100) | 89.0 % |

Numbers in parenthesis are percentages for the worst and best illumination within each probe set. The overall mean of the table is 92.1%.

## 5.3  Identification Confidence

In this section, we present an automated technique for assessing the quality of the fitting in terms of a fitting score (FS). We show that the fitting score is correlated with identification performance and hence, may be used as an identification confidence measure. This method was first presented by Blanz et al. [9]

A fitting score can be derived from the image error and from the model coefficients of each fitted segment from the average.

$$FS = f(\frac{E_I}{N_{vv}}, \boldsymbol{\alpha}_g, \boldsymbol{\beta}_g, \boldsymbol{\alpha}_{s_1}, \boldsymbol{\beta}_{s_1}, \ldots, \boldsymbol{\beta}_{s_4}) \tag{33}$$

Although the FS can be derived by a Bayesian method, we learned it using a support vector machine (SVM) (see Vapnik [31] for a general description of SVM and Blanz et al. [9] for details about FS learning).

Figure 10.13 shows the identification results for the PIE images varying in illumination across three poses, with respect to the FS for a gallery of side views. FS > 0 denotes good fittings and FS < 0 poor ones. We divided the probe images into eight bins of different FS and computed the percentage of correct rank 1 identification for each of these bins. There is a strong correlation between the FS and identification performance, indicating that the FS is a good measure of identification confidence.

## 5.4  Virtual Views as an Aid to Standard Face Recognition Algorithms

The face recognition vendor test (FRVT) 2002 [24] was an independently administered assessment, conducted by the U.S. government of the performance of commercially available automatic face recognition systems. The test is described in Section 2 of Chapter 14. It was realized that identification of face images significantly drops if the face image is nonfrontal. Hence, one of the questions addressed by FRVT02 is this: Do identification performances of nonfrontal face images improve if the pose is normalized by our 3D morphable model? To answer this question, we normalized the pose of a series of images [8]. Normalizing the pose means to fit an input image where the face is nonfrontal, thereby estimating its 3D structure, and to synthesize an image with a frontal view of the estimated face. Examples of pose-normalized images are shown in Figure 10.14. As neither the hair nor the shoulders are modeled, the synthetic images are rendered into a standard frontal face image of one person. This normalization is performed by the following steps.

**Fig. 10.13.** Identification results as a function of the fitting score.

1. Manually define up to 11 landmark points on the input image to ensure optimal quality of the fitting.
2. Run the SNO fitting algorithm described in Section 4.2 yielding a 3D estimation of the face in the input image.
3. Render the 3D face in front of the standard image using the rigid parameters (position, orientation, and size) and illumination parameters of the standard image. These parameters were estimated by fitting the standard face image.
4. Draw the hair of the standard face in front of the forehead of the synthetic image. This makes the transition between the standard image and the synthetic image smoother.

The normalization was applied to images of 87 individuals at five poses (frontal, two side views, one up view and a down view). Identifications were performed by the 10 participants to FRVT02 (see pages 31 and 32 of Phillips et al. [24]) using the frontal view images as gallery and nine probe sets: four probe sets with images of nonfrontal views, four probe sets with the normalized images of the nonfrontal views and one probe set with our preprocessing normalization applied to the front images. The comparison of performances between the normalized images (called morph images) and the raw images is presented on Figure 10.15 for a verification experiment (the hit rate is plotted for a false alarm rate of 1%).

The frontal morph probe set provides a baseline for how the normalization affects an identification system. In the frontal morph probe set, the normalization is applied to the gallery images. The results on this probe set are shown on the first column of Figure 10.15. The verification rates would be 1.0, if a system were insensitive to the artifacts introduced by the morphable model and did not rely on the person's hairstyle, collar, or other details that are exchanged by the normalization (which are, of course, no reliable features by which to identify one person). The sensitivity to the morphable model of the 10 participants ranges from 0.98 down to 0.45. The overall results showed that, with the exception of Iconquest, morphable models significantly improved (and usually doubled) performance.

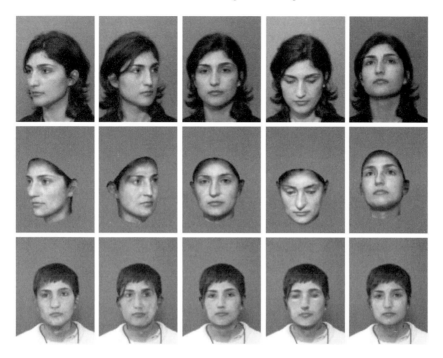

**Fig. 10.14.** From the original images (top row), we recover the 3D shape (middle row), by SNO fitting. Mapping the texture of visible face regions on the surface and rendering it into a standard background, which is a face image we selected, produces virtual front views (bottom row). Note that the frontal-to-frontal mapping, which served as a baseline test, involves hairstyle replacement (bottom row, center).

## 6 Conclusions

We have shown that 3D morphable models can be one way to approach challenging real world identification problems. They address in a natural way such difficult problems as combined variations of pose and illumination. Morphable models can be extended, in a straightforward way, to cope with other sources of variation such as facial expression or age.

Our focus wass mainly centered on improving the fitting algorithms with respect to accuracy and efficiency. We also investigated several methods for estimating identity from model coefficients. However, a more thorough understanding of the relation between these coefficients and identity might still improve recognition performance. The separation of identity from other attributes could be improved, for instance, by using other features made available by the fitting, such as the texture extracted from the image (after correspondences are recovered by model fitting). Improving this separation might even be more crucial when facial expression or age variation are added to the model.

To model fine and identity-related details such as freckles, birthmarks, and wrinkles, it might be helpful to extend our current framework for representing texture. Indeed, linear combination of textures is a rather simplifying choice. Hence improving the texture model is subject to future research.

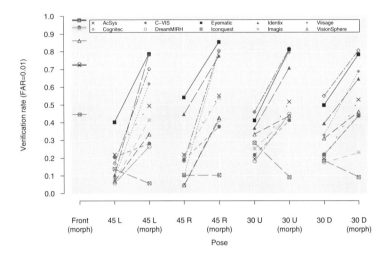

**Fig. 10.15.** The effect of the original images versus normalized images using the 3D morphable models. The verification rate at a false alarm rate of 1% is plotted. (Courtesy of Jonathon Phillips.)

Currently our approach is clearly limited by its computational load. However this disadvantage will evaporate with time as computer increase their clock speed. Adding an automatic landmark detection will enable 3D morphable models to compete with state of the art commercial systems such as those that took part in the Face Recognition Vendor Test 2002 [24].

# References

1. S. Baker and I. Matthews.  Equivalence and efficiency of image alignment algorithms.  In *CVPR*, 2001. http://www.ri.cmu.edu/projects/project_515.html.
2. B. Bascle and A. Blake. Separability of pose and expression in facial tracking and animation. In *Sixth International Conference on Computer Vision*, 1998.
3. J. Bergen and R. Hingorani.  Hierarchical motion-based frame rate conversion.  Technical report, David Sarnoff Research Center Princeton, NJ, 1990.
4. D. Beymer and T. Poggio. Image representations for visual learning. *Science* 272:1905–1909, 1996.
5. D. Beymer, A. Shashua, and T. Poggio.  Example based image analysis and synthesis.  Technical report, Artificial Intelligence Laboratory, MIT, Cambridge, MA, 1993.
6. V. Blanz and T. Vetter. A morphable model for the synthesis of 3D-faces. In *SIGGRAPH 99*, 1999.
7. V. Blanz and T. Vetter. Face recognition based on fitting a 3d morphable model. *PAMI*, 2003.
8. V. Blanz and T. Vetter.  Generating frontal views from single, non-frontal images. In: Face recognition vendor test 2002: Technical appendix O.  NISTIR 6965, National Institute of Standards and Technology, Gaithersburg, MD 2003.
9. V. Blanz, S. Romdhani, and T. Vetter.  Face identification across different poses and illuminations with a 3D morphable model. In *Auto. Face and Gesture Recognition*, 2002.
10. T. Cootes, K. Walker, and C. Taylor. View-based active appearance models. In *Automatic Face and Gesture Recognition*, 2000.

11. I. Craw and P. Cameron. Parameterizing images for recognition and reconstruction. In *Proc. BMVC*, 1991.

12. A. Dempster, N. Laird, and D. Rubin. Maximum likelihood from incomplete data via the EM algorithm. *Journal of the Royal Statistical Society B* 39:1–38, 1977.

13. R. Duda, P. Hart, and D. Stork. *Pattern classification*. Wiley, New-York, 2001.

14. J. Foley, A. van Dam, S. Feiner, and J. Hughes. *Computer Graphics: Principles and Practice*. Addison-Wesley, 1996.

15. P. Hallinan. *A deformable model for the recognition of human faces under arbitrary illumination*. PhD thesis, Harvard University, 1995.

16. R. Haralick and L. Shapiro. *Computer and robot vision*. Addison-Wesley, Reading, MA,1992.

17. B. Horn and B. Schunck. Determining optical flow. *Artificial Intelligence* 17:185–203, 1981.

18. A. Lanitis, C. Taylor, and T. Cootes. An automatic face identification system using flexible appearance models. In *Proc. British Machine Vison Conference*, 1994.

19. B. Lucas and T. Kanade. An iterative image registration technique with an application to stereo vision. In *Proc. Intl Joint Conf. Artificial Intelligence*, 1981.

20. I. Matthews and S. Baker. Active appearance models revisited. Technical report, Robotics Institute, Carnegie Mellon University, 2003.

21. T. Minka. Old and new matrix algebra useful for statistics. http://www.stat.cmu.edu/˜minka/papers/matrix.html, 2000.

22. H. Murase and S. Nayar. Visual learning and recognition of 3d objects from appearance. *IJCV* 14:5–24, 1995.

23. A. Pentland, B. Moghaddam, and T. Starner. View-based and modular eigenspaces for face recognition. In *Proc. of IEEE Conf. on Computer Vision and Pattern Recognition*, 1994.

24. P. Phillips, P. Grother, R. Michaels, D. Blackburn, E. Tabassi, and M. Bone. Face recognition vendor test 2002: evaluation report. NISTIR 6965, National Institute of Standards and Technology, Gaithersburg, MD, 2003.

25. W. Press, S. Teukolsky, W. Vetterling, and B. Flannery. *Numerical recipes in C: the art of Scientific Computing*. Cambridge University Press, Cambridge, UK, 1992.

26. S. Romdhani and T. Vetter. Efficient, robust and accurate fitting of a 3D morphable model. In *IEEE International Conference on Computer Vision*, 2003.

27. S. Romdhani, N. Canterakis, and T. Vetter. Selective vs. global recovery of rigid and non-rigid motion. Technical report, CS Dept, University of Basel, 2003.

28. L. Sirovich and M. Kirby. Low-dimensional procedure for the characterization of human faces. *Journal of the Optical Society of America A* 4:519–524, 1987.

29. M. Tipping and C. Bishop. Probabilistic principal component analysis. *Journal of the Royal Statistical Society, Series B*, 1999.

30. M. Turk and A. Pentland. Eigenfaces for recognition. *Journal of Cognitive Neuroscience* 3:71–86, 1991.

31. V. Vapnik. *The Nature of Statistical Learning*. Springer, New-York, 1995.

32. T. Vetter and N. Troje. Separation of texture and shape in images of faces for image coding and synthesis. *Journal of the Optical Society of America* 14:2152–2161, 1997.

33. T. Vetter, M. Jones, and T. Poggio. A bootstrapping algorithm for learning linear models of object classes. In *Proc. of IEEE Conf. on Computer Vision and Pattern Recognition*, 1997.

# Chapter 11. Facial Expression Analysis

Ying-Li Tian,[1] Takeo Kanade[2], and Jeffrey F. Cohn[2,3]

[1]  IBM T. J. Watson Research Center, Hawthorne, NY 10532, USA. yltian@us.ibm.com
[2]  Robotics Institute, Carnegie Mellon University, Pittsburgh, PA 15213, USA. tk@cs.cmu.edu
[3]  Department of Psychology, University of Pittsburgh, Pittsburgh, PA 15260, USA.
     jeffcohn@pitt.edu

## 1 Principles of Facial Expression Analysis

### 1.1 What Is Facial Expression Analysis?

Facial expressions are the facial changes in response to a person's internal emotional states, intentions, or social communications. Facial expression analysis has been an active research topic for behavioral scientists since the work of Darwin in 1872 [18, 22, 25, 71]. Suwa et al. [76] presented an early attempt to automatically analyze facial expressions by tracking the motion of 20 identified spots on an image sequence in 1978. After that, much progress has been made to build computer systems to help us understand and use this natural form of human communication [6, 7, 17, 20, 28, 39, 51, 55, 65, 78, 81, 92, 93, 94, 96].

In this chapter, facial expression analysis refers to computer systems that attempt to automatically analyze and recognize facial motions and facial feature changes from visual information. Sometimes the facial expression analysis has been confused with emotion analysis in the computer vision domain. For emotion analysis, higher level knowledge is required. For example, although facial expressions can convey emotion, they can also express intention, cognitive processes, physical effort, or other intra- or interpersonal meanings. Interpretation is aided by context, body gesture, voice, individual differences, and cultural factors as well as by facial configuration and timing [10, 67, 68]. Computer facial expression analysis systems need to analyze the facial actions regardless of context, culture, gender, and so on.

The accomplishments in the related areas such as psychological studies, human movement analysis, face detection, face tracking, and recognition make the automatic facial expression analysis possible. Automatic facial expression analysis can be applied in many areas such as emotion and paralinguistic communication, clinical psychology, psychiatry, neurology, pain assessment, lie detection, intelligent environments, and multimodal human-computer interface (HCI).

### 1.2 Basic Structure of Facial Expression Analysis Systems

Facial expression analysis includes both measurement of facial motion and recognition of expression. The general approach to automatic facial expression analysis (AFEA) consists of three steps (Figure 11.1): face acquisition, facial data extraction and representation, and facial expression recognition.

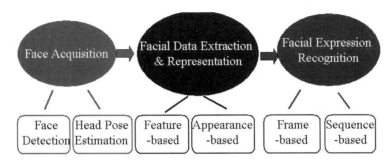

**Fig. 11.1.** Basic structure of facial expression analysis systems.

Face acquisition is a processing stage to automatically find the face region for the input images or sequences. It can be a detector to detect face for each frame or just detect face in the first frame and then track the face in the remainder of the video sequence. To handle large head motion, the the head finder, head tracking, and pose estimation can be applied to a facial expression analysis system.

After the face is located, the next step is to extract and represent the facial changes caused by facial expressions. In facial feature extraction for expression analysis, there are mainly two approaches: geometric feature-based methods and appearance-based methods. The geometric facial features present the shape and locations of facial components (including the mouth, eyes, brows, and nose). The facial components or facial feature points are extracted to form a feature vector that represents the face geometry. With appearance-based methods, image filters, such as Gabor wavelets, are applied to either the whole face or specific regions in a face image to extract a feature vector. Depending on the different facial feature extraction methods, the effects of in-plane head rotation and different scales of the faces can be eliminated by face normalization before the feature extraction or by feature representation before the step of expression recognition.

Facial expression recognition is the last stage of AFEA systems. The facial changes can be identified as facial action units or prototypic emotional expressions (see Section 2.1 for definitions). Depending on if the temporal information is used, in this chapter we classified the recognition approaches as frame-based or sequence-based.

## 1.3 Organization of the Chapter

This chapter introduces recent advances in facial expression analysis. The first part discusses general structure of AFEA systems. The second part describes the problem space for facial expression analysis. This space includes multiple dimensions: level of description, individual differences in subjects, transitions among expressions, intensity of facial expression, deliberate versus spontaneous expression, head orientation and scene complexity, image acquisition and resolution, reliability of ground truth, databases, and the relation to other facial behaviors or nonfacial behaviors. We note that most work to date has been confined to a relatively restricted region of this space. The last part of this chapter is devoted to a description of more specific approaches and the techniques used in recent advances. They include the techniques for face acquisition, facial data extraction and representation, and facial expression recognition. The chapter concludes with a discussion assessing the current status, future possibilities, and open questions about automatic facial expression analysis.

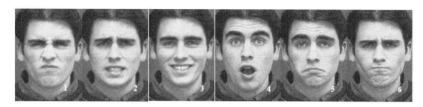

**Fig. 11.2.** Emotion-specified facial expression (posed images from database [43] ). 1, disgust; 2, fear; 3, joy; 4, surprise; 5, sadness; 6, anger. From Schmidt and Cohn [72], with permission.

## 2 Problem Space for Facial Expression Analysis

### 2.1 Level of Description

With few exceptions [17, 20, 30, 81], most AFEA systems attempt to recognize a small set of prototypic emotional expressions as shown in Figure 11.2, (i.e., disgust, fear, joy, surprise, sadness, anger). This practice may follow from the work of Darwin [18], and more recently Ekman and Friesen [23, 24] and Izard et al. [42], who proposed that emotion-specified expressions have corresponding prototypic facial expressions. In everyday life, however, such prototypic expressions occur relatively infrequently. Instead, emotion more often is communicated by subtle changes in one or a few discrete facial features, such as tightening of the lips in anger or obliquely lowering the lip corners in sadness [11]. Change in isolated features, especially in the area of the eyebrows or eyelids, is typical of paralinguistic displays; for instance, raising the brows signals greeting [21]. To capture such subtlety of human emotion and paralinguistic communication, automated recognition of fine-grained changes in facial expression is needed. The facial action coding system (the FACS: [25]) is a human-observer-based system designed to detect subtle changes in facial features. Viewing videotaped facial behavior in slow motion, trained observers can manually FACS code all possible facial displays, which are referred to as action units and may occur individually or in combinations.

FACS consists of 44 action units. Thirty are anatomically related to contraction of a specific set of facial muscles (Table 11.1) [22]. The anatomic basis of the remaining 14 is unspecified (Table 11.2). These 14 are referred to in FACS as miscellaneous actions. Many action units may be coded as symmetrical or asymmetrical. For action units that vary in intensity, a 5-point ordinal scale is used to measure the degree of muscle contraction. Table 11.3 shows some examples of combinations of FACS action units.

Although Ekman and Friesen proposed that specific combinations of FACS action units represent prototypic expressions of emotion, emotion-specified expressions are not part of FACS; they are coded in separate systems, such as the emotional facial action system (EMFACS) [37].

**Table 11.1.** FACS action units (AU). AUs with an askerik indicate that the criteria have changed for this AU, that is, AU 25, 26, and 27 are now coded according to criteria of intensity (25A-E), and AU 41, 42, and 43 are now coded according to criteria of intensity.

| Upper Face Action Units | | | | | |
|---|---|---|---|---|---|
| AU 1 | AU 2 | AU 4 | AU 5 | AU 6 | AU 7 |
| Inner Brow Raiser | Outer Brow Raiser | Brow Lowerer | Upper Lid Raiser | Cheek Raiser | Lid Tightener |
| *AU 41 | *AU 42 | *AU 43 | AU 44 | AU 45 | AU 46 |
| Lid Droop | Slit | Eyes Closed | Squint | Blink | Wink |
| Lower Face Action Units | | | | | |
| AU 9 | AU 10 | AU 11 | AU 12 | AU 13 | AU 14 |
| Nose Wrinkler | Upper Lip Raiser | Nasolabial Deepener | Lip Corner Puller | Cheek Puffer | Dimpler |
| AU 15 | AU 16 | AU 17 | AU 18 | AU 20 | AU 22 |
| Lip Corner Depressor | Lower Lip Depressor | Chin Raiser | Lip Puckerer | Lip Stretcher | Lip Funneler |
| AU 23 | AU 24 | *AU 25 | *AU 26 | *AU 27 | AU 28 |
| Lip Tightener | Lip Pressor | Lips Part | Jaw Drop | Mouth Stretch | Lip Suck |

FACS itself is purely descriptive and includes no inferential labels. By converting FACS codes to EMFACS or similar systems, face images may be coded for emotion-specified expressions (e.g., joy or anger) as well as for more molar categories of positive or negative emotion [56].

### 2.2 Individual Differences in Subjects

Face shape, texture, color, and facial and scalp hair vary with sex, ethnic background, and age [29, 99]. Infants, for instance, have smoother, less textured skin and often lack facial hair in the brows or scalp. The eye opening and contrast between iris and sclera differ markedly between Asians and Northern Europeans, which may affect the robustness of eye tracking and facial feature analysis more generally. Beards, eyeglasses, or jewelry may obscure facial features. Such individual differences in appearance may have important consequences for face analysis. Few attempts to study their influence exist. An exception was a study by Zlochower et al. [99], who found that algorithms for optical flow and high-gradient component detection that had been optimized for young adults performed less well when used in infants. The reduced texture

Table 11.2. Miscellaneous Actions.

| AU | Description |
|----|-------------|
| 8  | Lips toward |
| 19 | Tongue show |
| 21 | Neck tighten |
| 29 | Jaw thrust |
| 30 | Jaw sideways |
| 31 | Jaw clench |
| 32 | Bite lip |
| 33 | Blow |
| 34 | Puff |
| 35 | Cheek suck |
| 36 | Tongue bulge |
| 37 | Lip wipe |
| 38 | Nostril dilate |
| 39 | Nostril compress |

Table 11.3. Some examples of combination of FACS action units.

| AU 1+2 | AU 1+4 | AU 4+5 | AU 1+2+4 | AU 1+2+5 |
| AU 1+6 | AU 6+7 | AU 1+2+5+6+7 | AU 23+24 | AU 9+17 |
| AU 9+25 | AU 9+17+23+24 | AU 10+17 | AU 10+25 | AU 10+15+17 |
| AU 12+25 | AU 12+26 | AU 15+17 | AU 17+23+24 | AU 20+25 |

of infants' skin, their increased fatty tissue, juvenile facial conformation, and lack of transient furrows may all have contributed to the differences observed in face analysis between infants and adults.

In addition to individual differences in appearance, there are individual differences in expressiveness, which refers to the degree of facial plasticity, morphology, frequency of intense expression, and overall rate of expression. Individual differences in these characteristics are well established and are an important aspect of individual identity [53] (these individual differences in expressiveness and in biases for particular facial actions are sufficiently strong that they may be used as a biometric to augment the accuracy of face recognition algorithms [16]). An extreme example of variability in expressiveness occurs in individuals who have incurred damage either to the facial nerve or central nervous system [63, 85]. To develop algorithms that are robust to individual differences in facial features and behavior, it is essential to include a large sample of varying ethnic background, age, and sex, which includes people who have facial hair and wear jewelry or eyeglasses and both normal and clinically impaired individuals.

## 2.3 Transitions Among Expressions

A simplifying assumption in facial expression analysis is that expressions are singular and begin and end with a neutral position. In reality, facial expression is more complex, especially at the level of action units. Action units may occur in combinations or show serial dependence. Transitions from action units or combination of actions to another may involve no intervening neutral state. Parsing the stream of behavior is an essential requirement of a robust facial analysis system, and training data are needed that include dynamic combinations of action units, which may be either additive or nonadditive.

As shown in Table 11.3, an example of an additive combination is smiling (AU 12) with mouth open, which would be coded as AU 12+25, AU 12+26, or AU 12+27 depending on the degree of lip parting and whether and how far the mandible was lowered. In the case of AU 12+27, for instance, the facial analysis system would need to detect transitions among all three levels of mouth opening while continuing to recognize AU 12, which may be simultaneously changing in intensity.

Nonadditive combinations represent further complexity. Following usage in speech science, we refer to these interactions as co-articulation effects. An example is the combination AU 12+15, which often occurs during embarrassment. Although AU 12 raises the cheeks and lip corners, its action on the lip corners is modified by the downward action of AU 15. The resulting appearance change is highly dependent on timing. The downward action of the lip corners may occur simultaneously or sequentially. The latter appears to be more common [73]. To be comprehensive, a database should include individual action units and both additive and nonadditive combinations, especially those that involve co-articulation effects. A classifier trained only on single action units may perform poorly for combinations in which co-articulation effects occur.

## 2.4 Intensity of Facial Expression

Facial actions can vary in intensity. Manual FACS coding, for instance, uses a 3- or more recently a 5-point intensity scale to describe intensity variation of action units (for psychometric data, see Sayette et al. [70]). Some related action units, moreover, function as sets to represent intensity variation. In the eye region, action units 41, 42, and 43 or 45 can represent intensity variation from slightly drooped to closed eyes. Several computer vision researchers proposed methods to represent intensity variation automatically. Essa and Pentland [28] represented intensity variation in smiling using optical flow. Kimura and Yachida [44] and Lien et al. [50] quantified intensity variation in emotion-specified expression and in action units, respectively. These authors did not, however, attempt the more challenging step of discriminating intensity variation within types of facial actions. Instead, they used intensity measures for the more limited purpose of discriminating between different types of facial actions. Bartlett and colleagues [4] tested their algorithms on facial expressions that systematically varied in intensity as measured by manual FACS coding. Although they failed to report results separately for each level of intensity variation, their overall findings suggest some success. Tian et al. [83] may be the only group to compare manual and automatic coding of intensity variation. Using Gabor features and an artificial neural network, they discriminated intensity variation in eye closure as reliably as did human coders. These findings suggest that it is feasible to automatically recognize intensity variation within types of facial actions. Regardless of whether investigators attempt to discriminate intensity variation within facial actions, it is important that the range of variation be described adequately. Methods that work for intense expressions may generalize poorly to ones of low intensity.

## 2.5  Deliberate Versus Spontaneous Expression

Most face expression data have been collected by asking subjects to perform a series of expressions. These directed facial action tasks may differ in appearance and timing from spontaneously occurring behavior [27]. Deliberate and spontaneous facial behavior are mediated by separate motor pathways, the pyramidal and extrapyramidal motor tracks, respectively [63]. As a consequence, fine-motor control of deliberate facial actions is often inferior and less symmetrical than what occurs spontaneously. Many people, for instance, are able to raise their outer brows spontaneously while leaving their inner brows at rest; few can perform this action voluntarily. Spontaneous depression of the lip corners (AU 15) and raising and narrowing the inner corners of the brow (AU 1+4) are common signs of sadness. Without training, few people can perform these actions deliberately, which incidentally is an aid to lie detection [27]. Differences in the temporal organization of spontaneous and deliberate facial actions are particularly important in that many pattern recognition approaches, such as hidden Markov modeling, are highly dependent on the timing of the appearance change. Unless a database includes both deliberate and spontaneous facial actions, it will likely prove inadequate for developing face expression methods that are robust to these differences.

## 2.6  Head Orientation and Scene Complexity

Face orientation relative to the camera, the presence and actions of other people, and background conditions may influence face analysis. In the face recognition literature, face orientation has received deliberate attention. The FERET database [64], for instance, includes both frontal and oblique views, and several specialized databases have been collected to try to develop methods of face recognition that are invariant to moderate change in face orientation [86]. In the face expression literature, use of multiple perspectives is rare; and relatively less attention has been focused on the problem of pose invariance. Most researchers assume that face orientation is limited to in-plane variation [4] or that out-of-plane rotation is small [51, 58, 65, 81]. In reality, large out-of-plane rotation in head position is common and often accompanies change in expression. Kraut and Johnson [48] found that smiling typically occurs while turning toward another person. Camras et al. [9] showed that infant surprise expressions often occur as the infant pitches her head back. To develop pose invariant methods of face expression analysis, image data are needed in which facial expression changes in combination with significant nonplanar change in pose. Some efforts have been made to handle large out-of-plane rotation in head position [80, 90, 91].

Scene complexity, such as background and the presence of other people, potentially influences accuracy of face detection, feature tracking, and expression recognition. Most databases use image data in which the background is neutral or has a consistent pattern and only a single person is present in the scene. In natural environments, multiple people interacting with each other are likely, and their effects need to be understood. Unless this variation is represented in training data, it will be difficult to develop and test algorithms that are robust to such variation.

## 2.7  Image Acquisition and Resolution

The image acquisition procedure includes several issues, such as the properties and number of video cameras and digitizer, the size of the face image relative to total image dimensions, and the ambient lighting. All of these factors may influence facial expression analysis. Images acquired in low light or at coarse resolution can provide less information about facial features. Similarly, when the face image size is small relative to the total image size, less information is available. NTSC cameras record images at 30 frames per second, The implications of down-sampling from this rate are unknown. Many algorithms for optical flow assume that pixel displacement between adjacent frames is small. Unless they are tested at a range of sampling rates, the robustness to sampling rate and resolution cannot be assessed.

Within an image sequence, changes in head position relative to the light source and variation in ambient lighting have potentially significant effects on face expression analysis. A light source above the subject's head causes shadows to fall below the brows, which can obscure the eyes, especially for subjects with pronounced bone structure or hair. Methods that work well in studio lighting may perform poorly in more natural lighting (e.g., through an exterior window) when the angle of lighting changes across an image sequence. Most investigators use single-camera setups, which is problematic when a frontal orientation is not required. With image data from a single camera, out-of-plane rotation may be difficult to standardize. For large out-of-plane rotation, multiple cameras may be required. Multiple camera setups can support three dimensional (3D) modeling and in some cases ground truth with which to assess the accuracy of image alignment. Pantic and Rothkrantz [60] were the first to use two cameras mounted on a headphone-like device; one camera is placed in front of the face and the other on the right side of the face. The cameras are moving together with the head to eliminate the scale and orientation variance of the acquired face images.

**Table 11.4.** A face at different resolutions. All images are enlarged to the same size. At 48 x 64 pixels the facial features such as the corners of the eyes and the mouth become hard to detect. Facial expressions are not recognized at 24 x 32 pixels [80].

| Face Process | 96 x 128 | 69 x 93 | 48 x 64 | 24 x 32 |
|---|---|---|---|---|
| Detect? | Yes | Yes | Yes | Yes |
| Pose? | Yes | Yes | Yes | Yes |
| Recognize? | Yes | Yes | Yes | Maybe |
| Features? | Yes | Yes | Maybe | No |
| Expressions? | Yes | Yes | Maybe | No |

Image resolution is another concern. Professional grade PAL cameras, for instance, provide very high resolution images. By contrast, security cameras provide images that are seriously degraded. Although postprocessing may improve image resolution, the degree of potential improvement is likely limited. Also the effects of postprocessing for expression recognition are not known. Table 11.4 shows a face at different resolutions. Most automated face-processing tasks should be possible for a 69 x 93 pixel image. At 48 x 64 pixels the facial features such as the corners of the eyes and the mouth become hard to detect. The facial expressions may be recognized at 48 x 64 and are not recognized at 24 x 32 pixels. Algorithms that work well at optimal resolutions of full face frontal images and studio lighting can be expected to perform poorly when recording conditions are degraded or images are compressed. Without knowing the boundary conditions of face expression algorithms, comparative performance is difficult to assess. Algorithms that appear superior within one set of boundary conditions may perform more poorly across the range of potential applications. Appropriate data with which these factors can be tested are needed.

## 2.8  Reliability of Ground Truth

When training a system to recognize facial expression, the investigator assumes that training and test data are accurately labeled. This assumption may or may not be accurate. Asking subjects to perform a given action is no guarantee that they will. To ensure internal validity, expression data must be manually coded and the reliability of the coding verified. Interobserver reliability can be improved by providing rigorous training to observers and monitoring their performance. FACS coders must pass a standardized test, which ensures (initially) uniform coding among international laboratories. Monitoring is best achieved by having observers independently code a portion of the same data. As a general rule, 15% to 20% of data should be comparison-coded. To guard against drift in coding criteria [54], re-standardization is important. When assessing reliability, coefficient kappa [32] is preferable to raw percentage of agreement, which may be inflated by the marginal frequencies of codes. Kappa quantifies interobserver agreement after correcting for the level of agreement expected by chance.

## 2.9  Databases

Because most investigators have used relatively limited data sets, the generalizability of different approaches to facial expression analysis remains unknown. In most data sets, only relatively global facial expressions (e.g., joy or anger) have been considered, subjects have been few in number and homogeneous with respect to age and ethnic background, and recording conditions have been optimized. Approaches to facial expression analysis that have been developed in this way may transfer poorly to applications in which expressions, subjects, contexts, or image properties are more variable. In the absence of comparative tests on common data, the relative strengths and weaknesses of different approaches are difficult to determine. In the areas of face and speech recognition, comparative tests have proven valuable [64], and similar benefits would likely accrue in the study of facial expression analysis. A large, representative test-bed is needed with which to evaluate different approaches. We have built a common database (Cohn-Kanade AU-Coded Face Expression Image Database) with which multiple laboratories may conduct comparative tests of their methods [43]. The details of the Cohn-Kanade AU-Coded Face Expression Image Database can be found in Chapter 12.

## 2.10  Relation to Other Facial Behavior or Nonfacial Behavior

Facial expression is one of several channels of nonverbal communication. Contraction of the muscle zygomaticus major (AU 12), for instance, often is associated with positive or happy vocalizations, and smiling tends to increase vocal fundamental frequency [15]. Also facial expressions often occur during conversations. Both expressions and conversations can cause facial changes. Few research groups, however, have attempted to integrate gesture recognition broadly defined across multiple channels of communication. An important question is whether there are advantages to early rather than late integration [35]. Databases containing multimodal expressive behavior afford the opportunity for integrated approaches to analysis of facial expression, prosody, gesture, and kinetic expression.

## 2.11  Summary and Ideal Facial Expression Analysis Systems

The problem space for facial expression includes multiple dimensions. An ideal facial expression analysis system has to address all these dimensions, and it outputs accurate recognition results. In addition, the ideal facial expression analysis system must perform automatically and in realtime for all stages (Figure 11.1). So far, several systems can recognize expressions in real time [47, 58, 80]. We summarize the properties of an ideal facial expression analysis system in Table 11.5.

**Table 11.5.** Properties of an ideal facial expression analysis system

| Robustness | |
|---|---|
| Rb1 | Deal with subjects of different age, gender, ethnicity |
| Rb2 | Handle lighting changes |
| Rb3 | Handle large head motion |
| Rb4 | Handle occlusion |
| Rb5 | Handle different image resolution |
| Rb6 | Recognize all possible expressions |
| Rb7 | Recognize expressions with different intensity |
| Rb8 | Recognize asymmetrical expressions |
| Rb9 | Recognize spontaneous expressions |
| **Automatic process** | |
| Am1 | Automatic face acquisition |
| Am2 | Automatic facial feature extraction |
| Am3 | Automatic expression recognition |
| **Real-time process** | |
| Rt1 | Real-time face acquisition |
| Rt2 | Real-time facial feature extraction |
| Rt3 | Real-time expression recognition |
| **Autonomic Process** | |
| An1 | Output recognition with confidence |
| An2 | Adaptive to different level outputs based on input images |

# 3 Recent Advances in Automatic Facial Expression Analysis

For automatic facial expression analysis, Suwa et al. [76] presented an early attempt in 1978 to analyze facial expressions by tracking the motion of 20 identified spots on an image sequence. Considerable progress had been made since 1990 in related technologies such as image analysis and pattern recognition that make AFEA possible. Samal and Iyengar [69] surveyed the early work (before 1990) about automatic recognition and analysis of human face and facial expression. Recently, two survey papers summarized the work (before year 1999) of facial expression analysis [31, 59]. In this chapter, instead of giving a comprehensive survey of facial expression analysis literature, we explore the recent advances in facial expression analysis based on three problems: (1) face acquisition, (2) facial feature extraction and representation, and (3) facial expression recognition.

The most extensive work about facial expression analysis includes the systems of CMU (Carnegie Mellon University) [81, 82, 14, 57, 90] , UCSD (University of California, San Diego) [3, 20, 33], UIUC (University of Illinois at Urbana-Champaign) [13, 88], MIT (Massachusetts Institute of Technology) [28], UMD (University of Maryland) [7, 93], TUDELFT (Delft University of Technology) [60, 59], IDIAP (Dalle Molle Institute for Perceptual Artificial Intelligence) [30, 31], and others [52, 97]. Because most of the work of MIT, UMD, TUDELFT, IDIAP, and others are summarized in the survey papers [31, 59], here we summarize the systems of CMU, UCSD, and UIUC. We focus on the new developments after 2000. The recent research in automatic facial expression analysis tends to follow these directions:

- Build more robust systems for face acquisition, facial data extraction and representation, and facial expression recognition to handle head motion (in-plane and out-of-plane), occlusion, lighting changes, and lower intensity of expressions
- Employ more facial features to recognize more expressions and to achieve a higher recognition rate
- Recognize facial action units and their combinations rather than emotion-specified expressions
- Recognize action units as they occur spontaneously
- Develop fully automatic and realtime AFEA systems

Table 11.6 summarizes the basic properties of the systems from the above three universities. Altogether, six systems are compared. They are CMU S1 [81, 82, 83] and CMU S2 [14, 57, 90], UCSD S1 [33] and UCSD S2 [3], and UIUC S1 [13] and UIUC S2 [88]. For each system, we list the methods used for face acquisition, feature extraction, and facial expression recognition.

## 3.1 Face Acquisition

With few exceptions, most AFEA research attempts to recognize facial expressions only from frontal-view or near frontal-view faces [45, 60]. Kleck and Mendolia [45] first studied the decoding of profile versus full-face expressions of affect by using three perspectives (a frontal face, a $90°$ right profile, and a $90°$ left profile). Forty-eight decoders viewed the expressions from 64 subjects in one of the three facial perspectives. They found that the frontal faces elicited higher intensity ratings than profile views for negative expressions. The opposite was found for positive expressions. Pantic and Rothkrantz [60] used dual-view facial images (a full-face and

**Table 11.6.** Recent Advances of Facial Expression Analysis

| | Method | Property | | |
|---|---|---|---|---|
| | | Real time | Fully automatic | Others |
| CMU S1 [81, 82, 83] | Detect face in 1st frame | Yes | Yes | Handle limited head motion; |
| | Initialize features in 1st frame | No | No | faces with glasses and hair; |
| | Track geometric features | Yes | Yes | recognize more than 30 |
| | Extract appearance features | Yes | Yes | AUs and combinations; |
| | Neural network classifier | Yes | Yes | 1st frame is frontal and expressionless |
| CMU S2 [14, 57, 90] | Detect face in 1st frame | Yes | Yes | Handle large head motion; |
| | Map face model in 1st frame | Yes | Yes | handle lighting changes; |
| | Track 3D head | Yes | Yes | handle occlusions; |
| | Stabilize facial region | Yes | Yes | spontaneous expressions; |
| | Extract geometric features | Yes | Yes | 1st frame is frontal |
| | Rule-based classifier | Yes | Yes | and expressionless |
| UCSD S1 [33] | Detect face in each frame | Yes | Yes | Frontal view; |
| | Resize and crop face | Yes | Yes | recognize basic expressions; |
| | Extract appearance features | Yes | Yes | neutral face needed |
| | SVM classifier | Yes | Yes | |
| UCSD S2 [3] | Estimate 3D head pose | No | No | Handle large head motion; |
| | Stabilize facial region | Yes | Yes | neutral face needed; |
| | Extract appearance features | Yes | Yes | recognize single AUs; |
| | HMM-SVM classifier | Yes | Yes | spontaneous expressions |
| UIUC S1 [13] | Initialize face model | No | No | Handle limited head motion; |
| | Track face in 3D | Yes | Yes | recognize basic expressions; |
| | Extract geometric features | Yes | Yes | 1st frame is frontal |
| | HMM classifier | Yes | Yes | and expressionless |
| UIUC S2 [88] | Initialize face model | No | No | Handle limited head motion; |
| | Track face in 3D | Yes | Yes | handle lighting changes; |
| | Extract geometric features | Yes | Yes | recognize basic expressions; |
| | Extract appearance features | No | Yes | 1st frame is frontal |
| | NN-HMM classifier | Yes | Yes | and expressionless |

a 90° right profile) which are acquired by two cameras mounted on the user's head. They did not compare the recognition results by using only the frontal view and the profile. So far, it is unclear how many expressions can be recognized by side-view or profile faces. Because the frontal-view face is not always available in real environments, the face acquisition methods should detect both frontal and nonfrontal view faces in an arbitrary scene.

To handle out-of-plane head motion, face can be obtained by face detection, 2D or 3D face tracking, or head pose detection. Nonfrontal view faces are warped or normalized to frontal view for expression analysis.

## Face Detection

Many face detection methods has been developed to detect faces in an arbitrary scene [41, 49, 61, 66, 74, 75, 87]. Most of them can detect only frontal and near-frontal views of faces. Heisele et al. [41] developed a component-based, trainable system for detecting frontal and near-frontal views of faces in still gray images. Rowley et al. [66] developed a neural network based system to detect frontal-view face. Viola and Jones [87] developed a robust realtime face detector based on a set of rectangle features.

To handle out-of-plane head motion, some researchers developed face detectors to detect face from different views [61, 74, 49]. Pentland et al. [61] detected faces by using the view-based and modular eigenspace method. Their method runs realtime and can handle varying head positions. Schneiderman and Kanade [74] proposed a statistical method for 3D object detection that can reliably detect human faces with out-of-plane rotation. They represent the statistics of both *object* appearance and *nonobject* appearance using a product of histograms. Each histogram represents the joint statistics of a subset of wavelet coefficients and their position on the object. Li et al. [49] developed an AdaBoost-like approach to detect faces with multiple views. A detail survey about face detection can be found in paper [95]. Chapter 2 is about face detection, so we here do not describe the details.

The UCSD S1 uses the face detector developed by Viola and Jones [87] to detect faces for each frame. The CMU systems (CMU S1 and CMU S2) assume that the first frame of the sequence is frontal and expressionless. They detect faces only in the first frame by a neural network-based face detector [66]. Then they perform feature tracking or head tracking for the remaining frames of the sequence.

## Head Pose Estimation

In a real environment, out-of-plane head motion is common for facial expression analysis. To handle the out-of-plane head motion, head pose estimation can be employed. The methods for estimating head pose can be classified as a 3D model-based methods [1, 77, 84, 90] and 2D image-based methods [8, 80, 89, 98].

**3D Model-Based Method.** The CMU S2, UCSD S2, UIUC S1, and UIUC S2 systems employ a 3D model based method to estimate head pose. UCSD S2 uses a canonical wire-mesh face model to estimate face geometry and 3D pose from hand-labeled feature points [3]. The UIUC systems use an explicit 3D wireframe face model to track geometric facial features defined on the model [77]. The 3D model is fitted to the first frame of the sequence by manually selecting landmark facial features such as corners of the eyes and mouth. The generic face model, which consists of 16 surface patches, is warped to fit the selected facial features. To estimate the head motion and deformations of facial features, a two-step process is used. The 2D image motion is tracked using template matching between frames at different resolutions. From the 2D motions of many points on the face model, the 3D head motion then is estimated by solving an overdetermined system of equations of the projective motions in the least-squares sense [13].

In CMU S2 [90], a cylindrical head model is used to automatically estimate the 6 degrees of freedom (dof) of head motion in realtime. An active appearance model (AAM) method is used to automatically map the cylindrical head model to the face region, which is detected by face detection [66], as the initial appearance template. For any given frame, the template is the head image in the previous frame that is projected onto the cylindrical model. Then the template is registered with the head appearance in the given frame to recover the full motion of the head. They first use the iteratively reweighted least squares technique [5] to deal with nonrigid motion and occlusion. Second, they update the template dynamically in order to deal

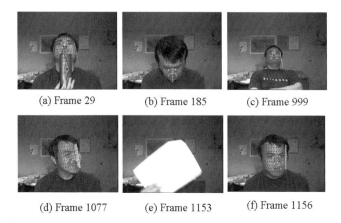

(a) Frame 29          (b) Frame 185          (c) Frame 999

(d) Frame 1077        (e) Frame 1153         (f) Frame 1156

**Fig. 11.3.** Example of the CMU S2 3D head tracking, including re-registration after losing the head [90].

with gradual changes in lighting and self-occlusion. This enables the system to work well even when most of the face is occluded. Because head poses are recovered using templates that are constantly updated and the pose estimated for the current frame is used in estimating the pose in the next frame, errors would accumulate unless otherwise prevented. To solve this problem, the system automatically selects and stores one or more frames and associated head poses from the tracked images in the sequence (usually including the initial frame and pose) as references. Whenever the difference between the estimated head pose and that of a reference frame is less than a preset threshold, the system rectifies the current pose estimate by re-registering this frame with the reference. The re-registration prevents errors from accumulating and enables the system to recover head pose when the head reappears after occlusion, such as when the head moves momentarily out of the camera's view. On-line tests suggest that the system could work robustly for an indefinite period of time. It was also quantitatively evaluated in image sequences that include maximum pitch and yaw as large as 40 and 75 degrees, respectively. The precision of recovered motion was evaluated with respect to the ground truth obtained by a precise position and orientation measurement device with markers attached to the head and found to be highly consistent (e.g., for maximum yaw of 75 degrees, absolute error averaged 3.86 degrees). An example of the CMU S2 3D head tracking is shown in Figure 11.3 including re-registration after losing the head. For details, see Xiao et al. [90].

**2D Image-Based Method.** To handle the full range of head motion for expression analysis, Tian et al. [80] detected the head instead of the face. The head detection uses the smoothed silhouette of the foreground object as segmented using background subtraction and computing the *negative curvature minima* (NCM) points of the silhouette. Other head detection techniques that use silhouettes can be found elsewhere [38, 40].

After the head is located, the head image is converted to gray-scale, histogram-equalized, and resized to the estimated resolution. Then a three-layer neural network (NN) is employed to estimate the head pose. The inputs to the network are the processed head image. The outputs are the three head poses: (1) frontal or near frontal view, (2) side view or profile, (3) others,

**Table 11.7.** Definitions and examples of the three head pose classes: frontal or near frontal view, side view or profile, and others, such as back of the head or occluded faces. The expression analysis process is applied to only the frontal and near-frontal view faces [80].

| Poses | Frontal or near frontal | Side view or profile | Others |
|---|---|---|---|
| Definitions | Both eyes and lip corners are visible | One eye or one lip corner is occluded | Not enough facial features |
| Examples | | | |

such as back of the head or occluded face (Table 11.7). In the frontal or near frontal view, both eyes and lip corners are visible. In the side view or profile, at least one eye or one corner of the mouth becomes self-occluded because of the head. The expression analysis process is applied only to the frontal and near-frontal view faces. Their system performs well even with very low resolution of face images.

## 3.2 Facial Feature Extraction and Representation

After the face is obtained, the next step is to extract facial features. Two types of features can be extracted: geometric features and appearance features. Geometric features present the shape and locations of facial components (including mouth, eyes, brows, nose). The facial components or facial feature points are extracted to form a feature vector that represents the face geometry. The appearance features present the appearance (skin texture) changes of the face, such as wrinkles and furrows. The appearance features can be extracted on either the whole face or specific regions in a face image.

To recognize facial expressions, an AEFA system can use geometric features only [13, 60], appearance features only [3, 33, 52], or hybrid features (both geometric and appearance features) [20, 81, 82, 88, 97]. The research shows that using hybrid features can achieve better results for some expressions.

To remove the effects of variation in face scale, motion, lighting, and other factors, one can first align and normalize the face to a standard face (2D or 3D) manually or automatically [3, 20, 33, 51, 88, 97] and then obtain normalized feature measurements by using a reference image (neutral face) [81].

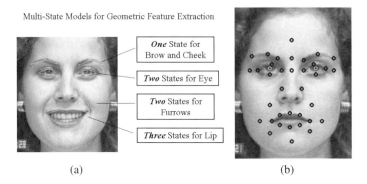

Fig. 11.4. Feature extraction of CMU S1. a. Multistate models for geometric feature extraction. b. Locations for calculating appearance features.

### Geometric Feature Extraction

In CMU S1, to detect and track changes of facial components in near frontal face images, multistate models are developed to extract the geometric facial features (Fig. 11.4). A three-state lip model describes the lip state: open, closed, tightly closed. A two-state model (open or closed) is used for each of the eyes. Each brow and cheek has a one-state model. Some appearance features, such as *nasolabial furrows* and *crows-feet wrinkles* (Fig. 11.5b), are represented explicitly by using two states: present and absent. Given an image sequence, the region of the face and approximate location of individual face features are detected automatically in the initial frame [66]. The contours of the face features and components then are adjusted manually in the initial frame. After the initialization, all face feature changes are automatically detected and tracked in the image sequence. CMU S1 system groups 15 parameters for the upper face and 9 parameters for the lower face, which describe shape, motion, and state of face components and furrows. To remove the effects of variation in planar head motion and scale between image sequences in face size, all parameters are computed as ratios of their current values to that in the reference frame. Details of geometric feature extraction and representation can be found in paper [81].

In CMU S2, the 3D head tracking is applied to handle large out-of plane head motion (Section 3.1) and track nonrigid features. The manual preprocessing of the geometric feature initialization in CMU S1 is reduced by using automatic active appearance model (AAM) mapping. Once the head pose is recovered, the face region is stabilized by transforming the image to a common orientation for expression recognition. Currently, only the geometric features of the eyebrow are extracted [14, 57].

The UIUC systems use an explicit 3D wireframe face model to track geometric facial features defined on the model [77]. The 3D model is fitted to the first frame of the sequence by manually selecting landmark facial features such as corners of the eyes and mouth. The generic face model, which consists of 16 surface patches, is warped to fit the selected facial features. Figure 11.6b shows an example of the geometric feature extraction of UIUC systems [88].

(a) Permanent features

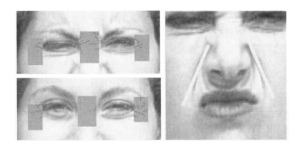

(b) Transient features

**Fig. 11.5.** Results of feature extraction in CMU S1 [81]. a. Permanent feature extraction (eyes, brows, and mouth). b. Transient feature extraction (crows-feet wrinkles, wrinkles at nasal root, and nasolabial furrows).

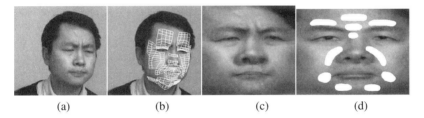

(a)                    (b)                    (c)                    (d)

**Fig. 11.6.** Feature extraction of UIUC S1. a. Input video frame. b. Snapshot of the geometric tracking system. c. Extracted texture map. d. Selected facial regions for appearance feature extraction [88].

## Appearance Feature Extraction

Gabor wavelets [19] are widely used to extract the facial appearance changes as a set of multiscale and multiorientation coefficients. The Gabor filter may be applied to specific locations on a face [52, 82, 83, 97] or to the whole face image [3, 20, 33]. Zhang et al. [97] was the first to compare two type of features to recognize expressions, the geometric positions of 34 fiducial points on a face and 612 Gabor wavelet coefficients extracted from the face image at these 34 fiducial points. The recognition rates for six emotion-specified expressions (e.g., joy and anger) were significantly higher for Gabor wavelet coefficients. Donato et al. [20] compared several techniques for recognizing six single upper face AUs and six lower face AUs.

These techniques include optical flow, principal component analysis, independent component analysis, local feature analysis, and Gabor wavelet representation. The best performances were obtained using a Gabor wavelet representation and independent component analysis. All of these systems [20, 97] used a manual step to align each input image with a standard face image using the center of the eyes and mouth.

In CMU S1, Tian et al. [82] studied geometric features and Gabor coefficients to recognize single AU and AU combinations. Following Zhang et al. [97], they used 480 Gabor coefficients in the upper face for 20 locations and 432 Gabor coefficients in the lower face for 18 locations (Figure 11.4). They found that Gabor wavelets work well for single AU recognition for homogeneous subjects without head motion. However, for recognition of AU combinations when image sequences include nonhomogeneous subjects with small head motions, the recognition results are relatively poor if we use only Gabor appearance features. Several factors may account for the difference. First, the previous studies used homogeneous subjects. For instance, Zhang et al. [97] included only Japanese and Donato et al. [20] included only Euro-Americans. The CMU S1 uses diverse subjects of European, African, and Asian ancestry. Second, the previous studies recognized emotion-specified expressions or only single AUs. The CMU S1 tested the Gabor-wavelet-based method on both single AUs and AU combinations, including nonadditive combinations in which the occurrence of one AU modifies another. Third, the previous studies manually aligned and cropped face images. The CMU S1 omitted this preprocessing step. In summary, using Gabor wavelets alone, recognition is adequate only for AU6, AU43, and AU0. Using geometric features alone, recognition is consistently good and shows high AU recognition rates with the exception of AU7. Combining both Gabor wavelet coefficients and geometric features, the recognition performance increased for all AUs.

In UCSD S1, the 2D frontal face image is detected by a face detector for each frame [87]. In UCSD S2, 3D pose and face geometry is estimated from hand-labeled feature points by using a canonical wire-mesh face model [62]. Once the 3D pose is estimated, faces are rotated to the frontal view and warped to a canonical face geometry. Then, the face images are automatically scaled and cropped to a standard face with a fixed distance between the two eyes in both UCSD S1 and S2. Difference images are obtained by subtracting a neutral expression face. UCSD S1 and S2 employed a family of Gabor wavelets at five spatial frequencies and eight orientations to a different image. Instead of specific locations on a face, they apply the Gabor filter to the whole face image. To provide robustness to lighting conditions and to image shifts they employed a representation in which the outputs of two Gabor filters in quadrature are squared and then summed. This representation is known as Gabor energy filters and it models complex cells of the primary visual cortex. Figure 11.7 shows an example of the UCSD systems Gabor appearance feature extraction [3].

In UIUC S2, Wen and Huang [88] use the ratio-image based method to extract appearance features, which is independent of a person's face albedo. To limit the effects of the noise in tracking and individual variation, they extracted the appearance features in facial regions instead of points, and then used the weighted average as the final feature for each region. Eleven regions were defined on the geometric-motion-free texture map of the face (Figure 11.6d). Gabor wavelets with two spatial frequency and six orientations are used to calculate Gabor coefficients. A 12-dimension appearance feature vector is computed in each of the 11 selected regions by weighted averaging of the Gabor coefficients. To track the face appearance variations, an appearance model (texture image) is trained using a Gaussian mixture model based on

Gabor Kernel          Output

Difference Image

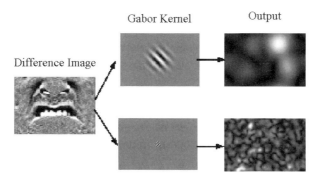

**Fig. 11.7.** Gabor appearance feature extraction in the UCSD systems. From Bartlett et al. [3], with permission.

exemplars. Then an online adaption algorithm is employed to progressively adapt the appearance model to new conditions such as lighting changes or differences in new individuals. See elsewhere for details [88].

### 3.3 Facial Expression Recognition

The last step of AFEA systems is to recognize facial expression based on the extracted features. Many classifiers have been applied to expression recognition such as neural network (NN), support vector machines (SVM), linear discriminant analysis (LDA), K-nearest neighbor, multinomial logistic ridge regression (MLR), hidden Markov models (HMM), tree augmented naive Bayes, and others. Some systems use only a rule-based classification based on the definition of the facial actions. Here, we summarize the expression recognition methods to frame-based and sequence-based expression recognition methods. The frame-based recognition method uses only the current frame with or without a reference image (mainly it is a neutral face image) to recognize the expressions of the frame. The sequence-based recognition method uses the temporal information of the sequences to recognize the expressions for one or more frames. Table 11.8 summarize of the recognition methods, recognition rates, recognition outputs, and the databases used in the most recent systems. For the systems that used more classifiers, the best performance for person-independent test has been selected.

**Frame-Based Expression Recognition.** Frame-based expression recognition does not use temporal information for the input images. It uses the information of current input image with/without a reference frame. The input image can be a static image or a frame of a sequence that is treated independently. Several methods can be found in the literature for facial expression recognition such as *neural networks* [81, 82, 97], *support vector machines* [3, 33], *linear discriminant analysis* [17], Bayesian network [13], and rule-based classifiers [60]. The CMU S1, UCSD S1, and UIUC S2 systems used frame-based classifiers.

CMU S1 employed a neural network-based recognizer to recognize FACS AUs. They used three-layer neural networks with one hidden layer to recognize AUs by a standard backpropagation method [66]. Separate networks are used for the upper and lower face. The inputs

**Table 11.8.** FACS AU or expression recognition of recent advances. SVM, support vector machines; MLR, multinomial logistic ridge regression; HMM, hidden Markov models; BN, Bayesian network; GMM, Gaussian mixture model.

| Systems | Recognition methods | Recognition rate | Recognized outputs | Databases |
|---|---|---|---|---|
| CMU S1 [81, 82, 83] | Neural network (frame) | 95.5% | 16 single AUs and their combinations | Ekman-Hager [26], Cohn-Kanade [43] |
| CMU S2 [14, 57] | Rule-based (sequence) | 100% | Blink, nonblink | Frank-Ekman [36] |
| | | 57% | Brow up, down, and non-motion | |
| UCSD S1 [33] | SVM+MLR (frame) | 91.5% | 6 Basic expressions | Cohn-Kanade [43] |
| UCSD S2 [3] | SVM + HMM (sequence) | 98% | blink, nonblink | Frank-Ekman [36] |
| | | 70% | brow up, down, and nonmotion | |
| UIUC S1 [13] | BN + HMM (frame & sequence) | 73.22% | 6 Basic expressions | Cohn-Kanade [43] |
| | | 66.53% | 6 Basic expressions | UIUC-Chen [12] |
| UIUC S2 [88] | NN + GMM (frame) | 71% | 6 Basic expressions | Cohn-Kanade [43] |

can be the normalized geometric features, the appearance feature, or both as shown in Figure 11.8. The outputs are the recognized AUs. The network is trained to respond to the designated AUs whether they occur alone or in combination. When AUs occur in combination, multiple output nodes are excited. To our knowledge, CMU S1 is the first system to handle AU combinations. Although several other systems tried to recognize AU combinations [17, 20, 51], they treated each combination as if it were a separate AU. More than 7,000 different AU combinations have been observed [71], and a system that can handle AU combinations is more efficient. A overall recognition rate of 95.5% had been achieved for neutral expression and 16 AUs whether they occurred individually or in combinations.

In UCSD S1 [33], they used a two-stage classifier to recognize neutral expression and six emotion-specified expressions. First, SVMs were used for the pairwise classifiers, i.e., each SVM is trained to distinguish two emotions. Then they tested several approaches, such as nearest neighbor, a simple voting scheme, and multinomial logistic ridge regression (MLR) to convert the representation produced by the first stage into a probability distribution over six emotion-specified expressions and neutral. The best performance at 91.5% was achieved by MLR.

UIUC S2 also employed a two-stage classifier to recognize neutral expression and six emotion-specified expressions. First, a neural network is used to classify *neutral* and *nonneutral* -like [79]. Then Gaussian mixture models (GMMs) were used for the remaining expressions. The overall average recognition rate was 71% for a people-independent test. See details elsewhere [88].

**Sequence-Based Expression Recognition.** The sequence-based recognition method uses the temporal information of the sequences to recognize the expressions of one or more frames. To use the temporal information, the techniques such as HMM [3, 13, 17, 51], recurrent neural networks [46, 65], and rule-based classifier [14] were used in facial expression analysis. The

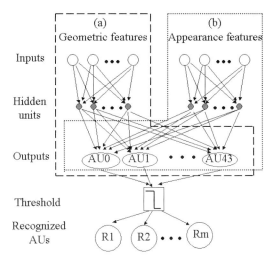

Fig. 11.8. Neural network-based recognizer for AU combinations in CMU S1. From Tian et al. [82], with permission.

CMU S2, UCSD S2, and UIUC S1 systems employed a sequence-based classifier. Note that the CMU S2 and UCSD S2 systems are comparative studies for FACS AU recognition in spontaneously occurring behavior by using the same database [36]. In that database, subjects were ethnically diverse, AUs occurred during speech, and out-of-plane motion and occlusion from head motion and glasses were common. So far, only several systems tried to recognize AUs or expression in spontaneously occurring behavior [3, 14, 80].

CMU S2 [14] employed a rule-based classifier to recognize AUs of eye and brow in spontaneously occurring behavior by using a number of frames in the sequence. The algorithm achieved an overall accuracy of 98% for three eye behaviors: blink (AU 45), flutter, and no blink (AU 0). *Flutter* is defined as two or more rapidly repeating blinks (AU 45) with only partial eye opening (AU 41 or AU 42) between them; 100% accuracy is achieved between blinks and nonblinks. Accuracy across the three categories in the brow region (brow-up, brow-down, nonbrow motion) was 57%. The number of brow-down actions was too small for reliable point estimates. Omitting brow-down from the analysis, recognition accuracy would increase to 80%. Human FACS coders had similar difficulty with brow-down, agreeing only about 50% in this database. The small number of occurrences was no doubt a factor for FACS coders as well. The combination of occlusion from eyeglasses and correlation of forward head pitch with brow-down complicated FACS coding. See Figure 11.9 for an example of the upper face in the database that shows the difficulties.

UCSD S2 [3] first employed SVMs to recognize AUs by using Gabor representations. Then they used hidden Markov models (HMMs) to deal with AU dynamics. HMMs were applied in two ways: (1) taking Gabor representations as input, and (2) taking the outputs of SVM as input. When they use Gabor representations as input to train HMMs, the Gabor coefficients were reduced to 100 dimensions per image using PCA. Two HMMs, one for blinks and one for nonblinks were trained and tested using leave-one-out cross-validation. A best performance of 95.7% recognition rate was obtained using five states and three Gaussians. They achieved

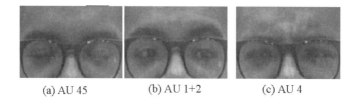

(a) AU 45        (b) AU 1+2        (c) AU 4

**Fig. 11.9.** An example of the Frank-Ekman database [36] was used by CMU S2 and UCSD S2 for spontaneous AU recognition. The cropped and stabilized upper face from the original video is displayed to show the difficulties. (From Bartlett et al. [3], with permission.)

a 98.1% recognition rate for blink and nonblink using SVM outputs as input to train HMMs for five states and three Gaussians. Accuracy across the three categories in the brow region (brow-up, brow-down, nonbrow motion) was 70.1% (HMMs trained on PCA-reduced Gabors) and 66.9% (HMMs trained on SVM outputs), respectively. Omitting brow-down, the accuracy increases to 90.9% and 89.5% respectively.

In UIUC S1, Cohen et al. [13] first evaluated Bayesian network (frame-based) classifiers such as Gaussian naive Bayes (NB-Gaussian), Cauchy naive Bayes (NB-Cauchy), and tree-augmented-naive Bayes (TAN), focusing on changes in distribution assumptions and feature dependency structures. They also proposed a new architecture of HMMs to segment and recognize neutral and six emotion-specified expressions from video sequences. For the person-independent test in the Cohn-Kanade database [43], the best performance at recognition rate of 73.2% was achieved by the TAN classifier. See details in Cohen et al. [13].

## 4 Discussion

Four recent trends in automatic facial expression analysis are (1) diversity of facial features in an effort to increase the number of expressions that may be recognized; (2) recognition of facial action units and their combinations rather than more global and easily identified emotion-specified expressions; (3) more robust systems for face acquisition, facial data extraction and representation, and facial expression recognition to handle head motion (both in-plane and out-of-plane), occlusion, lighting change, and low intensity expressions, all of which are common in spontaneous facial behavior in naturalistic environments; and (4) fully automatic and realtime AFEA systems. All of these developments move AFEA toward real-life applications. A public database (Cohn-Kanade AU-Coded Face Expression Image Database [43]) that addresses most problems for deliberate facial expression analysis has become widely used by many researchers to conduct comparative tests of their methods. Comparable image databases with ground-truth labels, preferably both action units and emotion-specified expressions, are needed for the next generation of systems, which are intended for naturally occurring behavior in real-life settings. For directed facial action tasks or other posed facial expressions, the CMU S1 system [81, 82, 83] can recognize the largest number of AUs whether they occur alone or in combinations. The system uses two neural networks (one for the upper face and one for the lower face). In recognizing whether AUs occur alone or in combinations, the system is performing a perceptual task analogous to that of human observers, who can recognize facial actions occurring in novel contexts. For spontaneous expression analysis, promising results have been achieved for a few AUs by CMU [14, 57] and UCSD [3] systems. Work in spontaneous facial expression analysis is just now emerging and potentially will have significant impact across a range of theoretical and applied topics.

Although many recent advances and successes in automatic facial expression analysis have been achieved, as described in the previous sections, many questions remain open, for which answers must be found. Some major points are considered here.

*1. How do humans correctly recognize facial expressions?*

Research on human perception and cognition has been conducted for many years, but it is still unclear how humans recognize facial expressions. Which types of parameters are used by humans, and how are they processed? By comparing human and automatic facial expression recognition we may be able advance our understanding of each and discover new ways of improving automatic facial expression recognition.

*2. Is it always better to analyze finer levels of expression?*

Although it is often assumed that more fine-grained recognition is preferable, the answer depends on both the quality of the face images and the type of application. Ideally, an AFEA system should recognize all action units and their combinations. In high quality images, this goal seems achievable; emotion-specified expressions then can be identified based on emotion prototypes identified in the psychology literature. For each emotion, prototypic action units have been identified. In lower quality image data, only a subset of action units and emotion-specified expression may be recognized. Recognition of emotion-specified expressions directly may be needed. We seek systems that become 'self aware' about the degree of recognition that is possible based on the information of given images and adjust processing and outputs accordingly. Recognition from coarse-to-fine, for example from emotion-specified expressions to subtle action units, depends on image quality and the type of application. Indeed, for some purposes, it may be sufficient that a system is able to distinguish between positive, neutral, and negative expression, or recognize only a limited number of target action units, such as brow lowering to signal confusion, cognitive effort, or negative affect.

*3. Is there any better way to code facial expressions for computer systems?*

Almost all the existing work has focused on recognition of facial expression, either emotion-specified expressions or FACS coded action units. The emotion-specified expressions describe expressions at a coarse level and are not sufficient for some applications. Although the FACS was designed to detect subtle changes in facial features, it is a human-observer-based system with only limited ability to distinguish intensity variation. Intensity variation is scored at an ordinal level; the interval level measurement is not defined, and anchor points may be subjective. Challenges remain in designing a computer-based facial expression coding system with more quantitative definitions.

*4. How do we obtain reliable ground truth?*

Whereas some approaches have used FACS, which is a criterion measure widely used in the psychology community for facial expression analysis, most vision-based work uses emotion-specified expressions. A problem is that emotion-specified expressions are not well defined. The same label may apply to very different facial expressions, and different labels may refer to the same expressions, which confounds system comparisons. Another problem is that the reliability of labels typically is unknown. With few exceptions, investigators have failed to report interobserver reliability and the validity of the facial expressions they have analyzed. Often there is no way to know whether subjects actually showed the target expression or whether two or more judges would agree that the subject showed the target expression. At a minimum, investigators should make explicit labeling criteria and report interobserver agreement for the labels. When the dynamics of facial expression are of interest, temporal resolution should be reported as well. Because intensity and duration measurements are critical, it is important to include descriptive data on these features as well. Unless adequate data about stimuli are reported, discrepancies across studies are difficult to interpret. Such discrepancies could be due to algorithms or to errors in ground truth determination.

## 5. How do we recognize facial expressions in real life?

Real-life facial expression analysis is much more difficult than the posed actions studied predominantly to date. Head motion, low resolution input images, absence of a neutral face for comparison, and low intensity expressions are among the factors that complicate facial expression analysis. Recent work in 3D modeling of spontaneous head motion and action unit recognition in spontaneous facial behavior are exciting developments. How elaborate a head model is required in such work is as yet a research question. A cylindrical model is relatively robust and has proven effective as part of a blink detection system [90], but highly parametric, generic, or even custom-fitted head models may prove necessary for more complete action unit recognition.

Most work to date has used a single, passive camera. Although there are clear advantages to approaches that require only a single passive camera or video source, multiple cameras are feasible in a number of settings and can be expected to provide improved accuracy. Active cameras can be used to acquire high resolution face images [40]. Also, the techniques of super-resolution can be used to obtain higher resolution images from multiple low resolution images [2]. At present, it is an open question how to recognize expressions in situations in which a neutral face is unavailable, expressions are of low intensity, or other facial or nonverbal behaviors, such as occlusion by the hands, are present.

## 6. How do we best use the temporal information?

Almost all work has emphasized recognition of discrete facial expressions, whether defined as emotion-specified expressions or action units. The timing of facial actions may be as important as their configuration. Recent work by our group has shown that intensity and duration of expression vary with context and that the timing of these parameters is highly consistent with automatic movement [73]. Related work suggests that spontaneous and deliberate facial expressions may be discriminated in terms of timing parameters [16], which is consistent with neuropsychological models [63] and may be important to lie detection efforts. Attention to timing also is important in guiding the behavior of computer avatars. Without veridical timing, believable avatars and ones that convey intended emotions and communicative intents may be difficult to achieve.

## 7. How may we integrate facial expression analysis with other modalities?

Facial expression is one of several modes of nonverbal communication. The message value of various modes may differ depending on context and may be congruent or discrepant with each other. An interesting research topic is the integration of facial expression analysis with that of gesture, prosody, and speech. Combining facial features with acoustic features would help to separate the effects of facial actions due to facial expression and those due to speech-related movements. The combination of facial expression and speech can be used to improve speech recognition and multimodal person identification [34].

## Acknowledgments

We sincerely thank Jing Xiao at Carnegie Mellon University, Dr. Marian Bartlett at MPLab of University of California San Diego, Zhen Wen at the University of Illinois at Urbana-Champaign for providing pictures and their permission to use them in this chapter. We also thank Dr. Zicheng Liu at Microsoft Research for reviewing this chapter.

## References

1. J. Ahlberg and R. Forchheimer. Face tracking for model-based coding and face animation. *International Journal of Imaging Systems and Technology*, pages 8–22, Vol. 13, Issue 1, 2003.
2. S. Baker and T. Kanade. Limits on super-resolution and how to break them. *IEEE Transactions on Pattern Analysis and Machine Intelligence*, 24(9):1167–1183, 2002.
3. M. Bartlett, B. Braathen, G. Littlewort-Ford, J. Hershey, I. Fasel, T. Marks, E. Smith, T. Sejnowski, and J. R. Movellan. Automatic analysis of spontaneous facial behavior: A final project report. Technical Report INC-MPLab-TR-2001.08, Machine Perception Lab, Institute for Neural Computation, University of California, San Diego, 2001.
4. M. Bartlett, J. Hager, P.Ekman, and T. Sejnowski. Measuring facial expressions by computer image analysis. *Psychophysiology*, 36:253–264, 1999.
5. M. Black. Robust incremental optical flow. In *PhD thesis, Yale University*, 1992.
6. M. Black and Y. Yacoob. Tracking and recognizing rigid and non-rigid facial motions using local parametric models of image motion. In *Proc. of International conference on Computer Vision*, pages 374–381, 1995.
7. M. Black and Y. Yacoob. Recognizing facial expressions in image sequences using local parameterized models of image motion. *International Journal of Computer Vision*, 25(1):23–48, October 1997.
8. L. Brown and Y.-L. Tian. Comparative study of coarse head pose estimation. In *IEEE Workshop on Motion and Video Computing, Orlando*, 2002.
9. L. Camras, L. Lambrecht, and G. Michel. Infant surprise expressions as coordinative motor structures. *Journal of Nonverbal Behavior*, 20:183–195, 1966.
10. J. Carroll and J. Russell. Do facial expression signal specific emotions? *Journal of Personality and Social Psychology.*, 70:205–218, 1996.
11. J. Carroll and J. Russell. Facial expression in hollywood's portrayal of emotion. *Journal of Personality and Social Psychology.*, 72:164–176, 1997.
12. L. Chen. Joint processing of ausio-visual information for the recognition of emotional expressions in human-computer interaction. In *PhD thesis, University of Illinois at Urbana-Champaign, Department of Electrical Engineering*, 2000.
13. I. Cohen, N. Sebe, F. Cozman, M. Cirelo, and T. Huang. Coding, analysis, interpretation, and recognition of facial expressions. *Journal of Computer Vision and Image Understanding Special Issue on Face Recognition*, 2003.
14. J. Cohn, T. Kanade, T. Moriyama, Z. Ambadar, J. Xiao, J. Gao, and H. Imamura. A comparative study of alternative facs coding algorithms. Technical Report CMU-RI-TR-02-06, Robotics Institute, Carnegie Mellon University, Pittsburgh, November 2001.

15. J. Cohn and G. Katz. Bimodal expression of emotion by face and voice. In *ACM and ATR Workshop on Face/Gesture Recognition and Their Applications*, pages 41–44, 1998.

16. J. Cohn, K. Schmidt, R. Gross, and P. Ekman. Individual differences in facial expression: stability over time, relation to self-reported emotion, and ability to inform person identification. In *Proceedings of the International Conference on Multimodal User Interfaces (ICMI 2002)*, pages 491–496, 2002.

17. J. Cohn, A. Zlochower, J. Lien, and T. Kanade. Automated face analysis by feature point tracking has high concurrent validity with manual facs coding. *Psychophysiology*, 36:35–43, 1999.

18. C. Darwin. *The Expression of Emotions in Man and Animals*. John Murray, reprinted by University of Chicago Press, 1965, 1872.

19. J. Daugmen. Complete discrete 2d gabor transforms by neutral networks for image analysis and compression. *IEEE Transaction on Acoustic, Speech and Signal Processing*, 36(7):1169–1179, 1988.

20. G. Donato, M. Bartlett, J. Hager, P. Ekman, and T. Sejnowski. Classifying facial actions. *IEEE Transaction on Pattern Analysis and Machine Intelligence*, 21(10):974–989, 1999.

21. Eihl-Eihesfeldt. *Human Ethology*. Aldine de Gruvter, New York, 1989.

22. P. Ekman. *The Argument and Evidence about Universals in Facial Expressions of Emotion*, pages 143–164. Wiley, New York, 1989.

23. P. Ekman. Facial expression and emotion. *American Psychologist*, 48:384–392, 1993.

24. P. Ekman and W. Friesen. *Pictures of Facial Affect*. Palo Alto, CA: Consulting Psychologist., 1976.

25. P. Ekman and W. Friesen. *The Facial Action Coding System: A Technique for the Measurement of Facial Movement*. Consulting Psychologists Press, San Francisco, 1978.

26. P. Ekman, J. Hager, C. Methvin, and W. Irwin. *Ekman-Hager Facial Action Exemplars*. Human Interaction Laboratory, University of California, San Francisco.

27. P. Ekman and E. e. Rosenberg. *What the Face Reveals*. Oxford University, New York, 1997.

28. I. Essa and A. Pentland. Coding, analysis, interpretation, and recognition of facial expressions. *IEEE Trans. on Pattern Analysis and Machine Intell.*, 19(7):757–763, 1997.

29. L. Farkas and I. Munro. *Anthropometric Facial Proportions in Medicine*. Charles C Thomas, Springfield, IL, 1987.

30. B. Fasel and J. Luttin. Recognition of asymmetric facial action unit activities and intensities. In *Proceedings of International Conference of Pattern Recognition*, 2000.

31. B. Fasel and J. Luttin. Automatic facial expression analysis: Survey. *Pattern Recognition*, 36(1):259–275, 2003.

32. J. Fleiss. *Statistical Methods for Rates and Proportions*. Wiley, New York, 1981.

33. G. Ford. Fully automatic coding of basic expressions from video. Technical Report INC-MPLab-TR-2002.03, Machine Perception Lab, Institute for Neural Computation, University of California, San Diego, 2002.

34. N. Fox, R. Gross, P. de Chazal, J. Cohn, and R. Reilly. Person identification using multi-modal features: speech, lip, and face. In *Proc. of ACM Multimedia Workshop in Biometrics Methods and Applications (WBMA 2003)*, CA, 2003.

35. N. Fox and R. Reilly. Audio-visual speaker identification. In *Proc. of the 4th International Conference on Audio-and Video-Based Biometric Person Authentication*, 2003.

36. M. Frank and P. Ekman. The ability to detect deceit generalizes across different types of high-stake lies. *Personality and Social Psychology*, 72:1429–1439, 1997.

37. W. Friesen and P. Ekman. Emfacs-7: emotional facial action coding system. *Unpublished manuscript, University of California at San Francisco*, 1983.

38. H. Fujiyoshi and A. Lipton. Real-time human motion analysis by image skeletonization. In *Proc. of the Workshop on Application of Computer Vision*, 1998.

39. K. Fukui and O. Yamaguchi. Facial feature point extraction method based on combination of shape extraction and pattern matching. *Systems and Computers in Japan*, 29(6):49–58, 1998.

40. A. Hampapur, S. Pankanti, A. Senior, Y. Tian, L. Brown, and R. Bolle. Face cataloger: multi-scale imaging for relating identity to location. In *Proceedings of IEEE Conference on Advanced Video and Signal Based Surveillance*, 2003.

41. B. Heisele, T. Serre, M. Pontil, and T. Poggio. Component-based face detection. In *Proc. IEEE Conf. on Computer Vision and Pattern Recogn. (CVPR)*, 2001.

42. C. Izard, L. Dougherty, and E. A. Hembree. A system for identifying affect expressions by holistic judgments. In *Unpublished Manuscript, University of Delaware*, 1983.

43. T. Kanade, J. Cohn, and Y.-L. Tian. Comprehensive database for facial expression analysis. In *Proceedings of International Conference on Face and Gesture Recognition*, pages 46–53, 2000.

44. S. Kimura and M. Yachida. Facial expression recognition and its degree estimation. In *Proc. Of the International Conference on Computer Vision and Pattern Recognition*, pages 295–300, 1997.

45. R. Kleck and M. Mendolia. Decoding of profile versus full-face expressions of affect. *Journal of Nonverbal Behavior*, 14(1):35–49, 1990.

46. H. Kobayashi, K. Tange, and F. Hara. Dynamic recognition of six basic facial expressions by discrete-time recurrent neural network. In *Proc. of the International Joint Conference on Neural Networks*, pages 155–158, 1993.

47. H. Kobayashi, K. Tange, and F. Hara. Real-time recognition of six basic facial expressions. In *Proc. IEEE Workshop on Robot and Human Communication*, pages 179–186, 1995.

48. R. Kraut and R. Johnson. Social and emotional messages of smiling: an ethological approach. *Journal of Personality and Social Psychology*, 37:1539–1523, 1979.

49. S. Li and L. Gu. Real-time multi-view face detection, tracking, pose estimation, alignment, and recognition. In *IEEE Conf. on Computer Visioin and Pattern Recognition Demo Summary*, 2001.

50. J.-J. Lien, T. Kanade, J. Cohn, and C. Li. Subtly different facial expression recognition and expression intensity estimation. In *Proceedings of the IEEE International Conference on Computer Vision and Pattern Recognition*, pages 853–859, 1998.

51. J.-J. Lien, T. Kanade, J. Cohn, and C. Li. Detection, tracking, and classification of action units in facial expression. *Journal of Robotics and Autonomous System*, 31:131–146, 2000.

52. M. Lyons, S. Akamasku, M. Kamachi, and J. Gyoba. Coding facial expressions with gabor wavelets. In *Proceedings of International Conference on Face and Gesture Recognition*, 1998.

53. A. Manstead. *Expressiveness as an individual difference*, pages 285–328. Cambridge University Press, Cambridge, UK, 1991.

54. P. Martin and P. Bateson. *Measuring behavior: An Introductory Guide*. Cambridge University Press, Cambridge, UK, 1986.

55. K. Mase. Recognition of facial expression from optical flow. *IEICE Transactions*, E. 74(10):3474–3483, 1991.

56. R. Matias, J. Cohn, and S. Ross. A comparison of two systems to code infants' affective expression. *Developmental Psychology*, 25:483–489, 1989.

57. T. Moriyama, T. Kanade, J. Cohn, J. Xiao, Z. Ambadar, J. Gao, and M. Imanura. Automatic recognition of eye blinking in spontaneously occurring behavior. In *Proceedings of the 16th International Conference on Pattern Recognition (ICPR '2002)*, volume 4, pages 78–81, 2002.

58. Y. Moses, D. Reynard, and A. Blake. Determining facial expressions in real time. In *Proc. of Int. Conf. On Automatic Face and Gesture Recognition*, pages 332–337, 1995.

59. M. Pantic and L. Rothkrantz. Automatic analysis of facial expressions: the state of the art. *IEEE Transaction on Pattern Analysis and Machine Intelligence*, 22(12):1424–1445, 2000.

60. M. Pantic and L. Rothkrantz. Expert system for automatic analysis of facial expression. *Image and Vision Computing*, 18(11):881–905, 2000.

61. A. Pentland, B. Moghaddam, and T. Starner. View-based and modular eigenspaces for face recognition. In *Proc. IEEE Conf. Computer Vision and Pattern Recognition*, pages 84–91, 1994.

62. F. Pighin, H. Szeliski, and D. Salesin. Synthesizing realistic facial expressions from photographs. In *Proc of SIGGRAPH*, 1998.

63. W. Rinn. The neuropsychology of facial expression: a review of the neurological and psychological mechanisms for producing facial expressions. *Psychological Bulletin*, (95):52–77, 1984.

64. S. Rizvi, P. Phillips, and H. Moon. The feret verification testing protocol for face recognition algorithms. In *Proceedings of the Third International Conference on Automatic Face and Gesture Recognition*, pages 48–55, 1998.

65. M. Rosenblum, Y. Yacoob, and L. Davis. Human expression recognition from motion using a radial basis function network architecture. *IEEE Transactions On Neural Network*, 7(5):1121–1138, 1996.

66. H. Rowley, S. Baluja, and T. Kanade. Neural network-based face detection. *IEEE Transactions On Pattern Analysis and Machine intelligence*, 20(1):23–38, 1998.

67. J. Russell. Culture and the categorization. *Psychological Bulletin*, 110:426–450, 1991.

68. J. Russell. Is there universal recognition of emotion from facial expression? a review of the cross-cultural studies. *Psychological Bulletin*, 115:102–141, 1991.

69. A. Samal and P. Iyengar. Automatic recognition and analysis of human faces and facil expressions: A survey. *Pattern Recognition*, 25(1):65–77, 1992.

70. M. Sayette, J. Cohn, J. Wertz, M. Perrott, and D. Parrott. A psychometric evaluation of the facial action coding system for assessing spontaneous expression. *Journal of Nonverbal Behavior*, 25:167–186, 2001.

71. K. Scherer and P. Ekman. *Handbook of Methods in Nonverbal Behavior Research*. Cambridge University Press, Cambridge, UK, 1982.

72. K. Schmidt and J. Cohn. Human facial expressions as adaptations: Evolutionary questions in facial expression. *Yearbook of Physical Anthropology*, 44:3–24, 2002.

73. K. Schmidt, J. F. Cohn, and Y.-L. Tian. Signal characteristics of spontaneous facial expressions: Automatic movement in solitary and social smiles. *Biological Psychology*, 2003.

74. H. Schneiderman and T. Kanade. A statistical model for 3d object detection applied to faces and cars. In *IEEE Conference on Computer Vision and Pattern Recognition*. IEEE, 2000.

75. K. Sung and T. Poggio. Example-based learning for view-based human face detection. *IEEE Transactions on Pattern Analysis and Machine intelligence*, 20(1):39–51, 1998.

76. M. Suwa, N. Sugie, and K. Fujimora. A preliminary note on pattern recognition of human emotional expression. In *International Joint Conference on Pattern Recognition*, pages 408–410, 1978.

77. H. Tao and T. Huang. Explanation-based facial motion tracking using a piecewise bezier volume deformation model. In *Proc. IEEE Conf. Computer Vision and Pattern Recognition*, 1999.

78. D. Terzopoulos and K. Waters. Analysis of facial images using physical and anatomical models. In *IEEE International Conference on Computer Vision*, pages 727–732, 1990.

79. Y.-L. Tian and R. Bolle. Automatic detecting neutral face for face authentication. In *Proceedings of AAAI-03 Spring Symposium on Intelligent Multimedia Knowledge Management, CA*, 2003.

80. Y.-L. Tian, L. Brown, A. Hampapur, S. Pankanti, A. Senior, and R. Bolle. Real world real-time automatic recognition of facial expressions. In *Proceedings of IEEE Workshop on Performance Evaluation of Tracking and Surveillance, Graz, Austria*, 2003.

81. Y.-L. Tian, T. Kanade, and J. Cohn. Recognizing action units for facial expression analysis. *IEEE Trans. on Pattern Analysis and Machine Intell.*, 23(2):1–19, 2001.

82. Y.-L. Tian, T. Kanade, and J. Cohn. Evaluation of gabor-wavelet-based facial action unit recognition in image sequences of increasing complexity. In *Proceedings of the 5th IEEE International Conference on Automatic Face and Gesture Recognition (FG'02), Washington, DC*, 2002.

83. Y.-L. Tian, T. Kanade, and J. Cohn. Eye-state action unit detection by gabor wavelets. In *Proceedings of International Conference on Multi-modal Interfaces (ICMI 2000)*, pages 143–150, Sept, 2000.

84. K. Toyama. look, ma–no hands! hands-free cursor control with real-time 3d face tracking. In *Proc. Workshop on Perceptual User Interfaces(PUI'98)*, 1998.

85. J. VanSwearingen, J. Cohn, and A. Bajaj-Luthra. Specific impairment of smiling increases severity of depressive symptoms in patients with facial neuromuscular disorders. *Journal of Aesthetic Plastic Surgery*, 23:416–423, 1999.

86. T. Vetter. Learning novels views to a single face image. In *Proceedings of the IEEE International Conference on Automatic Face and Gesture Recognition*, pages 22–29, 1995.

87. P. Viola and M. Jones. Robust real-time object detection. In *International Workshop on Statistical and Computational Theories of Vision - Modeling, Learning, Computing, and Sampling*, 2001.

88. Z. Wen and T. Huang. Capturing subtle facial motions in 3d face tracking. In *Proc. of Int. Conf. On Computer Vision*, 2003.

89. Y. Wu and K. Toyama. Wide-range person and illumination-insensitve head orientation estimation. In *Proceedings of International Conference on Automatic Face and Gesture Recognition*, pages 183–188, 2000.

90. J. Xiao, T. Kanade, and J. Cohn. Robust full motion recovery of head by dynamic templates and re-registration techniques. In *Proceedings of International Conference on Automatic Face and Gesture Recognition*, pages 163–169, 2002.

91. J. Xiao, T. Moriyama, T. Kanade, and J. Cohn. Robust full-motion recovery of head by dynamic templates and re-registration techniques. *International Journal of Imaging Systems and Technology*, September, 2003.

92. Y. Yacoob and M. Black. Parameterized modeling and recognition of activities. In *Proc. 6th IEEE Int. Conf. on Computer Vision*, pages 120–127, Bombay, 1998.

93. Y. Yacoob and L. Davis. Recognizing human facial expression from long image sequences using optical flow. *IEEE Trans. on Pattern Analysis and Machine Intell.*, 18(6):636–642, June 1996.

94. Y. Yacoob, H.-M. Lam, and L. Davis. Recognizing faces showing expressions. In *Proc. Int. Workshop on Automatic Face- and Gesture-Recognition*, pages 278–283, Zurich, Switserland, 1995.

95. M. Yang, D. Kriegman, and N. Ahuja. Detecting faces in images: a survey. *IEEE Trans. on Pattern Analysis and Machine Intell.*, 24(1), 2002.

96. Z. Zhang. Feature-based facial expression recognition: sensitivity analysis and experiments with a multi-layer perceptron. *International Journal of Pattern Recognition and Artificial Intelligence*, 13(6):893–911, 1999.

97. Z. Zhang, M. Lyons, M. Schuster, and S. Akamatsu. Comparison between geometry-based and gabor-wavelets-based facial expression recognition using multi-layer perceptron. In *International Workshop on Automatic Face and Gesture Recognition*, pages 454–459, 1998.

98. L. Zhao, G. Pingali, and I. Carlbom. Real-time head orientation estimation using neural networks. In *Proc of the 6th International Conference on Image Processing*, 2002.

99. A. Zlochower, J. Cohn, J. Lien, and T. Kanade. A computer vision based method of facial expression analysis in parent-infant interaction. In *International Conference on Infant Studies, Atlanta*, 1998.

# Chapter 12. Face Synthesis

Zicheng Liu[1] and Baining Guo[2]

[1] Microsoft Research, Redmond, WA 98052, USA. zliu@microsoft.com
[2] Microsoft Research Asia, Beijing 100080, China. bainguo@microsoft.com

## 1 Introduction

How to synthesize photorealistic images of human faces has been a fascinating yet difficult problem in computer graphics. Here, the term "face synthesis" refers to synthesis of still images as well as synthesis of facial animations. In general, it is difficult to draw a clean line between the synthesis of still images and that of facial animations. For example, the technique of synthesizing facial expression images can be directly used for generating facial animations, and most of the facial animation systems involve the synthesis of still images. In this chapter, we focus more on the synthesis of still images and skip most of the aspects that mainly involve the motion over time.

Face synthesis has many interesting applications. In the film industry, people would like to create virtual human characters that are indistinguishable from the real ones. In games, people have been trying to create human characters that are interactive and realistic. There are commercially available products [15, 16] that allow people to create realistic looking avatars that can be used in chatting rooms, e-mail, greeting cards, and teleconferencing. Many human-machine dialog systems use realistic-looking human faces as visual representation of the computer agent that interacts with the human user. Face synthesis techniques have also been used for talking head compression in the video conferencing scenario.

The techniques of face synthesis can be useful for face recognition too. Romdhani et al. [35] used their three dimensional (3D) face modeling technique for face recognition with different poses and lighting conditions. Qing et al. [32] used the face relighting technique as proposed by Wen et al. [40] for face recognition under a different lighting environment. Many face analysis systems use an analysis-by-synthesis loop where face synthesis techniques are part of the analysis framework.

In this chapter, we review recent advances on face synthesis including 3D face modeling, face relighting, and facial expression synthesis.

## 2 Face Modeling

In the past a few years, there has been a lot of work on the reconstruction of face models from images. There are commercially available software packages [15, 16] that allow a user to construct their personalized 3D face models. In addition to its applications in games and entertainment, face modeling techniques can also be used to help with face recognition tasks especially in handling different head poses (see Romdhani et al. [35] and Chapter 10). Face modeling techniques can be divided into three categories: face modeling from an image sequence, face modeling from two orthogonal views, and face modeling from a single image. An image sequence is typically a video of someone's head turning from one side to the other. It contains a minimum of two views. The motion between each two consecutive views is relatively small, so it is feasible to perform image matching.

## 2.1 Face Modeling from an Image Sequence

Given an image sequence, one common approach for face modeling typically consists of three steps: image matching, structure from motion, and model fitting. First, two or three relatively frontal views are selected, and some image matching algorithms are used to compute point correspondences. The selection of frontal views are usually done manually. Point correspondences are computed either by using dense matching techniques such as optimal flow or feature-based corner matching. Second, one needs to compute the head motion and the 3D structures of the tracked points. Finally, a face model is fitted to the reconstructed 3D points. People have used different types of face model representations including parametric surfaces [11], linear class face scans [5], and linear class deformation vectors [25].

Fua and Miccio [10, 11] computed dense matching using image correlations. They then used a model-driven bundle adjustment technique to estimate the motions and compute the 3D structures. The idea of the model-driven bundle adjustment is to add a regularizer constraint to the traditional bundle adjustment formulation. The constraint is that the reconstructed 3D points can be fit to a parametric face model. Finally, they fit a parametric face model to the reconstructed 3D points. Their parametric face model contains a generic face mesh and a set of control points each controlling a local area of the mesh. By adjusting the coefficients of the control points, the mesh deforms in a linear fashion. Denote $c_1, c_2, ..., c_m$ to be the coefficients of the control points. Let $R, T, s$ be the rotation, translation, and scaling parameters of the head pose. Denote the mesh of the face as $S = S(c_1, c_2, .., c_m)$. Let $\mathcal{T}$ denote the transformation operator, which is a function of $R, T, s$. The model fitting can be formulated as a minimization problem

$$min \sum_i Dist\,[P_i, \mathcal{T}(S)]\,, \tag{1}$$

where $P_i$ is the reconstructed 3D points, and $Dist(P_i, \mathcal{T}(S)$ is the distance from $P_i$ to the the surface $\mathcal{T}(S)$.

This minimization problem can be solved using an iterative closest point approach. First, $c_1, ..., c_m$ are initialized and fixed. For each point $P_i$, find its closest point $Q_i$ on the surface $S$. Then solve for the pose parameters $R, T, s$ to minimize $\sum_i ||P_i, \mathcal{T}(Q_i)||$ by using the quaternion-based technique [14]. The head pose parameters are then fixed. Because $S$ is a linear function of $c_1, .., c_m$, Eq. 1 becomes a linear system and can be solved through a least-square procedure. At the next iteration, the newly estimated $c_1, ...c_m$ are fixed, and we solve for $R, T, s$ again.

Liu et al. [23, 25] developed a face modeling system that allows an untrained user with a personal computer and an ordinary video camera to create and instantly animate his or her face model. The user first turns his or her head from one side to the other. Then two frames pop up, and the user is required to mark five feature points (two inner eye corners, two mouth corners, and the nose top) on each view. After that, the system is completely automatic. Once the process finishes, his or her constructed face model is displayed and animated. The authors used a feature-based approach to find correspondences. It consists of three steps: (1) detecting corners in each image; (2) matching corners between the two images; (3) detecting false matches based on a robust estimation technique. The reader is referred to Liu et al. [25] for details. Compared to the optical flow approach, the feature-based approach is more robust to intensity and color variations.

After the matching is done, they used both the corner points from the image matching and the five feature points clicked by the user to estimate the camera motion. Because of the matching errors for the corner points and the inaccuracy of the user-clicked points, it is not robust to directly use these points for motion estimation. Therefore they used the physical properties of the user-clicked feature points to improve the robustness. They used the face symmetry property to reduce the number of unknowns and put reasonable bounds on the physical quantities (such as the height of the nose). In this way, the algorithm becomes significantly more robust. The algorithm's details were described by Liu and Zhang [23].

For the model fitting, they used a linear class of face geometries as their model space. A face was represented as a linear combination of a neutral face (Fig. 12.1) and some number of face *metrics*, where a metric is a vector that linearly deforms a face in certain way, such as to make the head wider, the nose bigger, and so on. To be more precise, let us denote the face geometry by a vector $\mathcal{S} = (\mathbf{v}_1^T, \ldots, \mathbf{v}_n^T)^T$, where $\mathbf{v}_i = (X_i, Y_i, Z_i)^T$ ($i = 1, \ldots, n$) are the vertices, and a metric by a vector $\mathcal{M} = (\delta \mathbf{v}_1^T, \ldots, \delta \mathbf{v}_n^T)^T$, where $\delta \mathbf{v}_i = (\delta X_i, \delta Y_i, \delta Z_i)^T$. Given a neutral face $\mathcal{S}^0 = (\mathbf{v}_1^{0\,T}, \ldots, \mathbf{v}_n^{0\,T})^T$ and a set of $m$ metrics $\mathcal{M}^j = (\delta \mathbf{v}_1^{j\,T}, \ldots, \delta \mathbf{v}_n^{j\,T})^T$, the linear space of face geometries spanned by these metrics is

$$\mathcal{S} = \mathcal{S}^0 + \sum_{j=1}^{m} c_j \mathcal{M}^j \; subject \; to \; c_j \in [l_j, u_j] \tag{2}$$

where $c_j$ represents the metric coefficients, and $l_j$ and $u_j$ are the valid range of $c_j$.

The model fitting algorithm is similar to the approach by Fua and Miccio [10, 11], described earlier in this section. The advantage of using a linear class of face geometries is that it is guaranteed that every face in the space is a reasonable face, and, furthermore, it has fine-grain control because some metrics are global whereas others are only local. Even with a small number of 3D corner points that are noisy, it is still able to generate a reasonable face model. Figure 12.2 shows side-by-side comparisons of the original images with the reconstructed models for various people.

Note that in both approaches just described the model fitting is separated from the motion estimation. In other words, the resulting face model is not used to improve the motion estimation.

During motion estimation, the algorithm by Liu et al. [25] used only general physical properties about human faces. Even though Fua and Miccio [10, 11] used face model during motion estimation, they used it only as a regularizer constraint. The 3D model obtained with their model-driven bundle adjustment is in general inaccurate, and they have to throw away the model and use an additional step to recompute the 3D structure. The problem is that the camera mo-

**Fig. 12.1.** Neutral face.

**Fig. 12.2.** Side by side comparison of the original images with the reconstructed models of various people.

tions are fixed on the second step. It may happen that the camera motions are not accurate owing to the inaccurate model at the first stage, so the structure computed at the second stage may not be optimal either. What one needs is to optimize camera motion and structure together.

Shan et al. [36] proposed an algorithm, called model-based bundle adjustment, that combines the motion estimation and model fitting into a single formulation. Their main idea was to directly use the model space as a search space. The model parameters (metric coefficients) become the unknowns in their bundle adjustment formulation. The variables for the 3D positions of the feature points, which are unknowns in the traditional bundle adjustment, are eliminated. Because the number of model parameters is in general much smaller than the isolated points, it results in a smaller search space and better posed optimization system.

Figure 12.3 shows the comparisons of the model-based bundle adjustment with the traditional bundle adjustment. On the top are the front views, and on the bottom are the side views. On each row, the one in the middle is the ground truth, on the left is the result from the traditional bundle adjustment, and on the right is the result from the model-based bundle adjustment. By looking closely, we can see that the result of the model-based bundle adjustment is much closer to the ground truth mesh. For example, on the bottom row, the nose on the left mesh (traditional bundle adjustment) is much taller than the nose in the middle (ground truth). The nose on the right mesh (model-based bundle adjustment) is similar to the one in the middle.

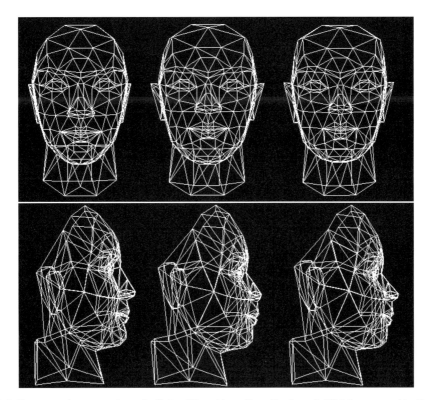

**Fig. 12.3.** Face mesh comparison. Left: traditional bundle adjustment; Middle: ground truth; Right: model-based bundle adjustment. (From Shan et al. [36], with permission.)

## 2.2 Face Modeling from Two Orthogonal Views

A number of researchers have proposed that we create face models from two orthogonal views [1, 7, 17]: one frontal view and one side view. The frontal view provides the information relative to the horizontal and vertical axis, and the side view provides depth information. The user needs to manually mark a number of feature points on both images. The feature points are typically the points around the face features, including eyebrows, eyes, nose, and mouth. Because of occlusions, the number of feature points on the two views are in general different. The quality of the face model depends on the number of feature points the user provides. The more feature points, the better the model, but one needs to balance between the amount of manual work required from the user and the quality of the model.

Because the algorithm is so simple to implement and there is no robustness issue, this approach has been used in some commercially available systems [16]. Some systems provide a semiautomatic interface for marking the feature points to reduce the amount of the manual work. The disadvantage is that it is not convenient to obtain two orthogonal views, and it requires quite a number of manual interventions even with the semiautomatic interfaces.

## 2.3 Face Modeling from a Single Image

Blanz and Vetter [5] developed a system to create 3D face models from a single image. They used both a database of face geometries and a database of face textures. The geometry space is the linear combination of the example faces in the geometry database. The texture space is the linear combination of the example texture images in the image database. Given a face image, they search for the coefficients of the geometry space and the coefficients of the texture space so the synthesized image matches the input image. More details can be found in Chapter 10 and in their paper [5]. One limitation of their current system is that it can only handle the faces whose skin types are similar to the examples in the database. One could potentially expand the image database to cover more varieties of skin types, but there would be more parameters and it is not clear how it is going to affect the robustness of the system.

Liu [22] developed a fully automatic system to construct 3D face models from a single frontal image. They first used a face detection algorithm to find a face and then a feature alignment algorithm to find face features. By assuming an orthogonal projection, they fit a 3D face model by using the linear space of face geometries described in Section 2.1. Given that there are existing face detection and feature alignment systems [20, 43], implementing this system is simple. The main drawback of this system is that the depth of the reconstructed model is in general not accurate. For small head rotations, however, the model is recognizable. Figure 12.4 shows an example where the left is the input image and the right is the feature alignment result. Figure 12.5 shows the different views of the reconstructed 3D model. Figure 12.6 shows the results of making expressions for the reconstructed face model.

# 3 Face Relighting

During the past several years, a lot of progress has been made on generating photo-realistic images of human faces under arbitrary lighting conditions. One class of method is inverse

**Fig. 12.4.** Left: input image. Right: the result from image alignment. (From Liu [22], with permission.)

**Fig. 12.5.** Views of the 3D model generated from the input image in Figure 12.4. (From Liu [22], with permission.)

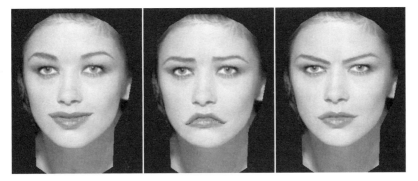

**Fig. 12.6.** Generating different expressions for the constructed face model. (From Liu [22], with permission.)

rendering [8, 9, 12, 26, 27, 45]. By capturing the lighting environment and recovering surface reflectance properties, one can generate photo-realistic rendering of objects including human faces under new lighting conditions. To recover the surface reflectance properties, one typically needs special setting and capturing equipment. Such systems are best suited for studio-like applications.

## 3.1 Face Relighting Using Ratio Images

Riklin-Raviv and Shashua [34] proposed a ratio-image technique to map one person's lighting condition to a different person. Given a face under two different lighting conditions, and another face under the first lighting condition, they used the color ratio (called the quotient image) to generate an image of the second face under the second lighting condition. For any given point on the face, let $\rho$ denote its albedo, and $\mathbf{n}$ its normal. Let $E(\mathbf{n})$ and $E'(\mathbf{n})$ be the irradiances under the two lighting conditions, respectively. Assuming a Lambertian reflectance model, the intensities of this point under the two lighting conditions are $I = \rho E(\mathbf{n})$ and $I' = \rho E'(\mathbf{n})$. Given a different face, let $\rho_1$ be its albedo. Then its intensities on the two lighting conditions are $I_1 = \rho E(\mathbf{n})$, and $I_1' = \rho E'(\mathbf{n})$. Therefore we have

$$\frac{I_1}{I} = \frac{I_1'}{I'} \tag{3}$$

Thus

$$I_1' = I' \frac{I_1}{I} \tag{4}$$

Equation 4 shows that one can obtain $I_1'$ from $I$, $I'$, and $I_1$. If we have one person's images under all possible lighting conditions and the second person's image under one of the lighting conditions, we can use Eq. 4 to generate the second person's images under all the other lighting conditions.

In many applications, we do not know in which lighting condition the second person's image is. Riklin-Raviv and Shashua [34] proposed that we use a database of images of different people under different lighting conditions. For any new person, if its albedo is "covered by" (formally called "rational span", see Riklin-Raviv and Shashua [34] for details) the albedos of the people in the database, it is possible to figure out in which lighting condition the new image was.

## 3.2 Face Relighting from a Single Image

Wen et al. [40] proposed a technique that does not require a database. Given a single image of a face, they first computed a special radiance environment map. For any point on the radiance environment map, its intensity is the irradiance at the normal direction multiplied by the average albedo of the face. In other words, the special radiance environment map is the irradiance map times a constant albedo.

This special radiance environment map is computed using spherical harmonic basis functions [3, 33] . Accordingly, the irradiance can be approximated as a linear combination of nine spherical harmonic basis functions [3, 33].

$$E(\mathbf{n}) \approx \sum_{l \leq 2, -l \leq m \leq l} \hat{A}_l \, L_{lm} \, Y_{lm}(\mathbf{n}). \tag{5}$$

Wen et al. [40] also expanded the albedo function $\rho(\mathbf{n})$ using spherical harmonics

$$\rho(\mathbf{n}) = \rho_{00} + \Psi(\mathbf{n}) \tag{6}$$

where $\rho_{00}$ is the constant component, and $\Psi(\mathbf{n})$ contains other higher order components.

From Eqs. 5 and 6, we have

$$\rho(\mathbf{n})E(\mathbf{n}) \approx \rho_{00} \sum_{l \leq 2, -l \leq m \leq l} \hat{A}_l \, L_{lm} \, Y_{lm}(\mathbf{n}) + \Psi(\mathbf{n}) \sum_{l \leq 2, -l \leq m \leq l} \hat{A}_l \, L_{lm} \, Y_{lm}(\mathbf{n})$$

If we assume $\Psi(\mathbf{n})$ does not have first four order ($l = 1, 2, 3, 4$) components, the second term of the righthand side in Eq. 7 contains components with orders equal to or higher than 3 (see Wen et al. [40] for the explanation). Because of the orthogonality of the spherical harmonic basis, the nine coefficients of order $l \leq 2$ estimated from $\rho(\mathbf{n})E(\mathbf{n})$ with a linear least-squares procedure are $\rho_{00} \hat{A}_l \, L_{lm}$, where $(l \leq 2, -l \leq m \leq l)$. Therefore we obtain the radiance environment map with a reflectance coefficient equal to the average albedo of the surface.

Wen et al. [40] argued that human face skin approximately satisfies the above assumption, that is, it does not contain low frequency components other than the constant term.

By using a generic 3D face geometry, Wen et al. [40] set up the following system of equations:

$$I(\mathbf{n}) = \sum_{l \leq 2, -l \leq m \leq l} x_{lm} \, Y_{lm}(\mathbf{n}) \tag{7}$$

They used a linear least-squares procedure to solve the nine unknowns $x_{lm}$, $l \leq 2, -l \leq m \leq l$, thus obtaining the special radiance environment map.

One interesting application is that one can relight the face image when the environment rotates. For the purpose of explanation, let us imagine the face rotates while the environment is static. Given a point on the face, its intensity is $I_f = \rho E(\mathbf{n})$. The intensity of the corresponding point on the radiance environment map is $I_s(\mathbf{n}) = \bar{\rho}E(\mathbf{n})$, where $\bar{\rho}$ is the average albedo of the face. After rotation, denote $\mathbf{n}'$ to be the new normal. The new intensity on the face is $I_f' = \rho E(\mathbf{n})$. The intensity on the radiance environment map corresponding to the $\mathbf{n}'$ is $I_s(\mathbf{n}') = \bar{\rho}E(\mathbf{n}')$. Therefore

$$I_f' = I_f \frac{I_s(\mathbf{n}')}{I_s(\mathbf{n})} \tag{8}$$

The bottom row of Figure 12.7 shows the relighting results. The input image is the one in the middle. The images at the top are the ground truth. We can see that the synthesized results match well with the ground truth images. There are some small differences mainly on the first and last images due to specular reflections. (According to Marschner et al. [28], human skin is almost Lambertian at small light incidence angles and has strong non-Lambertian scattering at higher angles.)

Another application is that one can modify the estimated spherical harmonic coefficients to generate radiance environment maps under the modified lighting conditions. For each new radiance environment map, one can use the ratio-image technique (see Eq. 8) to generate the face image under the new lighting condition. In this way, one can modify the lighting conditions

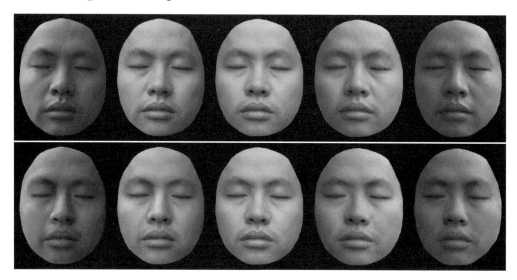

**Fig. 12.7.** Comparison of synthesized results and ground truth. The top row is the ground truth. The bottom row is the synthesized result, where the middle image is the input. (From Wen et al. [40], with permission.)

of the face. In addition to lighting editing, this can also be used to generate training data with different lighting conditions for face detection or face recognition applications.

Figure 12.8 shows four examples of lighting editing by modifying the spherical harmonics coefficients. For each example, the left image is the input image, and the right image is the result after modifying the lighting. In example (a), lighting is changed to attach shadow to the person's left face. In example (b), the light on the person's right face is changed to be more reddish, and the light on her left face becomes slightly more bluish. In (c), the bright sunlight move from the person's left face to his right face. In (d), we attach shadow to the person's right face and change the light color as well.

### 3.3 Application to Face Recognition under Varying Illumination

Qing et al. [32] used the face relighting technique as described in the previous section for face recognition under different lighting environments. For any given face image under unknown illumination, they first applied the face relighting technique to generate a new image of the face under canonical illumination. Canonical illumination is the constant component of the spherical harmonics, which can be obtained by keeping only the constant coefficient ($x_{00}$ in Eq. 7) while setting the rest of the coefficients to zero. The ratio-image technique of Eq. 8 is used to generate the new image under canonical illumination.

Image matching is performed on the images under canonical illumination. Qing et al. [32] performed face recognition experiments with the PIE database [37]. They reported significant improvement of the recognition rate after using face relighting. The reader is referred to their article [32] for detailed experimental results.

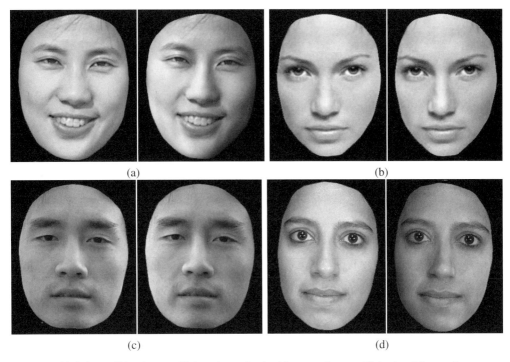

(a)                                              (b)

(c)                                              (d)

**Fig. 12.8.** Lighting editing by modifying the spherical harmonics coefficients of the radiance environment map. The left image in each pair is the input image and the right image is the result after modifying the lighting. (From Wen et al. [40], with permission.)

## 4 Facial Expression Synthesis

### 4.1 Physically Based Facial Expression Synthesis

One of the early physically based approaches is the work by Badler and Platt [2], who used a mass and spring model to simulate the skin. They introduced a set of muscles. Each muscle is attached to a number of vertices of the skin mesh. When the muscle contracts, it generates forces on the skin vertices, thereby deforming the skin mesh. A user generates facial expressions by controlling the muscle actions.

Waters [39] introduced two types of muscles: linear and sphincter. The lips and eye regions are better modeled by the sphincter muscles. To gain better control, they defined an influence zone for each muscle so the influence of a muscle diminishes as the vertices are farther away from the muscle attachment point.

Terzopoulos and Waters [38] extended Waters' model by introducing a three-layer facial tissue model. A fatty tissue layer is inserted between the muscle and the skin, providing more fine grain control over the skin deformation. This model was used by Lee et al. [19] to animate Cyberware scanned face meshes.

One problem with the physically based approaches is that it is difficult to generate natural looking facial expressions. There are many subtle skin movement, such as wrinkles and furrows, that are difficult to model with a mass-and-spring scheme.

## 4.2 Morph-Based Facial Expression Synthesis

Given a set of 2D or 3D expressions, one could blend these expressions to generate new expressions. This technique is called morphing or interpolation. This technique was first reported in Parke's pioneer work [29]. Beier and Neely [4] developed a feature-based image morphing technique to blend 2D images of facial expressions. Bregler et al. [6] applied the morphing technique to mouth regions to generate lip-synch animations.

Pighin et al. [30] used the morphing technique on both the 3D meshes and texture images to generate 3D photorealistic facial expressions. They first used a multiview stereo technique to construct a set of 3D facial expression examples for a given person. Then they used the convex linear combination of the examples to generate new facial expressions. To gain local control, they allowed the user to specify an active region so the blending affects only the specified region. The advantage of this technique is that it generates 3D photorealistic facial expressions. The disadvantage is that the possible expressions this technique can generate is limited. The local control mechanism greatly enlarges the expression space, but it puts burdens on the user. The artifacts around the region boundaries may occur if the regions are not selected properly. Joshi et al. [18] developed a technique to automatically divide the face into subregions for local control. The region segmentation is based on the analysis of motion patterns for a set of example expressions.

## 4.3 Expression Mapping

Expression mapping (also called performance-driven animation) has been a popular technique for generating realistic facial expressions. This technique applies to both 2D and 3D cases. Given an image of a person's neutral face and another image of the same person's face with an expression, the positions of the face features (e.g., eyes, eyebrows, mouths) on both images are located either manually or through some automatic method. The difference vector of the feature point positions is then added to a new face's feature positions to generate the new expression for that face through geometry-controlled image warping (we call it geometric warping ) [4, 21, 42]. In the 3D case, the expressions are meshes, and the vertex positions are 3D vectors. Instead of image warping, one needs a mesh deformation procedure to deform the meshes based on the feature point motions [13].

Williams [41] developed a system to track the dots on a performer's face and map the motions to the target model. Litwinowicz and Williams [21] used this technique to animate images of cats and other creatures.

Because of its simplicity, the expression mapping technique has been widely used in practice. One great example is the FaceStation system developed by Eyematic [16]. The system automatically tracks a person's facial features and maps his or her expression to the 3D model on the screen. It works in real time without any markers.

There has been much research done to improve the basic expression mapping technique. Pighin et al. [30] parameterized each person's expression space as a convex combination of a few basis expressions and proposed mapping one person's expression coefficients to those of another person. It requires that the two people have the same number of basis expressions and that there is a correspondence between the two basis sets. This technique was extended by Pyun et al. [31]. Instead of using convex combination, Pyun et al. [31] proposed to the use of radial basis functions to parameterize the expression space.

Noh and Neumann [44] developed a technique to automatically find a correspondence between two face meshes based on a small number of user-specified correspondences. They also developed a new motion mapping technique. Instead of directly mapping the vertex difference, this technique adjusts both the direction and the magnitude of the motion vector based on the local geometries of the source and target model.

**Mapping Expression Details**

Liu et al. [24] proposed a technique to map one person's facial expression details to a different person. Facial expression details are subtle changes in illumination and appearance due to skin deformations. The expression details are important visual cues, but they are difficult to model and synthesize. Given a person's neutral face image and an expression image, Liu et al. [24] observed that the illumination changes caused by the skin deformations can be extracted in a skin color independent manner using an expression ratio image (ERI) . The ERI can then be applied to a different person's face image to generate the correct illumination changes caused by the skin deformation of that person's face.

Let $I_a$ be person A's neutral face image, let $I'_a$ be A's expression image. Given a point on the face, let $\rho_a$ be its albedo, and let $\mathbf{n}$ be its normal on the neutral face. Let $\mathbf{n}'$ be the normal when the face makes the expression. By assuming Lambertian model, we have $I_a = \rho_a E(\mathbf{n})$ and $I'_a = \rho_a E(\mathbf{n}')$. Taking the ratio, we have:

$$\frac{I'_a}{I_a} = \frac{E(\mathbf{n}')}{E(\mathbf{n})} \tag{9}$$

Note that $\frac{I'_a}{I_a}$ captures the illumination changes due to the changes in the surface normals; furthermore, it is independent of A's albedo. $\frac{I'_a}{I_a}$ is called the expression ratio image. Let $I_b$ be person B's neutral face image. Let $\rho_b$ be its albedo. By assuming that $B$ and $A$ have similar surface normals on their corresponding points, we have $I_b = \rho_b E(n)$. Let $I'_b$ be the image of B making the same expression as A; then $I'_b = \rho_b E(\mathbf{n}')$. Therefore

$$\frac{I'_b}{I_b} = \frac{E(\mathbf{n}')}{E(\mathbf{n})} \tag{10}$$

and so

$$I'_b = I_b \frac{I'_a}{I_a} \tag{11}$$

Therefore, we can compute $I'_b$ by multiplying $I_b$ with the expression radio image.

Figure 12.9 shows a male subject's thinking expression and the corresponding ERI. Figure 12.10 shows the result of mapping the thinking expression to a female subject. The image in the middle is the result of using traditional expression mapping. The image on the right is the result generated using the ERI technique. We can see that the wrinkles due to skin deformations between the eyebrows are mapped well to the female subject. The resulting expression is more convincing than the result from the traditional geometric warping. Figure 12.12 shows the result of mapping the smile expression (Fig. 12.11) to Mona Lisa. Figure 12.13 shows the result of mapping the smile expression to two statues.

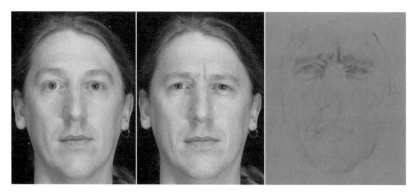

**Fig. 12.9.** Expression ratio image. Left: neutral face. Middle: expression face. Right: expression Ratio image. The ratios of the RGB components are converted to colors for display purpose. (From Liu et al. [24], with permission.)

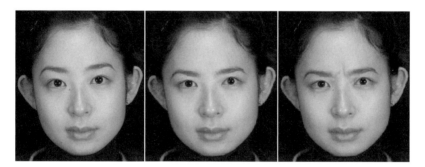

**Fig. 12.10.** Mapping a thinking expression. Left: neutral face. Middle: result from geometric warping. Right: result from ERI. (From Liu et al. [24], with permission.)

**Geometry-Driven Expression Synthesis**

One drawback of the ERI technique is that it requires the expression ratio image from the performer. Zhang et al. [46] proposed a technique that requires only the feature point motions from the performer, as for traditional expression mapping. One first computes the desired feature point positions (geometry) for the target model, as for traditional expression mapping. Based

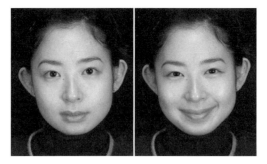

**Fig. 12.11.** Smile expression used to map to other people's faces.

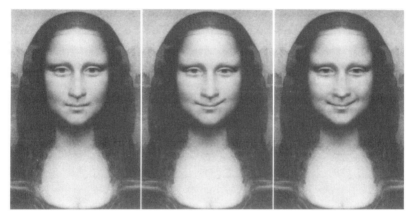

**Fig. 12.12.** Mapping a smile to Mona Lisa's face. Left: "neutral" face. Middle: result from geometric warping. Right: result from ERI. (From Liu et al. [24], with permission.)

on the desired feature point positions, the expression details for the target model are synthesized from examples.

Let $E_i = (G_i, I_i), i = 0, ..., m$, be the example expressions where $G_i$ represents the geometry and $I_i$ is the texture image ( assuming that all the texture images $I_i$ are pixel aligned). Let $H(E_0, E_1, ..., E_m)$ be the set of all possible convex combinations of these examples. Then

$$H(E_0, E_1, ..., E_m) = \tag{12}$$
$$\{(\sum_{i=0}^{m} c_i G_i, \sum_{i=0}^{m} c_i I_i) | \sum_{i=0}^{m} c_i = 1, c_i \geq 0, i = 0, ..., m\}.$$

Note that each expression in the space $H(E_0, E_1, ..., E_m)$ has a geometric component $G = \sum_{i=0}^{m} c_i G_i$ and a texture component $I = \sum_{i=0}^{m} c_i I_i$. Because the geometric component is much easier to obtain than the texture component, Zhang et al. [46] proposed using the geometric component to infer the texture component. Given the geometric component $G$, one can project $G$ to the convex hull spanned by $G_0, ..., G_m$ and then use the resulting coefficients to composite the example images and obtain the desired texture image.

(a)                                                    (b)

**Fig. 12.13.** Mapping expressions to statues. a. Left: original statue. Right: result from ERI. b. Left: another statue. Right: result from ERI. (From Liu et al. [24], with permission.)

To increase the space of all possible expressions, they proposed subdividing the face into a number of subregions. For each subregion, they used the geometry associated with this subregion to compute the subregion texture image. The final expression is then obtained by blending these subregion images together. Figure 12.14 is an overview of their system. It consists of an offline processing unit and a run time unit. The example images are processed offline only once. At run time, the system takes as input the feature point positions of a new expression. For each subregion, they solve the quadratic programming problem of Eq. 13 using the interior point method. They then composite the example images in this subregion together to obtain the subregion image. Finally they blend the subregion images together to produce the expression image.

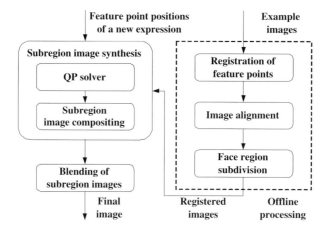

**Fig. 12.14.** Geometry-driven expression synthesis system. (From Zhang et al. [46], with permission.)

Figure 12.15a shows the feature points they used by Zhang et al. [46]. Figure 12.15b shows the face region subdivision. From Figure 12.15(a), we can see that the number of feature points used for their synthesis system is large. The reason is that more feature points are better for the image alignment and for the quadratic programming solver. The problem is that some feature points, such as those on the forehead, are quite difficult to obtain from the performer, and they are person-dependent. Thus these feature points are not suited for expression mapping. To address this problem, they developed a motion propagation technique to infer feature point motions from a subset. Their basic idea was to learn how the rest of the feature points move from the examples. To have fine-grain control, they divided the face feature points into hierarchies and performed hierarchical principal component analysis on the example expressions.

There are three hierarchies. At hierarchy 0, they used a single feature point set that controls the global movement of the entire face. There are four feature point sets at hierarchy 1, each controlling the local movement of facial feature regions (left eye region, right eye region, nose region, mouth region). Each feature point set at hierarchy 2 controls details of the face regions, such as eyelid shape, lip line shape, and so on. There are 16 feature point sets at hierarchy 2. Some facial feature points belong to several sets at different hierarchies, and they are used as bridges between global and local movement of the face, so the vertex movements can be propagated from one hierarchy to another.

For each feature point set, Zhang et al. [46] computed the displacement of all the vertices belonging to this feature set for each example expression. They then performed principal component analysis on the vertex displacement vectors corresponding to the example expressions and generated a lower dimensional vector space. The hierarchical principal component analysis results are then used to propagate vertex motions so that from the movement of a subset of feature points one can infer the most reasonable movement for the rest of the feature points.

Let $v_1$, $v_2$,..., $v_n$ denote all the feature points on the face. Let $\delta V$ denote the displacement vector of all the feature points. For any given $\delta V$ and a feature point set $F$ (the set of indexes of the feature points belonging to this feature point set), let $\delta V(F)$ denote the subvector of those vertices that belong to $F$. Let $Proj(\delta V, F)$ denote the projection of $\delta V(F)$ into the subspace spanned by the principal components corresponding to $F$. In other words, $Proj(\delta V, F)$ is the best approximation of $\delta V(F)$ in the expression subspace. Given $\delta V$ and $Proj(\delta V, F)$, let us say that $\delta V$ is *updated* by $Proj(\delta V, F)$ if for each vertex that belongs to $F$ its displacement in $\delta V$ has been replaced with its corresponding value in $Proj(\delta V, F)$.

The motion propagation algorithm takes as input the displacement vector for a subset of the feature points, say, $\Delta v_{i_1}, \Delta v_{i_2}, ..., \Delta v_{i_k}$. Denote $T = \{i_1, i_2, ..., i_k\}$. Below is a description of the motion propagation algorithm.

**MotionPropagation**

Begin

    Set $\delta V = 0$.

    While (stop-criteria is not met) Do

        For each $i_k \in T$, set $\delta V(i_k) = \Delta v_{i_k}$.

      For all Feature point set $F$, set $hasBeenProcessed(F)$ to be false.

        Find the feature point set $F$ with the lowest hierarchy such that $F \cap T \neq \emptyset$.

        MotionPropagationFeaturePointSet(F).

    End

End

The function MotionPropagationFeaturePointSet is defined as follows:

**MotionPropagationFeaturePointSet**($F^*$)
Begin
    Set $h$ to be the hierarchy of $F^*$.
    If $hasBeenProcessed(F^*)$ is true, return.
    Compute $Proj(\delta V, F^*)$.
    Update $\delta V$ with $Proj(\delta V, F^*)$.
    Set $hasBeenProcessed(F^*)$ to be true.
    For each feature set $F$ belonging to hierarchy $h - 1$ such that $F \cap F^* \neq \emptyset$.
        $MotionPropagation(F)$.
    For each feature set $F$ belonging to hierarchy h+1 such that $F \cap F^* \neq \emptyset$.
        $MotionPropagation(F)$.
  End

The algorithm initializes $\delta V$ to a zero vector. At the first iteration, it sets $\delta V(i_k)$ to be equal to the input displacement vector for vertex $v_{i_k}$. Then it finds the feature point set with the lowest hierarchy so it intersects with the input feature point set $T$ and calls $MotionPropagationFeaturePointSet$. The function uses principal component analysis to infer the motions for the rest of the vertices in this feature point set. It then recursively calls $MotionPropagation\text{-}FeaturePointSet$ on other feature point sets. At the end of the first iteration, $\delta V$ contains the inferred displacement vectors for all the feature points. Note that for the vertex in $T$ its inferred displacement vector may be different from the input displacement vector because of the principal component projection. At the second iteration, $\delta V(i_k)$ is reset to the input displacement vector for all $i_k \in T$. The process repeats.

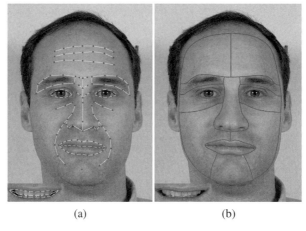

(a)                      (b)

**Fig. 12.15.** a. Feature points. b. Face region subdivision. (From Zhang et al. [46], with permission.)

Figure 12.17 shows the results of mapping a female subject's expressions to a male subject. The example images of the male subject are shown in Figure 12.16.

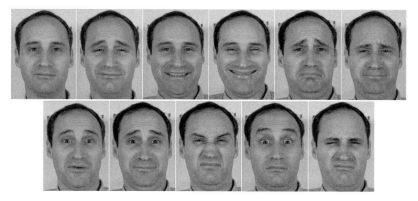

**Fig. 12.16.** Example images of the male subject. (From Zhang et al. [46], with permission.)

In addition to expression mapping, Zhang et al. [46] applied their techniques to expression editing. They developed an interactive expression editing system that allows a user to drag a face feature point, and the system interactively displays the resulting image with expression details. Figure 12.18 is a snapshot of their interface. The red dots are the feature points that the user can click and drag. Figure 12.19 shows some of expressions generated by the expression editing system.

## 5 Discussion

We have reviewed recent advances on face synthesis including face modeling, face relighting, and facial expression synthesis. There are many open problems that remain to be solved.

One problem is how to generate face models with fine geometric details. As discussed in Section 2, many 3D face modeling techniques use some type of model space to constrain the search, thereby improving the robustness. The resulting face models in general do not have the geometric details, such as creases and wrinkles. Geometric details are important visual cues for human perception. With geometric details, the models look more realistic; and for personalized face models, they look more recognizable to human users. Geometric details can potentially improve computer face recognition performance as well.

Another problem is how to handle non-Lambertian reflections. The reflection of human face skin is approximately specular when the angle between the view direction and lighting direction is close to $90^o$. Therefore, given any face image, it is likely that there are some points on the face whose reflection is not Lambertian. It is desirable to identify the non-Lambertian reflections and use different techniques for them during relighting.

How to handle facial expressions in face modeling and face relighting is another interesting problem. Can we reconstruct 3D face models from expression images? One would need a way to identify and undo the skin deformations caused by the expression. To apply face relighting techniques on expression face images, we would need to know the 3D geometry of the expression face to generate correct illumination for the areas with strong deformations.

One ultimate goal in face animation research is to be able to create face models that look and move just like a real human character. Not only do we need to synthesize facial expression,

**Fig. 12.17.** Results of the enhanced expression mapping. The expressions of the female subject are mapped to the male subject. (From Zhang et al. [46], with permission.)

we also need to synthesize the head gestures, eye gazes, hair, and the movements of lips, teeth, and tongue.

Face synthesis techniques can be potentially used for face detection and face recognition to handle different head poses, different lighting conditions, and different facial expressions. As we discussed earlier, some researchers have started applying some face synthesis techniques to face recognition [32, 35]. We believe that there are many more opportunities along this line, and that it is a direction worth exploring.

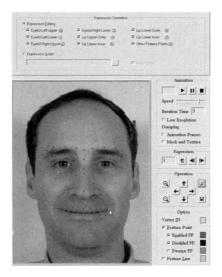

**Fig. 12.18.** The expression editing interface. The red dots are the feature points which a user can click on and drag. (From Zhang et al. [46], with permission.)

## Acknowledgments

We thank Ying-Li Tian for carefully reading our manuscripts and providing critical reviews. We also thank Zhengyou Zhang, Alex Acero, and Heung-Yeung Shum for their support.

## References

1. T. Akimoto, Y. Suenaga, and R. S. Wallace. Automatic 3D facial models. *IEEE Computer Graphics and Applications*, 13(5):16–22, 1993.
2. N. Badler and S. Platt. Animating facial expressions. In *Computer Graphics*, pages 245–252. Siggraph, 1981 (www.siggraph.org).
3. R. Basri and D. Jacobs. Lambertian reflectance and linear subspaces. In *Proc. ICCV'01*, pages 383–390, 2001.
4. T. Beier and S. Neely. Feature-based image metamorphosis. In *Computer Graphics*, pages 35–42. Siggraph, 1992 (www.siggraph.org).
5. V. Blanz and T. Vetter. A morphable model for the synthesis of 3d faces. In *Computer Graphics, Annual Conference Series*, pages 187–194. Siggraph, August 1999.
6. C. Bregler, M. Covell, and M. Slaney. Video rewrite: driving visual speech with audio. In *Computer Graphics*, pages 353–360. Siggraph, 1997 (www.siggraph.org).
7. B. Dariush, S. B. Kang, and K. Waters. Spatiotemporal analysis of face profiles: detection, segmentation, and registration. In *Proc. of the 3rd International Conference on Automatic Face and Gesture Recognition*, pages 248–253. IEEE, 1998.
8. P.E. Debevec. Rendering synthetic objects into real scenes: bridging traditional and image-based graphics with global illumination and high dynamic range photography. In *Computer Graphics, Annual Conference Series*, pages 189–198. Siggraph, 1998 (www.siggraph.org).

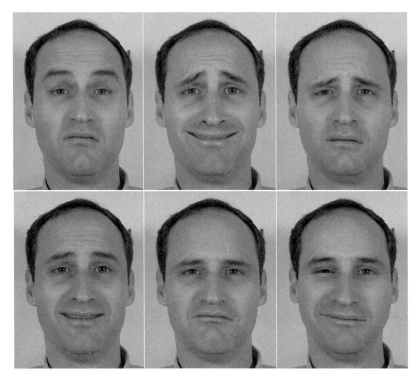

**Fig. 12.19.** Expressions generated by the expression editing system. (From Zhang et al. [46], with permission.)

9.  P.E. Debevec, T. Hawkins, C. Tchou, H.-P. Duiker, W. Sarokin, and M. Sagar. Acquiring the reflectance field of a human face. In *Computer Graphics, Annual Conference Series*, pages 145–156. Siggraph, 2000 (wwww.siggraph.org).
10. P. Fua and C. Miccio. Animated heads from ordinary images: a least-squares approach. *Computer Vision and Image Understanding*, 75(3):247–259, 1999.
11. P. Fua and C. Miccio. From regular images to animated heads: a least squares approach. In *Eurographics of Computer Vision*, pages 188–202, 1996.
12. A. Georghiades, P. Belhumeur, and D. Kriegman. Illumination-based image synthesis: creating novel images of human faces under differing pose and lighting. In *IEEE Workshop on Multi-View Modeling and Analysis of Visual Scenes*, pages 47–54, 1999.
13. B. Guenter, C. Grimm, D. Wood, H. Malvar, and F. Pighin. Making faces. In *Computer Graphics, Annual Conference Series*, pages 55–66. Siggraph, 1998 (www.siggraph.org).
14. B.K. Horn. Closed-form solution of absolute orientation using unit quaternions. *Journal of the Optical Society A*, 4(4):629–642, 1987.
15. http://www.digimask.com.
16. http://www.eyematic.com.
17. H.H.S.Ip and L. Yin. Constructing a 3D individualized head model from two orthogonal views. *Visual Computer*, (12):254–266, 1996.
18. P. Joshi, W.C. Tien, M. Desbrun, and F. Pighin. Learning controls for blend shape based realistic facial animation. In *Proc. Symposium on Computer Animation (SCA'03)*, pages 187–192, 2003.

19. Y. Lee, D. Terzopoulos, and K. Waters. Realistic modeling for facial animation. In *Computer Graphics*, pages 55–62. Siggraph, 1995 (www.siggraph.org).

20. S.Z. Li and and X.L. Zou and Y.X. Hu and Z.Q. Zhang and S.C. Yan and X.H. Peng and L. Huang and H.J. Zhang. Real-time multi-view face detection, tracking, pose estimation, alignment, and recognition. In *IEEE Conf. on Computer Visioin and Pattern Recognition Demo Summary*, 2001.

21. P. Litwinowicz and L. Williams. Animating images with drawings. In *Computer Graphics*, pages 235–242. Siggraph, 1994 (www.siggraph.org).

22. Z. Liu. A fully automatic system to model faces from a single image. In *Microsoft Research Technical Report: MST-TR-2003-55*, 2003.

23. Z. Liu and Z. Zhang. Robsut head motion computation by taking advantage of physical properties. In *IEEE Workshop on Human Motion (HUMO)*, pages 73–77, 2000.

24. Z. Liu, Y. Shan, and Z. Zhang. Expressive expression mapping with ratio images. In *Computer Graphics, Annual Conference Series*, pages 271–276. Siggraph, 2001 (www.siggraph.org).

25. Z. Liu, Z. Zhang, C. Jacobs, and M. Cohen. Rapid modeling of animated faces from video. *Journal of Visualization and Computer Animation*, 12(4):227–240, 2001.

26. S.R. Marschner and D.P. Greenberg. Inverse lighting for photography. In *IST/SID Fifth Colort Imaging Conference*, 1997.

27. S.R. Marschner, B. Guenter, and S. Raghupathy. Modeling and rendering for realistic facial animation. In *Rendering Techniques*, pages 231–242. Springer, New York, 2000.

28. S.R. Marschner, S.H. Westin, E.P.F. Lafortune, K.E. Torrance, and D.P. Greenberg. Image-based brdf measurement including human skin. In *Proceedings of 10th Eurographics Workshop on Rendering, Granada, Spain*, D. Lischinski and W. Larson, editors, Rendering Techniques, 1999.

29. F.I. Parke. Computer generated animation of faces. In *ACM National Conference*, 1972.

30. F. Pighin, J. Hecker, D. Lischinski, R. Szeliski, and D.H. Salesin. Synthesizing realistic facial expressions from photographs. In *Computer Graphics, Annual Conference Series*, pages 75–84. Siggraph, 1998 (www.siggraph.org).

31. H. Pyun, Y. Kim, W. Chae, H.W. Kang, and S.Y. Shin. An example-based approach for facial expression cloning. In *Proc. Symposium on Computer Animation (SCA'03)*, pages 167–176, 2003.

32. L. Qing, S. Shan, and W. Gao. Face recognition with harmonic de-lighting. In *Asian Conference on Computer Vision (ACCV)*, 2004.

33. R. Ramamoorthi and P. Hanrahan. An efficient representation for irradiance environment maps. In *Proc. SIGGRAPH 2001*, pages 497–500, 2001 (www.siggraph.org).

34. T. Riklin-Raviv and A. Shashua. The quotient image: class based re-rendering and recognition with varying illuminations. In *IEEE Conference on Computer Vision and Pattern Recognition*, pages 566–571, 1999.

35. S. Romdhani, V. Blanz, and T. Vetter. Face identification by fitting a 3D morphable model using linear shape and texture error functions. In *European Conference on Computer Vision (ECCV'2002)*, pages IV:3–19, 2002.

36. Y. Shan, Z. Liu, and Z. Zhang. Modle-based bundle adjustment with application to face modeling. In *International Conference on Computer Vision (ICCV'01)*, II 644–651, 2001.

37. T. Sim, S. Baker, and M. Bsat. The CMU pose, illumination, and expression (PIE) database. In *Face and Gesture'02*, 2002.

38. D. Terzopoulos and K. Waters. Physically-based facial modeling and animation. *Journal of Visualization and Computer Animation*, 1(4):73–80, March 1990.

39. K. Waters. A muscle model for animating three-dimensional facial expression. *Computer Graphics*, 22(4):17–24, 1987.

40. Z. Wen, Z. Liu, and T.S. Huang. Face relighting with radiance environment maps. In *IEEE Conference on Computer Vision and Pattern Recognition*, II 158–165, 2003.

41. L. Williams. Performace-driven facial animation. In *Computer Graphics*, pages 235–242. Siggraph, 1990 (www.siggraph.org).

42. G. Wolberg. *Digital Image Warping*. IEEE Computer Society Press, 1990.

43. S.C. Yan, M.J. Li, H.J. Zhang, and Q.S. Cheng. Ranking prior local confidence model for statistical shape localization. In *IEEE International Conference on Computer Vision*, pages 51-58, 2003.

44. J.Y. Noh and U. Neumann. Expression cloning. In *Computer Graphics, Annual Conference Series*, pages 277–288. Siggraph, 2001 (www.siggraph.org).

45. Y. Yu, P. Debevec, J. Malik, and T. Hawkins. Inverse global illumination: Recovering reflectance models of real scenes from photographs. In *Proc. SIGGRAPH 99*, pages 215–224, 1999 (www.siggraph.org).

46. Q. Zhang, Z. Liu, B. Guo, and H. Shum. Geometry-driven photorealistic facial expression synthesis. In *Proc. Symposium on Computer Animation (SCA'03)*, pages 177–186, 2003.

# Chapter 13. Face Databases

Ralph Gross

Robotics Institute, Carnegie Mellon University, Pittsburgh, PA 15213, USA.
`rgross@cs.cmu.edu`

Because of its nonrigidity and complex three-dimensional (3D) structure, the appearance of a face is affected by a large number of factors including identity, face pose, illumination, facial expression, age, occlusion, and facial hair. The development of algorithms robust to these variations requires databases of sufficient size that include carefully controlled variations of these factors. Furthermore, common databases are necessary to comparatively evaluate algorithms. Collecting a high quality database is a resource-intensive task: but the availability of public face databases is important for the advancement of the field. In this chapter we review 27 publicly available databases for face recognition, face detection, and facial expression analysis.

## 1 Databases for Face Recognition

Face recognition continues to be one of the most popular research areas of computer vision and machine learning. Along with the development of face recognition algorithms, a comparatively large number of face databases have been collected. However, many of these databases are tailored to the specific needs of the algorithm under development. In this section we review *publicly* available databases that are of demonstrated use to others in the community. At the beginning of each subsection a table summarizing the key features of the database is provided, including (where available) the number of subjects, recording conditions, image resolution, and total number of images. Table 13.1 gives an overview of the recording conditions for all databases discussed in this section. Owing to space constraints not all databases are discussed at the same level of detail. Abbreviated descriptions of a number of mostly older databases are included in Section 1.13. The scope of this section is limited to databases containing full face imagery. Note, however, that there are databases of subface images available, such as the recently released CASIA Iris database [23].

| Database | No. of subjects | Pose | Illumination | Facial Expressions | Time |
|----------|-----------------|------|--------------|--------------------|------|
| AR | 116 | 1 | 4 | 4 | 2 |
| BANCA | 208 | 1 | ++ | 1 | 12 |
| CAS-PEAL | 66 – 1040 | 21 | 9 – 15 | 6 | 2 |
| CMU Hyper | 54 | 1 | 4 | 1 | 1 – 5 |
| CMU PIE | 68 | 13 | 43 | 3 | 1 |
| Equinox IR | 91 | 1 | 3 | 3 | 1 |
| FERET | 1199 | 9 – 20 | 2 | 2 | 2 |
| Harvard RL | 10 | 1 | 77 – 84 | 1 | 1 |
| KFDB | 1000 | 7 | 16 | 5 | 1 |
| MIT | 15 | 3 | 3 | 1 | 1 |
| MPI | 200 | 3 | 3 | 1 | 1 |
| ND HID | 300+ | 1 | 3 | 2 | 10/13 |
| NIST MID | 1573 | 2 | 1 | ++ | 1 |
| ORL | 10 | 1 | ++ | ++ | ++ |
| UMIST | 20 | ++ | 1 | ++ | 1 |
| U. Texas | 284 | ++ | 1 | ++ | 1 |
| U. Oulu | 125 | 1 | 16 | 1 | 1 |
| XM2VTS | 295 | ++ | 1 | ++ | 4 |
| Yale | 15 | 1 | 3 | 6 | 1 |
| Yale B | 10 | 9 | 64 | 1 | 1 |

**Table 13.1.** Overview of the recording conditions for all databases discussed in this section. Cases where the exact number of conditions is not determined (either because the underlying measurement is continuous or the condition was not controlled for during recording) are marked with "++."

## 1.1 AR Database

| No. of subjects | Conditions | | Image Resolution | No. of Images |
|-----------------|------------|---|------------------|---------------|
| 116 | Facial expressions | 4 | $768 \times 576$ | 3288 |
| | Illumination | 4 | | |
| | Occlusion | 2 | | |
| | Time | 2 | | |
| | http://rvl1.ecn.purdue.edu/~aleix/aleix_face_DB.html | | | |

The AR database was collected at the Computer Vision Center in Barcelona, Spain in 1998 [25]. It contains images of 116 individuals (63 men and 53 women). The imaging and recording conditions (camera parameters, illumination setting, camera distance) were carefully controlled and constantly recalibrated to ensure that settings are identical across subjects. The resulting RGB color images are $768 \times 576$ pixels in size. The subjects were recorded twice at a 2–week interval. During each session 13 conditions with varying facial expressions, illumination and occlusion were captured. Figure 13.1 shows an example for each condition. So far, more than 200 research groups have accessed the database.

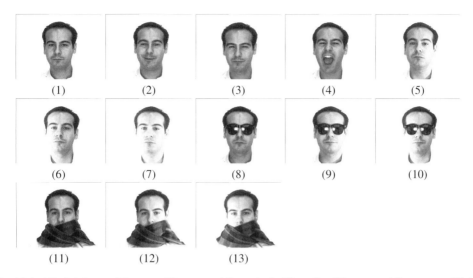

**Fig. 13.1.** AR database. The conditions are (1) neutral, (2) smile, (3) anger, (4) scream, (5) left light on, (6) right light on, (7) both lights on, (8) sun glasses, (9) sun glasses/left light (10) sun glasses/right light, (11) scarf, (12) scarf/left light, (13) scarf/right light

## 1.2 BANCA Database

| No. of Subjects | Conditions | | Image Resolution |
|---|---|---|---|
| 208 | Image quality | 3 | $720 \times 576$ |
| | Time | 12 | |
| http://www.ee.surrey.ac.uk/Research/VSSP/banca/ | | | |

The BANCA multi-modal database was collected as part of the European BANCA project, which aimed at developing and implementing a secure system with enhanced identification, authentication, and access control schemes for applications over the Internet [1]. The database was designed to test multimodal identity verification with various acquisition devices (high and low quality cameras and microphones) and under several scenarios (controlled, degraded, and adverse). Data were collected in four languages (English, French, Italian, Spanish) for 52 subjects each (26 men and 26 women). Each subject was recorded during 12 different sessions over a period of 3 months. Recordings for a true client access and an informed imposter attack were taken during each session. For each recording the subject was instructed to speak a random 12-digit number along with name, address, and date of birth (client or imposter data). Recordings took an average of 20 seconds. Figure 13.2 shows example images for all three recording conditions. The BANCA evaluation protocol specifies training and testing sets for a number of experimental configurations, so accurate comparisons between algorithms are possible.

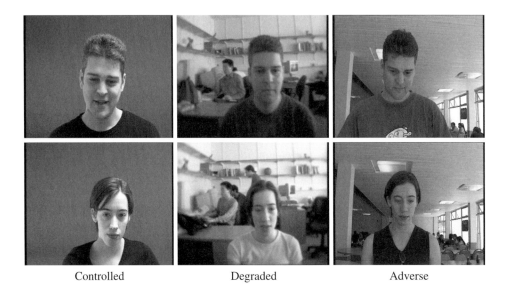

|  Controlled  |  Degraded  |  Adverse  |

**Fig. 13.2.** Images for the three recording conditions in the BANCA database. A high quality digital camera was used to record the images for the *controlled* and *adverse* conditions. The images of the *degraded* condition were taken with a low quality web cam.

### 1.3  CAS-PEAL Database

| No. of Subjects | Conditions | | Image Resolution | No. of Images |
|---|---|---|---|---|
| 1040 | Pose | 21 | | |
| 377 | Facial expressions | 6 | | |
| 438 | Accessory | 6 | | |
| 233 | Illumination | 9 – 15 | $360 \times 480$ | 30,900 |
| 297 | Background | 2 – 4 | | |
| 296 | Distance | 1 – 2 | | |
| 66 | Time | 2 | | |
| http://www.jdl.ac.cn/peal/index.html | | | | |

The CAS-PEAL (pose, expression, accessory, lighting) Chinese face database was collected at the Chinese Academy of Sciences (CAS) between August 2002 and April 2003.[1] It contains images of 66 to 1040 subjects (595 men, 445 women) in seven categories: pose, expression, accessory, lighting, background, distance, and time [12]. For the pose subset, nine cameras distributed in a semicircle around the subject were used. Images were recorded sequentially within a short time period (2 seconds). In addition, subjects were asked to look up and down (each time by roughly $30°$) for additional recordings resulting in 27 pose images. The current database release includes 21 of the 27 different poses. See Figure 13.3 for example images.

---

[1] The construction of the CAS-PEAL face database has been supported by the China National Hi-Tech Program 2001AA114010.

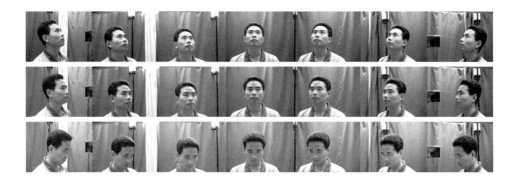

**Fig. 13.3.** Pose variation in the CAS-PEAL database. The images were recorded using separate cameras triggered in close succession. The cameras are each about $22.5°$ apart. Subjects were asked to look up, to look straight ahead, and to look down. Shown here are seven of the nine poses currently being distributed.

**Fig. 13.4.** Illumination variation in the CAS-PEAL database. The images were recorded with constant ambient illumination and manually triggered fluorescent lamps.

To record faces under varying yet natural looking lighting conditions, constant ambient illumination together with 15 manually operated fluorescent lamps were used. The lamps were placed at (-90°, -45°, 0°, 45°, 90°) azimuth and (-45°, 0°, 45°) elevation. Recording of the illumination images typically took around two minutes; therefore small changes between the images might be present. Example images for all illumination conditions are shown in Figure 13.4. For the expression subset of the database, subjects were asked to smile, to frown, to look surprised, to close their eyes, and to open the mouth. Images were captured using all nine cameras as described above. In the current database release only the frontal facial expres-

**Fig. 13.5.** Example release images of the pose subset of the CAS-PEAL database. Images are gray-scale and 360 × 480 in size.

sion images are included. A smaller number of subjects were recorded wearing three types of glasses and three types of hats. Again, images were captured using all nine cameras, with only the frontal images currently being distributed. To capture the effect of the camera auto white-balance, subjects were also recorded with five uniformly colored backgrounds (blue, white, black, red, and yellow). Furthermore, images were obtained at two distances (1.2 and 1.4 meters). Finally a small number of subjects returned 6 months later for additional recordings. Of the 99,594 images in the database, 30,900 images are available in the current release. To facilitate database distribution, the release images are stored as cropped gray-scale images of size 360 × 480. Figure 13.5 shows example images of the currently distributed images.

### 1.4 CMU Hyperspectral Face Database

| No. of Subjects | Conditions | | Spectral Range | Image Resolution |
|---|---|---|---|---|
| 54 | Illumination | 4 | 0.45 − 1.1 $\mu m$ | 640 × 480 |
| | Time | 1 − 5 | | |
| http://www.ri.cmu.edu/pubs/pub_4110.html | | | | |

The CMU Hyperspectral database, collected under the DARPA HumanID program [28], covers the visible to near-infrared range, from 0.45 to 1.1 $\mu m$ [7]. Using a CMU developed imaging sensor based on an Acousto-Optic-Tunable Filter (AOTF), the wavelength range is sampled in $10nm$ steps, resulting in 65 images. Acquisition of the 65 images took an average of 8 seconds. Because of the relative lack of sensitivity of the system (only 5 − 10% of light is used), comparatively strong illumination from one to three 600 W halogen lamps was used during data collection. The lamps were placed at -45°, 0°, and +45° with respect to the subject. Each of the 54 subjects was then imaged under four illumination conditions (three lamps individually and then combined). Subjects were recorded between one and five times over a 6–week period. Figure 13.6 shows example images for a selection of wavelengths between 0.5 and 1 $\mu m$.

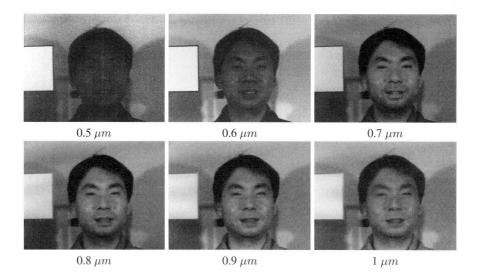

| 0.5 μm | 0.6 μm | 0.7 μm |

| 0.8 μm | 0.9 μm | 1 μm |

**Fig. 13.6.** Example images of the CMU Hyperspectral Face Database. Each recording produces images for every $10nm$ step in the range between $0.45$ and $1.1 \mu m$.

## 1.5 CMU Pose, Illumination, and Expression (PIE) Database

| No. of Subjects | Conditions | | Image Resolution | No. of Images |
|---|---|---|---|---|
| 68 | Pose | 13 | $640 \times 486$ | 41,368 |
| | Illumination | 43 | | |
| | Facial expressions | 3 | | |
| http://www.ri.cmu.edu/projects/project_418.html | | | | |

The CMU PIE database was collected between October and December 2000 [38]. It systematically samples a large number of pose and illumination conditions along with a variety of facial expressions. Although only available for 2 years, PIE has already made an impact on algorithm development for face recognition across pose [15, 33] and on the evaluation of face recognition algorithms [16]. So far the database has been distributed to more than 150 research groups.

The PIE database contains 41,368 images obtained from 68 individuals. The subjects were imaged in the CMU 3D Room [21] using a set of 13 synchronized high-quality color cameras and 21 flashes. The resulting RGB color images are 640 × 480 in size. Figure 13.7 shows example images of a subject in all 13 poses. In addition to the pose sequence, each subject was recorded under four additional conditions.

1. *Illumination 1*: A total of 21 flashes are individually turned on in rapid sequence. The images in the illumination 1 condition were captured with the room lights on, which produces more natural looking images than the second condition. Each camera recorded 24 images, 2 with no flashes, 21 with one flash firing, and then a final image with no flashes. Only the output of three cameras (frontal, three-quarter, and profile view) was kept.

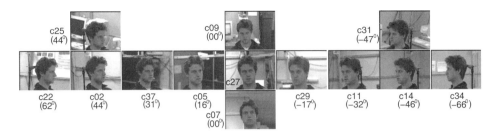

**Fig. 13.7.** Pose variation in the PIE database. The pose varies from full left profile (c34) over full frontal (c27) to full right profile (c22). Approximate pose angles are shown below the camera numbers.

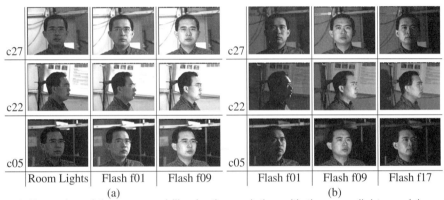

| | Room Lights | Flash f01 | Flash f09 | Flash f01 | Flash f09 | Flash f17 |
|---|---|---|---|---|---|---|
| | | (a) | | | (b) | |

**Fig. 13.8.** Examples of the pose and illumination variation with the room lights on (a), and the room lights off (b). Note how the combination of room illumination and flashes leads to much more natural looking images than with just the flash alone.

2. *Illumination 2*: The procedure of the illumination 1 condition was repeated with the room lights off. The output of all 13 cameras was retained in the database. Combining the two illumination settings, a total of 43 illumination conditions were recorded.

3. *Expression*: The subjects were asked to display a neutral face, to smile, and to close their eyes in order to simulate a blink. The images of all 13 cameras are available in the database.

4. *Talking*: Subjects counted starting at 1 for 2 seconds. Sixty frames of them talking were recorded using three cameras (frontal, three-quarter, and profile views).

Examples of the pose and illumination variation are shown in Figure 13.8. Figure 13.8a contains variations with the room lights on and Figure 13.8b with the lights off.

In addition to the raw image data, a variety of miscellaneous "meta-data" were also collected to aid in calibration and other processing.

Head, camera, and flash locations: Using a theodolite, the xyz locations of the head, the 13 cameras, and the 21 flashes were measured. The numerical values of the locations are

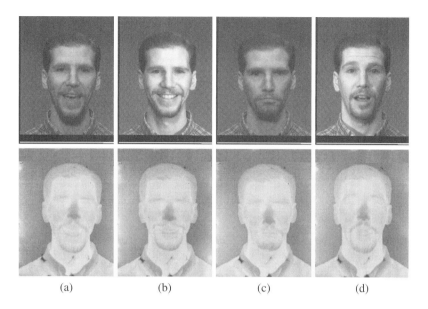

|  (a)  |  (b)  |  (c)  |  (d)  |

**Fig. 13.9.** Example images of the Equinox IR database. The upper row contains visible images and the lower row long-wave infrared images. The categories are (a) vowel (frontal illumination), (b) "smile" (right illumination), (c) "frown" (frontal illumination), (d) "surprise" (left illumination).

included in the database and can be used to estimate (relative) head poses and illumination directions.

Background images:  At the start of each recording session, a background image was captured from each of the 13 cameras. These images can be used for background subtraction to help localize the face region.

Color calibration images:  Although the cameras that were used are all of the same type, there is still a large amount of variation in their photometric responses due to their manufacture and to the fact that the aperture settings on the cameras were all set manually. The cameras were "auto white-balanced," but there is still some noticeable variation in their color response. To allow the cameras to be intensity (gain and bias)- and color-calibrated, images of color calibration charts were captured at the start of every session.

## 1.6  Equinox Infrared Face Database

| No. of Subjects | Conditions | | Spectral Range | Image Resolution |
|---|---|---|---|---|
| 91 | Illumination | 3 | $8 - 12\ \mu m$ <br> Visible | $240 \times 320$ |
| | Facial expressions | 3 | | |
| | Speech sequence | 1 | | |
| http://www.equinoxsensors.com/products/HID.html | | | | |

Various evaluations of academic and commercial face recognition algorithms give empirical evidence that recognizer performance generally decreases if evaluated across illumination

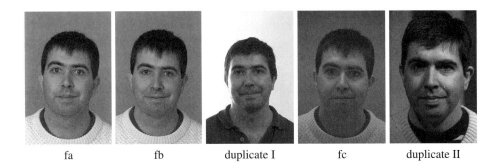

fa            fb         duplicate I        fc        duplicate II

**Fig. 13.10.** Frontal image categories used in the FERET evaluations. For images in the *fb* category a different facial expression was requested. The *fc* images were recorded with a different camera and under different lighting conditions. The duplicate images were recorded in a later session, with 0 and 1031 days (duplicate I) or 540 to 1031 days (duplicate II) between recordings.

conditions [4, 16, 30]. One way to address this problem is to use thermal infrared imagery, which has been shown to be nearly invariant to changes in ambient illumination [42]. As part of the DARPA HumanID program [28], Equinox Corporation collected a database of long-wave infrared (LWIR) imagery in the spectral range of $8 - 12$ $\mu m$ [39]. The database is unique in that the sensor used for the collection simultaneously records video sequences with a visible CCD array and LWIR microbolometer. The resulting image pairs are $240 \times 320$ pixels in size and co-registered to within 1/3 pixel. All LWIR images were radiometrically calibrated with a black-body radiator.

The database contains 91 subjects. For each subject, a 4-second (40 frames) video sequence was recorded while the subject pronounced the vowels. Additional still images were obtained in which the subjects display the facial expressions "smile," "frown," and "surprise." All images were recorded under three illumination conditions: frontal, left lateral, and right lateral. People wearing glasses were imaged twice: with and without glasses. Figure 13.9 shows example images of both the visual and LWIR imagery across all imaging conditions. For some subjects, additional boresighted short-wave infrared (SWIR) ($0.9 - 1.7$ $\mu m$) and middle-wave infrared (MWIR) ($3 - 5$ $\mu m$) data are available.

### 1.7 FERET

| No. of Subjects | Conditions | | Image Resolution | No. of Images |
|:---:|:---|:---:|:---:|:---:|
| 1199 | Facial expressions | 2 | $256 \times 384$ | 14,051 |
| | Illumination | 2 | | |
| | Pose | 9 – 20 | | |
| | Time | 2 | | |
| | http://www.nist.gov/humanid/feret/ | | | |

The Facial Recognition Technology (FERET) database was collected at George Mason University and the US Army Research Laboratory facilities as part of the FERET program,

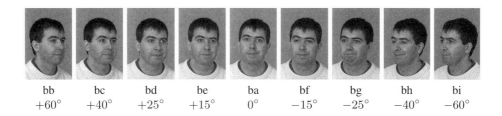

| bb | bc | bd | be | ba | bf | bg | bh | bi |
|----|----|----|----|----|----|----|----|----|
| $+60°$ | $+40°$ | $+25°$ | $+15°$ | $0°$ | $-15°$ | $-25°$ | $-40°$ | $-60°$ |

**Fig. 13.11.** Pose variation in the FERET database. The poses vary from $+60°$ (bb) to full frontal (ba) and on to -60° (bi). Images are available for 200 subjects.

sponsored by the US Department of Defense Counterdrug Technology Development Program [31, 32]. The FERET and facial recognition vender test (FRVT) 2000 [4] evaluations as well as independent evaluations [6] used the database extensively, so detailed performance figures are available for a range of research algorithms as well as commercial face recognition systems. The lists of images used in training, gallery, and probe sets are distributed along with the database, so direct comparisons of recognizer performance with previously published results are possible. To date, the database has been distributed to more than 460 research groups.

The FERET database documentation lists 24 facial image categories. The images were recorded in 15 sessions between August 1993 and July 1996. Because the recording equipment had to be reassembled for each session, slight variations between recording sessions are present. Images were recorded with a 35 mm camera, subsequently digitized, and then converted to 8-bit gray-scale images. The resulting images are $256 \times 384$ pixels in size. Figure 13.10 shows five frontal image categories of the database. The *fa* and *fb* images were obtained in close succession. The subjects were asked to display a different facial expression for the *fb* image. The resulting changes in facial expression are typically subtle, often switching between "neutral" and "smiling." The images in the *fc* category were recorded with a different camera and under different lighting. A number of subjects returned at a later date to be imaged again. For the images in the duplicate I set, 0 to 1031 days passed between recording sessions (median 72 days, mean 251 days). A subset of these images forms the duplicate II set, where at least 18 months separated the sessions (median 569 days, mean 627 days).

The remaining image categories cover a wide set of pose variations. Figure 13.11 shows categories *ba* through *bi*. The images were recorded by asking the subject to rotate the head and body. The pose angles range from $+60°$ to -60°. These pose data are available for 200 subjects.

A different set of pose images is shown in Figure 13.12. Here images were collected at the following head aspects: right and left profile (labeled *pr* and *pl*), right and left quarter profile (*qr*, *ql*) and right and left half profile (*hr*, *hl*). In these categories images were recorded for 508 to 980 subjects. In addition, five irregularly spaced views were collected for 264 to 429 subjects.

Ground-truth information, including the date of the recording and if the subject is wearing glasses, is provided for each image in the data set. In addition, the manually determined locations of left and right eye and the mouth center is available for 3816 images.

|   pr   |   hr    |    qr    |    ql    |    hl    |    pl   |
|  +90°  | +67.5°  |  +22.5°  |  −22.5°  |  −67.5°  |  −90°   |

**Fig. 13.12.** Additional set of pose images from the FERET database. Images were collected at the following head aspects: right and left profile (labeled *pr* and *pl*), right and left quarter profile (*qr, ql*), and right and left half profile (*hr, hl*).

|  +45°  |  +30°  |  +15°  |  +00°  |  −15°  |  −30°  |  −45°  |

**Fig. 13.13.** Pose variation in the Korean face database. The poses vary from +45° to full frontal and on to -45°.

In a new release of the FERET database, NIST is making higher resolution ($512 \times 768$) color images of most of the original gray-scale images available. More information about the color FERET dataset can be found at http://www.nist.gov/humanid/colorferet/.

## 1.8 Korean Face Database (KFDB)

| No. of Subjects | Conditions | | Image Resolution | No. of Images |
|:---:|:---|:---:|:---:|:---:|
| 1000 | Pose | 7 | $640 \times 480$ | 52,000 |
|  | Illumination | 16 |  |  |
|  | Facial expressions | 5 |  |  |

The Korean Face Database (KFDB) contains facial imagery of a large number of Korean subjects collected under carefully controlled conditions [19]. Similar to the CMU PIE database described in Section 1.5, images with varying pose, illumination, and facial expressions were recorded. The subjects were imaged in the middle of an octagonal frame carrying seven cameras and eight lights (in two colors: fluorescent and incandescent) against a blue screen background. The cameras were placed between 45° off frontal in both directions at 15° increments. Figure 13.13 shows example images for all seven poses. Pose images were collected in three styles: natural (no glasses, no hair band to hold back hair from the forehead), hair band, and glasses. The lights were located in a full circle around the subject at 45° intervals.

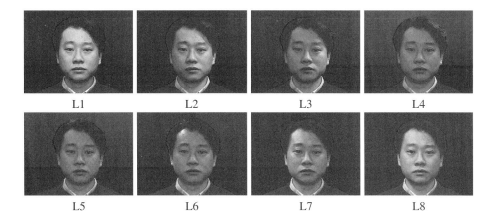

**Fig. 13.14.** Illumination variation in the Korean face database. Lights from eight different positions (L1 - L8) located in a full circle around the subject were used. For each position images with both fluorescent and incandescent lights were taken.

Separate frontal pose images were recorded with each light turned on individually for both the fluorescent and incandescent lights. Figure 13.14 shows example images for all eight illumination conditions. In addition, five images using the frontal fluorescent lights were obtained with the subjects wearing glasses. The subjects were also asked to display five facial expressions — neutral, happy, surprise, anger, and blink — which were recorded with two different colored lights, resulting in 10 images per subject. In total, 52 images were obtained per subject. The database also contains extensive ground truth information. The location of 26 feature points (if visible) is available for each face image.

## 1.9  Max Planck Institute for Biological Cybernetics Face Database

| No. of Subjects | Conditions | | Image Resolution |
|---|---|---|---|
| 200 | Modality | 2 | $256 \times 256$ |
| | Pose | 7 | |
| http://faces.kyb.tuebingen.mpg.de/ | | | |

The face database from the Max Planck Institute for Biological Cybernetics is unique, as it is based on 3D data collected with a *Cyberware* laser scanner [5]. The database contains 200 subjects (100 men, 100 women). In addition to the head structure data, which are stored in a cylindrical representation at a resolution of 512 sample points for both horizontal and vertical angles, color values are recorded at the same spatial resolution. Subjects were wearing bathing caps at the time of recording that are later automatically removed. The faces are free of makeup, accessories, or facial hair. A mostly automatic postprocessing procedure normalized the faces into a standard reference frame and removed shoulders and the region behind the ears. The face representation after all processing consists of approximately 70,000 vertices and a similar number of color values. For all subjects, 2D image data at seven face poses are available for

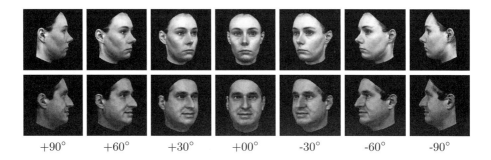

| +90° | +60° | +30° | +00° | -30° | -60° | -90° |

**Fig. 13.15.** Example images of the MPI face database. The images show seven different poses ranging from full left profile over frontal to full right profile for a female subject (first row) and a male subject (second row).

download. Figure 13.15 shows example images for both a female and a male subject. For 7 of the 200 subjects, the full 3D data are available.

## 1.10 Notre Dame HumanID Database

| No. of Subjects | Conditions | | Image Resolution | No. of Images |
|---|---|---|---|---|
| > 300 | Time | 10/13 | 1600 × 1200 | > 15,000 |
| | Illumination | 3 | | |
| | Facial Expressions | 2 | | |
| http://www.nd.edu/~cvrl/HID-data.html | | | | |

A number of evaluations of face recognition algorithms have shown that performance degrades if there is a time delay between the acquisition of gallery and probe images [4, 16, 30, 31]. Gross et al. [16] observed differences already for 2–week time laps. The face recognition vendor test 2002 measured a 5% decrease in recognizer performance for each year between recording the gallery and probe images [30]. To further investigate the time dependence in face recognition, a large database is currently being collected at the University of Notre Dame [11] under the DARPA HumanID program [28]. During the spring semester of 2002 approximately 80 subjects were imaged 10 times over an 11–week period. In the fall of 2002 a much larger pool of more than 300 subjects was recorded multiple times over 13 weeks. A minimum of four high-resolution color images are obtained during each session under controlled conditions. Subjects are recorded under two lighting configurations. The "FERET style lighting" uses two lights to the right and left of the subject. "Mugshot lighting" uses an additional third light directly opposite the subject's face. Also, two facial expression images ("neutral" and "smile") are recorded. Figure 13.16 shows the 10 images of a subject from weeks 1 through 10. In addition to the studio recordings, two images with "unstructured" lighting are obtained. These images were recorded in a hallway outside the laboratory with a different camera and weekly changing subject positions. Figure 13.17 shows examples of this condition. As part of the University of Notre Dame collection efforts, a number of additional images are recorded including infrared, range, hand, and ear images.

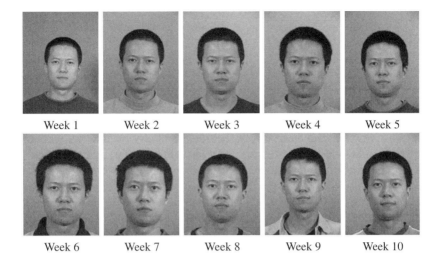

**Fig. 13.16.** Notre Dame HumanID database. The subjects are imaged on a weekly basis over 11- to 13–week periods. Example images show the subject under controlled studio lighting.

**Fig. 13.17.** Notre Dame HumanID database. Example images of the "unstructured" lighting condition recorded in the hallway outside of the laboratory.

## 1.11 University of Texas Video Database

| No. of Subjects | Conditions | Image Resolution |
|---|---|---|
| 284 | Pose (still and video)<br>Facial speech (video)<br>Facial expression (video) | 720 × 480 |
| http://www.utdallas.edu/dept/bbs/FACULTY_PAGES/otoole/database.htm | | |

Whereas the face recognition vendor test 2002 did not measure improvements in face recognition performance from video input [30] it is generally believed that the use of video data has considerable potential for improving face detection and recognition [44]. Recently, the collection of a large database of static digital images and video clips of faces at the University of

**Fig. 13.18.** University of Texas Video Database. Example images for the different recording conditions of the database. First row: Facial speech. Second row: Laughter. Third row: Disgust.

Texas has been completed [27]. The database contains a total of 284 subjects (208 female, 76 male). Most of the participants were Caucasians between the ages of 18 and 25. The subjects were imaged at close range in front of a neutral background under controlled ambient lighting. To cover up clothing each participant wore a gray smock. Data were collected in four different categories: *still facial mug shots*, *dynamic facial mug shots*, *dynamic facial speech*, and *dynamic facial expression*. For the still facial mug shots, nine views of the subject, ranging from left to right profile in equal-degree steps were recorded. The subjects were instructed to use markers suspended from the ceiling at the appropriate angles as guides for correct head positioning. For the dynamic facial mug shot category a moving version of the still facial mug shots was recorded. Aided by a metronome, the subjects rotated their heads from one position to the next in 1-second steps. The resulting sequences are 10 seconds in length. The dynamic facial speech sequences were recorded while the subjects responded to a series of mundane questions, eliciting head motions, and changes in facial expression and eye gaze direction. For most faces in the database, a "neutral" and an "animated" sequence are available. The sequence length is cropped to be 10 seconds. For the dynamic facial expression sequences, the subjects were recorded while watching a 10–minute video intended to elicit different emotions. After the recording, short 5-second clips with the subject displaying facial expressions corresponding to happiness, sadness, fear, disgust, anger, puzzlement, laughter, surprise, boredom, or disbelief were hand selected and included in the database along with a 5-second "blank stare" clip, which contains no facial motions but possibly other movements of the head or the eyes. Figure 13.18 shows example images from three of the four recording conditions.

## 1.12 Yale Face Database B

| No. of Subjects | Conditions | | Image Resolution | No. of Images |
|---|---|---|---|---|
| 10 | Pose | 9 | $640 \times 480$ | 5850 |
| | Illumination | 64 | | |
| http://cvc.yale.edu/projects/yalefacesB/yalefacesB.html | | | | |

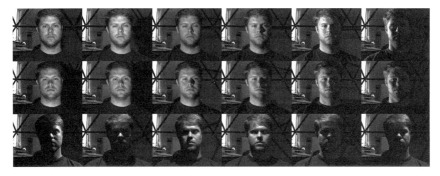

**Fig. 13.19.** Yale Face Database B: 18 example images from the 64 illumination conditions.

The Yale Face Database B [13] was collected to allow systematic testing of face recognition methods under large variations in illumination and pose. The subjects were imaged inside a geodesic dome with 64 computer-controlled xenon strobes. Images of 10 individuals were recorded under 64 lighting conditions in nine poses (one frontal, five poses at $12°$, and three poses at $24°$ from the camera axis). Because all 64 images of a face in a particular pose were acquired within about 2 seconds, only minimal changes in head position and facial expression are visible. The database is divided into four subsets according to the angle between the light source and the camera axis ($12°$, $25°$, $50°$, $77°$). Hand-labeled locations of the eyes and the center of the mouth are distributed along with the database. Example images of the database are shown in Figure 13.19.

## 1.13  Older Databases

### Harvard Robotics Lab (HRL) Database

| # Subjects | Conditions | | Image Resolution |
|:---:|:---|:---:|:---:|
| 10 | Illumination | 77–84 | $193 \times 254$ |
| ftp://cvc.yale.edu/CVC/pub/images/hrlfaces | | | |

The HRL database collected by Peter Hallinan was the first database to systematically sample a wide range of illumination conditions [17, 18]. The subjects were seated on a stool and instructed to maintain a constant head position (although slight movements were unavoidable). The face was then illuminated by a dominant light source whose positions sampled the hemisphere in front of the subject in $15°$ increments (longitude and latitude). In this way at least 75 images of each of 10 subjects were recorded.

## MIT Database

| No. of Subjects | Conditions | Image Resolution | No. of Images |
|---|---|---|---|
| 16 | Head orientation<br>Illumination<br>Scale | $120 \times 128$ | 433 |
| ftp://whitechapel.media.mit.edu/pub/images/ | | | |

The MIT database contains 16 subjects under three lighting conditions (head-on, $45°$, $90°$), three scale conditions, and three head tilt condition (upright, right, left) [41].

## NIST Mugshot Identification Database (MID)

| No. of Subjects | Conditions | Image Resolution | No. of Images |
|---|---|---|---|
| 1573 | Frontal and profile view | Varying | 3248 |
| http://www.nist.gov/srd/nistsd18.htm | | | |

The NIST Mugshot Identification Database contains frontal and profile views of 1573 (mostly male) subjects.

## Olivetti Research Lab (ORL) Database

| No. of Subjects | Image Resolution | No. of Images |
|---|---|---|
| 10 | $92 \times 110$ | 400 |
| http://www.uk.research.att.com/facedatabase.html | | |

The ORL database was collected between 1992 and 1994 [36]. It contains slight variations in illumination, facial expression (open/closed eyes, smiling/not smiling) and facial details (glasses/no glasses). However, the conditions were not varied systematically. As argued by Phillips and Newton [29] algorithm performance over this database has been saturated.

## UMIST Face Database

| No. of Subjects | Conditions | Face Resolution | No. of Images |
|---|---|---|---|
| 20 | Pose | $220 \times 220$ | 564 |
| http://images.ee.umist.ac.uk/danny/database.html | | | |

The UMIST Face Database [14] contains image sequences of subjects slowly rotating their head from profile to frontal view.

## University of Oulu Physics-Based Face Database

| No. of Subjects | Conditions | | Image Resolution |
|---|---|---|---|
| 125 | Camera calibration<br>Illumination | 16 | $428 \times 569$ |
| http://www.ee.oulu.fi/research/imag/color/pbfd.html | | | |

The University of Oulu Physics-based Face database contains color images of faces under different illuminants and camera calibration conditions as well as skin spectral reflectance measurements of each person [24]. Four Macbeth SpectraLight illuminants were used: horizon, incandescent, TL84 fluorescent, and daylight. Images were collected by white-balancing and linearizing the camera for one illumination condition and then recording the subject under all four illumination conditions without changing the camera setting. This results in 16 images per subject. If the subject was wearing glasses, an additional 16 images with the subject wearing them were recorded. Additional information such as camera spectral response and the spectral power distribution of the illuminants are provided.

**Yale Face Database**

| No. of Subjects | Conditions | | Image Resolution | No. of Images |
|---|---|---|---|---|
| 15 | W/ and w/o glasses | 2 | $320 \times 243$ | 165 |
| | Illumination | 3 | | |
| | Facial expressions | 6 | | |
| http://cvc.yale.edu/projects/yalefaces/yalefaces.html | | | | |

The Yale Face database [2] contains 11 images of 15 subjects in a variety of conditions including with and without glasses, illumination variation, and changes in facial expression.

**XM2VTS Database**

| No. of Subjects | Conditions | Image Resolution |
|---|---|---|
| 295 | Head rotation sequences | $720 \times 576$ |
| | Speech sequences | |
| | Time | |
| http://www.ee.surrey.ac.uk/Research/VSSP/xm2vtsdb/ | | |

The XM2VTS database [26] was collected for research and development of identity verification systems using multimodal (face and voice) input data. The database contains 295 subjects, each recorded at four sessions over a period of 4 months. At each session two head rotation shots and six speech shots (subjects reading three sentences twice) were recorded. 3D models of 293 subjects are available as well. The XM2VTS evaluation protocol specifies training, evaluation, and test sets, so detailed comparisons between algorithms are possible. A variety of subsets of the database are available for purchase from the University of Surrey. To date, the XM2VTS database has been distributed to more than 100 institutions.

## 2 Databases for Face Detection

Face detection algorithms typically have to be trained on face and nonface images to build up an internal representation of the human face. For this purpose the face databases listed in Section 1 are often used. According to a recent survey of face detection algorithms [43], popular choices are the FERET, MIT, ORL, Harvard, and AR databases. Along with these public databases, independently collected, nonpublic databases are often also employed. To

**Fig. 13.20.** Example images from the *Upright Test Set* portion of the MIT/CMU test set.

comparatively evaluate the performance of face detection algorithms, common testing data sets are necessary. These data sets should be representative of real-world data containing faces in various orientations against a complex background. In recent years two public data sets emerged as quasi-standard evaluation test sets: the combined MIT/CMU test set for frontal face detection [35, 40] and the CMU test set II for frontal and nonfrontal face detection [37]. In the following we describe both databases. They are available for download from http://www.ri.cmu.edu/projects/project_419.html.

## 2.1 Combined MIT/CMU Test Set

The combined MIT/CMU data set includes 180 images organized in two sets. The first group of 130 images contains 507 upright faces (referred to as the *Upright Test Set* [34]); 23 of the 130 images were collected by Sung and Poggio [40]. The images come from a wide variety of sources including the Internet, newspapers and magazines (scanned at low resolution), analog cameras, and hand drawings. Figure 13.20 shows example images from this set. A number of images are included that do not contain any faces in order to test tolerance to clutter.

The second set of data was collected to test detection of tilted faces. It contains 50 images with 223 faces, among which 210 are at angles of more than $10°$ from upright. This set is referred to as the *Tilted Test Set* [34]. Figure 13.21 shows example images from this set.

**Fig. 13.21.** Example images from the *Tilted Test Set* portion of the MIT/CMU test set.

**Fig. 13.22.** Images from the CMU Test Set II. Most of the faces in this test set are in profile view.

## 2.2  CMU Test Set II

This dataset was collected to test face detection algorithms that are able to handle out-of-plane rotation. It contains 208 images with 441 faces out of which 347 are in profile view. The images were all collected from the Internet. Figure 13.22 shows example images from this set.

## 2.3  Other Databases

### Nonface Images

Unlike the well defined class of face images, it is much more difficult if not impossible to characterize the class of nonface images. This task is important as face detection algorithms typically operate by discriminating between "images containing faces" and "images not containing faces." A popular source of nonface images other than the World Wide Web is the Washington University archive, which contains a wide variety of nonface images. The archive is accessible at http://wuarchive.wustl.edu/~aminet/pix/.

## BioID Face Database

The BioID database contains 1521 frontal view images of 23 subjects. Images are $384 \times 288$ in size. Because the images were recorded at different locations, significant variations in illumination, background, and face size are present. Manually marked eye locations are available for all images. The database can be downloaded from http://www.humanscan.de/support/downloads/facedb.php.

## MIT CBCL Face Database #1

The MIT Center for Biological and Computation Learning distributes a database of 2901 faces and 28,121 nonfaces. The images are $19 \times 19$ in size and gray-scale. The database is available for download from http://www.ai.mit.edu/projects/cbcl/software-datasets/FaceData2.html.

# 3 Databases for Facial Expression Analysis

The human face is able to display an astonishing variety of expressions. Collecting a database that samples this space in a meaningful way is a difficult task. Following the work on automated facial expression analysis, available databases cluster into two categories. In one group we find work that has concentrated on recognizing what Ekman and Friesen called the six *basic emotions* [8]—happiness, sadness, fear, disgust, surprise, and anger—from either single images or image sequences. In the other group research has focused on extracting a more fine-grained description of facial expressions. Here the underlying data are typically coded using the facial action coding system (FACS) [9], which was designed to describe subtle changes in facial features in terms of 44 distinct action units. Of the 44 action units, 30 are anatomically related to a specific set of facial muscles. For the remaining 14 units the anatomic basis is unspecified. The following section describes well known databases in both groups. A question unique to collecting data for facial expression analysis is how facial actions are elicited during data collection. To facilitate the collection process, subjects are usually asked to perform the desired actions. However, appearance and timing of these directed facial actions may differ from spontaneously occurring behavior [10]. Most of the databases collected primarily for face recognition also recorded subjects under changing facial expressions (see Section 1). The video database collected at the University of Texas [27] deserves special mention here, because it also contains a wide range of spontaneous facial expressions from a large number of subjects (see Section 1.11).

## 3.1 Japanese Female Facial Expression (JAFFE) Database

| No. of Subjects | Expressions | Image Resolution |
|---|---|---|
| 10 | 7 | $256 \times 256$ |
| http://www.mis.atr.co.jp/~mlyons/jaffe.html | | |

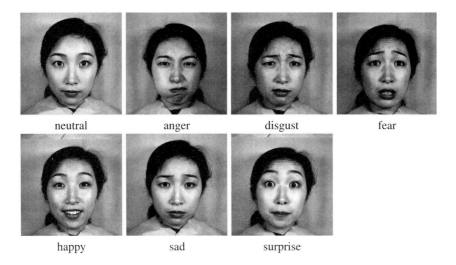

| neutral | anger | disgust | fear |

| happy | sad | surprise |

**Fig. 13.23.** Example images from the JAFFE database. The images in the database have been rated by 60 Japanese female subjects on a 5-point scale for each of the six adjectives. The majority vote is shown underneath each image (with neutral being defined through the absence of a clear majority) .

The JAFFE database contains 213 images of 10 Japanese female models obtained in front of a semireflective mirror [22]. Each subject was recorded three or four times while displaying the six basic emotions and a neutral face. The camera trigger was controlled by the subjects. The resulting images have been rated by 60 Japanese women on a 5-point scale for each of the six adjectives. The rating results are distributed along with the images. Figure 13.23 shows example images for one subject along with the majority rating. The images were originally printed in monochrome and then digitized using a flatbed scanner.

## 3.2 University of Maryland Database

| No. of Subjects | Expressions | Image Resolution |
|---|---|---|
| 40 | 6 | $560 \times 240$ |
| http://www.umiacs.umd.edu/users/yaser/DATA/index.html | | |

The University of Maryland database contains image sequences of 40 subjects of diverse racial and cultural backgrounds [3]. The subjects were recorded at a full frame rate while continuously displaying their own choice of expressions. In contrast to other databases the subjects were instructed to move their heads but avoid profile views. The resulting sequences were later ground-truthed manually. The database contains 70 sequences with a total of 145 expressions. Each sequence is about 9 seconds long and contains one to three expressions. Occurrences of the six basic emotions were not balanced, with "happiness," "surprise," "disgust," and "anger" being more frequent than "sadness" and "fear." Figure 13.24 shows peak frame examples from the database.

**Fig. 13.24.** Images from the University of Maryland database. The images show peak frames taken from an image sequence in which the subjects display a set of facial expressions of their choice.

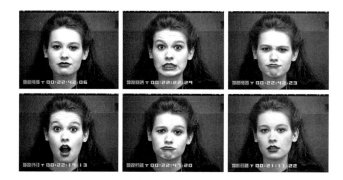

**Fig. 13.25.** Cohn-Kanade AU-Coded Facial Expression database. Examples of emotion-specified expressions from image sequences.

### 3.3 Cohn-Kanade AU-Coded Facial Expression Database

| No. of Subjects | Expressions | Image Resolution |
|---|---|---|
| 100 | 23 | $640 \times 480$ |
| http://vasc.ri.cmu.edu/idb/html/face/facial_expression/index.html | | |

The Cohn-Kanade AU-Coded Facial Expression Database is publicly available from Carnegie Mellon University [20]. It contains image sequences of facial expressions from men and women of varying ethnic backgrounds. The subjects perform a series of 23 facial displays that include single action units and combinations of action units. A total of 504 sequences are available for distribution. The camera orientation is frontal. Small head motion is present. There are three variations in lighting: ambient lighting, single-high-intensity lamp, and dual high-intensity lamps with reflective umbrellas. Facial expressions are coded using the facial action coding system [9] and assigned emotion-specified labels. Emotion expressions included happy, surprise, anger, disgust, fear, and sadness. Examples of the expressions are shown in Figure 13.25.

## Acknowledgments

We thank the following individuals for their help in compiling this chapter: Simon Baker, Kevin Bowyer, Jeffrey Cohn, Patrick Flynn, Athos Georghiades, Patrick Grother, Josh Harms, Bon-Woo Hwang, Stan Janet, Stan Li, Michael Lyons, Iain Matthews, Aleix Martinez, Jonathon Phillips, Michael Renner, Shiguang Shan, Henry Schneiderman, Diego Socolinsky, Tieniu Tan, Ying-Li Tian, Alice O'Toole, Christian Wallraven, and Yaser Yacoob. This work was supported by U.S. Office of Naval Research contract N00014-00-1-0915 and by U.S. Department of Defense contract N41756-03-C4024.

# References

1. E. Bailly-Bailliere, S. Bengio, F. Bimbot, M. Hamouz, J. Kittler, J. Mariethoz, J. Matas, K. Messer, V. Popovici, F. Poree, B. Ruiz, and J.-P. Thiran. The BANCA database and evaluation protocol. In *Audio- and Video-Based Biometric Person Authentication (AVBPA)*, pages 625–638, 2003.
2. P. N. Belhumeur, J. P. Hespanha, and D. J. Kriegman. Eigenfaces vs. fisherfaces: recognition using class specific linear projection. *IEEE Transactions on Pattern Analysis and Machine Intelligence*, 19(7):711–720, July 1997.
3. M. J. Black and Y. Yacoob. Recognizing facial expressions in image sequences using local parameterized models of image motion. *International Journal of Computer Vision*, 25(1):23–48, 1997.
4. D. Blackburn, M. Bone, and P. J. Phillips. Facial recognition vendor test 2000: evaluation report, 2000.
5. V. Blanz and T. Vetter. A morphable model for the synthesis of 3d faces. In *Computer Graphics Proceedings, Annual Conference Series (SIGGRAPH)*, 1999.
6. D. Bolme, R. Beveridge, M. Teixeira, and B. Draper. The CSU face identification evaluation system: its purpose, features and structure. In *International Conference on Vision Systems*, pages 304–311, 2003.
7. L. Denes, P. Metes, and Y. Liu. Hyperspectral face database. Technical report, Robotics Institute, Carnegie Mellon University, 2002.
8. P. Ekman and W. Friesen. Constants across cultures in the face and emotion. *Journal of Personality and Social Psychology*, 17(2):124–129, 1971.
9. P. Ekman and W. Friesen. *Facial Action Coding System*. Consulting Psychologist Press, Palo Alto, CA, 1978.
10. P. Ekman and E. Rosenberg, editors. *What the face reveals*. Oxford University Press, New York, 1997.
11. P. Flynn, K. Bowyer, and P. J. Phillips. Assesment of time dependency in face recognition: an initial study. In *Audio- and Video-Based Biometric Person Authentication (AVBPA)*, pages 44–51, 2003.
12. W. Gao, B. Cao, S. Shan, D. Zhou, X. Zhang, and D. Zhao. CAS-PEAL large-scale Chinese face database and evaluation protocols. Technical Report JDL-TR-04-FR-001, Joint Research & Development Laboratory, 2004.
13. A. Georghiades, D. Kriegman, and P. Belhumeur. From few to many: generative models for recognition under variable pose and illumination. *IEEE Transactions on Pattern Analysis and Machine Intelligence*, 23(6):643–660, 2001.

14. D. Graham and N. Allison. Characterizing virtual eigensignatures for general purpose face recognition. In H. Wechsler, P. J. Phillips, V. Bruce, F. Fogelman-Soulie, and T. Huang, editors, *Face Recognition: From Theory to Applications*, NATO ASI Series F. pages 446–456, 1998.

15. R. Gross, I. Matthews, and S. Baker. Eigen light-fields and face recognition across pose. In *Proceedings of the Fifth International Conference on Face and Gesture Recognition*, pages 1–7, 2002.

16. R. Gross, J. Shi, and J. Cohn. Quo vadis face recognition? In *Third Workshop on Empirical Evaluation Methods in Computer Vision*, 2001.

17. P. Hallinan. *A Deformable Model for Face Recognition under Arbitrary Lighting Conditions*. Ph.D. thesis, Harvard University, 1995.

18. P. Hallinan, G. Gordon, A. Yuille, P. Giblin, and D. Mumford. *Two- and Three-dimensional Patterns of the face*. A.K. Peters, Wellesley, MA, 1999.

19. B.-W. Hwang, H. Byun, M.-C. Roh, and S.-W. Lee. Performance evaluation of face recognition algorithms on the asian face database, KFDB. In *Audio- and Video-Based Biometric Person Authentication (AVBPA)*, pages 557–565, 2003.

20. T. Kanade, J. Cohn, and Y. Tian. Comprehensive database for facial expression analysis. In *Proceedings of the Fourth IEEE International Conference on Automatic Face and Gesture Recognition*, pages 46–53, 2000.

21. T. Kanade, H. Saito, and S. Vedula. The 3D room: digitizing time-varying 3D events by synchronized multiple video streams. Technical Report CMU-RI-TR-98-34, CMU Robotics Institute, 1998.

22. M. Lyons, S. Akamatsu, M. Kamachi, and J. Gyoba. Coding facial expressions with Gabor wavelets. In *3rd International Conference on Automatic Face and Gesture Recognition*, pages 200–205, 1998.

23. L. Ma, T. Tan, Y. Wang, and D. Zhang. Personal identification based on iris texture analysis. *IEEE Transactions on Pattern Analysis and Machine Intelligence*, 25(12):1519–1533, 2003.

24. E. Marszalec, B. Martinkauppi, M. Soriano, and M. Pietkainen. A physics-based face database for color research. *Journal of Electronic Imaging*, 9(1):32–38, 2000.

25. A. R. Martinez and R. Benavente. The AR face database. Technical Report 24, Computer Vision Center(CVC) Technical Report, Barcelona, 1998.

26. K. Messer, J. Matas, J. Kittler, J. Luettin, and G. Maitre. XM2VTSDB: the extended M2VTS database. In *Second International Conference on Audio and Video-based Biometric Person Authentication*, 1999.

27. A. O'Toole, J. Harms, S. Snow, D. R. Hurst, M. Pappas, and H. Abdi. A video database of moving faces and people. submitted, 2003.

28. P. J. Phillips. Human identification technical challenges. In *IEEE International Conference on Image Processing*, volume 1, pages 22–25, 2002.

29. P. J. Phillips and E. M. Newton. Meta-analysis of face recognition algorithms. In *5th IEEE Conf. on Automatic Face and Gesture Recognition*, Washington, DC, 2002.

30. P. J. Phillips, P. Grother, J. M. Ross, D. Blackburn, E. Tabassi, and M. Bone. Face recognition vendor test 2002: evaluation report, March 2003.

31. P. J. Phillips, H. Moon, S. Rizvi, and P. J. Rauss. The FERET evaluation methodology for face-recognition algorithms. *IEEE Transactions on Pattern Analysis and Machine Intelligence*, 22(10):1090–1104, 2000.

32. P. J. Phillips, H. Wechsler, and P. Rauss. The FERET database and evaluation procedure for face-recognition algorithms. *Image and Vision Computing*, 16(5):295–306, 1998.

33. S. Romdhani, V. Blanz, and T. Vetter. Face identification by matching a 3D morphable model using linear shape and texture error functions. In *Proceedings of the European Conference on Computer Vision*, pages 3–19, 2002.

34. H. Rowley. *Neural Network-Based Face Detection*. Ph.D. thesis, Carnegie Mellon University, 1999.

35. H. Rowley, S. Baluja, and T. Kanade. Neural network-based face detection. *IEEE Transactions on Pattern Analysis and Machine Intelligence*, 20(1):23–38, 1998.

36. F. Samaria and A. Harter. Parameterisation of a stochastic model for human face identification. In *2nd IEEE Workshop on Applications of Computer Vision*, Sarasota, FL, 1994.

37. H. Schneiderman and T. Kanade. A statistical method for 3D object detection applied to faces and cars. In *Proc. of the IEEE Conference on Computer Vision and Pattern Recognition*, pages 746–751, 2000.

38. T. Sim, S. Baker, and M. Bsat. The CMU pose, illumination, and expression database. *IEEE Transactions on Pattern Analysis and Machine Intelligence*, 25(12):1615–1618, 2003.

39. D. Socolinsky, L. Wolff, J. Neuheisel, and C. Eveland. Illumination invariant face recognition using thermal infrared imagery. In *Proceedings of the IEEE Conference on Computer Vision and Pattern Recognition*, 2001.

40. K.-K. Sung and T. Poggio. Example-based learning for view-based human face detection. *IEEE Transactions on Pattern Analysis and Machine Intelligence*, 20(1):39–51, 1999.

41. M. Turk and A. Pentland. Face recognition using eigenfaces. In *Proceedings of the IEEE Conference on Computer Vision and Pattern Recognition*, 1991.

42. L. Wolff, D. Socolinsky, and C. Eveland. Quantitative measurement of illumination invariance for face recognition using thermal infrared imagery. In *IEEE Workshop on Computer Vision Beyond The Visible Spectrum: Methods and Applications*, 2001.

43. M.-H. Yang, D. Kriegman, and N. Ahuja. Detecting faces in images: a survey. *IEEE Transactions on Pattern Analysis and Machine Intelligence*, 24(1):34–58, 2002.

44. W. Zhao, R. Chellappa, A. Rosenfeld, and P. J. Phillips. Face recognition: a literature survey. Technical Report CS-TR4167, University of Maryland, 2000.

# Chapter 14. Evaluation Methods in Face Recognition

P. Jonathon Phillips, Patrick Grother, and Ross Micheals

National Institute of Standards and Technology, Gaithersburg, MD 20899, USA.
jonathon@nist.gov, pgrother@nist.gov, rossm@nist.gov

Automatic face recognition has a long history of independent evaluations with the three FERET evaluations [13, 14, 15] and the two Face Recognition Vendor Tests (FRVT) [2, 11]. These five evaluations have provided a basis for measuring progress in face recognition, determining the most promising approaches and identifying future research directions.

The heart of designing and conducting evaluations is the experimental protocol. The protocol states how an evaluation is to be conducted and how the results are to be computed. In this chapter we concentrate on describing the FERET and FRVT 2002 protocols.[1] The FRVT 2002 evaluation protocol is based in the FERET evaluation protocols. The FRVT 2002 protocol is designed for biometric evaluations in general, not just for evaluating face recognition algorithms.

The FRVT 2002 protocol was designed to allow us to compute a wide range of performance statistics. This includes the standard performance tasks of open-set and closed-set identification as well as verification. It also allows resampling techniques, similarity score normalization, measuring the variability of performance statistics, and covariate analysis [1, 5, 6, 9].

## 1 Standard Performance Measures

In face recognition and biometrics, performance is reported on three standard tasks: verification and open-set and closed-set identification. Each task has its own set of performance measures. All three tasks are closely related, with open-set identification being the general case.

A biometric system works by processing biometric samples. *Biometric samples* are recordings of a feature of a person that allows that person to be recognized. Examples of biometric samples are facial images and fingerprints. A biometric sample can consist of multiple recordings: for example, five images of a person acquired at the same time or a facial image and a fingerprint.

Computing performance requires three sets of images. The first is a *gallery* $\mathcal{G}$ which contains biometric samples of the people known to a system. The other two are *probe sets*. A *probe*

---

[1] This chapter focuses on measures and protocols used in FERET and FRVT. There are other protocols as well, such as BANCA (see http://www.ee.surrey.ac.uk/banca/).

is a biometric sample that is presented to the system for recognition, where recognition can be verification or identification . The first probe set is $\mathcal{P}_\mathcal{G}$ which contains biometric samples of people in a gallery (these samples are different from those in the gallery). The other probe set is $\mathcal{P}_\mathcal{N}$, which contains biometric samples of people who are not in a gallery.

Closed-set identification is the classic performance measure used in the automatic face recognition community, where it is known as identification. With closed-set identification, the basic question asked is: Whose face is this? This question is a meaningful one for closed-set identification because a biometric sample in a probe is always that of someone in the gallery. The general case of closed-set identification is open-set identification. With open-set identification, the person in the probe does not have to be somebody in the gallery; and here the basic question asked is: Do we know this face? With open-set identification, a system has to decide if the probe contains an image of a person in the gallery. If a system decides that a person is in a gallery, the system has to report the identity of the person. When a gallery is small, open-set identification can be referred to as a watch list task. When the gallery is large, then open-set identification models mugshot book searching and the operation of large automatic fingerprint identification systems (AFIS as they are sometimes called). Open-set and closed-set identification are sometimes referred to as 1 to many matching or 1:N matching. Depending on the context and author, 1 to many matching or 1:N matching can refer to either open-set or closed-set identification.

In a verification task, a person presents a biometrics sample to a system and claims an identity. The system then has to decide if the biometric sample belongs to the claimed identity. During verification, the basic question asked is: Is this person who he claims to be? Verification is also called authentication and 1-to-1 matching.

## 1.1 Open-Set Identification

Open-set identification is the general case task, with verification and closed-set identification being special cases. In the open-set identification task, a system determines if a probe $p_j$ corresponds to a person in a gallery $\mathcal{G}$. If the probe is determined to be in the gallery, the algorithm identifies the person in the probe.

A gallery $\mathcal{G}$ consists of a set of biometric samples $\{g_1, \ldots, g_{|\mathcal{G}|}\}$, with one biometric sample per person. When a probe $p_j$ is presented to a system, it is compared to the entire gallery. The comparison between a probe $p_j$ and each gallery biometric sample $g_i$ produces a similarity score $s_{ij}$. Larger similarity scores indicate that two biometric samples are more similar. (A distance measure between biometric samples can be converted to a similarity score by negating the distance measure.) A similarity score $s_{ij}$ is a *match score* if $g_i$ and $p_j$ are biometric samples of the same person. A similarity score $s_{ij}$ is a *nonmatch score* if $g_i$ and $p_j$ are biometric samples of different people. If $p_j$ is a biometric sample of a person in the gallery, let $g^*$ be its unique match in the gallery. The similarity score between $p_j$ and $g^*$ is denoted by $s_{*j}$. The function id() returns the identity of a biometric sample, with $\text{id}(p_j) = \text{id}(g^*)$. For identification, all similarity scores between a probe $p_j$ and a gallery are examined and sorted. A probe $p_j$ has rank $n$ if $s_{*j}$ is the $n^{th}$ largest similarity score. This is denoted by $\text{rank}(p_j) = n$. Rank 1 is sometimes called the top match.

Performance for open-set identification is characterized by two performance statistics: the detection and identification rate and the false alarm rate. We first look at the case where the

identity of a probe is someone in the gallery (i.e., $p_j \in \mathcal{P}_\mathcal{G}$). A probe is detected and identified
if the probe is correctly identified and the correct match score is above an operating threshold
$\tau$. These conditions formally correspond to:

- rank$(p_j) = 1$ and
- $s_{*j} \geq \tau$ for the similarity match where id$(p_j) = $ id$(g^*)$

for operating threshold $\tau$. The detection and identification rate is the fraction of probes in $\mathcal{P}_\mathcal{G}$
that are correctly detected and identified. The detection and identification rate is a function of
the operating threshold $\tau$. The detection and identification rate at threshold $\tau$ is

$$P_{DI}(\tau, 1) = \frac{|\{p_j : \text{rank}(p_j) = 1, \ \text{and } s_{*j} \geq \tau\}|}{|\mathcal{P}_\mathcal{G}|} \tag{1}$$

The second performance statistic is false alarm rate. The false alarm rate provides perfor-
mance when a probe is not of someone in the gallery (i.e., $p_j \in \mathcal{P}_\mathcal{N}$). This type of probe is also
referred to as an imposter. A false alarm occurs when the top match score for an imposter is
above the operating threshold. Formally, a false alarm occurs when

$$\max_i s_{ij} \geq \tau$$

The false alarm rate is the fraction of probes in $p_j \in \mathcal{P}_\mathcal{N}$ that are false alarms. This is computed
by

$$P_{FA}(\tau) = \frac{|\{p_j : \max_i s_{ij} \geq t\}|}{|\mathcal{P}_\mathcal{N}|} \tag{2}$$

The ideal system would have a detection and identification rate of 1.0 and a false alarm rate
of 0; all people in the gallery are detected and identified, and there are no false alarms. However, in real-world systems there is a trade-off between the detection and identification, and
false alarm rates. By changing the operating threshold, the performance rates change. Increasing an operating threshold lowers both the false alarm rate and the detection and identification
rate. Both these performance rates cannot be maximized simultaneously; there is a trade-off between them. This trade-off is shown on a receiver operator characteristic (ROC). An example of
an ROC is shown in Figure 14.1. The horizontal axis is the false alarm rate (scaled logarithmi-
cally). A logarithmic axis emphasizes low false alarms rates, which are the operating points of
interest in applications. The vertical axis is the detection and identification rate. When reporting
performance, the size of the gallery and both probe sets must be stated.

In the general open-set identification case, a system examines the top $n$ matches between
a probe and a gallery. A probe of a person in the gallery is detected and identified at rank $n$
if the probe is of rank $n$ or less and the correct match is above the operating threshold. These
conditions formally correspond to:

- rank$(p_j) \leq n$ and
- $s_{*j} \geq \tau$ for the similarity match where id$(p_j) = $ id$(g^*)$

The detection and identification rate at rank $n$ is the fraction of probes in $\mathcal{P}_\mathcal{G}$ who are correctly
detected and identified at rank $n$. The detection and identification rate at rank $n$ and threshold
$\tau$ is

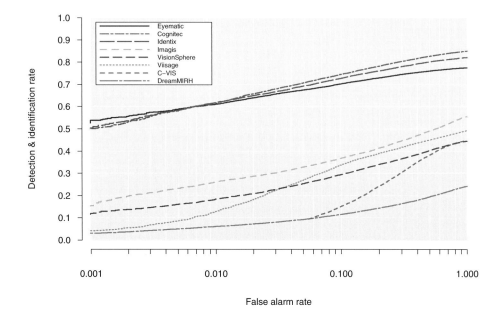

**Fig. 14.1.** Open-set identification performance reported on an ROC. The gallery consisted of 800 individuals. Performance is for FRVT 2002 and is explained in Section 3.3.

$$P_{DI}(\tau, n) = \frac{|\{p_j : \mathrm{rank}(p_j) \le n, \;\; \mathrm{and}\; s_{*j} \ge \tau\}|}{|\mathcal{P}_\mathcal{G}|} \tag{3}$$

The computation of $P_{FA}(\tau)$ at rank $n$ is the same as in the rank 1 case.

The general open-set identification performance can be plotted along three axes: detection and identification rate, false alarm rate, and rank. The performance of a system is represented as a surface in this three-dimensional parameter space. Instead of plotting the complete open-set identification performance as a surface, performance is usually plotted as two-dimensional slices. One example is Figure 14.1, where rank is held constant at 1, and the trade-off between the detection and identification rate and false alarm rate is shown. Figure 14.2 presents another format for reporting open-set identification performance. The vertical axis is the detection and identification rate, and the horizontal axis is rank on a logarithmic scale. Each curve is the performance of the same system at a different false alarm rate.

The method presented above for computing rank assumes that all the similarity scores between a probe and a gallery are unique. Special care must be taken if there are multiple similarity scores with the same value; we refer to these as tied similarity scores. There are three methods for handling tie scores: *optimistic*, *pessimistic*, and *average* rank. The optimistic rank is the number of similarity scores strictly greater than ($>$) $s_{*j} + 1$. In this case we assign a probe the highest possible rank. The pessimistic rank is the number of similarity scores greater than or equal to ($\ge$) $s_{*j} + 1$. In this case we assign a probe the lowest possible rank. The average rank is the average of the optimistic and pessimistic ranks. In the FRVT 2002 protocol the average rank was used. Resolving ties with the optimistic rank can lead to strange pathologies.

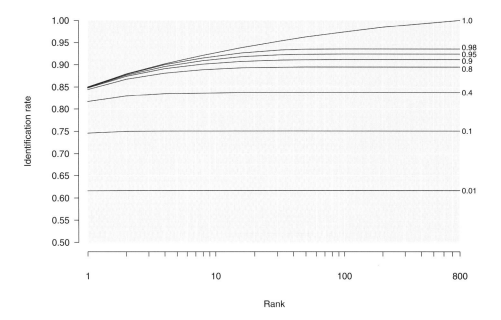

**Fig. 14.2.** Open-set identification performance as a function of rank for eight false alarm rates. The false alarm rate for each curve is on the right side of the graph. The gallery size is 800. The top curve is for a false alarm rate of 1.0.

For example, if a similarity matrix consisted of one value, the identification rate reported with the optimistic rank would be 100%.

## 1.2 Verification

Verification or authentication follows an operational model. During a typical verification task, a person presents his biometric sample to a system and claims to be a person in the system's gallery. The presented biometric sample is a probe. The system then compares the probe with the stored biometric sample of the person in the gallery. The comparison produces a similarity score. The system accepts the identity claim if the similarity score is greater than the system's operating threshold. The operational threshold is determined by the application, and different applications have different operational thresholds. Otherwise, the system rejects the claim.

There are two standard protocols for computing verification performance. The first is the round robin method. In the round robin protocol, both the probe set $\mathcal{P}_G$ and $\mathcal{P}_\mathcal{N}$ are the same set and are referred to as probe set $\mathcal{P}$. All scores between gallery and probe set samples are computed. All match scores between a gallery and a probe set are used to compute the verification rate, and all nonmatch scores are used to compute the false accept rate. Formally, for the round robin method, the verification rate is computed by

$$P_V(\tau) = \frac{|\{p_j : s_{ij} \geq \tau, \ \mathrm{id}(g_i) = \mathrm{id}(p_j)\}|}{|\mathcal{P}|} \tag{4}$$

and the false accept rate is computed by

$$P_{FA}(\tau) = \frac{|\{s_{ij} : s_{ij} \geq \tau \text{ and } \text{id}(g_i) \neq \text{id}(p_j)\}|}{(|\mathcal{P}| - 1)\,|\mathcal{G}|} \tag{5}$$

One complaint with the round robin protocol is that probes are used to generate both verification and false accept rates. There is a concern that this does not adequately model the situation where false identity claims are generated by people not in the gallery. The true imposter protocol addresses this concern. In the true imposter protocol, performance is computed from two probe sets, $\mathcal{P}_\mathcal{G}$ and $\mathcal{P}_\mathcal{N}$. The verification rate is computed from the match scores between a gallery and $\mathcal{P}_\mathcal{G}$. The number of match scores is the size of $\mathcal{P}_\mathcal{G}$. The false alarm rate is computed from all nonmatch scores between the gallery and $\mathcal{P}_\mathcal{N}$. These nonmatch scores are called true imposters because people in $\mathcal{P}_\mathcal{N}$ are not in the gallery. The number of nonmatch scores is $|\mathcal{P}_\mathcal{N}|\,|\mathcal{G}|$. Formally, for the true imposter method, the verification rate is computed by

$$P_V(\tau) = \frac{|\{p_j : s_{ij} \geq \tau, \ \text{id}(g_i) = \text{id}(p_j)\}|}{|\mathcal{P}_\mathcal{G}|} \tag{6}$$

and the false accept rate is computed by

$$P_{FA}(\tau) = \frac{|\{s_{ij} : s_{ij} \geq \tau\}|}{|\mathcal{P}_\mathcal{N}|\,|\mathcal{G}|} \tag{7}$$

## 1.3 Closed-Set Identification

Performance on the closed-set identification task is the classic performance statistic in face recognition. With closed-set identification, the question is not always "Is the top match correct?" but rather "Is the correct answer in the top $n$ matches?".

The first step in computing closed-set performance is to sort the similarity scores between $p_j$ and gallery $\mathcal{G}$, and compute the rank$(p_j)$. The identification rate for rank $n$, $P_I(n)$, is the fraction of probes at rank $n$ or lower. For rank $n$, let

$$C(n) = |\{p_j : \text{rank}(p_j) \leq n\}| \tag{8}$$

be the cumulative count of the number of probes of rank $n$ or less. The identification rate at rank $n$ is

$$P_I(n) = \frac{|C(n)|}{|\mathcal{P}_\mathcal{G}|} \tag{9}$$

The functions $C(n)$ and $P_I(n)$ are nondecreasing in $n$. The identification rate at rank 1, $P_I(1)$, is also called the correct identification rate and the top match rate or score.

Closed-set identification performance is reported on a cumulative match characteristic (CMC) . A CMC plots $P_I(n)$ as a function of rank $n$. Figure 14.3 shows a CMC. The horizontal axis is rank on a logarithmic scale, and the vertical axis is $P_I(n)$.

Closed-set identification performance is most often summarized with rank 1 performance, the other points such as rank 5, 10, or 20 are commonly used. The strength and weakness of the CMC is its dependence on gallery size, $|\mathcal{G}|$. To show the effect of gallery size on performance, rank 1 performance versus gallery size is plotted. To remove the effect of gallery size, one

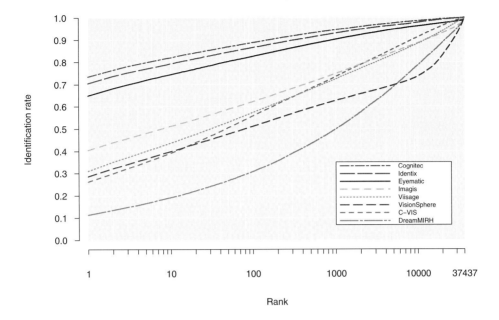

**Fig. 14.3.** Identification performance reported on a CMC. The gallery consisted of one image of 37,437 individuals. The probe set consisted of two images of each the 37,437 individuals in the gallery. Performance is for FRVT 2002 and is explained in Section 3.3.

can plot identification performance as a percentage of rank (i.e., performance when the correct answer is in the top 10%).

Closed-set identification is a special case of open-set identification where the probe set $\mathcal{P}_\mathcal{N}$ is empty and the operating threshold $\tau = -\infty$. An operating threshold of $\tau = -\infty$ corresponds to a false alarm rate of 1.0. This means that $s_{*j} \geq \tau$ for all match scores and all match scores are reported as alarms. Thus for any $n$, $P_{DI}(-\infty, n) = P_I(n)$. The curve in Figure 14.2 with a false alarm rate of 1.0 (top curve) is the CMC for the closed-set version of this experiment. The CMC for an open-set experiment is closed-set identification performance computed in the open-set gallery $\mathcal{G}$ and probe set $\mathcal{P}_\mathcal{G}$. In Figure 14.2, it is interesting to note the difference between the CMC and the performance curve with a false alarm rate of 0.98. This shows that there are a reasonable number of match scores with a low similarity score.

## 1.4 Normalization

The FRVT 2002 protocol introduced similarity score normalization procedures to biometric evaluations. Normalization is a postprocessing function $f$ that adjusts similarity scores based on a specific gallery. A normalization function is $f : R^{|\mathcal{G}|} \to R^{|\mathcal{G}|}$. The input to a normalization function is a vector $\mathbf{s} = (s_{1j}, \ldots, s_{|\mathcal{G}|j})$ of all similarity scores between a probe $p_j$ and a gallery $\mathcal{G}$. The output is a vector $\widehat{\mathbf{s}}$ of length $|\mathcal{G}|$ which is a new set of normalized similarity scores $\widehat{\mathbf{s}} = (\widehat{s_{1j}}, \ldots, \widehat{s_{|\mathcal{G}|j}})$ between a probe $p_j$ and a gallery $\mathcal{G}$. The normalization function attempts to adjust for variations among probes and to emphasize differences among the gallery signatures. The final performance scores are computed from the normalized similarity scores. An example of a normalization function is

$$\widehat{s_{ij}} = \frac{s_{ij} - \mathrm{mean}(\mathbf{s})}{\mathrm{sd}(\mathbf{s})}$$

where mean($\mathbf{s}$) is the sample mean of the components of $\mathbf{s}$ and sd($\mathbf{s}$) is the sample standard deviation of the componenets of $\mathbf{s}$. FRVT 2002 and the HumanID Gait Challenge problem demonstrated the effectiveness of normalization for verification [16].

If the gallery changes, similarity scores must be normalized again. This has implications for scoring techniques that require performance on multiple galleries. Traditionally, verification has been referred to as 1-to-1 matching. This is because, during verification, one probe is matched with one gallery signature. Normalization requires that a probe be compared with a gallery. When normalization is applied, is verification still 1-to-1 matching?

## 1.5 Variability

The variance of performance statistics in biometrics is an important but often overlooked subject in biometrics. We look at variations in verification performance. The first is how performance varies with different galleries. This models the performance of a system that is installed at different locations. The second is how performance varies for different classes of probes. For example, what is the difference in performance for male and female probes? Each combination of the gallery and probe sets generates a different ROC. To study the variation, it is necessary to combine results over a set of ROCs. One method of combining results is to measure the variation of the verification rate for each false alarm rate. This models the situation where one can readjust the operating threshold for each gallery or probe set. For many applications, this is not feasible or desirable. However, this is an appropriate technique for combining ROCs from multiple systems because it is not possible to set uniform operating thresholds across different systems. For the same system, it is possible to set one operating threshold across all galleries and probe sets. Using this *base-operating threshold*, one computes the verification and false accept rate for each gallery and probe set. The resulting verification and false alarm rates vary across different galleries and probe sets. This method for computing variance in performance models the situation in which the operating threshold is set once for an application. Setting the base-operating threshold can be based on an overall desired performance level for the population that uses the system. In the FRVT 2002 protocol, the base-operating threshold is set based on the system performance on an aggregate population. The base-operating threshold corresponds to a specific false accept rate on the aggregate population, which is referred to as the *nominal false accept rate*.

In most ROCs, verification performance is reported for a single large gallery. The results do not address the important question of how performance varies if the people in the gallery are different. This question was studied in FRVT 2002, and here we present the technique that was used. To measure variation due to gallery change, verification performance was computed for the 12 galleries (Fig. 14.4). Each of the 12 galleries consisted of 3000 different people. The probe set contained two images of each person in the gallery and 6000 true imposters (two images of 3000 individuals). The centerline is the aggregate performance for the 12 galleries.

For selected operating points, performance was computed for the 12 small galleries and probe sets. Verification rates and false accept rates were computed for each of the 12 galleries. Thus at each operating threshold there are 12 pairs of verification and false accept rates. A standard error ellipse was computed for each set of verification and false accept rates.

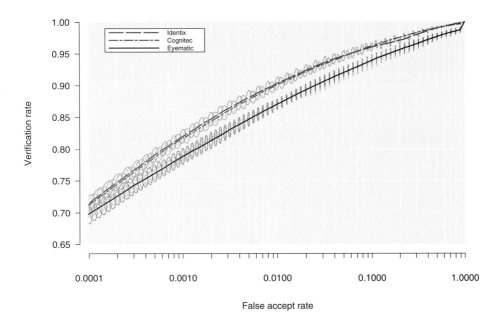

**Fig. 14.4.** Standard error ellipses for verification performance for Cognitec, Eyematic, and Identix. The standard error was computed for 12 galleries of size 3000. The center line is the ROC performance for the aggregate of all 12 galleries. The ellipses are two times the standard deviation at select performance points. Each ellipse is computed from the performance of the 12 small galleries at the selected performance points. Each point clustered around an ellipse corresponds to 1 of the 12 galleries. Performance is for FRVT 2002 and is explained in Section 3.3.

Error ellipses in Figure 14.4 are two times the standard deviation of the verification and false accept rates along the appropriate axes. An ellipse gives an estimate of the range in performance that could result if the people in the gallery are changed. If the large gallery were larger, it would be possible to compute performance for more small galleries of size 3000. A greater number of small galleries would increase the accuracy of the error ellipse. However, the size of the ellipses would not decrease as the number of small galleries is increased. This is because the error ellipses are a function of the multiple small galleries, and the composition of the small galleries reflects the natural variation in the population. The natural variation is always present: more small galleries increase the accuracy of the estimated variation in the performance owing to the natural composition of the population. In the HCInt the ellipses are estimated from disjoint galleries and probe sets. This avoids many of the issues associated with resampling techniques. Resampling techniques require making assumptions about the distributional properties of the similarity scores. Typical assumptions are that similarity scores are independent and identically distributed (iid). When interpreting the meaning of error ellipses, a number of subtle facts must be noted. The error ellipses are not error bounds on the ROC. Rather, error ellipses are a measure of the variance in performance that occurs by changing the gallery. The standard error is an empirical estimate of the variation. They are not confidence intervals. Confidence intervals decrease in size as the number of samples increase. Estimating confidence intervals requires that one knows or can estimate the underlying distribution.

## 2 FERET and FRVT 2002 Evaluation Protocols

A set of design principles and its associated testing protocol describe how evaluations are designed and conducted. Design principles outline the core philosophy and guiding beliefs when designing an evaluation; the evaluation protocol provides the implementation details.

The de facto evaluation protocol standards in face recognition and biometrics are the FRVT 2002 and FERET evaluation protocols [11, 13]. The FRVT 2002 evaluation protocol is based on the September 1996 evaluation protocol. The FRVT 2002 protocol added general biometric samples, normalization of similarity scores, and an XML-based specification [7]. The XML-based specification is extensible to other biometrics and is being used for fingerprint recognition evaluation.

The design of FRVT 2002, along with the FERET evaluations and FRVT 2000, followed the precepts for biometrics evaluations articulated by Phillips et al. [12]. Succinctly stated, the precepts are as follows:

1. Evaluations are designed and administered by groups that are independent of the algorithm developers and vendors being tested.
2. Test data are sequestered and not seen by the participants prior to an evaluation.
3. The evaluation test design, protocol, and methodology are published.
4. Performance results are spread in a manner that allows for meaningful differences among the participants.

Points 1 and 2 ensure fairness of an evaluation. Point 1 provides assurance that the test is not designed to favor one participant over another. Independent evaluations help enforce points 2 and 4. In addition, point 2 ensures that systems are evaluated for their ability to generalize performance to new data sets, not the ability of the system to be tuned to a particular set of biometric samples. When judging and interpreting results, it is necessary to understand the conditions under which algorithms and systems are tested. These conditions are described in the evaluation test design, protocol, and methodology. Tests are administered using an evaluation protocol that identifies the mechanics of the tests and the manner in which the tests will be scored. For face recognition, the protocol states the number and types of images of each person in the test, how the output from the algorithm is recorded, and how the performance results are reported. Publishing the evaluation protocol, as recommended in point 3, lets the readers of published results understand how the results were computed.

Point 4 addresses the *three bears* problem. Phillips et al. [13] first articulated the three bears problem when designing evaluations. The three bears problem sets guiding principles for designing an evaluation of the right level of difficulty. If all the scores for all algorithms are too high and within the same error margin, one cannot distinguish among the algorithms tested. In addition, if the scores are too high in an evaluation, it is an indication that the evaluation was in reality an exercise in "tuning" algorithm parameters. If the scores are too low, it is not possible to determine what problems have been solved. The goal in designing an evaluation is to have variation among the scores. There are two types of variation. The first is variation among the experiments in an evaluation. Most evaluations consist of a set of experiments where each experiment reports performance on different problems in face recognition. For example, experiments might look at changes in lighting or subject pose. The second type of variation is among algorithms for each experiment. The variation in performance among the experiments lets one know which problems are currently sufficiently solved for consideration in field testing, which problems are research problems, and which problems are beyond the capabilities of the field. The variation in algorithm performance lets one know which techniques are best for a particular experiment. If all the scores for all algorithms across all experiments are virtually the same, one cannot distinguish among the algorithms.

The key elements that ease adoption of points 3 and 4 can be incorporated into the evaluation protocol. For the FERET and FRVT evaluations, this was the FERET and FRVT 2002 evaluation protocol. It was designed to assess the state of the art, advance the state of the art, and point to future directions of research. The ability to accomplish these three goals simultaneously was through a protocol whose framework allows the computation of performance statistics for multiple galleries and probe sets; which, in turn, allows the FERET and FRVT 2002 evaluation protocol to solve the three bears problem by including galleries and probe sets of different levels of difficulty in the evaluation. It produces a comprehensive set of performance statistics that assess the state of the art and the progress in face recognition; it also points to future directions of research. The use of an XML-based specification allows this evaluation protocol to become a formal standard for biometric evaluation.

The solution to the three bears problem lies in the selection of images used for the evaluation. The characteristics and quality of the images are major factors in determining the difficulty of the problem being evaluated. For example, the location of the face in an image can affect problem difficulty. The problem is much easier to address if a face must be in the center of the image compared to the case where a face can be located anywhere within the image. In FERET and FRVT 2002 data sets, variability was introduced by the size of the database, inclusion of images obtained at different dates, and the use of both outdoor and indoor locations. This resulted in changes in lighting, scale, and background.

The testing protocol is based on a set of design principles. The design principles directly relate the evaluation to the face recognition problem being evaluated. In particular, for FERET and FRVT 2000, the driving applications were searching large databases and access control. Stating the design principles allows one to assess how appropriate the FERET tests and FRVT 2000 are for a particular face recognition algorithm. Also, design principles assist in determining if an evaluation methodology for testing algorithm(s) is appropriate for a particular application.

The FERET and FRVT 2002 evaluation protocols consist of two parts. The first is the rules for conducting an evaluation, and the second is the format of the results that allow scoring. For FERET this was file format-based, and for FRVT 2002 the file format specifications are XML-based.

The input to an algorithm or system being evaluated is two sets of biometrics samples: target set $\mathcal{T}$ and a query set $\mathcal{Q}$. Galleries and probe sets are constructed from the target and query sets, respectively. The output from an algorithm is a similarity measure $s_{ij}$ between all pairs of images $t_i$ from the target set and $q_j$ from the query set. A similarity measure is a numerical measure of how similar two faces are. Performance statistics are computed from the similarity measures. A complete set of similarity scores between all pairs of biometric samples from the target and query set is referred to as a *similarity matrix*. The first rule in the FERET and FRVT 2002 evaluation protocol is that a complete similarity matrix must be computed. This rule guarantees that performance statistics can be computed for all algorithms.

To be able to compute performance for multiple galleries and probe sets requires that multiple biometric samples of a person are placed in both the target and query sets. This leads to the second rule: Each biometrics sample in the target and query sets is considered to contain a unique sample. In practice, this rule is enforced by giving each sample in the target and query sets a unique random identifier.

The third rule is that training is completed prior to the start of an evaluation. This forces each algorithm to have a general representation for faces, not a representation tuned to a specific gallery. Also, if training were specific to a gallery, it would not be possible to construct multiple galleries and probe sets from a single run. An algorithm would have to be retrained and the evaluation rerun for each gallery. In the FRVT 2002 protocol, similarity score normalization is permitted. This allows adjustments based on the samples in a gallery.

Using target and query sets allows us to compute performance for different categories of biometric samples. Using face recognition as an example, possible probe categories include (1) gallery and probe images taken on the same day, (2) duplicates taken within a week of the gallery image, and (3) duplicates where the time between the images is at least 1 year. This is illustrated in the following example. A target and query set consists of the same set of facial images. Eight images of each face are taken, indoors and outdoors, with two different facial expressions on two different days. From these target and query sets, one can measure the effects of indoor versus outdoor illumination by constructing a gallery of indoor images and a probe set of outdoor images, both consisting of neutral expressions taken on the first day. Construction of similar galleries and probe sets would allow one to test the effects of temporal or expression changes. The effect of covariates such as the age and sex of a person can also be measured. It is the ability to construct virtual galleries from the target set and virtual probe sets from the query set that allows the FERET and FRVT 2002 protocol to perform detailed analysis.

The FERET and FRVT 2002 evaluation protocol allows computation of performance statistics for verification and open-set and closed-set identification tasks. The protocol is sufficiently flexible that one can estimate performance using subsampling and resampling techniques. For example, galleries of varying size are created to measure the effects of gallery size on performance. To estimate the variability of performance, multiple galleries are created.

## 3 Evaluation Reviews

Given the numerous theories and techniques that are applicable to face recognition, it is clear that evaluation and benchmarking of these algorithms is crucial. Evaluations and benchmarking allow testing of theories and identification of the most promising approaches. The most important face recognition evaluations are the three FERET evaluations and the two FRVT. All five evaluations build on each other. The three FERET evaluations were administered in August 1994, March 1995, and September 1996. The two FRVT evaluations were administered in 2000 and 2002.

## 3.1 FERET Evaluations

Until the FERET evaluations, there did not exist a common evaluation protocol that included a large data set and a standard evaluation method. This made it difficult to assess the status of face recognition technology, even though many existing systems reported almost perfect performance on small data sets.

The first FERET evaluation test was administered in August 1994 [14]. This evaluation established a baseline for face recognition algorithms and was designed to measure performance of algorithms that could automatically locate, normalize, and identify faces. This evaluation consisted of three tests, each with a different gallery and probe set. The first test measured identification performance from a gallery of 316 individuals with one image per person; the second was a false-alarm test; and the third measured the effects of pose changes on performance. The second FERET evaluation was administered in March 1995; it consisted of a single test that measured identification performance from a gallery of 817 individuals and included 463 duplicates in the probe set [14]. (A duplicate is a probe for which the corresponding gallery image was taken on a different day; there were only 60 duplicates in the Aug94 evaluation.) The third and last evaluation (Sep96) was administered in September 1996 and March 1997.

### Database

The FERET database was the first data set available to researchers. In terms of the number of people, it is the largest data set that is publically available. The images in the database were initially acquired with a 35 mm camera and then digitized.

The images were collected in 15 sessions between August 1993 and July 1996. Each session lasted 1 or 2 days, and the location and setup did not change during the session. Sets of 5 to 11 images of each individual were acquired under relatively unconstrained conditions. They included two frontal views; in the first of these (**fa**) a neutral facial expression was requested and in the second (**fb**) a different facial expression was requested (these requests were not always honored); (Fig. 14.5). For 200 individuals, a third frontal view was taken using a different camera and different lighting condition; this is referred to as the **fc** image. The remaining images were nonfrontal and included right and left profiles, right and left quarter profiles, and right and left half profiles. The FERET database consists of 1564 sets of images (1199 original sets and 365 duplicate sets), a total of 14,126 images. A development set of 503 sets of images were released to researchers; the remaining images were sequestered for independent evaluation. In late 2000 the entire FERET database was released along with the Sep96 evaluation protocols, evaluation scoring code, and baseline principal component analysis (PCA) algorithm.

### Evaluation

Details of the three FERET evaluations can be found elsewhere [13, 14, 15]. The results of the most recent FERET evaluation (Sep96) is briefly reviewed here. Because the entire FERET

| fa | fb | duplicate I | fc | duplicate II |

**Fig. 14.5.** Images from the FERET dataset. The **fa** and **fb** were taken with the same lighting condition with different expressions. The **fc** image has a different lighting condition than the **fa** and **fb** images. The duplicate I image was taken within 1 year of the **fa** image, and the duplicate II and **fa** image were taken at least 1 year apart.

data set has been released, the Sep96 protocol provides a good benchmark for performance of new algorithms. For the Sep96 evaluation, there was a primary gallery consisting of one frontal image (**fa**) per person for 1196 individuals. This was the core gallery used to measure performance for the following four different probe sets.

- **fb** probes – gallery and probe images of an individual taken on the same day with the same lighting (1195 probes)
- **fc** probes – gallery and probe images of an individual taken on the same day with different lighting (194 probes)
- Dup I probes – gallery and probe images of an individual taken on different days—duplicate images (722 probes)
- Dup II probes – gallery and probe images of an individual taken more than a year apart (the gallery consisted of 894 images; 234 probes)

The Sep96 evaluation tested the following 10 algorithms

- An algorithm from Excalibur Corporation (Carlsbad, CA)(September 1996)
- Two algorithms from MIT Media Laboratory (September 1996) [8, 18]
- Three linear discriminant analysis (LDA)-based algorithms from Michigan State University [17] (September 1996) and the University of Maryland  [4, 21] (September 1996 and March 1997)
- A gray-scale projection algorithm from Rutgers University [19] (September 1996)
- An elastic graph matching (EGM) algorithm from the University of Southern California [10, 20] (March 1997)
- A baseline PCA algorithm [9, 18]
- A baseline normalized correlation matching algorithm

Performance was computed for both closed-set identification and verification. Three of the algorithms performed very well: Probabilistic PCA from MIT [8], subspace LDA from UMD [21, 22], and EGM from USC [10, 20].

A number of lessons were learned from the FERET evaluations. The first is that performance depends on the probe category, and there is a difference between best and average algorithm performance. Another lesson is that the scenario has an impact on performance. For identification, on the **fb** and duplicate probes the USC scores were 94% and 59%, and the UMD scores were 96% and 47%.

**Summary**

The availability of the FERET database and evaluation technology has had a significant impact on progress in the development of face recognition algorithms. The FERET data set facilitated the development of algorithms, and the FERET series of tests has allowed advances in algorithm development to be quantified. This is illustrated by the performance improvements in the MIT algorithms between March 1995 and September 1996 and in the UMD algorithms between September 1996 and March 1997.

Another important contribution of the FERET evaluations is the identification of areas for future research. In general, the test results revealed three major problem areas: recognizing duplicates, people under illumination variations, and under pose variations.

**3.2  FRVT 2000**

The Sep96 FERET evaluation measured performance on prototype laboratory systems. After March 1997 there was rapid advancement in the development of commercial face recognition systems. This advancement represented both a maturing of face recognition technology and the development of the supporting system and infrastructure necessary to create commercial off-the-shelf (COTS) systems. By the beginning of 2000, COTS face recognition systems were readily available.

To assess the state of the art in COTS face recognition systems, the FRVT 2000 was organized [2]. FRVT 2000 was a technology evaluation that used the Sep96 evaluation protocol but was significantly more demanding than the Sep96 FERET evaluation.

Participation in FRVT 2000 was restricted to COTS systems, with companies from Australia, Germany, and the United States participating. The five companies evaluated were Banque-Tec International, C-VIS Computer Vision und Automation GmbH, Miros, Lau Technologies, and Visionics Corporation.

A greater variety of imagery was used in FRVT 2000 than in the FERET evaluations. FRVT 2000 reported results in eight general categories: compression, distance, expression, illumination, media, pose, resolution, and temporal. There was no common gallery across all eight categories; the sizes of the galleries and probe sets varied from one category to another.

We briefly summarize the results of FRVT 2000. Full details can be found in Blackburn et al. [2] and include identification and verification performance statistics. The media experiments showed that changes in media do not adversely affect performance. Images of a person were obtained simultaneously on conventional film and digital media. The compression experiments showed that compression does not adversely affect performance. Probe images compressed up to 40:1 did not reduce recognition rates. The compression algorithm was JPEG.

FRVT 2000 also examined the effect of the pose angle on performance. The results show that pose does not significantly affect performance up to $\pm 25°$, but that performance is significantly affected when the pose angle reaches $\pm 40°$.

In the illumination category, two key effects were investigated. The first was indoor lighting changes. This was equivalent to the **fc** probes in FERET. For the best system in this category, the indoor change of lighting did not significantly affect performance. In a second experiment, recognition with an indoor gallery and an outdoor probe set was computed. Moving from indoor to outdoor lighting significantly affected performance, with the best system achieving an identification rate of only 0.55.

The temporal category is equivalent to the duplicate probes in FERET. To compare progress since FERET, dup I and dup II scores were reported. For FRVT 2000 the dup I identification rate was 0.63 compared with 0.58 for FERET. The corresponding rates for dup II were 0.64 for FRVT 2000 and 0.52 for FERET. These results show that there was algorithmic progress between the FERET and FRVT 2000 evaluations. FRVT 2000 showed that two common concerns, the effects of compression and recording media, do not affect performance. It also showed that future areas of interest continue to be duplicates, pose variations, and illumination variations generated when comparing indoor images with outdoor images.

## 3.3  FRVT 2002

The FRVT 2002 was a large-scale evaluation of automatic face recognition technology. The primary objective of FRVT 2002 was to provide performance measures for assessing the ability of automatic face recognition systems to meet real-world requirements. Ten participants were evaluated under the direct supervision of the FRVT 2002 organizers in July and August 2002. Ten companies participated in FRVT 2002: AcSys Biometrics Corp., Cognitec Systems GmbH, C-VIS Computer Vision und Automation GmbH, Dream Mirh, Eyematics Interfaces, Iconquest, Identix, Imagis Technologies, Viisage Technology, and VisionSphere Technologies.

FRVT 2002 consisted of two parts: a high computational intensity test (HCInt) and a medium computational intensity test (MCInt). The heart of the FRVT 2002 was the HCInt, which consisted of 121,589 operational images of 37,437 people. The images were provided from the U.S. Department of State's Mexican nonimmigrant visa archive. From these data, real-world performance figures were computed on a very large data set. Performance statistics were computed for verification, closed-set identification, and open-set identification (watch list) tasks. Open-set identification performance is reported in Figure 14.1, closed-set identification performance is reported in Figure 14.3, and verification performance with error ellipses is given in Figure 14.2 for the HCInt (only 8 of the 10 companies took part in the HCInt portion of FRVT 2002). The MCInt measured performance on facial images from different categories. The categories included mugshot style images, still images taken outside, nonfrontal indoor images, and morphed nonfrontal images.

FRVT 2002 results show that normal changes in indoor lighting do not significantly affect performance of the top systems. Approximately the same performance results were obtained using two indoor data sets with different lighting in FRVT 2002. In both experiments, the best performer had a 90% verification rate at a false accept rate of 1%. Compared with similar experiments conducted 2 years earlier in FRVT 2000, the results of FRVT 2002 indicate there was a 50% reduction in error rates. For the best face recognition systems, the recognition rate for faces captured outdoors, at a false accept rate of 1%, was only 50%. Thus, face recognition from outdoor imagery remains a challenging area of research.

An important question for real-world applications is the rate of decrease in performance as time increases between the acquisition of the database of images and the new images presented to a system. FRVT 2002 found that for the top systems performance degraded at approximately 5% points per year.

One open question in face recognition is: How does the database and watch list size affect performance? Because of the large number of people and images in the FRVT 2002 data set, FRVT 2002 reported the first large-scale results on this question. For the best system, the top-rank identification rate was 85% on a database of 800 people, 83% on a database of 1600, and 73% on a database of 37,437. For every doubling of database size, performance decreases by two to three overall percentage points. More generally, identification performance decreases linearly in the logarithm of the database size.

Previous evaluations have reported face recognition performance as a function of imaging properties. For example, previous reports compared the differences in performance when using indoor versus outdoor images or frontal versus nonfrontal images. FRVT 2002, for the first time, examined the effects of demographics on performance. Two major effects were found. First, recognition rates for men were higher than for women. For the top systems, identification rates for men were 6% to 9% points higher than that of women. For the best system, identification performance on men was 78% and for women was 69%. Second, recognition rates for older people were higher than for younger people. For 18- to 22-year-olds the average identification rate for the top systems was 62%, and for 38- to 42-year-olds it was 74%. For every 10 years' increase in age, on average performance increases approximately 5% through age 63.

FRVT 2002 looked at two of these new techniques. The first was the three-dimensional morphable models technique of Blanz and Vetter [3]. Morphable models comprise a technique for improving recognition of nonfrontal images. FRVT 2002 found that Blanz and Vetter's technique significantly increased recognition performance. The second technique is recognition from video sequences. Using FRVT 2002 data, recognition performance using video sequences was the same as the performance using still images.

In summary, the key lessons learned in FRVT 2002 were (1) given reasonable controlled indoor lighting, the current state of the art in face recognition is 90% verification at a 1% false accept rate; (2) face recognition in outdoor images is a research problem; (3) the use of morphable models can significantly improve nonfrontal face recognition; (4) Identification performance decreases linearly in the logarithm of the size of the gallery; and (5) in face recognition applications, accommodations should be made for demographic information, as characteristics such as age and sex can significantly affect performance.


# 4 Conclusions

Periodic face recognition evaluations have advanced the field of face recognition from its infancy during the early 1990s to the deployment of systems. The periodic evaluations have developed standard evaluation protocols and methods for reporting performance scores. As the field of face recognition has advanced, there has been concomitant advancement in the evaluation techniques. This is leading to different styles of evaluations, each with its ability to answer different questions.

The face recognition community, and biometrics in general, has developed a range of evaluations in terms of number of people and images. To provide a rough guide to evaluation size, we introduce the following nomenclature

- Small: $\sim$1000 signatures and $\sim$330 individuals
- Medium: $\sim$10,000 signatures and $\sim$3300 individuals
- Large: $\sim$100,000 signatures and $\sim$33,000 individuals
- Very large: $\sim$1,000,000 signatures and $\sim$330,000 individuals
- Extremely large: $\sim$10,000,000 signatures and $\sim$3,300,000 individuals

Each size has its own role and place. A larger evaluation is not inherently better, especially when cost is considered. Most evaluations have been small, but they have had a positive impact on the development and assessment of biometrics.

The FERET, FRVT 2000, and FRVT 2002 MCInt evaluations were small to medium evaluations and were able to differentiate between large and small effects on performance. The FERET evaluations showed a big difference in performance between images taken on the same day and images taken on different days. This showed that the interesting problem for face recognition was images taken on different days. The FRVT 2002 MCInt results showed a large difference in performance between recognition of nonfrontal images and nonfrontal images that have been morphed. The MCInt results showed that morphable models improved performance for nonfrontal images. Evaluation such as FERET and FRVT 2002 MCInt are good for making an assessment on (1) a specified set of experiments, and (2) when one is looking to distinguish between large and small effects.

The FRVT 2002 HCInt allowed a more detailed analysis and was able to estimate the variance of performance statistics and measure the effects of covariates on performance. This analysis required not only large numbers of images and people but also an appropriate number of errors. If there had only been 10 or 100 errors, we would not have been able to perform a detailed covariate analysis. When designing very large and extremely large evaluations, one needs to state the objective of the evaluation and have an idea of the overall accuracy of the biometric being tested. For example, if a biometric has an identification rate of 0.9999 (error rate of one in 10,000), an evaluation on a data set of 100,000 images would, on average, produce 10 errors. To be able to perform a detailed analysis of performance, such as in the FRVT 2002 HCInt, we would require a test set several orders of magnitude larger.

Evaluations of all sizes are needed and have their role in assessing performance of biometrics. Factors affecting the size and design of an evaluation include the evaluation goals and the overall accuracy of a biometric: the greater the accuracy of the biometric, the larger the required size of an evaluation; and the more detailed analysis needed, the larger is the required size of an evaluation. At the other end of the scale, an evaluation with very specific and defined purposes maybe able to meet its goals with a small evaluation.

When research in automatic face recognition began, the primary goal was to develop recognition algorithms. With progress in face recognition, the goal of understanding the properties of face recognition algorithms has joined the goal of developing algorithms. Understanding the properties of face recognition lies in computational experiments.

Independent evaluations provide an assessment of the state-of-the-art, but do not provide an understanding of the fundamental properties of face recognition algorithms. The province of answering these types of question is computational experiments. For example, FRVT 2002 showed that men are easier to recognize than women. However, FRVT 2002 was not designed to answer the more fundamental question of why men are easier to recognize than women. The computational experiments are only beginning to be performed, but they are starting to have an effect. They will give greater understanding of face recognition and provide a strong scientific underpinning.

# References

1. J. R. Beveridge, K. She, B. A. Draper, and G. H. Givens. A nonparametric statistical comparison of principal component and linear discriminant subspaces for face recognition. In *Proceedings of IEEE Conference on Computer Vision and Pattern Recognition*, volume 1, pages 535–542, 2001.

2. D. Blackburn, M. Bone, and P. J. Phillips. Face recognition vendor test 2000. Technical report, http://www.frvt.org, 2001.

3. V. Blanz and T. Vetter. A morphable model for the synthesis of 3D faces. In *Proceedings, SIGGRAPH'99*, pages 187–194, 1999.

4. K. Etemad and R. Chellappa. Discriminant analysis for recognition of human face images. *J. Opt. Soc. Am. A*, 14:1724–1733, 1997.

5. G. H. Givens, J. R. Beveridge, B. A. Draper, and D. Bolme. A statistical assessment of subject factors in the PCA recognition of human faces. In *CVPR Workshop on Statistical Analysis in Computer Vision*, 2003.

6. R. J. Micheals and T. Boult. Efficient evaluation of classification and recognition systems. In *Proceedings of IEEE Conference on Computer Vision and Pattern Recognition*, volume 1, pages 50–57, 2001.

7. R. J. Micheals, P. Grother, and P. J. Phillips. The NIST HumanID evaluation framework. In J. Kittler and M. S. Nixon, editors, *Third Inter. Conf. on Audio- and Video-based Biometric Person Authentication*, volume LNCS 2688, pages 403–411. Springer, New York, 2003.

8. B. Moghaddam, C. Nastar, and A. Pentland. Bayesian face recognition using deformable intensity surfaces. In *Proceedings of IEEE Conference on Computer Vision and Pattern Recognition*, pages 638–645, 1996.

9. H. Moon and P. J. Phillips. Computational and performance aspects of PCA-based face-recognition algorithms. *Perception*, 30:303–321, 2001.

10. K. OkadaK. J. Steffens, T. Maurer, H. Hong, E. Elagin, H. Neven, and C. von der Malsburg. The Bochum/USC face recognition system. In H. Wechsler, P. J. Phillips, V. Bruce, F. Fogelman Soulie, and T. S. Huang, editors, *Face Recognition: From Theory to Applications*. Springer-Verlag, Berlin, 1998.

11. P. J. Phillips, P. Grother, R. Micheals, D. Blackburn, E. Tabassi, and J. Bone. Face recognition vendor test 2002: Evaluation report. Technical Report NISTIR 6965, National Institute of Standards and Technology, 2003 (http://www.frvt.org).

12. P. J. Phillips, A. Martin, C. L. Wilson, and M. Przybocki. An introduction to evaluating biometric systems. *Computer*, 33:56–63, 2000.

13. P. J. Phillips, H. Moon, S. Rizvi, and P. Rauss. The FERET evaluation methodology for face-recognition algorithms. *IEEE Trans. PAMI*, 22:1090–1104, 2000.

14. P. J. Phillips, H. Wechsler, J. Huang, and P. Rauss. The FERET database and evaluation procedure for face-recognition algorithms. *Image and Vision Computing*, 16(5):295–306, 1998.

15. S. Rizvi, P. J. Phillips, and H. Moon. A verification protocol and statistical performance analyis for face recognition algorithms. In *Proceedings of IEEE Conference on Computer Vision and Pattern Recognition*, pages 833–838, 1998.

16. S. Sarkar, P. J. Phillips, Z. Liu, I. Robledo, P. Grother, and K. W. Bowyer. The HumanID gait challenge problem: data sets, performance, and analysis. Technical report, 2003 (http://www.gaitchallenge.org).

17. D. Swets and J. Weng. Using discriminant eigenfeatures for image retrieval. *IEEE Trans. PAMI*, 18(8):831–836, 1996.
18. M. Turk and A. Pentland. Eigenfaces for recognition. *J. Cognitive Neuroscience*, 3(1):71–86, 1991.
19. J. Wilder. Face recognition using transform coding of gray scale projection projections and the neural tree network. In R. J. Mammone, editor, *Artifical Neural Networks with Applications in Speech and Vision*, pages 520–536. Chapman Hall, Lodon, 1994.
20. L. Wiskott, J.-M. Fellous, N. Kruger, and C. von der Malsburg. Face recognition by elasric bunch graph matching. *IEEE Trans. PAMI*, 17(7):775–779, 1997.
21. W. Zhao, R. Chellappa, and A. Krishnaswamy. Discriminant analysis of principal components for face recognition. In *3rd International Conference on Automatic Face and Gesture Recognition*, pages 336–341, 1998.
22. W. Zhao, A. Krishnaswamy, R. Chellappa, D. Swets, and J. Weng. Discriminant analysis of principal components for face recognition. In H. Wechsler, P. J. Phillips, V. Bruce, F. Fogelman Soulie, and T. S. Huang, editors, *Face Recognition: From Theory to Applications*, pages 73–85. Springer, Berlin, 1998.

# Chapter 15. Psychological and Neural Perspectives on Human Face Recognition

Alice J. O'Toole

School of Behavioral and Brain Sciences, University of Texas at Dallas

Human face "processing" skills can make simultaneous use of a variety of information from the face, including information about the age, sex, race, identity, and even current mood of the person. We are further able to track facial motions that alter the configuration of features, making it difficult to encode the structure of the face. Facial movements include the gestures we make when we speak, changes in our gaze direction or head pose, and expressions such as smiling and frowning. These movements play an important role in human social interactions and in the survival mechanisms that protect us from danger; they also indicate the presence of a potential mate and direct our attention to an object or event of importance in our environment.

We are capable of these impressive feats of visual information processing even when viewing conditions are variable or less than optimal — for example, when the face is poorly illuminated, viewed from an unusual vantage point or viewed from a distance so the resolution of the image on the retina is limited. These viewing parameters have proven challenging for computational models of face recognition.

Given the evolutionary importance of accurate, speedy recognition of human faces and recognition of the social information conveyed by expressions and movements, it is perhaps not surprising that the neural processing of faces has been studied intensively in recent decades. What is known to date indicates that several areas of the human brain are involved in the analysis of the human face and that these areas may distinguish processing according to the functions of information they analyze. The analysis of the static features of faces, which convey identity and categorical information about faces, is probably carried out in a different part of the brain than analysis of the motions that carry social information. The processing of emotional information from the face is further differentiated neurally.

From a combined psychophysical and neural perspective, human face recognition serves as an example to the developers of automatic face recognition algorithms that it is possible and indeed "easy" to recognize faces, even when viewing conditions are challenging. The human system, however, is not infallible. Errors of identification abound in circumstances that challenge the human system on its own terms. The purpose of this chapter is to provide an overview of the human face processing system from both a psychological and neural perspective. We hope that this overview and analysis of the human system may provide insights into successful strategies for dealing with the problem of automatic face recognition. We further hope that it will provide a useful guide for comparing the strengths and weaknesses of the human system with those of currently available face recognition and analysis algorithms.

In this chapter, we consider the psychological and neural aspects of face perception and recognition. For the psychological part, we first discuss the diversity of tasks humans perform with faces and link them to the kinds of information that supports each. Next, we consider the characteristics of human face recognition. In this section we address questions about the circumstances under which humans excel at face recognition and the circumstances under which recognition accuracy begins to fail. More specifically, we present an overview of the factors that affect human memory for faces. For the neural part of the chapter, we consider what is known about the neural processing of faces. We present a multiple systems model of neural processing that suggests a functional organization of facial analysis. This analysis distinguishes among the components of facial features and motions that subserve various tasks. Finally, we summarize the points of interest for algorithm developers in seeking solutions to the challenges of robust and accurate face recognition.

# 1 Psychological Aspects of Face Perception and Recognition

## 1.1 Extracting Information from the Human Face

Perhaps the most remarkable aspect of the human face is the diversity of information it provides to the human observer, both perceptually and socially. We consider, in turn, the major tasks that can be accomplished with this information.

### Identity

Each human face is unique and, as such, provides information about the identity of its owner. Humans can keep track of hundreds (if not thousands) of individual faces. This far exceeds our ability to memorize individual exemplars from any other class of objects (e.g., How many individual suitcases can we remember?).

To identify a face, we must locate and encode the information that makes the face *unique* or different from all other faces we have seen before and from all other unknown faces. As impressive as it is to be able to identify a face we have seen before, it is equally impressive to state with confidence that a face is one we have never seen before.

Computational models such as principal component analysis (PCA) have given insight into the nature of the information in faces that makes them unique. In a series of simulations, face recognition accuracy for sets of eigenvectors was found to be *highest* for eigenvectors with relatively *low* eigenvalues [34]. This may seem surprising from an engineering point of view, which suggests that low dimensional representations should be based on the eigenvectors with the largest eigenvalues. From a perceptual point of view, however, the finding makes sense. Eigenvectors with relatively small eigenvalues explain little variance in the set of faces. Indeed, to identify a face, we need to encode the information that a face shares with few other faces in the set. This information is captured in eigenvectors with small eigenvalues. A perceptual illustration of the finding may be seen in Figure 1. The original face appears on the left. The middle image is a reconstruction of the face using the first 40 eigenvectors. The rightmost image is reconstruction of the face with all but the first 40 eigenvectors. As can be seen, it is much easier to identify the face when it is reconstructed with eigenvectors with relatively smaller eigenvalues.

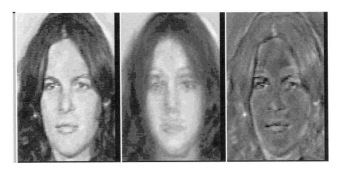

**Fig. 15.1.** Identity-specific information in faces using principal component analysis [34]. The original face appears on the left. The middle image is a reconstruction of the face using the first 40 eigenvectors. The rightmost image is reconstruction of the face with all but the first 40 eigenvectors. As can be seen, it is much easier to identify the face when it is reconstructed with eigenvectors with relatively smaller eigenvalues.

Because faces all share the same set of "features" (e.g.,eyes, nose, mouth) arranged in roughly the same configuration, the information that makes individual faces unique must be found in subtle variations in the form and configuration of the facial features. Data from human memory experiments suggest that humans use both feature-based and configural information to recognize faces (e.g., [2]), with perhaps special reliance on facial configurations (e.g., [45]). The reliance of the human perceptual system on configural information has been demonstrated using various experimental manipulations. These are aimed at perturbing the configuration of a face or at disrupting our ability to process its configural information. The manipulations used in previous work include distortions of the relative positions of the mouth, eyes, and nose [2], inverting a face [53], and altering the vertical alignment of the contours [54]. All of these manipulations strongly affect human recognition accuracy and processing speed.

An excellent example of the importance of configuration in human face perception can be illustrated with the classic "Thatcher illusion," so named because it was demonstrated first with Margaret Thatcher's face [47]. The illusion is illustrated in Figure 2. A face can be "Thatcherized" by inverting the eyes and the mouth, and then inverting the entire picture. Most people do not notice anything peculiar about the inverted face. Upright, however, we see a gross distortion of the configuration of the facial features. There is evidence that humans are highly sensitive to the configuration of the features in a face, but that the processing of configuration is limited to faces presented in an upright orientation. The phenomenon illustrates that human face perception has some important processing limits for nontypical views.

In the human memory literature, the terms *identification* and *recognition* are often distinguished. Recognition is the process by which a human observer judges whether a face has been seen before. This definition includes the two components of accuracy required for face recognition. First, a previously encountered face is "recognized" when it is judged as familiar or

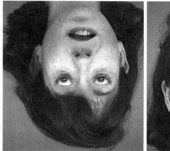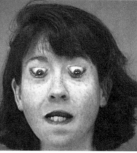

**Fig. 15.2.** Thatcher Illusion. The invertedface appears normal. Upright, however, the configural distortion is evident. The illusion illustrates the limits of configural processing for atypical views of the face.

"known." Second, a novel or previously unseen face is "correctly rejected" when it is judged as unfamiliar or "unknown". Correct judgments on the former component are referred to as "hits," and mistakes are referred to as "misses." Correct judgments on the latter component are referred to as "correct rejections," and mistakes are referred to as "false alarms." Recognition memory performance is generally measured using the signal detection theory measure of $d'$, which considers both hits and false alarms [18].

An important characteristic of human face recognition is that it can occur in the absence of the ability to *identify* a face. For example, one may be absolutely certain they recognize the grocery store clerk but may fail to retrieve a name or context of encounter (e.g., "He is in one of my classes" or "That's Bob from the gym"). The feeling of certainty that we recognize a face is therefore not linked inextricably to the memory of an individual person. This is a common perceptual phenomenon that occurs with stimuli in other modalities (e.g., a familiar tune or a familiar taste than is recognized but not identified).

In the human memory literature, identification presumes recognition but requires the retrieval of a semantic label such as a name or context of encounter. For face recognition algorithms, identification is the task most commonly performed. The retrieval process used by most algorithms is specific to an individual face rather than being a general judgment about whether the face is "in the database somewhere." Only a few algorithms allow recognition to occur independently of identification, and these tend to be models aimed at simulating human performance (e.g. [35]).

## Visually Derived Semantic Categories of Faces

In addition to our ability to recognize and identify faces, humans can also categorize faces along a number of dimensions referred to as "visually derived semantic categories" [8], including race, sex, and age. By a broader definition, one can also include other visually specified, albeit abstract, categories such as personality characteristics. For example, most humans happily make a judgment about whether a face looks "generous" or "extroverted." Faces can be categorized quickly and easily based on all of these dimensions. An intriguing aspect of this phenomenon is that making such judgments actually *increases* human accuracy when compared to making physical feature-based judgments (e.g., nose size) [6].

In contrast to the information needed to specify facial identity (i.e., what makes a face unique or different from all others), visually derived semantic categorizations are based on the features a face shares with an entire category of faces. To determine that a face is male, for example, we must locate and encode the features the face shares with other male faces. As was the case for identity-specific information, computational models such as PCA can provide insight into the nature of category-specific information from the face. Simulations to evaluate gender classification accuracy for individual eigenvectors showed that eigenvectors with relatively large eigenvalues contain the most useful information for this task [34]. This is illustrated in Figure 3. The top row (leftmost) shows the first eigenvector from a PCA from which the average face was not subtracted. This image approximates the average face. Next to it appears the second eigenvector. The images on the right were constructed by adding the second eigenvector to the average and by subtracting the second eigenvector from the average, respectively. The general male-female forms are contrasted in these combined images. Using the eigenvector weights for the second eigenvector alone achieved accuracy levels over 75%. An analogous demonstration using three-dimensional laser scans appears at the bottom of the figure [38]. This shows the average combined positively and negatively with the first eigenvector, which was the best predictor of the gender of the face.

There has been less research on the perception of visually derived semantic categories than on face recognition. Notwithstanding, research on the perception of face gender indicates that humans are highly accurate at sex classification [10, 1, 38], even when obvious "surface cues" such as facial and head hair are absent. They are also capable of making gender judgments on the faces of young children, which contain more subtle cues to gender than adult faces [52]. Male and female prototypes of this information appear in Figure 4. These prototypes were constructed by morphing pairs of boy's (or girl's) faces together, and then morphing together pairs of the pairs, and so on until reaching a single convergent image was reached [52]. Humans are also surprisingly good at estimating the age of a face ([9, 39]).

## Facial Expressions, Movement, and Social Signals

The human face moves and deforms in a variety of ways when we speak or display facial expressions. We can also orient ourselves within our environment by moving our head or eyes. We interpret these expressions and movements quickly and accurately. Virtually all of the face and head movements convey a social message. Rolling our eyes as we speak adds an element of disbelief or skepticism to what we are saying. Expressions of fear, happiness, disgust, and anger are readily and universally interpretable as conveying information about the internal state of another person [15]. Finally, the head movements that accompany changes in the focus of our attention provide cues that signal the beginning and end of social interactions.

The data in the psychological literature linking facial movements to social interpretations are limited. In general, except at the extremes, facial expressions and gestures are difficult to produce on demand and are further difficult to quantify as stimuli. There is also only limited ground truth available with facial expressions. This makes controlled experimentation difficult. Anecdotally, however, it is clear that these movements provide constant feedback to the perceiver that helps to guide and structure a social interaction.

It is possible, but not certain, that facial movements may also complicate the job of the perceiver for recognizing faces. It is likely that the information needed to recognize faces can

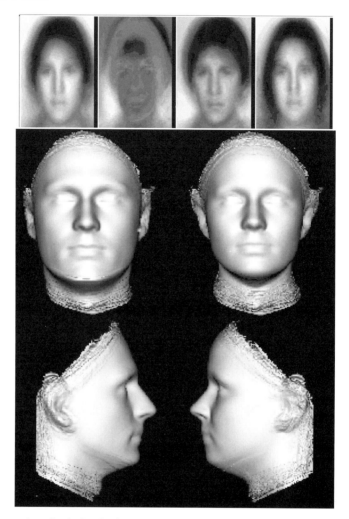

**Fig. 15.3.** Computationally-derived information in images [34] and three dimensional head models [38] that specifies the gender of a face. The top part of the figure shows the results of a principal component analysis of face images. Left to right: average face, second eigenvector, average face plus the second eigenvector, and average face minus the second eigenvector. Face projections onto this eigenvector predicted the sex of the face accurately. The bottom part of the figure shows an analogous analysis for laser-scanned heads. In the top row, the average plus and minus the first eigenvector are displayed. In the bottom row, the average plus and minus the sixth eigenvector are displayed.

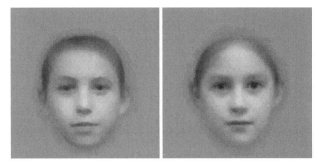

**Fig. 15.4.** Computationally-derived gender information in children's faces. At left is the male proto-type, made by morphing boys together (see text for details); and at right is the female prototype.

be found in the invariant or unique form and configuration of the features. Non rigid facial movements alter the configuration of facial features, often in a dramatic way. Research on the effects of various motions on recognition accuracy is just beginning, and complete answers to these questions are not yet available. A detailed discussion of these issues can be found in a recent review [37].

## 1.2  Characteristics of Human Face Recognition

Human face recognition accuracy varies as a function of *stimulus factors*, *subject factors*, and *photometric conditions*. All three of these factors, (including subject factors) are relevant for predicting the accuracy of automatic face recognition algorithms. We explain this point in more detail shortly. For humans, and perhaps also for machines, familiarity with the face can be an important predictor of the robustness of face recognition over changes in viewing parameters.

### Stimulus Factors

Not all faces are recognized equally accurately. Indeed, some people have highly unusual faces, with distinctive features or configurations of features. These faces seem, and are, easy to re-member. Specifically, distinctive faces elicit more hits and fewer false alarms than more typical faces, which have relatively few distinguishing characteristics. The negative correlation be-tween the typicality and recognizability of faces is one of the most robust findings in the face recognition literature (e.g., [27]). The finding is relevant for predicting face recognition success for human observers at the level of individual faces.

   More theoretically, the relationship between face typicality and recognizability has inter-esting implications for understanding the way human face recognition works. When a human observer judges a face to be unusual or distinctive, nominally it might be because "the nose is too big," or "the eyes are too close together." It is clear, however, that implicit in these judg-ments is a reference to internalized knowledge about how long a nose *should be* or how close together eyes *should be*. The typicality-recognizability finding has been interpreted as evidence that human observers store a representation of the average or *prototype* face, against which all other faces are compared [51]. This suggests that individual faces are represented, not in absolute terms, but in relative terms.

The typicality-recognizability relationship suggests that individual faces may be represented in human memory in terms of their deviation from the average. There are interesting computational models of face encoding and synthesis that share this kind of encoding. Specifically, algorithms that directly use the correspondence of features to an average ([4, 13, 25], share the basic principles of a prototype theory of human face recognition because the faces are encoded relative to one another via the prototype or average of the faces.

At a more concrete level, the prototype theory of face recognition has been modeled in the context of a multidimensional face space [51]. By this account, individual faces can be thought of metaphorically as points or vectors in the space, with the axes of this space representing the features on which faces vary. The prototype, or average face, is at the center of the space. The face space model predicts the typicality-recognizability relationship by assuming that the density of faces is highest near the center of the space and falls off as a function of the distance from the center. Typical faces, close to the center of the space, are easily confused with other faces, yielding a high probability of false alarms. Distinctive faces are found farther from the center of the space and are not easily confused with other faces.

Face space models have been implemented computationally as well and are currently the most common base for automatic face recognition algorithms. For example, the principal components model, or *eigenface model* [49], implements the the psychological face space model in a concrete fashion. Principal components form the statistically based feature axes in the space. The coordinates of individual faces with respect to the axes locate individual faces in the space. Principal component-based face recognition models can be shown to predict aspects of the typicality-recognizability relationship for human observers [35].

The typicality-recognizability finding also suggests a reason for the superior recognition of caricatures over veridical faces [42]. Artists draw caricatures in a way that exaggerates the distinctive features in a face. For example, Mick Jagger can be caricatured by making his already thick lips, even thicker. Computer-based caricatures are made by comparing the feature values for an individual face with feature values for an average face, and then redrawing the face, exaggerating features that deviate substantially from the average (see [39, 42] for a review). Several studies have shown that computer-generated caricatures are recognized more accurately and more quickly than veridical versions of the faces. This is a notable finding in that caricatures are clearly distorted versions of faces we have experienced. Thus, the finding suggests that a distorted version of a face is actually easier to recognize than the exact template stored.

A sophisticated method for producing caricatures from laser scans was developed recently [4]. The laser scans are put into point-by-point correspondence [4] with an alogorithm based on optic flow analysis. Once in correspondence, it is possible to create caricatures simply by increasing the distance from the average face in the face space and reconstructing the laser scan with the new "feature values." Note that "features" here means complex face shapes. An illustration of this appears in Figure 5, created using Blanz and Vetter's caricature generator for laser scan data [4]. The representation here includes both the surface map and the overlying texture map. It is clear that the distinctive and unique aspects of this individual are enhanced and exaggerated in the caricatured version of the face.

In fact, it is possible to create and display an entire trajectory of faces through the space, beginning at the average face and going toward the original (see Figure 6). The faces in between are called "anti-caricatures" and are recognized less accurately by humans than are veridical faces (see [39] for a review of studies).

**Fig. 15.5.** Computer-generated three-dimensional caricatures from Blanz and Vetter's caricature generator [4]. Both the surface and texture data are caricatured.

**Fig. 15.6.** Computer-generated three-dimensional anti-caricatures from Blanz and Vetter's caricature generator [4]. The average face is at the far left and the original face is at the far right. The faces in between lie along a trajectory from the average to the original face in face space.

The concept of a trajectory can be extended even further by imagining what a face would look like "on the other side of the mean." Thus if we extend the trajectory in Figure 5 in the *opposite direction*, (i.e., through the mean and out the other side), we would arrive at the "opposite" of the face (see Figure 7). This "anti-face" is one in which all of the "feature values" are inverted. So, the dark-skinned, dark-eyed, thin face becomes a light-skinned, light-eyed, round face [5]. The anti-face is linked perceptually to the face in an opponent fashion, suggesting that faces may be stored in the brain in relation to the existence of a prototype [26]. Staring at the anti-face for a short amount of time seems to facilitate identification of the real face [26]. This situation suggests a kind of excitory-inhibitory trade-off between feature values around the average.

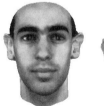

**Fig. 15.7.** Computer-generated three-dimensional anti-caricatures from Blanz and Vetter's caricature generator [4]. The veridical face is on the left and the *anti-face* is on the right. The anti-face lies on the other side of the mean, along a trajectory from the original face, through the mean, and out the other side [5].

There are also interesting additional perceptual dimensions to the caricatured faces. When a computer-based algorithm is applied to the three-dimensional shape information from laser scans omitting the surface texture, caricaturing actually increases the perceived *age* of the face [39], as illustrated in Figure 8. Again, the laser scans are put into correspondence [4] and are exaggerated simply by increasing the distance from the average face in the face space. Human subjects recognize the caricatured faces more accurately and judge these caricatured faces to be older (even decades older) than the original veridical face [39].

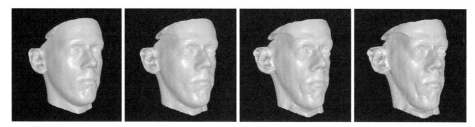

**Fig. 15.8.** Computer-generated three-dimensional charicatures from Blanz and Vetter's caricature generator [4]. When caricaturing is applied to three-dimensional head models, the face appears to age.

The robust relationship between the typicality of a face and its recognizability has practical implications for the accuracy of eyewitness identifications. Specifically, if we consider the effects of typicality, face recognition accuracy should be expected to vary with the face itself. In an eyewitness identification situation, therefore, typical suspects are more likely to be identified erroneously than distinctive suspects. This error bias for typical faces is also likely to be the case for automatic face recognition algorithms, many of which are based on statistical or multidimensional space-based models of faces [35].

**Interaction of Stimulus and Subject Factors**

The interaction of stimulus and subject factors in face recognition should be expected when one takes into account the likelihood that we encode faces in terms of their deviation from the average or prototype face. It seems highly unlikely that the "average" face, which we learn and internalize as we begin to experience faces, is the same for all groups of subjects. For example, the faces we might encounter growing up in Japan would yield a different average than those we might encounter growing up in India or the United States. In fact, as is well known anecdotally, there is good psychophysical evidence for an *other-race effect* [30, 28, 35]. The other-race effect is the phenomenon that we recognize faces of our own race more accurately than faces of other races.

There are a number of explanations for the other race effect, but they all involve the idea that there is an interaction between stimulus factors and subject experience factors. The *contact hypothesis* suggests that a subject's experience with faces of their own race biases for the encoding of features that are most useful for distinguishing among own-race race. This enables subjects to create a detailed and accurate representation of the distinctive features of own-race faces. It causes a problem with other-race faces, however, because they are not well character-ized by these features. A simple-minded example might go as follows. Caucasians might rely on eye color as an important facial feature. Although this would be a helpful feature for Cau-casian faces, it is likely to be far less helpful for Asian faces. A perceptual consequence of the failure to accurately encode the distinguishing facial characteristics of other-race faces is that these faces are then perceived as more similar, one to the next, than own-race faces. This yields the well-known feeling, and oft-quoted statement, that other-race faces "all look alike to me."

The other-race effect for humans is surprisingly relevant for computational algorithms of face recognition, which often rely on statistically based learning procedures. These procedures are used commonly for acquiring the basis set or principal components with which faces are encoded. It is clear that the racial composition of the training set of faces affect the performance of these algorithms depending on the race of the target face.

In a recent study, 13 automatic face recognition algorithms were tested for the presence of an other-race effect [16]. The results were interesting and in some ways surprising. First, algorithms based on generic PCA actually performed better on faces in the "minority race" than in the "majority race." Minority and majority refer to the relative numbers of faces of two races in the training set. This is because minority race faces are distinctive or unusual relative to the other faces in the database. These distinctive faces inhabit a less populated area of the face space and are thus less likely to have competing neighbors that might be mistaken for them. A second set of algorithms that linked PCA to a second-stage learning algorithm (e.g., Fischer discriminant analysis) showed the classic other-race effect, with performance better for majority race faces. This is likely to be due to the fact that the second stage training procedures serve to warp the space to maximize the distance between different faces in the space. This improves majority race face encoding at the cost of minority race face encoding.

## Face Representations, Photometric Factors, and Familiarity

Much recent research has been devoted to understanding how humans are able to recognize ob-jects and faces when there are changes in the photometric conditions between learning and test stimuli. The rationale for this research is as follows. Studying how well we generalize recog-nition of faces to novel viewing conditions may give insight into the representations our brains create of faces. This can occur via inferences about the way learned information can be used to recognize altered versions of a target stimulus. Thus, some representations (e.g., an object-centered three-dimensional representation) predict good generalization to novel views and il-lumination conditions. For this reason, the effects of photometric variables, such as changes in the illumination or viewpoint, have been studied in some detail. We consider only the effects of viewpoint and illumination change because they currently represent one of the most important challenges for algorithms to be able to function in real world conditions. In any case, the effects for other photometric changes are quite consistent with illumination and viewpoint effects.

We first present a brief overview of the psychological theories of face and object representa-tion. We then discuss the relevant data and its implications for the nature of face representations.

## Face Representation Debate

There are long-standing questions in the psychological literature about the nature of face repre-sentations. Much of this debate concerns differences in the extent to which psychologists posit two- versus three-dimensional representations of faces and objects. It is worth noting that these theories have been developed primarily to account for object recognition. There are important differences between face and object recognition, including the level of analysis required for tasks. Object recognition refers to the ability to classify individual objects as members of a category (e.g., "It is a chair"). Face recognition refers usually to a recognition or identity decision about a single exemplar of the face category (e.g., "I've met you before," "There's Bob!" ). Recent developments on refining computational models to simultaneously subserve performance at both of these levels can be found in a recent review [43]. For present purposes, we discuss only the history and rationale of the two competing approaches.

*Structural theories* suggest that recognition occurs by building a three-dimensional representation of faces and objects from the two-dimensional images that appear on the retina. The most well known of these theories is the "recognition by components" theory [3], based on the foundations laid in Marr's classic book on vision [31].

*Interpolation-based models* such as those advanced by Poggio and Edelman [41] posit two-dimensional representations of objects. By this theory, we can encode multiple view-based representations of faces and objects. Recognition of a novel view of an object or face occurs by interpolation to the closest previously seen view. Compromise or hybrid accounts of recognition posit a correspondence process by which novel views are aligned to view-based templates, and recognition occurs by a matching process [50]. More recent models have tackled the complex problem of affine tranformations with biologically plausible computational schemes, but these models retain the basic view-based nature of the encoding [43].

## Familiarity and Face Recognition over Photometric Inconsistencies

Under some circumstances, humans show a remarkable capacity to recognize people under very poor viewing conditions. We can all recognize the face of a friend from a single glance on a dark train platform or in a blurry low quality photograph. The psychological literature is clear, however, that this ability is limited to faces with which we have previous experience or familiarity. Burton et al. [11] recently reviewed the literature on familiar face recognition.

When psychologists discuss recognition of *unfamiliar faces*, they usually mean recognition of a face with which we have had only one previous encounter. This is the kind of performance we might expect from a security guard who is interested in recognizing people from the memory of a photograph he has viewed previously. Most experiments in the laboratory are done on relatively unfamiliar faces owing to the difficulties encountered when testing memory for familiar faces. For example, a familiar face recognition experiment requires a set of stimulus faces known to all subjects in the experiment (e.g., famous faces) or requires the construction of stimulus sets tailored to the experience of each subject. These difficulties in experimentation are the reason that the data on familiar face recognition are limited.

For unfamiliar faces, there is general agreement that recognition declines as a function of the difference between learning and testing conditions. Hancock et al. [19] recently reviewed the literature on unfamiliar face recognition. In most controlled human memory experiments, subjects learn previously unfamiliar faces from a single image and are asked to recognize the face from a second novel image of the person after a delay. When there are changes in the viewpoint between learning and test images, such as from frontal to profile views, accuracy declines as a function of the difference between learning and test images [36, 33, 48].

The difficulties over viewpoint change are seen also with perceptual matching experiments that do not involve a memory component. In matching experiments, subjects are asked to determine if the persons pictured in two simultaneously or sequentially presented images are the same or different. Match accuracy declines as a function of the difference in viewpoint [48, 14].

There are comparable deficits in recognition accuracy when the illumination conditions are changed. These too depend on the degree of change between the learning and test image. At one extreme, photographic negatives of people, which approximate the unusual condition of lighting a face from below, are difficult to recognize [53]. But even less extreme changes in illumination produce detrimental effects on accuracy (e.g., [7, 22]).

The debate about whether these results support a two-dimensional or three-dimensional representation of faces has evolved over the past decade. It is reasonable to assume that *view dependence* in recognition performance supports a two-dimensional representation hypothesis, under the assumption that one matches the target with the image previously learned. The greater the difference between the two images, the worse the performance. Alternatively, however, it is possible that view-dependent recognition performance may be indicative of a three-dimensional representation that is only poorly constructed because of a lack of data. In other words, a good three-dimensional representation may require exposure to more than a single view to be accurate enough to support view-independent performance.

In summary, there is a problem with using view independence to argue for a three-dimensional hypothesis and view dependence to argue for a two-dimensional hypothesis. Specifically, without familiarity, performance is usually view-dependent, and with experience or familiarity it is usually view-independent. A two-dimensional representation is consistent with view independence provided that one has experience with multiple views of a face. Likewise, a three-dimensional representation can yield view-dependent performance when one has not experienced a sufficient number of views to build a good structural representation. It may therefore be impossible to settle this issue using only psychological data. The addition of computational and neural data to make precise predictions about generalization and familiarity may be necessary to tease apart these hypotheses.

Before leaving the issue of recognizing familiar and unfamiliar faces, we note two recent experiments that speak to the robustness of familiar face recognition in a naturalistic setting. Burton and colleagues asked participants to pick out faces from poor quality videos similar to those used in low-cost security systems [12]. They used video footage of professors captured from university surveillance cameras. Burton et al. tested three groups of participants: students familiar with the professors; students unfamiliar with the professors; and a group of trained police officers who were unfamiliar with the professors. The performance of all but the familiar subjects was poor. To track down the source of the good performance by the familiar subjects, Burton et al. designed a second experiment to determine which aspect(s) of the stimuli contributed to the familiarity advantage. They did this by editing the videos to obscure either the body/gait or the face. They found that the "face-obscured" version of the tape resulted in much worse recognition performance than the "body-obscured" version. The authors concluded that face information plays the key role in identifying someone familiar, even when other informative and cues, such as body and gait are present.

In summary, human memory research indicates that memory for familiar faces (i.e., those with which we have experience) is robust against a variety of changes in photometric conditions. For relatively unfamiliar faces, recognition performance for humans suffers as a function of the difference between learning and test images. This makes human recognition performance for unfamiliar faces similar to the performance of most face recognition algorithms, which are similarly challenged by changes in photometric factors between learning and test. It is important to bear in mind that most algorithms are limited in terms of the number and type of views and illumination conditions available to train the model (see Riesenhuber and Poggio [43] for a discussion of this issue). When human observers are similarly limited, recognition accuracy is also poor. Understanding the process and representational advantages that humans acquire as they become familiar with a face may therefore be useful for extending the capabilities of algorithms in more naturalistic viewing conditions.

## 2 Neural Systems Underlying Face Recognition

The neural systems underlying face recognition have been studied over the past 30 years from the perspective of neuropsychology, neurophysiology, and functional neuroimaging. It is beyond the scope of this chapter to provide a comprehensive review of this extensive literature. Rather, we provide a brief sketch of the kinds of literature that have formed the foundations of the inquiry and then focus on a recent model that has begun to make sense of the diverse and plentiful findings from these various disciplines.

### 2.1 Diversity of Neural Data on Face Process

#### Neuropsychology

Studies of patients who suffer brain injuries after accidents or stroke have often provided important insights into the organization of neural function. For faces, neuropsychological data on *prosopagnosia* provided some of the first hints that brain processing of faces might be "special" in some way. Prosopagnosia is a rare condition in which a patient, after a brain injury or stroke, loses the ability to recognize faces, despite a preserved ability to recognize other visual objects. A person with prosopagnosia can recognize his car, his house, his clothes but fails to recognize the people he knows by their faces. Even more intriguing, some prosopagnosics can recognize facial expressions, while failing entirely to recognize the identity of the person displaying the facial expression [24].

It is worth noting that the problem in prosopagnosia is not a problem with identifying the person. Rather, prosopagnosics can identify people accurately using their voices or other cues such as the clothes they wear. They simply lack the ability to encode the identity-specific information in individual faces. In other words, they fail to encode the information that makes an individual face unique.

The existence of prosopagnosia suggests some localization of function in the brain for identifying faces. This general claim has been supported in functional neuroimaging studies as well, which we discuss shortly. It further suggests some modularity of processing. Modular processesing is used to refer to tasks that are encapsulated in the brain and are thought to function as relatively independent systems. Though there is still much controversy about the extent to which the processing of faces in the brain is modular (see [20, 44]), there is general agreement that at least some of the important processes are relatively local and primarily (if not exclusively) dedicated to analyzing faces.

## Neurophysiology

Over the last three decades or so, the function of individual neurons in the visual cortex of animals has been probed with single and multiple electrode recordings. Electrodes can record the activity of single neurons. Used in conjunction with a stimulus that activates the neuron, these methods can provide a catalog of the stimulus features that are encoded by neurons in the visual system. In these studies, neurophysiologists insert an electrode into an individual neuron in the brain while stimulating the animal with a visual stimulus(e.g., a moving bar of light). The "effective visual stimulus" causes the neurons to discharge and defines the receptive field properties of the neuron. With these methods, neurons selective for oriented lines, wavelengths, motion direction/speed, and numerous other features have been discovered in the occipital lobe of the brain. Beyond the primary visual areas in the occipital lobe of the brain, higher level visual areas in the temporal cortex have been found that are selective for complex visual forms and objects [46, 29], including faces and hands. Some of the *face-selective neurons* respond only to particular views of faces [40].

The selectivity of individual neurons for faces has lent support to the idea that face processing in the brain may be confined to a (or some) relatively local area(s) of the brain. It further supports the idea that face analysis may act as a special purpose system in the brain. The claim that face processing is "special" in this way, however, has been controversial for a number of reasons. To begin with, unlike object recognition, face recognition requires an ability to keep track of many individual exemplars from the category of faces. In other words, we require a level of visual expertise with faces that is not needed with most (or possibly any) other category of objects.

This second definition of "special" implies the need to process faces at a level of visual sophistication beyond that required for other objects. It has been hypothesized, therefore, that regions of the brain that appear to be selective only for faces may actually be selective for the *processes* needed to achieve the high level of expertise we show for faces [17]. This hypothesis has been examined with functional neuroimaging methods by looking at the responses of face-selective areas to other objects (e.g., birds) with which some subjects have perceptual expertise (e.g., bird watchers). Indeed, there is some evidence that a particular brain region that is selective for faces responds also to object categories with which a particular subject has perceptual expertise [17]. For reasons having to do with the complexity and nonuniformity of functional magnetic resonance imaging (fMRI) analyses, the question remains a topic of active debate.

Finally, we note that one must be cautious when interpreting neurophysiological data, which is always gathered using animals, usually primates, as subjects. Although the brains of primates are similar to those of humans, there are still important differences in the structure and function of the various brain areas. For this reason, functional neuroimaging analyses, applied to human brains, can be helpful in ascertaining critical differences between the brains of human and nonhuman primates.

## Functional Neuroimaging

A recent set of tools in the arsenal of brain study allows a glimpse of the human brain while it is working. Positron emission tomography (PET) and fMRI are two of the most common functional neuroimaging tools. Although they work in very different ways, both allow a high resolution spatial brain image to be overlaid with a high resolution temporal image of the activity levels of different parts of the brain as the subject engages in a task (e.g.,viewing a face, reading, or listening to music). Using this technology, neuroscientists have recently named a small area in the human inferior temporal lobe of the brain the "fusiform face area"(FFA) [23]. This area of the brain responds maximally and selectively to the passive viewing of faces [23].

Interestingly, other areas of the brain seem to respond to faces as well but are constrained by additional parameters of the stimulus such as expression or facial movement. We next consider these data in the context of a recent model of neural processing of faces.

## 2.2 Multiple Systems Model

As noted, the brain systems that process information about human faces have been studied for many decades using single-unit neurophysiology in primates and neuropsychological case studies of prosopgnosia. Neuroimaging studies from the past decade have enriched and extended our knowledge of the complex neural processing that underlies face perception. These studies allow researchers to examine the normal human brain as it carries out face processing tasks. The number of brain areas that respond to faces has made interpretation of the complete neural system for face processing challenging. The complexity of the problem is compounded by the difficulties encountered when comparing the nonhuman primate brain examined in single unit neurophysiology with the human brain, which is the subject of neuroimaging and neuropsychological studies.

Progress in this endeavor was made recently by Haxby and colleagues, who integrated extensive findings from across these diverse lines of research. They proposed a *distributed neural system* for human face perception [21]. Their model emphasizes a distinction between the representation of the invariant and changeable aspects of the face, both functionally and structurally. Where function is concerned, the model posits that the invariant aspects of faces contribute to face recognition, whereas the changeable aspects of faces serve social communication functions and include eye gaze direction, facial expression, and lip movements. The proposed neural system reflects an analogous structural split. The model includes three core brain areas and four areas that extend the system to a number of related specific tasks. The locations of these areas are displayed in Figure 9.

For the core system, the lateral fusiform gyrus is an area activated in many neuroimaging studies of face perception. As noted previously, this region is commonly known now as the *fusiform face area*. It is the site proposed to represent information about facial identity and other categorical properties of faces. In primate studies, the homologous area is the inferotemporal cortex. Though bilateral activations of this region are frequently found in human neuroimaging studies, the most consistent findings are lateralized in the right hemisphere. This is consistent with much previous neuropsychological data indicating the relative dominance of the right hemisphere in the analysis of faces.

The area Haxby et al. proposed as the site of encoding for the changeable aspects of the faces is the posterior superior temporal sulcus (pSTS). Studies of single unit physiology in nonhuman primates and neuroimaging studies in humans indicate that this area is important for detecting gaze information, head orientation, and expression. More generally, Haxby et al. noted that the perception of biologic motion, including motion of the whole body, the hand, and the eyes and mouth, has been shown consistently to activate the pSTS.

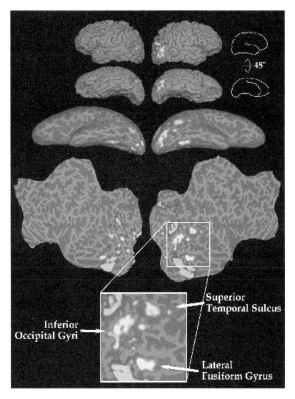

**Fig. 15.9.** Locations of the core areas of the distributed neural system for face processing are illustrated, using data from a functional magnetic imaging experiment [21]. The core areas include the fusiform gyrus, superior temporal sulcus, and inferior occipital gyri (see text). The upper rows show the folded surface of the cortex, with the second row tilted up to reveal the fusiform area below. The third row shows the brain "inflated" to reveal hidden areas within the sulci. The fourth row shows a flattened version of the brain with the areas of interest expanded. Orange areas indicate higher neural activity in response to faces over houses. Blue areas indicate less response to faces than to houses. (See insert for color reproduction of this figure)

The lateral inferior occipital gyri comprise the third component of the distributed neural system. Haxby et al. noted that this region abuts the lateral fusiform region ventrally and the superior temporal sulcal region dorsally, and it may provide input to both of these areas. The region is proposed to be a precursor area involved in the early perception of facial features and may transit information to the lateral fusiform area and the pSTS.

In addition to the three core regions of the distributed system, four brain regions have been proposed as part of an extended system for face processing: intraparietal sulcus, auditory cortex, anterior temporal area, and a set of limbic structures including the amygdala and insula. The intraparietal sulcus is involved in spatially directed attention; the auditory areas are involved in prelexical speech perception from lip movements; the anterior temporal area is involved in the retrieval of personal identity, name, and biographical information; and, the limbic structures are involved in the perception of emotion from expression. The limbic system is a part of the phylogenetically older mammilian brain that is closely tied to the survival mechanisms subserved by the emotions (e.g., fear, disgust).

Three of the four extender systems tie into specific tasks that we accomplish with various facial movements. The movements of the eyes and head direct our attention. The movements of the lips as we speak can increase the signal-to-noise ratio in understanding speech. Finally, the emotions are a critical output system for facial motions. The accurate perception of emotions, such as fear, from the faces of others is a necessary component for adaptive social interactions.

## Early Visual Processing and the Distributed Model

The functional and structural devisions proposed in the distributed model between the processing of the invariant and changeable aspects of faces map easily onto what is known about the channeling of information in early vision [32]. From the retina, through the lateral geniculate nucleus of the thalamus, and up to the visual cortical regions of the occipital/temporal lobes (V1, V2, V3, V4, and V5/MT), two primary processing streams can be distinguished. They are evident via both anatomic markers (e.g., the size and shape of the cells and the extent of their interconnections) and their receptive field properties.

The parvocellular stream begins with ganglion cells in the retina and is selective for the color and form, among other visual features. It projects ventrally toward the temporal cortex and ultimately toward brain regions such as the fusiform area, which are thought to be responsible for object and face recognition. The magnocelluar stream also begins with the ganglion cells in the retina but is selective for properties of motion, such as speed and direction. It is also sensitive to form information but not to color. The magnocellular stream projects to the parietal cortex and to regions close to the posterior superior temporal areas. In general, the magnocellular stream is thought to be important for processing motion information and for locating objects in the visual environment. It has also been implicated in functions that enable visual and motor coordination for action(e.g., picking up an object using vision to guide the action).

These parallel processing streams map easily onto the distributed model and are suggestive of a cortical organization that distinguishes between object properties that may change continually and object properties that remain invariant over time. This makes for a system that can functionally divide the processing of faces into two parts: identity analysis and social interaction-based analysis.

## 2.3  Conclusions

Human memory for faces is characterized by robust generalization to new viewing conditions for faces that are familiar to us. Similiar to many computational models, however, human abilities are far less impressive when faces are relatively new to them. Stimulus and subject factors such as the typicality of the face and the interaction between the observer's race and the face race are strong determinants of human accuracy at the level of individual faces. These combined findings are suggestive of a system that represents faces in an image-based fashion and operates on faces in the context of a particular subject's experience history with faces. The representation suggested is one that encodes faces relative to a global average and evaluates deviation from the average as an indication of the unique properties of individual faces. Although little is currently known about how facial movements affect the extraction and encoding of uniqueness information in a face, this topic is fast becoming a focus of many current studies in the literature.

The neural underpinnings of the face system are likewise complex and possibly divergent. The relatively local nature of the areas in the brain that respond to faces must be weighed against the findings that many parts of the brain are active. The variety of tasks we perform with faces may account for the need to execute, in parallel, analyses that may be aimed at extracting qualitatively different kinds of information from faces. The tracking and interpreting of facial motions of at least three kinds must occur while the human observer processes information about the identity and categorical status of the face. Each of these movements feeds an extended network of brain areas involved in everything from prelexical access of speech to lower order limbic areas that process emotion. The multifaceted nature of these areas suggests that the problem of face processing is actually comprised of many subunits that the brain may treat more or less independently.

# References

1. H. Abdi, D. Valentine, B. Edelman, and A.J. O'Toole. More about the difference between men and women: evidence from linear neural networks and the principal-component approach. *Perception*, 24 :539–562, 1995.

2. J.C. Bartlett and J. Searcy. Inversion and configuration of faces. *Cognitive Psychology*, 25:281–316, 1993.

3. I. Biederman and P. Gerhardstein. Recognizing depth-rotated objects: evidence and conditions for three-dimensional viewpoint invariance. *J. Exp. Psychol. Hum. Percept. Perform.*, 19:1162–1183, 1993.

4. V. Blanz and T. Vetter. A morphable model for the synthesis of 3D faces. In *SIGGRAPH'99 Proceedings*, ACM: Computer Society Press, 187–194, 1999.

5. V. Blanz, A.J. O'Toole, T. Vetter, and H.A. Wild. On the other side of the mean: The perception of dissimilarity in human faces. *Perception*, 29, 885–891, 2000.

6. G.H. Bower and M.B. Karlin. Depth of processing pictures of faces and recognition memory. *Journal of Experimental Psychology*. 103:751-757, 1974.

7. W. L. Braje, D.J. Kersten, M.J. Tarr, and N.F. Troje. Illumination effects in face recognition. *Psychobiology*, 26:371–380, 1999.

8. V. Bruce and A.W. Young. Understanding face recognition. *British Journal of Psychology*, 77(3):305–327, 1986.

9. D.M. Burt and D.I. Perrett. Perception of age in adult Caucasian male faces: Computer graphic manipulation of shape and colour information. In *Proceedings of the Royal Society London B*, 259:137–143, 1995.

10. A.M. Burton, V. Bruce, and N. Dench. What's the difference between men and women: Evidence from facial measurement. *Perception*, 22:(2)153–176, 1993.

11. A.M. Burton, V. Bruce, and P.J.B. Hancock. From pixels to people: a model of familiar face recognition. *Cognitive Science*, 23:1–31, 1999.

12. A.M. Burton, S. Wilson, M. Cowan, and V. Bruce. Face recognition in poor-quality video. *Psychological Science*, 10:243-248, 1999.

13. I. Craw and P. Cameron. Parameterizing images for recognition and reconstruction. In P. mowforth, editor *Proceedings of the British Machine Vision Conference* Springer, London, 1991.

14. S. Edelman and H.H. Bülthoff. Orientation dependence in the recognition of familiar and novel views of three-dimensional objects. *Vision Research*, 32(12):2385–2400, 1992.

15. P.J. Ekman and W.V. Friesen. *The Facial Action Coding System: A Technique for the Measurement of Facial Movement*. Consulting Psychology Press, San Francisco, 1978.

16. D.S. Furl, P. J. Phillips, and A.J. O'Toole. Face recognition algorithms as models of the other-race effect. *Cognitive Science*, 96:1–19, 2002.

17. I. Gauthier, M.J. Tarr, A.W. Anderson, P. Skudlarski, and J.C. Gore. Activation of the middle fusiform face area increases with expertise recognizing novel objects. *Nature Neuroscience,*, 2:568–, 1999.

18. D.M. Green and J.A. Swets. *Signal detection Theory and Psychophysics*. Wiley, New York, 1966

19. P.J.B. Hancock, V. Bruce, and A.M. Burton. Recognition of unfamiliar faces. *Trends in Cognitive Sciences*, 4:(9)263–266, 1991.

20. J.V. Haxby, M.I. Gobbini, M.L. Furey, A. Ishai, J.L. Shouten and J.L.Pietrini. Distributed and overlapping representations of faces and objects in ventral temporal cortex. *Science*, 293:2425–2430, 2001.

21. J.V. Haxby, E.A. Hoffman, and M.I. Gobbini. The distributed human neural system for face perception. *Trends in Cognitive Sciences*, 20(6):223–233, 2000.

22. H. Hill and V. Bruce. Effects of lighting on the perception of facial surface. *J. Exp. Psychol. : Hum. Percept. Perform.,*, 4:(9)263–266, 1991.

23. N. Kanwisher, J. McDermott, and M. Chun. The fusiform face area: a module in human extrastriate cortex specialized for face perception. *J. Neurosci.*, 17 :4302-4311, 1997.

24. J. Kurucz and J. Feldmar. Prosopo-affective agnosia as a symptom of cerebral organic brain disease, *Journal of the American Geriatrics Society*, 27:91-95, 1979.

25. A. Lanitis, C.J. Taylor, and T.F. Cootes. Automatic interpretation and coding of face imaging using flexible models. *IEEE Transactions Pat. Anal. Mach. Intell.*, 19: 743, 1997.

26. D. Leopold, A.J. O'Toole, T. Vetter, and V. Blanz. Prototype-referenced shape encoding revealed by high-level aftereffects. *Nature Neuroscience*, 4:89-94, 2001.

27. L. Light, F. Kayra-Stuart, and S. Hollander. Recognition memory for typical and unusual faces. *Journal of Experimental Psychology: Human Learning and Memory*, 5:212–228, 1979.

28. D.S. Lindsay, P.C. Jack, and M.A. Christian. Other-race face perception. *Journal of Applied Psychology*, 76:587–589, 1991.

29. N.K. Logothetis, J. Pauls, H.H. Bülthoff, and T. Poggio. Shape representation in the inferior temporal cortex of monkeys. *Current Biology*, 5:552–563, 1991.

30. R.S. Malpass and J. Kravitz. Recognition for faces of own and other race faces. *Journal of Personality and Social Psychology*, 13:330–334, 1969.

31. D. Marr. *Vision*. Freeman, San Francisco, 1982.

32. W.H. Merigan. P and M pathway specialization in the macaque. In A. Valberg and B.B. Lee, editors. *From Pigments to Perception*. Plenum, New York. pages 117–125, 1991.

33. Y. Moses, S. Edelman, and S. Ullman. Generalization to novel images in upright and inverted faces. *Perception*, 25:(4)443–461, 1996.

34. A.J. O'Toole, H., Abdi, K.A. Deffenbacher, and D. Valentin. Low dimensional representation of faces in high dimensions of the space. *Journal of the Optical Society of America A*, 10, 405–410, 1993.

35. A.J. O'Toole, K.A. Deffenbacher, and D. Valentine. Structural aspects of face recognition and the other-race. *Memory & Cognition*, 22: 208–224, 1994.

36. A.J. O'Toole, S.E. Edelman, and H.H. Bülthoff. Stimulus-specific effects in face recognition over changes in viewpoint. *Vision Research*, 38: 2351–2363, 1998.

37. A.J. O'Toole, D. Roark, and H. Abdi. Recognition of moving faces: a psychological and neural perspective. *Trends in Cognitive Sciences*, 6:261–266, 2002.

38. A.J. O'Toole, T. Vetter, N.F. Troje, and H.H. Buelthoff. Sex classification is better with three-dimensional head structure than with image intensity information. *Perception*, 26:75–84, 1997.

39. A.J. O'Toole, T. Vetter, H. Volz, and E.M. Salter. Three-dimensional caricatures of human heads: distinctiveness and the perception of facial age. *Perception*, 26:719–732, 1997.

40. D. Perrett, J. Hietanen, M. Oram, and P. Benson. Organization and function of cells responsive to faces in temporal cortex. *Phil. Trans. Roy. Soc. Lond. B Biol. Sci*, 335:23–30, 1992.

41. T. Poggio and S. Edelman. A network that learns to recognize 3D objects. *Nature*, 343:263–266, 1991.

42. G. Rhodes. *Superportraits: Caricatures and Recognition*. Psychology Press, Hove, UK, 1997.

43. M. Riesenhuber and T. Poggio. Models of object recognition. *Nature Neuroscience Supplement*, 3 :–1204, 2000.

44. M. Spiridon and N. Kanwisher. How distributed is visual category information in human occipito-temporal cortex? An fMRI study. *Neuron*, 35:1157, 1991.

45. J. W. Tanaka and M.J. Farah. Parts and wholes in face recognition. *Quarterly Journal of Psychology*, 46A:(2)225–245, 1993.

46. K. Tanaka. Neuronal mechanisms of object recognition. *Science*, 262:685–688, 1991.

47. P. Thompson. Margaret Thatcher: A new illusion. *Perception*, 9:483–484, 1980.

48. N.F. Troje and H.H. Bülthoff. Face recognition under varying pose: The role of texture and shape. Vision Research, 36:1761–1771, 1996.

49. M. Turk and A. Pentland. Eigenfaces for recoginition. *Journal of Cognitive Neuroscience*, 3:71–86, 1991.

50. S. Ullman. *High-Level Vision*, MIT Press, Cambridge, MA, 1996.

51. T. Valentine. A unified account of the effects of distinctiveness, inversion, and race in face recognition. *Quarterly Journal of Experimental Psychology*, 43A:161–204, 1991.

52. H. A. Wild, S.E. Barrett, M.J Spence, A.J. O'Toole, Y. Cheng, and J. Brooke. Recognition and categorization of adults' and children's faces: examining performance in the absence of sex-stereotyped cues. *Journal of Experimental Child Psychology*, 77:269–291, 2000.

53. R.K. Yin. Looking at upside-down faces. *Journal of Experimental Psychology*, 81:141–145, 1969.

54. A.W. Young, D. Hellawell, and D.C. Hay. Configurational information in face perception. *Perception*, 16:747–759, 1987.

# Chapter 16. Face Recognition Applications

Thomas Huang, Ziyou Xiong, and Zhenqiu Zhang

University of Illinois at Urbana-Champaign, Urbana, IL, 61801, USA. {huang, zxiong,
zzhang6}@ifp.uiuc.edu

## 1 Introduction

One of the reasons face recognition has attracted so much research attention and sustained
development over the past 30 years is its great potential in numerous government and commercial applications. In 1995, Chellappa et al. [5] listed a small number of applications of face
recognition technology and described their advantages and disadvantages. However, they did
not analyze any system deployed in real applications. Even the more recent review [35], where
the set of potential applications has been grouped into five categories, did not conduct such an
analysis. In 1997, at least 25 face recognition systems from 13 companies were available [3].
Since then, the numbers of face recognition systems and commercial enterprises have greatly
increased owing to the emergence of many new application areas, further improvement of the
face recognition technologies, and increased affordability of the systems. We have listed 10
of the representative commercial face recognition companies, their techniques for face detection, the face features they extract, and face similarity comparison methods in Table 1. These
10 companies are also the participants of the latest face recognition vendor test (FRVT 2002)
[27] carried out independently by the U.S. government to evaluate state-of-the-art face recognition technology. Although some of these techniques are not publicly available for proprietary
reasons, one can conclude that many others have been incorporated into commercial systems.

As one of the most nonintrusive biometrics, face recognition technology is becoming ever
closer to people's daily lives. Evidence of this is that in 2000 the International Civil Aviation
Organization endorsed facial recognition as the most suitable biometrics for air travel [11]. To
our knowledge, no review papers are available on the newly enlarged application scenarios since
then [3, 5, 35]. We hope this chapter will be an extension of the previous studies. We review
many face recognition applications that have already used face recognition technologies. This
set of applications is a much larger super-set of that reviewed in [3]. We also review some other
new scenarios that will potentially utilize face recognition technologies in the near future.

These scenarios are grouped into 10 categories, as shown in Table 16.2. Although we try to
cover as many categories as possible, these 10 categories are neither exclusive nor exhaustive.
For each category, some of the exemplar applications are also listed. The last category, called
"Others," includes future applications and some current applications that we have not looked
into. These 10 categories are reviewed from Section 3 to Section 11. In Section 12, some of the

**Table 16.1.** Comparison of face recognition algorithms from 10 commercial systems in FRVT 2002. N/A: not available.

| Company | Method for face detection | Face feature extraction method | Matching method |
|---|---|---|---|
| Acsys | N/A | Biometric templates | Template matching |
| Cognitec | N/A | Local discriminant analysis (LDA) | N/A |
| C-VIS | Fuzzy face model and neural net | N/A | Elastic net matching |
| Dream Mirh | N/A | N/A | N/A |
| Eyematic | General face model | Gabor wavelet | Elastic graph matching |
| IConquest | Fractal image comparison algorithm | | |
| Identix | N/A | Local feature analysis (LFA) | Neural network |
| Imagis | Deformable face model | Spectral analysis | N/A |
| Viisage | N/A | Eigenface | Euclidian distance |
| VisionSphere | N/A | Holistic feature code | N/A |

limitations of the face recognition technologies are reviewed. Concluding remarks are made in Section 13.

## 2 Face Identification

Face recognition systems identify people by their face images [6]. In contrast to traditional identification systems, face recognition systems establish the presence of an authorized person rather than just checking whether a valid identification (ID) or key is being used or whether the user knows the secret personal identification numbers (PINs) or passwords. The security advantages of using biometrics to check identification are as follows. It eliminates the misuse of lost or stolen cards, and in certain applications it allows PINs to be replaced with biometric characteristics, which makes financial and computer access applications more convenient and secure. In addition, in situations where access control to buildings or rooms is automated, operators may also benefit from improved efficiency. Face recognition systems are already in use today, especially in small database applications such as those noted in Section 3. In the future, however, the targeted face ID applications will be large-scale applications such as e-commerce, student ID, digital driver licenses, or even national ID.

Large-scale applications still face a number of challenges. Some of the trial applications are listed below.

1. In 2000 FaceIt technology was used for the first time to eliminate duplicates in a nationwide voter registration system because there are cases where the same person was assigned more than one identification number [11]. The face recognition system directly compares the face images of the voters and does not use ID numbers to differentiate one from the others. When the top two matched faces are extremely similar to the query face image, manual inspection is required to make sure they are indeed different persons so as to eliminate duplicates.

**Table 16.2.** Application categories

| Category | Exemplar application scenarios |
| --- | --- |
| Face ID | Driver licenses, entitlement programs, immigration, national ID, passports, voter registration, welfare registration |
| Access control | Border-crossing control, facility access, vehicle access, smart kiosk and ATM, computer access, computer program access, computer network access, online program access, online transactions access, long distance learning access, online examinations access, online database access |
| Security | Terrorist alert, secure flight boarding systems, stadium audience scanning, computer security, computer application security, database security, file encryption, intranet security, Internet security, medical records, secure trading terminals |
| Surveillance | Advanced video surveillance, nuclear plant surveillance, park surveillance, neighborhood watch, power grid surveillance, CCTV control, portal control |
| Smart cards | Stored value security, user authentication |
| Law enforcement | Crime stopping and suspect alert, shoplifter recognition, suspect tracking and investigation, suspect background check, identifying cheats and casino undesirables, post-event analysis, welfare fraud, criminal face retrieval and recognition |
| Face databases | Face indexing and retrieval, automatic face labeling, face classification |
| Multimedia management | Face-based search, face-based video segmentation and summarization, event detection |
| Human computer interaction (HCI) | Interactive gaming, proactive computing |
| Others | Antique photo verification, very low bit-rate image & video transmission, etc. |

2. Viisage's faceFinder system [30] has been supplied to numerous state corrections authorities and driver license bureaus. This face recognition technology has also been used by the U.S. Department of State for the Diversity Visa Program, which selects approximately 50,000 individuals to be considered for a permanent U.S. visa from millions of applications submitted each year. Each application includes a facial image. The system compares the image of every applicant against the database to reduce the potential of the same face obtaining multiple entries in the lottery program. Once enrolled in the Viisage system, images can also be used during the diversity visa application process to help identify known individuals who pose specific security threats to the nation.

# 3 Access Control

In many of the access control applications, such as office access or computer log-in, the size of the group of people that need to be recognized is relatively small. The face pictures are also captured under constrained conditions, such as frontal faces and indoor illumination. Face recognition-based systems in these applications can achieve high accuracy without much co-operation from the users; for example, there is no need to touch an object by fingers or palms, no need to present an eye to a detector. When combined with other forms of authentication schemes such as fingerprint or iris recognition, face recognition systems can achieve high accuracy. Thus the user satisfaction level is high. This area of application has attracted many commercial face recognition systems. The following are several examples.

- In 2000, IBM began to ship FaceIt [10] enabled screen saver with Ultraport camera for A, T, and X series Thinkpad notebook computers. Face recognition technology is used to monitor continuously who is in front of a computer terminal. It allows the user to leave the terminal without closing files and logging off. When the user leaves for a predetermined time, a screen saver covers the work and disables the keyboard and mouse. When the user returns and is recognized, the screen saver clears and the previous session appears as it was left. Any other user who tries to log in without authorization is denied.
- The University of Missouri-Rolla campus has chosen a face recognition system by Omron [26] to secure a nuclear reactor, which is a 200-kilowatt research facility that uses low-enriched uranium to train nuclear engineers. Visitors must pass through a staff-monitored lobby, a second door that is accessed with a key, and a third door that is secured with a keypad before getting to the face scanner, which regulates access to the reactor core.
- Another commercial access control system is called FaceGate [9]. Entering a building using FaceGate simply requires one to enter his entry code or a card and face a camera on the door entry system. Figure 16.1 is a snapshot of the system. By applying a mathematical model to an image of a face, FaceGate generates a unique biometric "key." Whenever one wishes to access a building, FaceGate verifies the person's entry code or card, then compares his face with its stored "key." It registers him as being authorized and allows him to enter the building. Access is denied to anyone whose face does not match.

**Fig. 16.1.** FaceGate access control system.

- The FaceKey standard biometric access control system combines face recognition and fingerprint recognition to provide a high level of security [12]. There is no need for cards, keys, passwords or keypads. The combination of the two biometrics makes it possible to have security with a low error rate. The system can operate as a stand-alone, one-door system, or it can be networked to interconnect multiple doors at multiple sites, domestically or internationally.
- "FaceVACS-Entry" [6] adds facial recognition to conventional access control systems. At the access point, the face of each person is captured by a video camera, and the facial features are extracted and compared with the stored features. Only if they match is access permitted. For high security areas, a combination with card terminals is possible, so each card can be used only by its owner. Flexible communication interfaces enable easy integration into existing access control or time and attendance systems. Terminals with FaceVACS-Entry can be networked together, so after central enrollment the face data are distributed automatically to all the terminals. In addition, visual control by security personnel can be supported. All facial images collected at the terminals can be stored in a log for later visual inspection via a standard browser.

In addition to commercial access control systems, many systems are being developed in university research laboratories that are exploring new face recognition algorithms. We give two examples.

1. At the University of Illinois [34] face recognition and speaker identification systems have been integrated to produce high recognition accuracy for a computer login system. Figure 16.2 shows the system interface where the upper-left corner displays the realtime video captured by a digital camcorder. The upper-center displays text or digits for the user to read aloud for speaker identification. At the upper-right corner are three buttons titled "Start Testing," "Add User," "Delete User," indicating three functionalities. Two bar charts in the lower-left corner display the face recognition and speaker identification likelihoods, respectively, for each user. In the lower-center, icon images of users that are currently in the database are shown in black and white and the recognized person has his image enlarged and shown in color. The lower-right of the screen displays all the names of the users currently in the database.
2. The second system [2] uses a multilayer perceptron for access control based on face recognition. The robustness of neural network (NN) classifiers is studied with respect to the false acceptance and false rejection errors. A new thresholding approach for rejection of unauthorized persons is proposed. Ensembles of NN with different architectures were also studied.

## 4 Security

Today more than ever, security is a primary concern at airports and for airline personnel and passengers. Airport security systems that use face recognition technology have been implemented at many airports around the globe. Figure 16.3 diagrams a typical airport security system that employs face recognition technology. Although it is possible to control lighting conditions and face orientation in some security applications, (e.g., using a single pedestrian lane with controlled lighting), one of the greatest challenges for face recognition in public places is the large

**Fig. 16.2.** A computer access control system using both face and speaker recognition.

number of faces that need to be examined, resulting in a high false alarm rate. Overall, the performance of most of the recognition systems has not met the very low false rejects goal with low false alarm requirements. The user satisfaction level for this area of application is quite low.

Some of the exemplar systems at airports, stadiums and for computer security are listed below.

1. In October, 2001, Fresno Yosemite International (FYI) airport in California deployed Viisage's face recognition technology for airport security purposes. The system is designed to alert FYI's airport public safety officers whenever an individual matching the appearance of a known terrorist suspect enters the airport's security checkpoint. Anyone recognized by the system would undergo further investigative processes by public safety officers.
2. At Sydney airport, Australian authorities are trying out a computerized face-recognition system called SmartFace by Visionics with cameras that have wide-angle lenses. The cameras sweep across the faces of all the arriving passengers and send the images to a computer, which matches the faces with pictures of wanted people stored in its memory. If the computer matches the face with that of a known person, the operator of the surveillance system receives a silent alarm and alerts the officers that the person should be questioned. The technology is also used at Iceland's Keflavik airport to seek out known terrorists.

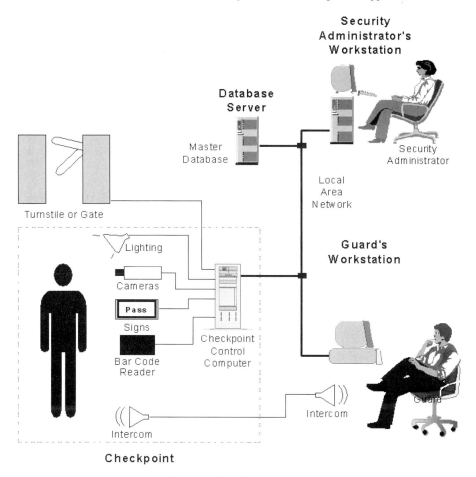

**Fig. 16.3.** An exemplar airport security system.

3. At Oakland airport (San Jose, California), a face recognition system by Imagis Technologies of Vancouver, British Columbia, Canada is used in interrogation rooms behind the scenes to match suspects brought in for questioning to a database of wanted criminals' pictures.

4. Malaysia'a 16 airports use a FaceIt-based security system to enhance passenger and baggage security. A lipstick-size camera at the baggage check-in desk captures a live video of the passengers and embeds the data on a smart-card chip. The chip is embedded on the boarding pass and on the luggage claim checks. The system ensures that only passengers who have checked their luggage can enter the departure lounge and board the aircraft, and that only the luggage from boarding passengers is loaded into the cargo area. During the boarding process, the system automatically checks a realtime image of a passenger's face against that on the boarding pass smart chip. No luggage is loaded unless there is a match.

5. Viisage's faceFINDER equipment and software were used to scan the stadium audience at the Super Bowl 2001 at the Raymond James Stadium in Tampa, Florida in search of criminals. Everyone entering the stadium was scanned by video cameras set up at the entrance turnstiles. These cameras were tied to a temporary law-enforcement command center that digitized their faces and compared them against photographic lists of known malefactors. The system is also used by South Wales Police in Australia to spot soccer hooligans who are banned from attending matches.

6. Computer security has also seen the application of face recognition technology. To prevent someone else from modifying files or transacting with others when the authorized individual leaves the computer terminal momentarily, users are continuously authenticated, ensuring that the individual in front of the computer screen or at a kiosk is the same authorized person who logged in.

# 5 Surveillance

Like security applications in public places, surveillance by face recognition systems has a low user satisfaction level, if not lower. Unconstrained lighting conditions, face orientations and other factors all make the deployment of face recognition systems for large scale surveillance a challenging task. The following are some examples of face-based surveillance.

1. In 1998 Visionics FaceIt technology was deployed for the first time to enhance town center surveillance in Newham Borough of London, which has 300 cameras linked to the closed circuit TV (CCTV) control room. The city council claims that the technology has helped to achieve a 34% drop in crime since its installation. Similar systems are in place in Birmingham, England. In 1999 Visionics was awarded a contract from National Institute of Justice to develop smart CCTV technology [11].

2. Tampa, Florida police use video cameras and face recognition software to scan the streets in search of sex offenders. FaceIt provided by Visionics quickly compares the face of a target against a database of people wanted on active warrants from the Hillsborough Sheriff's Office and a list of sex offenders maintained by the Florida Department of Law Enforcement. When the FaceIt system comes up with a close match, cops using it in a remote location can contact others on the street via radio and instruct them to do further checking.

3. Virginia Beach, Virginia is the second U.S. city to install the FaceIt system on its public streets to scan pedestrian's faces to compare with 2500 images of people with outstanding warrants, missing persons, and runaways.

4. In New York City, the National Park Service deployed a face recognition surveillance system for the security of the Statue of Liberty. The system, including two cameras mounted on tripods, at the ferry dock where visitors leave Manhattan for Liberty Island, takes pictures of visitors and compares them with a database of terror suspects. The cameras are focused on the line of tourists waiting to board the ferry, immediately before they pass through a bank of metal detectors.

## 6 Smart Cards

The Smart Card has an embedded microprocessor or memory chip that provides the processing power to serve many applications. Memory cards simply store data. A microprocessor card, on the other hand, can add, delete, and manipulate information in its memory on the card. A microprocessor card also has built-in security features. Contact-less smart cards contain a small antenna so the card reader detects the card from a distance. The Smart Card's portability and ability to be updated make it a technology well suited for securely connecting the virtual and physical worlds.

The application of face recognition technology in smart cards, in essence, is a combination of the two. This can be seen from the following two examples. Smart cards store the mathematical characteristics of the faces during the enrollment stage. The characteristics are read out during the verification stage for comparison with the live capture of the person's face. If granted, the person can have his stored facial characteristics updated in the card's memory.

1. Maximus [24] coupled face recognition system with fingerprint technology to construct a smart card designed to help airline passengers quickly clear security. To get a smart card, one needs to submit to a background check and register his or her facial and fingerprint characteristics. Biometric readers, presumably set up in specially designated "fast lanes," then verify his or her identification.
2. The ZN-Face system [17], which combines face recognition and smart card technology, is used for protecting secure areas at Berlin airports. Potential threats posed by criminals who often succeed in entering high security areas by means of a suitable disguise (e.g., pilot uniforms) are ruled out effectively. The individual's face characteristics are stored on a smart card; ZN-Face compares and verifies the card information with the face readings at each access station.

Smart cards are used mainly in a face verification scenario. The accuracy of the similarity calculation between the face characteristics stored in the cards and the live-captured face depends on the elapsed time between the two images. With a timely update of the face characteristics, this elapsed time can be kept short. High user satisfaction level can be achieved for a small database of faces.

## 7 Law Enforcement

With a face recognition and retrieval program, investigators can find a suspect quickly. Face recognition technology empowers the law enforcement agencies with the ability to search and identify suspects quickly even with incomplete information of their identity, sometimes even with a sketch from a witness's recollection. Owing to the difficulty of obtaining good-quality face images of the criminals, the system performance is rather low. However, automatic face recognition is playing increasingly important role in assisting the police departments. Some examples in this category of applications are as follows.

1. A law enforcement system by Imigis provides the Huntington Beach, California's police officers and detectives with current arrest information and photographs, readily available

by using laptops, Internet protocols, and secure wireless delivery and communication [16]. The Imagis system includes biometric facial recognition, and image and database management, giving officers invaluable investigative tools in their law enforcement and surveillance work. With this face recognition and retrieval program, investigators no longer have to spend hundreds of hours trying to identify a suspect. Now detectives can take a suspect composite and systematically search any digital database of booking images to identify possible suspects. Similarly, a suspect's image caught on a bank or convenience store surveillance video can be matched against a digital photo database for possible identification. With a face ID interface on a county booking system, officers are able to utilize this face-recognition technology at the time of booking to immediately identify a criminal with multiple identities or outstanding warrants. Detectives can also use face ID to search for suspects in a database of registered sex offenders. It allows witnesses to identify specific features of various faces as a means to query a large database of images. This function enhances the crime resolution process by eliminating the need for witnesses to search large mug-shot books one image at a time.

2. When deployed in a casino environment, an intelligent surveillance and patron management system supported by Imagis's face recognition technology [15] allows casino operators to identify and exclude certain individuals from specific properties. Using a database of North American undesirable patrons or self-barred gamblers, casinos receive a highly effective security solution that can rapidly identify persons entering or playing in casinos. It not only can conduct face recognition searches from images captured through existing surveillance cameras against an internal database, a casino can also widen the identification search to the national database.

## 8 Face Databases

During the early 1990s, because of the emergence of large image databases, difficulties faced by the text-based image retrieval became more and more acute [29]. Content-based image retrieval tries to solve the difficulties faced by text-based image retrieval. Instead of being manually annotated by text-based keywords, images would be indexed by their own visual content, such as color and texture. Feature vector is the basis of content-based image retrieval, which captures image properties such as color and texture. However, these general features have their own limitations. Recently, researchers have tried to combine it with other image analysis technologies, such as face detection and recognition, to improve the retrieval accuracy. Although face recognition techniques have been mainly used to retrieve and index faces in face-only databases (e.g., searching mug-shot databases of criminals), recently these techniques have also been used for other databases containing both faces and nonfaces (e.g., personal photo albums).

The performance of these retrieval systems is still low because the size of face database is normally large and the face pictures are captured under unconstrained conditions.

### 8.1 Using Faces to Assist Content-based Image Retrieval

A personal digital photo album has many images that have either human faces or no human faces. Deciding whether an image contains a face can be a preprocessing step to limit the range of search space for a given image query. FotoFile [18] is one of the systems that tries to support this functionality to make the management of personal photo albums easier. This system also blends human and automatic annotation methods. Fotofile offers a number of techniques that make it easier for a consumer to annotate the content manually and to fit the annotation task more naturally into the flow of activities that consumers find enjoyable. The use of automated feature extraction tools enables FotoFile to generate some of the annotation that would otherwise have to be manually entered. It also provides novel capabilities for content creation and organization.

When presented with photos that contain faces of new people, the face recognition system attempts to match the identity of the face. The user either corrects or confirms the choice; the system then can match faces to their correct identities more accurately in subsequent photos. Once a face is matched to a name, that name is assigned as an annotation to all subsequently presented photos that contain faces that match the original. To handle the false positives and false negatives of the face recognition system, a user must confirm face matches before the annotations associated with these faces are validated.

### 8.2 Using Content-Based Image Retrieval Techniques to Search Faces

The content-based retrieval of faces has multiple applications that exploit existing face databases. One of the most important tasks is the problem of searching a face without its explicit image, only its remembrance. Navarrete and del Solar [25] used the so-called relevance feedback approach. Under this approach, previous human computer interactions are employed to refine subsequent queries, which iteratively approximate the wishes of the user. This idea is implemented using self-organizing maps. In particular, their system uses a tree-structured self-organizing map (TS-SOM) for auto-organizing the face images in the database. Similar face images are located in neighboring positions of the TS-SOM.

To know the location of the requested face in the map, the user is asked to select face images he considers to be similar to the requested one from a given set of face images. The system then shows the new images, which have neighboring positions, with respect to the ones selected by the user. The user and the retrieval system iterate until the interaction process converges (i.e., the requested face image is found). This retrieval system in shown in Figure 16.4, and a real example of the interactive face-retrieval process is shown in Figure. 16.5.

Eickeler and Birlinghoven [8] explored the face database retrieval capabilities of a face recognition system based on the hdden Markov model. This method is able to work on a large database. Experiments carried out on a database of 25,000 face images show that this method is suitable for retrieval on a large face database. Martinez [23] presented a different approach to indexing face images. This approach is based on identifying frontal faces and allows reasonable variability in facial expressions, illumination conditions, and occlusions caused by eyewear or items of clothing such as scarves. The face recognition system of this approach is also based on the hidden Markov model [8].

## 9 Multimedia Management

Human faces are frequently seen in news, sports, films, home video, and other multimedia content. Indexing this multimedia content by face detection, face tracking, face recognition,

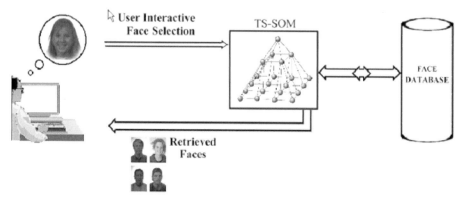

**Fig. 16.4.** Interface of the SOM system.

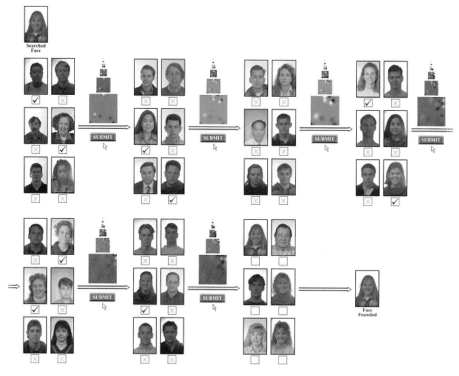

**Fig. 16.5.** Face retrieval using the SOM system.

and face change detection is important to generate segments of coherent video content for video browsing, skimming, and summarization. Together with speech recognition, natural language processing, and other image understanding techniques, face processing is a powerful tool for automatic indexing, retrieval, and access to the ever-growing digital multimedia content.

One difficulty of directly using face recognition in multimedia applications is that usually the gallery set is not available. The identity of the person whose face has been detected must be obtained through the multimedia content itself. Houghton [14] developed a "face-naming" method. His method finds names in Web pages associated with the broadcast television stations using three text processing methods and names in images using the optical character recognition (OCR) technique. The names are then linked to the faces detected in the images. The face detector is the FaceIt [10]. In this way, a gallery set is created. Queried about an image without a name, the "face-naming" system compares the faces in the image with the gallery and returns the identity of the face.

Ma and Zhang [22] developed an interactive user interface to let the user annotate a set of video segments that the face recognizer concludes to be belonging to the same nonenrolled person. They have used the face detection algorithm [28] to detect faces to help to extract key frames for indexing and browsing home video. Chan et al. [4] used face recognition techniques to browse video databases to find shots of particular people.

One integrated multimedia management system is the "Infomedia" project at Carnegie Mellon University [31]. This project aims to create an information digital video library to enhance learning for people of all ages. Thousands of hours of video content is indexed and archived for search and retrieval by users via desktop computers through computer networks. One of its indexing schemes is the face detection developed by Rowley et al. [28]. The detected human faces and text are used as a basis for significance during the creation of video segments. A small number of face images can be extracted to represent the entire segment of video containing an individual for video summarization purposes. It supports queries such as "find video with talking heads" supported by face detection, "find interviews by Tim Russert" supported by face detection and video text recognition, and so on.

Another system is a multilingual, multimodal digital video library system, called iVIEW, developed at the Chinese University of Hong Kong [21]. Its face recognition scheme is similar to the one in Houghton's article [14]. Faces detected are cross-referenced with the names detected by OCR on on-screen words. iVIEW is designed on Web-based architecture with flexible client server interaction. It supports access to both English and Chinese video contents. It also supports access via wired and wireless networks.

Wang and Chang [32] developed a system for realtime detection, tracking, and summarization of human faces in the video compressed domain at Columbia University. Their face detection component uses the MPEG compressed data to detect face objects and refine the results by tracking the movement of faces. The summaries of people appearance in the spatial and temporal dimensions help users to understand the interaction among people.

Because the orientation of faces or lighting conditions in most of the multimedia content is seldom controlled, face recognition accuracy is relatively low.

## 10  Human Computer Interaction

To achieve efficient and user-friendly human-computer interaction, human body parts (e.g., the face) could be considered as a natural input "device". This has motivated research on tracking, analyzing, and recognizing human body movements.

### 10.1  Face Tracking

Although the goal of such interfaces is to recognize and understand human body movements, the first step to achieve this goal is to reliably localize and track such human body parts as the face and the hand. Skin color offers a strong cue for efficient localization and tracking of human body parts in video sequences for vision-based human-computer interaction. Color-based target localization could be achieved by analyzing segmented skin color regions. Although some work has been done on adaptive color models, this problem still needs further study. Wu and Huang [33] presented their investigation of color-based image segmentation and nonstationary color-based target tracking by studying two representations for color distributions. Based on the so-called D-EM algorithm, they implemented a nonstationary color tracking system. Figure. 16.6 shows an example of face localization and tracking in a typical laboratory environment.

**Fig. 16.6.** Tracking results based on color model.

### 10.2  Emotion Recognition

It is argued that for the computer to be able to interact with humans it must have the communication skills of humans, and one of these skills is the ability to understand the emotional state of the person. The most expressive way humans display emotions is through facial expressions.

Cohen et al. [7] reported on several advances they have made in building a system for classifying facial expressions from continuous video input. They used Bayesian network classifiers for classifying expressions from video. Figure 16.7 shows four examples of realtime expression recognition. The labels show the recognized emotion of the user.

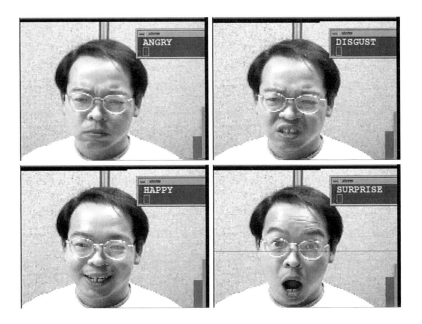

**Fig. 16.7.** Emotion recognition results.

## 10.3 Face Synthesis and Animation

A realistic three dimensional head model is one of the key factors in natural human-computer interaction. A graphics-based human model provides an effective solution for information display, especially in collaborative environments. Examples include 3D model-based very low bit-rate video coding for visual telecommunication, audio/visual speech recognition, and talking head representation of computer agents. In noisy environments, the synthetic talking face can help users understand the associated speech, and it helps people react more positively during interactive sessions. It has been shown that a virtual sales agent inspires confidence in customers in the case of e-commerce, and a synthetic talking face enables students to learn better in computer-aided education [13].

Hong et al.[13] have successfully designed a system, called iFACE, that provides functionalities for face modeling and animation. The 3D geometry of a face is modeled by a triangular mesh. A few control points are defined on the face mesh. By dragging the control points, the user can construct different facial shapes. Two kinds of media, text stream and speech stream, can be used to drive the face animation. A display of the speech-driven talking head is shown in Figure 16.8.

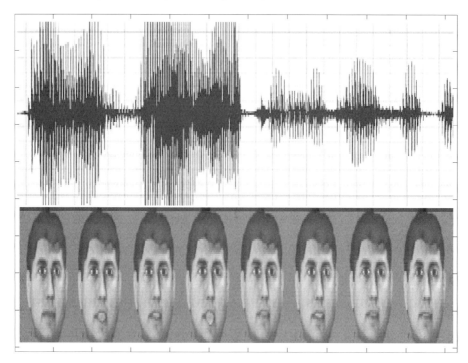

**Fig. 16.8.** Speech driven face animation.

## 11 Other Applications

Many of the application scenarios in this section require close collaboration between face recognition systems and domain experts. The face recognition systems assist the domain experts.

- **Antique photo verification.** It is of great value for historians, biographers, and antique collectors to verify whether an antique photo of a person is genuine, given a true photo taken when that person is much older. The age difference and sometimes the low quality of the antique photo pose a great challenge for the face recognition systems.
- **Face images transmission.** Li et al. [19] coded the face images with a compact parameterized model for low bandwidth communication applications, such as videophone and teleconferencing. Instead of sending face images or video, they send robust feature representation of the faces to the other end of the channel so that by fitting a generic face model to the face feature representation a good reconstruction of the original face images can be achieved. Similarly, Lyons et al. [20] developed an algorithm that can automatically extract a face from an image, modify it, characterize it in terms of high-level properties, and apply it to the creation of a personalized avatar in an online Japanese sumo game application. The algorithm has potential applications in educational systems (virtual museums or classrooms) and in entertainment technology (e.g., interactive movies, multiple user role-playing communities).

- Chellappa et al. [5] listed several application scenarios that involve close collaboration between the face recognition system and the user or image domain expert. The interaction between the algorithms and known results in psychophysics and neuroscience studies is needed in these applications. We summarize these applications below; for detailed information see Chellappa et al. [5].

  1. "Expert Identification": An expert confirms that the face in the given image corresponds to the person in question. Typically, in this application a list of similar looking faces is generated using a face identification algorithm. The expert then performs a careful analysis of the listed faces.

  2. "Witness Face Reconstruction": The witness is asked to compose a picture of a culprit using a library of features such as noses, eyes, lips, and so on. The "sketch" by the user is compared with all the images in the database to find the closest matches. The witness can refine the "sketch" based on these matches. A face recognition algorithm can recompute the closest matches in the hope of finding the real culprit.

  3. "Electronic Lineup": A witness identifies a face from a set of face images that include some false candidates. This set of images can be the results from the "Witness Face Reconstruction" application by the face recognition algorithm.

  4. "Reconstruction of Face from Remains" and "Computerized Aging": Available face images are transformed to what a face could have been or what the face will be after some time.

## 12  Limitations of Current Face Recognition Systems

Although face recognition technology has great potential in the applications reviewed above, currently the scope of the application is still quite limited. There are at least two challenges that need to be addressed to deploy them in large-scale applications.

1. Face recognition technology is still not robust, especially in unconstrained environments, and recognition accuracy is not acceptable, especially for large-scale applications. Lighting changes, pose changes, and time differences between the probe image and the gallery image(s) further degrade the performance. These factors have been evaluated in FRVT 2002 using some of the best commercial systems [27]. For example, in a verification test with reasonably controlled indoor lighting, when the gallery consisted of 37,437 individuals with one image per person and the probe set consisted of 74,854 probes with two images per person, the best three systems, on average, achieved a verification rate of 90% at a false alarm rate of 1%, 80% at a false alarm rate of 0.1%, and 70% at a false alarm rate of 0.01%. This level of accuracy may be (or may not be) suitable for an access control system with a small database of hundreds of people but not for a security system at airports where the number of passengers is much larger. When evaluating the performance with respect to pose change, with a database of 87 individuals the best system can achieve an identification rate of only 42% for faces with $\pm 45°$ left or right pose differences and 53% with $\pm 45°$ up or down pose differences. The elapsed time between the database and test images degrades performance at a rate of 5% per year of difference. Lighting changes between probe images obtained outdoors and gallery images taken indoors degrade the best systems, from

a verification rate of 90% to around 60% at a false accept rate of 1%. The test results in FRVT 2002 can partly explain why several systems installed at airports and other public places have not received positive feedback based on their poor performance. One example is that the crowd surveillance system tested by Tampa, Florida police reported 14 instances of a possible criminal match in a 4-day session, but they were all false alarms. The Tampa police department has abandoned the system.

2. The deployment of face recognition-based surveillance systems has raised concerns of possible privacy violation. For example, the American Civil Liberties Union (ACLU) opposes the use of face recognition software at airports due to ineffectiveness and privacy concern [1]. In addition to listing several factors affecting the face recognition accuracy, such as change of hairstyle, weight gain or loss, eye glasses or disguise, the ACLU opposes face recognition because "facial recognition technology carries the danger that its use will evolve into a widespread tool for spying on citizens as they move about in public places."

# 13 Conclusions

We reviewed many face recognition systems in various application scenarios. We also pointed out the limitations of the current face recognition technology. The technology has evolved from laboratory research to many small-, medium- or, large-scale commercial deployments. At present it is most promising for small- or medium-scale applications, such as office access control and computer log in; it still faces great technical challenges for large-scale deployments such as airport security and general surveillance. With more research collaborations worldwide between universities and industrial researchers, the technology will become more reliable and robust.

Another direction for improving recognition accuracy lies in a combination of multiple biometrics and security methods. It can work with other biometrics such as voice-based speaker identification, fingerprint recognition, and iris scans in many applications. For security purpose at airports, face recognition systems can also work together with x-ray luggage scanners, metal detectors, and chemical trace detectors at security checkpoints.

This chapter concludes with the following description of how face recognition could be used in our daily lives in the near future, although some of them are already in place.

If we drive to work, a face recognizer installed in the car will decide whether to authorize our usage of the vehicle before starting the engine. If we choose to take a bus or subway to work, our pre-paid boarding pass will be verified by a face recognizer comparing the photo on the pass and live captured pictures of our faces. At the entrance of the office building, we go through a face recognition based access control system that compares our face images with those in its database. We sit down in front of the office computer, a face recognizer in it runs its face recognition algorithm before we log on. when we go to a secure area in the office building, the security check is carried out by another face recognizer. On a business trip, when we use the smart ATM, we are subject to a face recognizer of the bank system. At the airport, our boarding pass and passport or identity card are screened by the airport's face recognizer for passenger security purpose. When we go back home, a face recognition based home security system makes sure we are living in the house before we open the door.

## Acknowledgments

We sincerely thank Dr. Ying Wu, Northwestern University, Dr. Lawrence Chen, Kodak Research Lab, Dr. Javier Ruiz-del-Solar, Universidad de Chile, Chile, and Dr. Julian L. Center, Jr., Lau Technologies for providing some of the pictures and their permission to use them in the paper. We also want to thank Dr. Anil K. Jain, Michigan State University for giving us helpful suggestions on improving the manuscript.

## References

1. ACLU. http://archive.aclu.org/features/f110101a.html.
2. D. Bryliuk and V. Starovoitov. Access control by face recognition using neural networks and negative examples. In *Proceedings of The 2nd International Conference on Artificial Intelligence*, pages 428–436, 2002.
3. C. Bunney. Survey: face recognition systems. *Biometric Technology Today*, pages 8–12, 1997.
4. Y. Chan, S.-H. Lin, and S. Kung. Video indexing and retrieval. In *Multimedia Technology for Applications*. B.J. Sheu, M. Ismail, M.Y. Wang, and R.H. Tsai, editors. Wiley, New York, 1998.
5. R. Chellappa, C. Wilson, and S. Sirohey. Human and machine recognition of faces: a survey. *Proceedings of the IEEE*, 83-5:704–740, 1995.
6. Cognitec. http://www.cognitec-systems.de/index.html.
7. I. Cohen, N. Sebe, F.G. Cozman, M.C. Cirelo, and T. Huang. Learning Bayesian network classifiers for facial expression recognition using both labeled and unlabeled data. In *Proceedings of the IEEE Int. Conf. on Computer Vision and Pattern Recognition (CVPR 2002)*, 2003.
8. S. Eickeler and S. Birlinghoven. Face database retrieval using pseudo 2D hidden Markov models. In *Proceeding of IEEE Int. Conf. on Face and Gestures (FG 2002)*, 2002.
9. FaceGate. http://www.premierelect.co.uk/faceaccess.html.
10. FaceIt. http://www.identix.com.
11. FaceIt-Hist. http://www.identix.com/company/comp_history.html.
12. FaceKey. http://www.facekey.com.
13. P. Hong, Z. Wen, and T. Huang. IFace: a 3D synthetic talking face. *International Journal of Image and Graphics*, 1(1):19–26, 2001.
14. R. Houghton. Named faces: putting names to faces. *IEEE Intelligence Systems*, 14-5:45–50, 1999.
15. Imagis. http://www.imagistechnologies.com.
16. Imagis-Beach. http://cipherwar.com/news/01/imagis_big_brother.htm.
17. W. Konen and E. Schulze-Krüger. ZN-face: a system for access control using automated face recognition. In *Proceedings of the International Workshop on Automatic Face and Gesture Recognition*, pages 18–23, 1995.
18. A. Kudhinsky, C. Pering, M.L. Creech, D. Freeze, B. Serra, and J. Gvvizdka. FotoFile: a consumer multimedia organization and retrieval system. In *Proceedings of CHI'99*, pages 496–503, 1999.
19. H. Li, P. Roivainen, and R. Forchheimer. 3D motion estimation in model-based facial image coding. *IEEE Trans. Pattern Analysis and Machine Intelligence*, 15-6:545–555, 1993.
20. M. Lyons, A. Plante, S. Jehan, S. Inoue, and S. Akamatsu. Avatar creation using automatic face recognition. In *Proceedings, ACM Multimedia 98*, pages 427–434, 1998.
21. M.R. Lyu, E. Yau, and S. Sze. A multilingual, multimodal digital video library system. In *ACM/IEEE Joint Conference on Digital Libraries, JCDL 2002, Proceedings*, pages 145–153, 2002.
22. W.-Y. Ma and H. Zhang. An indexing and browsing system for home video. In *Proc. of 10th European Signal Processing Conference*, 2000.

23. A. Martinez. Face image retrieval using HMMs. In *Proceedings of the IEEE Workshop on Content-Based Access of Image and Video Libraries*, 1999.

24. Maximus. http://www.maximus.com/corporate/pages/smartcardsvs.

25. P. Navarrcte and J. del Solar. Interactive face retrieval using self-organizing maps. In *Proceedings, 2002 Int. Joint Conf. on Neural Networks: IJCNN2002*, 2002.

26. Omron. http://www.omron.com.

27. P. Phillips, P. Grother, R. Michaels, D. Blackburn, E.Tabassi, and M. Bone. Face recognition vendor test 2002: evolution report. *http://www.frvt2002.org*.

28. H. Rowley, S. Baluja, and T. Kanade. Neural network-based face detection. *IEEE Patt. Anal. Mach. Intell.*, 20:22–38, 1998.

29. Y. Rui, T.S. Huang, and S.-F. Chang. Image retrieval: current techniques, promising directions and open issues. *J. Visual Communication and Image Representation*, 10-4:39–62, 1999.

30. Viisage. http://www.viisage.com.

31. H. Wactlar, T.K.M. Smith, and S. Stevens. Intelligence access to digital video: informedia project. *IEEE Computer*, 29-5:46–52, 1996.

32. H. Wang and S.-F. Chang. A highly efficient system for automatic face region detection in mpeg video sequences. *IEEE Trans. on Circuits and Systems for Video Technology, Special Issue on Multimedia Systems and Technologies*, 7-4:615–628, 1997.

33. Y. Wu and T. Huang. Nonstationary color tracking for vision-based human computer interaction. *IEEE Transactions on Neural Networks*, 13-4, 2002.

34. Z. Xiong, Y. Chen, R. Wang, and T. Huang. Improved information maximization based face and facial feature detection from real-time video and application in a multi-modal person identification system. In *Proceedings of the Fourth International Conference on Multimodal Interfaces (ICMI'2002)*, pages 511-516, 2002.

35. W. Zhao, R. Chellappa, A. Rosenfelda, and J. Phillips. Face recognition: a literature survey. Technical Report, CS-TR4167R, University of Maryland, 2000.

# Index